Pearson Education
Test Prep Series

M000273879

for AP® ECONOMICS
Macroeconomics and Microeconomics

To accompany:

BADE • PARKIN

Foundations of
Economics

AP® Edition, 7e

Robin **Bade**
Michael **Parkin**

Foundations of
Economics
Seventh Edition

Mark Rush, Editor
University of Florida

Ulrich Kleinschmidt
I.H. Kempner High School

AP® is a trademark registered and/or owned by the College Board, which was not involved in the production of, and does not endorse, this product.

PEARSON

Boston Columbus Indianapolis New York San Francisco Upper Saddle River
Amsterdam Cape Town Dubai London Madrid Milan Munich Paris Montreal Toronto
Delhi Mexico City Sao Paulo Sydney Hong Kong Seoul Singapore Taipei Tokyo

Executive Acquisitions Editor: Adrienne D'Ambrosio
Program Manager: Nancy Freihofer
Project Manager: Sarah Dumouchelle

Copyright © 2015, 2012, 2009, 2007, 2004 Pearson Education, Inc., publishing as Prentice Hall. All rights reserved. Manufactured in the United States of America. This publication is protected by Copyright, and permission should be obtained from the publisher prior to any prohibited reproduction, storage in a retrieval system, or transmission in any form or by any means, electronic, mechanical, photocopying, recording, or likewise. To obtain permission(s) to use material from this work, please submit a written request to Pearson Education, Inc., Permissions Department, Permissions Department, 221 River Street, Hoboken, New Jersey 07030.

10 9 8 7 6 5 4 3

ISBN-10:   0-13-381271-5
ISBN-13: 978-0-13-381271-8

www.pearsonschool.com/advanced

PEARSON

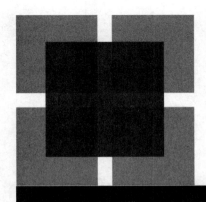

Table of Contents

© 2015 Pearson Education, Inc.

© 2015 Pearson Education, Inc.

Your Test for AP

■ Introduction

We know that when you use this workbook, you have one paramount goal: To pass your test for AP. However, after you finish your class, you will realize that much more has occurred. You will understand the language of economics, and you will be able to integrate economic concepts into your everyday experiences. You will make more informed personal decisions, and you will better understand economic issues highlighted in the media. In short, you will see the world in a fresh perspective and a new light. It is these facts that make economics so exciting and also a core competency for responsible citizens.

■ Your Textbook and Your Test Prep Workbook for AP

Each chapter in your textbook is divided into Checkpoint sections. These Checkpoints are smaller sections that revolve around a key point. These provide a logical and understandable framework for the material you are learning. At the end of each Checkpoint is a page that offers you Practice Problems to test your understanding of key ideas. There also are worked and illustrated solutions to the Practice Problems. The Checkpoints enable you to review material when it's fresh in your mind—the most effective and productive time to do so. The Checkpoints guide you through the material in a step-by-step approach that takes the guesswork out of learning. In addition to the Checkpoints, each chapter of your textbook also opens with a Chapter Checklist that tells you what you'll be able to do when you've completed the chapter.

This Test Prep Workbook for AP follows the same Checkpoint divisions. Each chapter in this workbook has a Chapter Summary that summarizes the material using the same Checkpoints. For each Checkpoint, the workbook has additional worked and illustrated Practice Problems to help ensure your grasp of the material. Following these are Self-Test questions. These questions are designed to help you learn the material to answer the questions you will encounter on your test. The test for AP consists of 60 multiple choice questions, two shorter free response questions, and one long free response question. So each Checkpoint contains multiple choice, short response and long response questions. There are also true and false questions. While the test for AP does not have true and false questions, the questions in your workbook are designed to tackle a definition or calculation that you might see on your AP® exam.

Make these Checkpoints and the Checklists work for you! To learn economics, you have to do economics. The Checklist-Checkpoint system provides you with a structure for doing just that. To make it work for you, start by familiarizing yourself with the Checklist at the beginning of each textbook chapter: it tells you where you'll be heading. As you progress through the chapter, you'll see that each ma-

© 2015 Pearson Education, Inc.

jor section corresponds to one of the Checklist items. After studying each section, be sure to work the Checkpoint in the textbook! That's the time to reinforce what you've just read—while it's still fresh in your mind. The number of tasks varies from two to five and most often is three or four.

After your work the Checkpoint in the text, you face a choice: For more immediate reinforcement, you can switch to the questions (and answers) for the Checkpoint in this workbook. Or you can use this workbook as a chapter review by working with it only after you have completed the chapter in the textbook. Which procedure will work best for you? That is a question you must answer. Perhaps you can try them both and see which is superior. But, regardless of the answer, remember the most important point: To learn economics you have to do economics!

This workbook contains an AP Test Hints section that can be of incredible worth. It includes a section of "AP Topics," a section of "AP Vocabulary," and a section of "Extra AP material." You should review each of these sections *very* carefully. They have hints and insights that may prove invaluable on your test for AP. The "AP Topics" tell you what the key points in the chapter are. There also is a brief summary of what you need to know about each topic. The "AP Vocabulary" gives you the main vocabulary items of the chapter, where they are found in the textbook, how they are defined, and often has a short explanation of their importance. The "Extra AP material" contains notes, updates, extra discussion, special AP references that students must know for the test for AP. In addition to these sections, *be sure* to work the problems in the last chapter of this workbook, the "AP Graphing Question," chapter. These problems will increase your skill in using what you have learned to answer questions that are similar to what you will be asked on your test for AP.

■ How to Use Your Test Prep Workbook for AP to Succeed on Your Test

No matter whether you choose to use this workbook while you are studying a chapter in the textbook or after you have completed the textbook chapter, there are a few hints we can offer about how to best use this book.

Chapter Checklist

This first section is a one-page summary of the key material. It is designed to focus you quickly and precisely on the core material that you must master. It is an excellent study aid for the night before your test. Think of it as notes that serve as a final check of the key concepts you have studied.

AP Test Hints

You may want to concentrate on this material because it will help you understand what your test will be like and therefore will give you confidence for the test. You can use the AP Topics and the AP Vocabulary to help focus your study time. Try covering the definitions and testing yourself to be sure that you know the material! The last section, Extra AP Material is crucial. Be *absolutely* certain to read it!

Additional Practice Problems

The practice problems in each Checkpoint in the textbook are extremely valuable because they help you do economics in order to grasp what you have just studied. This workbook provides additional Practice Problems to help you do more economics. Although the answer is given to the additional Practice Problems, try to solve it on your own before reading the answer.

Following the additional Practice Problem is the AP Self Test section. These questions are designed to give you practice and to test skills and techniques you must master to do well on your test. Before we describe the parts of the AP Self Test section, here are some general tips that apply to all parts.

© 2015 Pearson Education, Inc.

Use a pencil to write your answers. Write your answers in the workbook so you have neat, complete pages from which to study. Draw graphs wherever they are applicable. Some questions will ask explicitly for graphs; others will not but will require a chain of reasoning that involves shifts of curves on a graph. Always draw the graph. Don't try to work through the reasoning in your head — you are much more likely to make mistakes that way. Whenever you draw a graph, even in the margins of this book, label the axes. You might think that you can keep the labels in your head, but you will be confronting many different graphs with many different variables on the axes. Avoid confusion and label. As an added incentive, remember that on your AP® exam, you will lose points for unlabeled axes.

Take notes on your incorrect answers attempted and this will become a great study aid. It is hard to over-emphasize that you need to draw graphs of the concepts covered. Graphs are analyzed on the multiple choice questions and are required on the free response questions. As we said just before, practice the correct labeling of the graphs, as this is also required. Why are we repeating this suggestion? If you forget to label the axes on your graphs during the test, you will not earn points, and we *do not* want you to lose these points! One third of the test for AP is based on Free Response questions. Practice creating these graphs. Remember that the command in the question to *explain* means making *how* and *why* connections.

Do the AP Self Test questions as if they were real exam questions—do them without looking at the answers. This is the single most important tip we can give you about effectively using this workbook to improve your exam performance. Struggling for the answers to questions that you find difficult is one of the most effective ways to learn. The adage "no pain, no gain" applies well to studying. You will learn the most from right answers you had to struggle for and from your wrong answers and mistakes. Only after you have attempted all the questions should you look at the answers. When you finally do check the answers, be sure to understand where you went wrong and why the right answer is correct.

True or False

First in the AP Self Test section are a few true or false questions. The test for AP does *not* have true or false questions. But we think these questions are a highly effective way to learn important definitions or facts, so do not skip them. The answers to the questions are given at the end of the chapter. The answer also has a page reference to the textbook. If you missed the question or did not completely understand the answer, definitely turn to the textbook and study the topic so that you will not miss similar questions on your exams.

Multiple Choice

As we describe below, multiple choice questions are a major important component of your test, so pay particular attention to these questions. The answers are given at the end of the chapter. If you had any difficulty with a question, use the textbook page reference in the answer to look up the topic and then study it to remove this potential weakness.

Short Response and Long Response Questions

The other major component of your test for AP will be short response and long response questions. The last two sections of questions in this workbook are designed to ensure that you are well prepared to handle these questions. Most Checkpoints have both short response and long response questions, though a few have only one style of question. Although the answer is given at the end of the chapter, do *not* look at the answer before you attempt to solve the problem. It is much too easy to deceive yourself into thinking you understand the answer when you simply look at the question and then read the answer. Involve yourself in the material by answering the question and then

© 2015 Pearson Education, Inc.

looking at the answer. If you cannot answer the question or if you got the answer wrong, use the reference to the page number in the text to study the material.

These questions are also excellent for use in a study group. If you and several friends are studying, you can use these questions to quiz your understanding. If you have disagreements about the correct answers, use the page references to the text so that you can settle these disagreements and be sure that everyone has a solid grasp of the point!

It is an extremely safe bet that you will be expected to use graphs on at least some of the questions on your test. Because so many of these questions require that you use a graph as part of your answer, you might save the last chapter, Chapter 34, until a week or so before the end of your class or before your test. The broad questions in this chapter all require that you use a graph to answer them. They serve as the workbook's "final exam" and so should be among the last topics you study.

■ Your Test for AP

The AP® Economics Examinations make use of a variety of question types and graphical analysis to assess the skill level of students. The AP® examinations reflect the types of assessment that occur at the college level.

The AP® Economics Examinations are separated into two tests: a microeconomics test and a macroeconomics test. Each makes use of a variety of question types and graphical analysis requirements. Each test takes two hours and 10 minutes to complete. The multiple choice section has 60 questions and there are 70 minutes allowed for completion. The three free response questions are given 60 minutes of time for completion. The first free response question is the long question, usually contains 10 or more rubric points and usually requires the use of one or more graphs. The other two free response questions are the short questions and usually contain about 6 rubric points and often require the use of a graph. In both the multiple-choice and free-response sections of the exams, you can expect to work with graphs, charts, and tables.

The AP® Economics Examinations contain these distinct question types:
- Definition or identification questions
- Graph or table questions
- Analysis or cause and effect questions
- Multiple-choice questions

Multiple Choice

The multiple-choice section of each exam contains 60 questions, with 70 minutes allotted for Section I. The multiple-choice section accounts for 2/3 of your test score. As is the case for the multiple choice questions in this workbook, each question has five choices and only one choice is judged correct. The questions are straightforward, and many require analysis and interpretation. Some will require analysis of a graph, chart, or table.

The questions are machine scored. In all prior testing years there was a penalty for incorrect answers, but AP® has removed that penalty. Make sure to bubble in all questions before the end of the section time.

Free Response

This section is worth 1/3 of the total test score and students are expected to answer all three questions presented. The free-response section begins with a mandatory 10-minute reading period, during which you are encouraged to read the questions, sketch graphs, make notes, and plan answers.

© 2015 Pearson Education, Inc.

In your graphs, be careful when labeling the axes because this is a great way to earn easy rubric points. You should take this time to make sure you understand the question, check the expected rubric points, draft some responses, sketch any graph you think will be useful, and generally plan your answers. You then have 50 minutes to write your answers. There will be three questions, one longer and two shorter. The free-response questions in Section II of each exam will require you to analyze a given economic situation and use economic principles to explain answers. Using explanatory diagrams that clarify the analysis and clearly explain the reasoning results in the greatest number of points. Sometimes a graph is given as part of the question and your task is to derive the answer from the graph data. Generally, the longer free-response questions require you to interrelate several content areas, while the two shorter free-response questions focus on a specific topic in a given content area. The raw score for Section II is composed of the scores from the three questions and then apportioned according to value assigned to each (the larger question is 50 percent of the score and the two smaller questions are each 25 percent of score).

■ Taking Your Test for AP

Multiple Choice Hints

- Remember to sort through the choices. Eliminate quickly those answer choices you know are incorrect. You will feel comfortable with the test format if you have studied the questions in this book.

- You have 70 minutes to answer 60 multiple-choice questions, so don't spend too much time on any one question. You don't need to get every multiple-choice question right to score well on the AP® Economics exam.

- Make sure that you first answer all the questions that you know rather than answering the questions in consecutive order. Put a mark in the test booklet next to the questions that you cannot easily answer and return to them later. Often your subconscious will be working on these questions and you will see the answer the second time you look at the question, so make sure to give yourself enough time to return. Remember that questions are random and disconnected so do not carry an assumption from one question to the next.

- Practice all the assignments in this book and accompanying resources. That strategy will build your confidence on test day. With confidence, your mindset, your approach, and, most importantly, your score should benefit.

Free Response Hints

- A 10-minute reading period begins the free-response portion of the AP® Economics exam. This time gives you an opportunity to read the questions and plan for the answers. You can sketch an answer in the test booklet (this is the page with the question); however, you cannot open your answer book (blank pages for your answer) and write the answer. When planning, pay attention to how the parts of a question might influence or be related to sequential sub-questions. This might help you to confirm that you are answering a section completely or heading in the right direction.

- Remember that time might be an issue so allocate your time appropriately for the weighting of the questions asked. You have 25 minutes for the first essay and 12 minutes for each of the remaining two. If you used the 10-minute planning period well, you should have no problem finishing this section.

- Use correct terminology. Learn and use the correct language of economics.

© 2015 Pearson Education, Inc.

- You may answer the questions in any order, but clearly indicate which question is being addressed. If you answer the questions out of order, clearly mark in your test booklet which question is being presented. Use the same outline numbers or letters from the question in your answer, and answer them in the same order. The questions are divided into parts such as (a), (b), (c), and (d), with each part calling for a different response. Attempt to answer them all since points are earned independently. If the answer to a later part of a question depends on the answer to an earlier part, you may still be able to receive points for the later part, even if the earlier answer is wrong. If you write nothing for a subsection, you will receive nothing; if you write at least a partial answer, you may well receive partial credit.

- If the question requires you to draw a graph, it is important, if asked, to explain what the graph shows. Label graphs clearly, correctly, and fully. Label the curves and the axes. Changes in curves should be indicated clearly with arrows or clear sequencing, such as showing a change in a supply curve with the first curve labeled S or S_1 and the second curve labeled S' or S_2. You should also indicate the initial equilibrium and the final equilibrium by clearly labeling the points in the figure and then referring to them in your answer. More information about changes is good and helps the grader determine the kind of change you mean.

- Recall the terms used in your practice questions and exercises. All assertions, such as "the price increased," should explain the reason.

- If there is time, review your answer, always asking whether or not you have answered the question directly.

© 2015 Pearson Education, Inc.

■ AP® Economics Correlation Charts

This chart correlates the Advanced Placement® Microeconomics topics as outlined by The College Board with the corresponding chapters and section numbers in *Foundations of Economics*, AP® Edition. Use this chart to help you quickly find a topic you want to study or review.

AP® Microeconomic Topics	Textbook Chapters and Checkpoints
I. Basic Economic Concepts	**Chapters 1, 2, 3**
A. Scarcity, Choice, and Opportunity Costs	1.1, 1.2, 3.2
B. Production Possibility Curve	3.1
C. Comparative Advantage, Specialization, and Trade	3.5
D. Circular Flow	2.3
E. Property Rights and Role of Incentives	1.2, 11.1
F. Marginal Analysis	1.2
II. Nature and Functions of Product Markets	**Chapters 4, 5, 6, 7, 8, 12, 13, 14, 15, 16, 17**
A. Supply and Demand	Chapter 4
1. Market equilibrium	4.3
2. Determinants of supply and demand	4.1, 4.2
3. Price and quantity controls	Chapter 7
a. Price ceiling	7.1
b. Price floor	7.2
c. Production quota	7.3
4. Elasticity	Chapter 5
a. Price elasticity of demand	5.1
b. Income and cross-price	5.3
c. Price elasticity of supply	5.2
5. Consumer surplus, producer surplus, and market efficiency	Chapter 6
6. Tax incidence and deadweight loss	8.1
B. Theory of Consumer Choice	Chapter 13
1. Total utility and marginal utility	13.2
2. Utility maximization: equalizing marginal utility per dollar	13.2
3 Income and substitution effects	This *AP Test Prep Workbook*, Chapter 13
C. Production and Costs	Chapter 14
1. Production functions: short and long run	14.2, 14.3
2. Marginal product and diminishing returns	14.2
3. Short-run costs	14.3
4. Long-run costs and economies of scale	14.4
5. Cost minimizing input combination	This *AP Test Prep Workbook*, Chapters 14 and 19
D. Firm Behavior and Market Structure	Chapters 14, 15, 16, 17, 18
1. Profit	Chapters 14, 15, 16
a. Accounting versus economic profit	14.1

© 2015 Pearson Education, Inc.

© 2015 Pearson Education, Inc.

This chart correlates the Advanced Placement® Macroeconomics topics as outlined by The College Board with the corresponding chapters and section numbers in *Foundations of Economics*, AP® Edition. Use this chart to help you quickly find a topic you want to study or review.

AP® Macroeconomic Topics	**Textbook Chapters and Checkpoints**
I. Basic Economic Concepts	**Chapters 1, 3, 4, 5, 20, 21, 22, 24**
A. Scarcity, Choice, and Opportunity Cost	1.1, 1.2, 3.2
B. Production Possibilities Curve	3.1
C. Comparative Advantage, Specialization, and Exchange	3.4
D. Demand, Supply, and Market Equilibrium	Chapter 4
E. Macroeconomic Issues: Business Cycle, Unemployment, Inflation, Growth	Chapters 20, 21, 22, 24
II. Measurement of Economic Performance	**Chapters 2, 21, 22, 23**
A. National Income Accounts	Chapter 21
1. Circular flow	2.3, 21.1
2. Gross domestic product	21.2
3. Components of gross domestic product	21.2
4. Real versus nominal gross domestic product	21.2
B. Inflation Measurement and Adjustment	Chapters 23
1. Price indices	23.1, 23.2
2. Nominal and real values	Chapters 21 and 23, 23.3
3. Costs of inflation	28.3
C. Unemployment	Chapter 22
1. Definition and measurement	22.1, 22.2
2. Types of unemployment	22.3
3. Natural rate of unemployment	22.3, 24.1, 24.2
III. National Income and Price Determination	**Chapters 29, 30**
A. Aggregate Demand	Chapter 29
1. Determinants of aggregate demand	29.2
2. Multiplier and crowding-out effects	26.2, 29.2, 32.2, 32.3
B. Aggregate Supply	Chapter 29
1. Short-run and long-run analyses	29.1, 32.3
2. Sticky versus flexible wages and prices	Chapter 24, 29.1
3. Determinants of aggregate supply	29.1
C. Macroeconomic Equilibrium	Chapters 29
1. Real output and price level	29.3
2. Short and long run	Chapter 29
3. Actual versus full-employment output	Chapters 29, 32, 33
4. Economic fluctuations	29.3, 32.2, 33.2

© 2015 Pearson Education, Inc.

© 2015 Pearson Education, Inc.

■ Ending Thoughts

In writing this book, we had the privilege of working with many talented instructors. In past editions, we worked with and managed contributions from Carl Coates, Bruce L. Damasio, Joy Joyce, Vanessa Lal, Matt Pedlow, Peggy Pride, Amy Shrout, and Sandra Wright. Pamela Schmitt deserves special thanks for her accuracy checking of a previous edition. The sponsoring editor, Adrienne D'Ambrosio provided guidance and motivation for us. It is fair to say that without her help and insight, this workbook would never have been written. For this edition, the Project Manager, Sarah Dumouchelle, was a delight to work with. She provided ample motivation … and, surprisingly did so without the use of dire threats!

We have tried to make this Workbook for AP as helpful and useful as possible. Undoubtedly we have made some mistakes; mistakes that you may see. If you find any, we, and succeeding generations of students, would be grateful if you could point them out to us. If you have questions, suggestions, or simply comments, please let us know by emailing Mark Rush at Mark.Rush@Warrington.UFL.EDU.

Ulrich Kleinschmidt and Mark Rush

© 2015 Pearson Education, Inc.

Getting Started

Chapter 1

CHAPTER CHECKLIST

Chapter 1 defines economics, microeconomics and macroeconomics; discusses the three major questions of *what, how,* and *for whom*; covers the six core economic ideas that shape how economists think about issues; and, examines methods used by economists.

1 Define economics and explain the kinds of questions that economists try to answer.

Economic questions exist because of scarcity, the point that wants exceed the ability of resources to satisfy them. Economics is the social science that studies the choices that individuals, businesses, government, and entire societies make as they cope with scarcity, the incentives that influence those choices, and the arrangements that coordinate them. The field of economics is divided into microeconomics, the study of the choices that individuals and businesses make and the way these choices interact and are influenced by governments, and macroeconomics, the study of the aggregate effects on the national economy and the global economy of the choices that individuals, businesses, and governments make. Economics studies how choices wind up determining: *what* goods and services get produced?; *how* goods and services are produced?; and *for whom* goods and services are produced? Economics also studies when choices made in a person's self-interest also serve the social interest. For instance, do the self-interested choices made about globalization, the information age, climate change and social security also promote the social interest?

2 Explain the ideas that define the economic way of thinking.

The six ideas that are the core of the economic approach: a choice is a tradeoff; benefit is what you gain from something; cost is what you must give up to get something; people make rational choices by comparing benefits and costs; most choices are "how much" choices made at the margin; and choices respond to incentives. Choices are tradeoffs—giving up one thing to get another. The benefit from something is the gain or pleasure it brings. Benefit is measured by what someone is willing to give up to get something. The opportunity cost of something is the best thing that must be given up. A rational choice uses the available resources to most effectively meet the objective of the person making the choice. Making choices on the margin means comparing all the relevant alternatives systematically and incrementally to determine the best choice. The marginal cost is the opportunity cost of a one-unit increase in an activity; the marginal benefit is the gain from a one-unit increase in an activity. Rational choices compare the marginal benefit of an activity to its marginal cost and undertake the activity if the marginal benefit exceeds or equals the marginal cost. Statements about "what is" are positive statements; statements about "what ought to be" are normative statements. Economists are interested in positive statements about cause and effect so they develop economic models. Economists use natural experiments, statistical investigations, and economic experiments to test if their models are making correct predictions.

© 2015 Pearson Education, Inc.

YOUR AP TEST HINTS

AP Topics

Topic on your AP test	What to Know	Corresponding textbook section
What is economics?	The social science of choices made by societies facing unlimited and repeated wants with limited and scarce resources.	Checkpoint 1.1
What is the economic way of thinking?	Economists analyze choices, tradeoffs, benefits, and incentives, as well as government policies.	Checkpoint 1.2

AP Vocabulary Covered

Terms	What to Know	Text Section
Scarcity	Everything is scarce, all resources are limited	Checkpoint 1.1, p. 2
Choices	Selecting from available alternatives	Checkpoint 1.1, p. 2
Microeconomics	Choices that individual and businesses make	Checkpoint 1.1, p. 2
Macroeconomics	The study of the national and global economies	Checkpoint 1.1, p. 3
Goods and services	The objects and actions that satisfy wants	Checkpoint 1.1, p. 3
Self interest	What is best for each individual	Checkpoint 1.1, p. 4
Social interest	What is best for society as a whole	Checkpoint 1.1, p. 4
Globalization	The expansion of international trade	Checkpoint 1.1, p. 5
Government budget deficit	Annual expenditures greater than revenues	Checkpoint 1.1, p. 6
Government budget debt	The total of all prior deficits	Checkpoint 1.1, p. 6
Tradeoff	Giving up one thing to get another	Checkpoint 1.2, p. 8
Opportunity cost	What is given up when a tradeoff decision is made	Checkpoint 1.2, p. 8
Benefit	The gain of a decision measured by willingness	Checkpoint 1.2, p. 9
Rational choice	The best use of resources for achieving goals	Checkpoint 1.2, p. 9
Margin	Comparing choices for next decisions with benefits	Checkpoint 1.2, p. 10
Marginal cost	The opportunity cost of the next unit	Checkpoint 1.2, p. 10
Marginal benefit	The benefit of the next unit	Checkpoint 1.2, p. 10
Incentive	The reward or penalty of an action or decision	Checkpoint 1.2, p. 11
Economic model	Economic description of changes in economic facts	Checkpoint 1.2, p. 12
Normative statements	Statements of opinions and values	Checkpoint 1.2, p. 13
Positive statement	Statements of facts that can be tested	Checkpoint 1.2, p. 13

Extra AP material

- Economic structures have different ways to answer the "how," "what," and "for whom" questions. They can be classified as a "free market," "command," or "mixed" economies. A free market economy uses private ownership of capital (so that individuals own the business firms) and markets are left free of government regulations. A command economy answers the questions using public ownership of capital (so that the government owns the businesses) and government planners tell businesses what and how they will produce. A mixed economy uses both. Some mixed economies use more free market aspects and others use more command elements.

© 2015 Pearson Education, Inc.

CHECKPOINT 1.1

■ **Define economics and explain the kinds of questions that economist try to answer.**

Quick Review

- *Self-interest* The choices that people make that they think are the best for them.
- *Social interest* The choices that are best for society as a whole.

Additional Practice Problems 1.1

1. Which of the following headlines deals with *what, how,* and *for whom* questions?
   a. A new government program is designed to provide high-quality school lunches for children from poorer families.
   b. Intel researchers discover a new chip-making technology.
   c. Regis Hairstyling sets a record for hairstylings in month of July

2. Which of the following headlines concern social interest and self interest?
   a. A new government program is designed to provide high-quality school lunches for children from poorer families.
   b. Intel researchers discover a new chip-making technology.
   c. Regis Hairstyling sets a record for hairstylings in month of July.

Solutions to Additional Practice Problems 1.1

1a. "More lunches" is a *what* question and "for children from poorer families" is a *for whom* question.

1b. "New chip-making technology" is a *how* question because it deals with how computer chips will be manufactured.

1c. "Record for hairstylings" is a *what* question because it notes that a record number of hairstylings have taken place in July.

2a. The decision to implement a new government program is a decision that is most likely made in the social interest. The self-interest of the government bureaucrat who

made the decision might also be involved, particularly if the bureaucrat also will help manage the program.

2b. Intel's decision to research new chip-making technology is made in Intel's self-interest.

2c. Regis's decision to offer hairstylings is made in its self-interest as are the decisions of the people who had their hair styled by Regis.

■ **AP Self Test 1.1**

True or false

1. Faced with scarcity, we must make choices.

2. The question of *what* refers to what production method should a firm use?

3. The answers to the *what, how* and *for whom* questions depend on the interactions of the choices people, businesses, and governments make.

4. If Sam buys a pizza because she is hungry, her choice is made in the social interest.

5. Because everyone is a member of society, all choices made in self-interest are also in the social interest.

Multiple choice

1. The characteristic from which all economic problems arise is
   a. political decisions.
   b. providing a minimal standard of living for every person.
   c. how to make a profit.
   d. hunger.
   e. scarcity.

2. Scarcity results from the fact that
   a. people's wants exceed the resources available to satisfy them.
   b. not all goals are desirable.
   c. we cannot answer the major economic questions.
   d. choices made in self-interest are not always in the social interest.
   e. the population keeps growing.

© 2015 Pearson Education, Inc.

3. To economists, scarcity means that
   a. limited wants cannot be satisfied by the unlimited resources.
   b. a person looking for work is not able to find work.
   c. the number of people without jobs rises when economic times are bad.
   d. there can never be answers to the *what, how* or *for whom* questions.
   e. unlimited wants cannot be satisfied by the limited resources.

4. The question "Should we produce LCD televisions or computer monitors?" is an example of a ____ question.
   a. what
   b. how
   c. for whom
   d. where
   e. why

5. The question "Should we produce houses using bricks or wood?" is an example of a ____ question.
   a. what
   b. how
   c. for whom
   d. where
   e. why

6. The question "Should economics majors or sociology majors earn more after they graduate?" is an example of a ____ question.
   a. what
   b. how
   c. for whom
   d. where
   e. why

7. If a decision is made and it is the best choice for society, the decision is said to be
   a. a valid economic choice.
   b. made in self-interest.
   c. made in social interest.
   d. consistent with scarcity.
   e. a want-maximizing choice.

Short Response Questions

1. If there was no scarcity, would there be a need for economics?

2. What are the three major questions answered by people's economic choices?

Long Response Questions

1. Will there ever come a time without scarcity?

3. Why is the distinction between choices made in self-interest and choices made in social interest important?

Additional Exercises (also in MyEconLab Test A)

1. Every day, we make many choices. Why can't we avoid having to make choices?

2. Which of the following headlines deals with *what, how,* and *for whom* questions?
   a. "Major league baseball's turf keepers earn about $85,000, umpires earn about $350,000, and players make millions a year"
   b. "Many full-service gas stations are switching to self-serve"
   c. "Retail trends analysts make as much as $300,000 a year, while retail salespeople make less than $10 an hour"

3. Explain how the following headlines concern self-interest and social interest:
   a. "Former-president George W. Bush powers his Texas ranch with solar electricity"
   b. "Today's upper-class traveler goes on safari in southern Africa or stays at eco-resorts that cost $1,000 a night but do not have electricity"

CHECKPOINT 1.2

■ **Explain the ideas that define the economic way of thinking.**

Quick Review

- *Opportunity cost* The opportunity cost of something is the best thing you must give up to get it.

© 2015 Pearson Education, Inc.

- *Marginal cost* The opportunity cost from a one-unit increase in an activity.
- *Marginal benefit* The benefit that arises from a one-unit increase in an activity.
- *Rational choice* A choice that compares the marginal benefit and marginal cost of the activity and takes the action if the marginal benefit exceeds or equals the marginal cost.
- *Positive statement* A statement that tells what is currently believed about the way the world operates. Positive statements can be tested.
- *Normative statement* A statement that tells what ought to be. It depends on values and cannot be tested.

Additional Practice Problems 1.2

1. What are the opportunity costs of *using* this *Test Prep Guide*?

2. Kate usually plays tennis for two hours a week and her grade on each math test is usually 70 percent. Last week, after playing two hours of tennis, Kate thought long and hard about playing for another hour. She decided to play another hour of tennis and cut her study time by one additional hour. But the grade on last week's math test was 60 percent.

   a. What was Kate's opportunity cost of the third hour of tennis?

   b. Given that Kate made the decision to play the third hour of tennis, what can you conclude about the comparison of her marginal benefit and marginal cost of the second hour of tennis?

   c. Was Kate's decision to play the third hour of tennis rational?

3. Classify each of the following statements as positive or normative:

   a. There is too much poverty in the United States.

   b. An increase in the gas tax will cut pollution.

   c. Cuts to social security in the United States have been too deep.

Solutions to Additional Practice Problems 1.2

1. The opportunity cost is mainly the time spent using the *Test Prep Guide* because that time could be devoted to other activities. The best activity given up, be it studying for another class, or sleeping, or some other activity, which is lost because of the time spent using the *Test Prep Guide* is the opportunity cost. Once you have purchased this *Test Prep Guide*, its price is not an opportunity cost of *using* the *Test Prep Guide* because you have already paid the price.

2a. The opportunity cost of the third hour of tennis was the 10 percentage point drop on her math test grade because she cut her studying time by one hour to play an additional hour of tennis. If Kate had not played tennis for the third hour, she would have studied and her grade would not have dropped.

2b. Kate chose to play the third hour of tennis, so the marginal benefit of the third hour of tennis was greater than the marginal cost of the third hour. If the marginal benefit of the third hour of tennis was less than the marginal cost of the third hour, Kate would have chosen to study rather than play tennis.

2c. Even though her grade fell, Kate's choice used the available time to most effectively satisfy her wants because the marginal benefit of the third hour of playing tennis exceeded the marginal cost of the third hour. This was a choice made in her self-interest.

3a. A normative statement because it depends on the speaker's values and cannot be tested.

3b. A positive statement because it can be tested by increasing the gas tax and then measuring the change in pollution.

3c. A normative statement because it depends on the speaker's values (someone else might propose still deeper cuts) and cannot be tested.

© 2015 Pearson Education, Inc.

■ AP Self Test 1.2

True or false

1. Instead of attending his microeconomics class for two hours, Jim can play a game of tennis or watch a movie. For Jim the opportunity cost of attending class is forgoing the game of tennis *and* watching the movie.

2. Marginal cost is what you gain when you get one more unit of something.

3. A rational choice involves comparing the marginal benefit of an action to its marginal cost.

4. A change in marginal benefit or a change in marginal cost brings a change in the incentives that we face and leads us to change our actions.

5. The statement, "When more people volunteer in their communities, crime rates decrease" is a positive statement.

Multiple choice

1. Jamie has enough money to buy either a Mountain Dew, or a Pepsi, or a bag of chips. He chooses to buy the Mountain Dew. The opportunity cost of the Mountain Dew is
   a. the Pepsi and the bag of chips.
   b. the Pepsi or the bag of chips, whichever the best alternative given up.
   c. the Mountain Dew.
   d. the Pepsi because it is a drink, as is the Mountain Dew.
   e. zero because he enjoys the Mountain Dew.

2. The benefit of an activity is
   a. purely objective and measured in dollars.
   b. the gain or pleasure that it brings.
   c. the value of its opportunity cost.
   d. measured by what must be given up to get one more unit of the activity.
   e. not measurable on the margin.

3. The marginal benefit of an activity is
   i. the benefit from a one-unit increase in the activity.
   ii. the benefit of a small, unimportant activity.
   iii. measured by what the person is willing to give up to get one additional unit of the activity.
   a. i only.
   b. ii only.
   c. iii only.
   d. i and iii.
   e. ii and iii.

4. The cost of a one-unit increase in an activity
   a. is called the total one-unit cost.
   b. is called the marginal cost.
   c. decreases as more of the activity is done.
   d. is called the marginal benefit/cost.
   e. is called the unit cost.

5. If the marginal benefit of the next slice of pizza exceeds the marginal cost, you will
   a. eat the slice of pizza.
   b. not eat the slice of pizza.
   c. be unable to choose between eating or not eating.
   d. eat half the slice.
   e. More information is needed about how much the marginal benefit exceeds the marginal cost to determine if you will or will not eat the slice.

6. When people make rational choices, they
   a. behave selfishly.
   b. do not consider their emotions.
   c. weigh the costs and benefits of their options and act to satisfy their wants.
   d. necessarily make a decision in the social interest.
   e. are necessarily making the best decision.

7. A positive statement
   a. must always be right.
   b. cannot be tested.
   c. can be tested against the facts.
   d. depends on someone's value judgment.
   e. cannot be negative.

© 2015 Pearson Education, Inc.

Short Response Questions

1. What is benefit and how is it measured?

2. Identify each of the following as either a normative or a positive statement.

   a. The high temperature today was 15 degrees.

   b. It was too cold today.

   c. Government action is needed if the unemployment rate exceeds 6 percent.

   d. The government should decrease its tax on gasoline.

Long Response Questions

1. What is an opportunity cost?

2. You have $12 and can buy a pizza, a movie on a DVD, or a sketch pad for drawing. You decide to buy the pizza and think that if you hadn't been so hungry, you would have purchased the DVD. What is the opportunity cost of your pizza?

3. What is a marginal cost? A marginal benefit? How do they relate to rational choice?

4. Becky is writing an essay about the law that requires all passengers in a car to use a seat belt and its effectiveness. What might be a positive statement and a normative statement that she will include in her essay?

Additional Exercises (also in MyEconLab Test A)

1. Bill Gates has donated billions of dollars through the Bill and Melinda Gates Foundation to support universities, cancer research, a children's hospital, the Seattle Symphony, etc. Are his donations rational? In making these donations, might Bill Gates have responded to any incentive? Does he make his decision about his donations on the margin?

2. Tony is an engineering student, who is considering taking an extra course in history. What things might be part of his costs and benefits of the history course? Think of an incentive that might encourage him to take the course.

© 2015 Pearson Education, Inc.

SELF TEST ANSWERS

■ AP Self Test 1.1

True or false

1. True; page 2
2. False; page 3
3. True; page 4
4. False; page 4
5. False; page 5

Multiple choice

1. e; page 2
2. a; page 2
3. e; page 2
4. a; page 3
5. b; page 3
6. c; page 4
7. c; page 4

Short Response Questions

1. If there was no scarcity, then there likely would be no need for economics. Economics studies the choices that people make to cope with scarcity, so if there was no scarcity, then people's choices would not be limited by scarcity; page 2.

2. The questions are "*What* goods and services get produced and in what quantities?", "*How* are goods and services produced?", and "*For whom* are the goods and services produced?" pages 3-4.

Long Response Questions

1. There will never be a time without scarcity because human wants are unlimited. For instance, anyone daydreaming about what he or she wants can list a limitless number of goods and services. Clearly it is impossible for this person to ever attain all these wants. Similarly, it will be impossible for society to ever be able to meet everyone's wants. For instance, how many people want to ski on non-crowded, nicely groomed ski runs in Utah on a pleasant day? Because there are a limited number of nicely groomed ski runs in Utah, it is impossible for everyone who wants to ski there to do so much less to ski there on a non-crowded slope; page 2.

2. In general economists believe that people make choices according to their self-interest. These choices might or might not be in the social interest. Part of what economists study is when choices made in people's self-interest also further the social interest; page 5.

Additional Exercises (also in MyEconLab Test A)

1. The only way to avoid making choices is to either limit our wants or conjure up unlimited resources. Because neither is possible, we will always face choices; page 2.

2. a. The differences in incomes between turf keepers, umpires, and players is directly a *for whom* question. In addition, because it's likely that the consumption choices of the turf keepers, umpires, and players are different, there is also a *what* question involved; pages 3-4.

   b. The switch to self serve directly reflects a *how* question, that is, how will gasoline be delivered. In addition, because the switch means people previously employed at gas stations will be fired, there is a *for whom* question also involved; pages 3-4.

   c. The differences in incomes between retail trend analysts and retail salespeople is directly a *for whom* question. Because it's likely that the consumption choices of the analysts and salespeople are different, there is also a *what* question involved; pages 3-4.

3. a. Former-president Bush's decision to power his ranch with solar power is in his self interest because it affects what he pays for power; pages 4-5.

   b. The travelers' decisions are in their self interest. And, if they are also best for society, then they are in the social interest; pages 4-5.

© 2015 Pearson Education, Inc.

■ AP Self Test 1.2

True or false

1. False; page 9
2. False; page 10
3. True; page 11
4. True; page 11
5. True; page 13

Multiple choice

1. b; page 9
2. b; page 9
3. d; page 10
4. b; page 10
5. a; page 11
6. c; page 11
7. c; page 13

Short Response Questions

1. The benefit of something is the gain or pleasure that it brings. Economists measure the benefit of something by what a person is willing to give up to get it; pages 9-10.
2. a. Positive statement; page 13.
   b. Normative statement; page 13.
   c. Normative statement; page 13.
   d. Normative statement; page 13.

Long Response Questions

1. The opportunity cost of something is the best thing that must be given up. The opportunity cost is only the *single* best thing, not *all* the other things given up; page 9.
2. The opportunity cost of the pizza is the best thing given, which in this case is the DVD. The opportunity cost is *not* the DVD and the sketch pad because you would not have been able to purchase both of them with your $12; page 9.

3. Marginal cost is the cost of a one-unit increase in an activity. Marginal benefit is the benefit of a one-unit increase in an activity. A rational choice is made by comparing the marginal cost and marginal benefit, so that if the marginal benefit of an activity exceeds or equals the marginal cost, the activity is undertaken; pages 10-11.
4. A positive statement is "People who wear seat belts are involved in fewer road deaths." This statement can be tested. A normative statement is "People should be free to choose whether to wear a seat belt or not." This statement cannot be tested; page 13.

Additional Exercises (also in MyEconLab Test A)

1. As long as Mr. Gates compares the marginal benefits and marginal costs of his donations and made the best decision he could, his donations are the result of rational decisions. Mr. Gates perhaps responded to incentives when making these donations. For example, by making these donations, he reduced his taxable income. Mr. Gates made his decisions on the marginal as long as he compared all the alternatives available to him. For instance, he could consider giving more or less money to AIDs initiatives or more or less money to cancer research.
2. The costs of any extra course include the extra tuition as well as less time available for studying for other courses, for work, or for leisure. The benefits include increased knowledge of history. An incentive to taking the course might be the promise of a better job or perhaps the fact that he is required to take a history class as a general education requirement in order to graduate.

© 2015 Pearson Education, Inc.

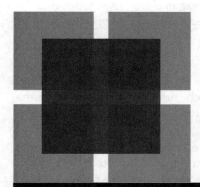

Chapter

1

Appendix: Making and Using Graphs

After you have completed the appendix, you will have thoroughly reviewed the graphs used in your economics course.

◼ Making and using graphs.

Graphs represent quantities as distances. The vertical axis is the *y*-axis and the horizontal axis is the *x*-axis. A scatter diagram plots a graph of one variable against the value of another variable. A time-series graph measures time along the *x*-axis and the variable (or variables) of interest along the *y*-axis. A cross-section graph shows the values of an economic variable for different groups in the population at a point in time. Graphs can show the relationship between two variables in an economic model. Variables that move in the same direction have a positive, or direct, relationship. Variables that move in the opposite direction have a negative, or inverse, relationship. Some relationships have minimum or maximum points. The slope of a relationship is the change in the value of the variable measured on the *y*-axis divided by the change in the value of the variable measured on the *x*-axis. Using the symbol "Δ" to mean "change in", the slope of a relationship equals $\Delta y \div \Delta x$. To graph a relationship among more than two variables, we use the *ceteris paribus* assumption and graph the relationship between two of the variables, holding the other variables constant.

YOUR AP TEST HINTS

AP Topics

Topic on your AP test	What to Know	Corresponding textbook section
Graphing	Axis labels used in economics, types of graphs used, direct and inverse relationships	Chapter 1, Appendix

AP Vocabulary Covered

Terms	What to Know	Text Section
y-axis	Vertical axis	Appendix, p. 21
x-axis	Horizontal axis	Appendix, p. 22
Scatter diagram	Two variables plotted on *y*-axis and *x*-axis	Appendix, p. 22
Time series graph	Variable plotted on *y*-axis, time plotted on *x*-axis	Appendix, p. 22
Cross section graph	Values of different population groups	Appendix, p. 22
Direct relationship	Variables that move in the same direction (positive relationship)	Appendix, p. 24
Inverse relationship	Variables that move in opposite directions (negative relationship)	Appendix, p. 24

© 2015 Pearson Education, Inc.

| Slope | Change in y-axis variable divided by change in x-axis variable | Appendix, p. 27 |
| *Ceteris paribus* | An assumption meaning "other things remaining the same" | Appendix, p. 28 |

Extra AP material

- Your AP test probably will not ask strictly mathematical questions such as in this appendix, but this material will be important in answering some of the questions. Be sure to understand changes of 10%, 20%, 25%, and 50% without the use of a calculator. Such numbers do show up in the Multiple Choice and Free Response questions and must be done quickly off the top of your head.

- *Macroeconomics* students will discover that there are fewer graphs that require specific numbers on the y-axis and x-axis. The main exception will be with multipliers, where specific numbers will be given on the exam. Be sure to check the notes for Chapter 29. Students will be required to create graphs on the Free Response questions, so learn the key macroeconomic graphs thoroughly.

- *Microeconomics* students will use actual numbers on the x-axis and y-axis more often. The chapter and checkpoints on elasticity will be important for micro topics. Be sure to check the notes for Chapter 5. Students will also be required to create graphs on the Free Response questions and should be prepared to use graphs to manipulate specific numeric changes in markets.

- As you'll soon see, the most fundamental graphs used in economics are supply and demand graphs. For these figures be sure to measure price along the y-axis and quantity along the x-axis.

CHECKPOINT 1

■ Making and using graphs.

Additional Practice Problems

1. You have data on the average monthly rainfall and the monthly expenditure on umbrellas in Seattle, Washington. What sort of graph would be the best to reveal if any relationship exists between these variables?

■ FIGURE A1.1

2. In Figure A1.1, draw a straight line showing a positive relationship and another straight line showing a negative relationship.

Year	Price (dollars per gallon)
1998	1.12
1999	1.22
2000	1.56
2001	1.53
2002	1.44
2003	1.64
2004	1.92
2005	2.34
2006	2.64
2007	2.85
2008	3.32

■ FIGURE A1.2

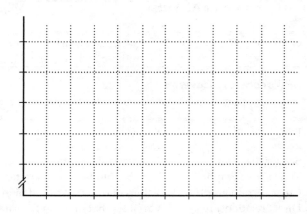

3. The table has the average price of a gallon of

© 2015 Pearson Education, Inc.

gasoline, including taxes, for eleven years. In Figure A1.2, measuring years along the horizontal axis, label the axes and then plot these data. What type of graph are you creating? What is the general trend of gas prices during this decade?

■ **FIGURE A1.3**

Price (dollars per paperback book)

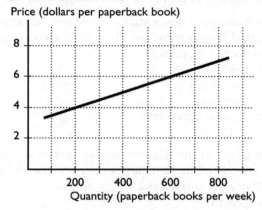

4. Figure A1.3 shows the relationship between the price of a paperback book and the quantity of paperback books a publisher is willing to sell. What is the slope of the line in Figure A1.3?

Solutions to Additional Practice Problems I

1. A scatter diagram would be the best graph to use. A scatter diagram would plot the monthly value of, say, rainfall along the vertical axis (the y-axis) and the monthly value of umbrella expenditure along the horizontal axis (the x-axis).

2. Figure A1.4 has two lines, one showing a positive relationship and the other showing a negative relationship. Your figure does not need to have identical lines. The key point your figure needs is that the line for the positive relationship slopes up as you move rightward along it and the line for the negative relationship slopes down as you move rightward along it.

3. Figure A1.5 labels the axes and plots the data in the table. The graph is a time-series graph. The trend is positive because gas prices generally increased during these years

■ **FIGURE A1.4**

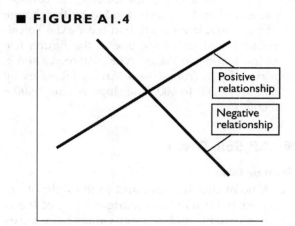

■ **FIGURE A1.5**

Price (dollars per gallon)

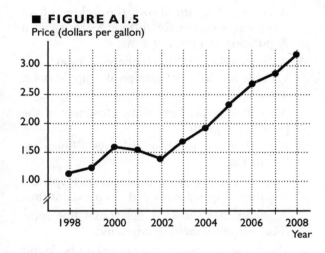

■ **FIGURE A1.6**

Price (dollars per paperback book)

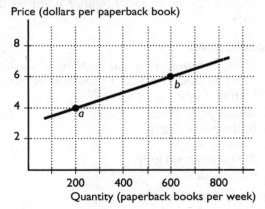

© 2015 Pearson Education, Inc.

4. The slope of a line is the change the variable measured on the y-axis divided by the change in the variable measured on the x-axis. To calculate the slope of the line in the figure, use points a and b in Figure A1.6. Between a and b, y rises by 2, from 4 to 6. And x increases by 400, from 200 to 600. The slope equals $2/400 = 0.005$.

■ AP Self Test I

True or false

1. A point that is above and to the right of another point will have a larger value of the x-axis variable and a larger value of the y-axis variable.

2. A scatter diagram shows the values of an economic variable for different groups in a population at a point in time.

3. A time-series graph compares values of a variable for different groups at a single point in time.

4. A trend is a measure of the closeness of the points on a graph.

5. A positive relationship is always a linear relationship.

6. A relationship that starts out sloping upward and then slopes downward has a maximum.

7. A graph that shows a horizontal line indicates variables that are unrelated.

8. The slope at a point on a curve can be found by calculating the slope of the line that touches the point and no other point on the curve.

Multiple choice

1. Demonstrating how an economic variable changes from one year to the next is best illustrated by a
   a. scatter diagram.
   b. time-series graph.
   c. linear graph.
   d. cross-section graph.
   e. trend-line.

2. To show the values of an economic variable for different groups in a population at a point in time, it is best to use a
   a. scatter diagram.
   b. time-series graph.
   c. linear graph.
   d. cross-section graph.
   e. trend diagram.

3. If whenever one variable increases, another variable also increases, then these two variables are ____ related.
   a. positively
   b. negatively
   c. inversely
   d. cross-sectionally
   e. not

4. A graph of the relationship between two variables is a line that slopes down to the right. These two variables are ____ related.
   a. positively
   b. directly
   c. negatively
   d. not
   e. trend-line

5. Two variables are unrelated if their graph is
   i.   a vertical line.
   ii. a 45 degree line.
   iii. a horizontal line.
   a. i only.
   b. ii only
   c. iii only
   d. i and iii.
   e. i, ii, and iii.

© 2015 Pearson Education, Inc.

■ FIGURE A1.7

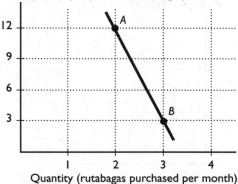

Price (dollars per pound of rutabagas)

Quantity (rutabagas purchased per month)

6. In figure A1.7, between points *A* and *B*, what is the slope of the line?

  a. 12
  b. 3
  c. 9
  d. –9
  e. 0

■ FIGURE A1.8

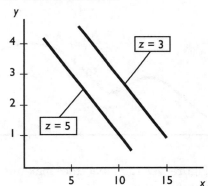

7. In Figure A1.8, an increase in z leads to a

  a. movement up along one of the lines showing the relationship between *x* and *y*.
  b. movement down along one of the lines showing the relationship between *x* and *y*.
  c. rightward shift of the line showing the relationship between *x* and *y*.
  d. leftward shift of the line showing the relationship between x and y.
  e. trend change in both *x* and *y*.

8. In Figure A1.8, *ceteris paribus*, an increase in *x* is associated with

  a. an increase in *y*.
  b. a decrease in *y*.
  c. an increase in z.
  d. a random change in z.
  e. no change in either *y* or z.

Short Response Questions

1. What are the three types of graphs?

Year	Workers (millions)
2004	8.7
2005	9.0
2006	9.2
2007	9.5
2008	9.6
2009	9.5
2010	9.3
2011	9.5
2012	9.8
2013	10.1

■ FIGURE A1.9

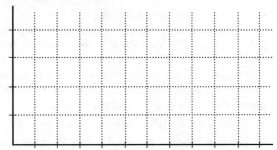

2. The table above gives the number of people working in restaurants and bars in the United States during 10 previous years. In Figure A1.9, measure time on the horizontal axis and the number of workers on the vertical axis, and then plot these data.

  a. What type of graph are you creating?
  b. Using your figure, what was the trend in the number of people working in restaurants and bars during these years?

© 2015 Pearson Education, Inc.

Year	Revenue (billions of dollars)	Workers (millions)
1999	285	7.9
2000	306	8.1
2001	318	8.3
2002	332	8.4
2003	350	8.5
2004	372	8.7
2005	393	9.0
2006	418	9.2
2007	438	9.5
2008	453	9.6

■ **FIGURE A1.10**

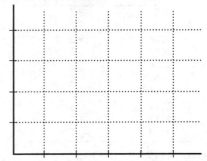

3. The table above gives the annual revenue for restaurants and bars and the number of people employed in restaurants and bars in the United States during 10 previous years. In Figure A1.10, measure the revenue along the horizontal axis and the number of workers along the vertical axis and plot the data.

   a. What type of graph are you creating?

   b. What relationship do you see in your figure between the revenue and the number of workers?

Price (dollars per sack of cat food)	Quantity (sacks of cat food per month)
1	10,000
2	8,000
3	7,000
4	4,000

4. The number of sacks of premium cat food that cat lovers will buy depends on the price of a sack of cat food. The relationship is given in the table above. In Figure A1.11, plot this relationship, putting price on the vertical

■ **FIGURE A1.11**

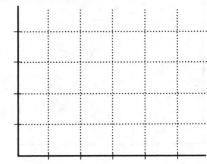

axis and the quantity on the horizontal axis

   a. If the price of a sack of cat food is $2, how many sacks will be purchased?

   b. If the price of a sack of cat food is $3, how many sacks will be purchased?

   c. Is the relationship between the price and the quantity positive or negative?

■ **FIGURE A1.12**

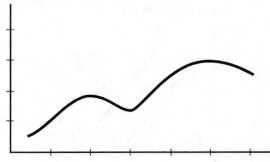

5. In Figure A1.12, label the maximum and minimum points.

6. In Figure A1.13 (on the next page), draw a line through point A with a slope of 2. Label the line "1." Draw another line through point A with a slope of –2. Label this line "2."

© 2015 Pearson Education, Inc.

■ **FIGURE A1.13**

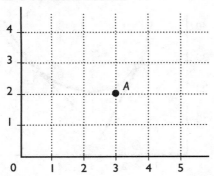

7. If two variables are positively related, will the slope of a graph of the two variables be positive or negative? If two variables are negatively related, will the slope of a graph of the two variables be positive or negative?

8. If a line slopes upward to the right, is its slope positive or negative? If a line slopes downward to the right, is its slope positive or negative?

x	y	z
1	4	0
2	3	2
3	1	6
4	0	8

■ **FIGURE A1.14**

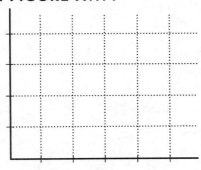

9. The table above contains data for three variables.

a. In Figure A1.14, put y on the vertical axis and x on the horizontal axis. Show the relationship between x and y. Is this relationship positive or negative?

b. What is the slope between $x = 2$ and $x = 3$?

c. In Figure A1.15, put z on the vertical axis and x on the horizontal axis. Show the relationship between x and z. Is this relationship positive or negative?

■ **FIGURE A1.15**

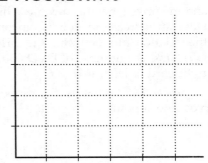

Price (dollars per DVD)	Quantity of DVDs purchased, low income	Quantity of DVDs purchased, high income
11	4	5
12	3	4
13	1	3
14	0	2

■ **FIGURE A1.16**

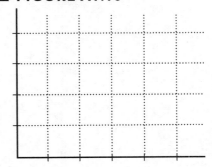

10. Bobby says that he buys fewer DVDs when the price of a DVD is higher. Bobby also says that he will buy more DVDs after he graduates and his income is higher. The table above shows the number of DVDs Bobby buys in a month at different prices when his income is low and when his income is high.

a. In Figure A1.16, put price on the vertical

© 2015 Pearson Education, Inc.

axis and the quantity purchased on the horizontal axis. Show the relationship between the number of DVDs purchased and the price when Bobby's income is low.

b. On the same figure, draw the relationship between the number of DVDs purchased and the price when his income is high.

c. Does an increase in Bobby's income shift the relationship between the price of a DVD and the number of DVDs purchased rightward or leftward?

11. In Figure A1.17, what is the slope of the curved line at point *A*? At point *B*?

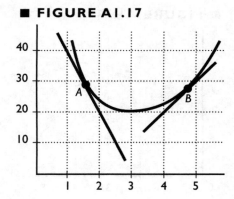

■ **FIGURE A1.17**

© 2015 Pearson Education, Inc.

SELF TEST ANSWERS

■ AP Self Test 1

True or false

1. True; page 21
2. False; page 22
3. False; page 22
4. False; page 22
5. False; page 24
6. True; page 26
7. True; page 26
8. True; page 27

Multiple choice

1. b; page 22
2. d; page 22
3. a; page 24
4. c; page 25
5. d; page 26
6. d; page 27
7. d; page 28
8. b; page 28

Short Response Questions

1. The three types of graphs are scatter diagram, time-series graph, and cross-section graph; page 22.

■ FIGURE A1.18

Workers (millions)

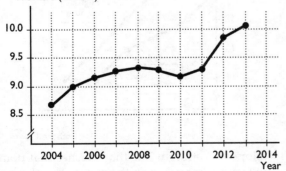

2. Figure A1.18 plots the data.
   a. This is a time-series graph; page 22.
   b. The trend is positive. During these 10 years there is an increase in the number of people working in restaurants and bars; page 22.

■ FIGURE A1.19

Workers (millions)

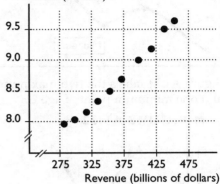

Revenue (billions of dollars)

3. Figure A1.19 plots the data.
   a. The figure is a scatter diagram; page 22.
   b. The relationship between the revenue and the number of workers is positive; page 24.

■ FIGURE A1.20

Price (dollars per sack)

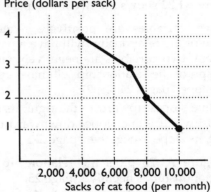

Sacks of cat food (per month)

4. Figure A1.20 plots the relationship.
   a. If the price is $2 per sack, 8,000 sacks are purchased; page 21.
   b. If the price is $3 per sack, 7,000 sacks are purchased; page 21.
   c. The relationship between the price and quantity of sacks is negative; page 25.

© 2015 Pearson Education, Inc.

■ **FIGURE A1.21**

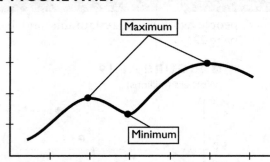

5. Figure A1.21 labels the two maximum points and one minimum point; page 26.

■ **FIGURE A1.22**

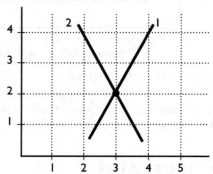

6. Figure A1.22 shows the two lines; page 27.

7. If two variables are positively related, a graph of the relationship will have a positive slope. If two variables are negatively related, a graph of the relationship will have a negative slope; pages 24, 25, 27.

8. If a line slopes upward to the right, its slope is positive. If a line slopes downward to the right, its slope is negative; page 27.

9. a. Figure A1.23 plots the relationship. The relationship is negative; page 25.
   b. The slope equals $(3 - 1) \div (2 - 3)$, which is -2; page 27.
   c. Figure A1.24 plots the relationship. The relationship is positive; page 24.

10. a. Figure A1.25 plots the relationship; page 28.
    b. Figure A1.25 plots the relationship; page 28.
    c. An increase in Bobby's income shifts the relationship rightward; page 28.

11. The slope of a curved line at a point equals the

■ **FIGURE A1.23**

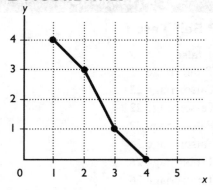

■ **FIGURE A1.24**

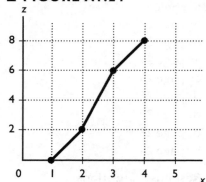

■ **FIGURE A1.25**

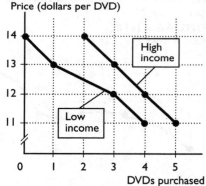

slope of a straight line that touches that point and no other point on the curve. The slope of the curved line at point *A* is -20 and the slope of the curved line at point *B* is 10; page 27.

© 2015 Pearson Education, Inc.

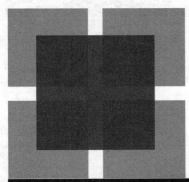

The U.S. and Global Economies

Chapter 2

Chapter 2 introduces the circular flow model which shows how goods and services and expenditures flow from and to households, firms, the government, and the rest of the world.

1 Describe what, how, and for whom goods and services are produced in the United States.

The production of goods and services, the "what" question, is divided into two broad categories: consumption goods and services, and capital goods. Consumption goods and services are bought by individuals and governments and used in the current period. Capital goods are bought by businesses and government to use over future periods to produce other goods and services. The "how" of production involves the factors of production: land, labor, capital, and entrepreneurship. Goods and services are sold to those who have income, so the personal distribution of income is one way of showing who ends up with our national output. The functional distribution of income shows how much is paid to the owners of each type of productive resource. The largest share of national income is wages, so workers get the largest share of our nation's goods and services.

2 Describe what, how, and for whom goods and services are produced in the global economy.

Countries are divided into advanced economies (the richest 29 countries) and emerging market and developing economies. The advanced economies produce 50 percent of the world's total output, with 19 percent produced in the United States. China produces 15 percent of world output. The advanced economies have more human capital and physical capital than the developing countries. In the world, the lowest-paid 20 percent of the population receives 2 percent of world income and the highest-paid 20 percent receives 70 percent of world income. Inequality of incomes across the entire world has decreased during the past twenty years, primarily because incomes in China have grown rapidly

3 Explain the circular flow model of the U.S. economy and the global economy.

Markets are any arrangement that brings buyers and sellers together to do business with each other. The circular flow model shows that households provide the services from the factors of production, and firms hire these services in factor markets. The circular flow also shows that households purchase goods and services and firms sell goods and services in goods markets. In the circular flow, the government purchases goods and services in goods markets. It makes transfers to firms and households and also taxes them. The decisions made by households and firms in these markets determine the answers to the "what," "how," and "for whom" questions. Households and firms in the United States buy goods and services from firms in other countries (U.S. imports) and U.S. firms sell goods and services to households and firms in other countries (U.S. exports). Using financial inflows, we borrow from other countries (when the value of imports exceeds that of exports) and using financial outflows, we lend to other countries (when the value of exports exceeds that of imports).

© 2015 Pearson Education, Inc.

YOUR AP TEST HINTS

AP Topics

Topic on your AP test	What to Know	Corresponding textbook section
Goods and services U.S.	What, how, and for whom production occurs	Checkpoint 2.1
Goods and services Global	What, how, and for whom production occurs	Checkpoint 2.2
Circular flow model	Households, firms, flow of factors of production, flow of goods and services in the U.S. and the global markets	Checkpoint 2.3

AP Vocabulary Covered

Terms	What to Know	Text Sections
Consumption goods and services	Items that individuals and governments use up in the immediate time frame	Checkpoint 2.1, p. 32
Capital goods	Materials used by businesses to create productive resources for future goods and services	Checkpoint 2.1, p. 32
Factors of production	Land, labor, capital, and entrepreneurship	Checkpoint 2.1, p. 34
Land	Any resource from nature	Checkpoint 2.1, p. 34
Labor	Human effort to produce goods and services	Checkpoint 2.1, p. 35
Human capital	Knowledge and skills possessed by people	Checkpoint 2.1, p. 35
Capital	Tools, instruments, machines, buildings, etc.	Checkpoint 2.1, p. 35
Financial capital	Money, stocks, bonds for financial resources	Checkpoint 2.1, p. 35
Entrepreneurship	Human resource that organizes businesses	Checkpoint 2.1, p. 36
Rent	Income paid for the use of land	Checkpoint 2.1, p. 37
Wages	Income paid for the use of labor	Checkpoint 2.1, p. 37
Interest	Income paid for the use of capital	Checkpoint 2.1, p. 37
Profit (or loss)	Income earned by entrepreneurs	Checkpoint 2.1, p. 37
Advanced economies	Wealthiest 29 countries	Checkpoint 2.2, p. 39
Emerging markets	28 Central, Eastern European, and Asian countries	Checkpoint 2.2, p. 39
Developing markets	119 Asian, African, and other region's countries	Checkpoint 2.2, p. 39
BRICS	Brazil, Russia, India, China, South Africa	Checkpoint 2.2, p. 39
Households (in the U.S.)	Individuals who own the factors of production	Checkpoint 2.3, p. 46
Firms	Institutions that organize production	Checkpoint 2.3, p. 46
Market	An arrangement where buyers meet sellers	Checkpoint 2.3, p. 46
Goods markets	Buying and selling goods and services	Checkpoint 2.3, p. 46
Factor markets	Buying and selling services of factors of production	Checkpoint 2.3, p. 46

Extra AP material

- The AP test will refer to different "types" of economic activities. The *private economy* refers to individual and business decisions of households and firms. The *public economy* refers to the actions of the government being added to the analysis. A *closed economy* refers to the domestic economy of a specific country because the economy is "closed" to trade. An *open economy* adds the effects of international trade to the closed economy.

© 2015 Pearson Education, Inc.

CHECKPOINT 2.1

■ **Describe what, how, and for whom goods and services are produced in the United States.**

Quick Review

- *Consumption goods and services* Goods and services that are bought by individuals and the government and used in the current period.
- *Capital goods* Goods that are bought by businesses to increase their productive resources and to use over future periods to produce other goods and services.

Additional Practice Problems 2.1

1. Tell whether the following goods and services are consumption goods and services or capital goods.
   a. A taco at Taco Bell purchased for lunch by Shaniq.
   b. A new grill purchased by Taco Bell.
   c. A tour down the Colorado river from Rimrock Adventures purchased by the Miller family.
   d. CamelBak drinking packs purchased by the U.S. Marine Corp.
   e. CamelBak drinking packs purchased by Rimrock Adventures for use by their customers during tours.
   f. A CamelBak drinking pack purchased by Anne for use while mountain biking.
   g. A smart phone tablet purchased by Sebastian so he can always keep in touch with his friends' Facebook posts.

2. How much labor is there in the United States? What determines the quantity of labor?

Solutions to Additional Practice Problems 2.1

1a. Shaniq's taco is a consumption good.
1b. The new grill is a capital good.
1c. The tour is a consumption service.
1d. The drinking pack purchased by the Marines is a consumption good because it is purchased by the government.

1e. The drinking pack purchased by Rimrock Adventures is a capital good because it is purchased by a business.
1f. The drinking pack purchased by Anne is a consumption good.
1g. The smart phone pack purchased by Sebastian is a consumption good.

2. In the United States, in 2013 about 155 million people had jobs or were available for work and they provided about 275 billion hours of labor a year. The quantity of labor depends on the size of the population, the percentage of the population that takes jobs, and on social relationships that influence things such as how many women take paid work. An increase in the proportion of women who have taken paid work has increased the quantity of labor in the United States over the past 50 years.

■ **AP Self Test 2.1**

True or false

1. Consumption goods and services include a slice of pizza purchased to eat at home.
2. A gold mine is included in the "land" category of productive resources.
3. Michael Dell, the person who founded and manages Dell computers, is an example of an entrepreneur.
4. In the United States, the factor of production that earns the most income is labor.
5. In the United States, the richest 20 percent of individuals earn approximately 30 percent of total income.

Multiple choice

1. When the total U.S. production of goods and services is divided into consumption goods and services, and capital goods,
   a. by far the largest component is consumption goods and services.
   b. by far the largest component is capital goods.
   c. the quantities of the two groups are almost exactly equal.
   d. the quantities are not comparable.
   e. None of the above are correct.

© 2015 Pearson Education, Inc.

2. An example of a capital good is
   a. a fiber optic cable TV system.
   b. an insurance policy.
   c. a hair cut.
   d. an iPod.
   e. a slice of pizza.

3. The quantity of health services produced in the United States is
   a. about equal to the quantity of produce produced by the nation's farms.
   b. second in size to only education.
   c. considered a capital good because it helps restore and retain people's human capital.
   d. the largest component of production.
   e. None of the above are correct.

4. Which of the following correctly lists the factors of production?
   a. machines, buildings, land, and money
   b. hardware, software, land, and money
   c. capital, money, and labor
   d. owners, workers, and consumers.
   e. land, labor, capital, and entrepreneurship

5. Human capital is
   a. solely the innate ability we are born with.
   b. the money humans have saved.
   c. the knowledge people accumulate through education and experience.
   d. machinery that needs human supervision.
   e. any type of machinery.

6. Wages are paid to _____ and interest is paid to _____.
   a. entrepreneurs; capital
   b. labor; capital
   c. labor; land
   d. entrepreneurs; land
   e. labor; entrepreneurs

7. Dividing the nation's income among the factors of production, the largest percentage is paid to
   a. labor.
   b. land.
   c. capital.
   d. entrepreneurship.
   e. labor and capital, with each receiving about 41 percent of the total income.

8. The personal distribution of income shows
   a. that labor earn the largest percentage of total income.
   b. how profit accounts for the largest fraction of total income.
   c. that the richest 20 percent of households earn 23 percent of total income.
   d. that interest accounts for most of the income of the richest 20 percent of households.
   e. that the poorest 20 percent of households earn 3 percent of total income.

Short Response Questions

1. Is an automobile a consumption good or a capital good?

2. Compare the incomes received by the poorest and richest 20 percent of individuals.

Additional Exercises (also in MyEconLab Test A)

1. What is the distinction between consumption goods and services and capital goods? Which one of them brings an increase in productive resources?

2. If everyone in the United States were to consume an equal quantity of goods and services, what percentage of total income would the poorest 20 percent of households have to receive from higher-income groups?

3. Compare the percentage of total U.S. income that labor earns to the percentage earned by all the other factors of production combined.

CHECKPOINT 2.2

■ **Describe what, how, and for whom goods and services are produced in the global economy.**

Quick Review

- *Advanced economies* The 29 countries (or areas) that have the highest living standards.

- *Emerging markets and Developing economies* Emerging markets are the 28 countries in Europe and Asia that were until the early 1990s part of the Soviet Union or its satellites and are changing the way

© 2015 Pearson Education, Inc.

they organize their economies. Developing economies are the 119 countries in Africa, the Middle East, Europe, and Central and South America that have not yet achieved a high standard of living for their people.

Additional Practice Problems 2.2

1. What percentage of the world's population live in developing economies? In places such as China, India, and Africa, what was the average income per day?

2. What percentage of the world's population live in advanced economies? In the United States what is the average income per day?

3. Which BRICS country has the highest average income per person?

4. How does the total production within the advanced economies, the BRICS nations, and the emerging and developing economies compare?

5. How is it possible that income inequality within most countries has increased in recent years yet income inequality across the whole world has decreased in recent years?

Solutions to Additional Practice Problems 2.2

1. The world's population is about 7 billion. More than 5 billion of the people live in developing economies. So, approximately 80 percent of the world's population lives in developing economies. Average daily income in China is $25, in India is $10, and in Africa is $7. Because these are the average, many people live on less than these amounts.

2. About 1 billion people, or 15 percent of the world's population live in the 28 advanced economies. The average income per day in the United States was $137.

3. Russia's average income per person is the highest.

4. Of the world's total production, the advanced economies produce 50 percent (19 percent is produced in the United States). The BRICS economies produce 28 percent of the world's production, and the emerging and developing economies produce the remainder, 22 percent.

5. While income inequality within nations has been increasing, the difference in incomes among different nations has been decreasing. In particular, China has seen extremely rapid growth in income. The growth in income for this poor but populous nation has decreased income inequality in the world as a whole.

■ AP Self Test 2.2

True or false

1. About 50 percent of the world's population lives in the advanced economies.

2. Mexico is classified as an emerging market economy.

3. Taken as a group, the 119 developing economy nations produce a larger percentage of total world production than do the 29 advanced economy nations.

4. Most of the world's electricity is generated by coal.

5. Workers in the advanced economies have much more human capital than workers in the developing economies.

6. Income inequality within most nations has increased over the past years.

Multiple choice

1. The world population is approximately ____ people.
   a. 7 million
   b. 2 trillion
   c. 7 billion
   d. 1.4 trillion
   e. 70 million

2. The percentage of the world's population that lives in the advanced economies is
   a. more than 71 percent.
   b. between 51 percent and 70 percent.
   c. between 31 percent and 50 percent.
   d. between 20 percent and 30 percent.
   e. less than 20 percent.

© 2015 Pearson Education, Inc.

3. Which of following groups of countries are *all* advanced economies?
   a. Australia, Brazil, and the United States
   b. Hong Kong, Japan, France, and the United Kingdom
   c. Italy, the United States, China, and Russia
   d. Singapore, Russia, France, and Chad
   e. Mexico, Canada, Germany, and Egypt

4. The emerging market economies are
   a. the largest grouping including the nations of China and India.
   b. in transition from state-owned production to free markets.
   c. most of the nations of Western Europe.
   d. the nations that are currently agricultural in nature.
   e. the nations with the highest standards of living.

5. Production in the advanced economies is about ____ percent of total world production and in the emerging market and developing economies is about ____ percent of total world production.
   a. 50; 39
   b. 23; 62
   c. 50; 22
   d. 30; 46
   e. 20; 73

6. Compared to the developing economies, the advanced economies have ____ human capital and ____ physical capital.
   a. more; more
   b. more; less
   c. the same; the same
   d. less; more
   e. less; less

7. In the advanced economies, ____ of the factories use advanced capital equipment and in the developing economies ____ of the factories use advanced capital equipment.
   a. virtually all; virtually all
   b. some; some
   c. virtually all; none
   d. some; none of
   e. virtually all; some

8. Among the United States, China, Russia, India, and Brazil, the country with the highest average income per person is
   a. the United States.
   b. Russia.
   c. India.
   d. China.
   e. Brazil.

Long Response Questions

1. What are the groups the International Monetary Fund uses to classify countries? Describe each group. Which group has the largest number of countries? The largest number of people?

2. As a fraction of total world production, how does production within the advanced economies compare to production within the emerging market and developing economies? As a fraction of total population, how does the population within the advanced economies compare to the population within the emerging market and developing economies?

3. How does the amount of human capital in the advanced economies compare to that in the developing economies?

4. How does the distribution of income within the United States compare to the distribution of income in the world economy?

Additional Exercises (also in MyEconLab Test A)

1. Describe how inequality around the world has changed over the past few decades.

CHECKPOINT 2.3

■ **Explain the circular flow model of the U.S. economy and the global economy.**

Quick Review

- *Circular flow model* A model of the economy, illustrated in Figure 2.1, that shows the circular flow of expenditures and incomes that result from firms', households', and governments' choices.

© 2015 Pearson Education, Inc.

■ FIGURE 2.1

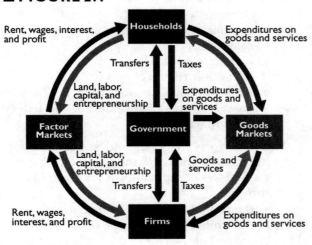

Additional Practice Problems 2.3

1. Describe where the following money flows fit in the circular flow.
   a. Shaniq pays for a taco at Taco Bell.
   b. Sam receives his monthly Social Security payment.
   c. Jennifer gets a $10,000 end of the year bonus from Bank of America, where she works.
   d. Exxon pays landowners in Texas $20,000 for the oil under their land.
   e. Bill pays property tax of $6,000.

2. In the circular flow, what is the relationship between the flow of expenditures into the goods markets (from households and the government) and the flow of revenues out of the goods markets to firms?

Solutions to Additional Practice Problems 2.3

1a. Shaniq's payment is an expenditure on a good that flows from households through the goods market to Taco Bell, a firm.

1b. Sam's check is a transfer payment from the government to households.

1c. Jennifer's payment is wages flowing from a firm, Bank of America, through the factor market to households.

1d. Exxon's payment is rent flowing from a firm, Exxon, through the factor market to households.

1e. Bill's payment is a tax flowing from households to government.

2. The flow of expenditures into the goods markets–the funds that households and the government spend on the goods and services they purchase–equals the flow of revenue out of the goods markets.

■ AP Self Test 2.3

True or false

1. Firms own the factors of production.

2. A market is any arrangement where buyers and sellers meet face-to-face.

3. Factors of production flow from households to firms through goods markets.

4. Rent, wages, interest, and profit are the payments made by firms to households through factor markets.

5. Social security payments are made by state and local governments.

6. Because government impose only taxes, in the circular flow their actions do not affect the goods market.

Multiple choice

1. Within the circular flow model, economists define households as
   a. families with at least 2 children.
   b. families living in their own houses.
   c. individuals or groups living together.
   d. married or engaged couples.
   e. individuals or groups within the same legally defined family.

2. A market is defined as
   a. the physical place where goods (but not services) are sold.
   b. the physical place where goods *and* services are sold.
   c. any arrangement that brings buyers and sellers together.
   d. a place where money is exchanged for goods.
   e. another name for a store.

© 2015 Pearson Education, Inc.

3. In the circular flow model,
   a. only firms sell in markets.
   b. only households buy from markets.
   c. some firms only sell and some firms only buy.
   d. the money used to buy goods and the goods themselves travel in the same direction.
   e. both firms and households buy or sell in different markets.

4. ____ choose the quantities of goods and services to produce, while ____ choose the quantities of goods and services to buy.
   a. Households; firms
   b. Firms; households and the government
   c. The government; firms
   d. Firms; only households
   e. Households; the government

5. A circular flow model shows the interrelationship between the ____ market and the ____ markets.
   a. household; goods
   b. household; factor
   c. business; household
   d. expenditure; income
   e. goods; factor

6. In the circular flow model, the expenditures on goods and services flow in the
   a. same direction as goods and services in all cases.
   b. same direction as goods and services *only if* they both flow through the goods market.
   c. same direction as goods and services *only if* they both flow through the factor market.
   d. opposite direction as goods and services.
   e. same direction as factor markets.

7. Of the following, which is *not* a source of revenue for the federal government?
   a. personal income taxes.
   b. sales taxes.
   c. corporate income taxes.
   d. Social Security taxes.
   e. None of the above are correct; that is, they are *all* sources of revenue for the federal government.

8. U.S. exports of goods and services flow to households and firms in ____ and U.S. financial inflows of capital flow to households and firms in ____.
   a. the United States; the United States
   b. the United States; the rest of the world
   c. the rest of the world; the United States
   d. the rest of the world; the rest of the world
   e. the United States; the rest of the world and the United States

Short Response Questions

1. The circular flow reveals that which two groups interact to determine what will be the payments to the factors of production?

2. In the circular flow model, what are the sources of expenditures on goods and services?

3. In recent years, which spent more: the federal government or state and local governments?

Long Response Questions

■ **FIGURE 2.2**

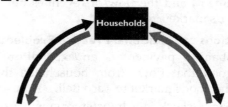

1. Figure 2.2 ignores the government and shows the flows into and out of households. Label the flows and identify who they come from and who they go to.

© 2015 Pearson Education, Inc.

■ FIGURE 2.3

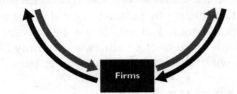

2. Figure 2.3 ignores the government and shows the flows into and out of firms. Label the flows and identify who they come from and who they go to.

■ FIGURE 2.4

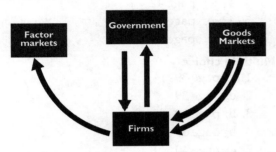

3. Figure 2.4 now includes the government and shows the money flows into and out of firms. Label the money flows.

4. Ignoring taxes and transfer payments, what funds flow into firms and what funds flow out of them?

5. Is it possible for something to affect households and not firms? To affect firms and not households? Explain your answers.

Additional Exercises (also in MyEconLab Test A)

1. What are the choices made by households and firms that determine what, how, and for whom goods and services are produced? Where, in the circular flow model, do those choices appear?

2. How do the actions of governments modify what, how, and for whom goods and services are produced? Where, in the circular flow model, do those choices appear?

© 2015 Pearson Education, Inc.

SELF TEST ANSWERS

■ AP Self Test 2.1

True or false
1. True; page 32
2. True; page 34
3. True; page 36
4. True; page 37
5. False; page 37

Multiple choice
1. a; page 32
2. a; page 32
3. d; pages 32, 33
4. e; page 34
5. c; page 35
6. b; page 37
7. a; page 37
8. e; page 37

Short Response Questions
1. An automobile might be either a consumption or a capital good. It is a consumption good if it is purchased by a household. It is a capital good if it is purchased by a business for use within the business; page 32.
2. The richest 20 percent of households earn 51 percent of the total U.S. income. The poorest 20 percent of households earn 3 percent of the total U.S. income; page 37.

Additional Exercises (also in MyEconLab Test A)
1. Consumption goods and services are items that are bought by individuals and governments and used in the current period. Capital goods are goods that are bought by businesses to increase their productive resources and thereby help produce additional goods and services. Capital goods increase the nation's capital, which is a productive resource; page 32.
2. If everyone were to consume an equal quantity of goods and services, the poorest 20 percent of individuals would need to receive about 17 percent of total income from the higher-income groups; page 37.

3. Labor earns by far the largest share of the nation's total income, about 69 percent. The other factors of production earn only 31 percent of the nation's total income; page 37.

■ AP Self Test 2.2

True or false
1. False; page 39
2. False; page 39
3. False; page 40
4. True; page 42
5. True; page 42
6. True; page 44

Multiple choice
1. c; page 39
2. e; page 39
3. b; page 39
4. b; page 39
5. c; page 40
6. a; pages 42-43
7. e; page 43
8. a; pages 43-44

Long Response Questions
1. The groups are the advanced economies and the emerging market and developing economies. Advanced economies have the highest standard of living. Emerging market and developing economies have yet to achieve a high standard of living. The emerging market economies are changing their economies from government management and state-ownership of capital to market-based economies similar to that in the United States. There are more nations, 119, and more people, almost 5 billion, in developing economies; page 39.
2. Production in the advanced economies accounts for 50 percent of world production and production in the emerging market and developing economies accounts for 22 percent. (The remainder is produced in the BRICS economies.) The population within

© 2015 Pearson Education, Inc.

the advanced economies accounts for 15 percent of the world's population and the emerging market and developing economies account for 43 percent of the world's population; page 40.

3. The human capital possessed by workers in the advanced economies is *much* larger than that in the developing economies. People in the advanced economies have vastly more education, more on-the-job training and, in general, better health than in the developing economies; page 42.

4. The distribution of income within the United States is more equal than the distribution of income in the world economy. In the United States, the poorest 20 percent of households receive about 3 percent of the total income and the richest 20 percent of households receive about 50 percent of total income. In the world economy, the poorest 20 percent of households receive about 2 percent of total income and the richest 20 percent receive about 70 percent of total income; page 43.

Additional Exercises (also in MyEconLab Test A)

1. Inequality around the world has decreased over the past few decades. Extreme poverty has fallen, largely because of income growth in China, the largest nation in the world and a nation that was the source of much of the extreme poverty of a few decades ago; page 44.

■ AP Self Test 2.3

True or false

1. False; page 46
2. False; page 46
3. False; pages 46-47
4. True; pages 46-47
5. False; page 48
6. False; page 49

Multiple choice

1. c; page 46
2. c; page 46
3. e; pages 46-47

4. b; pages 47, 49
5. e; pages 46-47
6. d; page 47
7. b; page 48
8. c; page 51

Short Response Questions

1. Payments to the factors of production are determined by the interaction of households, who own and provide the services from the factors of production, and firms, who employ the services from these factors; page 47.

2. The circular flow identifies two sources of expenditures on goods and services: expenditures by households and expenditures by the government; page 49.

3. In 2012, the federal government spent $3 trillion and in 2012 state and local governments spent $2.2 trillion. The federal government spends significantly more than state and local governments; page 48.

Long Response Questions

■ FIGURE 2.5

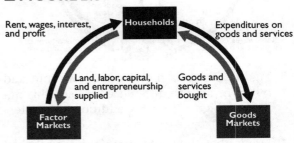

1. Figure 2.5 labels the flows. Rent, wages, interest, and profits (or losses) flow from the factor markets while the services from land, labor, capital, and entrepreneurship flow to the factor markets. In addition, expenditures on goods and services flow to the goods market, and goods and services flow from the goods market; page 47.

© 2015 Pearson Education, Inc.

■ FIGURE 2.6

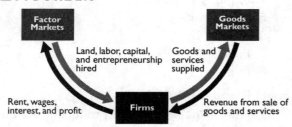

2. Figure 2.6 labels the flows. Revenue from the sale of goods and services, which are the expenditures on goods and services, flow to firms from the goods market and payments of rent, wages, interest, and profit (or loss) flow from firms into the factor market. The services from land, labor, capital, and entrepreneurship flow to firms from the factor markets, and goods and services flow from firms into the goods markets; page 47.

■ FIGURE 2.7

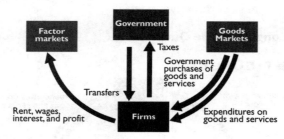

3. Figure 2.7 labels the money flows into and out of firms. The difference between this figure and Figure 2.6 is the addition of transfers and taxes; page 49.

4. Funds that flow into firms are households' expenditures and government expenditures on goods and services. Funds that flow out of firms are payments for rent, wages, interest, and profit (or loss) to households in exchange for the factors of production; pages 47, 49.

5. The circular flow shows that at the macroeconomic level it is impossible for something to influence only firms or only households. An influence that changes households' buying behavior in goods markets affects firms because they sell to households in goods markets; page 47.

Additional Exercises (also in MyEconLab Test A)

1. Households choose the quantities of land, labor, capital, and entrepreneurship services to provide to firms. Households decide what goods and services they will buy. Firms choose the quantities of services of the factors of production to hire and the quantities of goods and services to produce. Households decide what to buy in goods markets and what quantities of the services of factors of production to provide in factor markets. Firms decide the quantities of services of factors of production to hire in factor markets and the quantity of goods and services to produce in goods markets; pages 46-47.

2. Governments modify the answers to the "what," "how," and "for whom" questions by their interactions with firms and households. In the goods market, governments decide what goods to buy, thereby affecting the "what" question. Governments also tax firms and households and give firms and households transfer payments. These directly effect the "for whom" question because taxes decrease the payer's ability to buy goods and services while transfers enhance the recipient's buying power. The taxes and transfer payments also affect households' and firms' decisions about what services of the factors of production to provide and what services to buy, so these taxes and transfer payments also affect the "how" question; page 49.

© 2015 Pearson Education, Inc.

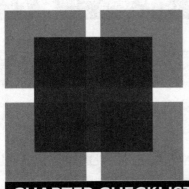

Chapter

3

The Economic Problem

Chapter 3 develops an economic model, the production possibilities frontier, or *PPF*, model. The *PPF* shows how the opportunity cost of a good or service increases as more of the good or service is produced. It can be used to illustrate economic growth and to demonstrate societies and individuals gain by specializing according to comparative advantage.

1 Explain and illustrate the concepts of scarcity, production efficiency, and tradeoff using the production possibilities frontier.

The production possibilities frontier, *PPF*, is the boundary between the combinations of goods and services that can be produced and those that cannot be produced, given the available factors of production and technology. Production points outside the *PPF* are unattainable. Points on and inside the *PPF* are attainable. Production points on the *PPF* are production efficient while production points within the *PPF* are inefficient. Moving along the *PPF* producing more of one good, less of another good is produced—a tradeoff. Moving from inside the *PPF* to a point on the *PPF*, more of some goods and services can be produced without producing less of others—a free lunch.

2 Calculate opportunity cost.

Along the *PPF* all choices involve a tradeoff. Along the *PPF*, the opportunity cost of the good on the *x*-axis is the loss of the good measured along the *y*-axis and is equal to the decrease in the good on the *y*-axis divided by the increase in the good on the *x*-axis. As more of a good is produced, its opportunity cost increases, so the *PPF* is bowed outward. The opportunity cost increases because resources are not equally productive in all activities. In the real world, most activities have increasing opportunity cost.

3 Explain what makes production possibilities expand.

Economic growth is the sustained expansion of production possibilities. If more capital is accumulated production possibilities increase and the *PPF* shifts outward. The (opportunity) cost of economic growth is that resources used to increase capital cannot be used to produce current consumption goods and services.

4 Explain how people gain from specialization and trade.

A person (or nation) has an absolute advantage when the person (or nation) is more productive than another—needs fewer inputs or less time to produce the good. A person (or nation) has a comparative advantage in an activity or producing a good if the person (or nation) can perform the activity or produce the good at lower opportunity cost than another. A person (or nation) can have an absolute advantage in all activities but cannot have a comparative advantage in all activities. People can gain from specializing in production according to comparative advantage and then trading with others. In this situation people (and nations) can consume combinations of goods and services that lie beyond their production possibilities frontiers.

© 2015 Pearson Education, Inc.

YOUR AP TEST HINTS

AP Topics

Topic on your AP test	What to Know	Corresponding textbook section
Production possibilities frontier (*PPF*)	Scarcity, efficiency, tradeoffs being graphed	Checkpoint 3.1
Opportunity costs	How to calculate these concepts	Checkpoint 3.2
Expanding PPFs	What can expand production possibilities	Checkpoint 3.3
Trade specialization	Comparative advantages and gaining from trade	Checkpoint 3.4

AP Vocabulary Covered

Terms	What to Know	Text Sections
Production Possibilities Frontier (*PPF*)	The boundary of combinations of production between 2 goods or services using factors of production	Checkpoint 3.1, p. 58
Production efficiency	Production on the production possibility frontier	Checkpoint 3.1, p. 60
Unattainable production	Production points beyond the production possibilities	Checkpoint 3.1, p. 60
Inefficient production	Production inside the frontier, wasting resources	Checkpoint 3.1, p. 61
Tradeoff (exchange)	Opportunity cost of moving along the *PPF*	Checkpoint 3.1, p. 61
Increasing opportunity cost	Demonstrated by the bowed outward *PPF*	Checkpoint 3.2, p. 65
Economic growth	Demonstrated by the *PPF* shifting outward	Checkpoint 3.3, p. 68
Absolute advantage	Can produce more using the same resources	Checkpoint 3.4, p. 71
Comparative advantage	Producing at a lower opportunity cost	Checkpoint 3.4, p. 71
Gains from international trade	Both countries end up with more goods or services due to using comparative advantages for trade	Checkpoint 3.4, p. 74

Extra AP material

- The production possibilities frontier is often referred to as the *production possibility curve* or *PPC*.

- A common production possibilities frontier figure measures *capital goods* along the *y*-axis and *consumer goods* along the *x*-axis. However, production of any two sets of goods can be illustrated using a production possibilities frontier.

- If the opportunity cost of a good along the *PPF* is constant as more of the good is produced, then the *PPF* is a straight line.

- If the opportunity cost of a good along the *PPF* increases as more of the good is produced, then the *PPF* is a bowed outward.

- All the production points on the production possibilities frontier are called *production efficient*. But not all production efficient points are equally valued by society. The production efficient point at which the goods and services most highly valued by society are produced is called *allocative efficient* (sometimes just called *efficient* for short). The concept of allocative efficiency is covered in Chapter 6.

- When questions cover the concept of *absolute advantage*, there will be a description of two countries having *similar resources* but one is able to produce more with those resources than the other country.

© 2015 Pearson Education, Inc.

CHECKPOINT 3.1

- **Explain and illustrate the concepts of scarcity, production efficiency, and tradeoff using the production possibilities frontier.**

Quick Review

- *Production possibilities frontier* The boundary between combinations of goods and services that can be produced and combinations that cannot be produced, given the available factors of production and the state of technology.
- *Unattainable points* Production points outside the *PPF* are unattainable.
- *Tradeoff* A constraint or limit to what is possible that forces an exchange or a substitution of one thing for something else.

Additional Practice Problem 3.1

Possibility	Fish (pounds)	and	Fruit (pounds)
A	0.0	and	36.0
B	4.0	and	35.0
C	7.5	and	33.0
D	10.5	and	30.0
E	13.0	and	26.0
F	15.0	and	21.0
G	16.5	and	15.0
H	17.5	and	8.0
I	18.0	and	0.0

1. The table above shows Crusoe's *PPF*. Can Crusoe gather 21 pounds of fruit and catch 30 pounds of fish? Explain your answer. Suppose that Crusoe discovers another fishing pond with more fish, so that he can catch twice as many fish as before. Now can Crusoe gather 21 pounds of fruit and catch 30 pounds of fish? Explain your answer.

Solution to Additional Practice Problem 3.1

1. Initially, Crusoe cannot gather 21 pounds of fruit and catch 30 pounds of fish. This production point lies outside his *PPF* and so is unattainable. Once Crusoe discovers the new pond, however, he can gather 21 pounds of fruit and catch 30 pounds of fish. (In Row *F*, double the

amount of Crusoe's fish.) The *PPF* depends on the available factors of production and when the factors of production increase, Crusoe's production possibilities change.

- **AP Self Test 3.1**

True or false

1. A point outside the production possibilities frontier is unattainable.
2. If all the factors of production are fully employed, the economy will produce at a point on the production possibilities frontier.
3. Moving from one point on the *PPF* to another point on the *PPF* illustrates a free lunch.
4. All production points on the *PPF* are production efficient.

Multiple choice

1. The production possibilities frontier is a graph showing the
   a. exact point of greatest efficiency for producing goods and services.
   b. tradeoff between free lunches.
   c. maximum combinations of goods and services that can be produced.
   d. minimum combinations of goods and services that can be produced.
   e. resources available for the economy's production uses.

2. The production possibilities frontier is a boundary that separates
   a. the combinations of goods that can be produced from the combinations of services.
   b. attainable combinations of goods and services that can be produced from unattainable combinations.
   c. equitable combinations of goods and services that can be produced from inequitable combinations.
   d. fair combinations of goods and services that can be consumed from unfair combinations.
   e. affordable production points from unaffordable points.

© 2015 Pearson Education, Inc.

3. Points inside the *PPF* are all
   a. unattainable and have fully employed resources.
   b. attainable and have fully employed resources.
   c. unattainable and have some unemployed resources.
   d. attainable and have some unemployed resources.
   e. unaffordable.

4. Points on the *PPF* are all
   a. unattainable and have fully employed resources.
   b. free lunches.
   c. inefficient.
   d. attainable and have some unemployed resources.
   e. production efficient.

5. During a time with high unemployment, a country can increase the production of one good or service
   a. without decreasing the production of something else.
   b. but must decrease the production of something else.
   c. and must increase the production of something else.
   d. by using resources in the production process twice.
   e. but the opportunity cost is infinite.

6. Moving along the production possibilities frontier itself illustrates
   a. the existence of tradeoffs.
   b. the existence of unemployment of some factors of production.
   c. the benefits of free lunches.
   d. how free lunches can be exploited through trade.
   e. how tradeoffs need not occur if the economy is efficient.

Short Response Questions

■ FIGURE 3.1

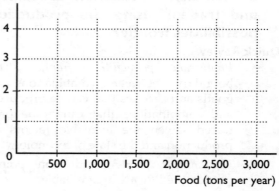
Computers (millions per year)

1. In Figure 3.1, draw a production possibilities frontier showing combinations of computers and food. Label the points that are attainable and unattainable. Label the points that have full employment and the points that have unemployment.

2. What factors limit the amount of production in the United States?

3. What points are production efficient? Moving between these points, is there a tradeoff or a free lunch?

Long Response Question

1. What is the relationship between unemployment of a resource and a free lunch? Between full employment of all factors of production and a tradeoff?

Additional Exercises (also in MyEconLab Test A)

The table shows the production possibilities frontier of a small Pacific island economy.

Possibility	Fish (pounds)		Berries (pounds)
A	0	and	20
B	1	and	18
C	2	and	15
D	3	and	11
E	4	and	6
F	5	and	0

Use this table to work these exercises.

1. Explain why this economy cannot produce 2 pounds of fish and 18 pounds of berries.

© 2015 Pearson Education, Inc.

2. Explain why 3 pounds of fish and 11 pounds of berries achieves production efficiency.

3. Explain why it would be inefficient to produce 4 pounds of fish and 5 pounds of berries.

4. Explain why moving from row A to row B of the table involves a tradeoff.

5. Explain why the citizens of this economy could enjoy a free lunch if they were producing 4 pounds of fish and 5 pounds of berries.

CHECKPOINT 3.2

■ Calculate opportunity cost.

Quick Review

- *Opportunity cost is a ratio* Along a *PPF*, the opportunity cost of one good equals the quantity of the other good forgone divided by the increase in the first good.

Additional Practice Problem 3.2

Possibility	Fish (pounds)		Fruit (pounds)
A	0.0	and	36.0
B	4.0	and	35.0
C	7.5	and	33.0
D	10.5	and	30.0
E	13.0	and	26.0
F	15.0	and	21.0
G	16.5	and	15.0
H	17.5	and	8.0
I	18.0	and	0.0

1. The table above shows Robinson Crusoe's production possibilities. How does Crusoe's opportunity cost of a pound of fish change as he catches more fish?

Solution to Additional Practice Problem 3.2

Move from	Increase in fish (pounds)	Decrease in fruit (pounds)	Opportunity cost of fish (pounds of fruit)
A to B	4.0	1.0	0.25
B to C	3.5	2.0	0.57
C to D	3.0	3.0	1.00
D to E	2.5	4.0	1.60
E to F	2.0	5.0	2.50
F to G	1.5	6.0	4.00
G to H	1.0	7.0	7.00
H to I	0.5	8.0	16.00

1. The table above shows Crusoe's opportunity cost of a pound of fish. His opportunity cost of a pound of fish increases as he catches more fish. As he moves from point A to point B and catches his first fish, the opportunity cost is only 0.25 pounds of fruit per pound of fish. But as he moves from point H to point I and catches only fish, the opportunity cost has increased to 16.0 pounds of fruit per pound of fish.

■ AP Self Test 3.2

True or false

1. Moving from one point on the *PPF* to another point on the *PPF* has no opportunity cost.

2. When moving along the *PPF*, the quantity of CDs increases by 2 and the quantity of DVDs decreases by 1, so the opportunity cost is 2 CDs minus 1 DVD.

3. Increasing opportunity costs are common.

© 2015 Pearson Education, Inc.

Multiple choice

1. The opportunity cost of one more slice of pizza in terms of sodas is the
   a. number of pizza slices we have to give up to get one extra soda.
   b. number of sodas we have to give up to get one extra slice of pizza.
   c. total number of sodas that we have divided by the total number of pizza slices that we have.
   d. total number of pizza slices that we have divided by the total number of sodas that we have.
   e. price of a pizza slice minus the price of a soda.

2. Moving between two points on a *PPF*, a country gains 6 automobiles and forgoes 3 trucks. The opportunity cost of 1 automobile is
   a. 3 trucks.
   b. 6 automobiles – 3 trucks.
   c. 2 trucks.
   d. 1/2 of a truck.
   e. 1 automobile.

3. Moving between two points on a *PPF*, a country gains 8 desktop computers and forgoes 4 laptop computers. The opportunity cost of 1 desktop computer is
   a. 4 laptops.
   b. 8 desktops.
   c. 1 desktop.
   d. 2 laptops.
   e. 1/2 of a laptop.

4. A country produces only cans of soup and ink pens. If the country produces on its bowed outward *PPF* and increases the production of cans of soup, the opportunity cost of additional
   a. cans of soup is increasing.
   b. cans of soup is decreasing.
   c. cans of soup remain unchanged.
   d. ink pens is increasing.
   e. More information is needed to determine what happens to the opportunity cost.

5. Moving along a country's *PPF*, a reason opportunity costs increase is that
   a. unemployment decreases as a country produces more and more of one good.
   b. unemployment increases as a country produces more and more of one good.
   c. technology declines as a country produces more and more of one good.
   d. some resources are better suited for producing one good rather than the other.
   e. technology must advance in order to produce more and more of one good.

6. Increasing opportunity costs exist
   a. in the real world.
   b. as long as there is high unemployment.
   c. only in theory but not in real life.
   d. for a country but not for an individual.
   e. inside the *PPF* but not on the *PPF*.

Short Response Questions

Production point	MP3 players (millions per year)		DVD players (millions per year)
A	4.0	and	0.0
B	3.0	and	3.0
C	2.0	and	4.0
D	1.0	and	4.7
E	0.0	and	5.0

1. The table shows the production possibilities for a nation.
   a. Placing MP3 players on the vertical axis, label the axes in Figure 3.2 and graph the production possibilities frontier.

■ **FIGURE 3.2**

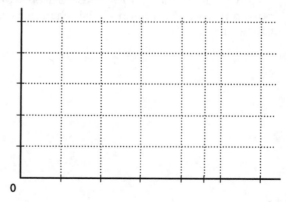

© 2015 Pearson Education, Inc.

b. What is the opportunity cost per DVD player of moving from point *A* to point *B*? *B* to *C*? *C* to *D*? *D* to *E*? How does the opportunity cost change as more DVD players are produced?

2. What does it mean for the opportunity cost to be a ratio?

Long Response Questions

Production point	Cans of soda (millions per year)		Candy bars (millions per year)
A	8.0	and	0.0
B	6.0	and	4.0
C	4.0	and	6.0
D	2.0	and	7.0
E	0.0	and	7.5

1. The table above shows the production possibilities for Sweetland.
   a. What is the opportunity cost per candy bar player of moving from point *A* to point *B*? *B* to *C*? *C* to *D*? *D* to *E*?
   b. What is the opportunity cost per can of soda of moving from point *E* to point *D*? *D* to *C*? *C* to *B*? *B* to *A*?
   c. How does the opportunity cost of a candy bar change as more candy bars are produced? How does the opportunity cost of a soda change as more sodas are produced?

2. What is the opportunity cost of increasing the production of a good while moving along a *PPF*? Why does this opportunity cost increase?

Additional Exercises (also in MyEconLab Test A)

Possibility	Fish (pounds)		Berries (pounds)
A	0	and	20
B	3.0	and	18
C	5.5	and	15
D	7.5	and	11
E	9.0	and	6
F	10.0	and	0

The table shows Robinson Crusoe's production possibilities in winter. Use the information in this table to work the exercises.
1. If Crusoe currently catches 5.5 pounds of fish and picks 11 pounds of berries a day, what is his opportunity cost of an extra pound of berries? And what is his opportunity cost of an extra pound of fish? Explain your answers.

2. If Crusoe produces efficiently, does his opportunity cost of a pound of berries increase as he spends more time picking berries? Explain.

CHECKPOINT 3.3

■ **Explain what makes production possibilities expand.**

Quick Review
• *Opportunity cost of growth* The opportunity cost of economic growth is the current consumption goods and services forgone.

Additional Practice Problem 3.3
1. Does economic growth eliminate scarcity?

Solution to Additional Practice Problem 3.3
1. Economic growth does not eliminate scarcity. Scarcity exists as long as people's wants exceed what can be produced. Economic growth increases the goods and services that can be produced but people's wants will continue to outstrip the ability to produce. While economic growth means that additional wants can be satisfied, people's wants are infinite and so scarcity will continue to be present even with economic growth.

■ **AP Self Test 3.3**

True or false
1. Economic growth abolishes scarcity.
2. The opportunity cost of economic growth is less consumption goods in the future.
3. Production possibilities per person in the United States have remained constant during the last 30 years.

© 2015 Pearson Education, Inc.

Multiple choice

1. To increase its economic growth, a nation should
   a. limit the number of people in college because they produce nothing.
   b. encourage spending on goods and services.
   c. encourage education because that increases the quality of labor.
   d. increase current consumption.
   e. eliminate expenditure on capital goods.

2. Other things equal, if Mexico devotes more resources to train its population than Spain,
   a. Mexico will be able to eliminate opportunity cost faster than Spain.
   b. Mexico will be able to eliminate scarcity faster than Spain.
   c. Spain will grow faster than Mexico.
   d. Mexico will grow faster than Spain.
   e. Mexico will have more current consumption than Spain.

3. If a nation devotes a larger share of its current production to consumption goods, then
   a. its economic growth will slow down.
   b. its *PPF* will shift outward.
   c. its *PPF* will shift inward.
   d. some productive factors will become unemployed.
   e. it must produce at a point within its *PPF*.

4. Which of the following is correct?
   i.   As an economy grows, the opportunity costs of economic growth decrease.
   ii. Economic growth has no opportunity cost.
   iii. The opportunity cost of economic growth is current consumption forgone.
   a. i only.
   b. ii only.
   c. iii only.
   d. i and iii.
   e. i and ii.

5. When a country's production possibilities frontier shifts outward over time, the country is experiencing
   a. no opportunity cost.
   b. economic growth.
   c. higher unemployment of resources.
   d. a decrease in unemployment of resources.
   e. an end to opportunity cost.

6. The opportunity cost of economic growth is ____ and the benefit of economic growth is ____.
   a. increased current consumption; increased future consumption
   b. increased current consumption; decreased future consumption
   c. decreased current consumption; increased future consumption
   d. decreased current consumption; decreased future consumption
   e. nothing; increased future consumption

Long Response Questions

■ FIGURE 3.3

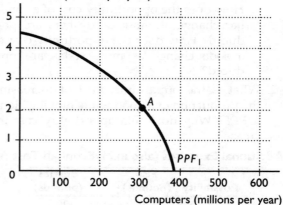

Automobiles (millions per year)

1. In the above figure, illustrate what happens if there is a technological breakthrough in the production of computers but not in the production of automobiles.
   a. Suppose the economy was initially producing at point *A*. After the breakthrough, is it possible for the economy to produce more computers *and* more automobiles?

© 2015 Pearson Education, Inc.

2. What is the opportunity cost of economic growth?

3. What is the benefit of economic growth?

Additional Exercises (also in MyEconLab Test A)

Possibility	Education services (graduates)		Consumption goods (units)
A	1,000	and	0
B	750	and	1,000
C	500	and	2,000
D	0	and	3,000

1. If the nation shown in the table above uses all its resources to produce consumption goods, at what rate will the nation grow? If the nation increases the number of graduates from 0 to 750, will the nation experience economic growth? Explain your answer.

CHECKPOINT 3.4

■ **Explain how people gain from specialization and trade.**

Quick Review

- *Comparative advantage* The ability of a person to perform an activity or produce a good or service at a lower opportunity cost than someone else.

Additional Practice Problem 3.4

1. Tony and Patty produce scooters and snowboards. The figure shows their production possibilities per day. With these production possibilities, the opportunity cost of a snowboard for Patty is 1/2 a scooter and for Tony is 2 scooters. Patty has a lower opportunity cost and therefore she has the comparative advantage in snowboards. The opportunity cost of a scooter for Patty is 2 snowboards and for Tony is 1/2 of a snow-

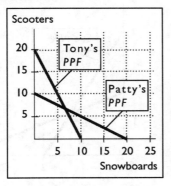

board. Tony has a lower opportunity cost and so he has the comparative advantage in scooters.

Suppose Patty acquires new equipment for scooter production that lets her produce a maximum of 60 rather than 10 scooters a day, should Patty and Tony specialize and trade?

Solution to Additional Practice Problem 3.4

1. Once Patty can produce 60 scooters a day, her opportunity costs change. Her opportunity cost of a scooter falls to 1/3 of a snowboard per scooter and her opportunity cost of a snowboard rises to 3 scooters per snowboard. With these opportunity costs, the comparative advantages have switched: Patty now has a comparative advantage in scooters and Tony in snowboards. Patty and Tony should still specialize and trade, only now Patty will specialize in scooters and Tony will specialize in snowboards. Comparative advantage can switch as the production possibilities frontier shifts outward.

■ **AP Self Test 3.4**

True or false

1. A person has an absolute advantage in an activity if the person can perform the activity at lower opportunity cost than someone else.

2. To achieve the gains from trade, a producer specializes in the product in which he or she has a comparative advantage and then trades with others.

3. Specialization and trade can make both producers better off even if one of them has an absolute advantage in producing all goods.

Multiple choice

1. "Comparative advantage" is defined as a situation in which one person can produce
   a. more of all goods than another person.
   b. more of a good than another person.
   c. a good for a lower dollar cost than another person.
   d. a good for a lower opportunity cost than another person.
   e. all goods for lower opportunity costs than another person.

© 2015 Pearson Education, Inc.

For the next three questions, use the following information: Scott and Cindy both produce only pizza and tacos. In one hour, Scott can produce 20 pizzas or 40 tacos. In one hour, Cindy can produce 30 pizzas or 40 tacos.

2. Scott's opportunity cost of producing 1 taco is
   a. 1/2 of a pizza.
   b. 1 pizza.
   c. 2 pizzas.
   d. 20 pizzas.
   e. 2 tacos.

3. Cindy's opportunity cost of producing 1 taco is
   a. 3/4 of a pizza.
   b. 1 pizza.
   c. 30 pizzas.
   d. 40 pizzas.
   e. 1 taco.

4. Based on the data given,
   a. Cindy has a comparative advantage in producing tacos.
   b. Scott has a comparative advantage in producing tacos.
   c. Cindy and Scott have the same comparative advantage in producing tacos.
   d. neither Cindy nor Scott has a comparative advantage in producing tacos.
   e. Cindy and Scott have the same comparative advantage in producing pizzas.

5. In one hour John can produce 20 loaves of bread or 8 cakes. In one hour Phyllis can produce 30 loaves of bread or 15 cakes. Which of the following statements is true?
   a. Phyllis has a comparative advantage in producing bread.
   b. John has a comparative advantage in producing cakes.
   c. Phyllis has an absolute advantage in both goods.
   d. John has an absolute advantage in both goods.
   e. Phyllis has a comparative advantage in producing both cakes and bread.

6. In one hour John can produce 20 loaves of bread or 16 cakes. In one hour Phyllis can produce 30 loaves of bread or 15 cakes. Which of the following statements is true?
   a. Phyllis has a comparative advantage in producing cakes.
   b. John has a comparative advantage in producing cakes.
   c. Phyllis has an absolute advantage in both goods.
   d. John has an absolute advantage in both goods.
   e. Phyllis has a comparative advantage in producing both cakes and bread.

7. In one hour John can produce 20 loaves of bread or 16 cakes. In one hour Phyllis can produce 30 loaves of bread or 15 cakes. John and Phyllis will reap the largest gains from specialization and trade if John produces _____ and Phyllis produces _____.
   a. only bread; only cakes
   b. only cakes; only bread
   c. both bread and cakes; only loaves
   d. only cakes; both bread and cakes
   e. both bread and cake; both bread and cake

Short Response Question

■ **FIGURE 3.4**

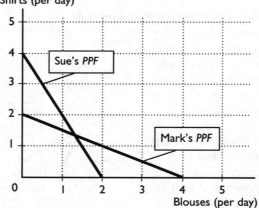

1. Figure 3.4 shows Mark and Sue's *PPFs*.
   a. What is Sue's opportunity cost of producing a shirt? What is Mark's opportunity cost of producing a shirt?

© 2015 Pearson Education, Inc.

b. Who has the comparative advantage in producing shirts?

c. What is Sue's opportunity cost of producing a blouse? What is Mark's opportunity cost of producing a blouse?

d. Who has the comparative advantage in producing blouses?

e. Who should specialize in producing blouses and who should specialize in producing shirts?

f. If Mark and Sue specialize according to their comparative advantage, indicate the total production of shirts and blouses by putting a point in Figure 3.4 showing the total production. Label the point A.

g. How does point A show the gains from trade?

Long Response Questions

1. Why should people specialize according to their comparative advantage?

2. When it comes to trading one good for another, why is comparative advantage crucial and absolute advantage unimportant?

Additional Exercises (also in MyEconLab Test A)

Sara and Fran produce boards and sails for windsurfing. The tables show their production possibilities. Each week Sara produces 6 boards and 6 sails, and Fran produces 24 boards and 24 sails.

Sara's Production Possibilities		
Boards (per week)		**Sails (per week)**
15	and	0
12	and	2
9	and	4
6	and	6
3	and	8
0	and	10

Fran's Production Possibilities		
Boards (per week)		**Sails (per week)**
40	and	0
32	and	12
24	and	24
16	and	36
8	and	48
0	and	60

1. Who has a comparative advantage in producing boards? And who has a comparative advantage in producing sails?

2. Can Sara and Fran gain by changing their production and trading 1 board for 1 sail? Explain why or why not.

© 2015 Pearson Education, Inc.

SELF TEST ANSWERS

■ AP Self Test 3.1

True or false
1. True; page 60
2. True; page 60
3. False; page 61
4. True; pages 60-61

Multiple choice
1. c; page 58
2. b; pages 59-60
3. d; page 60
4. e; pages 60-61
5. a; page 62
6. a; pages 61-62

Short Response Questions

■ FIGURE 3.5

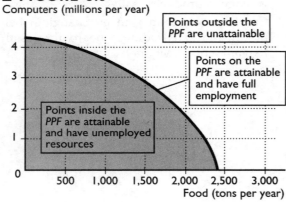

Computers (millions per year)

1. Figure 3.5 shows a *PPF* between computers and food; pages 59-60.
2. The factors that limit the amount of production in *any* economy are the available resources and the state of technology; page 58.
3. All points *on* the production possibilities frontier are production efficient. Moving from one point to another incurs an opportunity cost so there is tradeoff; pages 60-62.

Long Response Question
1. When the nation is producing at a point with unemployment of a resource, there are free lunches available because the production of some goods and services can be increased without decreasing the production of anything else. When the nation is producing at full employment of all factors of production, the production point is on the *PPF* and so only tradeoffs are available: If the production of one good or service is increased, the production of something else must be decreased; pages 61-62.

Additional Exercises (also in MyEconLab Test A)
1. The combination of 2 pounds of fish and 18 pounds of berries is not attainable. After the economy produces 2 pounds of fish, the maximum amount of berries it can produce is 15 pounds, not 18 pounds; page 60.
2. The combination of 3 pounds of fish and 11 pounds of berries is production efficient because it lies on the nation's production possibilities frontier. After producing 3 pounds of fish, the production possibilities frontier indicates that the maximum amount of berries that can be produced is 11 pounds, which is the amount produced in the question; pages 60-61.
3. It is inefficient to produce 4 pounds of fish and 5 pounds of berries because it is possible to more berries (or more fish). In particular, after producing 4 pounds of fish the production possibilities frontier indicates that it is possible to produce 6 pounds of berries, 1 pound *more* than the (inefficient) amount in the question, 5 pounds of berries; page 61.
4. Moving from row *A* to row *B* involves a tradeoff because the production of more fish is traded off against the production of fewer berries; pages 61-62.
5. The citizens could enjoy a free lunch if they were producing 4 pounds of fish and 5 pounds of berries because this production combination is inefficient. According to the production possibilities frontier, after producing 4 pounds of fish if resource use is rearranged so that it efficient, the nation could produce 6 pounds of berries, 1 pound *more*

© 2015 Pearson Education, Inc.

than the (inefficient) amount in the question, 5 pounds of berries. Hence by using resources more efficiently, the citizens could have more berries and not lose any fish, a free lunch; pages 61-62.

■ AP Self Test 3.2

True or false

1. False; page 64
2. False; page 65
3. True; page 66

Multiple choice

1. b; page 64
2. d; page 64
3. e; page 64
4. a; page 65
5. d; page 66
6. a; page 66

Short Response Questions

■ FIGURE 3.6

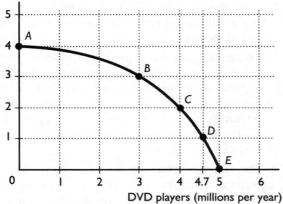

MP3 players (millions per year)

DVD players (millions per year)

1. a. Figure 3.6 illustrates the production possibilities frontier; page 64.
   b. The opportunity cost of moving from point *A* to point *B* to is 0.33 MP3 players per DVD player; from *B* to *C* is 1.00 MP3 player per DVD player; from *C* to *D* is 1.43 MP3 players per DVD player; and, from *D* to *E* is 3.33 MP3 players per DVD player. The opportunity cost increases; page 64.

2. The opportunity cost is the amount of a good forgone to gain an additional unit another good. We divide the quantity of the good forgone by the increase in the other good. So opportunity cost is a ratio—the change in the quantity of one good divided by the change in the quantity of another good; page 66.

Long Response Questions

1. a. The opportunity cost of moving from point *A* to point *B* to is 0.5 cans of soda per candy bar; from *B* to *C* is 1.0 can of soda per candy bar; from *C* to *D* is 2.0 cans of soda per candy bar; and, from *D* to *E* is 4.0 cans of soda per candy bar; page 64.
   b. The opportunity cost of moving from point *E* to point *D* to is 0.25 candy bars per can of soda; from *D* to *C* is 0.50 candy bars per can of soda; from *C* to *B* is 1.00 candy bar per can of soda; and, from *B* to *A* is 2.00 candy bars per can of soda; page 64.
   c. As more candy bars are produced, the opportunity cost increases. As more cans of soda are produced, the opportunity cost increases; page 65.

2. The opportunity cost of increasing production of one good is the production of some other good forgone. The opportunity cost increases, so that increasingly large amounts of the other good are forgone, because resources are not equally productive in all activities. When initially increasing the production of one good, resources that are well suited for its production are used. When still more of the good is produced, resources that are less well suited must be used. Because the resources are ill suited, more are necessary to increase the production of the first good, and the forgone amount of the other good increases; page 66.

Additional Exercises (also in MyEconLab Test A)

1. His opportunity cost of a pound of berries and a pound of fish are both zero. The opportunity cost is zero because he is operating inside his production possibilities frontier. He could pick 4 more pounds of berries

© 2015 Pearson Education, Inc.

without giving up any fish or catch 2 more fish without giving up any berries; page 62.

Move from	Increase in berries picked (pounds)	Decrease in fish caught (pounds)	Opportunity cost of berries (pounds of fish)
F to E	6.0	1.0	0.17
E to D	5.0	1.5	0.30
D to C	4.0	2.0	0.50
C to B	3.0	2.5	0.83
B to A	2.0	3.0	1.50

2. Crusoe's opportunity cost of a pound of berries is the fish he forgoes. To calculate the opportunity cost, compute the increase in fruit and the decrease in fish as he increases the time he spends picking berries and decreases the time he spends catching fish. Then, divide the decrease in fish by the increase in berries to get the opportunity cost of a pound of berries. The table above shows the opportunity cost of a pound of berries moving along the *PPF*. As Crusoe moves from point *F* to point *E* and then to point *D* and so forth, his opportunity cost of a pound of berries increases. His opportunity cost increases as he picks more berries because initially he picks from the most productive bushes and so must spend a short period of time picking berries, that is, a short period of time away from fishing. But as he picks more berries, he must pick from less productive bushes and so spends increasing more time away from fishing; pages 64, 66.

■ AP Self Test 3.3

True or false
1. False; page 68
2. False; pages 68, 70
3. False; page 70

Multiple choice
1. c; page 68
2. d; pages 68, 70
3. a; page 68
4. d; page 68
5. b; page 68
6. c; page 68

Long Response Questions

■ FIGURE 3.7

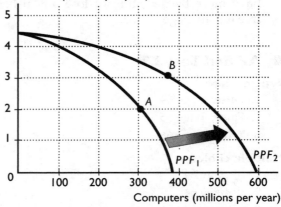

Automobiles (millions per year)

1. Figure 3.7 illustrates the new production possibilities frontier. Because the technological breakthrough did not affect automobile production, the maximum amount of automobiles that can be produced on the vertical axis does not change; pages 68-69.
   a. Figure 3.7 shows that it is possible for the production of *both* automobiles and computers to increase, as a movement from the initial point *A* to a possible new point *B* illustrates; pages 69-70 .

2. Economic growth requires developing new technologies, accumulating more human capital, or accumulating more capital. All of these avenues require resources, so the opportunity cost of economic growth is the decrease in the current production of goods and services; page 68.

3. The benefit from economic growth is increased consumption per person in the future after the production possibilities frontier has expanded; page 68.

Additional Exercise (also in MyEconLab Test A)

1. If the nation uses all of its resources to produce consumption goods, it will not grow because it does not increase its human capital, which is its only source of economic growth. If the nation increases its graduates from 0 to 750, the nation will experience eco-

© 2015 Pearson Education, Inc.

nomic growth because its human capital increases; page 68.

■ AP Self Test 3.4

True or false

1. False; pages 71-72
2. True; page 74
3. True; pages 74-75

Multiple choice

1. d; page 72
2. a; page 72
3. a; page 72
4. b; pages 73-74
5. c; pages 73-74
6. b; pages 73-74
7. a; pages 73-74

Short Response Question

1. a. Sue's opportunity cost of a shirt is 1/2 of a blouse because, when moving along her *PPF* to produce 1 more shirt she gives up 1/2 of a blouse. Mark's opportunity cost of a shirt is 2 blouses; page 73

   b. Sue has the comparative advantage in producing shirts because her opportunity cost is lower; pages 73-74.

   c. Sue's opportunity cost of a blouse is 2 shirts because, when moving along her *PPF*, to produce 1 more blouse she gives up 2 shirts. Mark's opportunity cost of a blouse is 1/2 of a shirt; page 73.

   d. Mark has the comparative advantage in producing blouses because his opportunity cost is lower; pages 73-74.

   e. Mark should specialize in producing blouses and Sue should specialize in producing shirts; page 74.

   f. Mark produces 4 blouses and Sue produces 4 shirts, so a total of 4 shirts and 4 blouses are produced. Figure 3.8 shows this production as point *A*; pages 74-75.

   g. If Mark and Sue agree that the total production at point *A* should be divided evenly, then both Mark and Sue will receive 2 shirts and 2 blouses. When both

were producing only for themselves, neither could produce 2 shirts and 2 blouses because this point is beyond both their *PPF*s. By specializing and trading, *both* Mark and Sue can consume at a point outside of their *PPF*s; page 75.

■ FIGURE 3.8

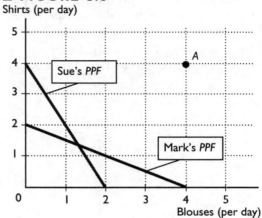

Long Response Questions

1. A person's comparative advantage is the good that the person can produce at a lower opportunity cost than can other people. When this person specializes in the production of the good, it is produced at the lowest cost; page 73.

2. People are willing to trade if they can obtain a good at lower opportunity cost than what it costs them to produce the good. Comparative advantage tells which person has a lower opportunity cost. Even if a person has an absolute advantage in all goods, he or she does not have a comparative advantage in all goods. So comparative advantage determines who produces a product and who does not; page 73.

Additional Exercises (also in MyEconLab Test A)

1. For each board Sara makes, she forgoes 2/3 of a sail, so for her the opportunity cost of 1 board is 2/3 of a sail. For each board Fran makes, she forgoes 1½ sails, so for her the opportunity cost of 1 board is 1½ sails. The opportunity cost of producing a board is

© 2015 Pearson Education, Inc.

lower for Sara, so she has the comparative advantage in producing boards.

For each sail Sara makes, she forgoes 1½ boards, so for her the opportunity cost of 1 sail is 1½ boards. For each sail Fran makes, she forgoes 2/3 of a board, so for her the opportunity cost of 1 sail is 2/3 of a board. The opportunity cost of producing a sail is lower for Fran, so she has the comparative advantage in producing sails; pages 73-74.

2. Yes, Sara and Fran can gain by changing their production and then trading 1 board for 1 sail. Sara will trade boards with Fran in exchange for sails. With trade, each sail has the opportunity cost for Sara of 1 board, less than her opportunity cost of 1½ boards if she does not trade. Fran will trade sails with Sara in exchange for boards. With trade, each board has the opportunity cost for Fran of 1 sail, less than her opportunity cost of 1½ sails if she does not trade. Sara and Fran can both have more boards and more sails if they specialize and trade; pages 74-75.

© 2015 Pearson Education, Inc.

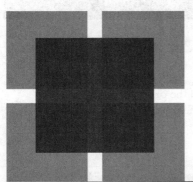

Demand and Supply

Chapter 4

Demand and supply determine the quantities and prices of goods and services.

1 Distinguish between quantity demanded and demand, and explain what determines demand.

The quantity demanded is the amount of any good, service, or resource that people are willing and able to buy during a specified period at a specified price. Demand is the relationship between the quantity demanded and the price of a good when all other influences on buying plans remain the same. The law of demand states: Other things remaining the same, if the price of a good rises, the quantity demanded of that good decreases; and if the price of a good falls, the quantity demanded of that good increases. A demand curve is a graph of the relationship between the quantity demanded of a good and its price when all other influences on buying plans remain the same. The market demand is the sum of the demands of all the buyers in a market. A change in price leads to a *change in the quantity demanded* and a movement along the demand curve. Factors that *change demand* and shift the demand curve are: prices of related goods; expected future prices; income; expected future income and credit; number of buyers; and preferences. If demand increases, the demand curve shifts rightward.

2 Distinguish between quantity supplied and supply, and explain what determines supply.

The quantity supplied is the amount of any good, service, or resource that people are willing and able to sell during a specified period at a specified price. Supply is the relationship between the quantity supplied and the price of a good when all other influences on selling plans remain the same. The law of supply states that other things remaining the same, if the price of a good rises, the quantity supplied of that good increases; and if the price of a good falls, the quantity supplied of that good decreases. A supply curve is a graph of the relationship between the quantity supplied of a good and its price when all other influences on selling plans remain the same. A change in price leads to a *change in the quantity supplied* and a movement along the supply curve. Factors that *change supply* and shift the supply curve are: prices of related goods; prices of resources and other inputs; expected future prices; number of sellers; and productivity. If supply increases, the supply curve shifts rightward.

3 Explain how demand and supply determine price and quantity in a market, and explain the effects of changes in demand and supply.

The equilibrium price and equilibrium quantity occur when the quantity demanded equals the quantity supplied. An increase in demand raises the price and increases the quantity. An increase in supply lowers the price and increases the quantity. An increase in both demand and supply increases the quantity but the price might rise, fall, or not change. An increase in demand and a decrease in supply raises the price but the quantity might increase, decrease, or not change. Changes in demand and supply in the opposite direction to those given above lead to opposite changes in price and quantity.

© 2015 Pearson Education, Inc.

YOUR AP TEST HINTS

AP Topics

Topic on your AP test	What to Know	Corresponding textbook section
Demand	Relationship between the quantity demanded and the price	Checkpoint 4.1
Supply	Relationship between the quantity supplied and the price	Checkpoint 4.2
Price and Quantity	Where the demand and supply curves intersect	Checkpoint 4.3

AP Vocabulary Covered

Terms	What to Know	Text Sections
Markets	Goods, services, resources, inputs, money, virtual space	Checkpoint 4.1, p. 82
Quantity demanded	The amount willing and able to buy at a specified price	Checkpoint 4.1, p. 83
Law of Demand	Price rises, the quantity demanded decreases; price falls, the quantity demanded increases	Checkpoint 4.1, p. 83
Demand	The relationship between quantity demanded and price	Checkpoint 4.1, p. 83
Demand schedule	A list of quantities demanded at various prices	Checkpoint 4.1, p. 84
Demand curve	A graph showing quantity demanded at various prices	Checkpoint 4.1, p. 84
Market demand	Sum of demands from all buyers in the market	Checkpoint 4.1, p. 85
Changes in demand	The movement of the demand curve due to changes in any factor other than the price	Checkpoint 4.1, p. 86
Substitute (in demand)	A good consumed instead of another good	Checkpoint 4.1, p. 86
Complement (in demand)	A good consumed with another good	Checkpoint 4.1, p. 86
Normal good	Demand for the good increases as income increases	Checkpoint 4.1, p. 87
Inferior good	Demand for the good decreases as income increases	Checkpoint 4.1, p. 87
Change in quantity demanded	Changes in purchases due to price changes	Checkpoint 4.1, p. 88
Quantity supplied	The amount willing and able to supply at a specified price	Checkpoint 4.2, p. 90
Law of Supply	Price rises, the quantity supplied increases; price falls, the quantity supplied decreases	Checkpoint 4.2, p. 90
Supply	The relationship between quantity of supply and price	Checkpoint 4.2, p. 90
Supply schedule	A list of quantities supplied at different prices	Checkpoint 4.2, p. 91
Supply curve	A graph showing quantity supplied at various prices	Checkpoint 4.2, p. 91
Market supply	The sum of supplies from all sellers in the market	Checkpoint 4.2, p. 92
Changes in supply	The movement of the supply curve due to changes in any factor other than price	Checkpoint 4.2, p. 93
Substitute (in supply)	A good produced in place of another good	Checkpoint 4.2, p. 93
Complement (in supply)	A good produced along with another good	Checkpoint 4.2, p. 93
Change in quantity supplied	A change in quantity suppliers are willing to supply at different market prices	Checkpoint 4.2, p. 95

© 2015 Pearson Education, Inc.

Market equilibrium	Where quantity demand and quantity supplied meet	Checkpoint 4.3, p. 98
Equilibrium Price	Quantity demanded equals quantity supplied (y-axis)	Checkpoint 4.3, p. 98
Equilibrium Quantity	Quantity demanded equals quantity supplied (x-axis)	Checkpoint 4.3, p. 98
Surplus	Quantity supplied exceeds quantity demanded	Checkpoint 4.3, p. 98
Shortage	Quantity demanded exceeds quantity supplied	Checkpoint 4.3, p. 98

Extra AP material

- On the AP test, factors that change demand are often said to be "determinants of demand." On the AP test, factors that change supply are often referred to as "determinants of supply."
- When a problem on the AP test describes any change in a market *other than a change in the price of the good itself,* refer to the determinants of demand or supply and shift either the demand curve or the supply curve.
- When supply determinants are mentioned, they often focus on *input cost changes, input availability, worker productivity changes,* or *technological developments.*
- The phrase, "other things remaining the same" is typically expressed on the AP test as "other things constant." See prior notes on *Ceteris paribus.*
- When both the demand and supply curves shift, the result that you cannot tell if the price or quantity rises, falls, or stays the same is expressed on the AP test by saying there is an "indeterminate result."
- Consumer information, both favorable and not, can be a factor that changes demand. For instance, favorable information increases the demand and shifts the demand curve rightward.
- The time period available for production can be a factor that changes supply. The longer the time available, the greater the supply, so the supply curve shifts rightward as more time passes.

CHECKPOINT 4.1

■ **Distinguish between quantity demanded and demand, and explain what determines demand.**

Quick Review

- *Change in the quantity demanded* A change in the quantity of a good that people plan to buy that results from a change in the price of the good.
- *Law of demand* If the price of a good rises, the quantity demanded of that good decreases, and if the price of a good falls, the quantity demanded of that good decreases.
- *Change in demand* A change in the quantity that people plan to buy when any influence on buying plans, other than the price of the good, changes. These other influences include: prices of related goods, expected future prices, income, expected future income and credit, number of buyers, and preferences.

Additional Practice Problems 4.1

1. In the market for motor scooters, several events occur, one at a time. Explain the influence of each event on the quantity demanded of scooters and on the demand for scooters. Illustrate the effects of each event either by a movement along the demand curve or a shift in the demand curve for scooters and say which event (or events) illustrates the law of demand in action. These events are:
   a. The price of a scooter falls.
   b. The price of a car falls.
   c. Citing rising injury rates, cities and towns ban scooters from busy streets.
   d. Scooters are a normal good and income increases.

© 2015 Pearson Education, Inc.

e. Scooters become unfashionable and the number of buyers decreases.

2. Suppose that each year Anna, Ben, Carol, and Dana are willing and able to buy scooters as shown in the table.

Price (dollars per scooter)	Quantity demanded			
	Anna	Ben	Carol	Dana
100	0	0	0	0
75	1	0	0	0
50	2	1	1	0
25	2	1	2	1

■ **FIGURE 4.1**

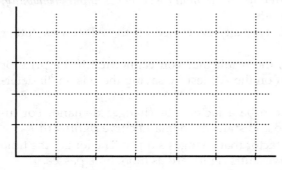

Using the information in the table:
  a. Label the axes in Figure 4.1 above.
  b. Graph the market demand curve.

Solutions to Additional Practice Problems 4.1

1a. This problem emphasizes the distinction between a change in the quantity demanded and a change in demand. A fall in the price of a scooter brings an increase in the quantity

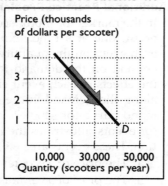

demanded of scooters, which is illustrated by a movement down along the demand curve for scooters as shown in the figure. This event illustrates the law of demand in action.

1b. A car is a substitute for a scooter. With the lower price of a car, some people who previously would have bought a scooter will now buy a car instead. So a fall in the price of cars decreases the demand for scooters. The demand curve for scooters shifts leftward, as shown in the figure on the following page.

1c. Rising injury rates and banning scooters from streets changes preferences and makes scooters less desirable. The demand for scooters decreases and the demand curve

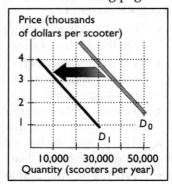

for the scooters shifts leftward as shown in the figure leftward as shown in the figure by the shift from demand curve D_0 to demand curve D_1.

1d. A scooter is a normal good, so people will buy more scooters when their income increases. The demand for scooters increases and the demand curve shifts rightward as illustrated in the figure.

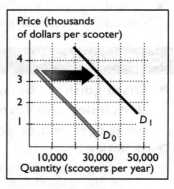

1e. A decrease in the number of buyers decreases the demand for scooters. The demand curve shifts leftward.

© 2015 Pearson Education, Inc.

■ FIGURE 4.2

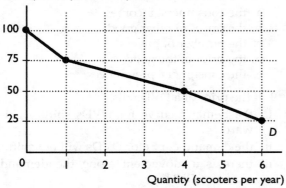

Price (dollars per scooter)

2a. Figure 4.2 labels the axes.

2b. The market demand curve is derived by adding the quantities demanded by Anna, Ben, Carol, and Dana at each price. The market demand curve is illustrated in Figure 4.2.

■ AP Self Test 4.1

True or false

1. The law of demand states that other things remaining the same, if the price of a good rises, the quantity demanded of that good increases.

2. If the quantity of ice cream demanded at each price increases, there is a movement along the demand curve for ice cream.

3. When Sue's income increases, her demand for movies increases. For Sue, movies are a normal good.

4. A rise in the price of a computer increases the demand for computers because a computer is a normal good.

5. If people's incomes fall and all other influences on buying plans remain the same, the demand for computers will decrease and there will be a movement along the demand curve.

Multiple choice

1. The "law of demand" indicates that if the University of Maine increases its tuition, all other things remaining the same,
   a. the demand for classes will decrease at the University of Maine.
   b. the demand for classes will increase at the University of Maine.
   c. the quantity of classes demanded will increase at the University of Maine.
   d. the quantity of classes demanded will decrease at the University of Maine.
   e. both the demand for and the quantity of classes demanded will decrease at the University of Maine.

2. Other things remaining the same, the quantity of a good or service demanded will increase if the price of the good or service
   a. rises.
   b. falls.
   c. does not change.
   d. rises or does not change.
   e. rises or falls.

3. Teenagers demand more soda than other age groups. If the number of teenagers increases, everything else remaining the same,
   a. market demand for soda increases.
   b. market demand for soda decreases.
   c. market demand for soda does not change.
   d. there is a movement along the market demand curve for soda.
   e. None of the above answers is correct because the effect on the demand depends whether the supply curve shifts.

4. One reason the demand for laptop computers might increase is a
   a. fall in the price of a laptop computers.
   b. fall in the price of a desktop computer.
   c. a change in preferences as laptops have become more portable, with faster processors and larger hard drives.
   d. poor quality performance record for laptop computers.
   e. a decrease in income if laptops are a normal good.

© 2015 Pearson Education, Inc.

5. The number of buyers of sport utility vehicles, SUVs, decreases sharply. So the
   a. demand curve for SUVs shifts leftward.
   b. demand curve for SUVs shifts rightward.
   c. demand curve for SUVs does not shift nor is there a movement along the demand curve.
   d. demand curve for SUVs does not shift but there is a movement downward along it.
   e. the supply curve for SUVs shifts rightward.

■ **FIGURE 4.3**
Price (dollars per pizza)

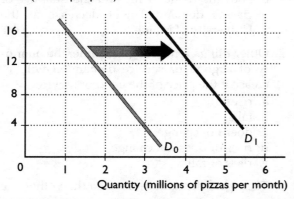

6. The shift of the demand curve for pizza illustrated in Figure 4.3 could be the result of
   a. a rise in income if pizza is a normal good.
   b. a fall in the price of fried chicken, a substitute for pizza.
   c. consumers coming to believe that pizza is unhealthy.
   d. the belief that pizza will fall in price next month.
   e. a fall in the price of a pizza.

7. The shift of the demand curve for pizza illustrated in Figure 4.3 could be the result of
   a. a rise in income if pizza is an inferior good.
   b. a fall in the price of soda, a complement for pizza.
   c. a decrease in the number of college students if college students eat more pizza than other age groups.
   d. a rise in the price of a pizza.
   e. a fall in the price of a pizza.

8. When moving along a demand curve, which of the following changes?
   a. the consumers' incomes
   b. the prices of other goods
   c. the number of buyers
   d. the price of the good
   e. the consumers' preferences

9. If the price of a DVD falls,
   i. the demand curve for DVDs shifts rightward.
   ii. the demand curve for DVDs will not shift.
   iii. there is a movement along the demand curve for DVDs.
   a. i only.
   b. ii only.
   c. iii only.
   d. ii and iii.
   e. i and iii.

10. Pizza and tacos are substitutes and the price of a pizza increases. Which of the following correctly indicates what happens?
    a. The demand for pizzas decreases and the demand for tacos increases.
    b. The demand for both goods decreases.
    c. The quantity of tacos demanded increases and the quantity of pizza demanded decreases.
    d. The quantity of pizza demanded decreases and the demand for tacos increases.
    e. The demand for each decreases because both are normal goods.

Short Response Questions

Price (dollars per bundle of cotton candy)	Quantity (bundles of cotton candy per month)
1	10,000
2	8,000
3	7,000
4	4,000

1. The demand schedule for cotton candy is given in the following table. In Figure 4.4 (on the next page), draw the demand curve. Label the axes.
   a. If the price of cotton candy is $2 a bundle, what is the quantity demanded?

© 2015 Pearson Education, Inc.

■ **FIGURE 4.4**

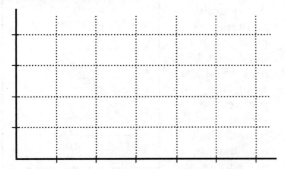

    b. If the price of cotton candy is $3 a bundle, what is the quantity demanded?

    c. Does the demand curve you drew slope upward or downward?

■ **FIGURE 4.5**

Price (dollars per pound of butter)

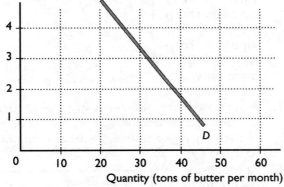

Quantity (tons of butter per month)

2. Butter is a normal good and margarine is substitute for butter. Figure 4.5 shows the demand curve for butter.

    a. In Figure 4.5, show how the demand curve shifts if incomes rise. Label this demand curve D_1.

    b. In Figure 4.5, show how the demand curve shifts if margarine falls in price. Label this demand curve D_2.

    c. If the price of butter falls from $4 a pound to $3 a pound, does the demand curve shift toward demand curve D_1, D_2, or neither? Explain your answer.

Long Response Questions

1. Explain the difference between a change in quantity demanded and a change in demand.

2. What is the difference between a movement along a demand curve and a shift in a demand curve?

Additional Exercises (also in MyEconLab Test A)

The following events occur one at a time in the market for Caribbean cruises.

    a. Caribbean cruises become more popular.

    b. The price of a Caribbean cruise rises.

    c. The price of a cruise to Asia falls.

    d. Celebrity Cruises launches its new "students only" Caribbean cruises.

    e. People expect the price of a Caribbean cruise to fall next season.

    f. Cruise companies increase the number of leading rock artists booked for their onboard entertainment.

1. Explain the effect of each event on the demand for Caribbean cruises.

2. Use a graph to illustrate the effect of each event.

3. Does any event (or events) illustrate the law of demand?

CHECKPOINT 4.2

■ **Distinguish between quantity supplied and supply, and explain what determines supply.**

Quick Review

- *Change in quantity supplied* A change in the quantity of a good that suppliers plan to sell that results from a change in the price of the good.

- *Change in supply* A change in the quantity that suppliers plan to sell when any influence on selling plans other than the price of the good changes.

© 2015 Pearson Education, Inc.

Additional Practice Problems 4.2

1. In the market for motor scooters, several events occur, one at a time. Explain the effect of each on the quantity supplied of scooters and on the supply of scooters. Illustrate the effects of each either by a movement along the supply curve or a shift in the supply curve and say which illustrate the law of supply. These events are:

   a. The price of a scooter rises.

   b. The price of the steel used to make scooters rises.

   c. The number of firms making scooters decreases.

   d. Technological change increases the productivity of the factories making scooters.

Price (dollars per ton of plywood)	Quantity supplied (tons of plywood per month)			
	Eddy	Franco	George	Helen
100	2	2	1	1
75	2	1	1	1
50	1	1	1	0
25	0	0	1	0

2. Each month Eddy, Franco, George, and Helen are willing and able to sell plywood as shown in the table above.

   a. Label the axes in Figure 4.6.

   b. Graph the market supply curve.

■ FIGURE 4.6

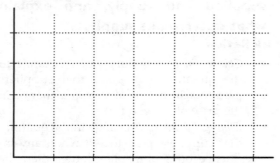

Solutions to Additional Practice Problems 4.2

1a. This problem emphasizes the distinction between a change in the quantity supplied and a change in supply. A rise in the price of a scooter increases the quantity of scooters supplied, which is illustrated by a movement up along the supply curve as shown in the figure. There is no change in the supply and the supply curve does not shift. This event illustrates the law of supply in action.

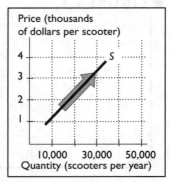

1b. When the price of the steel used to make scooters rises, the cost to produce scooters increases, which decreases the supply of scooters. The supply curve shifts leftward as shown.

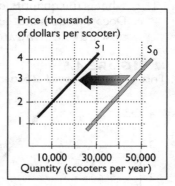

1c. A decrease in the number of firms producing scooters decreases the supply of scooters. The supply curve shifts leftward, as illustrated in the figure above.

1d. An increase in the productivity of the factories making scooters lowers the costs of producing scooters. The supply of scooters increases and the supply curve shifts rightward, as illustrated in the figure.

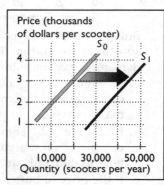

© 2015 Pearson Education, Inc.

■ FIGURE 4.7
Price (dollars per ton of plywood)

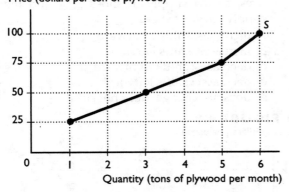

Quantity (tons of plywood per month)

Price (dollars per ton of plywood)	Quantity supplied (tons per month)
100	6
75	5
50	3
25	1

2a. The axes are labeled in Figure 4.7.

2b. The market supply curve is derived by adding the quantities supplied by Eddy, Franco, George, and Helen at each price. The table above gives the resulting sum and the market supply curve is illustrated in Figure 4.7.

■ AP Self Test 4.2

True or false

1. The law of supply states that other things remaining the same, if the price of a good rises, the supply of the good increases.

2. When new technology for producing computers is used by manufacturers, the supply of computers increases.

3. If the wage rate paid to chefs rises and all other influences on selling plans remain the same, the supply of restaurant meals will increase.

4. If the price of coffee is expected to rise next month, the supply of coffee this month will decrease.

5. The supply of a good will increase and there will be a movement up along the supply

curve of the good if the price of one of its substitutes in production falls.

Multiple choice

1. The quantity supplied of a good, service, or resource is _____ during a specified period and at a specified price.
   a. the amount that people are able to sell
   b. the amount that people are willing to sell
   c. the amount that people are able and willing to sell
   d. the amount that people are willing and able to buy
   e. the amount sold

2. One reason supply curves have an upward slope is because
   a. increased supply will require increased technology.
   b. people will pay a higher price when less is supplied.
   c. a higher price brings a greater profit, so firms want to sell more of that good.
   d. to have more of the good supplied requires more firms to open.
   e. None of the above answers is correct because supply curves have a downward slope.

3. Which of the following indicates that the law of supply applies to makers of soda?
   a. An increase in the price of a soda leads to an increase in the demand for soda.
   b. An increase in the price of a soda leads to an increase in the supply of soda.
   c. An increase in the price of a soda leads to an increase in the quantity of soda supplied.
   d. A decrease in the price of a soda leads to an increase in the quantity of soda demanded.
   e. A decrease in the price of a soda leads to an increase in the supply of soda.

© 2015 Pearson Education, Inc.

4. The market supply curve is the ____ of the ____.
   a. horizontal sum; individual supply curves
   b. vertical sum; individual supply curves
   c. horizontal sum; individual supply curves minus the market demand
   d. vertical sum; individual supply curves minus the market demand
   e. vertical average; individual supply curves

5. If the costs to produce pizza increase, which will occur?
   a. The supply of pizza will decrease.
   b. The quantity of pizzas supplied will increase as sellers try to cover their costs.
   c. Pizza will cease to be produced and sold.
   d. The demand curve for pizza will shift leftward when the price of a pizza increases.
   e. The demand curve for pizza will shift rightward when the price of a pizza increases.

6. A rise in the price of a substitute in production for a good leads to
   a. an increase in the supply of that good.
   b. a decrease in the supply of that good.
   c. no change in the supply of that good.
   d. a decrease in the quantity of that good supplied.
   e. no change in either the supply or the quantity supplied of the good.

7. An increase in the productivity of producing jeans results in
   a. the quantity of jeans supplied increasing.
   b. the supply of jeans increasing.
   c. buyers demanding more jeans because they are now more efficiently produced.
   d. buyers demanding fewer jeans because their price will fall, which signals lower quality.
   e. some change but the impact on the supply of jeans is impossible to predict.

8. The price of leather used to produce shoes rises, so the supply of shoes ____ and the supply curve of shoes ____.
   a. increases; shifts rightward
   b. increases; shifts leftward
   c. decreases; shifts rightward
   d. decreases; shifts leftward
   e. does not change; does not shift

■ **FIGURE 4.8**

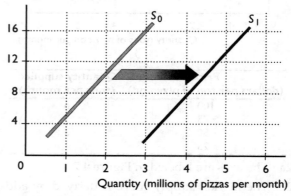
Price (dollars per pizza)

Quantity (millions of pizzas per month)

9. The shift of the supply curve of pizza illustrated in Figure 4.8 could be the result of
   a. a rise in the price of cheese used to produce pizza.
   b. a decrease in the number of firms producing pizza.
   c. an increase in the productivity of the firms producing pizza.
   d. a rise in the price of a substitute in production.
   e. a rise in the price of a pizza.

10. The shift of the supply curve of pizza illustrated in Figure 4.8 could be the result of
    a. a rise in income if pizza is a normal good.
    b. a fall in the price of soda, a consumer complement for pizza.
    c. an increase in the number of firms producing pizza.
    d. a rise in the price of a pizza.
    e. a rise in the wage paid the workers who make pizza.

© 2015 Pearson Education, Inc.

Short Response Questions

1. What is the law of supply?

Price (dollars per bundle of cotton candy)	Quantity (bundles of cotton candy per month)
I	4,000
2	8,000
3	10,000
4	12,000

2. The supply schedule for cotton candy is given in the table above. In Figure 4.4, you previously drew a demand curve for cotton candy. Now use the supply schedule to draw the supply curve in Figure 4.4.

   a. If the price of cotton candy is $2 a bundle, what is the quantity supplied?

   b. If the price of cotton candy is $3 a bundle, what is the quantity supplied?

   c. Does the supply curve you drew slope upward or downward?

Price (dollars per pizza)	Quantity supplied (pizza per day)			
	Tom	Bob	Kate	Market supply
I4	20	12	15	_____
12	16	10	10	_____
10	12	8	5	_____
8	8	6	0	_____

3. The table gives the supply schedules for the three pizza producers in a small town. Calculate the market supply schedule.

4. Figure 4.9 shows a supply curve for rubber bands. Suppose the productivity of producing rubber bands increases. In Figure 4.9, illustrate the effect of this event.

Long Response Question

1. What influence(s) lead to a change in the quantity supplied? A change in supply?

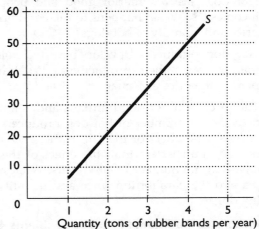

■ FIGURE 4.9
Price (dollars per ton of rubber bands)

Additional Exercises (also in MyEconLab Test A)

Factories can use their resources to produce either DVDs or CDs. In the market for DVDs, the following events occur one at a time:

   a. The price of a CD falls.

   b. A new robot technology lowers the cost of producing DVDs.

   c. The price of a DVD falls.

   d. The price of a DVD is expected to rise next year.

   e. The wage rate paid to DVD factory workers increases.

1. Explain the effect of each event on the supply of DVDs.

2. Show on a graph the effect of each event.

3. Does any event (or events) illustrate the law of supply?

CHECKPOINT 4.3

■ Explain how demand and supply determine the price and quantity in a market, and explain the effects of changes in demand and supply.

Quick Review

• *Market equilibrium* When the quantity demanded equals the quantity supplied.

© 2015 Pearson Education, Inc.

Additional Practice Problems 4.3

1. Hot dogs are an inferior good and people's incomes rise. What happens to the equilibrium price and quantity of hot dogs?

2. Hot dog producers develop new technology that increases their productivity. What happens to the price and quantity of hot dogs?

3. The price of a hot dog bun falls and, simultaneously, the number of hot dog producers increases. The effect of the fall in the price of a hot dog bun is less than the effect of the increase in the number of producers. What happens to the equilibrium price and quantity of hot dogs?

Solutions to Additional Practice Problems 4.3

1. When income increases, the demand for an inferior good decreases and the demand curve shifts leftward. The supply does not change and the sup- 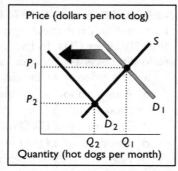 ply curve does not shift. The equilibrium price of a hot dog falls and the equilibrium quantity decreases, as illustrated in the figure.

2. When the productivity of producing a good increases, the supply of the good increases and the supply curve shifts rightward. So the supply 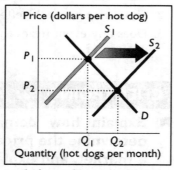 curve of hot dogs shifts rightward. The demand does not change and so the demand curve does not shift. As illustrated, the price of a hot dog falls and the quantity increases.

3. The fall in the price of a complement, hot dog buns, increases the demand for hot dogs and the demand curve for hot dogs shifts rightward. The increase in the number of producers increases the supply of hot dogs and the supply curve shifts rightward. Because the increase in sup- 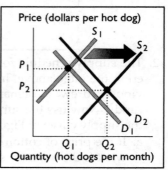 ply exceeds the increase in demand, the price of a hot dog falls and the quantity increases, as shown in the figure.

■ AP Self Test 4.3

True or false

1. If the price of asparagus is below the equilibrium price, there is a shortage of asparagus and the price of asparagus will rise until the shortage disappears.

2. When the demand for skateboards decreases and the supply of skateboards remains unchanged, the quantity supplied of skateboards decreases as the price rises.

3. Gasoline refiners expect the price of oil will fall next month. If the supply of oil does not change, the equilibrium price of oil today falls and the equilibrium quantity today decreases.

4. As summer comes to an end and winter sets in, the demand for and supply of hamburger buns decrease. The price of a hamburger bun definitely remains the same.

5. The number of buyers of grapefruit juice increases and at the same time severe frost decreases the supply of grapefruit juice. The price of grapefruit juice will rise.

© 2015 Pearson Education, Inc.

Multiple choice

1. The equilibrium price of a good occurs if the
   a. quantity of the good demanded equals the quantity of the good supplied.
   b. quantity of the good demanded is greater than the quantity of the good supplied.
   c. quantity of the good demanded is less than the quantity of the good supplied.
   d. demand for the good is equal to the supply of the good.
   e. price of the good seems reasonable to most buyers.

2. Which of the following is correct?
   i. A surplus puts downward pressure on the price of a good.
   ii. A shortage puts upward pressure on the price of a good
   iii. There is no surplus or shortage at equilibrium.
   a. i and ii..
   b. i and iii.
   c. ii and iii.
   d. i, ii, and iii.
   e. only iii.

3. The number of people looking to buy ceiling fans increases, so there is an increase in the
   a. quantity of ceiling fans demanded and a surplus of ceiling fans.
   b. demand for ceiling fans and a rise in the price of a ceiling fan.
   c. demand for ceiling fans and a surplus of ceiling fans.
   d. supply of ceiling fans and no change in the price of a ceiling fan.
   e. demand for ceiling fans and in the supply of ceiling fans.

4. Which of the following is the best explanation for why the price of gasoline increases during the summer months?
   a. Oil producers have higher costs of production in the summer.
   b. Sellers have to earn profits during the summer to cover losses in the winter.
   c. There is increased driving by families going on vacation.
   d. There is less competition among oil refineries in the summer.
   e. The number of gas stations open 24 hours a day rises in the summer months and so the price must rise to cover the higher costs.

5. Suppose that the price of lettuce used to produce tacos increases. This change means that the equilibrium price of a taco ____ and the equilibrium quantity ____.
   a. rises; increases
   b. rises; decreases
   c. falls; increases
   d. falls; decreases
   e. does not change; decreases

6. The technology associated with manufacturing computers has advanced enormously. This change has led to the price of a computer ____ and the quantity ____.
   a. rising; increasing
   b. rising; decreasing
   c. falling; increasing
   d. falling; decreasing
   e. falling; not changing

7. Candy makers accurately anticipate the increase in demand for candy for Halloween so that the supply of candy and the demand for candy increase the same amount. As a result, the price of candy ____ and the quantity of candy ____.
   a. rises; does not change
   b. falls; increases
   c. does not change; increases
   d. does not change; does not change
   e. rises; rises

© 2015 Pearson Education, Inc.

8. During 2011 the supply of gasoline decreased while at the same time the demand for gasoline increased. If the magnitude of the increase in demand was greater than the magnitude of the decrease in supply, then the equilibrium price of gasoline ____ and the equilibrium quantity ____.
   a. increased; increased
   b. increased; decreased
   c. increased; did not change
   d. decreased; did not change
   e. did not change; increased

Short Response Questions

1. In Checkpoint 4.1 you drew a demand curve in Figure 4.4; in Checkpoint 4.2, you drew a supply curve in that figure. Return to Figure 4.4 and answer the following questions.
   a. If the price of cotton candy is $1, what is the situation in the market?
   b. If the price of cotton candy is $3, what is the situation in the market?
   c. What is the equilibrium price and equilibrium quantity of cotton candy?

Price (dollars per sweatshirt)	Quantity demanded (sweatshirts per season)		Quantity supplied (sweatshirts per season)
	Hockey team	Soccer team	
35	5	8	32
30	6	9	25
25	8	11	19
20	12	15	12
15	17	20	8

2. The table gives the demand and supply schedules for sweatshirts. What is the market demand schedule? At what price will the quantity demanded be equal to the quantity supplied? What is the equilibrium quantity?

■ **FIGURE 4.10**

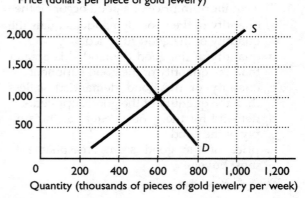

Price (dollars per piece of gold jewelry)

Quantity (thousands of pieces of gold jewelry per week)

3. Figure 4.10 shows the supply and demand for gold jewelry. In the figure, show what happens to the price and quantity if gold jewelry is a normal good and people's incomes rise.

■ **FIGURE 4.11**

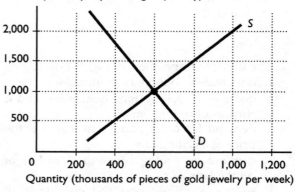

Price (dollars per piece of gold jewelry)

Quantity (thousands of pieces of gold jewelry per week)

4. Figure 4.11 shows the supply and demand for gold jewelry. Suppose that consumers think that silver jewelry is a substitute for gold jewelry. In Figure 4.12, show what happens to the price and quantity if the price of silver jewelry falls.

© 2015 Pearson Education, Inc.

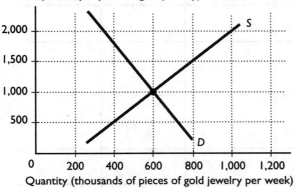

■ FIGURE 4.12

Price (dollars per piece of gold jewelry)

Quantity (thousands of pieces of gold jewelry per week)

5. Figure 4.12 shows the supply and demand for gold jewelry. Suppose the price of the gold that is used to produce gold jewelry rises. In the figure, show what happens to the price and quantity of gold jewelry.

6. These conditions in the table on the next page are changing in the market for oranges. Taking each change separately, complete the table. Use + for increase, — for decrease or NC for no change.

Long Response Questions

1. Consumers' incomes rise and steaks are a normal good. The supply of beef cattle has fallen recently due to a harsh winter in the western United States.
   a. Explain how these two events will impact the steak market.
   b. Use a correctly labeled graph of the steak market and show the price of a steak and the quantity of steaks after the incomes of consumers rise and the supply problem with cattle occurs.

2. Consumer information becomes available that there is a shock hazard with hair dryers. Workers who produce hair dryers have signed a wage agreement that gives them a 10 percent pay increase. The effect of the new information is greater than the effect of the wage hike.
   a. Explain how these two events will impact the market for hair dryers.
   b. Use a correctly labeled graph of the hair dryer market and show the price of a hair dryer and the quantity of hair dryers following the new consumer information and the increase in the workers' wages.

3. New cars are a normal good and people's incomes increase. Simultaneously, auto manufacturers must pay more for their workers' health insurance. What is the effect on the price and quantity of new cars?

Additional Exercises (also in MyEconLab Test A)

Price (dollars per bar)	Quantity demanded	Quantity supplied
	(bars per week)	
1.00	3,000	1,000
1.50	2,500	1,500
2.00	2,000	2,000
2.50	1,500	2,500
3.00	1,000	3,000

The table shows the demand and supply schedules for energy bars.

1. What is the market equilibrium?

2. If the price of bar is $1.50, describe the situation in the energy bar market. Explain how market equilibrium is restored.

3. A rise in income increases the quantity demanded by 1,000 bars a week at each price. Explain how the market adjusts to its new equilibrium.

4. A fire knocks out a large energy-bar factory and a fitness craze sends more people to the gym. How do these events influence demand and supply? Describe how the equilibrium price and equilibrium quantity change.

© 2015 Pearson Education, Inc.

	Change in Demand	Change in Supply	Effect on Price	Effect on Quantity
a. The growing season in Florida is shortened by 20 days of frost				
b. The price of tangerines (a close substitute for consumers) falls by 20 percent				
c. An announcement by the Surgeon General that oranges are a healthy source of nutrition				
d. The wages paid to orange grove workers increase by 10 percent				
e. Technology gains are made in harvesting equipment for oranges				
f. Consumers anticipate an increase in the price of oranges in the near future.				
g. Consumers' incomes fall by10 percent and oranges are a normal good				
h. The "Sunshine" ads promoting oranges as a quick snack are paying off for sellers.				

© 2015 Pearson Education, Inc.

SELF TEST ANSWERS

■ AP Self Test 4.1

True or false
1. False; page 83
2. False; page 82
3. True; page 87
4. False; page 87
5. False; page 88

Multiple choice
1. d; page 83
2. b; page 83
3. a; page 87
4. c; page 87
5. a; page 87
6. a; page 87
7. b; page 87
8. d; page 88
9. d; page 88
10. d; pages 87-88

Short Response Questions
1. Figure 4.13 illustrates the demand curve, labeled D in the diagram. (The supply curve is from the first "Complete the Graph" question in Checkpoint 4.2.)
   a. 8,000 bundles per month
   b. 7,000 bundles per month
   c. The demand curve slopes downward; page 88.

2. a. The demand increases and the demand curve shifts rightward, as shown in Figure 4.14 by the shift to D_1; page 88
   b. The demand decreases and the demand curve shifts leftward, as shown in Figure 4.14 by the shift to D_2; page 88
   c. The demand curve does not shift. The fall in the price of butter leads to an increase in the quantity demanded and a movement along the demand curve, not a shift of the demand curve; page 88.

■ FIGURE 4.13
Price (dollars per bundle of cotton candy)

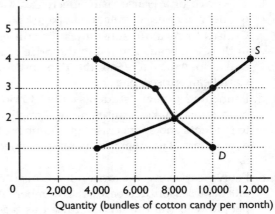

■ FIGURE 4.14
Price (dollars per pound of butter)

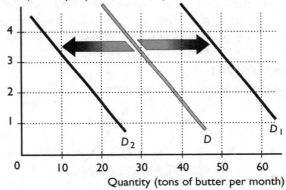

Long Response Questions
1. A change in the quantity demanded occurs when the price of the good changes. A change in demand occurs when any other influence on buying plans other than the price of the good changes; page 86.

2. A movement along a demand curve reflects a change in the quantity demanded and is the result of a change in the price of the product. A shift in a demand curve reflects a change in demand and is the result of a change in any factor, other than the price, that affects demand; page 88.

© 2015 Pearson Education, Inc.

Additional Exercises (also in MyEconLab Test A)

1. a. Caribbean cruises becoming more popular reflects a change in preferences. The demand increases; page 87.

   b. The price of a cruise rising decreases the quantity of cruises demanded; page 88.

   c. Cruises to Asia are substitutes for cruises in the Caribbean. The fall in the price of a cruise to Asia decreases the demand for Caribbean cruises; page 86.

   d. Launching a new "students only" Caribbean cruise makes cruises more attractive to students and so increases the number of demanders. The demand increases; page 87.

   e. People expecting the price of a cruise to fall next season decreases the number of people who want to take a cruise this season. The fall in the expected future price decreases the demand today; page 87.

   f. Increasing the number of leading rock artists performing on cruses increases people's preferences to take a cruise. The demand increases; page 87.

■ **FIGURE 4.15**

Price (thousands of dollars per cruise)

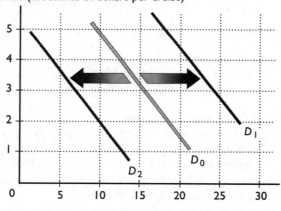

Quantity (millions of cruises per year)

2. a. Caribbean cruises becoming more popular increases demand and the demand curve shifts rightward. Figure 4.15 illustrates this change with the rightward shift of the demand curve from D_0 to D_1; page 88.

■ **FIGURE 4.16**

Price (thousands of dollars per cruise)

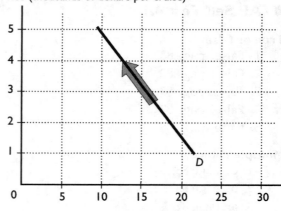

Quantity (millions of cruises per year)

   b. The price of a cruise rising decreases the quantity of cruises demanded. There is a movement up along the demand curve as illustrated in Figure 4.16 by the gray arrow. This change reflects the law of demand; page 88.

   c. The fall in the price of a cruise to Asia decreases the demand for Caribbean cruises and the demand curve shifts leftward. Figure 4.15 illustrates this change with the leftward shift of the demand curve from D_0 to D_2; page 87.

   d. Launching a new "students only" Caribbean cruise makes cruises more attractive to students so demand increases and the demand curve shifts rightward. Figure 4.15 illustrates this change with the rightward shift of the demand curve from D_0 to D_1; page 88.

   e. People expecting the price of a cruise to fall next season decreases demand today so the demand curve shifts leftward, from D_0 to D_2 in Figure 4.15; page 88.

   f. Increasing the number of leading rock artists performing on cruses increases demand so the demand curve shifts rightward, as illustrated in Figure 4.15 by the shift from D_0 to D_1; page 88.

© 2015 Pearson Education, Inc.

3. Only the second event, the rise in the price of a Caribbean cruise, reflects the law of demand. All the other events reflect a change in demand; page 90.

■ AP Self Test 4.2

True or false

1. False; page 90
2. True; page 94
3. False; page 94
4. True; page 94
5. False; page 94

Multiple choice

1. c; page 90
2. c; page 90
3. c; page 90
4. a; page 92
5. a; page 94
6. b; page 94
7. b; page 94
8. d; page 95
9. c; page 94
10. c; page 94

Short Response Questions

1. If other things remain the same, when the price of a good falls (rises), sellers decrease (increase) the quantity supplied; page 90.

2. The supply curve is illustrated in Figure 4.13, labeled S in the diagram.
   a. 8,000 bundles per month.
   b. 10,000 bundles per month.
   c. The supply curve slopes upward; page 91.

Price (dollars per pizza)	Market supply (pizzas per day)
14	47
12	36
10	25
8	14

3. The market supply schedule is in the table above; page 92.

4. Figure 4.17 illustrates the shift; pages 94-95.

■ FIGURE 4.17

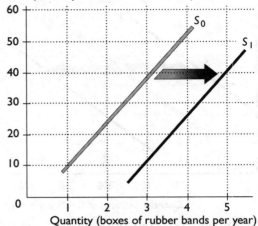

Price (dollars per box of rubber bands)

Quantity (boxes of rubber bands per year)

Long Response Questions

1. A change in the price of the product leads to a change in the quantity supplied. Changes in: prices of related goods; prices of resources and other inputs; expectations; number of sellers; and productivity lead to changes in supply; page 95.

Additional Exercises (also in MyEconLab Test A)

1. a. CDs and DVDs are substitutes in production. When the price of a CD falls, the supply of DVDs increases; page 93.
   b. The new robot technology lowers the cost of producing DVDs and increases the supply of DVDs; page 94.
   c. When the price of a DVD falls, the quantity of DVDs supplied decreases and there is a movement down along the supply curve of DVDs; page 95.
   d. If the price of a DVD is expected to rise next year, supply decreases now; page 94.
   e. If the wage rate paid to DVD factory workers increases, the supply of DVDs decreases because the price of a resource used to produce DVDs has risen; page 94.

2. a. When the price of a CD falls, the supply of DVDs increases and the supply curve of DVDs shifts rightward. In Figure 4.18 (on the next page) the supply curve shifts from S_0 to S_1; page 95.

© 2015 Pearson Education, Inc.

■ **FIGURE 4.18**

Price (dollars per DVD)

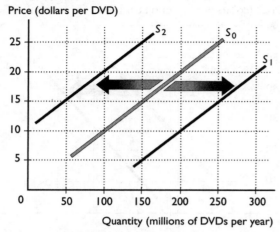

b. The new robot technology lowers the cost of producing DVDs and shifts the supply curve of DVDs rightward. In Figure 4.18 this shift is illustrated by the shift from S_0 to S_1; page 95.

■ **FIGURE 4.19**

Price (dollars per DVD)

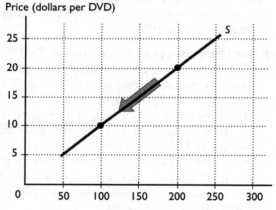

c. When the price of a DVD falls, the quantity of DVDs supplied decreases and there is a movement down along the supply curve of DVDs. In Figure 4.19 as the price falls from $20 per DVD to $10 per DVD the arrow shows that quantity supplied decreases from 200 million to 100 million; page 95.

d. If the price of a DVD is expected to rise next year, the supply curve shifts leftward, as illustrated in Figure 4.18 by the shift

from S_0 to S_2; page 95.

e. If the wage rate paid to DVD factory workers increases, the supply curve shifts leftward, as illustrated in Figure 4.18 by the shift from S_0 to S_2; page 95.

3. Only the third event, the fall in the price of a DVD, reflects the law of supply. All the other events reflect a change in supply; page 95.

■ **AP Self Test 4.3**

True or false

1. True; page 98
2. False; page 100
3. True; page 102
4. False; page 104
5. True; page 105

Multiple choice

1. a; page 98
2. d; page 99
3. b; page 100
4. c; page 100
5. b; page 102
6. c; page 102
7. c; page 104
8. a; page 105

Short Response Questions

1. a. A shortage of 6,000 bundles a month; page 99.
   b. A surplus of 3,000 bundles a month; page 99.
   c. The equilibrium price is $2 a bundle of cotton candy and the equilibrium quantity is 8,000 bundles a month; page 99.

Price (dollars per sweatshirt)	Quantity demanded (sweatshirts per season)
35	13
30	15
25	19
20	27
15	37

2. In the table, the market demand schedule is

© 2015 Pearson Education, Inc.

obtained by summing the Hockey team's demand and the Soccer team's demand. The equilibrium price is $25 and the equilibrium quantity is 19 sweatshirts; page 99.

■ **FIGURE 4.20**

Price (dollars per piece of gold jewelry)

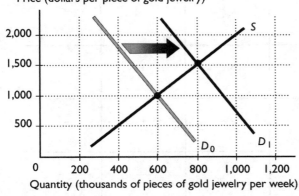

3. Figure 4.20 shows the effect of the increase in income. The increase in income increases the demand for normal goods, such as gold jewelry. The demand curve shifts rightward and the supply curve does not shift. The price of gold jewelry rises, to $1,500 in the figure, and the quantity increases, to 800,000 pieces per week in the figure; page 100.

■ **FIGURE 4.21**

Price (dollars per piece of gold jewelry)

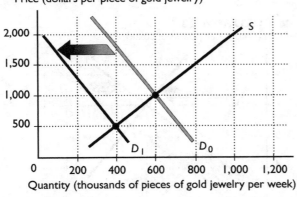

4. Figure 4.21 shows the effect of the fall in price of silver jewelry. A fall in the price of a substitute decreases the demand gold jewelry. The demand curve shifts leftward and the supply curve does not shift. The price of gold

jewelry falls, to $500 in the figure, and the quantity decreases, to 400,000 pieces per week in the figure; page 100.

■ **FIGURE 4.22**

Price (dollars per piece of gold jewelry)

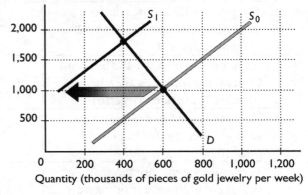

5. Figure 4.22 shows the effect of the fall in the price of gold. The price of gold is a cost to the producers of gold jewelry. A rise in the cost decreases the supply of the good. The supply curve shifts leftward and the demand curve does not shift. The price of gold jewelry rises, to $1,750 in the figure, and the quantity decreases, to 400,000 pieces per week in the figure; page 102.

6. These answers are in the table on the next page.

Long Response Questions

1. a. When incomes rise, consumers purchase more steaks. The demand for beef increases and the demand curve shifts rightward. At the same time, the supply of beef decreases because the harsh winter weather has lowered the stock of cattle below normal. The supply curve shifts leftward; pages 100-101.

   b. Because both the demand and supply change and we do not know the relative sizes of the two changes, either the price or the quantity will be indeterminate. In this case, the increase in demand leads to a higher price *and* the decrease in supply also leads to a higher price. So the combined effect of the two raises the price of

© 2015 Pearson Education, Inc.

	Change in Demand	Change in Supply	Effect on Price	Effect on Quantity
a. The growing season in Florida is shortened by 20 days of frost; page 102	NC	—	+	—
b. The price of tangerines (a close substitute for consumers) falls by 20 percent; page 101	—	NC	—	—
c An announcement by the Surgeon General that oranges are a healthy source of nutrition; page 101	+	NC	+	+
d. The wages paid to orange grove workers increase by 10 percent; page 102	NC	—	+	—
e. Technology gains are made in harvesting equipment for oranges; page 102	NC	+	—	+
f. Consumers anticipate an increase in the price of oranges in the near future; page 101	+	NC	+	+
g. The incomes of consumers fall by10 percent and oranges are a normal good; page 101	—	NC	—	—
h. The "Sunshine" ads promoting oranges as a quick snack are paying off for sellers; page 101	+	NC	+	+

steak. However, the increase in demand leads to a higher quantity and the decrease in supply leads to a lower quantity. So the combined effect of the two changes is indeterminate unless we know which change is larger. Figure 4.23 illustrates the case in which the change in demand exceeds the change in supply. In Figure 4.23, the demand curve shifts rightward from D to D_1 and the supply curve shifts leftward from S to S_1. The equilibrium price of a steak rises from $4 per pound to $12 per pound and the equilibrium quantity increases from 20,000 pounds per month to 40,000 pounds per month; page 103.

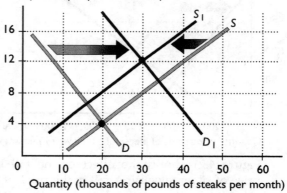

■ **FIGURE 4.23**

Price (dollars per pound of steak)

Quantity (thousands of pounds of steaks per month)

© 2015 Pearson Education, Inc.

2. a. The market for hairdryers is impacted by shifts in both the demand curve and the supply curve. The additional consumer information regarding the shock hazard decreases the demand for hairdryers and the demand curve shifts leftward. The wage hike increases the cost of producing hairdryers, so the supply decreases and the supply curve shifts leftward; pages 100-101.

■ **FIGURE 4.24**

Price (dollars per hair dryer)

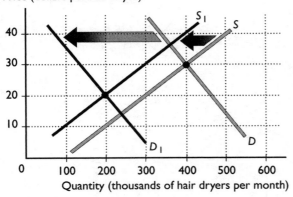

b. In Figure 4.24 the demand curve shifts leftward from D to D_1 and the supply curve shifts leftward from S to S_1. The decreases in both demand and supply lead to a decrease in the quantity of hairdryers. But the decrease in demand leads to a lower price while the decrease in supply leads to a higher price. In this case, however, we are told that the effect of the additional information exceeds the effect of the wage hike. So, as Figure 4.24 illustrates, the quantity falls from 400,000 hair dryers per month to 200,000 hair dryers per month and the price falls from $30 per hair dryer to $20 per hair dryer; page 104.

3. The increase in income increases the demand for normal goods and shifts the demand curve for new cars rightward. The increase in health insurance premiums decreases the supply of new cars and shifts the supply curve of new cars leftward. The price of a new car definitely rises. The effect on the quantity is ambiguous: it rises if the demand effect is larger, falls if the supply effect is larger, and does not change if the two effects are the same size; page 105.

Additional Exercises (also in MyEconLab Test A)

1. The market equilibrium is a price of $2.00 a bar and a quantity of 2,000 bars a week; page 98.

2. If the price of an energy bar is $1.50, the quantity demanded, 2,500 bars, is greater than the quantity supplied, 1,500 bars, so there is a shortage of 1,000 bars a week and the price rises. As the price rises, the quantity demanded decreases, the quantity supplied increases, and the shortage decreases. The price rises until it reaches $2.00, when the shortage disappears; page 98.

3. If the demand for energy bars increases by 1,000 bars at each price, the new equilibrium price is $2.50 a roll of film and the new equilibrium quantity is 2,500 bars a week. There is a shortage of energy bars at the original equilibrium price of $2.00 a bar, after the increase in demand. The shortage leads to the price rising. As the price rises, the quantity demanded decreases, the quantity supplied increases, and the shortage decreases. The price rises until the shortage disappears at a price of $2.50 a bar; page 100.

4. The fire decreases the supply and shifts the supply curve leftward. The fitness craze increases demand and shifts the demand curve rightward. At the initial equilibrium price, there is a shortage of energy bars and the price rises. If the magnitude of the decrease in supply is greater than the magnitude of the increase in demand, the equilibrium quantity decreases. If the magnitude of the decrease in supply is less than the magnitude of the increase in demand, the equilibrium quantity increases. In both cases the price rises; page 102.

© 2015 Pearson Education, Inc.

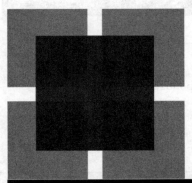

Elasticities of Demand and Supply

Chapter 5

CHAPTER CHECKLIST

In Chapter 5 we study the price elasticity of demand, the price elasticity of supply, the cross elasticity of demand, and the income elasticity of demand.

1 Define and calculate the price elasticity of demand, and explain the factors that influence it.

The price elasticity of demand is a measure of the responsiveness of the quantity demanded of a good to a change in its price when all other influences on buyers' plans remain the same. The price elasticity of demand equals the percentage change in the quantity demanded divided by the percentage change in price, with the negative sign ignored. When the percentage change in the quantity demanded exceeds the percentage change in price, demand is elastic and the elasticity of demand is greater than 1. When the percentage change in the quantity demanded equals the percentage change in price, demand is unit elastic and the elasticity of demand is equal to 1. When the percentage change in the quantity demanded is less than the percentage change in price, demand is inelastic and the elasticity of demand is less than 1. The more substitutes available for the good and the larger the proportion of income spent on the good, the larger the elasticity of demand. The total revenue from the sale of a good equals the price of the good multiplied by the quantity sold. If price and total revenue change in the opposite direction, demand is elastic. If a price change does not change total revenue, demand is unit elastic. If price and total revenue change in the same direction, demand is inelastic.

2 Define and calculate the price elasticity of supply, and explain the factors that influence it.

The price elasticity of supply is a measure of the responsiveness of the quantity supplied of a good to a change in its price when all other influences on sellers' plans remain the same. The two main influences on the price elasticity of supply are production possibilities and storage possibilities. If the good can be stored, supply is more elastic. The price elasticity of supply equals the percentage change in the quantity supplied divided by the percentage change in the price. If the price elasticity of supply is greater than 1, supply is elastic. If the price elasticity of supply equals 1, supply is unit elastic. If the price elasticity of supply is less than 1, supply is inelastic.

3 Define the cross elasticity of demand and the income elasticity of demand, and explain the factors that influence them.

The cross elasticity of demand is a measure of the responsiveness of the demand for a good to a change in the price of a substitute or complement when other things remain the same. The cross elasticity of demand is positive for substitutes and negative for complements. The income elasticity of demand is a measure of the responsiveness of the demand to a change in income when other things remaining the same. The income elasticity of demand equals the percentage change in the quantity demanded divided by the percentage change in income. It is positive for a normal good and negative for an inferior good.

© 2015 Pearson Education, Inc.

YOUR AP TEST HINTS

AP Topics

Topic on your AP test	What to Know	Corresponding textbook section
Price elasticity of demand	Measures how strongly quantity demanded responds to a change in price	Checkpoint 5.1
Price elasticity of supply	Measures how strongly quantity supplied responds to a change in price	Checkpoint 5.2
Cross elasticity of demand	Measures how strongly quantity demanded responds to a change in the price of another good	Checkpoint 5.3

AP Vocabulary Covered

Terms	What to Know	Text Sections
Price elasticity of demand	Percentage change in quantity demanded divided by percentage change in price	Checkpoint 5.1, p. 112
Midpoint method	Divide change in quantity (price) by the *average* quantity (price) then multiply by 100	Checkpoint 5.1, p. 112
Elastic demand	% change in Q^D exceeds the % change in price	Checkpoint 5.1, p. 114
Unit elastic demand	% change in Q^D equals the % change in price	Checkpoint 5.1, p. 114
Inelastic demand	% change in Q^D is less than the % change in price	Checkpoint 5.1, p. 114
Price elasticity of demand	% change in Q^D divided by % change in price	Checkpoint 5.1, p. 116
Total Revenue (*TR*)	Price of the good multiplied by number sold	Checkpoint 5.1, p. 120
Total revenue test	Demand is elastic if price and total revenue change in opposite direction; demand is inelastic if price and total revenue change in same direction; demand is unit elastic if change in price does not change total revenue	Checkpoint 5.1, p. 121
Price elasticity of supply	Percentage change in quantity supplied divided by percentage change in price	Checkpoint 5.2, p. 124
Factors influencing price elasticity of supply	Production possibilities and storage	Checkpoint 5.2, p. 126
Cross elasticity of demand	Percentage change in quantity demanded divided by percentage change in price of another good	Checkpoint 5.3, p. 129
Income elasticity of demand	Percentage change in quantity demanded divided by percentage change in income	Checkpoint 5.3, p. 130

Extra AP material

- On the AP test, the elasticity of demand is sometimes referred to as E_P, the elasticity of supply is E_S, the income elasticity of demand is E_I, and the cross elasticity of demand is E_X.
- The concept of elasticity is generally a microeconomic topic. The only point that elasticity appears on the AP macroeconomic test is the illustration of perfectly inelastic supply (a vertical supply curve) in figures of the money market.
- Perfectly elastic demand (a horizontal demand curve) is a key feature in the analysis of perfectly competitive firms.

© 2015 Pearson Education, Inc.

CHECKPOINT 5.1

■ **Define and calculate the price elasticity of demand, and explain the factors that influence it.**

Quick Review

- *Price elasticity of demand* The price elasticity of demand equals the magnitude of the percentage change in the quantity demanded divided by the percentage change in the price.
- *Elastic demand* When the percentage change in the quantity demanded exceeds the percentage change in price. The elasticity of demand is greater than 1 in value.
- *Inelastic demand* When the percentage change in the quantity demanded is less than the percentage change in price. The elasticity of demand is less than 1 in value.
- *Factors affecting elasticity* The demand for a good is more elastic if a large proportion of income is spent on it and if substitutes for it are easy to find. The factors that influence the ability to find substitutes for a good are whether the good is a luxury or a necessity, how narrowly it is defined, and the amount of time available to find substitutes for it.

Additional Practice Problems 5.1

1. For each of the following price changes, calculate the price elasticity of demand. Is the demand elastic, unit elastic, or inelastic?

   a. A 10 percent increase in price results in a 5 percent decrease in the quantity demanded.

   b. A 6 percent increase in price results in a 12 percent decrease in the quantity demanded.

   c. A 4 percent increase in price results in a 4 percent decrease in the quantity demanded.

Price (dollars per bag of cat food)	Quantity (bags of cat food per year)	Total revenue (dollars)
5	4	___
4	8	___
3	12	___
2	16	___
1	20	___

2. The table above gives the demand schedule for bags of cat food. A graph of this demand schedule gives a linear demand curve.

   a. Finish the table by calculating the total revenue for each row.

   b. When is the demand elastic? Inelastic? Unit elastic?

   c. Explain your answers to part (b).

Solutions to Additional Practice Problems 5.1

1a. The price elasticity of demand equals the magnitude of the percentage change in the quantity demanded divided by the percentage change in the price. So the elasticity of demand equals (5 percent) ÷ (10 percent) = 0.5. Because the elasticity of demand is less than 1, demand is inelastic.

1b. The price elasticity of demand equals (12 percent) ÷ (6 percent) =2.0. Because the elasticity of demand is greater than 1, demand is elastic.

1c. The price elasticity of demand equals (4 percent) ÷ (4 percent) = 1.0. Because the elasticity of demand equals 1, demand is unit elastic.

Price (dollars per bag of cat food)	Quantity (bags of cat food per year)	Total revenue (dollars)
5	4	20
4	8	32
3	12	36
2	16	32
1	20	20

2a. The completed table is above. Total revenue equals the price times the quantity sold.

2b. The demand is elastic at prices greater than $3 a bag. The demand is inelastic at prices less than $3 a bag. The demand is unit elastic at a price of $3 a bag.

2c. Demand is unit elastic at the midpoint of the demand curve. When demand is unit elastic,

© 2015 Pearson Education, Inc.

a price change leaves total revenue unchanged. The midpoint of the curve occurs when the price is $3 a bag, so demand is unit elastic at a price of $3 a bag.

Demand is elastic at all points above the midpoint of the demand curve. So when the price is greater than $3 a bag, demand is elastic. When demand is elastic, price and total revenue change in opposite directions. For example, when the price *rises* from $4 to $5, total revenue *decreases* from $32 to $20.

Demand is inelastic at all points below the midpoint of the demand curve. So when the price is less than $3 a bag, demand is inelastic. When demand is inelastic, price and total revenue change in the same direction. For example, when the price *rises* from $1 to $2, total revenue *increases* from $20 to $32.

■ AP Self Test 5.1

True or false

1. The price elasticity of demand equals the magnitude of the slope of the demand curve.

2. If the price increases by 10 percent and the quantity demanded decreases by 8 percent, the price elasticity of demand equals 1.25.

3. As the price of a good increases, if the quantity demanded of it remains the same, then demand for the good is perfectly inelastic.

4. Above the midpoint of a straight-line demand curve, demand is elastic.

5. When the price of a service increases by 5 percent and the quantity demanded decreases by 5 percent, total revenue remains unchanged.

6. If the price of tuna increases by 5 percent and the total revenue of tuna producers increases, then the demand for tuna is inelastic.

Multiple choice

1. The price elasticity of demand is a measure of the extent to which the quantity demanded of a good changes when _____ changes and all other influences on buyers' plans remain the same.
   a. income
   b. the price of a related good
   c. the price of the good
   d. the demand alone
   e. both the demand and supply simultaneously

2. Suppose the price of a movie falls from $9 to $7. Using the midpoint method, what is the percentage change in price?
   a. 33 percent
   b. −33 percent
   c. 25 percent
   d. −25 percent
   e. −97 percent

3. Suppose the price of a tie rises from $45 to $55. Using the midpoint method, what is the percentage change in price?
   a. 10 percent
   b. −10 percent
   c. 20 percent
   d. −20 percent
   e. 100 percent

4. Demand is elastic if
   a. consumers respond strongly to changes in the product's price.
   b. a large percentage change in price brings about a small percentage change in quantity demanded.
   c. a small percentage change in price brings about a small percentage change in quantity demanded.
   d. the quantity demanded is not responsive to price changes.
   e. the demand curve is vertical.

© 2015 Pearson Education, Inc.

5. During the winter of 2011–2012, the price of fuel oil increased enormously but the quantity demanded decreased only a little. This response indicates that the demand for fuel oil was
   a. inelastic.
   b. elastic.
   c. unit elastic.
   d. perfectly elastic.
   e. perfectly inelastic.

6. If substitutes for a good are readily available, the demand for that good
   a. does not change substantially if the price rises.
   b. does not change substantially if the price falls.
   c. is inelastic.
   d. is elastic.
   e. Both answers (a) and(b) are correct.

7. If the price of a product increases by 5 percent and the quantity demanded decreases by 5 percent, then the elasticity of demand is
   a. 0.
   b. 1.
   c. indeterminate.
   d. 5.
   e. 25.

8. The price of a bag of pretzels rises from $2 to $3 and the quantity demanded decreases from 100 to 60. What is the price elasticity of demand?
   a. 1.0
   b. 1.25
   c. 40.0
   d. 20.0
   e. 0.80

9. When a firm raises the price of its product, what happens to total revenue?
   a. If demand is elastic, total revenue decreases.
   b. If demand is unit elastic, total revenue increases.
   c. If demand is inelastic, total revenue decreases.
   d. If demand is elastic, total revenue increases.
   e. If demand is unit elastic, total revenue decreases.

Short Response Questions

■ **FIGURE 5.1**

1. In Figure 5.1, label the axes and then draw a demand curve for a good that has a perfectly elastic demand.

■ **FIGURE 5.2**

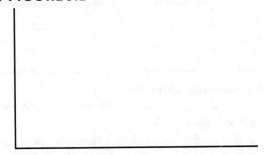

2. In Figure 5.2, label the axes and then draw a demand curve for a good that has a perfectly inelastic demand.

© 2015 Pearson Education, Inc.

3. Complete the table above by calculating the price elasticity of demand.
   a. Which row has the most elastic demand?
   b. Which row has the least elastic demand?

4. Suppose the price elasticity of demand for oil is 0.3. If the quantity of oil decreases by 6 percent, what is the effect on the price of oil?

■ **FIGURE 5.3**

Price (dollars per unit)

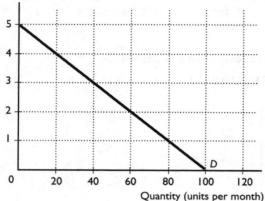

5. In Figure 5.3, darken the part of the demand curve along which demand is elastic. Label the point on the demand curve at which demand is unit elastic.

	Percentage change in price	Percentage change in quantity demanded	Price elasticity of demand
A	5	10	____
B	8	4	____
C	3	0	____
D	6	6	____
E	1	8	____

Long Response Questions

1. What does it mean when the demand for a good is inelastic?

2. What is the relationship between how narrowly a good is defined and the number of substitutes it has?

3. The Eye on Your Life explains how you can use elasticity in your personal life. You can also use it in your business life. Suppose you are a brand manager for Crest toothpaste and you are thinking about raising its price. How will this price hike affect the total revenue from sales of Crest?

Additional Exercises (also in MyEconLab Test A)

When the price of Internet service rises from $24 to $26 a month, the quantity demanded decreases from 204 million to 196 million subscribers.

1. Calculate the percentage change in the price of Internet service, the percentage change in the quantity demanded of Internet service, and the price elasticity of demand for Internet service.

2. Is the demand for Internet services elastic or inelastic? Would the demand for AOL service be more elastic or less elastic than the demand for Internet service? Why?

3. What is the change in the total revenue of Internet service providers? Why is the concept of price elasticity of demand useful to Internet service providers? If the demand curve for Internet service is a straight line, is the price at which the demand for Internet service is unit elastic above or below $25 a month? Why?

CHECKPOINT 5.2

■ **Define and calculate the price elasticity of supply, and explain the factors that influence it.**

Quick Review

- *Price elasticity of supply* A measure of the extent to which the quantity supplied of a good changes when the price of the good changes and all other influences on sellers' plans remain the same.

Additional Practice Problems 5.2

1. For each of the following price changes, calculate the price elasticity of supply.
   a. A 10 percent increase in price results in a 15 percent increase in the quantity supplied.
   b. A 6 percent increase in price results in a 3 percent increase in the quantity supplied.

© 2015 Pearson Education, Inc.

c. A 7 percent increase in price results in a 7 percent increase in the quantity supplied.

2. Over one month the elasticity of supply of avocados is 0.1 and over 5 years the elasticity of supply of avocados is 2.0. If the price of avocados rises 10 percent, what is the increase in the quantity supplied in one month and in 5 years? Why is there a difference in the quantities?

Solutions to Additional Practice Problems 5.2

1a. The elasticity of supply equals the percentage change in the quantity supplied divided by the percentage change in price, which is (15 percent) ÷ (10 percent) = 1.5.

1b. The elasticity of supply equals (3 percent) ÷ (6 percent) = 0.5.

1c. The elasticity of supply equals (7 percent) ÷ (7 percent) = 1.0.

2. The increase in the quantity supplied equals the percentage change in the price times the elasticity of supply. In one month the quantity supplied increases by (10 percent) × (0.1), which is 1 percent. In 5 years the quantity supplied increases by (10 percent) × (2.0), which is 20 percent. The increase in the quantity supplied is much greater after 5 years because more changes can be made as more time passes. Existing avocado trees can be more carefully cultivated and additional fertilizer used. Eventually additional avocado trees can be planted, mature, and then be harvested. The supply of avocados increases as time passes, making the supply more elastic.

■ AP Self Test 5.2

True or false

1. If the percentage change in the quantity supplied is zero when the price changes, supply is perfectly elastic.

2. Goods that can be produced at a constant (or very gently rising) opportunity cost have an elastic supply.

3. The supply of apples is perfectly elastic on the day of a price change.

4. The supply of a storable good is perfectly inelastic.

5. When the price of a pizza is $20, 10 pizzas are supplied and when the price rises to $30 a pizza, 14 pizzas are supplied. The price elasticity of supply of pizzas is 0.83.

6. If a 5 percent increase in price increases the quantity supplied by 10 percent, the elasticity of supply equals 2.0.

Multiple choice

1. The price elasticity of supply is a measure of the extent to which the quantity supplied of a good changes when only the
   a. cost of producing the product increases.
   b. quantity of the good demanded increases.
   c. supply increases.
   d. price of the good changes.
   e. number of firms changes.

2. When the percentage change in the quantity supplied exceeds the percentage change in price, then supply is
   a. elastic.
   b. inelastic.
   c. unit elastic.
   d. perfectly inelastic.
   e. perfectly elastic.

3. The supply of beachfront property on St. Simon's Island is
   a. elastic.
   b. unit elastic.
   c. negative.
   d. inelastic.
   e. perfectly elastic.

4. For a product with a rapidly increasing opportunity cost of producing additional units,
   a. demand is price elastic.
   b. supply is price elastic.
   c. demand is price inelastic.
   d. supply is price inelastic.
   e. the demand curve is vertical.

© 2015 Pearson Education, Inc.

5. The greater the amount of time that passes after a price change, the
   a. less elastic supply becomes.
   b. more elastic supply becomes.
   c. more negative supply becomes.
   d. steeper the supply curve becomes.
   e. more vertical the supply curve becomes.

6. The price elasticity of supply equals the percentage change in the
   a. quantity demanded divided by the percentage change in the price of a substitute or complement.
   b. quantity supplied divided by the percentage change in price.
   c. quantity demanded divided by the percentage change in price.
   d. supply divided by the percentage change in the demand.
   e. quantity supplied divided by the percentage change in income.

7. If a firm supplies 200 units at a price of $50 and 100 units at a price of $40, using the midpoint formula what is the price elasticity of supply?
   a. 0.33
   b. 1.00
   c. 3.00
   d. 5.00
   e. 8.50

8. If the quantity supplied increases by 8 percent when the price rises by 2 percent, the price elasticity of supply is _____ percent.
   a. 10.0
   b. 6.0
   c. 0.25
   d. 16.0
   e. 4.0

9. If the price of a good increases by 10 percent and the quantity supplied increases by 5 percent, then the elasticity of supply is
   a. greater than one and supply is elastic.
   b. negative and supply is inelastic.
   c. less than one and supply is elastic.
   d. less than one and supply is inelastic.
   e. greater than one and supply is inelastic.

Short Response Questions

■ **FIGURE 5.4**

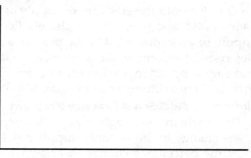

1. In Figure 5.4, label the axes and then draw a supply curve for a good that has a perfectly inelastic supply.

2. The elasticity of supply of wheat is 0.3 and the elasticity of supply of magazines is 1.3. If the prices of wheat and magazines both rise 10 percent, what is the increase in the quantity of wheat supplied and the increase in the quantity of magazines supplied?

	Price (dollars)	Quantity supplied (units per week)
A	5	10
B	15	30
C	25	50
D	35	90

3. The table above gives a supply schedule. Calculate the price elasticity of supply between points A and B; between points B and C; and between points C and D.

	Percentage change in price	Percentage change in quantity supplied	Price elasticity of supply
A	6	8	____
B	8	4	____
C	4	8	____

4. Complete the table above by calculating the price elasticity of supply.

Long Response Questions

1. Describe the elasticity of supply of a good that can be stored.

2. Why does the elasticity of supply increase as time passes after a price change?

© 2015 Pearson Education, Inc.

Additional Exercises (also in MyEconLab Test A)

In 2002, the price of asparagus crashed from $45 a crate to $15 a crate. A typical Californian asparagus farmer would have supplied 2,000 crates a day at $45 a crate but at $15 a crate would plow the crop into the ground and supply nothing.

1. Is the Californian supply of asparagus elastic, unit elastic, or inelastic? How do you think production possibilities and storage possibilities influence the price elasticity of supply of asparagus?

2. Calculate the price elasticity of supply of Californian asparagus. If the price of asparagus remains at $15 a crate, do you think the elasticity of supply will change over the coming years? Explain your answer.

CHECKPOINT 5.3

■ **Define the cross elasticity of demand and the income elasticity of demand, and explain the factors that influence them.**

Quick Review

- *Cross elasticity of demand* A measure of the extent to which the demand for a good changes when the price of a substitute or complement changes, other things remaining the same.

- *Income elasticity of demand* A measure of the extent to which the demand for a good changes when income changes, other things remaining the same.

Additional Practice Problems 5.3

1. For each of the following, calculate the cross elasticity of demand. Are the goods substitutes or complements?

   a. A 10 percent increase in the price of lettuce results in a 15 percent increase in the quantity of spinach demanded.

   b. A 5 percent increase in the price of beef results in a 10 percent increase in the quantity of pork demanded.

   c. A 4 percent increase in the price of a golf club results in a 2 percent decrease in the quantity of golf balls demanded.

2. For each of the following, calculate the income elasticity of demand. Are the goods normal or inferior goods?

   a. A 3 percent increase in income results in a 1 percent increase in the quantity demanded.

   b. A 6 percent increase in income results in a 3 percent decrease in the quantity demanded.

   c. A 2 percent increase in income results in a 4 percent increase in the quantity demanded.

3. Pepsi and Coke are substitutes. Pepsi and Tropicana orange juice also are substitutes. But quite likely the two cross elasticities of demand differ in size. Which cross elasticity do you think is larger and why?

Solutions to Additional Practice Problems 5.3

1a. The cross elasticity of demand equals the percentage change in the quantity demanded of one good divided by the percentage change in the price of the other good, which is (15 percent) ÷ (10 percent) = 1.5. The cross elasticity of supply is positive for substitute and negative for complements, so lettuce and spinach are substitutes.

1b. The cross elasticity of demand equals (10 percent) ÷ (5 percent) = 2.0. Beef and pork are substitutes.

1c. The cross elasticity of demand equals (−2 percent) ÷ (4 percent) = −0.5. Golf clubs and golf balls are complements.

2a. The income elasticity of demand equals the percentage change in the quantity demanded divided by the percentage change in income, which is (1 percent) ÷ (3 percent) = 0.33. The income elasticity is positive for a normal good and negative for an inferior good, so this good is a normal good.

2b. The income elasticity of demand equals (−3 percent) ÷ (6 percent) = −0.5. The good is an inferior good.

© 2015 Pearson Education, Inc.

2c. The income elasticity of demand equals (4 percent) ÷ (2 percent) = 2.0. The good is a normal good.

3. The cross elasticity between Pepsi and Coke is likely much larger than the cross elasticity between Pepsi and Tropicana orange juice. For many people, Pepsi and Coke are close to indistinguishable. Even a slight rise in the price of a Coke will increase the quantity of Pepsi demanded significantly, so their cross elasticity is large. Pepsi and Tropicana orange juice are less close substitutes. So, although an increase in the price of Tropicana orange juice will increase the demand for Pepsi, the increase will be relatively slight and the cross elasticity will be small.

■ AP Self Test 5.3

True or false
1. If the cross elasticity of demand is negative, the two goods are substitutes.

2. If the cross elasticity between hamburgers and hot dogs is positive, then hamburgers and hot dogs are substitutes.

3. An inferior good has a negative income elasticity of demand.

4. When the income elasticity of demand is positive, the good is a normal good.

5. A normal good is a good that has a positive cross elasticity of demand.

Multiple choice
1. The measure used to determine whether two goods are complements or substitutes is called the
   a. price elasticity of supply.
   b. cross elasticity of demand.
   c. price elasticity of demand.
   d. income elasticity.
   e. substitute elasticity of demand.

2. If beef and pork are substitutes, the cross elasticity of demand between the two goods is
   a. negative.
   b. positive.
   c. indeterminate.
   d. elastic.
   e. greater than one.

3. When the price of a pizza is $10, the quantity of soda demanded is 300 drinks. When the price of pizza is $15, the quantity of soda demanded is 100 drinks. The cross elasticity of demand equals
   a. –0.25.
   b. –0.40.
   c. –2.50.
   d. –25.00.
   e. 4.00.

4. When the price of going to a movie rises 5 percent, the quantity of DVDs demanded increases 10 percent. The cross elasticity of demand equals
   a. 10.0.
   b. 0.5.
   c. –0.5.
   d. –2.0.
   e. 2.0.

5. If two goods have a cross elasticity of demand of –2, then when the price of the one increases, the demand curve of the other good
   a. shifts rightward.
   b. shifts leftward.
   c. remains unchanged.
   d. may shift rightward, leftward, or remain unchanged.
   e. remains unchanged but the supply curve shifts leftward.

© 2015 Pearson Education, Inc.

6. The income elasticity of demand is the percentage change in the _____ divided by the percentage change in _____.
   a. quantity demanded; the price of a substitute or complement
   b. quantity supplied; price
   c. quantity demanded; price
   d. quantity demanded; income
   e. quantity demanded; the quantity supplied

7. When income increases from $20,000 to $30,000 the number of home-delivered pizzas per year increases from 22 to 40. The income elasticity of demand for home-delivered pizza equals
   a. 1.45.
   b 0.69.
   c. 0.58.
   d. 0.40.
   e. 2.86.

8. When income increases by 6 percent, the demand for potatoes decreases by 2 percent. The income elasticity of demand for potatoes equals
   a. −2.00.
   b. 3.00.
   c. −3.00.
   d. 0.33.
   e. −0.33.

9. If a product is a normal good, then its income elasticity of demand is
   a. zero.
   b. positive.
   c. negative.
   d. indeterminate.
   e. greater than one.

10. The income elasticity of demand for used cars is less than zero. So, used cars are
   a. an inferior good.
   b. a normal good.
   c. an inelastic good.
   d. a perfectly inelastic good.
   e. substitute goods.

Short Response Questions

■ FIGURE 5.5

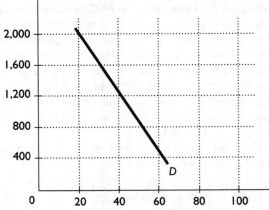

Price (dollars per large screen television)

Quantity (millions of large screen televisions per year)

1. The income elasticity of demand for large screen televisions is positive. In Figure 5.5, show the change when income increases.

	Percentage change in price of good A	Percentage change in quantity demanded of good B	Cross elasticity of demand
A	3	6	____
B	5	−10	____
C	−4	−8	____
D	8	4	____

2. Complete the table above. Which row has substitutes and which row has complements?

	Percentage change in income	Percentage change in quantity demanded	Income elasticity of demand
A	5	10	____
B	5	−10	____
C	5	2	____
D	6	6	____

3. Complete the table above. Which row indicates an inferior good and which row indicates a good that is income elastic?

Long Response Questions

1. Do you think the cross elasticity of demand between Pepsi and Coke is positive or negative, large or small? Why?

© 2015 Pearson Education, Inc.

2. The income elasticity of demand for inter-city bus trips is negative. What does this fact tell you about inter-city bus trips?

Additional Exercises (also in MyEconLab Test A)

When the price of a pizza falls from $9 to $7 and other things remain the same, the quantity demanded of pizza increases from 100 to 200 an hour, the quantity demanded of burgers decreases from 200 to 100 an hour, and the quantity demanded of cola increases from 150 to 250 cans an hour. Use this information to answer Exercises 1, 2, and 3.

1. Calculate the cross elasticity of demand for cola with respect to pizza.

2. Calculate the cross elasticity of demand for burgers with respect to pizza.

3. Of what use are these two cross elasticities of demand to the owner of a business that sells burgers and cola?

When incomes in Miami rise by 10 percent and other things remain the same, the quantity demanded of frozen fish cakes decreases by 5 percent and the quantity demanded of fresh fish increases by 15 percent. Use this information to answer Exercises 4, 5, and 6.

4. Calculate the income elasticity of demand for frozen fish cakes.

5. Calculate the income elasticity of demand for fresh fish.

6. How could a fish shop owner in Miami use these two income elasticities?

© 2015 Pearson Education, Inc.

SELF TEST ANSWERS

■ AP Self Test 5.1

True or false
1. False; page 116
2. False; page 116
3. True; page 114
4. True; page 118
5. True; page 120
6. True; page 120

Multiple choice
1. c; page 112
2. d; page 112
3. c; page 113
4. a; page 114
5. a; page 114
6. d; page 114
7. b; page 116
8. b; page 116
9. a; page 120

Short Response Questions
1. Figure 5.6 labels the axes and illustrates a demand curve for a good with a perfectly elastic demand; page 115.

2. Figure 5.7 labels the axes and illustrates a demand curve for a good with a perfectly inelastic demand; page 115.

■ FIGURE 5.6
Price (dollars)

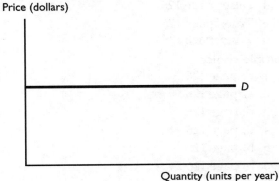

Quantity (units per year)

■ FIGURE 5.7
Price (dollars)

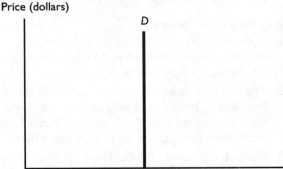

Quantity (units per year)

	Percentage change in price	Percentage change in quantity demanded	Price elasticity of demand
A	5	10	2.0
B	8	4	0.5
C	3	0	0.0
D	6	6	1.0
E	1	8	8.0

3. The complete table is above; page 116.
   a. The most elastic demand is in row E; page 116.
   b. The least elastic demand is in row C (the demand is perfectly inelastic); page 116.

4. The price rises by 20 percent; page 116.

■ FIGURE 5.8
Price (dollars per unit)

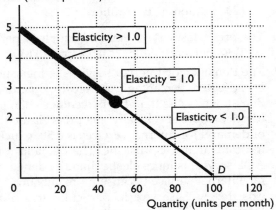

Quantity (units per month)

5. In Figure 5.8, demand is elastic along the dark portion of the demand curve. Demand

© 2015 Pearson Education, Inc.

is unit elastic at the midpoint of curve. Demand is inelastic along the demand curve below the midpoint; page 118.

Long Response Questions

1. Demand is inelastic if the percentage change in the quantity demanded is less than the percentage change in the price; page 114.

2. The more narrow the definition of the good, the more substitutes exist. For example, there are more substitutes for a slice of Pizza Hut pizza than for pizza in general; page 116.

3. When the price of a good rises, total revenue increases if demand is inelastic, does not change if demand is unit elastic, and decreases if demand is elastic. As brand manager, you can use this relationship to predict whether the total revenue from Crest will rise, fall, or stay the same if you boost its price; page 120.

Additional Exercises (also in MyEconLab Test A)

1. The percentage change in price is 8 percent. The midpoint formula shows the percentage change is:

$$\left(\frac{\$26 - \$24}{(\$24 + \$26) \div 2} \right) \times 100.$$

The percentage change in the quantity demanded is 4 percent. The percentage is:

$$\left(\frac{196 \text{ million} - 204 \text{ million}}{(204 \text{ million} + 196 \text{ million}) \div 2} \right) \times 100.$$

The price elasticity of demand equals (4 percent)÷(8 percent), which is 0.50; page 113.

2. The demand for Internet services is inelastic because the percentage change in quantity demanded is less than the percentage change in price. More specifically, the price elasticity of demand for Internet services is 0.50, which indicates that it is inelastic. The demand for AOL service is more elastic than the demand for Internet service because more substitutes exist for AOL service in particular than for Internet service in general. AOL service is a more narrowly defined service; pages 114, 116.

3. The initial total revenue is $24 a month × 204 million subscribers, which is $4,896 million a month. The new total revenue is $26 a month × 196 million subscribers, which is $5,096 million a month. So total revenue increases by $5,096 million a month − $4,896 million a month, which is $200 million a month.

The price elasticity of demand is useful because it allows us to make precise predictions about how much demanders change the quantity they demand when the price changes. For instance, if the price elasticity of demand for AOL is 0.5, then AOL can determine that a 10 percent increase in the price of their service will decrease the quantity that people demand by 5 percent; page 122.

The demand for Internet service is unit elastic at a price higher than $25 a month. At $25 a month, the elasticity equals 0.5. As we move up along a linear demand curve, the price elasticity of demand increases. So the demand for Internet service is unit elastic at the midpoint of the demand curve, which is at a price greater than $25 a month; page 118.

■ AP Self Test 5.2

True or false

1. False; page 124
2. True; page 124
3. False; page 126
4. False; page 126
5. True; page 126
6. True; page 126

Multiple choice

1. d; page 126
2. a; page 126
3. d; page 126
4. d; page 126
5. b; page 126
6. b; page 126
7. c; page 126
8. e; page 126
9. d; page 126

© 2015 Pearson Education, Inc.

Short Response Questions

■ **FIGURE 5.9**

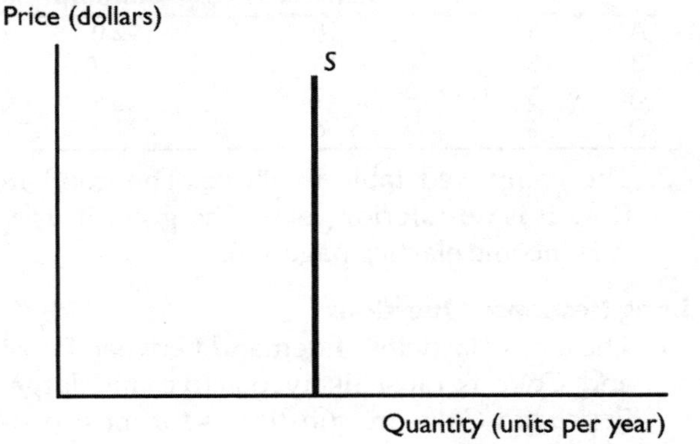

Price (dollars)

Quantity (units per year)

1. Figure 5.9 labels the axes and illustrates a supply curve for a good with a perfectly inelastic supply; page 125.

2. If the price of wheat rises 10 percent, the increase in the quantity supplied is (10 percent) × (0.3), which is 3 percent. If the price of a magazine rises 10 percent, the increase in the quantity supplied is (10 percent) × (1.3), which is 13 percent; pages 124, 126.

3. The price elasticity of supply between points A and B is 1.00; between points B and C is 1.00; and between points C and D is 1.71; page 126.

	Percentage change in price	Percentage change in quantity supplied	Price elasticity of supply
A	6	8	1.33
B	8	4	0.50
C	4	8	2.00

4. The completed table is above; page 126.

Long Response Questions

1. The elasticity of supply of a good that can be stored depends on the decision to keep the good in storage or offer it for sale. A small price change can make a big difference to this decision, so the supply of a storable good is highly elastic; page 126.

2. As time passes after a price change, it becomes easier to change production plans and supply becomes more elastic. For example, many manufactured goods have an inelastic supply if production plans have had only a short period in which to change. But after all the technologically possible ways of adjusting production have been exploited, supply is extremely elastic for most manufactured items; page 126.

Additional Exercises (also in MyEconLab Test A)

1. The supply of asparagus is elastic. The percentage change in the quantity supplied is greater than the percentage change in the price. The supply of asparagus over this large price range is elastic because there is the possibility of plowing the crop under and producing nothing. Once harvested, asparagus is not very storable, which makes supply more inelastic; pages 124-125.

2. The percentage change in the quantity supplied of asparagus is:

$$\left(\frac{2{,}000 - 0}{(2{,}000 + 0) \div 2} \right) \times 100,$$

which is 200 percent. The percentage change in the price of asparagus is

$$\left(\frac{\$45 \text{ a crate} - \$15 \text{ a crate}}{(\$45 \text{ a crate} + \$15 \text{ a crate}) \div 2} \right) \times 100,$$

which is 100 percent. So the price elasticity of supply = (200 percent) ÷ (100 percent) = 2.0.

As time passes, the elasticity of supply increases. After all the technologically possible ways of adjusting production have been exploited, the supply of asparagus becomes extremely elastic; pages 126-127.

■ **AP Self Test 5.3**

True or false

1. False; page 129
2. True; page 129
3. True; page 130
4. True; page 130
5. False; page 130

Multiple choice

1. b; page 129

© 2015 Pearson Education, Inc.

2. b; page 129

3. c; page 129

4. e; page 129

5. b; page 130

6. d; page 130

7. a; page 130

8. e; page 130

9. b; page 130

10. a; page 130

Short Response Questions

■ FIGURE 5.10

Price (dollars per large screen television)

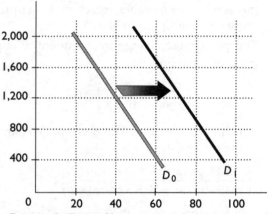

Quantity (millions of large screen televisions per year)

1. Because the income elasticity of demand is positive, we know that large screen televisions are a normal good. In Figure 5.10 an increase in income shifts the demand curve rightward from D_0 to D_1; page 130.

	Percentage change in price of good A	Percentage change in quantity demanded of good B	Cross elasticity of demand
A	3	6	2.0
B	5	−10	−2.0
C	−4	−8	2.0
D	8	4	0.5

2. The completed table is above. The goods in row B are complements; the goods in rows A, C, and D are substitutes; page 129.

	Percentage change in income	Percentage change in quantity demanded	Income elasticity of demand
A	5	10	2.0
B	5	−10	−2.0
C	5	2	0.4
D	6	6	1.0

3. The completed table is above. The good in Row B is an inferior good. The good in row A is income elastic; page 130.

Long Response Questions

1. The cross elasticity of demand between Pepsi and Coke is most likely positive and large. Pepsi and Coke are substitutes for most people, so their cross elasticity of demand is positive. They are close substitutes for many people, so their cross elasticity of demand is large; page 129.

2. The fact that the income elasticity of demand for inter-city bus trips is negative indicates that an inter-city bus trip is an inferior good. When people's incomes increase, they take fewer inter-city bus trips and instead fly, drive, or take the train; page 130.

Additional Exercises (also in MyEconLab Test A)

1. The cross elasticity of demand for cola with respect to pizza equals the percentage change in the quantity of cola divided by the percentage change in the price of a pizza. The percentage change in the quantity of cola equals

$$\left(\frac{250 \text{ an hour} - 150 \text{ an hour}}{(150 \text{ an hour} + 250 \text{ an hour}) \div 2}\right) \times 100,$$

which is 50 percent. The percentage change in the price of a pizza is

$$\left(\frac{\$7 \text{ a pizza} - \$9 \text{ a pizza}}{(\$9 \text{ a pizza} + \$7 \text{ a pizza}) \div 2}\right) \times 100,$$

which is −25 percent. So the cross elasticity of demand for cola with respect to pizza is (50 percent) ÷(−25 percent), which is −2.00. Because the cross elasticity of demand for the two is negative the two are complements; page 129.

© 2015 Pearson Education, Inc.

2. The cross elasticity of demand for burgers with respect to pizza equals the percentage change in the quantity of burgers divided by the percentage change in the price of a pizza. Part (a) shows that the percentage change in the price of pizza is −25 percent. The percentage change in the quantity of burgers is

$$\left(\frac{100 \text{ an hour} - 200 \text{ an hour}}{(200 \text{ an hour} + 100 \text{ an hour}) \div 2} \right) \times 100,$$

or −66.67 percent. The cross elasticity of demand for burgers with respect to pizza is equal to (−66.67 percent) ÷ (−25 percent), which is 2.67. Because the cross elasticity of demand for the two is positive the two are substitutes; page 129.

3. The owner can determine how the quantities of burgers and cola he or she sells will change if the price of a nearby pizza place changes the price of its pizza; pages 129-130.

4. The income elasticity of demand for frozen fish cakes is (−5 percent) ÷ (10 percent) = −0.50. The income elasticity is negative and the negative elasticity indicates that frozen fish cakes are an inferior good; page 130.

5. The income elasticity of demand for fresh fish is (15 percent) ÷(10 percent) = 1.50; page 130.

6. The owner of a fresh fish shop can use these two elasticities to predict how sales of fresh and frozen fish change when people's incomes change. For instance, if the economy in Miami goes into a recession so that people's incomes generally fall, the owner can predict that the quantity of frozen fish demanded will increase and the quantity of fresh fish demanded will decrease. As a result, the owner can stock more frozen fish and less fresh fish; page 131.

© 2015 Pearson Education, Inc.

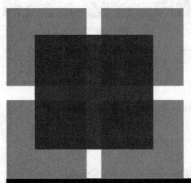

Efficiency and Fairness of Markets

Chapter 6

CHAPTER CHECKLIST

1 Describe the alternative methods of allocating scarce resources and define and explain the features of an efficient allocation.

Ways of allocating resources include: market price; command; majority rule; contest; first-come, first-served; sharing equally; lottery; personal characteristics; and force. Allocative efficiency occurs when we produce the quantities of goods and services on the *PPF* that people value most highly. Marginal benefit is the benefit that people receive from consuming one more unit of the product; marginal cost is the opportunity cost of producing one more unit of the product. The marginal benefit curve is downward sloping and the marginal cost curve is upward sloping. Allocative efficiency requires producing where the curves intersect, at the quantity that makes the marginal benefit equal the marginal cost.

2 Distinguish between value and price and define consumer surplus.

Value is what buyers get and price is what buyers pay. The value is the *marginal benefit,* which is the maximum price that buyers are willing to pay for another unit of the good. The demand curve is the marginal benefit curve. Consumer surplus is the marginal benefit from a good or service in excess of the price paid for it, summed over the quantity consumed.

3 Distinguish between cost and price and define producer surplus.

Cost is what a seller gives up to produce a good and price is what a seller receives when the good is sold. The cost of producing one more unit of a good or service is its *marginal cost.* The supply curve is the marginal cost curve. Producer surplus is the price of a good or service in excess of the marginal cost of producing it, summed over the quantity produced.

4 Evaluate the efficiency of the alternative methods of allocating resources.

When marginal benefit equals the marginal cost, the efficient quantity is produced. The sum of consumer surplus and producer surplus is maximized at a competitive equilibrium. According to Adam Smith, each participant in a competitive market is "led by an invisible hand" to promote the efficient use of resources. Market failure—underproduction or overproduction relative to the efficient quantity—creates a deadweight loss. Government imposed price and quantity regulations, taxes and subsidies, externalities, public goods, common resources, monopoly, and high transactions costs are obstacles to efficiency. Other means of allocation sometimes are efficient.

5 Explain the main ideas about fairness and evaluate the fairness of the alternative methods of allocating scarce resources.

Two views of fairness are: it's not fair if the *rules* aren't fair and it's not fair if the *result* isn't fair. When private property and property rights are protected and exchanges are voluntary is a fair rules approach. The fair results idea of income equality ignores the Big Tradeoff between efficiency and fairness. The Big Tradeoff points out the cost in terms of inefficiency of making income transfers that increase fairness.

© 2015 Pearson Education, Inc.

YOUR AP TEST HINTS

AP Topics

Topic on your AP test	What to Know	Corresponding textbook section
Resource allocation	Methods of scarce and efficient allocation	Checkpoint 6.1
Consumer surplus	Paying less than the maximum willing to pay; the area under the demand curve and above the price	Checkpoint 6.2
Producer surplus	Selling for more than the minimum willing to sell; the area under the price and above the supply curve	Checkpoint 6.3
Efficiency in markets	Marginal benefit equals marginal cost; competitive markets are efficient in the absence of the obstacles to efficiency	Checkpoint 6.4
Fairness of markets	Alternative methods of allocating scarce resources	Checkpoint 6.5

AP Vocabulary Covered

Terms	What to Know	Text Sections
Allocative efficiency	The most highly valued production point on the *PPF*; determined by the intersection of the marginal benefit curve and marginal cost curve ($MB = MC$)	Checkpoint 6.1, p. 141
Marginal benefit (*MB*)	The benefit of consuming one more unit	Checkpoint 6.1, p. 142
Marginal cost (*MC*)	The opportunity cost of producing one more unit	Checkpoint 6.1, p. 142
Efficient allocation	The highest valued allocation comparing *MB* and *MC*	Checkpoint 6.1, p. 143
Consumer surplus	Marginal benefit minus price paid, summed over the quantity consumed	Checkpoint 6.2, p. 147
Producer surplus	Price minus marginal cost, summed over the quantity produced	Checkpoint 6.3, p. 150
Market efficiency	$MB = MC$	Checkpoint 6.4, p. 152
Total surplus	The sum of producer surplus and consumer surplus	Checkpoint 6.4, p. 153
Market failure	An inefficient use of resources in the market	Checkpoint 6.4, p. 155
Deadweight loss	Loss from underproduction or overproduction	Checkpoint 6.4, p. 155
Externality	A cost or benefit that affects someone other than buyers or sellers	Checkpoint 6.4, p. 156
Public good	A good that benefits everyone	Checkpoint 6.4, p. 156
Monopoly	A firm as a sole provider of a good or service	Checkpoint 6.4, p. 156
Transaction cost	The opportunity cost of making trades	Checkpoint 6.4, p. 157
Tradeoff (Big tradeoff)	The decision to get results rather than just fairness	Checkpoint 6.5, p. 159

Extra AP material

- Allocative efficiency and the basics of $MB = MC$ are central to microeconomics questions and concepts.
- The AP test calls the situation in a market in which the marginal benefit equals marginal cost *allocative efficiency*. This refers to the point where this market outcome is allocating resources so that the efficient quantity is being produced. This is also the quantity that the society values the most.
- *Market fairness* concepts have not appeared on the AP test. The fairness concept of *utilitarianism* is not included on the test

© 2015 Pearson Education, Inc.

CHECKPOINT 6.1

■ **Describe the alternative methods of allocating scarce resources and define and explain the features of an efficient allocation.**

Quick Review

- *Allocation methods* Resources can be allocated by: using the market price; command; majority rule; a contest, first-come, first served; sharing equally; lottery; personal characteristics; and force.
- *Marginal benefit* The benefit that a person receives from consuming one more unit of a good or service.
- *Marginal cost* The opportunity cost of producing one more unit of a good or service.
- *Allocative efficiency* When the quantities of the goods and services produced are those that people value most highly because it is impossible to produce more of a good or service without giving up some of the another good or service that people value more highly. Allocative efficiency occurs when production is at the point where marginal benefit equals marginal cost.

Additional Practice Problems 6.1

1. Why is it necessary to allocate resources?
2. What is the command method of allocating resources?
3. Explain the relationship between production efficiency and allocative efficiency.

Solutions to Additional Practice Problems 6.1

1. Resources are scarce, so not everyone's wants can be fulfilled. Because not everyone can get everything he or she wants, *some* method must be used to determine whether or not resources are to be allocated to fulfill each specific want.
2. The command method of allocating resources relies upon someone in authority to order how resources shall be allocated. The former

Soviet Union and currently North Korea and Cuba are examples of entire economies in which command was (and still is for North Korea and Cuba) the major allocation method.

3. Production efficiency is a situation in it is impossible to produce more of one good or service without producing less of some other good or service—production is at a point on the *PPF*. Allocative efficiency is the most highly valued combination of goods and services on the *PPF*.

■ AP Self Test 6.1

True or false

1. When market prices are used to allocate resources, only the people who are able and willing to pay get the resources.
2. All combinations of goods and services on the production possibilities frontier are combinations of allocative efficiency.
3. The marginal benefit of a good increases as more of the good is consumed.
4. A production point can be allocatively efficient but not be production efficient.

Multiple choice

1. If a landlord will rent an apartment only to married couples over 30 years old, the landlord is allocating resources using a _____ allocation method.
   a. first-come, first-served
   b. market price
   c. contest
   d. personal characteristics
   e. command

2. Allocative efficiency occurs when
   a. the most highly valued goods and services are produced.
   b. all citizens have equal access to goods and services.
   c. the environment is protected at all cost.
   d. goods and services are free.
   e. production takes place at any point on the *PPF*.

© 2015 Pearson Education, Inc.

3. Marginal benefit equals the
   a. benefit that a person receives from consuming another unit of a good.
   b. additional efficiency from producing another unit of a good.
   c. increase in profit from producing another unit of a good.
   d. cost of producing another unit of a good.
   e. total benefit from consuming all the units of the good or service.

4. In general, the marginal cost curve
   a. has a positive slope.
   b. has a negative slope.
   c. is horizontal.
   d. is vertical.
   e. is U-shaped.

5. Allocative efficiency is achieved when the marginal benefit of a good
   a. exceeds the marginal cost by as much as possible.
   b. exceeds the marginal cost but not by as much as possible.
   c. is less than the marginal cost.
   d. equals the marginal cost.
   e. equals zero.

Short Response Questions

1. Only one person can become President of Sony, yet many of Sony's top executives would like that job. What allocation method is typically used to determine who becomes President? How does this allocation method benefit Sony?

2. Along a production possibilities frontier, to produce the first skateboard, 1 pair of roller blades must be forgone. To produce the second skateboard, 2 more pairs of roller blades must be forgone. Is the marginal cost of the second skate board 2 or 3 pairs of roller blades?

3. An economy produces only trucks and tractors and Figure 6.1 shows the marginal benefit and marginal cost of tractors. How many tractors are produced at the point of allocative efficiency?

■ **FIGURE 6.1**

Marginal benefit and marginal cost (trucks per tractor)

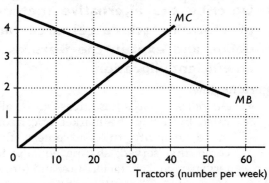

Long Response Questions

1. Suppose the price of a new BMW is $50,000. Which two kinds of people decide not to buy these BMWs? Is it true that when resources are allocated by market price, the rich always consume everything?

2. Why does allocative efficiency require producing where marginal benefit equals marginal cost rather than where marginal benefit exceeds marginal cost?

Additional Exercises (also in MyEconLab Test A)

1. Which method is used to allocate the following scarce resources?
   a. Airline tickets on the eve of Thanksgiving
   b. Goods at JCPenney in the January sales
   c. Presidency of the Students' Union
   d. The first serve in the final at the U.S. Open

Possibility	Bananas (pounds)	Coffee (pounds)
A	80	20
B	60	60
C	40	120
D	20	150

Bananas (pounds)	Willing to give up	Must give up
	(pounds of coffee per pound of bananas)	
20	3	1
40	2	2
60	1	3

2. The first table shows a nation's production possibilities of bananas and coffee. The sec-

© 2015 Pearson Education, Inc.

ond table shows the nation's marginal benefit schedule and marginal cost schedule. What is the marginal cost of growing 120 pounds of coffee? Calculate the quantity of coffee produced and the marginal benefit from coffee when the nation uses its resources efficiently.

CHECKPOINT 6.2

■ **Distinguish between value and price and define consumer surplus.**

Quick Review

- *Value* In economics the idea of value is called marginal benefit, which we measure as the maximum price that people are willing to pay for another unit of a good or service.
- *Consumer surplus* Consumer surplus is the marginal benefit from a good or service in excess of the price paid for it, summed over the quantity consumed.

Additional Practice Problems 6.2

1. The figure shows the demand curve for magazines and the market price of a magazine. Use the figure to answer the following questions.

   a. What is the value of the 1st magazine? What is the marginal benefit of the 1st magazine? What is the consumer surplus of the 1st magazine?

   b. What is the marginal benefit of the 2nd magazine? What is the consumer surplus of the 2nd magazine?

   c. What is the total quantity of magazines bought and the consumer surplus?

   d. If the price of a magazine rises to $10, what is the quantity bought and what is the consumer surplus?

2. Your friend paid a lawyer $50 for the hour it took the lawyer to write a letter to settle a rent dispute. Your friend wonders if the concepts of value, marginal benefit, and consumer surplus apply not only to goods but also to services, such as the lawyer's letter. What do you tell your friend?

Solutions to Additional Practice Problems 6.2

1a. The value of the 1st magazine equals the maximum price a consumer is willing to pay for the magazine. The figure shows that the maximum price for the 1st magazine is $15, so

the value of the magazine equals $15. The marginal benefit of the magazine is equal to the maximum price the consumer will pay, which is $15. The consumer surplus is equal to the marginal benefit of the 1st magazine ($15) minus the price of the magazine ($5) so the consumer surplus is $10.

1b. The marginal benefit of the magazine is equal to the maximum price the consumer will pay. The figure shows that the maximum price for the 2nd magazine is $10, so the marginal

benefit of the magazine equals $5. The consumer surplus is equal to $5.

1c. The quantity bought is 3 magazines because the demand curve shows that the quantity

© 2015 Pearson Education, Inc.

demanded at the price of $5 is 3 magazines. The consumer surplus equals the area of the darkened triangle in the figure. Calculating the area of the consumer surplus triangle, which is equal

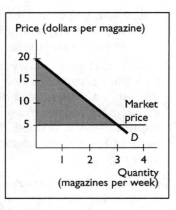

to one half the base of the triangle multiplied by the height or 1/2 × (3 − 0) × ($20 − $5), which is $22.50.

1d. If the price of a magazine rises to $10, the quantity bought is 2 magazines. The consumer surplus now equals 1/2 × (2 − 0) × ($20 − $10), which is $10.00.

2. All the concepts of value, marginal benefit, and consumer surplus apply to services as well as to goods. In your friend's case, there was some maximum amount your friend was willing to pay the attorney to write the letter. This maximum amount was the value to your friend of the letter. It is also the marginal benefit of the letter. Presumably your friend got the letter for some amount less than the maximum your friend was willing to pay. The difference between the marginal benefit of the letter and the price paid it is the consumer surplus your friend enjoyed from the letter.

■ AP Self Test 6.2

True or false

1. In economics, value and price refer to the same thing.

2. A demand curve is a marginal benefit curve.

3. The consumer surplus from one unit of a good is the marginal benefit from the good minus the price paid for it.

4. Consumer surplus always equals zero because consumers always pay for the goods and services they consume.

Multiple choice

1. Value is
   a. the price we pay for a good.
   b. the cost of resources used to produce a good.
   c. objective so that it is determined by market forces, not preferences.
   d. the marginal benefit we get from consuming another unit of a good or service.
   e. the difference between the price paid for a good and the marginal cost of producing that unit of the good.

2. A marginal benefit curve
   a. is the same as a demand curve.
   b. is the same as a supply curve.
   c. slopes upwards.
   d. is a vertical line at the efficient quantity.
   e. is U-shaped.

3. In general, as the consumption of a good or service increases, the marginal benefit from consuming that good or service
   a. increases.
   b. decreases.
   c. stays the same.
   d. at first increases and then decreases.
   e. at first decreases and then increases.

4. The difference between the marginal benefit from a new pair of shoes and the price of the new pair of shoes is
   a. the consumer surplus from that pair of shoes.
   b. what we get.
   c. what we have to pay.
   d. the price when the marginal benefit is maximized.
   e. the consumer's expenditure on the shoes.

5. Suppose the price of a scooter is $200 and Cora Lee is willing to pay $250. Cora Lee's
   a. consumer surplus from that scooter is $200.
   b. consumer surplus from that scooter is $50.
   c. marginal benefit from that scooter is $200.
   d. consumer surplus from that scooter is $150.
   e. consumer surplus from that scooter is $250.

© 2015 Pearson Education, Inc.

6. If the price of a pizza is $10 per pizza, the consumer surplus from the first pizza consumed ____ the consumer surplus from the second pizza consumed.
   a. is greater than
   b. equals
   c. is less than
   d. cannot be compared to
   e. None of the above answers is correct because more information is needed about the marginal cost of producing the pizzas to answer the question.

Short Response Questions

1. Define consumer surplus

Price (dollars per tablet)	Quantity (millions of tablets per year)	Consumer surplus (dollars)
500	4	___
400	8	___
300	12	___
200	16	___
100	20	___

2. The table above gives the demand schedule for tablets. The price of a tablet is $200.
   a. Complete the table by calculating the consumer surplus. In the first row, calculate the consumer surplus for the 4 millionth tablet; in the second row, calculate the consumer surplus for the 8 millionth tablet; and so on.
   b. As more tablets are purchased, what happens to the consumer surplus of the last unit purchased? Why?

3. Figure 6.2 shows the demand curve for roller blades.
   a. What is the marginal benefit of the 20,000th pair of roller blades?
   b. What is the marginal benefit of the 40,000th pair of roller blades?
   c. If the price of a pair of roller blades is $100, what is the consumer surplus on the 20,000th pair of roller blades?
   d. If the price of a pair of roller blades is $100, what is the quantity of roller blades purchased? What is the amount of the consumer surplus?

■ **FIGURE 6.2**

Price (dollars per pair of roller blades)

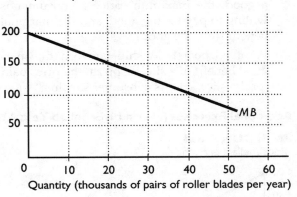

Quantity (thousands of pairs of roller blades per year)

■ **FIGURE 6.3**

Price (dollars per bag of potato chips)

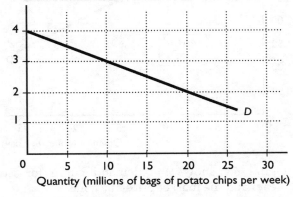

Quantity (millions of bags of potato chips per week)

4. Figure 6.3 shows the demand curve for bags of potato chips.
   a. What is the maximum price a consumer is willing to pay for the 10 millionth bag of chips?
   b. What is the marginal benefit from the 10 millionth bag of chips? What is the relationship between your answer to part (a) and your answer to this part?
   c. If the price of a bag of chips equals $2, in Figure 6.3 shade the area that equals the amount of the consumer surplus.
   d. If the price of a bag of chips equals $2, what is the amount of consumer surplus?

© 2015 Pearson Education, Inc.

Long Response Questions

1. What is the relationship between the value of a good, the maximum price a consumer is willing to pay for the good, and the marginal benefit from the good?

2. What is the relationship between the marginal benefit of a slice of pizza, the price paid for the slice, and its consumer surplus?

Additional Exercises (also in MyEconLab Test A)

■ **FIGURE 6.4**

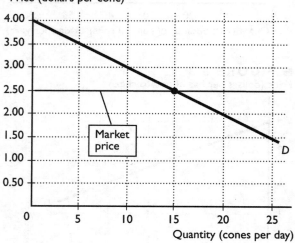

Price (dollars per cone)

Figure 6.4 shows the demand curve for ice cream and the market price of a cone.

1. What is the value of the 15th cone, the willingness to pay for the 5th cone, and the consumer surplus on the 5th cone?

2. How many ice cream cones are bought? Calculate the consumer surplus, the total expenditure on ice cream, and the total benefit from ice cream.

3. If demand for ice cream doubles, what is the change in total expenditure on ice cream and the change in consumer surplus?

CHECKPOINT 6.3

■ **Distinguish between cost and price and define producer surplus.**

Quick Review

- *Cost* Cost is what the seller must give up to produce a good.
- *Producer surplus* The producer surplus equals the price of a good in excess of the marginal cost of producing it, summed over the quantity produced.

Additional Practice Problems 6.3

1. The figure shows the supply curve and the market price of a magazine. Use the figure to answer the following questions.

a. What is the marginal cost of the 10 millionth magazine?

b. What is the minimum supply price of the 10 millionth magazine?

c. What is the producer surplus on the 10 millionth magazine?

d. What are the quantity of magazines sold and the total producer surplus?

2. Why is the minimum price for which a seller will produce a product equal to the product's marginal cost?

© 2015 Pearson Education, Inc.

Solutions to Additional Practice Problems 6.3

1a. The marginal cost of the 10 millionth magazine is equal to the minimum supply price of the 10 millionth magazine. The supply curve, which is also the marginal cost curve, shows  this price. In the figure, the supply curve shows that the marginal cost of 10 millionth magazine is $2.50.

1b. The minimum supply price of the 10 millionth magazine equals its marginal cost, $2.50.

1c. The producer surplus on the 10 millionth magazine is equal to its market price minus its marginal cost, which is $5 − $2.50 = $2.50.

1d. At the market price of $5, 20 million magazines are sold. The producer surplus equals the area of the grey triangle in the figure. Calculating the area of the triangle as one half  the base multiplied by the height, or 1/2 × (20 million − 0) × ($5 − 0), the producer surplus equals $50 million.

2. A seller is willing to produce a good as long as the price the seller receives covers all the costs of producing the good. So the minimum price for which a seller is willing to produce a unit of the good must be the amount that just equals the cost of the producing that unit. But the cost of producing any unit of a good is its marginal cost, so the minimum supply price equals the good's marginal cost.

■ AP Self Test 6.3

True or false

1. In economics, cost and price are the same thing.

2. The minimum price for which Bobby will grow another pound of rice is 20¢, so the marginal cost of an additional pound of rice is 20¢.

3. A supply curve is a marginal benefit curve.

4. Producer surplus equals the marginal benefit of a good minus the cost of producing it.

Multiple choice

1. Cost
   a. is what the buyer pays to get the good.
   b. is always equal to the marginal benefit for every unit of a good produced.
   c. is what the seller must give up to produce the good.
   d. is greater than market price, which results in a profit for firms.
   e. means the same thing as price.

2. If a firm is willing to supply the 1,000th unit of a good at a price of $23 or more, we know that $23 is the
   a. highest price the seller hopes to realize for this output.
   b. minimum price the seller must receive to produce this unit.
   c. average price of all the prices the seller could charge.
   d. price that sets the marginal benefit equal to the price.
   e. only price for which the seller is willing to sell this unit of the good.

3. A supply curve shows the ____ of producing one more unit of a good or service.
   a. producer surplus
   b. consumer surplus
   c. total benefit
   d. marginal cost
   e. marginal benefit to the producer

© 2015 Pearson Education, Inc.

4. The producer surplus on a unit of a good is
   a. equal to the marginal benefit from the good minus its price.
   b. equal to the price of the good minus the marginal cost of producing it.
   c. always equal to consumer surplus.
   d. Both answers (a) and (c) are correct.
   e. Both answers (b) and (c) are correct.

5. Suppose you're willing to tutor a student for $10 an hour. The student pays you $15 an hour. What is your producer surplus?
   a. $5 an hour
   b. $10 an hour
   c. $15 an hour
   d. $25 an hour
   e. more than $25 an hour

6. In a figure that shows a supply curve and a demand curve, producer surplus is the area
   a. below the demand curve and above the market price.
   b. below the supply curve and above the market price.
   c. above the demand curve and below the market price.
   d. above the supply curve and below the market price.
   e. between the demand curve and the supply curve.

Short Response Questions
■ FIGURE 6.5
Price (dollars per bag of potato chips)

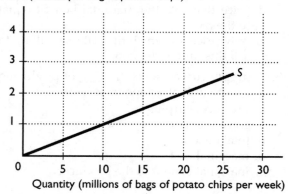

1. Figure 6.5 shows the supply curve for bags of potato chips.

a. What is the minimum price for which a supplier is willing to produce the 10 millionth bag of chips?
b. What is the marginal cost of the 10 millionth bag of chips? What is the relationship between your answer to part (a) and your answer to this part?
c. If the price of a bag of chips equals $2, in Figure 6.5 shade the area that equals the amount of the producer surplus.
d. If the price of a bag of chips equals $2, calculate the producer surplus.

Long Response Questions
1. What is the relationship between the minimum price a supplier must receive to produce a slice of pizza and the marginal cost of the slice of pizza? What is the relationship between the marginal cost curve and the supply curve?

2. What is producer surplus? As the price of a good or service rises and the supply curve does not shift, what happens to the amount of the producer surplus?

Additional Exercises (also in MyEconLab Test A)
■ FIGURE 6.6
Price (dollars per cone)

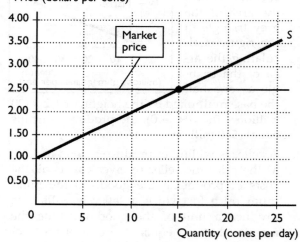

Quantity (cones per day)

Figure 6.6 shows the supply curve of ice cream and the market price of a cone.

1. What is the opportunity cost of the 15th cone, the minimum supply price of the 5th cone,

© 2015 Pearson Education, Inc.

and the producer surplus on the 5th cone?

2. What are the quantity of ice cream cones sold, the producer surplus on ice cream cones, the total revenue from the ice cream cones sold, and the total cost of producing ice cream cones?

3. If the price falls to $2.00 a cone, calculate the change in total revenue and the change in producer surplus?

CHECKPOINT 6.4

■ Evaluate the efficiency of the alternative methods of allocating resources.

Quick Review

- *Efficiency of competitive equilibrium* The condition that marginal benefit equals marginal cost delivers an efficient use of resources. It allocates resources to the activities that create the greatest possible value. Marginal benefit equals marginal cost at a competitive equilibrium, so a competitive equilibrium is efficient.

- *Deadweight loss* The decrease in consumer surplus and producer surplus that results from an inefficient level of production.

Additional Practice Problems 6.4

1. The figure shows the market for paper. Use the figure to answer the following questions.

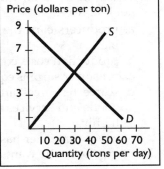

a. What are the equilibrium price and the equilibrium quantity of paper? What is the efficient quantity of paper?

b. In the market equilibrium, use the figure above to shade the consumer surplus and the producer surplus.

c. What does the consumer surplus equal? What does the producer surplus equal? What does the total surplus equal?

d. Is the market for paper efficient? Why or why not? Can the total surplus be any larger at any other level of production?

2. Who benefits from a deadweight loss?

Solutions to Additional Practice Problems 6.4

1a. The equilibrium is shown in the figure and is where the supply and demand curves intersect. The equilibrium price is $5 a ton and the equilibrium quantity is 30 tons a day. The efficient quantity is where the marginal benefit and marginal cost curves intersect. Because the demand curve is the marginal benefit curve and the supply curve is the marginal cost curve, the efficient quantity is 30 tons a day.

1b. The consumer surplus is illustrated in the figure as the area of the top, dark triangle. The producer surplus equals the area of the lower, lighter triangle.

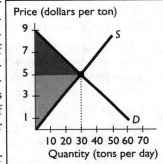

1c. The consumer surplus equals the area of the darker triangle, or $1/2 \times$ (30 tons) $\times$ ($4 per ton) = $60, where $4 a ton is the height of the triangle, $9 a ton − $5 a ton. The producer surplus equals the area of the lighter triangle, or $1/2 \times$ (30 tons) $\times$ ($5 per ton) = $75, where $5 a ton is the height of the triangle, $5 a ton − $0 a ton. The total surplus equals the sum of the consumer surplus plus the producer surplus, which is $135.

1d. The efficient use of resources occurs when marginal benefit equals marginal cost. The market equilibrium is efficient because the marginal benefit of a ton of paper equals its marginal cost. The sum of the consumer surplus and producer surplus, which equals the total surplus, is at its maximum at the effi-

© 2015 Pearson Education, Inc.

cient level of production so the total surplus cannot be larger at any other amount of production.

2. No one gains from a deadweight loss created by a market failure. Deadweight loss is a decrease in consumer surplus and producer surplus that results from an inefficient level of production. The deadweight loss is borne by the entire society. It is not a loss for the consumers and a gain for the producer. It is a social loss.

■ AP Self Test 6.4

True or false

1. When the demand curve is the marginal benefit curve and the supply curve is the marginal cost curve, the competitive equilibrium is efficient.

2. When the efficient quantity of a good is produced, the consumer surplus is always zero.

3. According to Adam Smith, the invisible hand suggests that competitive markets require government action to ensure that resources are allocated efficiently.

4. Market failure occurs if less than the efficient quantity of a good is produced but producing more than the efficient quantity does not result in market failure.

Multiple choice

1. When a market is efficient the
   a. sum of consumer surplus and producer surplus is maximized.
   b. deadweight gain is maximized.
   c. quantity produced is maximized.
   d. marginal benefit of the last unit produced exceeds the marginal cost by as much as possible.
   e. total benefit equals the total cost.

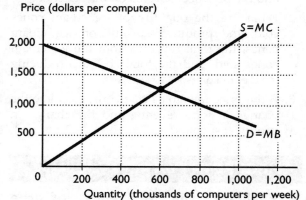

■ **FIGURE 6.7**
Price (dollars per computer)

2. Figure 6.7 shows the market for computers. What is the equilibrium quantity of computers?
   a. 0 computers per week
   b. 200,000 computers per week
   c. 400,000 computers per week
   d. 600,000 computers per week
   e. more than 600,000 computers per week

3. Figure 6.7 shows the market for computers. What is the efficient quantity of computers?
   a. 0 computers per week
   b. 200,000 computers per week
   c. 400,000 computers per week
   d. 600,000 computers per week
   e. more than 600,000 computers per week

4. Which of the following occurs when a market is efficient?
   a. producers earn the highest income possible
   b. production costs equal total benefit
   c. consumer surplus equals producer surplus
   d. scarce resources are used to produce the goods and services that people value most highly
   e. every consumer has all of the good or service he or she wants.

© 2015 Pearson Education, Inc.

5. The concept of "the invisible hand" suggests that markets
   a. do not produce the efficient quantity.
   b. are always fair.
   c. produce the efficient quantity.
   d. are unfair though they might be efficient.
   e. allocate resources unfairly and inefficiently.

6. When underproduction occurs,
   a. producers gain more surplus at the expense of consumers.
   b. marginal cost is greater than marginal benefit.
   c. consumer surplus increases to a harmful amount.
   d. there is a deadweight loss that is borne by the entire society.
   e. the deadweight loss harms only consumers.

7. When production moves from the efficient quantity to a point of overproduction,
   a. consumer surplus definitely increases.
   b. the sum of producer surplus and consumer surplus increases.
   c. there is a deadweight loss.
   d. consumers definitely lose and producers definitely gain.
   e. consumers definitely gain and producers definitely lose.

8. Which of the following can result in market failure?
   i. competition
   ii. an external cost or an external benefit
   iii. a tax
   a. i only.
   b. ii only.
   c. iii only.
   d. ii and iii.
   e. i and iii.

Short Response Questions

■ FIGURE 6.8

Price (thousands of dollars per automobile)

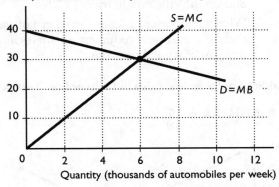

1. In Figure 6.8, what is the equilibrium quantity of automobiles? What is the efficient quantity of automobiles? Shade the consumer surplus and the producer surplus and calculate their amounts.

■ FIGURE 6.9

Price (thousands of dollars per automobile)

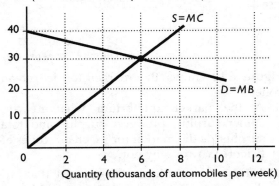

2. Figure 6.9 is identical to Figure 6.8.
   a. Suppose that 8,000 automobiles are produced. Shade the deadweight loss light grey and calculate its amount.
   b. Suppose that 4,000 automobiles are produced. Shade the deadweight loss dark grey and calculate its amount.

Long Response Questions

1. What is the relationship between a competitive market, efficiency, and the invisible hand?

© 2015 Pearson Education, Inc.

2. Suppose the demand for cotton clothing increases. What effect does the increase in demand have on the equilibrium quantity and on the efficient quantity?

3. What factors might lead a market failure, that is a market producing an inefficient amount of a good or service?

Additional Exercises (also in MyEconLab Test A)

■ **FIGURE 6.10**
Price (dollars per cone)

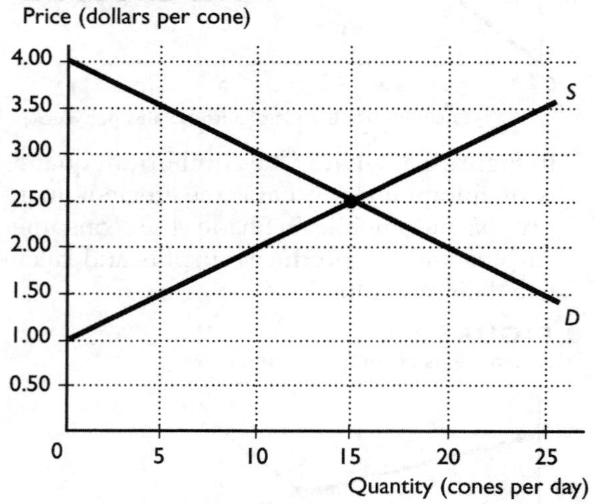

Figure 6.10 shows the market for ice cream cones.

1. At the market equilibrium, what are consumer surplus, producer surplus and total surplus? Is the market for ice cream cones efficient? Why or why not?

2. The government limits the quantity that producers can sell to 10 cones a day. Is the market for ice cream cones efficient? Explain. Calculate the deadweight loss.

3. The government passes a law requiring producers to sell 20 ice cream cones a day. Is the market for ice cream cones efficient? Explain. Calculate the deadweight loss.

CHECKPOINT 6.5

■ **Explain the main ideas about fairness and evaluate the fairness of alternative methods of allocating scarce resources.**

Quick Review

• *Big tradeoff* The big tradeoff is the tradeoff between efficiency and fairness that results when income transfers are made.

Additional Practice Problem 6.5

1. If Bill Gates gives $1,000 to a homeless person, would the transaction be fair? If Mr. Gates is taxed $1,000 by the government and the government gives the $1,000 to the same homeless person, would the transaction be fair? Comment on your answers.

Solution to Additional Practice Problem 6.5

1. If Mr. Gates gives $1,000 to a homeless person, the action is considered fair. The exchange is fair according to the fair rules principle because the exchange is voluntary. And the outcome is fair according to the fair results principle because there is more equality of income. If Mr. Gates is taxed by the government, the outcome is fair according to the fair results principle because there is more equality of income. But the transaction is not fair according to the fair rules principle because the exchange does not occur voluntarily.

■ **AP Self Test 6.5**

True or false

1. The principle that "it's not fair if the result isn't fair" can conflict with the principle that "it's not fair if the rules aren't fair."

2. The big tradeoff is the tradeoff between efficiency and happiness.

3. According to the "fair-rules" view of fairness, in times of natural disasters it is fair to force people to make available necessary goods and services at lower than usual prices.

© 2015 Pearson Education, Inc.

Multiple choice

1. The "fair-rules" view of fairness is based on
   a. income transfers from the rich to the poor.
   b. property rights and voluntary exchange.
   c. efficiency.
   d. the big tradeoff.
   e. allocating resources using majority rule.

2. The idea that unequal incomes are unfair generally uses the ____ principle of fairness.
   a. big tradeoff
   b. involuntary exchange
   c. voluntary exchange
   d. it's not fair if the result isn't fair
   e. it's not fair if the rules aren't fair

3. Which of the following is an example in which "the big tradeoff" can occur?
   a. the government redistributes income from the rich to the poor
   b. Ford increases the price of a pickup truck
   c. a basketball player signs a $5 million contract
   d. a college lowers tuition
   e. the price of personal computers falls year after year

Short Response Questions

1. In the United States, richer people generally pay a larger fraction of their income as taxes than do poorer people. Is this arrangement fair? Answer from a fair-results view and from a fair-rules view.

2. Suppose that during their working lifetimes, Matt and Pat have earned identical incomes as computer programmers. The only difference between the two is that Matt spent all of his income while Pat saved a large portion of hers. Now that they are retired, Pat's income is substantially higher than Matt's because of Pat's saving. Is it fair for Pat's income to be higher than Matt's? Answer from a fair results and from a fair rules perspective.

Long Response Questions

1. What is the effect of the big tradeoff in transferring income from people with high incomes to people with low incomes?

2. According to the "fair rules" approach to fairness, is it fair for the government to limit the prices sellers charge for bottled water after a flood destroys a town's water supply? Why or why not?

Additional Exercises (also in MyEconLab Test A)

An earthquake destroys the homes of a quarter of a city's population. People who are lucky enough to own one of the remaining homes offer rooms for rent at the highest amount that people are willing to pay.

1. Who gets to occupy the available rooms? Who receives the consumer surplus and who receives the producer surplus on rooms?

2. Is the allocation of rooms efficient? By what principle of fairness is the allocation fair or unfair.

© 2015 Pearson Education, Inc.

SELF TEST ANSWERS

■ AP Self Test 6.1

True or false

1. True; page 138
2. False; page 141
3. False; page 142
4. False; page 138

Multiple choice

1. d; page 140
2. a; page 141
3. a; page 142
4. a; page 143
5. d; pages 143-144

Short Response Questions

1. Sony is using a contest allocation method. Sony benefits from this allocation scheme because all the top executives who want to be President will work extremely hard for Sony in an effort to win the contest; page 139.

2. The marginal cost of the second skate board is 2 pairs roller blades. Marginal cost is the opportunity cost of producing one more unit of a good or service. It is not the cost of all the units produced; pages 142-143.

3. Allocative efficiency is the most highly valued combination of goods and services on the *PPF*. It is the combination where marginal cost equals marginal benefit. In Figure 6.1, allocative efficiency is achieved when 30 tractors a week are produced; page 144.

Long Response Questions

1. The people who do not buy these BMWs are the people cannot afford to pay $50,000 for the new BMW and the people who can afford to pay but choose not to pay it. The point that people can decide not to buy a particular good or service shows that the rich do not necessary consume everything; they buy and consume only the goods and services for which they choose to pay the market price; page 138.

2. If the marginal benefit from an additional unit of a good or service exceeds its marginal cost, the unit should be produced because its production benefits society more than it costs society to produce. Producing where marginal benefit equals marginal cost insures that *all* units that have a net benefit for society are produced, so this level of production is the point of allocative efficiency; page 144.

Additional Exercises (also in MyEconLab Test A)

1. a. Market price; page 138.
   b. First-Come, First-Serve and Market Price; pages 139, 140.
   c. Majority rule; page 139.
   d. Contest; page 139.

2. If 120 pounds of coffee are grown, the first table, which shows the nation's production possibilities, indicates that 40 pounds of bananas are produced. The marginal cost when this many bananas are produced is in the second table, which shows that the marginal cost of another pound of bananas is 2 pounds of coffee per pound of bananas. (This result is from the "Must give up" column because what must be given shows the marginal cost; the "Willing to give up" column shows the marginal benefit.) If the marginal cost of another pound of bananas is 2 pounds of coffee, then the marginal cost of another pound of coffee is 1/2 of a pound of bananas. In other words, to gain another pound of coffee, the nation must forgo 1/2 of a pound of bananas. Resources are used efficiently when the marginal benefit of a pound of coffee equals the marginal cost of a pound of coffee. When 120 pounds of coffee are grown, 40 pounds of bananas are grown the marginal cost of pound of coffee is 1/2 of a pound of bananas. The table also shows that at this quantity, the marginal benefit of a pound of bananas is 2 pounds of coffee, so the marginal benefit of a pound of coffee is 1/2 of a pound of bananas. Thus when 120 pounds of coffee are produced, the nation is producing the efficient quantity of coffee and the marginal benefit of a pound of coffee is 1/2 of a pound of bananas; pages 143-144 .

© 2015 Pearson Education, Inc.

■ AP Self Test 6.2

True or false
1. False; page 146
2. True; page 146
3. True; page 147
4. False; page 147

Multiple choice
1. d; page 146
2. a; page 146
3. b; page 146
4. a; page 147
5. b; page 147
6. a; page 147

Short Response Questions
1. Consumer surplus is the marginal benefit from a good or service minus the price paid for it, summed over the quantity consumed; page 147.

Price (dollars per tablet)	Quantity (millions of tablets per year)	Consumer surplus (dollars)
500	4	300
400	8	200
300	12	100
200	16	0
100	20	0

2. a. The table above has the consumer surpluses. The consumer surplus is zero for the 20 millionth tablet because when the price is $200, the 20 millionth tablet is not purchased. For the remaining quantities, the consumer surplus is the marginal benefit, which equals the maximum price consumers are willing to pay minus the price; page 147.

   b. The consumer surplus decreases as more tablets are purchased because the value of an additional tablets decreases as more are purchased; page 147.

3. a. The marginal benefit of the 20,000th pair of roller blades is the maximum price a consumer is willing to pay for that pair, which is $150; page 146.

   b. The marginal benefit of the 40,000th pair of roller blades is the maximum price a consumer is willing to pay for that pair, which is $100; page 146.

   c. The consumer surplus is the difference between the marginal benefit, $150, minus the price paid, $100, or $50; page 147.

   d. If the price is $100, then 40,000 pairs of roller blades will be purchased. The consumer surplus equals 1/2 × ($200 − $100) × (40,000 − 0), or $40,000,000; page 147.

4. a. The maximum price is $3; page 146.

   b. The marginal benefit is $3. The marginal benefit is the maximum price a consumer is willing to pay for another bag of potato chips; page 146.

■ FIGURE 6.11

Price (dollars per bag of potato chips)

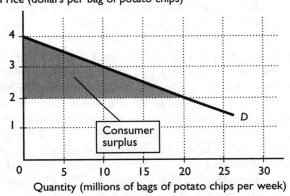

Quantity (millions of bags of potato chips per week)

   c. Figure 6.11 shades the area of the consumer surplus; page 147.

   d. The consumer surplus equals the area of the shaded triangle in Figure 6.11, which is 1/2 × ($4 − $2) × 20 million = $20 million; page 147.

Long Response Questions
1. The value of a good is equal to the maximum price a buyer is willing to pay, which also equals the marginal benefit; page 146.

2. The marginal benefit of the slice of pizza equals the price paid plus the consumer surplus on that slice; page 147.

© 2015 Pearson Education, Inc.

Additional Exercises (also in MyEconLab Test A)

1. The value of the 15th cone is $2.50. A consumer is willing to pay $3.50 for the 5th cone. The consumer surplus is the difference between the marginal benefit, which is what a consumer is willing to pay for the 5th cone, and the price paid for the cone. The consumer's marginal benefit for the 5th cone is $3.50 and the price is $2.50, so the consumer surplus equals $1.00; pages 146-147.

2. Fifteen cones are bought. The consumer surplus is the triangular area below the demand curve and above the market price. The area of a triangle equals 1/2 × base × height, which is 1/2 × 15 cones × $1.50 per cone = $11.25. The total expenditure on cones is 15 cones × $2.50 per cone, which equals $37.50. The total benefit from the cones is the area under the demand curve, composed of total expenditure of $37.50 plus consumer surplus of $11.25, which equals $48.75; page 147.

3. If demand doubles, the total expenditure increases. At every price consumers now buy double the quantity of cones they had previously purchased, so the total number of cones purchased is 30. The total expenditure on cones is 30 cones × $2.50 per cone, or $75.00. The vertical intercept does not change (doubling zero is still zero), so the area of the consumer surplus triangle is 1/2 × (30 cones) × ($1.50 per cone)= $22.50; page 147.

■ AP Self Test 6.3

True or false

1. False; page 149
2. True; page 149
3. False; page 149
4. False; page 150

Multiple choice

1. c; page 149
2. b; page 149
3. d; page 149
4. b; page 150
5. a; page 150
6. d; page 150

Short Response Question

■ FIGURE 6.12

Price (dollars per bag of potato chips)

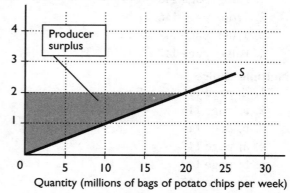

Quantity (millions of bags of potato chips per week)

1. a. As Figure 6.12 shows, the minimum price is $1; page 149.

   b. The marginal cost is $1. The marginal cost of the 10 millionth bag is the minimum price for which a supplier is willing to produce that bag of chips; page 149.

   c. Figure 6.12 shades the area of the producer surplus; page 150.

   d. The producer surplus equals the area of the shaded triangle in Figure 6.12, so producer surplus is 1/2 × ($2 − $0) × 20 million, which equals $20 million; page 150.

Long response Questions

1. The minimum price for which a firm will produce a slice of pizza equals the marginal cost of producing that slice. It is just worth producing one more slice of pizza if the price for which it can be sold equals its marginal cost. The supply curve tells us this price. So the supply curve is the same as the marginal cost curve; page 149.

2. Producer surplus equals the price of a good or service minus the marginal cost of producing it. As the price of a good or service rises and the supply curve does not shift, the producer surplus increases; page 150.

Additional Exercises (also in MyEconLab Test A)

1. The opportunity cost of the 15th cone is $2.50. The minimum supply price of the 5th cone is $1.50. Producer surplus is the price of

a good minus the marginal cost of producing it, which is its opportunity cost. On the 5th cone, the producer surplus is $2.50 − $1.50, which is $1.00; pages 149-150.

2. Fifteen cones are sold. The producer surplus is the triangular area above the supply curve and below the market price. The area of a triangle equals 1/2 × base × height, which is 1/2 × 15 cones × $1.50 per cone = $11.25. The total revenue from ice cream cones is 15 cones × $2.50 per cone, which equals $37.50. Total cost can be calculated as the area under the supply curve between the y-axis and the quantity of 15 ice cream cones. Alternatively, this area equals total revenue minus producer surplus, $37.50 − $11.25, which is $26.25; page 150.

3. If the price of a cone falls to $2.00 per cone, the number of cones sold decreases to 10. The total revenue from ice cream cones is 10 cones × $2.00 per cone, which equals $20.00. The producer surplus is the triangular area above the supply curve and below the (new) market price. The area of this triangle equals is 1/2 × 10 cones × $1.00 per cone = $5.00. The change in producer surplus is $11.25 − $5.00, which equals $6.25; page 150.

■ AP Self Test 6.4

True or false

    1. True; page 152
    2. False; page 152
    3. False; page 153
    4. False; page 155

Multiple choice

    1. a; page 153
    2. d; page 152
    3. d; page 152
    4. d; page 152
    5. c; page 153
    6. d; page 155
    7. c; page 155
    8. d; page 156

Short Response Questions

■ FIGURE 6.13

Price (thousands of dollars per automobile)

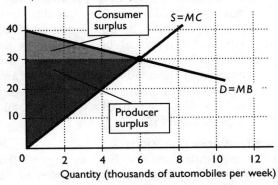

1. In Figure 6.13 the equilibrium quantity of automobiles is 6,000 a week. The efficient quantity of automobiles is also 6,000 a week because that is the quantity at which the marginal benefit equals the marginal cost. The consumer surplus and producer surplus are the shown in the figure. The consumer surplus is the area of the light grey triangle, which is 1/2 × ($40.00 − $30.00) × (6,000) = $60,000. The producer surplus is the area of the dark grey triangle, which is 1/2 × ($30.00 − $0.00) × (60,000) = $90,000; page 152.

■ FIGURE 6.14

Price (thousands of dollars per automobile)

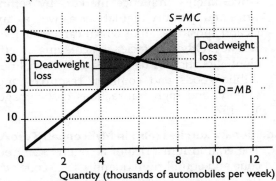

2. a. When 8,000 automobiles are produced, there is a deadweight loss from overproduction because for the last 2,000 automobiles, the marginal cost exceeds the marginal benefit. The deadweight loss is the

© 2015 Pearson Education, Inc.

area of the light grey triangle in Figure 6.14, which is 1/2 × ($40.00 − $26.67) × (8,000 − 6,000) = $1,330; page 155.

b. If 4,000 automobiles are produced, there again is a deadweight loss, this time from underproduction, because automobiles for which the marginal benefit exceeds the marginal cost are not produced. The amount of the deadweight loss is the area of dark grey triangle in Figure 6.14, which is 1/2 × ($33.33 − $20.00) × (6,000 − 4,000) = $1,330; page 155.

Long Response Questions

1. Adam Smith was the first to suggest that competitive markets send resources to the uses in which they have the highest value so that competitive markets are efficient. Smith said that each participant in a competitive market is "led by an invisible hand to promote an end [the efficient use of resources] which is no part of his intention;" page 153.

2. If the demand for cotton clothing increases, the demand curve for cotton clothing shifts rightward and the equilibrium quantity increases. The demand curve is the marginal benefit curve, so when the demand curve shifts rightward, the marginal benefit curve also shifts rightward. The efficient quantity also increases; page 152.

3. Governments influence markets by setting price and quantity regulations as well as taxes and subsidies, all of which can create inefficiency. Other obstacles to achieving an efficient allocation of resources are externalities, public goods and common resources, monopoly, and high transactions costs; pages 156-157.

Additional Exercises (also in MyEconLab Test A)

1. The equilibrium price of a cone is $2.50 per cone and equilibrium quantity is 15 cones. At the market equilibrium, consumer surplus is $11.25 and the producer surplus is $11.25. The total surplus is $22.50. The market for ice cream cones is efficient because 15 cones are produced and this is the quantity for which the marginal cost equals marginal benefit so

that the sum of consumer surplus and producer surplus is a maximum; page 152.

2. If output is limited to 10 cones per day, the market is not efficient; there is market failure. When 10 cones per day are produced, the marginal cost of the 10th cone, $2.00, does not equal the marginal benefit from the 10th cone, $3.00. The market is underproducing cones.

The deadweight loss is equal to the triangular area between demand and supply curves from 10 cones per day to 15 cones per day. The area of the triangle equals 1/2 × base × height, which is 1/2 × 5 cones × $1.00 per cone = $2.50; page 155.

3. If the government requires 20 cones to be produced per day, the market is not efficient. When 20 cones are produced, the marginal cost of the 20th cone, $3.00, does not equal marginal benefit from the 10th cone, $2.00. The market is overproducing.

The deadweight loss is equal to the triangular area between the supply and demand curves from 15 cones per day to 20 cones per day. The area of a triangle equals 1/2 × base × height, which is 1/2 × 5 cones × $1.00 per cone = $2.50; page 155.

■ AP Self Test 6.5

True or false
1. True; page 159
2. False; page 159
3. False; page 160

Multiple choice
1. b; page 159
2. d; page 159
3. a; page 161

Short Response Questions
1. The tax arrangement is fair from a fair-results view because it leads to a greater equality of income. The tax arrangement is not fair from a fair-results view because the tax is not a voluntary exchange; page 159.
2. From a fair-results view, it is not fair for Pat's income to be substantially higher than

Matt's. From a fair-rules view, it is fair because Pat and Matt had the same opportunities; page 159.

Long Response Questions

1. Income can be transferred from people with high incomes to people with low incomes only by taxing incomes, which discourages work. This tax results in the quantity of labor being less than the efficient quantity. Similarly, taxing income from capital discourages saving, which results in the quantity of capital being less than the efficient quantity. With less labor and less capital than the efficient amounts, the total amount of production is less than the efficient amount. So the greater the amount of income redistribution through income taxes, the greater is the inefficiency and the smaller is the economic pie; page 161.

2. Limiting the price that can be charged is unfair because it compels the seller to help and such compulsion is unfair since the seller is not engaging in a voluntary transaction; page 159.

Additional Exercises (also in MyEconLab Test A)

1. The people who value the rooms the most will occupy the rooms because they will be the people willing to pay the highest price for the rooms.

The consumers who occupy the rooms are the consumers who receive the consumer surplus.

Presuming there is no resale of rooms from one renter to another at a higher rent than the homeowner charges, the homeowners renting the rooms receive the producer surplus. If there is resale, then the reselling renters also receive producer surplus; pages 138 and 152.

2. The outcome is efficient. The outcome is unfair based on the fair-results principle because poor people can't afford to rent a room. So, the rooms will be shared unequally. The outcome is fair based on the fair-rules principle because the homeowners' property rights are enforced and there is voluntary exchange between the homeowners and renters. So the outcome is fair based on the fair-rules idea and unfair based on the fair results idea; page 159.

© 2015 Pearson Education, Inc.

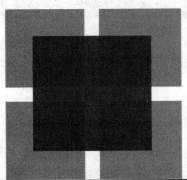

Government Actions in Markets

Chapter 7

In Chapter 7 we look at the inefficiency that is created when the government imposes a rent ceiling in the housing market, a minimum wage in the labor market, and a price support in an agricultural market.

1 Explain how a price ceiling works and show how a rent ceiling creates a housing shortage, inefficiency, and unfairness.

A price ceiling is an *upper* limit on the price at which a particular good, service, or factor of production may be traded. A rent ceiling is an example of a price ceiling. A rent ceiling set above the equilibrium rent is ineffective. A housing shortage occurs when a rent ceiling is set below the equilibrium rent because the quantity of housing demanded exceeds the quantity of housing supplied. A shortage results in black markets and search activity. A black market is an illegal market that operates alongside a government regulated market and search activity is the time spent looking for someone with whom to do business, increases. A rent ceiling creates a deadweight loss and decreases consumer surplus and producer surplus. Resources are also used in search. Rent ceilings violate the fair-rules view of fairness because they block voluntary exchange and they violate the "fair results" view because housing is generally *not* allocated to the poorest. Rent ceilings exist because of political support from current renters.

2 Explain how a price floor works and show how the minimum wage creates unemployment, inefficiency, and unfairness.

A price floor is a government regulation that sets a *lower* limit on the price at which a particular good, service, or factor of production may be traded. A minimum wage law is an example of a price floor. A minimum wage law is a government regulation that makes hiring labor services for less than a specified wage illegal. When a minimum wage is set above the equilibrium wage rate the quantity of labor supplied exceeds the quantity of labor demanded so that unemployment results. A minimum wage increases job search activity and illegal hiring. The minimum wage creates a deadweight loss. The minimum wage is unfair because it delivers an unfair result and blocks voluntary exchange.

3 Explain how a price support in the market for an agricultural product creates a surplus, inefficiency, and unfairness.

When governments intervene in agricultural markets, they isolate the domestic market from global competition by limiting imports. The government introduces a price floor, which in an agricultural market is called a price support. The price support leads to a surplus, so the government pays the farmers a subsidy by purchasing the surplus to keep the price at the support level. Buyers are worse off because the price rises and the quantity they purchase decreases and they must pay taxes to the government for the subsidy. Farmers are better off, but a deadweight loss is created because buyers' losses exceed farmers' gains. Farmers in developing economies are harmed two ways: First, their exports to the domestic nation are limited and, second the domestic government sells the surplus it has purchased in the rest of the world, thereby lowering the price received by farmers in developing countries.

© 2015 Pearson Education, Inc.

YOUR AP TEST HINTS

AP Topics

Topic on your AP test	What to Know	Corresponding textbook section
Price ceilings	Price control that sets an upper limit on the price for which the good may be sold	Checkpoint 7.1
Price floor	Price control that sets a lower limit on the price for which the good may be sold	Checkpoint 7.2
Price support	Price floor in an agricultural (farm) market	Checkpoint 7.3

AP Vocabulary Covered

Terms	What to Know	Text Sections
Price ceiling (Price cap)	A government imposed upper limit on a price; has an effect only if it is set *below* the equilibrium price	Checkpoint 7.1, p. 168
Rent ceiling	A price ceiling in a housing market; sets the highest legal rent that may be charged; creates shortages	Checkpoint 7.1, p. 168
Black market	An illegal market created to avoid government regulated markets	Checkpoint 7.1, p. 169
Search activity	The cost of time looking for someone to do business with	Checkpoint 7.1, p. 170
Price floor	A government imposed lower limit on a price, has an effect only if it is set *above* the equilibrium price	Checkpoint 7.2, p. 174
Minimum wage	A price floor in a labor market; sets the lowest legal wage that may be paid	Checkpoint 7.2, p. 175
Effect of a minimum wage	If set above the equilibrium wage, a minimum wage creates a surplus (unemployment) and leads to a deadweight loss	Checkpoint 7.2, p. 179
Price support	Government intervention in agricultural markets. Three parts: ▪ Isolate the domestic market from foreign competition; ▪ Introduce a price floor (called a price support); ▪ Pay farmers a subsidy	Checkpoint 7.3, p. 181
Subsidy	A government payment to a producer that pays some of the production costs	Checkpoint 7.3, p. 181
Effect of price support	If set above the equilibrium price, a price support leads to a surplus and a deadweight loss	Checkpoint 7.3, p. 183

Extra AP material

- Another term for rent ceiling is *rent control*.
- When a price control is imposed by a government and a shortage results, some sort of method must be applied to ration the goods. Examples can include a first-come first-served system, favoritism, rationing, or black markets.

© 2015 Pearson Education, Inc.

CHECKPOINT 7.1

■ **Explain how a price ceiling works and show how a rent ceiling creates a housing shortage, inefficiency, and unfairness.**

Quick Review

- *Price ceiling* A government regulation that places an *upper* limit on the price at which a particular good, service, or factor of production may be traded.
- *Rent ceiling* A government regulation that makes it illegal to charge more than a specified rent for housing.
- *Effective rent ceiling* When a rent ceiling is set below the equilibrium rent, the quantity of housing demanded is greater than the equilibrium quantity and the quantity of housing supplied is less than the equilibrium quantity. A housing shortage occurs.

Additional Practice Problems 7.1

1. The figure shows the rental market for apartments in Ocala, Florida.

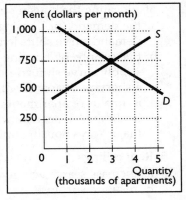

   a. With no government intervention, what is the rent and how many apartments are rented?
   b. If the government imposes a rent ceiling of $500 a month, what is the rent and how many apartments are rented?
   c. With a strictly enforced $500 rent ceiling, why is the housing market inefficient? What does the deadweight loss equal?
   d. With a strictly enforced $500 rent ceiling, is there a shortage or surplus of apartments?

Price (dollars per round of golf)	Quantity demanded	Quantity supplied
	(rounds per week)	
50	2,000	2,800
40	2,300	2,700
30	2,600	2,600
20	2,900	2,500
10	3,200	2,400

2. The table above gives the supply and demand schedules for rounds of golf at a golf course.
   a. What is the equilibrium price and equilibrium quantity of rounds of golf?
   b. Suppose the city government imposes a price ceiling of $40 a round of golf. What will be the price and quantity of rounds of golf? Is there a shortage?
   c. Suppose the city government imposes a price ceiling of $20 a round of golf. What will be the price and quantity of rounds of golf? Is there a shortage?

Solutions to Additional Practice Problems 7.1

1a. In the figure, the equilibrium rent and the equilibrium quantity are determined at the point where the demand curve and the supply curve intersect. The rent is $750 a month and 3,000 apartments are rented.

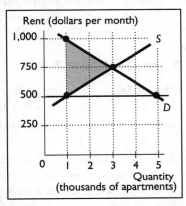

1b. To answer this practice problem remember that a rent ceiling is effective only when it is set below the equilibrium price. The rent ceiling of $500 per month is below the equilibrium rent, so it has an effect. The quantity of apartments rented decreases to 1,000 and the rent is $500.

1c. The market is inefficient because the marginal benefit of the last apartment rented, the 1,000th apartment, exceeds the marginal cost of the apartment. Because the housing mar-

© 2015 Pearson Education, Inc.

ket is inefficient a deadweight loss arises. In the figure the deadweight loss is shown by the grey triangle. The amount of the deadweight loss equals the area of the grey triangle. This area is $1/2 \times (\$1,000 - \$500) \times (3,000 - 1,000) = \$500,000$.

1d. There is a shortage of apartments. At the $500 rent ceiling, the quantity of apartments demanded is 5,000 and the quantity supplied is 1,000. So there is a shortage of 4,000 apartments.

2a. The equilibrium price is $30 a round of golf and the equilibrium quantity is 2,600 rounds a week.

2b. The price ceiling is above the equilibrium price, so the price remains at $30 a round and the quantity remains at 2,600 rounds a week. There is no shortage.

2c. The price ceiling is below the equilibrium price. The price falls to $20 a round. The quantity played equals the quantity supplied at $20, which is 2,500 rounds a week. There is a shortage of 400 rounds a week.

■ AP Self Test 7.1

True or false

1. A rent ceiling always lowers the rent paid.

2. When a rent ceiling is higher than the equilibrium rent, a black market emerges.

3. The opportunity cost of a dorm room is equal to its rent plus the value of the search time spent finding the dorm room.

4. Rent ceilings are efficient because they lower the cost of housing to low-income families.

5. The total loss from a rent ceiling exceeds the deadweight loss.

Multiple choice

1. A price ceiling is a government regulation that makes it illegal to charge a price
   a. below the equilibrium price.
   b. above the equilibrium price.
   c. for a good or service.
   d. above some specified level.
   e. below some specified level.

2. When a price ceiling is set below the equilibrium price, the quantity supplied ____ the quantity demanded and ____ exists.
   a. is less than; a surplus
   b. is less than; a shortage
   c. is greater than; a surplus
   d. is greater than; a shortage
   e. equals; an equilibrium

3. In a housing market with a rent ceiling set below the equilibrium rent,
   a. some people seeking an apartment to rent will not be able to find one.
   b. the total cost of renting an apartment will decrease for all those seeking housing.
   c. some landlords will not be able to find renters to fill available apartments.
   d. search will decrease because renters no longer need to search for less expensive apartments.
   e. None of the above answers is correct because to have an impact the rent ceiling must be set *above* the equilibrium rent.

4. A rent ceiling on housing creates a problem of allocating the housing units because
   a. the demand for housing decreases and the demand curve shifts leftward.
   b. the supply of housing increases and the supply curve shifts rightward.
   c. a shortage of apartments occurs.
   d. a surplus of apartments occurs.
   e. it eliminates search, which is one of the major ways housing units are allocated.

5. Rent ceilings
   a. increase search activity.
   b. result in surpluses.
   c. are efficient.
   d. benefit producers.
   e. have no effect if they are set below the equilibrium rent.

© 2015 Pearson Education, Inc.

■ **FIGURE 7.1**

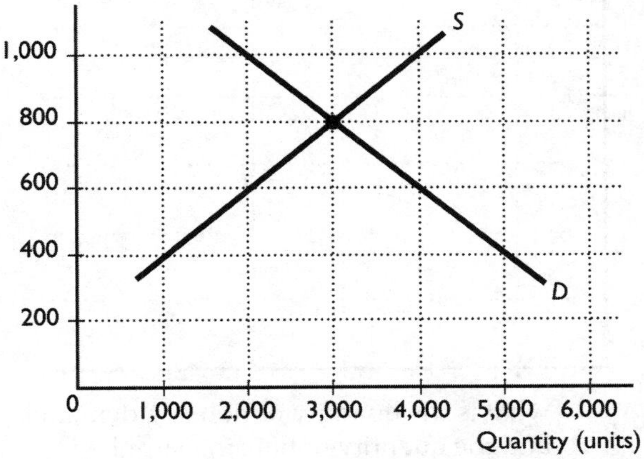

Rent (dollars per month)

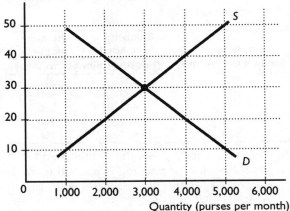

6. Figure 7.1 shows a housing market. If the government imposes a rent ceiling of $1,000 per month, there will be a
   a. surplus of 2,000 units.
   b. shortage of 2,000 units.
   c. surplus of 4,000 units.
   d. shortage of 1,000 units.
   e. neither a shortage nor a surplus of units.

7. Figure 7.1 shows a housing market. If the government imposes a rent ceiling of $400 per month, there will be a
   a. shortage of 1,000 units.
   b. shortage of 2,000 units.
   c. shortage of 3,000 units.
   d. shortage of 4,000 units.
   e. neither a shortage nor a surplus of units.

8. Figure 7.1 shows a housing market. Of the rent ceilings listed below, the deadweight loss from a rent ceiling is largest when the rent ceiling equals ____ per month.
   a. $1,000
   b. $800
   c. $600
   d. $400
   e. More information is needed to determine which of the rent ceilings has the largest deadweight loss.

9. Suppose that the government imposes a price ceiling on gasoline that is below the equilibrium price. The black market for gas-

oline is ____ market in which the price ____ the ceiling price.
   a. a legal; exceeds
   b. an illegal; exceeds
   c. a legal; is less than
   d. an illegal; is less than
   e. an illegal; equals

10. A rent ceiling creates a deadweight loss
    a. if it is set below the equilibrium rent.
    b. if it is set equal to the equilibrium rent.
    c. if it set above the equilibrium rent.
    d. if it decreases the taxes the government collects in the housing market.
    e. never, because if it did create a deadweight loss, the government would not impose it.

11. Rent ceilings
    a. eliminate the problem of scarcity.
    b. allocate resources efficiently.
    c. ensure that housing goes to the poor.
    d. benefit renters living in rent-controlled apartments.
    e. benefit landlords because the landlords know what rent to charge their renters.

Short Response Questions

■ **FIGURE 7.2**

Price (dollars per purse)

1. Figure 7.2 shows the market for purses.
   a. What is the equilibrium price and quantity of purses?

© 2015 Pearson Education, Inc.

b. Suppose the government imposes a $20 price ceiling. With the price ceiling, what is the quantity of purses demanded and the quantity of purses supplied? What is the shortage? Indicate the shortage in the figure.

c. The price ceiling creates a deadweight loss. Show the deadweight loss in the figure.

Price (dollars per carton)	Quantity demanded	Quantity supplied
	(cartons per day)	
1.00	200	110
1.25	175	130
1.50	150	150
1.75	125	170
2.00	100	190

2. The table above gives the demand and supply schedules for milk.

   a. What is the market equilibrium in the milk market?

   b. Suppose the government imposes a price ceiling of $1.25 per carton. What is the price of a carton of milk and what quantity is purchased? Is there a shortage or surplus of milk?

   c. Suppose the government imposes a price ceiling of $1.75 per carton. What is the price of a carton of milk and what quantity is purchased? Is there a shortage or surplus of milk?

Rent (dollars per month)	Quantity demanded	Quantity supplied
	(housing units per month)	
900	200	350
800	300	300
700	400	250
600	500	200
500	600	150

3. The table above gives the demand and supply schedules for housing in a small town. In Figure 7.3, graph the demand and supply curves. Label the axes.

   a. What is the equilibrium rent and quantity of housing?

   b. Suppose the government imposes a $600 a month rent ceiling. With the rent ceiling,

■ **FIGURE 7.3**

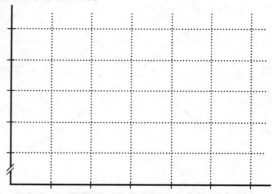

what is the quantity of housing demanded and the quantity of housing supplied?

c. Does the rent ceiling result in a shortage or a surplus of housing? Indicate the shortage or surplus in Figure 7.3.

Long Response Questions

1. What is a price ceiling? In your answer, discuss whether an effective price ceiling is above, below, or equal to the equilibrium price, who is helped and who is harmed by a price ceiling, and the relationship between a price ceiling and a black market.

2. Are rent ceilings efficient?

Additional Exercises (also in MyEconLab Test A)

■ **FIGURE 7.4**

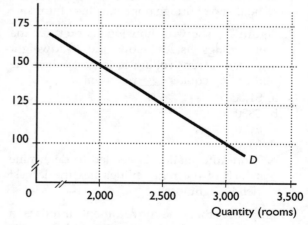

Figure 7.4 shows the demand for on-campus housing at the University of Idaho, in Moscow,

© 2015 Pearson Education, Inc.

Idaho. The college has 2,000 rooms for rent.

1. What is the equilibrium rent and how many rooms are rented? If the college sets a rent ceiling on on-campus housing of $125 a month, how would you describe the on-campus housing market? Would the allocation of housing be efficient? Would it be fair?

2. If the rent ceiling of $125 a month is strictly enforced and there is no black market, who would gain and who would lose?

3. If a black market developed as a result of the $125 a month rent ceiling, what range of rents would be offered for a room? Would the allocation of housing be efficient? Would it be fair? Explain.

CHECKPOINT 7.2

■ **Explain how a price floor works and show how the minimum wage creates unemployment, inefficiency, and unfairness.**

Quick Review

- *Price floor* A government regulation that places a *lower* limit on the price at which a particular good, service, or factor of production may be traded.

- *Minimum wage law* A government regulation that makes hiring labor services for less than a specified wage illegal.

- *Effective minimum wage law* When the minimum wage is set above the equilibrium wage rate, the quantity of labor demanded is less than the equilibrium quantity and the quantity of labor supplied is greater than the equilibrium quantity. Unemployment occurs.

Additional Practice Problems 7.2

1. The figure shows the market for fast food workers in Ocala, Florida.

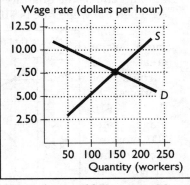

a. What is the equilibrium wage rate and what is the equilibrium quantity of employment?

b. If Ocala introduces a minimum wage for fast food workers of $10 an hour, how many fast food workers are employed?

c. With the minimum wage, is there a surplus or a shortage of fast food workers? Indicate the amount of any shortage or surplus in the figure.

d. Is the minimum wage of $10 an hour efficient? Is it fair?

Price (cents per pound)	Quantity demanded	Quantity supplied
	(tons of sugar per year)	
10	300	225
15	275	275
20	250	325
25	225	375

2. The above table gives the supply and demand schedules for sugar.

a. What is the equilibrium price and quantity of sugar?

b. If the government imposes a price floor of 25¢ a pound, what is the quantity demanded and the quantity supplied? Is there a shortage or surplus? How much?

Solutions to Additional Practice Problems 7.2

1a. The equilibrium wage rate and the equilibrium quantity of the workers are determined where the labor demand curve and the labor supply curve intersect. The equilibrium wage rate is $7.50 an hour and the equilibrium quantity of workers is 150.

© 2015 Pearson Education, Inc.

1b. 50 fast food workers are employed. This amount equals the quantity of labor demanded when the wage rate is $10 an hour.

1c. The minimum wage creates a surplus of workers. At the $10 wage rate, 200 workers are willing to work but firms are willing to hire only 50 workers. There is a surplus of 150 workers, that is, there are 150 workers unemployed. In the figure, the length of the arrow shows the 150 unemployed workers.

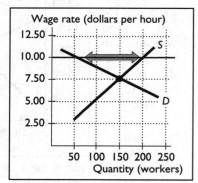

1d. The minimum wage of $10 an hour is not efficient because the marginal benefit to restaurants who demand workers exceeds the marginal cost borne by the workers who supply work. A deadweight loss is created. An additional loss arises as unemployed workers search for jobs. The minimum wage is not fair. It violates the "fair-rules" view of fairness because it prevents voluntary exchange. It violates the "fair-results" view of fairness because 100 workers lose their jobs and are made poorer.

2a. The equilibrium price is 15¢ a pound and the equilibrium quantity is 275 tons a year.

2b. The quantity demanded at 25¢ a pound is 225 tons and the quantity supplied is 375 tons. There is a surplus of 150 tons.

■ AP Self Test 7.2

True or false

1. Firms hire labor, so they determine how much labor to supply in a market.

2. A minimum wage has an impact when it is set above the equilibrium wage rate.

3. A minimum wage law can lead to increased job search activity and illegal hiring.

4. When a minimum wage is set above the equilibrium wage rate, the employee's marginal cost of working exceeds the employer's marginal benefit from hiring labor.

5. A minimum wage is fair because low-income workers receive an increase in take-home pay.

Multiple choice

1. A price floor is
   a. the highest price at which it is legal to trade a particular good, service, or factor of production.
   b. the lowest price at which it is legal to trade a particular good, service, or factor of production.
   c. an illegal price to charge.
   d. the price when the stock market crashes.
   e. the lowest price for which the quantity demanded equals the quantity supplied.

2. To be effective in raising people's wages, a minimum wage must be set
   a. above the equilibrium wage rate.
   b. below the equilibrium wage rate.
   c. equal to the equilibrium wage rate.
   d. below $7.
   e. either above or below the equilibrium wage depending on whether the supply curve of labor shifts rightward or leftward in response to the minimum wage.

3. A minimum wage set above the equilibrium wage rate
   a. increases the quantity of labor services supplied.
   b. decreases the quantity of labor services supplied.
   c. has no effect on the quantity of labor services supplied.
   d. shifts the labor supply curve rightward.
   e. shifts the labor supply curve leftward.

© 2015 Pearson Education, Inc.

4. Suppose the current equilibrium wage rate for lifeguards in Houston is $7.85 an hour. A minimum wage law that creates a price floor of $8.50 an hour leads to
   a. a surplus of lifeguards in Houston.
   b. a shortage of lifeguards in Houston.
   c. no changes in the lifeguard market.
   d. a change in the quantity of lifeguards supplied but no change in the quantity of lifeguards demanded.
   e. an increase in the number of lifeguards employed.

5. If the minimum wage is above the equilibrium wage rate, then an increase in the minimum wage ____ employment and ____ unemployment.
   a. increases; increases
   b. increases; decreases
   c. decreases; increases
   d. decreases; decreases
   e. does not change; increases

■ **FIGURE 7.5**
Wage rate (dollars per hour)

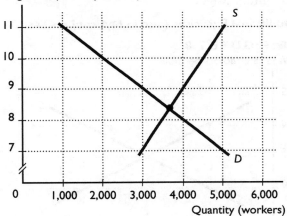

6. Figure 7.5 shows the market for fast food workers in San Francisco. A minimum wage of $11 per hour leads to unemployment of ____ workers.
   a. 1,000
   b. 2,000
   c. 3,000
   d. 4,000
   e. 5,000

7. In Figure 7.5, which of the following minimum wages creates the most unemployment?
   a. $7 an hour
   b. $8 an hour
   c. $9 an hour
   d. $10 an hour
   e. $11 an hour

8. If a minimum wage is introduced that is above the equilibrium wage rate,
   a. the quantity of labor services demanded increases.
   b. job search activity increases.
   c. the supply of labor increases and the supply of labor curve shifts rightward.
   d. unemployment decreases because more workers accept jobs at the higher minimum wage rate.
   e. the quantity of labor supplied decreases because of the increase in unemployment.

9. The minimum wage is set above the equilibrium wage rate. Does the minimum wage create inefficiency?
   a. Yes.
   b. No.
   c. Only if the supply of labor is perfectly inelastic.
   d. Only if the supply of labor is perfectly elastic.
   e. Only if employment exceeds the efficient amount.

10. When the minimum wage is raised, the ____ union labor ____.
    a. demand for; increases
    b. demand for; decreases
    c. supply of; increases
    d. supply of; decreases
    e. demand for; does not change

© 2015 Pearson Education, Inc.

Short Response Questions

Wage rate (dollars per hour)	Quantity demanded	Quantity supplied
	(workers per day)	
6	3,500	2,750
7	3,000	3,000
8	2,500	3,250
9	2,000	3,500
10	1,500	3,750

■ **FIGURE 7.6**

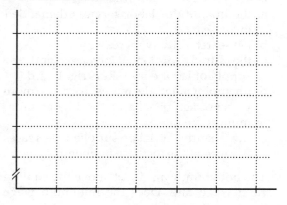

1. The table above gives the demand and supply schedules for labor in a small town.

   a. In Figure 7.6, at the top of the next column, label the axes. Draw the labor demand and labor supply curves. What is the equilibrium wage rate and employment?

   b. Suppose the government imposes a $6 an hour minimum wage. What is the effect on the wage rate and levels of employment and unemployment?

   c. Suppose the government raises the minimum wage from $6 an hour to $9 an hour. What is the effect on the wage rate and levels of employment and unemployment? Indicate any unemployment.

2. Figure 7.7 shows the labor demand and labor supply curves for Rochester, New York. Suppose the city is considering instituting a minimum wage. Indicate the minimum wages that lead to unemployment by darkening the vertical axis for all the minimum wages that create unemployment.

■ **FIGURE 7.7**

Wage rate (dollars per hour)

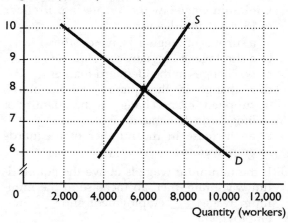

Long Response Questions

1. What is the effect of a minimum wage set below the equilibrium wage rate?

2. How does a minimum wage affect the time needed to find a job?

3. Do all low-wage workers benefit from a minimum wage?

Additional Exercises (also in MyEconLab Test A)

■ **FIGURE 7.8**

Wage rate (dollars per hour)

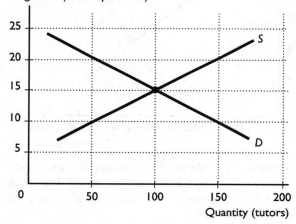

Figure 7.8 shows a market for private math tutors in College Station organized by the Students' Union.

1. What is the wage rate that math tutors earn and how many are employed? If the Stu-

© 2015 Pearson Education, Inc.

dents' Union sets the minimum wage for private math tutors at $20 an hour, how many tutors are unemployed?

2. If the Students' Union sets the minimum wage for private tutors at $12 an hour, is this minimum wage efficient? Is it fair?

3. Is a minimum wage of $20 an hour efficient? Is it fair? If a black market gets going, what wage rate might some tutors earn?

CHECKPOINT 7.3

■ **Explain how a price support in the market for an agricultural product creates a surplus, inefficiency, and unfairness.**

Quick Review

• *Price support* A price support is a price floor in an agricultural market maintained by a government guarantee to buy any surplus output at that price. The price support is the minimum price for which the product may be sold.

Additional Practice Problems 7.3

1. The figure shows the market for sugar.

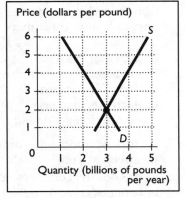

a. What is the equilibrium price and quantity of sugar?

b. If the government imposes a price support for sugar at $4 per pound, in the figure above, indicate this price support.

c. With the price support, how much sugar is produced? How much sugar is purchased by private consumers? How much is purchased by the government?

d. With the price support, what is the subsidy received by sugar producers?

e. Are consumers made better off or worse off with the price support?

f. Without the price support, is the market efficient? With the price support, is the market efficient?

2. With a price support, the government pays a subsidy to farmers by buying part of the crop. Why is this purchase necessary?

Solutions to Additional Practice Problems 7.3

1a. The equilibrium price and the equilibrium quantity of sugar are determined where the demand curve and the supply curve intersect. The figure shows that the equilibrium price is $2 a pound and the equilibrium quantity is 3 billion pounds a year.

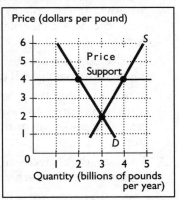

1b. The price support is shown in the figure as the solid line at $4 per pound.

1c. With the price support, the supply curve shows that at $4 per pound, 4 billion pounds of sugar are produced. The demand curve shows that at this price consumers buy 2 billion pounds. The government buys the surplus quantity of sugar, 2 billion pounds.

1d. The government buys 2 billion pounds of sugar at $4 per pound, so the subsidy is 2 billion pounds × $4 per pound, $8 billion.

1e. Consumers are worse off with the price support. With the price support the price they must pay for sugar increases, from $2 per pound to $4 per pound. In response consumers decrease the quantity of sugar they consume from 3 billion pounds to 2 billion pounds.

1f. Without the price support, the market is efficient. With the price support, the market is not efficient.

© 2015 Pearson Education, Inc.

2. The price support leads to a surplus of the crop. If the government did not buy the surplus, the farmers would not be able to cover their costs because there would be part of the crop left unsold.

■ AP Self Test 7.3

True or false

1. In order to have an effective price support, the government isolates the domestic market from the world market by restricting imports.

2. A price support sets the maximum price for which farmers may sell their crop.

3. In order to keep the price of a crop above the equilibrium price and equal to the supported price, the government must buy some of the crop.

4. Because they decrease production, price supports decrease farmers' total revenue.

5. Price supports are efficient because they guarantee production of the good.

Multiple choice

1. Price supports are generally used in
   a. labor markets.
   b. industrial markets.
   c. housing markets.
   d. markets for services.
   e. agricultural markets.

2. To have an effective price support program, the government must
   i.   isolate the domestic market from the world market
   ii. pay the farmers a subsidy
   iii. introduce a price floor
   a. i only.
   b. ii only.
   c. iii only.
   d. ii and iii.
   e. i, ii, and iii.

3. A price support directly sets the
   a. amount of production.
   b. subsidy the government must receive from producers.
   c. equilibrium quantity.
   d. lowest price for which the good may be sold.
   e. highest price for which the good may be sold.

4. To keep the price at the level set by the price support, the government must
   a. buy some of the good.
   b. sell some of the good.
   c. receive a subsidy from the producers.
   d. insure that imports are readily available.
   e. be careful to always set the price support below the equilibrium price.

5. With a price support program, who receives a subsidy?
   a. only consumers
   b. only producers
   c. the government
   d. importers
   e. both consumers and producers receive a subsidy

6. When a price support is set above the equilibrium price, producers ____ the quantity supplied and consumers ____ the quantity demanded.
   a. increase; increase
   b. increase; decrease
   c. decrease; increase
   d. decrease; decrease
   e. do not change; do not change

7. A price support ____ producers and ____ a deadweight loss.
   a. has no effect on; does not create
   b. benefits; creates
   c. harms; creates
   d. benefits; does not create
   e. harms; does not create

© 2015 Pearson Education, Inc.

■ **FIGURE 7.9**

Price (dollars per ton)

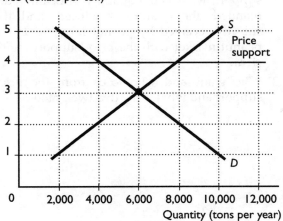

8. Figure 7.9 shows a price support program in an agricultural market. The amount of the subsidy necessary to keep the price at the price support is
   a. $4.
   b. $32,000.
   c. $8,000.
   d. $16,000.
   e. $24,000.

Short Response Questions

Price (dollars per bushel)	Quantity demanded	Quantity supplied
	(millions of bushels per year)	
3	3,500	2,000
4	3,000	3,000
5	2,500	4,000
6	2,000	5,000
7	1,500	6,000

1. The table gives the demand and supply schedules for wheat.
   a. In Figure 7.10 label the axes. Draw the demand curve and supply curve and indicate the equilibrium price and quantity.
   b. Suppose the government imposes a price support of $5 per bushel. What is the effect on the price of wheat, the quantity of wheat produced and the marginal cost of a bushel of wheat? Is there a deadweight loss?

■ **FIGURE 7.10**

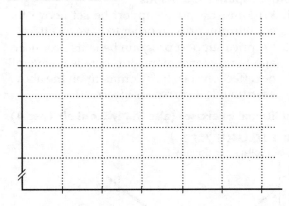

c. With the $5 per bushel price support, how much wheat do consumers buy? What is the subsidy the government must pay to producers?

■ **FIGURE 7.11**

Price (dollars per ton)

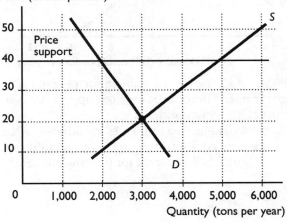

2. Figure 7.11 shows the demand and supply curves for peanuts. There is a price support of $40 per ton of peanuts.
   a. At the support price, what is the quantity of peanuts produced? What is the quantity consumers buy? How many tons of peanuts must the government buy? Indicate the amount the government must buy in Figure 7.11.
   b. How much is the subsidy paid by the government to producers?

© 2015 Pearson Education, Inc.

Long Response Questions

1. Why must a price support be set above the equilibrium price in order to have an effect?

2. "A price support program benefits producers and harms consumers. But there is no overall net effect on society." Comment on the above assertion. Is it correct or incorrect?

Additional Exercises (also in MyEconLab Test A)

■ **FIGURE 7.12**

Price (dollars per pound)

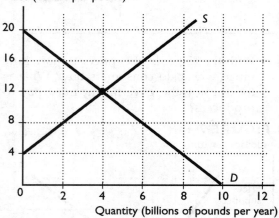

Quantity (billions of pounds per year)

Figure 7.12 shows the market for peanuts. The government introduces a price support for peanuts at $16 per pound.

1. Before the price support is introduced, what are the equilibrium price and quantity of peanuts? Is the market for peanuts efficient?

2. After the government introduces the price support, what is the quantity of peanuts demanded, the quantity produced, and the subsidy received by peanut farmers? Is the peanut market with the price support inefficient?

3. Who gains and who loses from the price support and what is the deadweight loss?

© 2015 Pearson Education, Inc.

SELF TEST ANSWERS

■ AP Self Test 7.1

True or false

1. False; page 168
2. False; page 168-169
3. True; page 170
4. False; page 171
5. True; page 171

Multiple choice

1. d; page 168
2. b; pages 169
3. a; page 169
4. c; page 169
5. a; page 170
6. e; page 168
7. d; pages 168-169
8. d; page 171
9. b; page 169
10. a; page 171
11. d; page 172

Short Response Questions

1. a. The equilibrium price is $30 per purse and the equilibrium quantity is 3,000 purses.

   b. The quantity of purses demanded is 4,000, the quantity of purses supplied is 2,000, and the shortage equals 2,000 purses. In Figure 7.13, the shortage equals the length of the double-headed arrow; page 169.

   c. The deadweight loss is shown in the figure; page 171.

2. a. The equilibrium price is $1.50 a carton and the quantity is 150 cartons a day.

   b. The price is $1.25 a carton and 130 cartons a day are purchased. There is a shortage of 45 cartons a day; page 169.

   c. The price ceiling is above the equilibrium price, and is ineffective. The price is $1.50 a carton, 150 cartons a day are purchased, and there is neither a shortage nor a surplus; page 168.

3. a. Figure 7.14 shows the demand curve and supply curve. The equilibrium rent is $800

■ FIGURE 7.13

Price (dollars per purse)

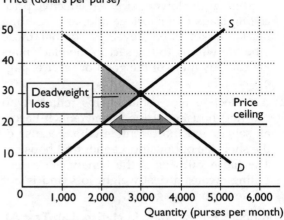

■ FIGURE 7.14

Rent (dollars per month)

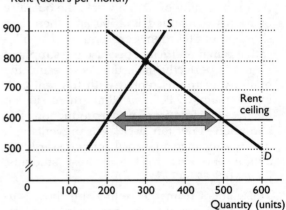

   a month and the quantity is 300 housing units a month.

   b. The quantity of housing demanded is 500 units a month; the quantity supplied is 200 units a month; page 169.

   c. The shortage of 300 units a month is indicated by the arrow; page 169.

Long Response Questions

1. A price ceiling is the highest price at which it is legal to trade a particular good, service, or factor of production. Price ceilings are designed to lower the price paid by consumers, so to be effective a price ceiling is set below

© 2015 Pearson Education, Inc.

the equilibrium price. Price ceilings help consumers who can buy at the lower price and harm all producers and consumers who cannot buy at the lower price. An effective price ceiling leads to a shortage and, as a result, a black market often develops so that those who are willing to transact in the black market can buy more of the good or service; pages 168-173.

2. An effective rent ceiling helps renters who can find housing at the lower rent. It harms all sellers and those renters who, because of the shortage of housing, cannot find housing. The harm outweighs the benefit, so a rent ceiling creates a deadweight loss and is not efficient; page; page 172.

Additional Exercises (also in MyEconLab Test A)

1. The equilibrium rent is $150 a week and the equilibrium quantity is 2,000 rooms rented. At a rent ceiling of $125 a week, the quantity of rooms demanded is 2,500 and there is a shortage of 500 rooms on campus. The allocation remains efficient because the supply of rooms is perfectly inelastic. As a result, the quantity of rooms rented with the rent ceiling remains 2,000 so that there is no deadweight loss from underproduction. The allocation is not fair because it prevents voluntary exchange and does not necessarily reallocate housing to the poorest students; pages 168, 171-172.

2. The gainers from the ceiling are those students who get the cheaper apartments on campus. The losers include those students who are unable to rent on campus at the $125 ceiling. The university also loses because it charges a lower rent; pages 171-172.

3. If a black market develops, rents will range from $125 a week to $150 a week. The highest rent that someone would offer is $150 a week. This rent equals the willingness of someone to pay for the 2,000th room. This market is efficient because the supply is perfectly inelastic, so 2,000 rooms are rented, the same as the efficient equilibrium quantity with no rent ceiling. (Generally a black mar-

ket is inefficient because marginal benefit exceeds marginal cost and a deadweight loss arises.) A black market is not fair because it does not provide rooms to the students who are most in need; pages 169-170, 172.

■ AP Self Test 7.2

True or false

1. False; page 174
2. True; page 175
3. True; page 176
4. False; page 178
5. False; page 179

Multiple choice

1. b; page 174
2. a; page 175
3. a; page 175
4. a; page 175
5. c; page 175
6. d; page 175
7. e; page 175
8. b; page 176
9. a; page 178
10. a; page 179

Short Response Questions

■ FIGURE 7.15

Wage rate (dollars per hour)

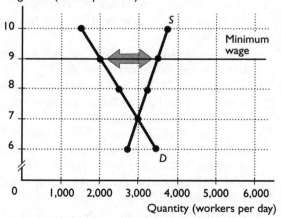

1. a. Figure 7.15 shows the demand and supply curves. The equilibrium wage rate is $7 an

© 2015 Pearson Education, Inc.

hour and the equilibrium employment is 3,000 workers a day.

b. The $6 minimum wage is below the equilibrium wage and has no effect; page 175.

c. The $9 minimum wage raises the wage rate to $9. Employment decreases to 2,000 workers. The number of workers looking for work is 3,500. Unemployment equals 3,500 − 2,000, which is 1,500 people. The amount of unemployment is shown by the arrow in Figure 7.15; page 175.

■ FIGURE 7.16

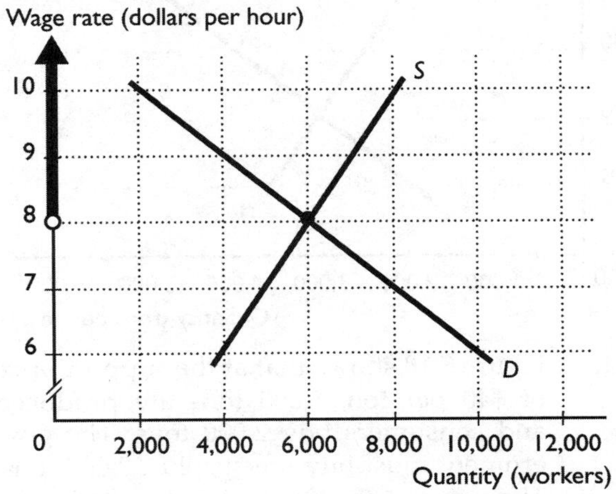

Wage rate (dollars per hour)

2. In order to have an effect in the market, the minimum wage must be set above the equilibrium wage. As Figure 7.16 shows, any minimum wage above $8 per hour creates unemployment; page 175.

Long Response Questions

1. A minimum wage set below the equilibrium wage rate has no effect on the wage rate or amount of employment. A minimum wage has an effect *only* when it exceeds the equilibrium wage rate because only in this case does it make the equilibrium wage rate illegal. If the minimum wage is set below the equilibrium wage rate, then the equilibrium wage rate remains legal and no changes occur in the market; page 175.

2. A minimum wage set above the equilibrium wage rate decreases the quantity of labor demand and increases the quantity of labor

supplied, thereby creating unemployment. As a result, it increases the time spent unemployed workers spend searching for a job; page 176.

3. A minimum wage does not help all low-wage workers. In particular, it harms low-wage workers who lose their jobs or cannot find jobs because of the minimum wage; page 178.

Additional Exercises (also in MyEconLab Test A)

1. The equilibrium wage rate is $15 an hour and the equilibrium quantity is 100 tutors. At a minimum wage of $20 an hour, only 50 tutors are hired and 150 people want to work as tutors. 100 tutors are unemployed; pages 174-176.

2. A $12 an hour minimum wage has no effect because it is below the equilibrium wage. The equilibrium wage rate remains at $15 an hour and the equilibrium quantity remains at 100. No tutors are unemployed. The $12 an hour minimum wage is efficient because it has no effect on the market equilibrium. According to the "fair results" view, it is unfair because some students have different income than other students. According to the "fair rules" view, it is fair as a competitive equilibrium; pages 178-179.

3. The minimum wage rate of $20 is inefficient because marginal benefit exceeds the marginal cost and there is a deadweight loss. The outcome is unfair. It benefits only the tutors who get the jobs and the unemployed tutors earn nothing. Students are unable to hire the tutors they want. If a black market develops and some tutors charge below the minimum wage, the supply curve shows that some are willing to tutor for $10 (or slightly more) an hour; pages 176, 178.

■ AP Self Test 7.3

True or false

1. True; page 181
2. False; page 181
3. True; page 182

© 2015 Pearson Education, Inc.

4. False; page 183
5. False; page 183

Multiple choice

1. e; page 181
2. e; page 181
3. d; page 181
4. a; page 182
5. b; page 182
6. b; page 182
7. b; page 183
8. d; page 182

Short Response Questions

■ **FIGURE 7.17**

Price (dollars per bushel)

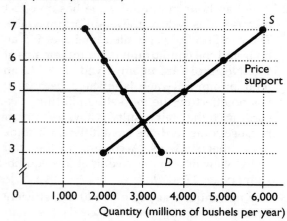

Quantity (millions of bushels per year)

1. a. Figure 7.17 shows the demand and supply curves. The equilibrium price is $4 a bushel and the equilibrium quantity is 3,000 million bushels a year.

   b. The $5 per bushel price support is illustrated in the figure. This price support raises the price of wheat to $5 per bushel. The quantity of wheat produced increases to 4,000 million bushels per year and the marginal cost of the last bushel of wheat produced increases to $5. There is a deadweight loss because the marginal cost exceeds the marginal benefit; pages 182-183.

   c. With the price support, consumers buy only 2,500 million bushels per year. There

is a surplus of 1,500 million bushels (4,000 million bushels produced minus $2,500 million purchased by consumers) that the government must buy. The government pays a subsidy of $5 per bushel × 1,500 million bushels, which is $7.5 billion; page 182.

■ **FIGURE 7.18**

Price (dollars per ton)

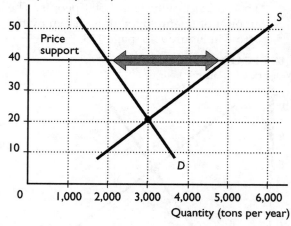

Quantity (tons per year)

2. a. Figure 7.18 shows that at the support price of $40 per ton, 5,000 tons are produced and consumers buy 2,000 tons. The government must buy the surplus, 3,000 tons. The amount the government must buy is equal to the length of the arrow in Figure 7.15; page 182.

   b. To buy the surplus, the government pays a subsidy to producers of $40 per ton × 3,000 tons, which is $120,000; page 182.

Long Response Questions

1. If a price support is set below the equilibrium price, it does not make the equilibrium price illegal and so is ineffective. If a price support is set above the equilibrium price, it makes the equilibrium price illegal and is effective; pages 181-182.

2. The first assertion is correct: a price support program increases producer surplus (which benefits producers) and decreases consumer surplus (which harms consumers). But the second assertion is incorrect. There is a net effect on society because a deadweight loss is created, which harms society; page 183.

© 2015 Pearson Education, Inc.

Additional Exercises (also in MyEconLab Test A)

1. The equilibrium price is $12 a pound and the equilibrium quantity is 4 billion pounds a year. If this price is the same as the world price, the market is efficient because marginal benefit equals marginal cost.

2. The price support of $16 per pound leads to a quantity demanded of 2 billion pounds of peanuts and a quantity produced of 6 billion pounds of peanuts. There is surplus of 4 billion pounds of peanuts. With the price support of $16 per pound, the government must buy the 4 billion pound surplus, so the total subsidy paid to peanut farmers is $16 per pound multiplied by 4 billion pounds, or $64 billion.

The market with the price support is inefficient because marginal cost exceeds marginal benefit. There is overproduction and a deadweight loss is created; pages 181-182.

3. Consumers lose because they must pay a higher price for a reduced quantity. Producers gain. Taxpayers lose because they must pay $64 billion in subsidies to suppliers. The deadweight loss is equal to $1/2 \times 2$ billion pounds of peanuts × ($16 per pound − $8 per pound), or $8 billion; pages 182-183.

© 2015 Pearson Education, Inc.

Chapter

Taxes

8

In Chapter 8 we study how taxes affect markets, who actually pays the tax, and the effect of an income tax and a Social Security tax, and we review ideas about the fairness of taxes.

1 Explain how taxes change prices and quantities, are shared by buyers and sellers, and create inefficiency.

Taxes raise the price paid by buyers, lower the price received by sellers, and decrease the quantity of the good. Tax incidence is the division of the burden of a tax between the buyers and the sellers; generally sellers and buyers both pay part of a tax. The incidence of a tax depends on the elasticities of demand and supply and *not* upon whom, the buyers or sellers, the government levies the tax. For a given elasticity of supply, buyers pay a larger share of the tax the more inelastic the demand for the good. Buyers pay the entire tax when demand is perfectly inelastic or supply is perfectly elastic. Similarly, for a given elasticity of demand, sellers pay a larger share of the tax the more inelastic the supply of the good. Sellers pay the entire tax when demand is perfectly elastic or supply is perfectly inelastic. The excess burden of a tax is the amount by which the burden of a tax exceeds the tax revenue received by the government—the deadweight loss from a tax. The more inelastic the demand or supply, the smaller the excess burden of the tax, that is, the smaller the deadweight loss from the tax.

2 Explain how income taxes and Social Security taxes change wage rates and employment, are shared by employers and workers, and create inefficiency.

The marginal tax rate is the percentage of an additional dollar that is paid in tax; the average tax rate is the percentage of income that is paid in tax. With a progressive tax, the average tax rate rises as income increases; with a proportional tax, the average tax rate is constant at all income levels; with a regressive tax, the average tax rate decreases as income increases. A tax on labor income decreases employment and creates a deadweight loss. Both the employer and the worker pay part of the tax. A tax on capital income decreases the quantity of capital and creates a deadweight loss. The supply of capital is highly elastic. If the supply of capital is perfectly elastic, then the demanders, that is, firms, pay the entire tax. A tax on land or other unique resources does not decrease the quantity and creates no deadweight loss because supply is perfectly inelastic. The entire burden of the tax falls on the owner of the resource. Social Security tax laws are written so that both workers and employers pay equal shares but the incidence *actually* depends on the elasticities of the demand for labor and the supply of labor.

3 Review ideas about the fairness of the tax system.

The benefits principle is the proposition that people should pay taxes equal to the benefits received from public services. This taxing principle means that those who benefit the most pay the most. The ability-to-pay principle is the proposition that people should pay taxes according to how easily they can bear the burden. For fairness, the ability-to-pay principle compares people along vertical and horizontal dimensions. The fairness and efficiency of taxes can conflict, leading to the big tradeoff.

© 2015 Pearson Education, Inc.

YOUR AP TEST HINTS

AP Topics

Topic on your AP test	What to Know	Corresponding textbook section
Taxes on goods and services	Effects on buyers and sellers; tax incidence	Checkpoint 8.1
Income tax and social security tax	Progressive and regressive taxes; tax incidence	Checkpoint 8.2
Fairness of tax	Effects of the "Big Tradeoff"	Checkpoint 8.3

AP Vocabulary Covered

Terms	What to Know	Text Sections
Tax incidence	Division of tax burden shared by buyers or sellers, based on elasticity of demand and supply	Checkpoint 8.1, p. 190
Excess burden	The amount by which the burden of taxation exceeds tax revenue; a deadweight loss	Checkpoint 8.1, p. 192
Taxable income	A person's taxable income minus exemptions and deductions	Checkpoint 8.2, p. 196
Marginal tax rate	Percent of an additional dollar of income paid in tax	Checkpoint 8.2, p. 197
Average tax rate	Percent of income paid in tax	Checkpoint 8.2, p. 197
Progressive tax	Average tax rate rises as income increases	Checkpoint 8.2, p. 197
Proportional tax	Average tax rate is constant at all income levels	Checkpoint 8.2, p. 197
Regressive tax	Average tax rate decreases as income increases	Checkpoint 8.2, p. 197
Benefit principal	Those who benefit from a program should pay the tax that funds the program	Checkpoint 8.3, p. 206
Ability-to-pay principle	Those more able to pay the tax should pay more	Checkpoint 8.3, p. 206
Horizontal equity	Taxpayers with the same ability to pay, pay the same	Checkpoint 8.3, p. 206
Vertical equity	Taxpayers with a greater ability to pay, pay a larger share	Checkpoint 8.3, p. 207
Marriage tax problem	Tax on a married couple that is greater than the tax for a couple filing as two single people	Checkpoint 8.3, p. 207

Extra AP material

- The federal system of taxation is progressive because people with higher incomes have higher average tax rates than people with lower incomes.
- Most states have sales taxes (and other similar taxes) that are regressive because people with lower incomes pay a higher percentage of their incomes to this tax than people with higher incomes.
- The AP test has not asked questions about capital income or land income taxation. But understanding these topics will help you better grasp the effects of income and social security taxes on wage income

© 2015 Pearson Education, Inc.

CHECKPOINT 8.1

■ **Explain how taxes change prices and quantities, are shared by buyers and sellers, and create inefficiency.**

Quick Review

- *Effect of a sales tax on the supply curve* A sales tax decreases the supply of the good and the supply curve shifts leftward. The vertical distance between the supply curve without the tax and the supply curve with the tax equals the amount of the tax.

- *Tax incidence and elasticities of demand and supply* For a given elasticity of supply, the more inelastic the demand, the larger the share of a tax paid by the buyer. And, for a given elasticity of demand, the more inelastic the supply, the larger the share of a tax paid by the seller.

Additional Practice Problem 8.1

1. The figure illustrates the initial equilibrium in the markets for Coke and Pepsi. The price of a 2 liter bottle of a Coke and a Pepsi are the same, $1.50, and the quantity of each are the same, 12 million bottles a week. The supply of Coke is identical to the supply of Pepsi and both are given by supply curve *S* in the figure. However, as shown in the figure with the demand curve *Dc* for Coke and *Dp* for Pepsi, the demand for Coke is more elastic than the demand for Pepsi. The government now imposes a $1 per bottle sales tax on Coke and Pepsi.

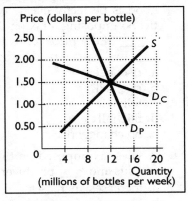

a. Does the price paid by consumers for a Coke rise by more than, less than, or the same amount as the price paid for a Pepsi?

b. Do the consumers of Coke pay more of the tax than do consumers of Pepsi? Do the producers of Coke pay more of the tax than do the producers of Pepsi?

c. Does the quantity of Coke decrease by more, less, or the same amount as the quantity of Pepsi?

d. Does the government collect more, less, or the same amount of tax revenue from the tax on Coke as it does from the tax on Pepsi?

e. Is the deadweight loss from the tax on Coke larger, smaller, or the same amount as the deadweight loss from the tax on Pepsi?

Solution to Additional Practice Problem 8.1

1a. A tax is like an increase in the suppliers' costs, so a tax decreases the supply and shifts the supply curve leftward. The vertical distance between the

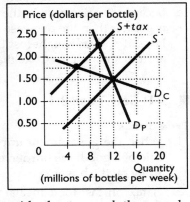

supply curve with the tax and the supply curve without the tax is equal to the amount of the tax, $1 per bottle in this problem. The figure shows this effect, with the supply curves for Coke and Pepsi both shifting to the curve labeled *S+tax*. The demand for Coke is more elastic, so the price paid by consumers for a Coke rises only to $1.75, a 25¢ increase. The demand for Pepsi is less elastic, so the price paid by consumers for a Pepsi rises to $2.25, a 75¢ increase.

1b. The demand for Coke is more elastic, so consumers pay less of the tax imposed on Coke. The price paid by consumers for a Coke rises 25¢, so consumers pay 25¢ of this tax and producers pay the remaining 75¢. The demand for Pepsi is more inelastic, so consumers pay more of the tax imposed on Pepsi.

© 2015 Pearson Education, Inc.

The price paid by consumers for a Pepsi rises 75¢, so consumers pay 75¢ of this tax and producers pay 25¢.

1c. The quantity of Coke decreases by more than the quantity of Pepsi because the demand for Coke is more elastic than the demand for Pepsi. In the figure, the equilibrium quantity of Coke decreases to 6 million bottles per week and the equilibrium quantity of Pepsi decreases only to 10 million bottles per week.

1d. The total amount of tax revenue equals the tax multiplied by the quantity sold. Because the decrease in the quantity of Coke sold is greater than the decrease in the quantity of Pepsi sold, less Coke than Pepsi is sold after the tax is imposed, so the government collects less tax revenue from the tax on Coke.

1e. Because the decrease in the quantity of Coke is greater than the decrease in the quantity of Pepsi, the deadweight loss of the tax is greater in the market for Coke than that for Pepsi.

■ AP Self Test 8.1

True or false

1. When the government imposes a tax on the sale of a good, the burden of the tax falls entirely on the buyer.

2. A tax on fast-food meals does not create a deadweight loss because the elasticity of supply of fast-food meals equals 1.0.

3. The excess burden of a tax is the deadweight loss from the tax.

4. For a given elasticity of supply, the more inelastic the demand for a good, the smaller the share of the tax paid by the buyer.

5. When the government taxes a good that has a perfectly elastic supply, the buyer pays the entire tax.

Multiple choice

1. Tax incidence refers to
   a. how government taxes are spent by the government.
   b. the incidences of tax revolts by the tax payers.
   c. the amount of a tax minus its burden.
   d. the division of the burden of a tax between the buyers and the sellers.
   e. tax revenue minus excess burden.

2. Neither the supply of nor demand for a good is perfectly elastic or perfectly inelastic. So imposing a tax on the good results in a ____ in the price paid by buyers and ____ in the equilibrium quantity.
   a. rise; an increase
   b. rise; a decrease
   c. fall; an increase
   d. fall; a decrease
   e. rise; no change

3. Neither the supply of nor demand for a good is perfectly elastic or perfectly inelastic. So imposing a tax on the good results in a ____ in the price received by sellers and a ____ in the price paid by buyers.
   a. rise; rise
   b. rise; fall
   c. fall; rise
   d. fall; fall
   e. no change; rise

4. A sales tax imposed on tires ____ consumer surplus and ____ producer surplus.
   a. increases; increases
   b. increases; decreases
   c. decreases; increases
   d. decreases; decreases
   e. does not change; does not change

© 2015 Pearson Education, Inc.

■ FIGURE 8.1

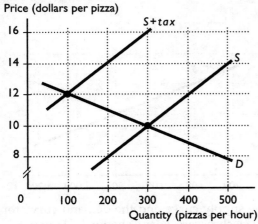

Price (dollars per pizza)

5. Figure 8.1 shows the market for delivered pizza. The government has imposed a tax of _____ per pizza.
   a. $6
   b. $8
   c. $10
   d. $12
   e. $16

6. In Figure 8.1, before the tax was imposed consumers paid _____ for a pizza and after the tax is imposed consumers pay _____ for a pizza.
   a. $10: $16
   b. $12; $16
   c. $10; $12
   d. $12; $16
   e. $10; $6

7. In Figure 8.1, the division of the tax is that consumers pay _____ of the tax and suppliers pay _____ of the tax.
   a. $6: $0
   b. $3; $3
   c. $0; $6
   d. $4; $2
   e. $2; $4

8. The deadweight loss from a tax is called the
   a. marginal benefit of the tax.
   b. marginal cost of the tax.
   c. excess burden of the tax.
   d. net gain from taxation.
   e. net loss from taxation.

9. A sales tax creates a deadweight loss because
   a. the sellers must complete paperwork when they sell an item.
   b. demand and supply both decrease.
   c. less is produced and consumed.
   d. citizens value government goods less than private goods.
   e. the government spends the tax revenue it collects.

10. To determine who bears the greater share of a tax, we compare the
    a. number of buyers to the number of sellers.
    b. elasticity of supply to the elasticity of demand.
    c. size of the tax to the price of the good.
    d. government tax revenue to the revenue collected by the suppliers.
    e. pre-tax quantity to the post-tax quantity.

11. Suppose the demand for barley is perfectly inelastic. The supply curve of barley is upward sloping. If a tax is imposed on barley,
    a. barley sellers pay the entire tax.
    b. barley buyers pay the entire tax.
    c. the government pays the entire tax.
    d. the tax is split evenly between barley buyers and sellers.
    e. who pays the tax depends on whether the government imposes the tax on barley sellers or on barley buyers.

Short Response Questions

1. Define the term "incidence of a tax."

2. What is the relationship between the deadweight loss from a tax and the excess burden of a tax? Why does a tax create a deadweight loss?

© 2015 Pearson Education, Inc.

Long Response Questions

■ **FIGURE 8.2**

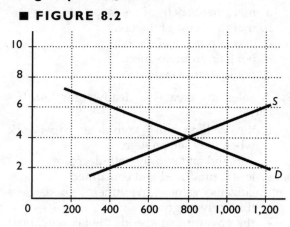

1. The supply curve and the demand curve for pizza slices are shown in Figure 8.2. The price is in dollars per slice and the quantity is pizza slices per day. Label the axes.
   a. What is the equilibrium price and quantity of pizza slices?
   b. Suppose the government imposes a sales tax of $4 a slice of pizza. In Figure 8.2, draw the new supply curve after the tax is imposed.
   c. After the tax is imposed, what is the price paid by buyers for a slice of pizza? What is the price received by sellers for a slice of pizza? What is the incidence of the tax?
   d. In Figure 8.2, darken the area of the deadweight loss from the tax.

■ **FIGURE 8.3**

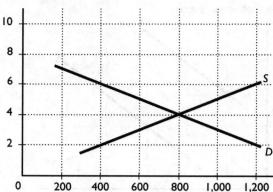

2. The supply curve and the demand curve for pizza slices are again shown in Figure 8.3. The price is in dollars per slice and the quantity is pizza slices per day. Once again, label the axes.
   a. Suppose the government imposes a tax on buyers of $4 a slice of pizza. In Figure 8.3, draw the new demand curve after the tax is imposed.
   b. After the tax is imposed, what is the price paid by buyers for a slice of pizza? What is the price received by sellers for a slice of pizza? What is the incidence of the tax?
   c. How do the prices paid and the tax incidence in this question compare to those in question 1? What general principle does your answer uncover?

3. The government decides to tax high blood pressure medicine. The supply by drug companies is elastic; the demand by patients is inelastic. Do the drug companies bear the entire tax burden? Is there much deadweight loss from this tax?

© 2015 Pearson Education, Inc.

Additional Exercises (also in MyEconLab Test A)

With the increased popularity of cell phones, the government imposes a tax of $20 a cell phone and a tax of 10¢ a call made on a cell phone. Suppose that the supply of cell phones is elastic, the demand for cell phones is inelastic, the supply of calls is perfectly elastic, and the demand for calls is elastic. Use this information to answer exercises 1 and 2.

1. Does the buyer or the seller pay more of the tax on a phone? Who pays more of the tax on a call? Would the taxes reduce the number of cell phones bought and the number of calls made from cell phones?

2. Which tax would raise more revenue for the government? Why? Which tax do you think would have the greater excess burden? Why?

3. The supply of apartments in New York City is inelastic, and the demand for apartments is elastic. The city introduces a tax on apartment rentals. Explain why the landlord would pay more of the tax than the renter and why the government would collect a large revenue from this tax.

CHECKPOINT 8.2

■ **Explain how income taxes and Social Security taxes change wage rates and employment, are shared by employers and workers, and create inefficiency.**

Quick Review

- *Progressive tax* A tax is progressive if the average tax rate increases as income increases.

- *Proportional tax* A tax is proportional if the average tax rate remains constant at all income levels.

- *Regressive tax* A tax is regressive if the average tax rate decreases as income increases.

Additional Practice Problems 8.2

1. The supply of capital is perfectly elastic. The income from capital is the interest received. If a tax is imposed on the income from capital, who pays the tax: the firms who demand capital or the suppliers of capital? Explain your answer.

2. The supply of land is perfectly inelastic. The income from land is rent. If a tax is imposed on the income from land, who pays the tax: the demanders of land or the suppliers? Explain your answer.

3. In Hong Kong, the marginal tax rates on salaries ranges from 2 percent to 20 percent with a maximum average tax of 15 percent, which is reached on incomes of about $59,000. Compare the tax rates in Hong Kong with the U.S. federal tax rate. In which country is the personal income tax (tax on salaries) more progressive? Why?

Solutions to Additional Practice Problems 8.2

1. Because the supply of capital is perfectly elastic, the suppliers pay none of the tax. The entire tax is paid by the demanders. Supply being perfectly elastic means that the suppliers have a huge number of options where to supply their capital, with all the options paying the same interest rate. If one of these options imposes a tax, suppliers will not supply any capital there unless the interest rate rises to compensate them fully for the tax. When the interest rate rises by the full amount of the tax, suppliers pay none of the tax. The interest rate must rise by the full amount of the tax because that is the only way that the return from supplying capital to this option equals the return from supplying capital to all the other options.

2. Because the supply of land is perfectly inelastic, the suppliers pay all of the tax. The demanders pay none of the tax. Supply being perfectly inelastic means that suppliers have no other choice but to supply their land. Demanders determine the maximum price they are willing to pay for this quantity of land and that is the price. If a tax is imposed on land, demanders will not pay any of the tax

© 2015 Pearson Education, Inc.

because they are already paying the maximum price they are wiling to pay. So suppliers pay the entire tax.

3. The personal income tax in the United States is more progressive because the average tax rate increases to higher levels in the United States. Hong Kong's marginal tax rates are lower than U.S. marginal tax rates, so Hong Kong's average tax rate remains lower than the U.S. average tax rate.

■ AP Self Test 8.2

True or false

1. When Hank earns an additional dollar, he pays 30 cents in additional tax. Hank's marginal tax rate is 30 percent.

2. If the average tax rate increases as income increases, the tax is a progressive tax.

3. Sam has $40,000 of taxable income and pays $4,000 income tax. Bert has $50,000 of taxable income and pays $4,500 income tax. Sam and Bert live in a country with a progressive income tax.

4. An income tax on labor creates a deadweight loss.

5. If the supply of capital is perfectly elastic, a tax on capital income decreases the demand for capital and decreases the interest rate.

Multiple choice

1. The percentage of an additional dollar of income that is paid in tax is the
   a. sales tax.
   b. excise tax.
   c. marginal tax rate.
   d. personal income tax.
   e. regressive tax.

2. If the average tax rate is constant as income increases, then the tax is called
   a. regressive.
   b. progressive.
   c. proportional.
   d. an average tax.
   e. efficient.

3. A tax on labor income
   a. increases the quantity employed because the demand for labor increases.
   b. decreases the quantity employed because the supply of labor decreases.
   c. increases the quantity employed because the supply of labor increases.
   d. decreases the quantity employed because the demand for labor increases.
   e. does not change the quantity employed because people must have jobs in order to earn any income.

4. The incidence of an income tax on labor income is generally that the tax is
   a. paid only by workers.
   b. paid only by employers.
   c. shared equally between workers and employers.
   d. shared but not necessarily equally between workers and employers.
   e. funded by the deadweight loss.

5. When governments tax capital income, the equilibrium quantity of capital
   a. increases because of the international mobility of capital.
   b. does not change because the supply of capital is perfectly elastic.
   c. decreases.
   d. does not change because the supply of capital is perfectly inelastic.
   e. might increase or decrease depending on whether the demand for capital is inelastic or elastic.

6. If the supply of capital is perfectly elastic, the incidence of a tax on capital income is
   a. paid entirely by the suppliers of capital.
   b. paid entirely by firms that demand capital.
   c. shared between firms that demand capital and the suppliers of capital.
   d. shared but not equally between firms that demand capital and the suppliers of capital.
   e. unknown.

© 2015 Pearson Education, Inc.

■ FIGURE 8.4

Interest rate (percent per year)

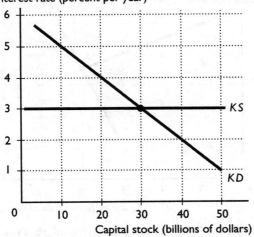

Capital stock (billions of dollars)

7. Figure 8.4 shows the capital market. If the government imposes a 2 percent tax on capital income, the interest rate ____.
   a. stays at 3 percent
   b. rises to 4 percent
   c. rises to 5 percent
   d. falls to 2 percent
   e. falls to 1 percent

8. Figure 8.4 shows the capital market. If the government imposes a 2 percent tax on capital income, the equilibrium quantity of capital becomes
   a. $10 billion.
   b. $20 billion.
   c. $30 billion.
   d. $40 billion.
   e. $50 billion.

9. A tax on income from land in Montana is borne entirely by landowners because the
   a. demand for land is perfectly inelastic.
   b. supply of land is perfectly inelastic.
   c. supply of land is perfectly elastic.
   d. demand for land is perfectly elastic.
   e. deadweight loss from the tax would otherwise be infinite.

10. When a social security tax is imposed on workers, employment ____ and when a social security tax is imposed on employers, employment ____.
    a. increases; increases
    b. increases; decreases
    c. decreases; increases
    d. decreases; decreases
    e. decreases; does not change

Short Response Question

1. Why is the supply of capital highly elastic? Who pays the tax on capital income if the supply of capital is perfectly elastic?

Long Response Questions

■ FIGURE 8.5

Wage rate (dollars per hour)

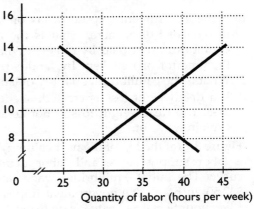

Quantity of labor (hours per week)

1. Figure 8.5 shows the labor market.
   a. Label the curves. What is the equilibrium wage rate and quantity of labor?
   b. Suppose the government imposes an income tax of $4 an hour on labor income. Illustrate the effect of this tax in the figure.
   c. After the tax is imposed, what is the wage rate paid by firms and what is the amount received by households?
   d. If a deadweight loss is created, shade its area. If a deadweight loss is not created, explain why not.

© 2015 Pearson Education, Inc.

■ **FIGURE 8.6**

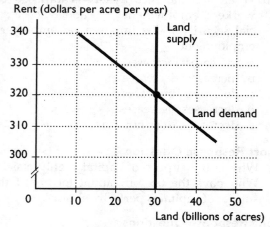

■ **FIGURE 8.7**

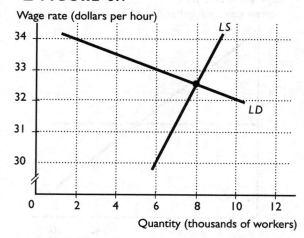

2. Figure 8.6 shows the market for land.
   a. What is the equilibrium rent and quantity of land?
   b. If the government imposes a tax on land income of $10 an acre, what is the new equilibrium rent paid by renters? What is the amount of rent kept by landowners? What is the equilibrium quantity of land?
   c. If a deadweight loss is created, shade its area. If a deadweight loss is not created, explain why not.

3. Figure 8.7 (at the top of the next column) has a labor supply curve and labor demand curve. The initial equilibrium wage rate is $32.50 an hour. The government imposes a $3 an hour Social Security tax on firms.
   a. In the figure, show the effect of this tax. What is the wage that workers receive before the tax and after the tax?
   b. Even though the Social Security tax has been imposed on the firms, how is the burden of the tax split?

4. The government mandates that half of a Social Security tax has to be paid by the employer and the other half has to be paid by the worker. Does this law mean that the burden of the tax is shared equally by the employer and worker?

Additional Exercise (also in MyEconLab Test A)

1. California taxes personal incomes, and in 2004, there were six tax brackets that ranged from 1.0 percent on a taxable income of $6,146 to 8.3 percent on taxable incomes above $40,345. California has an 8.84 percent corporate income tax. California has a 7.25 percent sales tax. Other taxes are 18 cents a gallon on gasoline, 87 cents a pack on cigarettes, and $0.20 per gallon on beer and wine. Property taxes vary across the counties and range from 1 percent to 2 percent of property values.
   a. Classify California's taxes into progressive, proportional, and regressive taxes.
   b. Which of California's taxes creates the biggest excess burden? Explain.

CHECKPOINT 8.3

■ **Review ideas about the fairness of the tax system.**

Quick Review
- *Benefits principle* People should pay taxes equal to the benefits they receive from public services.
- *Ability-to-pay principle* People should pay taxes according to how easily they can bear the burden.

© 2015 Pearson Education, Inc.

Additional Practice Problem 8.3

1. "The only fair taxes are user fees, such as toll roads. The gas tax is fair because the funds raised go for road maintenance. All government-provided services need to be funded through user fees. To pay for parks, we need to charge entrance fees. The cost of garbage collection must be based on how much garbage the household creates. Any tax except a user fee is unfair and must be abolished!" Comment on the fairness principle being used. Is it possible for *all* government programs to be funded through user fees?

Solution to Additional Practice Problem 8.3

1. The speaker is advocating the benefits principle of taxation, which is the proposition that people should pay taxes equal to the benefits they receive from public services. Although user fees have merit, it is not possible to fund all government programs through user fees. First, for public goods such as national defense, everyone consumes the same amount. It is impossible to determine how much any particular person benefits and therefore not possible to determine the proper fee. Second, some programs are designed to redistribute income to poorer people. It would be ludicrous to tax welfare recipients an amount equal to the benefits they received, which is the case under a user-fee arrangement.

■ AP Self Test 8.3

True or false

1. The benefits principle asserts that those people who are harmed by the deadweight loss of a tax should not pay the tax.

2. If the revenue from gasoline taxes is used to pay for road repairs, the tax reflects the ability-to-pay principle.

3. The U.S. income tax, which uses progressive income taxes, can be considered fair based on the principle of vertical equity.

4. Both vertical and horizontal equity can be achieved and the marriage tax problem eliminated if married couples are taxed as two single persons.

5. The taxes with the largest deadweight loss are taxes on capital income, and the people who pay these taxes generally have the greatest ability to pay taxes.

Multiple choice

1. Which of the following taxes best illustrates the benefits principle of taxation?
   a. sales tax on clothing used to fund food stamps
   b. state income tax used to fund state universities
   c. medicare tax imposed on all workers used to fund medical care for the elderly
   d. gasoline tax used to fund road repairs
   e. federal income tax used to fund NASA spending

2. The proposition that people should pay taxes according to how easily they can bear the burden is the ____ principle
   a. regressive tax
   b. benefits
   c. ability-to-pay
   d. fairness
   e. incidence of fairness

3. The government once imposed a luxury tax on very expensive jewelry. This tax followed the ____ principle.
   a. benefits
   b. ability-to-pay
   c. vertical equity
   d. horizontal equity
   e. fair-tax incidence

4. The proposition that taxpayers with the same ability to pay should pay the same taxes is called
   a. the benefits principle.
   b. the ability-to-pay imperative.
   c. vertical equity.
   d. horizontal equity.
   e. fair-tax incidence principle.

© 2015 Pearson Education, Inc.

5. Vertical equity implies that
   i. tax rates should be equal for all tax payers.
   ii. people with higher incomes should pay more in taxes.
   iii. people with higher incomes should pay a lower average tax rate.
   a. i only.
   b. ii only.
   c. iii only.
   d. i and ii.
   e. ii and iii.

6. Joan's income is $60,000 and she pays $6,000 in taxes. Juan's income is $40,000 and he pays $7,000 in taxes. This situation violates
   a. the benefits principle.
   b. the big tradeoff.
   c. vertical equity.
   d. horizontal equity.
   e. the fair-tax incidence principle.

7. Because the U.S. income tax is a progressive tax, taxing married couples as two single persons can violate
   a. the benefits principle.
   b. the ability-to-pay imperative.
   c. vertical equity.
   d. horizontal equity.
   e. the government's need for more revenue.

8. Compared to taxes on labor income, taxes on capital income generate _____ deadweight loss and are paid by people who generally have the _____ ability to pay.
   a. a larger; most
   b. a larger; least
   c. a smaller; most
   d. a smaller; least
   e. no; least

Short Response Questions

1. Define the benefits principle of taxation.

2. Define the ability-to-pay principle of taxation.

3. Is a tax on gasoline used to build roads an example of the benefits principle of taxation or the ability-to-pay principle of taxation? Is the federal income tax an example of the benefits principle of taxation or the ability-to-pay principle of taxation?

Long Response Questions

1. There are a variety of welfare programs, such as food stamps, designed to boost the income of poor families. Does it make sense to raise the tax revenue necessary to fund these programs by using the benefits principle of taxation?

2. What is the marriage tax problem? If a married couple is taxed as two single individuals, what problem is created?

Additional Exercise (also in MyEconLab Test A)

1. In Canada, the marginal income tax rates range from 22 percent to 40 percent. Does Canada place greater weight on the ability-to-pay principle than does the United States? Does Canada place a greater weight on efficiency and a smaller weight on fairness than does the United States?

© 2015 Pearson Education, Inc.

SELF TEST ANSWERS

■ AP Self Test 8.1

True or false
1. False; pages 190-191
2. False; page 192
3. True; page 192
4. False; page 193
5. True; page 194

Multiple choice
1. d; page 190
2. b; page 191
3. c; page 191
4. d; page 192
5. a; page 191
6. c; page 191
7. e; page 191
8. c; page 192
9. c; page 192
10. b; page 193
11. b; page 193

Short Response Questions
1. Tax incidence is the division of a tax between the buyers and the sellers; page 190.

2. The excess burden of a tax is the same as the deadweight loss. The deadweight loss arises because the tax leads to less of the good or service being produced and consumed; page 192.

Long Response Questions
1. The axes are labeled in Figure 8.8.
   a. The price is $4 a slice and the quantity is 800 slices a day; page 191.
   b. Figure 8.8 shows the supply curve after the tax is imposed; page 191.
   c. Buyers pay $6 a slice; sellers receive $2 a slice. The tax is split equally; page 191.
   d. The deadweight loss is the grey triangle in Figure 8.8; page 192.

2. The axes are labeled in Figure 8.9.
   a. Figure 8.9 shows the demand curve after the tax is imposed; page 191.

■ FIGURE 8.8

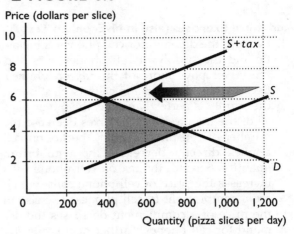

Price (dollars per slice)

■ FIGURE 8.9

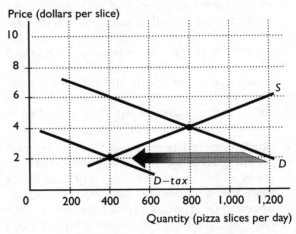

Price (dollars per slice)

b. Buyers pay $6 a slice; sellers receive $2 a slice. The tax is split equally; page 191.

c. The price paid and the tax incidence is the same in problem 1, when the tax is imposed on sellers, and in problem 2, when the tax is imposed on buyers. The general principle is that the tax incidence depends on the elasticity of demand and the elasticity of supply, not on who sends the tax to the government; pages 191, 193.

3. The burden of the tax will fall mainly upon buyers, not the drug companies, because

© 2015 Pearson Education, Inc.

demand is inelastic and supply is elastic. Because the demand is inelastic, the decrease in the quantity will not be large and so the deadweight loss from the tax is small; page 193.

Additional Exercises (also in MyEconLab Test A)

1. Because the demand for cell phones is inelastic and the supply of cell phones is elastic, the buyer pays more of the tax on phones. Because the demand for calls is elastic and the supply is perfectly elastic, the buyer pays *all* of the tax on calls. The taxes decrease the number of cell phones. First, the tax on cell phones directly decreases the equilibrium quantity. Second, the tax on cell phone calls increases the price of cell phone calls, which are a complement to cell phones. The rise in the price of a complement decreases the demand for cell phones, further decreasing the equilibrium quantity of cell phones. The taxes decrease the number of cell phone calls. First, the tax on cell phone calls directly decreases the equilibrium quantity. Second, the tax on cell phones increases the price of cell phones, which are a complement to cell phone calls. The rise in the price of a complement decreases the demand for cell phone calls, further decreasing the equilibrium quantity of cell phone calls; pages 193-194.

2. The tax on cell phones raises more revenue for the government because the decrease in the equilibrium quantity of cell phones is less than the decrease in the quantity of cell phone calls. The tax on cell phones is paid only partly by the buyers, so the price does not rise by the full amount of the tax. And, the demand for cell phones is inelastic, so the higher price of a cell phone decreases the quantity by a relatively small proportion. The tax on cell phone calls is totally paid by the buyers, so the price rises by the full amount of the tax. And, the demand for cell phone calls is elastic, so the (much) higher price of a cell phone call decreases the quantity by a relatively large proportion. The excess burden is greatest on cell phone calls because both the rise in price and the decrease

in quantity are greater for cell phone calls than for cell phones; pages 193-194.

3. The landlords pay a greater share of the tax because the supply of apartments is inelastic and the demand for apartments is elastic. The government will collect a large revenue from the tax because the equilibrium quantity does not decrease by much since the supply is inelastic. Even though the tax means that the suppliers receive less, with an inelastic supply the quantity supplied does not decrease substantially; page 194.

■ AP Self Test 8.2

True or false

1. True; page 197
2. True; page 197
3. False; page 197
4. True; page 198
5. False; page 199

Multiple choice

1. c; page 197
2. c; page 197
3. b; page 198
4. d; page 198
5. c; page 198
6. b; page 198
7. c; page 198
8. a; page 198
9. b; page 199
10. d; pages 200-201

Short Response Question

1. Because capital is internationally mobile, its supply is highly (perhaps perfectly) elastic. If the supply of capital is perfectly elastic, firms pay the entire tax on capital income; page 199.

Long Response Questions

1. a. The curves are labeled *LD* and *LS* in Figure 8.10 (on the next page). The equilibrium wage rate is $10 an hour and the equilibrium quantity of labor is 35 hours a week; page 198.

© 2015 Pearson Education, Inc.

■ FIGURE 8.10

Wage rate (dollars per hour)

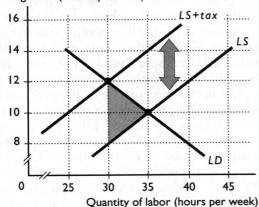

Quantity of labor (hours per week)

■ FIGURE 8.11

Wage rate (dollars per hour)

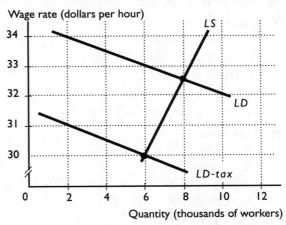

Quantity (thousands of workers)

b. The income tax decreases the supply of labor services. The labor supply curve shifts leftward from *LS* to *LS + tax*. The vertical distance between the two supply curves, indicated by the arrow, is equal to the $4 tax; page 198.

c. Firms pay a wage rate of $12 an hour; workers receive a wage rate of $8 an hour; page 198.

d. The deadweight loss is the grey triangle in Figure 8.10; page 198.

2. a. The equilibrium rent is $320 an acre per year and the equilibrium quantity of land is 30 billion acres; page 199.

b. After the tax, renters pay $320 an acre and landowners keep $310 an acre. The equilibrium quantity of land is 30 billion acres, the same as before the tax was imposed; page 199.

c. There is no deadweight loss created because the equilibrium quantity does not change. The amount produced remains the efficient quantity; page 199.

3. a. Figure 8.11 shows the effect of the tax. Because the tax is imposed on firms, the tax decreases the demand for labor services and shifts the labor demand curve leftward. The vertical distance between the initial supply curve, *LD*, and the new supply curve, *LD + tax*, is the amount of the tax, $3 an hour. The workers received $32.50

per hour before the tax and $30.00 after the tax; page 202.

b. Even though the tax is imposed on firms, the workers pay $2.50 of the $3.00 Social Security tax and the firms pay $0.50; page 202.

4. The burden of the Social Security tax is determined by the elasticity of supply and the elasticity of demand of labor, not by the law splitting the tax. If the demand for labor is more elastic than supply, the burden falls more on the worker and less on the employer. The government can legislate how the tax is collected, but cannot legislate the division of the tax's burden; pages 202-203.

Additional Exercise (also in MyEconLab Test A)

1. a. California's personal income tax is progressive; its corporate income tax is proportional; its sales tax and taxes on cigarettes and liquor are regressive. California's property taxes are progressive if the counties with higher property tax rates also have higher property values; page 197.

b. For two reasons, the tax that has the largest excess burden is probably the personal income tax. First, it has the highest marginal tax rate. Second, it is the largest tax, accounting for much more revenue than any of the other taxes. As a result, it probably has a large effect on the equilibrium quantity of labor and therefore a large excess burden; page 198.

© 2015 Pearson Education, Inc.

■ AP Self Test 8.3

True or false

1. False; page 206
2. False; page 206
3. True; page 207
4. False; pages 207-208
5. True; page 208

Multiple choice

1. d; page 206
2. c; page 206
3. b; page 206
4. d; page 206
5. b; page 207
6. c; page 207
7. d; page 207
8. a; page 208

Short Response Questions

1. The benefits principle of taxation is that people should pay taxes equal to the benefits they receive from public goods and services; page 206.

2. The ability-to-pay principle of taxation is that people according to how easily they can bear the tax burden; page 206.

3. The gasoline tax is an example of the benefits principle because the people who pay the tax benefit from the roads funded by the tax. The federal income tax is an example of the ability-to-pay principle because higher income people pay more taxes; page 206.

Long Response Questions

1. If the taxes necessary to fund the various welfare programs, such as food stamps, were assessed using the benefits principle of taxation, poor families would be required to pay the tax because they are the ones who benefit from the programs. But this outcome would defeat the purpose of the programs, which are designed to increase these families' incomes. The benefits principle of taxation does not work for government programs designed to increase the incomes of the poor; page 206.

2. The marriage tax problem is that a working couple pays more taxes if they are married than if they are single. Taxing the couple as single taxpayers violates horizontal equity because then two married couples with the same total income could pay different taxes depending on how much each partner earned; pages 207-208.

Additional Exercise (also in MyEconLab Test A)

1. The lowest marginal tax rate in Canada is higher than the lowest marginal tax rate in the United States. The highest marginal tax rates are almost the same. Because the tax rate is higher in Canada than in the United States, Canada places more weight on the ability-to-pay principle. Because the Canadian tax rate exceeds the U.S. tax rate, Canada places less weight on efficiency and more weight on fairness than does the United States; pages 206-208.

© 2015 Pearson Education, Inc.

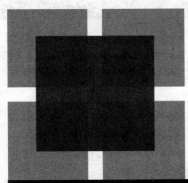

Global Markets in Action

Chapter 9

1 Explain how markets work with international trade.

The goods and services that we buy from people in other countries are our imports and those we sell to people in other countries are our exports. Comparative advantage enables countries to gain from trade. A nation has a comparative advantage in producing a good if it can produce that good at a lower opportunity cost than another country. In this case, the domestic no-trade price is lower than the world price so with international trade the country exports this good. However if the domestic no-trade price is higher than the world price, with international trade the country imports the good.

2 Identify the gains from international trade and its winners and losers.

International trade lowers the prices of the goods and services imported into the country. The lower prices for imported goods mean that consumers gain additional consumer surplus from imports but the lower prices also mean that producers lose producer surplus. The gain to consumers, however, exceeds the loss to producers. International trade raises the prices of the goods and services exported from the country. The higher prices for exported goods mean that producers gain additional producer surplus from exports, but the higher prices also mean that consumers lose consumer surplus. The gain to producers, however, exceeds the loss to consumers.

3 Explain the effects of international trade barriers.

A tariff is a tax imposed on a good when it is imported. A tariff raises the domestic price of the good and reduces imports of it. A tariff increases domestic production of the good, decreases domestic consumption, and yields revenue for the government. It decreases consumer surplus, increases producer surplus and creates a deadweight loss. An import quota is a quantitative restriction on the import of a good that limits the maximum quantity of a good that may be imported in a given period of time. Voluntary export restraints are like an import quota given to exporters of the good. Import quotas and voluntary export restraints (VER) reduce imports, decrease domestic consumption, and increase domestic production. Both decrease consumer surplus, increase producer surplus, and create a deadweight loss. A subsidy is a payment by the government to a producer. Some countries subsidize products which are then exported. Export subsidies increase domestic production of the good but create deadweight losses.

4 Explain and evaluate arguments used to justify restricting international trade.

The three main arguments for protection and restriction of trade are the national security argument, the infant-industry argument, and the dumping argument. Each of these arguments is flawed. Other flawed arguments for protection are that protection saves jobs, allows us to compete with cheap foreign labor, brings diversity and stability, and penalizes lax environmental standards. Tariffs are imposed in some nations to gain revenue for the government. More generally, trade is restricted because of rent seeking from those who benefit from trade restrictions.

© 2015 Pearson Education, Inc.

YOUR AP TEST HINTS

AP Topics

Topic on your AP test	What to Know	Corresponding textbook section
International trade and Comparative advantage	Effects on import and export markets	Checkpoint 9.1
Gains from international trade	Gains from exports and imports	Checkpoint 9.2
Trade restrictions	Effects from tariffs, quotas, and other trade restrictions	Checkpoint 9.3
Case against protectionism	Arguments against protectionism	Checkpoint 9.4

AP Vocabulary Covered

Terms	What to Know	Text Sections
Imports	Goods U.S. residents buy from other countries	Checkpoint 9.1, p. 214
Exports	U.S.-produced goods sold to other countries	Checkpoint 9.1, p. 214
Comparative advantage	Producing a good or service at a lower opportunity cost than another nation	Checkpoint 9.1, p. 214
Gain from international trade	Imports lead to lower prices and increased consumer surplus and total surplus; exports lead to higher prices and increased producer surplus and total surplus	Checkpoint 9.2, p. 220
Tariff	Tax on imported goods	Checkpoint 9.3, p. 223
Import quota	Quantitative restriction on amount of an import	Checkpoint 9.3, p. 227
Export subsidy	Government payments to exporters	Checkpoint 9.3, p. 229
Infant-industry argument	Protecting new industries to help prepare for world competition	Checkpoint 9.4, p. 231
Dumping	Foreign companies selling below cost to reduce international competition	Checkpoint 9.4, p. 232
Rent seeking	Political maneuvering to gain trade advantages	Checkpoint 9.4, p. 235

Extra AP material

- The textbook shows the effect of a tariff as raising the world price that the domestic country must pay. The AP test often shows the effect of a tariff as a leftward shift of the supply curve. The textbook assumes that the country is a small player in the world market, so it can import whatever quantity it wants at the going world price plus the tariff. The AP test assumes that the country is a large player in the world market so that its tariff affects not only the price within the country but also the world price. With the AP assumption, a tariff is similar to a cost increase insofar as it decreases the supply of the good or service and thereby shifts the supply curve leftward.

- The textbook illustrates the effect of a quota by adding the quota amount to the domestic supply curve so that total supply curve—domestic plus quota—is upward sloping. The AP test often illustrates a quota using an upward sloping supply curve that becomes vertical at the quota quantity. The AP test assumes that none of the good or service is produced domestically so there is no domestic supply curve. In this case, the supply curve to the country is the supply curve from foreign producers. This supply curve is upward sloping until it reaches the quota quantity. Once at this quantity, no further amount may be imported and so the supply curve becomes vertical.

© 2015 Pearson Education, Inc.

CHECKPOINT 9.1

■ **Explain how markets work with international trade.**

Quick Review

- *Imports* The goods and services that firms in one country buy from people and firms in other countries.
- *Exports* The goods and services that people and firms in one country sell to firms in other countries.
- *Comparative advantage* A nation has a comparative advantage in a good when its opportunity cost of producing the good is lower than any other nation's opportunity cost of producing the good.

Additional Practice Problem 9.1

1. The figure shows the market for CPU chips in the United States with no international trade. The world price for a CPU chip is $150.

Price (dollars per CPU chip)

   a. Does the United States have a comparative advantage in producing CPU chips? How can you tell?
   b. If international trade is allowed, will the United States import or export CPU chips?
   c. Will the quantity of CPU chips produced in the United States increase or decrease? By how much?
   d. Will the quantity of CPU chips consumed in the United States increase or decrease? By how much?
   e. How many CPU chips will the United States import or export?

Solution to Additional Practice Problem 9.1

1a. Because the price of a CPU chip in the United States is lower than the world price, the United States has a comparative advantage in producing CPU chips.

1b. Because the United States has a comparative advantage in producing CPU chips, the United States will export CPU chips.

1c. With international trade, the price of a CPU chip in the United States will be $150. At this price, the supply curve shows that the quantity of chips produced will equal 20 million per year. With no international trade, the equilibrium quantity of CPU chips produced is 15 million, so international trade leads to 5 million more chips being produced.

1d. With international trade, the price of a CPU chip in the United States will be $150. At this price, the demand curve shows that the quantity of chips demanded will equal 10 million per year. With no international trade, the equilibrium quantity of CPU chips consumed is 15 million, so international trade leads to 5 million fewer chips being consumed.

1e. The quantity of CPU chips exported equals the difference between the quantity of CPU chips produced, 20 million per year, and the quantity consumed, 10 million per year. So the United States will export 20 million CPU chips − 10 million CPU chips, which is 10 million CPU chips.

■ **AP Self Test 9.1**

True or false

1. The United States is the world's largest international trader.

2. If a nation can produce a service at a lower opportunity cost than any other nation, the nation has a national comparative advantage in producing that service.

3. If the price of a good in the United States with no international trade is higher than the world price, then with international trade the United States will export that good.

4. As a result of international trade, the U.S. production of goods exported from the United States increases and the U.S. production of goods imported into the United States decreases.

© 2015 Pearson Education, Inc.

Multiple choice

1. Goods and services that we buy from people and firms in other countries are called our
   a. imports.
   b. exports.
   c. inputs.
   d. raw materials.
   e. obligations.

2. If the United States exports planes to Brazil and imports ethanol from Brazil, the price received by U.S. producers of planes ____ and the price received by Brazilian producers of ethanol ____.
   a. does not change; does not change
   b. rises; rises
   c. rises; falls
   d. falls; rises
   e. falls; falls

3. When Italy buys Boeing jets, the price Italy pays is ____ if it produced its own jets and the price Boeing receives is ____ than it could receive from an additional U.S. buyer.
   a. lower than; lower
   b. higher than; higher
   c. lower than; higher
   d. higher than; lower
   e. the same as; higher

4. A nation will import a good if its no-trade, domestic
   a. price is equal to the world price.
   b. price is less than the world price.
   c. price is greater than the world price.
   d. quantity is less than the world quantity.
   e. quantity is greater than the world quantity.

5. When a good is imported, the domestic production of it ____ and the domestic consumption of it ____.
   a. increases; increases
   b. increases; decreases
   c. decreases; increases
   d. decreases; decreases
   e. increases; does not change

6. The United States exports a good if its no-trade U.S. price is ____ its world price. With international trade, U.S. production of the good ____ compared to the level of no-trade production.
   a. higher than; does not change
   b. higher than; increases
   c. lower than; increases
   d. the same as; increases
   e. the same as; does not change

Short Response Questions

1. French cheese is flown to the United States abroad a United Airlines plane. Classify these transactions from the vantage point of the United States and from the vantage point of France.

■ **FIGURE 9.1**

Price (dollars per bushel)

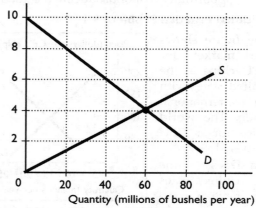

Quantity (millions of bushels per year)

2. Figure 9.1 shows the U.S. demand and supply curves for wheat.
   a. In the absence of international trade, what is the price of a bushel of wheat in the United States?
   b. If the world price of a bushel of wheat is $6 a bushel, will the United States import or export wheat? Above what world price for wheat will the United States export wheat? Below what world price for wheat will the United States import wheat?

© 2015 Pearson Education, Inc.

Price (dollars per ton)	Quantity supplied (tons per year)	Quantity demanded (tons per year)
400	38	58
500	42	52
600	46	46
700	50	40
800	54	34
900	58	28

3. The table above has the U.S. demand and supply schedules for potatoes.

a. If there is no international trade, what is the equilibrium price and quantity of potatoes?

b. If the world price of potatoes is $800 a ton, what is the quantity supplied and the quantity demanded in the United States? Does the United States import or export potatoes? What quantity?

c. If the world price of potatoes rises to $900 a ton, what are the quantity supplied and the quantity demanded in the United States? Does the United States import or export potatoes? What quantity?

d. Would the United States ever import potatoes?

4. How does international trade affect the domestic production and domestic consumption of goods imported into the country?

Additional Exercises (also in MyEconLab Test A)

1. Suppose that the world price of bananas is 18 U.S. cents a pound and that when Australia does not trade bananas internationally, their equilibrium price in Australia is 12 U.S. cents a pound. If Australia opens up to international trade, does it export or import bananas? Explain how the price of bananas in Australia changes. How does the quantity of bananas consumed in Australia change? How does the quantity of bananas grown in Australia change?

2. Both the United States and Canada produce lumber and wine. Canada exports lumber and imports wine. The United States imports lumber and exports wine. If the United States and Canada did not trade internationally, compare the equilibrium prices of lumber and wine in the two countries with the world prices of lumber and wine. Compare the quantities of lumber that Americans buy with and without international trade, and compare the quantities of wine that Canadians buy with and without international trade. Also compare the quantities of lumber that Americans produce with and without international trade, and compare the quantities of wine that Canadians produce with and without international trade.

CHECKPOINT 9.2

■ **Identify the gains from international trade and its winners and losers.**

Quick Review

- *Consumer surplus* Consumer surplus is the marginal benefit from a good or service minus the price paid for it, summed over the quantity consumed.

- *Producer surplus* The producer surplus of a good equals the price of a good minus the marginal cost of producing it summed over the quantity produced.

Additional Practice Problem 9.2

1. The figure shows the U.S. market for CPU chips with no international trade. The world price for a CPU chip is $150.

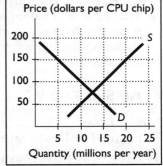

a. Does the United States import or export CPU chips and how many chips are imported or exported?

b. In the United States, tell who gains and who loses from the international trade and explain why they gain or lose. In the figure show the gains, the losses, and the net gain or net loss.

© 2015 Pearson Education, Inc.

Solution to Additional Practice Problem 9.2

1a. The United States exports 15 million CPU chips per year. (20 million are produced in the United States and 5 million are consumed in the United States.)

1b. Producers of CPU chips gain and consumers of CPU chips lose. The gains and loses are in the figure. Producers gain because the price of a CPU chip with international trade is higher than the price without international trade, so the producer surplus increases. The increase in producer surplus is equal to the sum of the area of the dark grey triangle and the light grey trapezoid. Consumers lose for precisely the same reason producers gain: The price of a CPU chip is higher with international trade than without international trade, so the consumer surplus decreases. The decrease in consumer surplus is equal to the area of the light grey trapezoid. On net, the economy gains from international trade. The increase in producer surplus is larger than the decrease in consumer surplus, as shown in the figure by the area of the dark grey triangle.

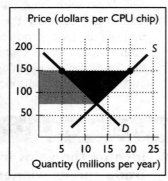

■ AP Self Test 9.2

True or false

1. International trade harms the nation.

2. Imports increase consumer surplus and decrease producer surplus.

3. The nation's total surplus increases when goods are exported.

4. Everyone in a nation gains from exports.

Multiple choice

1. International trade is definitely in the social interest if
   a. consumer surplus increases.
   b. producer surplus increases.
   c. consumer surplus does not decrease.
   d. producer surplus does not decrease.
   e. total surplus increases.

2. Imports ____ consumer surplus, ____ producer surplus, and ____ total surplus
   a. decrease; decrease; decrease
   b. increase; increase; increase
   c. increase; decrease; decrease
   d. increase; decrease; increase
   e. decrease; increase; increase

3. When a country imports a good, the ____ in consumer surplus is ____ the ____ in producer surplus.
   a. decrease; larger than; increase
   b. decrease; smaller than; increase
   c. increase; smaller than; decrease
   d. increase; equal to; decrease
   e. increase; larger than; decrease

4. When a country exports a good, the country's producer surplus ____, consumer surplus ____, and the country ____ from the trade.
   a. increases; increases; gains
   b. decreases; increases; gains
   c. increases; decreases; gains
   d. decreases; decreases; loses
   e. increases; decreases; loses

5. Which of the following is correct?
   i. U.S. total surplus decreases when the United States exports a good.
   ii. U.S. total surplus decreases when the United States imports a good.
   iii. U.S. total surplus increases when the United States imports a good and when the United States exports a good.
   a. i only.
   b. iii only.
   c. i and ii.
   d. ii only.
   e. None of the above because the U.S. total surplus does not change as a result of trade.

© 2015 Pearson Education, Inc.

Short Response Questions

1. How are the gains from international trade measured?

2. Why do consumers gain from imports?

3. Suppose the U.S. price of sugar without any international trade is 30¢ a pound. If the United States allows international trade, when would the U.S. gain be the largest: when the international price is 20¢ a pound or when the international price is 10¢ a pound? Explain your answer.

4. Why doesn't everyone in a nation gain from exporting a good?

Long Response Questions

■ **FIGURE 9.2**

Price (cents per pound)

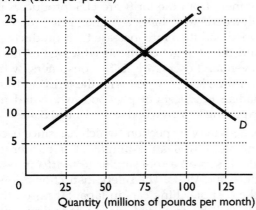

1. Figure 9.2 shows the supply of and demand for sugar in the United States.

    a. If the world price of sugar is 10¢ a pound, draw the world price line in the figure. What is the quantity consumed in the United States, the quantity produced in the United States, and the quantity imported?

    b. Show the changes in consumer surplus, producer surplus, and total surplus once the United States imports sugar.

■ **FIGURE 9.3**

Price (dollars per bushel)

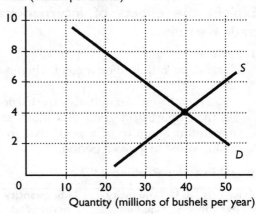

2. Figure 9.3 shows the supply of and demand for wheat in the United States.

    a. If the world price of wheat is $6 a bushel, draw the world price line in the figure. What is the quantity consumed in the United States, the quantity produced in the United States, and the quantity exported?

    b. Show the changes in consumer surplus, producer surplus, and total surplus once the United States exports wheat.

Additional Exercises (also in MyEconLab Test A)

The United States does not trade with Cuba. The price of a fine cigar is $20 in the United States and $2 in Cuba. The price of a basic car is $10,000 in the United States and $25,000 in Cuba. The world price of a fine cigar is $10 and the world price of a basic car is $15,000. Suppose that the two countries began to trade.

1. What would Cuba import and export? Who, in Cuba, would gain and who would lose from trade with the United States? Would Cuba gain from international trade? Draw graphs to illustrate your answer.

2. What would the United States import and export? Who in the United States would gain who would lose from trade with Cuba? Would the United States gain from international trade? Draw graphs to illustrate your answer.

© 2015 Pearson Education, Inc.

CHECKPOINT 9.3

■ Explain the effects of international trade barriers.

Quick Review

- *Tariff* A tax imposed on a good when it is imported.
- *Import Quota* A quantitative restriction on the import of a good that limits the maximum quantity of a good that may be imported in a given period.

Additional Practice Problems 9.3

Price (dollars per ton of plywood)	U.S. quantity supplied (tons per month)	U.S. quantity demanded (tons per month)
1,000	600	1,400
750	500	1,600
500	300	1,800
250	100	2,000

1. The table above shows the U.S. supply and demand schedules for plywood. The United States also can buy plywood from Canada at the world price of $500 per ton.

   a. If there are no tariffs or other barriers to trade, what is the price of a ton of plywood in the United States? How much plywood is produced in the United States and how much is consumed? How much plywood is imported from Canada?

   b. Suppose that the United States imposes a $250 per ton tariff on all plywood imported into the country. What now is the price of a ton of plywood in the United States? How much plywood is produced in the United States and how much is consumed? How much plywood is imported from Canada?

   c. Who has gained from the tariff and who has lost?

2. For many years Japan conducted extremely slow, detailed, and costly safety inspections of *all* U.S. cars imported into Japan. In terms of trade, what was the effect of this inspection? How did the inspection affect the price and quantity of cars in Japan?

Solutions to Additional Practice Problems 9.3

1a. With no tariffs or nontariff barriers, the price of a ton of plywood is equal to the world price, $500 per ton. At this price, 300 tons per month are produced in the United States and 1,800 tons per month are consumed. The difference between the quantity consumed and the quantity produced, which is 1,500 tons per month, is imported from Canada.

1b. If a $250 per ton tariff is imposed, the price in the United States rises to $750 per ton. At this price, 500 tons per month are produced in the United States and 1,600 tons per month are consumed. The difference between the quantity consumed and the quantity produced, which is 1,100 tons per month, is imported from Canada.

1c. Gainers from the tariff are U.S. producers of plywood, who have a higher price for plywood and therefore increase their production, and the U.S. government, which gains tariff revenue. Losers are U.S. consumers, who consume less plywood with the tariff, and Canadian producers of plywood, who wind up exporting less plywood to the United States.

2. Japan's safety inspection (which has since been eliminated) was an example of a barrier to trade. It served a role similar to tariffs, import quotas, and VERs. The safety inspection added to the cost of selling cars in Japan. It raised the price of U.S. produced cars in Japan and decreased the quantity of U.S. cars sold.

■ AP Self Test 9.3

True or false

1. If the United States imposes a tariff, the price paid by U.S. consumers does not change.

2. If a country imposes a tariff on rice imports, domestic production of rice will increase and domestic consumption of rice will decrease.

3. A tariff increases the gains from trade for the exporting country.

4. An import quota on a particular good specifies the minimum quantity of that good that can be imported in a given period.

© 2015 Pearson Education, Inc.

Multiple choice

1. A tax imposed on a good when it is imported is called
   a. an import tax quota.
   b. a VER.
   c. a tariff.
   d. a sanction.
   e. a border tax.

2. The average U.S. tariff was highest in the
   a. 1930s.
   b. 1940s.
   c. 1970s.
   d. 1980s.
   e. 1990s.

3. Suppose the world price of a shirt is $10. If the United States imposes a tariff of $5 a shirt, then the price of a shirt in the
   a. United States falls to $5.
   b. United States rises to $15.
   c. world falls to $5.
   d. world rises to $5.
   e. world rises to $15.

4. When a tariff is imposed on a good, the ____ increases.
   a. domestic quantity purchased
   b. domestic quantity produced
   c. quantity imported
   d. quantity exported
   e. world price

5. When a tariff is imposed on a good, domestic consumers of the good ____ and domestic producers of the good ____.
   a. win; lose
   b. lose; win
   c. win; win
   d. lose; lose
   e. lose; neither win nor lose

6. Which of the following parties benefits from an import quota but not from a tariff?
   a. the domestic government
   b. domestic producers
   c. domestic consumers
   d. the person with the right to import the good
   e. the foreign government

Short Response Questions

■ **FIGURE 9.4**

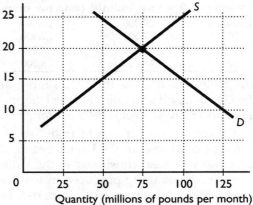

Price (cents per pound)

Quantity (millions of pounds per month)

1. Figure 9.4 shows the supply of and demand for sugar in the United States.

   a. If the world price of sugar is 10¢ a pound, draw the world price line in the figure. What is the quantity consumed in the United States, the quantity produced in the United States, and the quantity imported?

   b. Suppose the government imposes a 5¢ a pound tariff on sugar. Show the effect of the tariff in Figure 9.4. After the tariff, what is the quantity consumed in the United States, the quantity produced in the United States, and the quantity imported?

   c. Who wins and who loses from this tariff?

2. Suppose the U.S. government imposes a tariff on sugar. How does the tariff affect the price of sugar, U.S. sugar consumers, and U.S. sugar producers?

3. Suppose the U.S. government imposes an import quota on sugar. How does the import quota affect the price of sugar, U.S. sugar consumers, and U.S. sugar producers?

4. Why do consumers lose from a tariff?

© 2015 Pearson Education, Inc.

Long Response Questions

Price (dollars per ton of steel)	U.S. quantity supplied (tons per month)	U.S. quantity demanded (tons per month)
1,000	20,000	20,000
750	17,000	22,000
500	14,000	24,000
250	11,000	26,000

1. The table above gives the U.S. supply and the U.S. demand schedules for steel. Suppose the world price of steel is $500 per ton.

    a. If there are no barriers to trade, what is the price of steel in the United States, the quantity of steel consumed in the United States, the quantity produced in the United States, and the quantity imported into the United States?

    b. If the U.S. government imposes a tariff of $250 per ton of steel, what is the price of steel in the United States, the quantity of steel consumed in the United States, the quantity produced in the United States, and the quantity imported into the United States?

    c. Instead of a tariff, if the U.S. government imposes an import quota of 5,000 tons of steel per month, what is the price of steel in the United States, the quantity of steel consumed in the United States, the quantity produced in the United States, and the quantity imported into the United States?

    d. Comparing your answers to parts (b) and (c), are U.S. consumers better off with the tariff or the import quota? Are U.S. producers better off with the tariff or the import quota?

Additional Exercises (also in MyEconLab Test A)

Suppose that in response to huge job losses in the U.S. textile industry, Congress imposes a 100 percent tariff on imports of textiles from China. Use this formation to answer exercises 1 and 2.

1. Explain how the tariff on textiles will change the price of textiles, the quantity of textiles imported, and the quantity of textiles produced in the United States.

2. Explain how the U.S. and Chinese gain from trade will change. Who in the United States will lose and who will gain?

3. With free international trade between Australia and the United States, Australia would export beef to the United States. But the United States imposes an import quota on Australia beef. Explain how this import quota influences the price that U.S. consumers pay for beef, the quantity of beef produced in the United States, and the U.S. and Australian gains from trade. Who in the United States gains from the import quota on beef imports and who loses?

CHECKPOINT 9.4

■ **Explain and evaluate arguments used to justify restricting international trade.**

Quick Review

* *Rent seeking* Lobbying and other political activity that seeks to capture the gains from trade.

Additional Practice Problems 9.4

1. Pork is a popular food in China. China has occasionally limited U.S. exports of pork to China, most recently when swine flu was in the news. What argument might China make to limit imports of pork? Who in China would lose from this restriction of trade? Who would gain?

2. The United States has, from time to time, limited imports of lumber from Canada. What is the argument that the United States has used to justify this import quota? Who wins from this restriction? Who loses?

3. In each of the first two Practice Problems, identify who is rent seeking.

Solutions to Additional Practice Problems 9.4

1. The primary argument China has made involves the health of Chinese consumers. In particular, China argues that it must prohibit pork imports from the United States because Chinese consumers might catch swine flu from it.

© 2015 Pearson Education, Inc.

This argument is scientifically flawed because swine flu is not transmitted through pork products. The losers from the Chinese limitations are Chinese consumers who must pay a higher price for the pork they buy. The gainers are the Chinese pork farmers and processors who enjoy a higher price for pork.

2. In past decades, the United States asserted that the lumber industry was needed because it played a major role in national defense. With the use of more exotic materials in defense armaments, the national defense argument has passed into history. More recently, the United States has set import quotas and tariffs allegedly for environmental reasons and allegedly because the Canadian government was subsidizing the production of lumber. Both of these arguments are probably not the true reason for the restrictions. The import quotas and tariffs are the result of political lobbying by lumber producers and lumber workers. The winners from the import quotas and tariffs are the lumber producers and lumber workers. The losers are all U.S. lumber consumers.

3. Rent seeking is lobbying and other political activity that seeks to capture the gains from trade. In Practice Problem 1, the Chinese producers of pork are rent seeking. In Practice Problem 2, the U.S. lumber producers and U.S. lumber workers are rent seeking. It is important to keep in mind that free trade promotes prosperity for all countries. Protection reduces the potential gains from trade

■ AP Self Test 9.4

True or false

1. The national security argument is the only valid argument for protection.

2. Dumping by a foreign producer is easy to detect.

3. Protection saves U.S. jobs at no cost.

4. International trade is an attractive source for tax collection in developing countries

Multiple choice

1. The national security argument is used by those who assert they want to
   a. increase imports as a way of strengthening their country.
   b. increase exports as a way of earning money to strengthen their country.
   c. limit imports that compete with domestic producers important for national defense.
   d. limit exports to control the flow of technology to third world nations.
   e. limit all imports.

2. The argument that it is necessary to protect a new industry to enable it to grow into a mature industry that can compete in world markets is the
   a. national security argument.
   b. diversity argument.
   c. infant-industry argument.
   d. environmental protection argument.
   e. national youth protection argument.

3. ____ occurs when a foreign firm sells its exports at a lower price than its cost of production.
   a. Dumping
   b. The trickle-down effect
   c. Rent seeking
   d. Tariff avoidance
   e. Nontariff barrier protection

4. The United States
   a. needs tariffs to allow us to compete with cheap foreign labor.
   b. does not need tariffs to allow us to compete with cheap foreign labor.
   c. should not trade with countries that have cheap labor.
   d. will not benefit from trade with countries that have cheap labor.
   e. avoids trading with countries that have cheap labor.

© 2015 Pearson Education, Inc.

5. Why do governments in less-developed nations impose tariffs?
   a. The government gains revenue from the tariff.
   b. The government's low-paid workers are protected from high-paid foreign workers.
   c. The nation's total income is increased.
   d. The national security of the country definitely is improved.
   e. The government helps diversify its economy.

6. What is a major reason international trade is restricted in developed countries?
   a. rent seeking
   b. to allow competition with cheap foreign labor
   c. to save jobs
   d. to prevent dumping
   e. for national security

Short Response Question

1. How do you respond to a speaker who says that we need to limit auto imports from China in order to save U.S. jobs?

Long Response Questions

1. What is the dumping argument for protection? What is its flaw?

2. Why is it incorrect to assert that trade with countries that have lax environmental standards needs to be restricted?

3. The Eye on Your Life discusses the role international trade plays in your life. Suppose you get a job working for Frito Lay, the maker of corn chips (and other snacks). Frito Lay is a big user of corn. Corn can also be used to produce ethanol and increasingly more ethanol is being used as a replacement (or additive) fuel for gasoline. Currently the U.S. government places no tariff on ethanol imported from Brazil. Suppose a (hefty) tariff is proposed. As a representative of Frito Lay, would you be in favor of this tariff? Explain your answer.

Additional Exercises (also in MyEconLab Test A)

1. Venezuelan president Hugo Chavez opposed the creation of a Free Trade Area of the Americas (FTAA). Why? Who did he think will gain and lose? Do you think he is correct?

2. Hong Kong has never restricted trade. What gains has Hong Kong reaped by unilaterally adopting free trade with all nations? Is there any argument for restricted trade that might have benefited Hong Kong?

© 2015 Pearson Education, Inc.

SELF TEST ANSWERS

■ AP Self Test 9.1

True or false

1. True; page 214
2. True; page 214
3. False; pages 216-217
4. True; page 216

Multiple choice

1. a; page 214
2. b; page 214
3. c; page 214
4. c; page 216
5. c; page 216
6. c; page 217

Short Response Questions

1. From the U.S. vantage, the cheese is an imported good and the air transportation is an exported service. From the French vantage, the cheese is an exported good and the air transportation is an imported service; page 214.

2. a. In the absence of international trade, the equilibrium price of a bushel of wheat in the United States is $4; pages 216-217.

   b. If the world price of a bushel of wheat is $6 a bushel, the United States will export wheat because the world price exceeds the no-trade price. If the price of wheat exceeds $4 a bushel, the United States will export wheat. If the price of wheat is less than $4 a bushel, the United States will import wheat; pages 216-217.

3. a. In the absence of international trade, the equilibrium price is $600 a ton and the equilibrium quantity is 46 tons; pages 216-217.

   b. In the United States, the quantity supplied is 54 tons and the quantity demanded is 34 tons. The United States exports 20 tons of potatoes; page 217.

   c. In the United States, the quantity supplied is 58 tons and the quantity demanded is 28 tons. The United States exports 30 tons of potatoes; page 217.

   d. The United States would import potatoes if the world price is less than $600 a ton; page 216.

4. International trade lowers the domestic price of imported goods. The lower price increases the quantity domestic demanders consume and decreases the quantity domestic suppliers produce; page 216.

Additional Exercises (also in MyEconLab Test A)

1. With no international trade, the price in Australia is less than that in the world, so Australia has a comparative advantage in producing bananas. As a result, if Australia opens up to international trade, it will export bananas. With international trade, the price of bananas in Australia rises. The higher price leads to a decrease in the quantity of bananas consumed in Australia. The higher price also leads to an increase in the quantity of bananas grown in Australia; page 217.

2. Canada exports wood, so Canada has a comparative advantage in producing wood. If Canada did not trade internationally, the price of wood in Canada would be less than the world price. Canada imports wine, so Canada does *not* have a comparative advantage in producing wine. If Canada did not trade internationally, the price of wine in Canada would be higher than the world price. The United States exports wine, so the United States has a comparative advantage in producing wine. If the United States did not trade internationally, the price of wine in the United States would be less than the world price. The United States imports wood, so the United States does *not* have a comparative advantage in producing wood. If the United States did not trade internationally, the price of wood in the United States would be higher than the world price.

   With international trade, Americans buy more wood because the price of wood is lower in the United States with international trade than it would be without international trade. With international trade, Canadians

© 2015 Pearson Education, Inc.

buy more wine because the price of wine is lower in Canada with international trade than it would be without international trade. With international trade, the quantity of wood produced in the United States is less than it would be without international trade because international trade lowers the price of wood in the United States. With international trade, the quantity of wine produced in Canada is less than it would be without international trade because international trade lowers the price of wine in Canada; pages 216-217.

■ AP Self Test 9.2

True or false

1. False; pages 220-221
2. True; page 220
3. True; page 221
4. False; page 221

Multiple choice

1. e; page 219
2. d; page 220
3. e; page 220
4. c; page 221
5. b; pages 220-221

Short Response Questions

1. The gains from international trade are measured as increases in consumer surplus or in producer surplus. The net gain from international trade is measured as the gain in the total surplus; page 219.

2. Consumers gain from imports because international trade lowers the prices of imported goods and services. Consumer surplus increases because the price is lower and because the lower price leads consumers to buy more of the good or service; page 220.

3. Consumers are the group that gains from imports. Consumers gain because international trade lowers the prices of imported goods and services, which then increases their consumer surplus. The increase in consumer surplus will be larger the lower the

price. So the United States gains more if the international price of sugar is 10¢ a pound rather than 20¢ a pound; page 220.

4. When a good is exported, its domestic price rises. Producers gain from the higher price but consumers lose. (The gain to the producers, however, is larger than the loss to consumers.) So not everyone gains when a good is exported because consumers of that good lose; page 221.

Long Response Questions

■ FIGURE 9.5

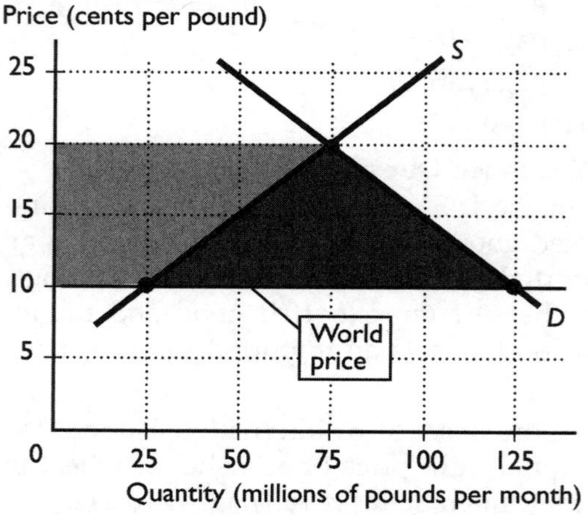

Price (cents per pound)

1. a. Figure 9.5 shows the world price line. At this price, 125 million pounds of sugar per month are consumed in the United States and 25 million pounds of sugar are produced in the United States. The difference, 100 million pounds of sugar per month, is imported into the United States; page 220.

   b. Consumer surplus increases. The increase in consumer surplus is equal to the sum of the area of the lighter grey trapezoid plus the area of the dark grey triangle in Figure 9.5. The producer surplus decreases. The decrease is equal to the area of the light grey trapezoid. On net, total surplus increases. The net increase is equal to the area of the dark grey triangle; page 220.

© 2015 Pearson Education, Inc.

■ **FIGURE 9.6**

Price (dollars per bushel)

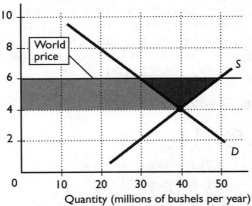

■ **FIGURE 9.7**

Price (thousands of dollars per car)

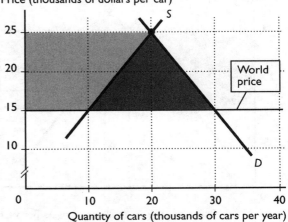

2. a. Figure 9.6 shows the world price line. At this price, 30 million bushels of wheat per year are consumed in the United States and 50 million bushels of wheat are produced in the United States. The difference, 20 million bushels of wheat per year, is exported from the United States; page 221.

b. Consumer surplus decreases. The decrease in consumer surplus is equal to the area of the lighter grey trapezoid in Figure 9.6. The producer surplus increases. The increase is equal to the sum of the area of the light grey trapezoid plus the area of the dark grey triangle. On net, total surplus increases. The increase is equal to the area of the dark grey triangle; page 221.

Additional Exercises (also in MyEconLab Test A)

1. Cuba would import cars and export cigars. Producers of cigars and consumers of cars would gain from international trade. Producers of cars and consumers of cigars would lose from international trade.

With the world price of a car of $15,000, Figure 9.7 shows the situation in Cuba in the market for cars. Producers of cars lose producer surplus equal to the lighter gray area. Consumers of cars gain this gray area as additional consumer surplus *and* they also gain the dark grey area as still more consumer surplus. So the net gain for the Cuban economy is the dark grey area.

With the world price of a cigar of $10, Figure 9.8 shows the situation in Cuba in the market for cigars. Consumers of cigars lose consumer surplus equal to the lighter grey area. Producers of cigars gain this gray area as additional producer surplus *and* they also gain the dark grey area as still more producer surplus. So the net gain for the Cuban economy is the dark grey area.

The Cuban economy, overall, would gain from international trade; pages 220-221.

■ **FIGURE 9.8**

Price (dollars per cigar)

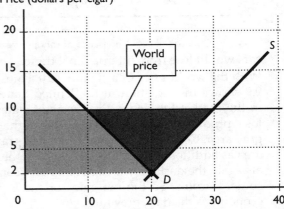

2. The United States would import cigars and export cars. Producers of cars and consumers of cigars would gain from international trade. Producers of cigars and consumers of

© 2015 Pearson Education, Inc.

■ **FIGURE 9.9**

Price (dollars per cigar)

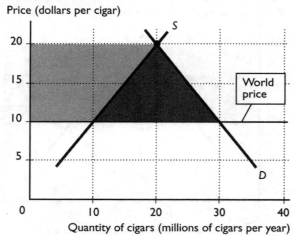

Quantity of cigars (millions of cigars per year)

■ **FIGURE 9.10**

Price (thousands of dollars per car)

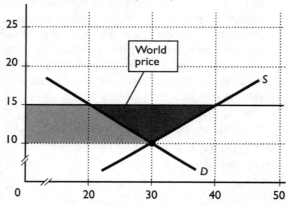

Quantity of cars (thousands of cars per year)

cars would lose from international trade.

With the world price of a cigar of $10, Figure 9.9 shows the situation in the United States in the market for cigars. Producers of cigars lose producer surplus equal to the lighter gray area. Consumers of cigars gain this gray area as additional consumer surplus *and* they also gain the dark grey area as still more consumer surplus. So the net gain for the U.S. economy is the dark grey area.

With the world price of a car of $15,000, Figure 9.10 shows the situation in the United States in the market for cars. Consumers of cars lose consumer surplus equal to the

lighter gray area. Producers of cars gain this gray area as additional producer surplus *and* they also gain the dark grey area as still more producer surplus. So the net gain for the U.S. economy is the dark grey area. The U.S. economy would gain from this international trade; pages 220-221.

■ **AP Self Test 9.3**

True or false

1. False; page 224
2. True; page 224
3. False; page 226
4. False; page 227

Multiple choice

1. c; page 223
2. a; page 223
3. b; page 224
4. b; page 224
5. b; pages 225-226
6. d; page 227

Short Response Questions

■ **FIGURE 9.11**

Price (cents per pound)

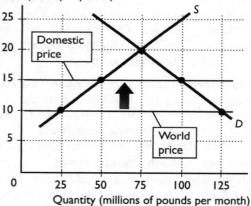

Quantity (millions of pounds per month)

1. a. The world price line is shown in Figure 9.11. 125 million pounds of sugar are consumed in the United States, 25 million pounds are produced in the United States, and 100 million pounds are imported into the United States; page 224.

© 2015 Pearson Education, Inc.

b. The tariff increases the domestic price, as shown in the figure. The quantity consumed in the United States decreases to 100 million pounds, the quantity produced in the United States increases to 50 million pounds, and the amount imported decreases to 50 million pounds; page 224.

c. Consumers lose because consumer surplus decreases. Producers gain because producer surplus increases. The government also gains because it raises revenue from the tariff; page 226.

2. The tariff raises the price of sugar. U.S. sugar consumers decrease the quantity they purchase and U.S. sugar producers increase the quantity they produce; pages 224-226.

3. The import quota has the same effects as the tariff in the previous question. The import quota raises the price of sugar. U.S. sugar consumers decrease the quantity purchased and U.S. sugar producers increase the quantity produced; page 227.

4. Consumers lose from a tariff because the tariff raises the price they pay and the quantity bought decreases. The tariff makes people pay more than the opportunity cost of the good. Society also loses because the tariff creates a deadweight loss; page 226.

Long Response Question

1. a. The price is the world price, $500 per ton. At this price, the quantity consumed in the United States is 24,000 tons per month, the quantity produced in the United States is 14,000 tons per month, and the quantity imported is the difference, 10,000 tons per month; page 224.

b. With a $250 per ton tariff, the price is $750 per ton. At this price, the quantity consumed in the United States is 22,000 tons per month, the quantity produced in the United States is 17,000 tons per month, and the quantity imported is the difference, 5,000 tons per month; page 224.

c. With an import quota of 5,000 tons per month, the total supply schedule equals the U.S. supply schedule plus an addition-

al 5,000 tons per month. The price of steel is $750 per ton because this is the price that sets the U.S. quantity demanded (22,000 tons) equal to the U.S. quantity supplied (17,000 tons) plus the quantity that can be imported (5,000 tons). At this price, the quantity consumed in the United States is 22,000 tons per month and the quantity produced in the United States is 17,000 tons per month; page 227.

d. U.S. consumers are no better off or worse off with the tariff or the import quota because both raise the price to $750 per ton and decrease the quantity consumed to 22,000 tons. U.S. producers are no better off or worse off with the tariff or the import quota because both raise the price to $750 per ton and increase the quantity produced to 17,000 tons; page 227.

Additional Exercises (also in MyEconLab Test A)

1. Higher tariffs increase the price U.S. consumers pay for textiles imported from China. Because the price of Chinese imported textiles rises, the quantity imported decreases. The quantity of textiles produced in the United States increases; page 224.

2. This trade restriction means that the U.S. and Chinese gains from trade definitely decrease. Textile workers and owners of textile firms will gain from the higher price. Textile consumers will lose from the higher price; pages 225-226.

3. By restricting the amount of beef imported into the United States, the import quota raises the price of beef to U.S. consumers. The quantity of beef produced in the United States increases. The U.S. and Australian gains from trade are reduced by the U.S. import quota. U.S. beef producers and their workers gain from the import quota on beef. In addition, the importers who have the right to import beef gain. U.S. consumers lose from the higher price of beef; pages 227-228.

© 2015 Pearson Education, Inc.

■ AP Self Test 9.4

True or false

1. False; page 231
2. False; page 232
3. False; page 233
4. True; page 234

Multiple choice

1. c; page 231
2. c; page 231
3. a; page 232
4. b; page 233
5. a; page 234
6. a; page 235

Short Response Question

1. Saving jobs is one of the oldest arguments in favor of protection. It is also incorrect. Protecting a particular industry will likely save jobs in that industry but will cost many other jobs in other industries. The cost to consumers of saving a job is many times the wage rate of the job saved; page 233.

Long Response Questions

1. Dumping occurs when a foreign firm sells its exports at a lower price than its cost of production. The dumping argument is flawed for the following reasons. First, it is virtually impossible to detect dumping because it is hard to determine a firm's costs and the fair market price. Second, it is hard to think of a good that is produced by a global natural monopoly. Third, if a firm truly was a global natural monopoly, the best way to deal with it would be by regulation; page 232.

2. The assertion that trade with developing countries that have lax environmental standards should be restricted to "punish" the developing nation for its lower standards is weak. Everyone wants a clean environment, but not every country can afford to devote resources toward this goal. The rich nations can afford this expenditure of resources, but for many poor nations protecting the environment takes second place to more pressing problems such as feeding their people. These nations must develop and grow economically in order to be able to afford to protect their environment. One important way to help these poorer nations grow is by trading with them. Through trade these nations' incomes increase and with this increase also increases their ability and willingness to protect the environment; page 234.

3. The tariff on ethanol imported from Brazil would severely limit the quantity of ethanol that can be imported and, by so doing, would push the price of ethanol in the United States higher. The high price for ethanol would increase the demand for U.S. corn to be processed into ethanol. The higher demand for corn means that the tariff on ethanol pushes the price of corn in the United States higher than it would be in the absence of the tariff. As a representative of Frito Lay, your interest lies in lowering the price of corn. Consequently you would not be in favor of the proposed tariff; page 224.

Additional Exercises (also in MyEconLab Test A)

1. Mr. Chavez argued against the Free Trade Area of the Americas because he thought that poor workers in nations such as Venezuela and other countries would be harmed by the trade. He also worried that U.S. firms would come to dominate markets in other countries. He was incorrect on both counts. First, poor workers in Venezuela would benefit from increased trade with the United States because the trade would increase the demand for their labor and thereby lead to higher wage rates. Second, it was unlikely U.S. firms would be able to dominate markets in other countries because to do so U.S. firms would need some sort of cost advantage over their foreign rivals, which was unlikely; pages 232-234.

2. Hong Kong has one of the most successful economies in the world as a result of adopting unilateral free trade. Both its exports and imports increased a result. There really isn't any argument for restricted free trade that might have benefited Hong Kong; page 235.

© 2015 Pearson Education, Inc.

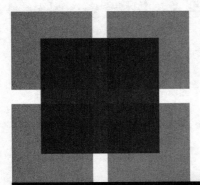

Externalities

Chapter 10

An externality is a cost or benefit that arises from production and that falls on someone other than its producer, or a cost or benefit that arises from consumption and that falls on someone other than the consumer. A negative externality imposes an external cost, and a positive externality provides an external benefit. Externalities in an unregulated market lead to inefficiency and create a deadweight loss.

1 Explain why negative externalities lead to inefficient overproduction and how property rights, pollution charges, and taxes can achieve a more efficient outcome.

Marginal private cost (*MC*) is the cost of producing an additional unit of a good or service that is borne by the producer of that good or service. Marginal external cost is the cost of producing an additional unit of a good or service that falls on people other than the producer. Marginal social cost (*MSC*), the marginal cost incurred by society, is the sum of marginal private cost and marginal external cost. Producers take account only of marginal private cost and overproduce if there is a marginal external cost. Sometimes it is possible to reduce the inefficiency arising from an externality by establishing a property right where one does not currently exist. When firms face an opportunity cost for what had been an external cost, they can produce less and/or use an abatement technology. The Coase theorem is the proposition that if property rights exist, only a small number of parties are involved, and transactions costs are low, then private transactions are efficient and the outcome is not affected by who is assigned the property right. The government can mandate that producers use clean technology. Governments also can impose a pollution tax (equal to the marginal external cost of the pollution), or use a cap-and-trade policy (firms are issued emission permits that allow them to emit a certain amount of pollution; the firms can buy and sell the permits).

2 Explain why positive externalities lead to inefficient underproduction and how public provision, subsidies, and vouchers can achieve a more efficient outcome.

Marginal private benefit (*MB*) is the benefit from an additional unit of a good or service that the consumer of that good or service receives. Marginal external benefit is the benefit from an additional unit of a good or service that people other than the consumer of the good or service enjoy. Marginal social benefit (*MSB*), the marginal benefit enjoyed by society, is the sum of marginal private benefit and marginal external benefit. External benefits from education arise because better-educated people are better citizens, commit fewer crimes, and support social activities. When people make decisions about how much schooling to obtain, they neglect its external benefit. The result is that if education were provided only by private schools that charged full-cost tuition, we would produce too few graduates. Three devices that governments can use to overcome the inefficiency created by external benefits are public provision, subsidies (payments to the producers by the government), and vouchers.

© 2015 Pearson Education, Inc.

YOUR AP TEST HINTS

AP Topics

Topic on your AP test	What to Know	Corresponding textbook section
Negative externality	Why inefficient overproduction occurs with negative externalities	Checkpoint 10.1
Positive externality	Why inefficient underproduction occurs with positive externalities	Checkpoint 10.2

AP Vocabulary Covered

Terms	What to Know	Text Sections
Externality	A cost or benefit from production or consumption that affects others besides the direct producers or consumers	Checkpoint 10.1, p. 242
Negative externality	A production or consumption event that creates an external cost	Checkpoint 10.1, p. 242
Positive externality	A production or consumption event that creates an external benefit	Checkpoint 10.1, p. 242
Marginal private cost (*MC*)	The cost of one more unit for the producer (*MC*)	Checkpoint 10.1, p. 244
Marginal external cost	The cost of one more unit for those other than the producer	Checkpoint 10.1, p. 244
Marginal social cost	The sum of all marginal private and external costs = (*MC* + *Marginal external cost*)	Checkpoint 10.1, p. 244
Property rights	Titles to ownership, use, and disposal of goods and services	Checkpoint 10.1, p. 247
Abatement technology	Anti-pollution technology	Checkpoint 10.1, p. 247
Coase theorem	Efficiency is reached if property rights and enforcement costs are low	Checkpoint 10.1, p. 247
Cap-and-Trade	Sellable pollution amounts for companies operating below maximum pollution limits	Checkpoint 10.1, p. 250
Marginal private benefit (*MB*)	The benefit of one more unit being consumed (*MB*)	Checkpoint 10.2, p. 254
Marginal external benefit	The benefit for people other than the consumers of one more unit	Checkpoint 10.2, p. 254
Marginal social benefit (*MSB*)	Benefit *enjoyed by all of society* from an additional unit of a good; (*MSB* = *MB* + *Marginal external benefit*)	Checkpoint 10.2, p. 254
Public provision	A good or service created by public authority and receiving revenue from the government	Checkpoint 10.2, p. 256
Subsidy	Producers receive payments from the government for some production costs	Checkpoint 10.2, p. 257
Voucher	Governmental funds the public can use for certain goods or services	Checkpoint 10.2, p. 258

Extra AP material

- Marginal costs and benefits are common AP test topics, but specifics about political issues like abatement technologies and vouchers have not appeared on the exams.

© 2015 Pearson Education, Inc.

CHECKPOINT 10.1

■ **Explain why negative externalities lead to inefficient overproduction and how property rights, pollution charges, and taxes can achieve a more efficient outcome.**

Quick Review

- *Marginal external cost* The cost of producing an additional unit of a good or service that falls on people other than the producer.
- *Efficiency* Efficiency is achieved when the marginal social benefit equals the marginal social cost.
- *Coase theorem* If property rights exist, only a small number of parties are involved, and transactions costs are low, then private transactions are efficient and the outcome is not affected by who is assigned the property right.

Additional Practice Problems 10.1

1. The figure illustrates the unregulated market for paper. When factories produce paper, they also create air pollution. The cost of the pollution is $1,500 per ton. The pollution is a marginal external cost.

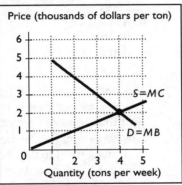

   a. What is the quantity of paper produced in an unregulated market? What is the price of a ton of paper?
   b. Draw the marginal social cost curve in the figure. What is the efficient quantity of paper to produce?
   c. If the government imposed a tax on the firms, what must the tax equal to have the efficient quantity of paper produced? With this tax imposed, what is the equilibrium price of a ton of paper?

2. Two factories each emit 10 tons of the pollutant sulfur dioxide a week. The cost to eliminate a ton of sulfur dioxide to Firm A is $4 and the cost to Firm B is $2. The government wants to eliminate 10 tons of sulfur dioxide a week.

   a. If the government requires that Firm A decrease emissions by 10 tons a week, what is the cost of eliminating the pollution?
   b. If the government requires that Firm B decrease emissions by 10 tons a week, what is the cost of the eliminating the pollution?
   c. If the government gives each firm 5 emission permits, each permit allowing 1 ton of pollution, what will occur?

Solutions to Additional Practice Problems 10.1

1a. The equilibrium is determined by the intersection of the demand and supply curves. So the equilibrium quantity is 4 tons of paper per week and the equilibrium price is $2,000 per ton.

1b. The figure shows the marginal social cost curve, labeled *MSC*. At 1 ton of paper this curve lies $1,500 above the supply curve; at 2 tons of paper it lies $3,000 above the supply curve; and so on. The efficient quantity is where the marginal social cost equals the marginal benefit, which the figure shows, is 2 tons of paper.

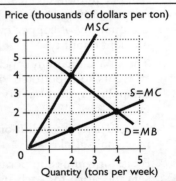

1c. To lead to efficiency, the tax must equal the marginal external cost. So the tax should be $1,500 per ton. At the efficient quantity of 2 tons, the tax is $3,000. With this tax, the equilibrium price is $4,000 per ton of paper.

2a. The cost for Firm A to decrease emissions is $4 a ton multiplied by 10 tons, which is $40 a week.

© 2015 Pearson Education, Inc.

2b. The cost for Firm B to decrease emissions is $2 a ton multiplied by 10 tons, which is $20 a week.

2c. Firm A is willing to buy permits from Firm B for any price less than $4 per permit; Firm B is willing to sell permits to Firm A for any price greater than $2 per permit. The two companies will settle on a price and Firm A will buy 5 permits from Firm B. Only Firm B will decrease its pollution and incur a cost of $20 a week.

■ AP Self Test 10.1

True or false

1. All externalities are negative.

2. Smoking on a plane creates a negative externality.

3. Marginal social cost equals marginal private cost minus marginal external cost.

4. Copper mining creates land pollution. If the copper mining industry is unregulated, then the quantity of copper mined is less than the efficient quantity.

5. The Coase theorem concludes that if property rights to a polluted river are assigned to the polluter, the quantity of pollution will increase.

6. For efficiency, a pollution tax must equal the marginal social cost.

7. By issuing emission permits, the government sets the price for each unit of pollution produced.

8. If the government imposes a pollution tax on lead mining equal to its marginal external cost, the quantity of lead mined will be the efficient quantity.

Multiple choice

1. Which of the following best describes an externality?
   a. something that is external to the economy
   b. a sales tax on a good in addition to the market price
   c. an effect of a transaction felt by someone other than the consumer or producer
   d. anything produced in other countries
   e. a change from what is normal

2. Pollution is an example of a ____ externality.
   a. negative production
   b. positive production
   c. negative consumption
   d. positive consumption
   e. Coasian

3. Which of the following is an example of an external cost?
   i. second-hand smoke
   ii. sulfur emitting from a smoke stack
   iii. garbage on the roadside
   a. i only.
   b. ii only.
   c. iii only.
   d. ii and iii.
   e. i, ii, and iii.

4. The cost of producing one more unit of a good or service that is borne by the producer of that good or service
   a. always equals the benefit the consumer derives from that good or service.
   b. equals the cost borne by people other than the producer.
   c. is the marginal private cost.
   d. is the external cost.
   e. is the marginal social cost.

5. The cost of producing an additional unit of a good or service that falls on people other than the producer is
   a. the marginal cost.
   b. represented by the demand curve.
   c. represented by the supply curve.
   d. the marginal external cost.
   e. the marginal social cost.

© 2015 Pearson Education, Inc.

6. The marginal cost of production that is borne by the entire society is the marginal
   a. private cost.
   b. social cost.
   c. external cost.
   d. public cost.
   e. user cost.

7. If the marginal private cost of producing one kilowatt of power in California is 8¢ and the marginal social cost of each kilowatt is 13¢, then the marginal external cost equals ____ a kilowatt.
   a. 8¢
   b. 13¢
   c. 5¢
   d. 0¢
   e. 21¢

8. When the production of a good has a marginal external cost, which of the following will occur in an unregulated market?
   i. Overproduction relative to the efficient level will occur.
   ii. The market price will be less than the marginal social cost at the equilibrium quantity.
   iii. A deadweight loss will occur.
   a. i only.
   b. ii only.
   c. iii only.
   d. i and ii.
   e. i, ii, and iii.

■ **FIGURE 10.1**

Price (dollars per ton)

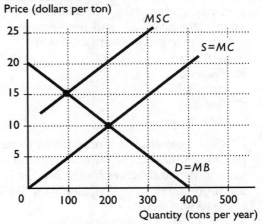

9. Figure 10.1 shows the market for a good with an external cost. The external cost equals ____.
   a. $5
   b. $10
   c. $15
   d. $20
   e. $25

10. Figure 10.1 shows the market for a good with an external cost. If the market is unregulated, the equilibrium quantity is ____ tons per year.
    a. 0
    b. 100
    c. 200
    d. 300
    e. 400

11. Figure 10.1 shows the market for a good with an external cost. The efficient quantity is ____ tons per year.
    a. 0
    b. 100
    c. 200
    d. 300
    e. 400

© 2015 Pearson Education, Inc.

12. The Coase theorem is the proposition that if property rights exist, a small number of people are involved, and transactions costs are low, then private transactions are
    a. inefficient.
    b. efficient.
    c. inequitable.
    d. illegal.
    e. unnecessary.

13. If polluting producers are required to pay a pollution tax, what is the effect on the supply and demand curves for the product?
    a. The quantity supplied along the supply curve will increase.
    b. The demand curve shifts leftward.
    c. The supply curve shifts rightward.
    d. The supply curve shifts leftward.
    e. *Both* the supply curve and the demand curve shift leftward.

14. In a cap-and-trade policy, a pollution permit
    a. allows firms to pollute all they want without any cost.
    b. allows firms to buy additional rights to pollute from the government.
    c. eliminates pollution by setting the price of pollution permits above the marginal cost of polluting.
    d. allows firms to buy and sell the right to pollute from other firms.
    e. is the Coase solution to pollution.

15. A Pigovian tax _____ producers to decrease their pollution and emissions permits _____ producers to decrease their pollution.
    a. motivates; motivates
    b. motivates; sometimes motivates
    c. motivates; does not motivate
    d. does not motivate; motivates
    e. does not motivate; does not motivate

Short Response Questions

Quantity (megawatts per day)	Marginal private cost (dollars)	Marginal social cost (dollars)	Marginal benefit (dollars)
1	5	10	50
2	10	20	40
3	15	30	30
4	20	40	20

1. The table above shows the marginal private cost, marginal social cost, and marginal benefit schedules for generating electricity.
    a. In Figure 10.2, label the axes and then plot the marginal private cost curve, the marginal social cost curve, and the marginal benefit curve.

■ **FIGURE 10.2**

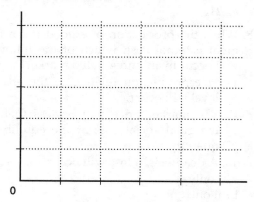

    b. How much electricity will an unregulated market produce? What is the marginal external cost at this amount of production?
    c. What is the efficient amount of electricity? Illustrate the deadweight loss resulting from the unregulated market equilibrium.
    d. At the efficient quantity of electricity, what is the marginal external cost? If the government imposes a pollution tax on producing electricity, in order to eliminate the deadweight loss, what should be the amount of tax? How much electricity is generated and what is its price?

© 2015 Pearson Education, Inc.

Quantity (tons per day)	Marginal private cost (dollars)	Marginal benefit (dollars)
1	200	600
2	300	500
3	400	400
4	500	300

2. The table above shows the marginal private cost and marginal benefit schedules for producing PBDE, a chemical flame retardant. Suppose that there is an external cost of $100 per ton of PBDE produced.

  a. In Figure 10.3, label the axes and then plot the marginal private cost curve, the marginal social cost curve, and the marginal benefit curve.

■ **FIGURE 10.3**

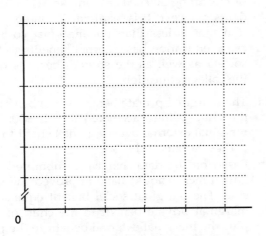

  b. How much PBDE will an unregulated market produce? What is the equilibrium price? What is the amount of the marginal external cost at the equilibrium quantity?

  c. What is the efficient amount of PBDE? At the efficient quantity, what is the amount of the marginal external cost?

  d. If the government set a pollution tax for producing PBDE, what must the tax equal to lead to the efficient quantity of PBDE?

3. The table at the top of the next column shows the costs of producing pesticide. Complete it.

4. According to the Coase theorem, when are private transactions efficient?

Quantity (tons of pesticide per day)	Marginal private cost (dollars per ton)	Marginal external cost (dollars per ton)	Marginal social cost (dollars per ton)
1	100	___	130
2	120	40	___
3	___	60	210
4	190	___	280
5	240	120	___

Long Response Questions

1. The production of fertilizer creates water pollution. How does a tax result in an efficient quantity of production? What information must the government possess to use a tax effectively?

2. What is an emissions permit? What advantage do emissions permits have over the government assigning each firm a limit on how much it can pollute?

CHECKPOINT 10.2

■ **Explain why positive externalities lead to inefficient underproduction and how public provision, subsidies, and vouchers can achieve a more efficient outcome.**

Quick Review
- *Marginal external benefit* The benefit from an additional unit of a good or service that people other than the consumer of the good or service enjoy.

Additional Practice Problems 10.2

1. The figure shows the marginal private benefit, marginal social benefit, and marginal cost of college education.

  a. What does the marginal external benefit equal when there

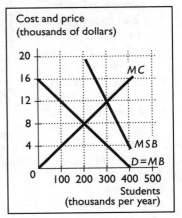

© 2015 Pearson Education, Inc.

are 300,000 students per year?

b. If colleges are private and government has no involvement in college education, how many people will undertake a college education and what will be the tuition?

c. What is the efficient number of students?

d. If the government decides to provide public colleges, what tuition will these colleges charge to achieve the efficient number of students? What is the marginal cost of educating this many students? Why is it justified to charge a tuition that is less than the marginal cost?

2. A vaccine for chicken pox was recently developed. The company that developed the vaccine, Merck Incorporated, was required to submit a document comparing the costs and benefits of vaccinating children. The government would approve the drug only if the benefit of vaccination exceeded the cost. The producer reports that the marginal cost of a dose of vaccine is $80. The marginal benefit to the child being vaccinated is estimated to be $30 and an additional marginal benefit to the child's parents is estimated at $60.

a. How much is the marginal private benefit and the marginal external benefit?

b. Based on these data, should the government have approved the vaccine?

Solutions to Additional Practice Problems 10.2

1a. The marginal external benefit equals the vertical distance between the marginal social benefit curve, *MSB*, and the marginal private benefit curve, *MB*. In the figure the difference is $8,000, so the marginal external benefit equals $8,000.

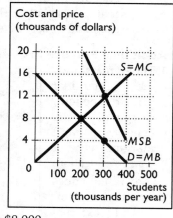

1b. If the government has no involvement, the equilibrium tuition and number of students is determined by the equilibrium between supply and demand. The supply curve is the marginal private cost curve, $S = MC$, and the demand curve is the marginal private benefit curve, *MB*. The figure shows that the equilibrium tuition equals $8,000 a year and the equilibrium enrollment is 200,000 students a year.

1c. The efficient number of students is 300,000 because this the quantity at which the marginal cost equals the marginal social benefit.

1d. The demand curve, which is the same as the marginal private benefit curve, shows that tuition must be $4,000 in order for 300,000 students to attend college. The marginal cost of educating 300,000 students is $12,000 students per year. It is justified to charge a tuition that is less than the marginal cost because education has external benefits so that society as well as the student benefits from the college education.

2a. The marginal private benefit is the benefit to the child being vaccinated and is $30. The marginal external benefit is the benefit to the child's parents and is $60.

2b. Based on the data that were submitted, the government should have approved the vaccine. The marginal social benefit equals the marginal private benefit to the child of $30 plus the marginal external benefit to the parent of $60, which is $90. The marginal social benefit from the vaccine is greater than the marginal cost.

■ AP Self Test 10.2

True or false

1. The marginal private benefit from a good or service must exceed the marginal external benefit.

2. The expanded job opportunities from a college degree are a marginal private benefit enjoyed by college graduates.

3. A flu vaccination has an external benefit, so the marginal private benefit curve for flu

© 2015 Pearson Education, Inc.

vaccinations lies above the marginal social benefit curve for flu vaccinations.

4. An unregulated market underproduces products with external benefits, such as education.

5. A public community college is an example of public provision of a good that has an external benefit.

6. To overcome the inefficiency in the market for a good with an external benefit, the government can either tax or subsidize the good.

7. Vouchers can help overcome the inefficiency created by a good with an external cost but not the inefficiency created by a good with an external benefit.

Multiple choice

1. The benefit the consumer of a good or service receives is the
   a. social benefit.
   b. external benefit.
   c. private benefit.
   d. public benefit.
   e. consumption benefit.

2. An external benefit is a benefit from a good or service that someone other than the _____ receives.
   a. seller of the good or service
   b. government
   c. foreign sector
   d. consumer
   e. market maker

3. When Ronald takes another economics class, other people in society benefit. The benefit to these other people is called the marginal _____ benefit of the class.
   a. social
   b. private
   c. external
   d. opportunity
   e. extra

4. Marginal social benefit equals
   a. marginal external benefit.
   b. marginal private benefit.
   c. marginal private benefit minus marginal external benefit.
   d. marginal private benefit plus marginal external benefit.
   e. marginal external benefit minus marginal private benefit.

5. If an external benefit is present, then the
   a. marginal private benefit curve lies above the marginal private cost curve.
   b. marginal social benefit curve lies above the marginal private benefit curve.
   c. marginal social cost curve lies above the marginal private benefit curve.
   d. marginal social benefit is equal to the marginal social cost.
   e. marginal social benefit curve is the same as the marginal private benefit curve.

■ **FIGURE 10.4**

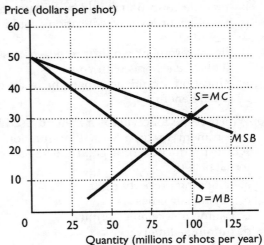

6. Figure 10.4 shows the market for flu vaccination, which has _____.
   a. only external costs
   b. only external benefits
   c. both external costs and external benefits
   d. neither external costs nor external benefits
   e. might have external benefits or external costs, but more information is needed

© 2015 Pearson Education, Inc.

7. Figure 10.4 shows the market for flu vaccination. If the market is unregulated, the equilibrium quantity of vaccinations is _____ shots per year.
   a. 0
   b. 50 million
   c. 75 million
   d. 100 million
   e. 125 million

8. Figure 10.4 shows the market for flu vaccination. The efficient quantity of vaccinations is _____ shots per year.
   a. 0
   b. 50 million
   c. 75 million
   d. 100 million
   e. 125 million

9. If all education in the United States were provided by private, tuition-charging schools,
   a. too much education would be consumed.
   b. too little education would be consumed.
   c. the efficient level of education would be provided.
   d. the government would provide *both* students and schools with vouchers.
   e. education would no longer have an external benefit.

10. Which of the following is a method used by government to cope with the situation in which production of a good creates an external benefit?
    a. removing property rights
    b. paying subsidies
    c. issuing marketable permits
    d. running a lottery
    e. imposing a Coasian tax

11. Which of the following is an example of a voucher?
    a. the postal service
    b. police services
    c. social security
    d. food stamps
    e. a tax on gasoline

12. If tuition at a college is $30,000 and the external benefit of graduating from this college is $10,000, then
    i. in the absence of any government intervention, the number of students graduating is less than the efficient number.
    ii. the government could increase the number of graduates by giving the college a $10,000 subsidy per student.
    iii. the government could increase the number of graduates by giving the students $10,000 vouchers.
    a. i only.
    b. i and ii.
    c. i and iii.
    d. ii and iii.
    e. i, ii, and iii.

Short Response Questions

■ **FIGURE 10.5**

Price (dollars per pound of honey)

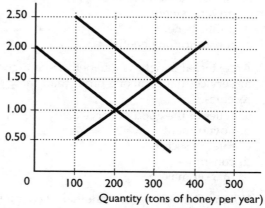

1. Figure 10.5 illustrates the market for honey.
   a. Label the curves in the figure.
   b. Based on Figure 10.5, does the production of honey create an external cost? An external benefit?
   c. What is the efficient quantity of honey? What is the quantity that will be produced in an unregulated market?
   d. Shade the area that equals the deadweight loss in an unregulated market.

© 2015 Pearson Education, Inc.

Quantity (millions of students per year)	Marginal private cost (thousands of dollars per student)	Marginal private benefit (thousands of dollars per student)	Marginal social benefit (thousands of dollars per student)
10	10	25	34
20	12	20	29
30	15	15	24
40	19	10	19
50	24	5	14

2. The table above shows the benefits and costs of a college education.

a. Based on the table, what is the amount of the marginal external benefit?

b. If the market for education was left unregulated, what would be the number of students educated per year?

c. What is the efficient number of students educated per year?

d. Would a subsidy or a tax be the proper government policy to make the market for education more efficient? What must the subsidy or tax equal to have the efficient number of students being educated?

3. Is efficiency guaranteed when production is such that the marginal private benefit equals the marginal private cost? Or does efficiency require that the marginal social benefit equal the marginal social cost?

Long Response Questions

1. Most elementary schools require that children be vaccinated before allowing the child to attend school. Can this policy be justified using economic analysis?

2. What is a voucher? How do vouchers work? Why is a voucher a proper policy to deal with the inefficiency created by a good or service that has an external benefit?

SELF TEST ANSWERS

■ AP Self Test 10.1

True or false

1. False; page 242
2. True; page 243
3. False; page 244
4. False; page 246
5. False; page 248
6. False pages 249-250
7. False; page 250
8. True; page 250

Multiple choice

1. c; page 242
2. a; page 242
3. e; pages 242-243
4. c; page 244
5. d; page 244
6. b; page 244
7. c; page 244
8. e; page 246
9. b; page 245
10. c; page 246
11. b; page 246
12. b; page 248
13. d; page 250
14. d; page 250
15. a; pages 249-251

Short Response Questions

1. a. Figure 10.6 shows the *MSC*, *MC*, and *MB* curves; page 246.
   b. An unregulated market produces 4 megawatts of electricity a day. The marginal external cost at this production is $20 per megawatt; page 246.
   c. The efficient amount of electricity is 3 megawatts a day. The deadweight loss is illustrated in the figure; page 246.
   d. At the efficient quantity of electricity, the marginal external cost is $15 a megawatt. The tax is $15 a megawatt. With the tax, 3

■ FIGURE 10.6
Price (dollars per megawatt)

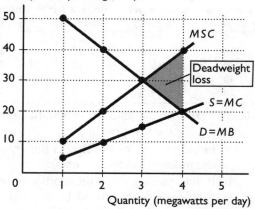

megawatts of electricity are produced. The price is $30 per megawatt; pages 249-250.

■ FIGURE 10.7
Price (dollars per ton)

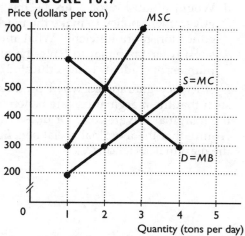

megawatts of electricity are produced. The price is $30 per megawatt; pages 249-250

2. a. Figure 10.7 shows the *MSC*, *MC*, and *MB* curves; page 246.
   b. An unregulated market produces 3 tons of PBDE a day. At this quantity the marginal external cost is $300; page 246.
   c. The efficient quantity of PBDE is 2 tons per day. At this quantity the marginal external cost is $200; page 246.
   d. The pollution tax equals $100 per ton of PBDE; pages 249-250.

© 2015 Pearson Education, Inc.

Quantity (tons of pesticide per day)	Marginal private cost (dollars per ton)	Marginal external cost (dollars per ton)	Marginal social cost (dollars per ton)
1	100	<u>30</u>	130
2	120	40	<u>160</u>
3	<u>150</u>	60	210
4	190	<u>90</u>	280
5	240	120	<u>360</u>

3. The completed table is above; page 244.

4. According to the Coase theorem, if property rights are assigned, the number of people involved is small, and transactions costs are low, then private transactions are efficient; page 248.

Long Response Questions

1. Pollution taxes are designed to charge polluting firms the cost of their pollution. By forcing firms to pay this cost, the firms' marginal private cost becomes equal to the marginal social cost. To use pollution taxes to overcome the problem of pollution, the government must know the marginal external cost at different levels of output; pages 249-250.

2. An emissions permit is part of a cap-and-trade policy. The permit is issued by the government and allows firms to pollute up to the limit of the permit. Firms can buy and sell emissions permits. The advantage emissions permits have over assigning each firm a limit for its pollution is the incentive it gives firms. When firms are assigned a limit, the price exceeds their marginal private so each firm has an incentive to increase its production past its limit. The government must monitor firms' compliance, which can be difficult and costly. Emissions permits, however, give the firms an incentive to increase their producer surplus by developing new, low-cost technology to limit pollution and thereby sell their pollution permits; page 250.

■ AP Self Test 10.2

True or false

1. False; page 254
2. True; page 254
3. False; page 254
4. True; page 255
5. True; page 256
6. False; page 256
7. False; page 258

Multiple choice

1. c; page 254
2. d; page 254
3. c; page 254
4. d; page 254
5. b; page 254
6. b; page 255
7. c; page 255
8. d; page 255
9. b; page 255
10. b; page 256
11. d; page 258
12. e; pages 255-258

Short Response Questions

■ **FIGURE 10.8**

Price (dollars per pound of honey)

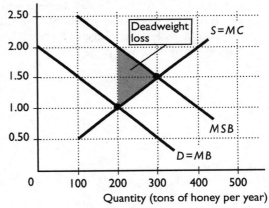

1. a. Figure 10.8 labels the curves; page 255.
   b. The production of honey has an external benefit but no external cost; page 255.
   c. The efficient quantity of honey is 300 tons, a year, at the intersection of the *MSB* curve and the *S = MC* curve. In an unregulated market, the equilibrium quantity is 200 tons a year, at the intersection of the

© 2015 Pearson Education, Inc.

$D = MB$ curve and the $S = MC$ curve; page 255.

d. Figure 10.8 shades the deadweight loss; page 255.

2. a. The marginal external benefit equals the difference between the marginal social benefit and the marginal private benefit, so it is $9,000 per student; page 254.

b. The competitive equilibrium is where the marginal private cost (which determines the supply) equals the marginal private benefit (which determines the demand), so the equilibrium number of students is 30 million per year; page 255.

c. The efficient quantity is produced when the marginal social benefit equals the marginal cost, so the efficient amount is 40 million students per year; page 255.

d. A subsidy would be a proper government policy. The subsidy would equal $9,000 per student, the amount of the marginal external benefit at the efficient quantity; page 257.

3. Efficiency is not guaranteed when production sets the marginal private benefit equal to the marginal cost. The efficient quantity is produced when the marginal social benefit equals marginal cost; page 255.

Long Response Questions

1. Vaccination protects not only the child who is vaccinated, but also makes it less likely for classmates to catch the disease. So a vaccination has an external benefit. Although at some number of vaccinations, the marginal cost of a vaccination is greater than the marginal private benefit of a vaccination, because the marginal social benefit exceeds the marginal private benefit the market will provide too few vaccinations. The market might be efficient when vaccination is required; page 255.

2. A voucher is a token that the government gives to households which they can use to buy specified goods or services. Vouchers increase the demand for the product and shift the demand curve (which is the same as the marginal private benefit curve, or MB curve) rightward, closer to the marginal social benefit curve. Vouchers reduce the inefficiency created by a good or service with an external benefit; page 258.

© 2015 Pearson Education, Inc.

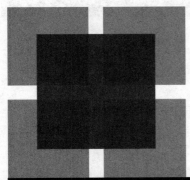

Public Goods and Common Resources

Chapter 11

1 Distinguish among private goods, public goods, and common resources.

An excludable good, service, or resource is one whose benefits you can prevent someone from enjoying; a nonexcludable good, service, or resource is one whose benefits you cannot prevent someone from enjoying. The sue of a rival good, service, or resource by one person decreases the quantity available for someone else; the use of a nonrival good, service, or resource by one person does not decrease the quantity available to someone else. A private good is excludable and rival. A public good can be consumed simultaneously by everyone and from which no one can be excluded. A public good is nonexcludable and nonrival. A common resource is a resource that is nonexcludable and rival. A natural monopoly is excludable and nonrival.

2 Explain the free-rider problem and how public provision might help to overcome it and deliver an efficient quantity of pubic goods.

Public goods create a free-rider problem: People enjoy the benefits of a good or service without paying for it. The marginal social benefit curve for a public good is the vertical sum of the individual marginal benefit curves. The efficient quantity of a public good sets marginal social benefit equal to marginal social cost. Because of the free-rider problem, public goods are under-provided by private firms so public provision of public goods might lead efficiency. The tendency for political parties to propose identical policies in order to appeal to the maximum number of voters is an example of the principle of minimum differentiation. Rational ignorance is the decision not to acquire information because the marginal cost of doing so exceeds the expected marginal benefit. Rational ignorance, combined with the bureaucratic desire to maximize budgets, can lead to inefficient overprovision of public goods.

3 Explain the tragedy of the commons and review its possible solutions.

Common resources suffer from the tragedy of the commons: the overuse of a common resource that arises when its users have no incentive to conserve it and use it sustainably. Fish are an example of a common resource. If the catch rate of a species of fish exceeds renewal rate, the stock of the fish decreases. The marginal private cost of fishing is the additional cost incurred to catch additional fish. Fishers, however, create an external cost because each boat makes it more costly for other fishers to catch fish so $MSC > MC$. The marginal social benefit is the same as the marginal private benefit. Efficiency occurs when the marginal social benefit from a resource equals its marginal social cost. But the marginal private cost is less than the marginal social cost, so in an unregulated market overuse of the resource occurs. The government can bring about an efficient use of the common resource by assigning property rights to the resource; by setting a production quota on the amount of the resource that can be used; or by creating a program of individual transferable quotas (ITQ). An individual transferable quota is a production limit that the owner can transfer to someone else.

© 2015 Pearson Education, Inc

YOUR AP TEST HINTS

AP Topics

Topic on your AP test	What to Know	Corresponding textbook section
Private, public, common resources	What distinguishes these goods and resources?	Checkpoint 11.1
Free-rider problem	How to solve the issue with a public provision	Checkpoint 11.2
Tragedy of the commons	What is it and are there solutions?	Checkpoint 11.3

AP Vocabulary Covered

Terms	What to Know	Text Sections
Excludable	When a good, service, or resource is set to block someone from using it without fees	Checkpoint 11.1, p. 266
Nonexcludable	When a good, service, or resource cannot be blocked from being used without paying fees	Checkpoint 11.1, p. 266
Rival	If a good, service, or resource is used by one person then the quantity for others is reduced	Checkpoint 11.1, p. 266
Nonrival	If a good, service, or resource is used by one person then the quantity for others is not reduced	Checkpoint 11.1, p. 266
Private good	A good only available to one purchaser	Checkpoint 11.1, p. 266
Public good	A good consumed by everyone at once, not excluded from anyone	Checkpoint 11.1, p. 267
Common resource	A resource used once, but all have access	Checkpoint 11.1, p. 267
Natural monopoly	A good that is both nonrival and excludable	Checkpoint 11.1, p. 267
Free rider	The person who gets a benefit from a good or service but doesn't have to pay	Checkpoint 11.2, p. 269
Principle of minimum differentiation	The trend that competitors make themselves similar in order to capture the maximum number of clients or voters	Checkpoint 11.2, p. 274
Rational ignorance	Deciding to stop gathering information because the marginal cost exceeds the marginal benefit	Checkpoint 11.2, p. 274
Tragedy of the commons	Overusing a popular resource because there is no incentive to conserve	Checkpoint 11.3, p. 278
Individual transferable quota (*ITQ*)	An individual quota for use that can be transferred by the person not using all of the quota	Checkpoint 11.3, p. 284

Extra AP material

* Another term for *tragedy of the commons* is *problem of the commons*.

© 2015 Pearson Education, Inc.

CHECKPOINT 11.1

■ **Distinguish among private goods, public goods, and common resources.**

Quick Review

- *Public good* A public good is nonrival and nonexcludable.
- *Private good* A private good is rival and excludable.
- *Common resource* A common resource is rival and nonexcludable.

Additional Practice Problem 11.1

1. It's a balmy, pleasant Sunday afternoon on a fall day on Long Island, where the U.S. Open Tennis Men's Singles Finals are being played. A variety of goods and services are being consumed. Classify each of the list of goods and services as rival, nonrival, excludable, and nonexcludable. State if they are a public good, a private good, or a common resource.

    a. U.S. Lawn Tennis Association membership

    b. tennis lessons

    c. racquets

    d. watching the Men's Singles Championship

    e. a pleasant, sunny afternoon

    f. sunset seen over Fire Island

    g. shrimp eaten at a tailgate party

Solution to Additional Practice Problem 11.1

1a. Membership in the U.S. Lawn Tennis Association is nonrival and excludable.

1b. Tennis lessons are rival and excludable and are a private good.

1c. Racquets are rival and excludable and hence are a private good.

1d. Watching the Men's Singles Championship is excludable. Whether it is rival depends on whether the match is a sell out. If it is a sell out, then watching the championship is rival and it is a private good; in the event that it is not sold out and seats remain available, it is nonrival.

1e. The pleasant afternoon is nonrival and nonexcludable and so is a public good.

1f. The sunset is nonrival and nonexcludable and so is a public good.

1g. The shrimp are rival and excludable and so are a private good.

■ AP Self Test 11.1

True or false

1. A good is nonexcludable if it is impossible to prevent someone from benefiting from it.

2. A private good is nonrival and nonexcludable.

3. A taco from Taco Bell is a public good.

4. A common resource is nonrival and excludable.

5. Fish in the ocean are rival and nonexcludable.

Multiple choice

1. The fact that Heidi's enjoyment of a sunset on Saint Simon's Island does not preclude Mounette from enjoying the same sunset is an example of
   a. a good that is nonrival.
   b. a good that is excludable.
   c. a private good.
   d. the rival nature of consumption.
   e. a common resource.

2. When use of a good decreases the quantity available for someone else, the good is
   a. rival.
   b. nonrival.
   c. excludable.
   d. nonexcludable.
   e. a public good.

3. A private good is ____ and ____.
   a. rival; excludable
   b. rival; nonexcludable
   c. nonrival; excludable
   d. nonrival; nonexcludable
   e. scarce; expensive

© 2015 Pearson Education, Inc.

4. If I order a pizza and invite my neighbors to eat it, the pizza is
   a. a private good.
   b. a common resource.
   c. a public good because many people ate it.
   d. either a common resource or a public good depending on whether it is overused.
   e. produced by a natural monopoly.

5. A public good is ____ and ____.
   a. rival; excludable
   b. rival; nonexcludable
   c. nonrival; excludable
   d. nonrival; nonexcludable
   e. cheap; available

6. A public good
   a. can only be consumed by one person at a time.
   b. can be consumed simultaneously by many people.
   c. is any good provided by a company owned by a member of the public.
   d. is any good provided by government.
   e. is both rival and excludable.

7. Which of the following is the best example of a public good?
   a. national defense
   b. a Ford Thunderbird
   c. Yosemite national park
   d. a Mountain Dew
   e. a satellite radio

8. Which of the following is the best example of a common resource?
   a. national defense
   b. a Ford Thunderbird
   c. Yosemite national park
   d. a can of Mountain Dew
   e. a cable television network

Short Response Question

1. Goods can be excludable or nonexcludable, rival or nonrival. Using these criteria, what is a public good, a private good, and a common resource?

Long Response Question

1. What does it mean for a good to be nonexcludable? Nonrival?

CHECKPOINT 11.2

■ **Explain the free-rider problem and how public provision might help to overcome it and deliver an efficient quantity of public goods.**

Quick Review

- *Free rider* A free rider enjoys the benefits of a good or service without paying for the good or service.

Additional Practice Problems 11.2

Quantity (square miles per day)	Abe's marginal benefit (dollars per day)	Bee's marginal benefit (dollars per day)	Kris's marginal benefit (dollars per day)
1	20	20	30
2	35	35	50
3	48	42	60
4	60	45	65
5	70	47	68

1. A (small) city that is exactly 5 square miles in size has three people in it, Abe, Bee, and Kris. The table above gives the marginal benefit of each from a mosquito control program.
   a. Is mosquito spraying a public good or a private good? Explain your answer.
   b. Calculate the marginal social benefit for spraying 1, 2, 3, 4, and 5 square miles a day.
   c. If the marginal cost of spraying was constant at $150 for a square mile, what is the efficient number of miles that should be sprayed?
   d. How many square miles would the bureau head of the city's mosquito control project lobby the city commissioners to spray?

2. How do rational ignorance and bureaucrats' goal of budget maximization combine to lead to inefficient overprovision of public goods?

© 2015 Pearson Education, Inc.

Solutions to Additional Practice Problems 11.2

1a. Mosquito spraying is a public good because it's both nonrival—everyone can simultaneously enjoy not being bitten—and nonexcludable—even if one of the residents does not pay, the mosquitoes still do not bite that resident.

1b. The marginal benefit is equal to the sum of benefits of all residents for each quantity. So the marginal social benefit for spraying 1 square mile is equal to $20 + $20 + $30 = $70. The rest of the answers in the table are calculated similarly.

Quantity (square miles per day)	Marginal social benefit (dollars per day)
1	70
2	120
3	150
4	170
5	185

1c. The marginal social cost equals the marginal social benefit when 3 square miles are sprayed, so 3 square miles is the efficient quantity of spraying.

1d. The head of the city's mosquito control commission wants to maximize the budget of the commission, so the head will lobby to spray 5 square miles.

2. If voters knew the marginal social benefit and marginal social cost of a public good, they could elect politicians who would deliver the efficient quantity. But voters generally are rationally ignorant about the marginal social benefit and marginal social cost of most public goods. So bureaucrats, who want to increase their budget, and special interest groups, such as the producers of a public good, lobby politicians to provide more than the efficient amount of public goods. Politicians accede to the lobbying because they know that (rationally ignorant) voters will not realize that too much of the public good is provided.

■ AP Self Test 11.2

True or false

1. Beth is a free rider when she is protected by the nation's military but does not pay anything for the protection.

2. The marginal social benefit curve for a public good slopes downward.

3. The efficient quantity of a public good is the quantity at which marginal social benefit equals marginal social cost.

4. A private firm would produce too much of a public good.

5. Rational ignorance can lead to the provision of more than the efficient amount of a public good.

Multiple choice

1. When someone enjoys the benefit of a good or service but does not pay for it, that person
   a. is a free range consumer.
   b. is a free rider.
   c. receives no marginal benefit from the good.
   d. must be consuming an excludable good
   e. is contributing to the tragedy of the commons.

2. The marginal social benefit of a public good is the
   a. sum of the marginal benefits of all the individuals at each quantity.
   b. marginal benefit of the individual person who places the lowest value on the good, multiplied by the number of people in the economy.
   c. marginal benefit of the individual person who places the highest value on the good, multiplied by the number of people in the economy.
   d. benefit of the last person's consumption.
   e. average of the marginal benefits of all the individuals at each quantity.

© 2015 Pearson Education, Inc.

3. The marginal social benefit curve of a public good
   a. slopes downward.
   b. slopes upward.
   c. is vertical.
   d. is horizontal.
   e. is U-shaped.

4. Sue and Mark are the only two members of a community. Sue's marginal benefit from one lighthouse is $2,000 and Mark's marginal benefit is $1,000. If the marginal social cost of one lighthouse is $2,500 and if a lighthouse is a public good, then for efficiency the lighthouse should
   a. be built but only Sue should be allowed to use it.
   b. be built but only Mark should be allowed to use it.
   c. be built and both Sue and Mark should be allowed to use it.
   d. not be built because its marginal cost exceeds Sue's marginal benefit.
   e. not be built because its marginal cost exceeds both Sue's and Mark's marginal benefit.

5. The efficient quantity of a public good is
   a. the quantity produced by private firms.
   b. the quantity at which the marginal social benefit equals the marginal social cost.
   c. impossible to determine because each person's marginal benefit is different.
   d. the quantity at which the marginal social benefit exceeds the marginal social cost by as much as possible.
   e. where the demand curve and supply curve of the good intersects.

6. The efficient quantity of a public good can't be produced by private firms because
   a. only government has the necessary resources.
   b. it is impossible to determine the efficient amount.
   c. consumers have an incentive to free ride and not pay for their share of the good.
   d. private firms aren't large enough.
   e. the price would be too high if private firms produced the goods.

7. If the two political parties propose similar or identical policies, they are following the principle of
   a. rational ignorance.
   b. inefficient overprovision.
   c. free riding.
   d. minimum differentiation.
   e. the commons.

8. ____ is the decision not to acquire information because the marginal cost of doing so exceeds expected marginal benefit.
   a. Rational ignorance
   b. The principle of minimum differentiation
   c. A free rider
   d. Consumer ignorance
   e. The tragedy of the commons

9. Government bureaucracies over-provide public goods and grow larger because of their goal of ____ combined with ____ of the voters.
   a. budget maximization; rational ignorance
   b. budget minimization; irrational intelligence
   c. budget maximization; minimum differentiation
   d. budget maximization; irrational exuberance
   e. minimum differentiation; budget maximization

© 2015 Pearson Education, Inc.

Short Response Question

Quantity (lighthouses)	Marginal benefit, Firm A (dollars)	Marginal benefit, Firm B (dollars)	Marginal benefit, Firm C (dollars)
1	50,000	50,000	50,000
2	45,000	45,000	45,000
3	40,000	40,000	40,000
4	35,000	35,000	35,000

1. Three shipping firms serve the west coast of a nation. The table has the firms' marginal benefit schedules for lighthouses. Lighthouses are a public good and the marginal social cost of constructing a lighthouse is constant at $120,000.

    a. Complete the table below. Then graph the economy's marginal social benefit and marginal social cost curves in Figure 11.1.

Quantity (lighthouses)	Marginal social benefit, (dollars per lighthouse)
1	
2	
3	
4	

    b. What is the efficient number of lighthouses to build?

    c. If all three firms agree to split the cost of building lighthouses equally, how much would each firm pay per lighthouse and how many lighthouses will be built?

    d. Suppose that one firm decides to free ride and not pay for the construction of any lighthouses. How much would each of the two other firms pay per lighthouse and how many lighthouses will be built?

    e. In the situation described in part (d), how might government action overcome the problem?

Long Response Questions

1. What is a free rider? Why is free riding not a problem for private goods?

2. A very small (!) nation has 10 citizens. Each resident has a $10 marginal benefit from 1 unit of a private good. In addition, each has a $10 marginal benefit from 1 unit of a public good. What is one combination of marginal

■ **FIGURE 11.1**

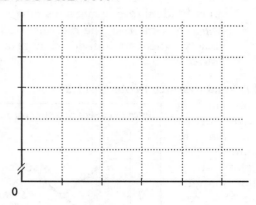

social benefit and quantity on the economy's marginal social benefit curve for the private good and what is one combination on the economy's marginal social benefit curve for the public good? Explain the difference.

3. How does free riding affect the private provision of a public good? How does rational ignorance affect the public provision of a public good?

4. The Eye on Your Life in the book explains how MP3 files have a free rider problem. One of the most common instances of free riding amongst students comes when a group of students are assigned to complete a project. Explain how free riding can occur in this situation. Occasionally instructors grade a group project by basing each student's grade, in part, on the group member's evaluations of each other. Explain how this technique can overcome the free rider problem.

CHECKPOINT 11.3

■ **Explain the tragedy of the commons and review its possible solutions.**

Quick Review

- *Tragedy of the commons* The absence of incentives to prevent the overuse and depletion of a commonly owned resource.

© 2015 Pearson Education, Inc.

- *Marginal private cost* The cost incurred by an individual from using a resource.
- *Marginal social cost* The cost incurred by society when an individual uses a resource.

Additional Practice Problem 11.3

1. Cod in the ocean are a common resource. The figure shows the marginal private cost, marginal social cost, and marginal social benefit of fishing.

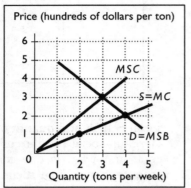

Price (hundreds of dollars per ton)

Quantity (tons per week)

a. What is the marginal external cost when 2 tons of cod are caught? Why is there an external cost from catching cod?
b. If fishing is unregulated, what will be the quantity of cod caught?
c. What is the efficient quantity of cod?
d. Is cod fishing subject to the tragedy of commons?

Solution to Additional Practice Problem 11.3

1a. The marginal external cost at any quantity is equal to the difference between the marginal social cost and the marginal private cost. At 2 tons of cod, the marginal external cost is $100 per ton. Cod fishing is subject to this external cost because it is a common resource. As a new boat starts to fish, by catching some of the fish stock, the new boat makes it more difficult, and therefore more costly, for the boats already fishing to catch fish. The increase in the other boats' costs is the external cost created by the new boat's catch of fish.

1b. The equilibrium quantity is where the marginal private cost curve (the supply curve) and marginal social benefit curve (the demand curve) cross, or 4 tons of fish.

1c. The efficient quantity is where the marginal social cost curve and marginal social benefit curve cross, or 3 tons of fish.

1d. Similar to other common resources, cod fishing is subject to the tragedy of commons because the equilibrium quantity of cod caught exceeds the efficient quantity of cod.

■ AP Self Test 11.3

True or false

1. The tragedy of the commons is the absence of incentives that prevent the overuse and depletion of a commonly owned resource.

2. The efficient use of a common resource occurs when the marginal private benefit equals the marginal private cost.

3. At the efficient level of use, the marginal private cost of a common resource exceeds the marginal social cost.

4. Property rights and production quotas are potential solutions to the tragedy of the commons.

Multiple choice

1. The tragedy of the commons is the absence of incentives to
   a. correctly measure the marginal benefit.
   b. prevent under use of the common resource.
   c. prevent overuse and depletion of the common resource.
   d. discover the resource.
   e. prevent the free-rider problem.

2. If the renewal rate of a common resource equals its rate of use, then the resource use is *definitely* ____ and *might* be ____.
   a. unsustainable; efficient
   b. unsustainable; at its maximum
   c. sustainable; efficient
   d. at its maximum; efficient
   e. None of the above answers is correct.

3. For a common resource such as fish, the marginal private benefit ____ the marginal

© 2015 Pearson Education, Inc.

social benefit and the marginal private cost ____ the marginal social cost.
a. equals; is less than
b. is greater than; equals
c. equals; equals
d. is less than; is less than
e. is greater than; is greater than

4. For a common resource, the marginal private cost curve ____ and the marginal social cost curve ____.
a. slopes upward; slopes upward
b. slopes upward; slopes downward
c. slopes downward; slopes upward
d. slopes downward; slopes downward
e. is vertical; is horizontal

5. For a common resource, the equilibrium with no government intervention is such that marginal ____ equals marginal ____.
a. private benefit; social cost
b. social benefit; private cost
c. social benefit; social cost
d. external benefit; external cost
e. social benefit; external cost

6. For a common resource, efficiency requires that the marginal ____ equals the marginal ____.
a. private benefit; private cost
b. social benefit; private cost
c. social benefit; social cost
d. external benefit; external cost
e. social benefit; external cost

7. Which of the following is *not* a potential solution to the tragedy of the commons?
a. Subsidizing use of the resource
b. Setting a production quota
c. Granting individual transferable quotas
d. Establish property rights to the resource
e. None of the above are correct because they are all potential solutions to the tragedy of the commons.

■ **FIGURE 11.2**
Price (dollars per ton of lumber)

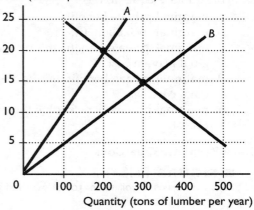

8. Figure 11.2 shows a market for logging in a tropical rainforest, which is a common resource. In the figure, curve *A* is the ____ and curve *B* is the ____.
a. *MSC*; *MC*
b. *MSB*; *MB*
c. *MB*; *MSB*
d. *MC*; *MSC*
e. *MC*; *MB*

9. Figure 11.2 shows a market for logging in a tropical rainforest, which is a common resource. The efficient quantity of timber is ____ and if the market is unregulated, the equilibrium quantity of timber is ____.
a. 0 tons; 500 tons
b. 0 tons; 300 tons
c. 300 tons; 200 tons
d. 300 tons; 0 tons
e. 200 tons; 300 tons

10. If the government assigns private property rights to a common resource, then the
a. resource is under-utilized.
b. marginal private cost becomes equal to the marginal social cost.
c. government needs to set a quota to achieve efficiency.
d. resource becomes subject to the free riding problem.
e. resource cannot be utilized.

© 2015 Pearson Education, Inc.

11. The market price of an individual transferable quota is equal to the
    a. marginal private benefit.
    b. marginal social benefit.
    c. marginal private benefit minus the marginal private cost.
    d. marginal social benefit minus the marginal cost.
    e. marginal private benefit plus the marginal cost.

Long Response Questions

■ **FIGURE 11.3**

Price (thousands of dollars per ton of swordfish)

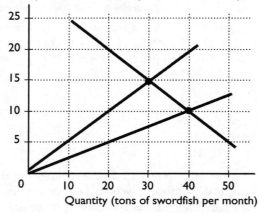

Quantity (tons of swordfish per month)

1. Figure 11.3 shows the marginal social cost, marginal private cost, and marginal social benefit curves for swordfish, a common resource. Label each curve.
   a. What is the equilibrium catch and what is the efficient catch?
   b. If the government sets a quota, what quota achieves the efficient outcome?
   c. If the government issues individual transferable quotas (ITQ), each good for one ton of swordfish, how many ITQs does the government issue? What is the market price of an ITQ?

2. What is the tragedy of the commons and why does it occur? Give an example of how the tragedy of the commons affects the world's fisheries.

3. For a common resource, why does the marginal private cost not equal the marginal social cost? Which is smaller?

4. Shrimp are now farmed in ponds belonging to individual owners. Is this shrimp farming subject to the tragedy of the commons? Why or why not?

© 2015 Pearson Education, Inc.

SELF TEST ANSWERS

■ AP Self Test 11.1

True or false
1. True; page 266
2. False; page 266
3. False; pages 266-267
4. False; page 267
5. True; page 267

Multiple choice
1. a; page 266
2. a; page 266
3. a; pages 266-267
4. a; page 266
5. d; page 267
6. b; page 267
7. a; page 267
8. c; page 267

Short Response Question
1. A public good is nonrival and nonexcludable. A private good is rival and excludable. A common resource is rival and nonexcludable; pages 266-267.

Long Response Question
1. A good is nonexcludable if it is impossible (or extremely costly) to prevent someone from benefiting from it. For example, the national defense provided by a fighter plane benefits everyone and so is nonexcludable. A good is nonrival if its use by one person does not decrease the quantity available for someone else. For example, the national defense provided by a fighter plane to you does not decrease the amount of defense it provides to your neighbor and so is nonrival; page 266.

■ AP Self Test 11.2

True or false
1. True; page 269
2. True; pages 270-271
3. True; page 272
4. False; page 272
5. True; pages 274-275

Multiple choice
1. b; page 269
2. a; pages 270-271
3. a; page 271
4. c; page 272
5. b; page 272
6. c; page 272
7. d; page 274
8. a; pages 274-275
9. a; page 275

Short Response Question

Quantity (lighthouses)	Marginal social benefit (dollars)
1	150,000
2	135,000
3	120,000
4	105,000

1. a. The complete table is above and the completed figure is Figure 11.4 (on the next page); pages 270-271.

■ FIGURE 11.4
Marginal social benefit and marginal social cost (thousands of dollars per lighthouse)

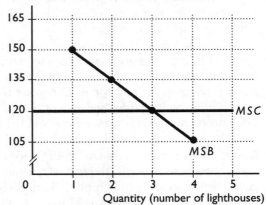

b. The efficient number of lighthouses to build is 3; page 272.
c. Each firm pays $40,000 per lighthouse and three lighthouses are built; page 272.
d. If one firm free rides, the other firms would need to pay $60,000 a lighthouse. No lighthouses would be built because

© 2015 Pearson Education, Inc.

$60,000 exceeds each firm's marginal benefit from any lighthouse; page 272.

e. The government could tax each firm $40,000 per lighthouse and use the tax revenue to build three lighthouses; pages 273-274.

Long Response Questions

1. A free rider is a person who enjoys the benefits of a good or service without paying for it. Free riding is not a problem for private goods because private goods are excludable; page 269.

2. For the private good, one combination on the economy's marginal social benefit curve is: $10 marginal social benefit and 10 units. For the public good, one combination is: $100 marginal social benefit and 1 unit. The difference occurs because for the rival private good, all residents need their own unit of the good in order to consume it, whereas for the nonrival public good, each citizen will consume the same unit. So to obtain the economy's marginal social benefit curve for a private good, we sum the quantities demanded at each price. To obtain the economy's marginal social benefit curve for a public good, we sum the marginal benefits of all individuals at each quantity; pages 270-271.

3. Because everyone can consume the same quantity of a public good and no one can be excluded from enjoying its benefits, no one has an incentive to pay for it. Everyone has an incentive to free ride. Because of the free-rider problem, the market would provide too small a quantity of a public good.
Bureaucrats who maximize their budgets and voters who work in the industry exert a larger influence on public policy than voters who are rationally ignorant. This set of circumstances leads to overprovision; pages 272, 275.

4. The free rider problem in student groups is that a student might try to avoid all work and rely on the other students to complete the assignment. The grading technique in which group members assign grades to other

members can overcome this free rider problem because each of the other group members can assign the free rider a grade of F. In order to avoid this grade, the potential free rider now is given the incentive to work and not free ride; page 269.

■ AP Self Test 11.3

True or false
1. True; page 278
2. False; pages 280-281
3. False; page 281
4. True; page 282

Multiple choice
1. c; page 278
2. c; pages 278-279
3. a; pages 279-281
4. a; page 281
5. b; page 281
6. c; page 281
7. a; page 282
8. a; page 281
9. e; page 281
10. b; page 282
11. d; page 285

Long Response Questions
■ FIGURE 11.5
Price (thousands of dollars per ton of swordfish)

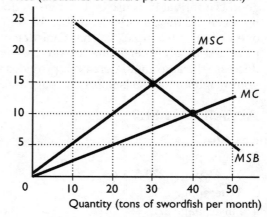

1.   Figure 11.5 labels the curves.; page 281.

© 2015 Pearson Education, Inc.

a. The equilibrium catch is determined by the intersection of the marginal cost curve, *MC*, and the marginal social benefit curve, *MSB*, so the equilibrium catch is 40 tons of swordfish. The efficient catch is determined by the intersection of the marginal social cost curve and the marginal social benefit curve, so the efficient catch is 30 tons of swordfish per month; page 281.

b. If the government sets the quota at the efficient quantity, the quota for the catch is 30 tons of swordfish per month; pages 283-284.

c. The efficient catch is 30 tons per month, so the government would issue 30 ITQs, each good for one ton per month. The market price of an individual transferable quota (ITQ) equals the marginal social benefit (which will equal the price) minus the marginal cost at the quota level of fish. The government issues ITQs for 30 tons, so the market price of an ITQ is $15,000, the marginal social benefit, minus $7,500, the marginal private cost, which equals a market price of $7,500; pages 284-285.

2. The tragedy of the commons is that there is no incentive to prevent the overuse and depletion of a commonly used resource. For example, as a new boat fishes a common resource fishing ground, the quantity of fish that the other boats can catch in an hour decreases. Their catch decreases because the new boat lands some of the fish that the other boats would have caught, which means that the initial boats' marginal cost of catching fish increases. But no individual boat owner takes account of the increase in the costs of the other boats because this is an external cost to the boat owner. Each owner is concerned with his or her costs and what he or she catches. Additional boats continue to fish until their marginal private benefit equals their marginal private cost of fishing. Each boat considers only its marginal private cost and ignores the external cost. With this many boats fishing, marginal private cost is greater than marginal social benefit and the fish stock is depleted; pages 278-280.

3. The marginal private cost of using a common resource does not equal the marginal social cost because the marginal private cost does not take account of the effect that using the resource has on others. As a common resource is used more intensively, each additional person's use increases everyone else's cost of using the resource. For instance, one person pumping water from an underground water pool—a common resource—decreases the total amount of water available and thereby increases the other users' costs of pumping water. Marginal private cost ignores the increase in other people's costs. The marginal social cost takes account of *both* the added cost to the new user (the marginal private cost) *and* the increase in everyone else's costs. So the marginal social cost exceeds the marginal private cost; pages 279-280.

4. The farmed shrimp are not subject to the tragedy of the commons because the shrimp are no longer a common resource. Because the shrimp belong to an individual farmer, the shrimp are now excludable; that is, the individual farmer decides what to do with his or her shrimp. Effectively the tragedy of the commons has been overcome because the farmer has the property right to the shrimp; pages 282-283.

© 2015 Pearson Education, Inc.

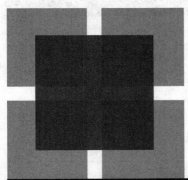

Markets with Private Information

Chapter 12

1 Describe the lemons problem and explain how the used-car market solves it.

In some markets, either the buyer or seller might have some relevant information that the other side lacks. This information is called private information. Asymmetric information is a situation in which the person on one side of a transaction has private information about things that are relevant to the transaction. The used car market is one with private information: The sellers *but not the buyers*, know if the car they are selling is a lemon. This market is subject to adverse selection, the tendency for people to enter into transactions that bring them benefits from their private information and impose costs on the uninformed party. In the used car market, adverse selection can result in only lemons being sold. The used car market overcomes this problem using signals, when an informed person takes an action that sends information to uninformed people. Warranties are an example of a signal that can allow the used car market to operate efficiently. Without warranties, the outcome will be a pooling equilibrium: when an uninformed person cannot determine quality so only lemons are traded. With warranties, the outcome will be a separating equilibrium: when the messages signaled provide full information to a previously uninformed party so that both lemons and good cars trade, with different prices.

2 Describe the asymmetric information problems in the insurance market and explain how they are solved.

People buy insurance to reduce risk. Insurance works by pooling a large number of risks so that the total number of adverse outcomes is relatively certain. The company uses the payments from all policy holders to compensate the few that suffer losses. But there is asymmetric information in the insurance market because the policy holders have private information. The asymmetric information creates two problems: moral hazard (an incentive after making an agreement to behave in a way that imposes costs on the other party to the agreement, for example an insured driver driving more aggressively) and adverse selection (for example, risky drivers are more inclined to buy insurance). Insurance companies use screens, which occur when an uninformed person creates an incentive for an informed person to reveal relevant private information. Offering no-claim bonuses and policies with high deductibles screen drivers and create a separating equilibrium because safe drivers will prefer these policies.

3 Explain the information problems and other economic problems in health-care markets.

Health-care markets suffer from asymmetric information (adverse selection means less healthy people are more inclined to buy insurance; moral hazard means that insured people are less careful); from a missing insurance market (people with a pre-existing health issue cannot buy insurance); and from public-health externalities (vaccination and treatment help prevent disease from spreading). The U.S. health system is higher cost and less efficient than health-care systems in other rich nations.

© 2015 Pearson Education, Inc.

YOUR AP TEST HINTS

AP Topics

Topic on your AP test	What to Know	Corresponding textbook section
The lemons problem	How some markets, like used cars, solve it	Checkpoint 12.1
Asymmetric information problems	How such market problems are solved	Checkpoint 12.2
Health care markets	Information problems and economic problems in this market	Checkpoint 12.3

AP Vocabulary Covered

Terms	What to Know	Text Sections
Private information	Market information available to some but not all	Checkpoint 12.1, p. 292
Asymmetric information	Either a buyer or a seller possesses private information that the other doesn't have	Checkpoint 12. 1, p. 292
Lemons problem	Some of the products are not of quality, some are, but it is not possible to distinguish them in the market	Checkpoint 12.1, p. 292
Adverse selection	Individuals using private information to get benefits and pass the costs on to those who don't have the information	Checkpoint 12.1, p. 295
Signaling	An informed person sending information to an uninformed person through an action	Checkpoint 12.1, p. 296
Pooling equilibrium	An uninformed person cannot determine quality in a market where only one piece of information is given	Checkpoint 12. 1, p. 297
Separating equilibrium	Signaling provides full information to an uninformed person in a market	Checkpoint 12.1, p. 297
Moral hazard	A person or company that uses private information that causes others, like the government, to pay costs	Checkpoint 12.2, p. 301
Screening	The ability of the uninformed to get information from the informed in order to access private information	Checkpoint 12.2, p. 302

Extra AP material

- Topics in this chapter are specific to industries like used cars and health care; where the AP exams will focus on more generic issues like market and business decision making in the areas of efficiency. Use this chapter as examples of issues facing certain inefficiencies and how they are approached.

© 2015 Pearson Education, Inc.

CHECKPOINT 12.1

■ **Describe the lemons problem and explain how the used-car market solves it.**

Quick Review

- *Private information* Information relevant to a transaction possessed by some market participants but not all.

- *Asymmetric information* A situation in which either the buyers or sellers have private information.

- *Adverse selection* The tendency for people to enter into transactions that bring them benefits from their private information.

- *Signal* When an informed person takes an action that sends information to uninformed persons.

Additional Practice Problems 12.1

1. What role does private information and adverse selection play in the fact that salespeople are often paid a commission that depends on their sales rather than a flat salary?

2. Suppose a teacher has an announced policy of giving all students a grade of A regardless of their effort or test scores. What sort of students will enroll in this instructor's class? How does this policy affect hard-working students in the class?

3. Which is preferable: a pooling equilibrium in the used car market or a separating equilibrium in the used car market? Why?

Solutions to Additional Practice Problems 12.1

1. Salespeople can either work hard to make sales or take it easy by shirking on the job. If a company offered its salespeople a flat salary, it would tend to attract salespeople who do not want to work hard. In other words, it would adversely select lazy salespeople. To overcome this adverse selection problem, most companies offer their salespeople a commission that depends on their sales.

2. This class will have a severe adverse selection problem: Largely lazy students who do not study and do not work hard will enroll in this class. The instructor's policy harms hard-working students in the class. A student's GPA sends a signal to potential employers and other schools about the student's ability to work hard and learn new material. Without this signal, these abilities remain the student's private information. By giving everyone in the class an A, this instructor degrades the information provided by his or her grade and makes it more difficult for hard working students to convey this information to others.

3. The separating equilibrium is preferable. In the pooling equilibrium, the price of a used car is low and only lemons are sold. Buyers who would prefer to pay a higher price to buy a good car cannot do so. There is a deadweight loss from the over-supply of lemons and the under-supply of good used cars. In the separating equilibrium, there are two prices: a low price for lemons and a higher price for good used cars. The deadweight losses are eliminated.

■ **AP Self Test 12.1**

True or false

1. Asymmetric information means that either the buyer or seller has private information.

2. Adverse selection occurs when one person enters into a contract with private information that will enable him or her to increase his or her benefits at the cost of decreasing the other party's benefits.

3. In the used car market, a warranty is an example of a signal.

4. In the used car market, warranties can lead to an equilibrium in which good cars have higher prices than lemons do.

5. In a pooling equilibrium, the price of a good used car is the same as the price of a lemon.

© 2015 Pearson Education, Inc.

Multiple choice

1. Asymmetric information means that
   a. the buyer *must* have information that the seller does not have.
   b. the seller *must* have information that the buyer does not have.
   c. either the buyer has information that the seller does not have *or* the seller has information that the buyer does not have.
   d. the buyer and seller have the same information.
   e. None of the above is correct.

2. The lemons problem in the used car market is that
   a. the price of a lemon is too high.
   b. the price of a lemon is too low.
   c. no lemons are bought or sold.
   d. only lemons are bought and sold.
   e. Both answers a and d are correct.

3. The fact that people who know they are risky drivers are more likely to buy auto insurance reflects
   a. adverse selection.
   b. moral hazard.
   c. a separating equilibrium.
   d. signaling.
   e. the lemons problem.

4. JCPenney guarantees to refund a customer's money if the customer returns poorly made clothing. This guarantee is an example of
   a. the adverse selection problem.
   b. the moral hazard problem.
   c. the cost of risk.
   d. signaling.
   e. a lemon problem.

5. If buyers cannot assess the quality of used cars and there are no warranties,
   a. only lemons are sold.
   b. only good used cars are sold.
   c. good cars are sold at a higher price than bad cars.
   d. there is no adverse selection problem.
   e. lemons and good cars sell for the same price.

6. In the used car market, with a pooling equilibrium the price of a lemon is ____ the price of a good used car and with a separating equilibrium the price of a lemon is ____ the price of a good used car.
   a. less than; equal to
   b. equal to; less than
   c. equal to; more than
   d. more than; more than
   e. equal to; equal to

Long Response Questions

1. What is the lemons problem? What role does asymmetric information play in the lemons problem?

2. Explain the relationship between asymmetric information and adverse selection.

3. How does signaling affect the equilibrium in a market with asymmetric information?

4. How does a pooling equilibrium differ from a separating equilibrium? Which is more efficient?

CHECKPOINT 12.2

■ **Describe the asymmetric information problems in the insurance market and explain how they are solved.**

Quick Review

- *Moral hazard* The tendency for a person with private information to use it in ways that impose costs on an uninformed party with whom they have made an agreement.

- *Screening* When an uninformed person creates an incentive for an informed person to reveal relevant private information.

Additional Practice Problem 12.2

1. How do insurance companies "pool risks?" Can insurance make people better off?

© 2015 Pearson Education, Inc.

Solutions to Additional Practice Problem 12.2

1. Insurance companies pool risks by insuring many people and thereby sharing risk. Take auto insurance. In any given year, an individual driver might or might not have an accident. There is significant uncertainty for the driver. But if the insurance company insures many drivers, while the company cannot predict *which* driver *will* have an accident, the company can forecast *how many* drivers will have accidents. The company can set its premium at a level that allows it to pay the amount it expects to pay and be reasonably certain that this amount is what it will pay.

   Insurance decreases the risks that the buyer faces and this effect makes people better off. Once again, take auto insurance. Without insurance, the buyer faces the risk of an accident which would decrease his or her wealth significantly. By purchasing insurance, the buyer eliminates the risk of a large fall in wealth from an accident by replacing it with a small, certain fall in wealth from the insurance premium. This decrease in risk can make the buyer better off.

■ AP Self Test 12.2

True or false

1. Buying insurance reduces the purchasers' risk.

2. Insurance companies pool risks.

3. If Kevin buys auto insurance, Kevin has decreased the risk that he will have an auto accident.

4. Adverse selection means that people who are at greater risk are more likely to buy insurance.

5. The number of traffic tickets a driver has accumulated is an example of a signal.

6. Aggressive drivers will buy insurance with a high deductible and low premium.

Multiple choice

1. In the United States, of all types of insurance, people spend the most on ____ insurance.
   a. auto
   b. property and casualty
   c. life
   d. health
   e. hurricane

2. Insurance companies
   a. pool risk and enable everyone to share the costs of bad outcomes.
   b. never can earn a profit because they accept risk.
   c. eliminate the risk of a bad outcome.
   d. know who will have a bad outcome.
   e. are risk averse.

3. When Sam makes an agreement and then behaves after the agreement in a way to increase his benefits and harm the other party to the agreement, Sam is illustrating
   a. signaling.
   b. adverse selection.
   c. moral hazard.
   d. the cost of contracting.
   e. a pooling equilibrium.

4. Ben is an aggressive driver so he is more likely to buy auto insurance. This situation illustrates the idea of
   a. moral hazard.
   b. adverse selection.
   c. the lemons problem.
   d. inefficiency.
   e. a separating equilibrium.

5. If you have private information that you are a riskier driver than your record indicates, you are likely to buy from your insurance company a policy that has a ____ deductible and a ____ premium.
   a. high; high
   b. high; low
   c. low; high
   d. low; low
   e. None of the above answers is correct because private information has no effect in the market for auto insurance.

© 2015 Pearson Education, Inc.

6. Screening
    a. leads to a pooling equilibrium in the insurance market.
    b. means an uninformed person passes knowledge to an informed person.
    c. makes no-claim bonuses unnecessary.
    d. explains why insurance companies offer low-premium, high-deductible policies and high-premium, low-deductible policies.
    e. makes the insurance market inefficient.

Short Response Question

1. Which of the following are examples of adverse selection and which are examples of moral hazard?

    a. A skier takes additional risks once she has health insurance.

    b. A baseball player takes more days off for minor injuries after signing a long-term contract.

    c. A person who is a poor credit risk is more likely to use pay-day advance loans.

    d. A student who is likely to work little in a class signs up for a section that has extensive group work rather than a section that is graded solely on the basis of exams.

    e. A lazy used car salesperson applies for a job with a car dealership where the pay is a fixed amount rather than based on sales.

    f. A realtor shows a house for sale only once a month rather than once a week as was verbally promised before the sales contract was signed.

Long Response Questions

1. The risk of an auto accident is always present, so how does auto insurance increase a driver's well-being?

2. Igor owns a pet bat. Sadly, this species has a 20 percent annual probability of dying. Igor buys insurance from the All Bat Insurance Company, which will pay Igor in case his bat dies. Suppose that Igor knew his bat was already sickly and had a higher than normal chance of dying but All Bat did not know this, and so charged Igor the premium that applies to healthy bats. Who expects to gain more than usual from this policy? What does this situation illustrate?

3. Larry and Harry have private information about their safety as drivers. Larry is a safe driver; he never speeds and comes to a full stop at every red light. Harry believes that speed limit signs are the minimum speed and that yellow lights mean full speed ahead.

    a. If you owned an automobile insurance company and had to charge everyone the same rate, who do you want to insure?

    b. You want to sell insurance to safe drivers, like Larry, for $500 a year and to risky drivers, like Harry, for $1,500 a year. If you cannot determine who is safe and who is risky, you offer both Larry and Harry insurance for $1,000 a year with no deductible. Is Harry likely to buy the insurance? Is Larry? Does Larry's decision depend on whether he can convince another insurance company that he is a safe driver?

    c. Suppose that you decide to sell two types of insurance policies: one costs $1,300 a year and has a $100 deductible and the other costs $300 a year and has a $1,500 deductible. Which type of insurance is Harry most likely to buy? Larry? Why?

    d. What do your answers to part (c) tell you about the role played by deductibles?

CHECKPOINT 12.3

■ **Explain the information problems and other economic problems in health-care markets.**

Quick Review

- *Moral hazard in the health-care market* Once insured, a person has less incentive to adopt a healthy life style.

- *Adverse selection in the health-care market* The healthiest people are less likely to buy health insurance.

© 2015 Pearson Education, Inc.

Additional Practice Problem 12.3

1. How does the health-care system in the United States compare to health-care systems in other major countries?

Solutions to Additional Practice Problem 12.3

1. The health-care system in the United States is unique compared to that in other major countries. All other major countries have a comprehensive national health-care system in which everyone is insured by a government-funded national insurance program. Health-care services are provided by private physicians, clinics, and so on but are paid for by the government. Patient care is allocated by urgency of need, so there are frequently long-waiting lists for treatment. In some nations people are permitted to buy private insurance and private health care. But in a few countries, no one is allowed to buy private insurance or private treatment.

   The United States has no comprehensive national health-care system and has no government-funded national insurance program. In the United States, people choose whether to buy health insurance. Treatment is allocated by price; those who can pay the price receive treatment.

■ AP Self Test 12.3

True or false

1. The market for health-care insurance is characterized by the absence of asymmetric information.

2. Health Maintenance Organizations help address the moral hazard problem in the market for health-care services.

3. The total expenditure by Medicaid and Medicare is determined by the decisions of Congress.

4. Vaccination against disease has a positive externality.

5. Most major nations do not have comprehensive national health-care systems.

6. The expenditure per person in the United States on health care is larger than in other major nations.

7. The Obama Affordable Care Act addresses the issue of over-expenditure on health care.

Multiple choice

1. Which of the following is *not* a problem in health-care markets?
   a. hospitals are not trying to maximize their profit.
   b. asymmetric information
   c. public-health externalities
   d. a missing insurance market
   e. None of the above answers are correct; that is, all the answers are problems in health-care markets.

2. Moral hazard in the market for health-care services leads
   a. patients to adopt healthy life styles.
   b. to a separating equilibrium.
   c. to all people buying health insurance
   d. to healthy people not buying health insurance.
   e. to providers over treating patients.

3. The missing insurance market is the insurance market for
   a. young healthy people.
   b. infectious diseases.
   c. people who have pre-existing health problems.
   d. people in Health Maintenance Organizations.
   e. vaccinations.

4. Vaccination against infectious diseases ___, so private markets will provide ____ efficient quantity of vaccination.
   a. is a public good; less than the
   b. is a public good; the
   c. leads to adverse selection; less than the
   d. has a positive externality; less than the
   e. has a positive externality; the

© 2015 Pearson Education, Inc.

5. Compared to other major nations, the United States spends ____ on health care and achieves ____ efficiency.
   a. less; greater
   b. more; about the same
   c. less; less
   d. more; less
   e. about the same amount; less

Long Response Questions

1. What is the missing insurance market in health care?

2. Describe the public-health externalities. Do they mean that health care would be over-provided or under-provided by private markets?

3. How can health care be under-provided in the United States yet face a problem of over-expenditure?

4. The Eye on Your Life discusses the role grades and a college education play in signaling your ability. Signals also play a role in assigning grades. Frequently instructors who assign group projects base some of the grade on grades each group participant assigns to the other participants. Using the concepts discussed in this chapter, explain why instructors use this method rather than assign everyone in the project the same grade.

© 2015 Pearson Education, Inc.

SELF TEST ANSWERS

■ AP Self Test 12.1

True or false
1. True; page 292
2. True; page 295
3. True; page 296
4. True; page 297
5. True; page 297

Multiple choice
1. c; page 292
2. d; pages 294-295
3. a; page 295
4. d; page 296
5. a; pages 294-295, 297
6. b; page 297

Long Response Questions
1. The lemons problem is an issue that arises in the used car market from asymmetric information. Sellers of used cars have private information about the quality of the car they are selling. If buyers cannot determine the quality of the car, they realize that owners of lemons are more likely to sell their car than owners of good used cars. In this case buyers will be willing to pay only a low price, the price they are willing to pay for a lemon. Sellers of good cars cannot receive the higher price their car is worth, so they are unwilling to sell their (good) used cars. Hence only lemons are bought and sold; pages 292-295.

2. Adverse selection is one of the issues asymmetric information creates. Adverse selection is the tendency for people to enter into transactions when their private information indicates to them that they will receive additional benefits than the other party expected. For instance, people who have private information that they are more prone to illness than the typical person are more likely to buy health insurance; page 295.

3. Signaling can change the equilibrium from a pooling equilibrium to a separating equilibrium. In a pooling equilibrium, buyers can-

not tell the difference between a high-quality item and a low-quality item. Both will trade for the same price which means that mainly (or only) low-quality items will trade. Signaling enables buyers to tell a high-quality item from a low-quality item and leads to a separating equilibrium: high-quality items sell for a higher price and low-quality items sell for a lower price. Both high- and low-quality items are traded; pages 296-297.

4. In a pooling equilibrium, high-quality items sell for the same price as low-quality items, so generally only low-quality items are traded. In a separating equilibrium, high-quality items sell for a higher price than low-quality items, so both high-and low-quality items are traded. The pooling equilibrium has a deadweight loss because too many low-quality items are traded and too few high-quality items are traded. The separating equilibrium does not have a deadweight loss; page 297.

■ AP Self Test 12.2

True or false
1. True; page 300
2. True; page 300
3. False; page 300
4. True; page 301
5. True; page 302
6. False; page 302

Multiple choice
1. d; page 299
2. a; page 300
3. c; page 301
4. b; page 301
5. c; page 302
6. d; pages 302-303

Short Response Question
1 a. Moral hazard; because the skier is changing behavior after the health insurance was purchased; page 301.

© 2015 Pearson Education, Inc.

b. Moral hazard, because the ball player's behavior is changing after the contract was signed; page 301.

c. Adverse selection, because the pay-day loan company is attracting poor credit risks; page 301.

d. Adverse selection, because the class section based on group work is attracting lazy students; page 301.

e. Adverse selection, because the car dealership is attracting lazy salespeople; page 301.

f. Moral hazard, because the realtor's behavior is changing after the contract was signed; page 301.

Long Response Questions

1 While the risk of an auto accident is always present, auto insurance removes the financial risk. Auto insurance means that the driver no longer faces the possibility of a large loss because if the driver has an accident, the insurance company reimburses the driver. However the driver must pay the insurance company its premium, so the driver has traded the risky possibility of a large loss for the certain case of a small loss. By reducing the driver's financial risk, the driver is made better off; pages 299-300.

2. Igor expects to gain more from the policy because the probability of his bat dying exceeds the normal probability. Thus the probability that All Bat will need to pay off on the policy exceeds normal. This situation illustrates the adverse selection problem: The people who most want to buy bat insurance are those who have sickly bats; page 301.

3. a. You want to sell insurance to Larry because you expect that his policy will be more profitable than Harry's policy; pages 300-303.

b. Harry is likely to buy the policy. If Harry does not buy the policy, he expects to pay $1,500 a year for his accidents. If he buys the policy, he pays only $1,000, a saving to Harry of $500. Larry may or may not buy a policy. If he is very risk averse and can-

not obtain a lower price from another company, he will buy your insurance. But, if he is only a little risk averse, he may decide to do without insurance. If another company can recognize him as a safe driver, it will therefore offer him a less expensive policy. Larry then will buy from your competitor; pages 302-303.

c. Harry probably will buy the first policy; Larry likely will buy the second. From Harry's standpoint, the second policy is more expensive than the first. Harry, the risky driver, is likely to have an accident and thereby incur the $1,500 deductible. Larry realizes that he is unlikely to have an accident and is not likely to have to pay the deductible. Larry is more likely to opt for the second policy because, if he has no accident, he pays only $300 rather than $1,300 for his insurance; pages 302-303.

d. Insurance companies use deductibles to separate risky and safe drivers. Safe drivers prefer a low premium and high deductible because they realize that they are not likely to have an accident and be forced to pay the deductible. Risky drivers prefer a high premium and low deductible because they know that an accident is probable and they do not want to be hit with a high deductible payment. High-risk drivers know that they are accident prone and they are willing to pay higher premiums for nearly full coverage, but low-risk drivers know that they seldom have accidents and they will choose lower premiums with lower coverage; page 302.

■ AP Self Test 12.3

True or false

1. False; page 305
2. True; page 306
3. False; page 306
4. True; page 307
5. False; page 307
6. True; page 308
7. False; page 309

Multiple choice

1. a; page 305
2. e; pages 305-306
3. c; page 306
4. d; page 307
5. d; page 308

Long Response Questions

1. The missing insurance market is the market for insurance for people who have pre-existing medical conditions. These people can either get no insurance or else get insurance that excludes their pre-existing condition. Hence the people with the greatest want for health insurance are often unable to obtain it; page 306.

2. There are two public health externalities. The first is that the control of infectious diseases is often a public good. For example, public sanitation, which helps control infectious diseases, is a public good and so is provided by the government to avoid the free-rider problem. The second externality arises from vaccination against infectious diseases, which has a positive externality. If a person is vaccinated, that person enjoys a gain from the vaccination, but so do his or her friends who become less likely to catch the disease; page 307.

3. Medicare and Medicaid are government programs that cover health care for the aged and those too poor to buy health insurance. Even with these programs, health care in the United States is under-provided because there are still millions of people without health-care insurance. Over-expenditure remains a problem, however, because insurance means that patients do not bear the full cost of their treatment. For instance, the total expenditure made under the Medicare and Medicaid programs is determined by the patients and not set by governmental decisions; pages 306, 309.

4. The group members have private information about each member's contribution, that is, who worked hard and who shirked. The instructor would like to know this private information, so the instructor allows the group members to signal this information by the grades they assign the other members. By acquiring this information, the instructor helps overcome the moral hazard created by the group members' incentives to not work and count on the other members to carry the load; page 301.

© 2015 Pearson Education, Inc.

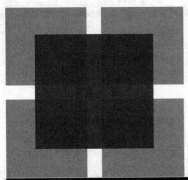

Consumer Choice and Demand

Chapter 13

Chapter 13 presents a model of consumer choice based on marginal utility. We use marginal utility theory to derive a demand curve and explain the paradox of value.

1 Calculate and graph a budget line that shows the limits to a person's consumption possibilities.

The budget line describes the limits to a consumer's consumption possibilities. A consumer can afford any combination on the budget line and inside it, but cannot afford any combination outside the budget line. When the price of a good changes, the slope of the budget line changes. A relative price is the price of one good in terms of another good—an opportunity cost. It equals the price of one good divided by the price of another good. The slope of the budget line equals the relative price of the good on the x-axis. An increase in the budget shifts the budget line rightward, and a decrease shifts the budget line leftward. An increase in the price of the good measured along the horizontal axis rotates the budget line inward around the vertical intercept and a decrease in the price rotates the budget line outward.

2 Explain marginal utility theory and use it to derive a consumer's demand curve.

Utility is the benefit or satisfaction a person gets from the consumption of a good or service. Total utility is the total benefit that a person gets from the consumption of a good or service; marginal utility is the change in total utility that results from a one-unit increase in the quantity of a good consumed. As more of a good is consumed, its total utility increases but its marginal utility decreases. A consumer maximizes total utility when he or she allocates his or her entire available budget and makes the marginal utility per dollar the same for all goods. The marginal utility per dollar is the marginal utility from the good relative to the price of the good. It equals the marginal utility divided by the price. If the price of a good falls, the marginal utility per dollar for that good rises at the current consumption level and the consumer buys more of that good. So when the price of a good falls, there is an increase in the quantity demanded and a movement down along the demand curve.

3 Use marginal utility theory to explain the paradox of value: why water is vital but cheap while diamonds are relatively useless but expensive.

The paradox of value is that water, which is essential to life, is cheap, while diamonds, which are relatively useless, are expensive. We solve this puzzle by distinguishing between total utility and marginal utility. The total utility from water is enormous. But we use so much water that its marginal utility is a small value. The total utility from diamonds is small. But we have few diamonds so their marginal utility is high. Diamonds have a high price and a high marginal utility while water has a low price and a low marginal utility. When the (high) marginal utility of diamonds is divided by the (high) price of a diamond, the result equals the (low) marginal utility of water divided by the (low) price of water so the marginal utility per dollar of diamonds equals that of water. Water is cheap but provides a large consumer surplus; diamonds are expensive but provide a small consumer surplus.

© 2015 Pearson Education, Inc.

YOUR AP TEST HINTS

AP Topics

Topic on your AP test	What to Know	Corresponding textbook section
Personal consumption possibilities	Calculating and graphing	Checkpoint 13.1
Marginal utility theory	Deriving a consumer demand curve	Checkpoint 13.2
Paradox of value	Why some products are cheap, others expensive	Checkpoint 13.3

AP Vocabulary Covered

Terms	What to Know	Text Sections
Budget line	The limits of consumption possibilities based on budget constraints and prices of goods and services	Checkpoint 13.1, p. 316
Utility	The benefit or satisfaction gotten from the consumption of a good or service	Checkpoint 13.2, p. 322
Total utility	The total benefit of consumption that generally increases as the quantity consumed of a good increases.	Checkpoint 13.2, p. 322
Marginal utility	The change in total utility from a one unit increase in consumption of the good	Checkpoint 13.2, p. 322
Diminishing marginal utility	Marginal utility decreases as the quantity consumed increases	Checkpoint 13.2, p. 322
Utility-maximizing rule	The greatest total utility from all goods and services consumed is reached when the entire budget is allocated and the marginal utility per dollar for all goods is equal	Checkpoint 13.2, p. 324
Marginal utility per dollar	The marginal utility from a good relative to the price paid for the good	Checkpoint 13.2, p. 324
Paradox of value	Why is an essential good like water cheap, when a non-essential good like a diamond expensive?	Checkpoint 13.3, p. 329

Extra AP material

- The material on *budget lines* in Checkpoint 13.1 and on indifference curves in the Appendix is not covered on the AP test.
- The more of a good that is consumed the *total utility* rises and the *marginal utility* falls.
- The *utility maximizing rule* might be used on the AP test to create the consumer equilibrium.
- The principle of *diminishing marginal utility* is one of the explanations of the downward sloping demand curve. The test might also ask about two other factors: the "income effect" and the "substitution effect".

The income effect is the impact of a change in the price of a good on a consumer's real income. When the price falls, consumers' real incomes or purchasing power will increase. They are able to buy more goods than before and will be able to buy more normal goods. The substitution effect is the impact of a change in the price of a good relative to potential substitutes. If the price falls the price is now relatively lower compared to substitutes. Consumers can respond by purchasing more of the relatively cheaper good. Both of these changes are shown with movements along the demand curve.

© 2015 Pearson Education, Inc.

CHECKPOINT 13.1

■ **Calculate and graph a budget line that shows the limits to a person's consumption possibilities.**

Quick Review

- *Budget line* A line that describes the limits to consumption choices and that depends on a consumer's budget and the prices of goods and services.

Additional Practice Problems 13.1

1. Mark, a chemistry major at Cal State East Bay, dines by himself at the local Olive Garden. He has $30 per week to spend. Pizza is $15 and a salad is $5.

   a. List the combinations of pizza and salads he can buy.

   b. Graph Mark's budget line in the figure to the right.

   c. What is the opportunity cost of a pizza?

   d. What is the relative price of a pizza?

   Quantity (salads)

   8
   6
   4
   2

   1   2
   Quantity (pizzas)

Solutions to Additional Practice Problems 13.1

Pizza	Salads
0	6
1	3
2	0

1a. The combinations of pizza and salads that Mark can afford are listed in the table. To construct this table, select the combinations of pizza and salad that spend all of Mark's $30 budget.

1b. The figure shows Mark's budget line. The maximum number of pizzas he can buy is 2; the maximum number of salads he can buy is 6.

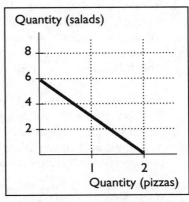

Quantity (salads)

8
6
4
2

1   2
Quantity (pizzas)

1c. The slope of the budget line is the opportunity cost of a pizza. The slope is (6 salads) ÷ (2 pizzas), which equals 3 salads per pizza. So consuming 1 pizza means Mark forgoes 3 salads.

1d. The opportunity cost of a pizza is also its relative price. The relative price of a pizza is 3 salads per pizza.

■ **AP Self Test 13.1**

True or false

1. Dian's budget line shows the limits to what Dian can consume.

2. When Stan's budget increases, his budget line shifts outward.

3. The slope of the budget line measures the opportunity cost of one more unit of the good plotted on the *x*-axis.

Multiple choice

1. A budget line shows the
   a. limits to production possibilities.
   b. limits to production opportunities.
   c. the slope of the demand curve.
   d. limits to consumption possibilities.
   e. way the demand curve shifts if the consumer's budget changes.

© 2015 Pearson Education, Inc.

2. Linda has $10 a month to spend on ice cream cones and chocolate bars. If the price of an ice cream cone is $2 a cone and the price of a chocolate bar is $1 a bar, which of the following is a point on Linda's budget line?
   a. 4 cones and 0 chocolate bars
   b. 1 cone and 8 chocolate bars
   c. 3 cones and 1 chocolate bar
   d. 5 cones and 10 chocolate bars
   e. 0 cones and 0 chocolate bars

3. If a consumer's budget increases, the budget line
   a. rotates outward and its slope changes.
   b. rotates inward and its slope changes.
   c. shifts outward and its slope does not change.
   d. shifts inward and its slope does not change.
   e. does not change.

■ **FIGURE 13.1**

Quantity (movies per month)

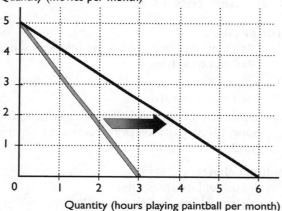

Quantity (hours playing paintball per month)

4. _____ will change Bobby's budget line as shown by the change from the gray budget line to the black budget line in Figure 13.1.
   a. An increase in Bobby's budget
   b. A decrease in Bobby's budget
   c. A fall in the price of playing paintball
   d. A rise in the price playing paintball
   e. A rise in the price of a movie

5. A relative price is the
   a. price of a substitute.
   b. price of a related good.
   c. price of one good divided by the price of another.
   d. absolute price of a good.
   e. price of one good multiplied by the price of another.

Short Response Question

■ **FIGURE 13.2**

Quantity (magazines per week)

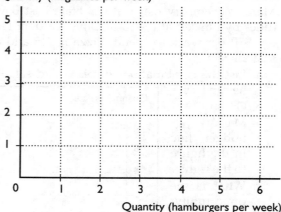

Quantity (hamburgers per week)

1. Jack buys two things: magazines, which have a price of $3 each, and hamburgers, which have a price of $4 each. Jack's income is $12.
   a. In Figure 13.2, draw Jack's budget line.
   b. Can Jack buy 2 magazines and 1 hamburger? Can he buy 2 magazines and 3 hamburgers?

Long Response Question

1. How is a budget line similar to a production possibilities frontier? How is it dissimilar?

Additional Exercises (also in MyEconLab Test A)

Jenny's burger and salad budget is $36 a week. The price of a burger is $3, and the price of a salad is $2.

1. List the combinations of burgers and salads that Jenny can afford.

2. Draw a graph of Jenny's budget line with the quantity of burgers plotted on the x-axis. Describe how Jenny's budget line changes if,

© 2015 Pearson Education, Inc.

other things remaining the same, the following changes occur one at a time:

a. The price of a salad rises.

b. Jenny's burger and salad budget decreases.

3. How does the relative price of a salad change if the price of a salad falls to $1? Explain your answer.

CHECKPOINT 13.2

■ **Explain marginal utility theory and use it to derive a consumer's demand curve.**

Quick Review

- *Marginal utility* The change in total utility that results from a one-unit increase in the quantity of a good consumed.
- *Marginal utility per dollar* The increase in total utility that comes from the last dollar spent on the good.

Additional Practice Problems 13.2

Orange juice		Cookies	
Quantity per week	Total utility	Quantity per week	Total utility
0	0	0	0
1	20	1	60
2	32	2	100
3	40	3	120
4	44	4	130
5	46	5	145

1. The table above shows Tommy's total utility from orange juice and cookies.

a. Calculate Tommy's marginal utility schedule from orange juice and from cookies by completing the table above in the next column.

b. If the price of a carton of orange juice is $2, what is Tommy's marginal utility per dollar for orange juice when Tommy buys 2 cartons of orange juice a week?

c. If the price of a box of cookies is $4, what is Tommy's marginal utility per dollar for cookies when Tommy buys 3 boxes of cookies a week?

Orange juice		Cookies	
Quantity per week	Marginal utility	Quantity per week	Marginal utility
0	XX	0	XX
1	___	1	___
2	___	2	___
3	___	3	___
4	___	4	___
5	___	5	___

d. If Tommy's budget for orange juice and cookies is $10 per week and orange juice is $2 per carton and cookies are $4 per box, what combination of orange juice and cookies will Tommy buy? Why does Tommy buy this combination? What is his total utility?

e. Tommy could afford to buy 5 cartons of orange juice a week. Why does he not buy 5 cartons?

2. If Jenny is allocating her entire available budget on movies and popcorn, explain the rule she follows to maximize her total utility.

Solutions to Additional Practice Problems 13.2

Orange juice		Cookies	
Quantity per week	Marginal utility	Quantity per week	Marginal utility
0	XX	0	XX
1	20	1	60
2	12	2	40
3	8	3	20
4	4	4	10
5	2	5	5

1a. The completed table is above. Marginal utility equals the change in total utility from a one-unit increase in the quantity of the good consumed. So the marginal utility of the second box of cookies equals 100 − 60, which is 40.

1b. The marginal utility per dollar is 12 ÷ $2 = 6.

1c. The marginal utility per dollar is 20 ÷ $4 = 5.

1d. Tommy buys 2 boxes of cookies and 1 carton of orange juice. This combination allocates his entire budget and the marginal utility per dollar for orange juice, 10, equals the marginal utility per dollar for cookies, 10. This combination gives Tommy total utility of 120.

© 2015 Pearson Education, Inc.

1e. Tommy does not buy 5 cartons of orange juice because his total utility would be only 46, well less than his total utility from the utility-maximizing combination derived in the answer to part (d).

2. If the marginal utility per dollar from movies exceeds the marginal utility per dollar from popcorn, then Jenny sees more movies and buys less popcorn because this action increases her total utility; if the marginal utility per dollar from popcorn exceeds the marginal utility per dollar from movies, Jenny buys more popcorn and sees fewer movies because this action increases her total utility. More generally, if the marginal gain from an action exceeds the marginal loss, take the action. Jenny is maximizing her total utility when the marginal utility per dollar from movies equals the marginal utility per dollar from popcorn.

■ AP Self Test 13.2

True or false

1. As Katie consumes more sushi, her total utility from sushi increases.

2. As Katie consumes more sushi, her marginal utility from sushi increases.

3. Bobby maximizes his utility whenever he allocates his entire available budget.

4. Tommy is allocating his entire available budget. If Tommy's marginal utility per dollar for tacos is 8 and the marginal utility per dollar from burritos is 10, then Tommy is NOT maximizing his total utility.

5. Marginal utility theory implies that other things remaining the same, the higher the price of a good, the greater is the quantity demanded of that good.

Multiple choice

1. In economics, utility
   a. always decreases as income increases.
   b. equals opportunity cost.
   c. is an index of satisfaction.
   d. is measured by the same units as relative price.
   e. and relative price are the same thing.

2. Marginal utility is the
   a. change in total utility that results from a one-unit increase in the quantity of a good consumed.
   b. total benefit from the consumption of a good or service.
   c. quantity of a good a consumer prefers.
   d. average utility per unit consumed.
   e. change in total utility that results from a one dollar increase in the price of a good consumed.

3. Sushi costs $3 per piece. Cynthia's total utility after eating one piece is 30 and her total utility after eating 2 pieces is 51, so her marginal utility from the second piece is
   a. 17.
   b. 10.
   c. 51.
   d. 7.
   e. 21.

4. As Shaniq drinks additional cups of tea at breakfast, Shaniq's
   a. marginal utility from tea decreases.
   b. total utility from tea increases.
   c. total utility from tea decreases.
   d. Both answers (a) and (b) are correct.
   e. Both answers (b) and (c) are correct.

5. Marginal utility per dollar is calculated by _____ the price of the good.
   a. multiplying the marginal utility from a good by
   b. dividing the marginal utility from a good by
   c. multiplying the total utility from a good by
   d. dividing the total utility from a good by
   e. None of the above answers is correct.

© 2015 Pearson Education, Inc.

6. Sushi costs $3 per piece. Cynthia's total utility after eating one piece is 30 and her total utility after eating 2 pieces is 51, so her marginal utility per dollar from the second piece is
   a. 17.
   b. 10.
   c. 51.
   d. 7.
   e. 21.

7. When Chris maximizes his total utility, then his entire available budget is allocated in such a way that the
   a. marginal utility from all goods is equal.
   b. marginal utility per dollar is equal for all goods.
   c. marginal utility is as large as possible for goods.
   d. marginal utility will start decreasing if it consumes fewer goods.
   e. quantities consumed of each good are equal.

8. Suppose that Misty likes pizza and hotdogs. If her marginal utility per dollar from pizza is 6 and from hotdogs is 5, Misty
   a. is maximizing her total utility.
   b. could increase her total utility by buying more hotdogs and less pizza.
   c. could increase her total utility by buying more pizza and fewer hotdogs.
   d. is maximizing her marginal utility.
   e. must obtain more income in order to reach her consumer equilibrium.

9. You can use marginal utility theory to find the demand curve by changing
   a. only the price of one good.
   b. only income.
   c. the utility schedule.
   d. only the prices of both goods.
   e. income and the prices of both goods.

10. Suppose that Hank consumes only Mountain Dew and pizza. If Hank's total utility from all amounts of both Mountain Dew and pizza double from what they were before, then Hank's demand for
    a. both goods must double.
    b. one of the goods must double.
    c. both goods must decrease by one-half.
    d. one of the goods must decrease by one-half.
    e. neither good changes.

Short Response Questions

Quantity (bottles of Aquafina per day)	Total utility	Marginal utility
0	0	
1	25	___
2	45	___
3	60	___
4	70	___
5	75	___
6	76	___

1. Carlos drinks Aquafina bottled water. The table above gives his total utility from this water. Calculate his marginal utility.

	Pizza			Soda	
Quantity (slices per day)	Total utility, pizza	Marginal utility, pizza	Quantity (cans per day)	Total utility, soda	Marginal utility, soda
0	0		0	0	
1	45	___	1	25	___
2	85	___	2	45	___
3	120	___	3	60	___
4	150	___	4	70	___
5	175	___	5	75	___
6	195	___	6	76	___

2. Bertha consumes only soda and pizza. The table above gives Bertha's total utility from soda and pizza slices.
   a. Complete the marginal utility columns of the table.
   b. The price of a can of soda is $1 and the price of a slice of pizza is $2. If Bertha's budget is $6, how many cans of soda and slices of pizza will she consume?
   c. Suppose the price of a slice of pizza rises to $3, while the price of a can of soda and

© 2015 Pearson Education, Inc.

■ **FIGURE 13.3**

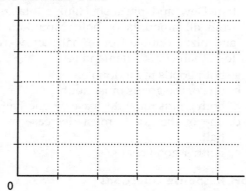

Bertha's budget does not change. Now how many cans of soda and slices of pizza will she consume?

d. What are two points on Bertha's demand curve for slices of pizza? Assuming her demand curve is a straight line, label the axes and then draw her demand curve in Figure 13.3.

Long Response Questions

Quantity (tacos per week)	Marginal utility	Quantity (hamburgers per week)	Marginal utility
0	0	0	0
1	50	1	80
2	40	2	40
3	30	3	20
4	20	4	10
5	10	5	5

1. Lisa eats tacos and hamburgers. The quantities and marginal utilities from each are in the table above. Lisa's budget is $8.

   a. If the price of taco is $1 and the price of a hamburger is $2, what quantity of tacos and hamburgers will Lisa purchase?

   b. If the price of a taco rises to $2 while neither Lisa's income nor the price of a hamburger change, what quantity of tacos and hamburgers will Lisa purchase?

   c. How does Lisa respond to a change in the price of a taco?

2. What does it mean to "allocate the entire available budget?" How does saving fit into the picture?

3. What is marginal analysis? Why is making the marginal utility per dollar necessary for a consumer to maximize his or her utility?

4. How do the income and substitution effects of a price change lead to the negative slope of a demand curve?

Additional Exercises (also in MyEconLab Test A)

Juice		Pasta	
Cans per week	Total utility	Dishes per week	Total utility
0	0	0	0
1	22	1	64
2	40	2	120
3	54	3	168
4	60	4	208
5	62	5	240
6	62	6	264

The table above shows Wanda's total utility for juice and pasta. The price of a can of juice is $1, the price of a dish of pasta is $4, and Wanda has $11 a week to spend.

1. Calculate Wanda's marginal utility and marginal utility per dollar from pasta when she buys 3 dishes a week. Calculate Wanda's marginal utility and marginal utility per dollar from juice when she buys 2 cans a week.

2. If Wanda buys 2 cans of juice and 2 dishes of pasta a week, is she maximizing her total utility? If Wanda is not maximizing her total utility, explain how she must adjust her consumption of juice and pasta to do so.

CHECKPOINT 13.3

■ **Use marginal utility theory to explain the paradox of value: why water is vital but cheap while diamonds are relatively useless but expensive.**

Quick Review

• *The paradox of value* Why is water, which is essential to life, cheap, but diamonds,

© 2015 Pearson Education, Inc.

which are useless compared to water, expensive?

Additional Practice Problem 13.3

1. Anthony buys 30,000 gallons of water a month. His marginal utility from a gallon of water is 100 units. The price of a gallon of water is $0.001. Anthony also buys 4 boxes of Krispy Kreme doughnuts a month. He pays $5 for a box. Anthony is maximizing his utility.

    a. What is the marginal utility from a box of Krispy Kreme doughnuts?

    b. Why does Anthony receive a lower marginal utility from his consumption of water?

Solution to Additional Practice Problem 13.3

1a. Because Anthony is maximizing his utility, the marginal utility per dollar he spends on water equals the marginal utility per dollar he spends on doughnuts. The marginal utility per dollar for water equals 100 units ÷ $0.001 = 100,000. So the marginal utility of a box of doughnuts divided by the price of a box of doughnuts ($5) must equal 100,000. In terms of a formula, $MU ÷ 5 = 100,000$, so the marginal utility of a box of doughnuts equals 5 ×100,000, which is 500,000.

1b. Anthony buys 30,000 gallons of water a month and (only) 4 boxes of doughnuts a month. As the quantity of a good consumed increases, the marginal utility decreases. Because Anthony is consuming much more water than doughnuts, his total utility from water is almost surely greater than his total utility from doughnuts, but his marginal utility from water is much less than his marginal utility from doughnuts.

■ AP Self Test 13.3

True or false

1. Susan's demand curve for curry shows the quantity of curry she demands at each price when her total utility is maximized.

2. Marginal benefit is the maximum price a consumer is willing to pay for an extra unit of a good or service when total utility is maximized.

3. The paradox of value is that water, which is essential to life, is plentiful, while diamonds, which are not essential to life, are much less plentiful.

4. The paradox of value is solved by noting that the total utility from water is small while the marginal utility from water is large.

5. The consumer surplus from water is greater than the consumer surplus from diamonds.

Multiple choice

1. At all points on a demand curve, the
    i. consumer's budget has been allocated to maximize total utility.
    ii. the quantity demanded at each price is determined by maximizing the consumer's total utility.
    iii. price represents the marginal benefit the consumer gets from an extra unit of a good.
    a. i only.
    b. ii only.
    c. i and ii.
    d. i and iii.
    e. i, ii, and iii.

2. As more of a good is consumed, the marginal utility of an additional unit ____, so consumers are willing to pay ____ for an additional unit.
    a. decreases; less
    b. increases; less
    c. decreases; more
    d. increases; more
    e. does not change; less

3. The paradox of value refers to the
    a. utility maximizing rule.
    b. fact that water is vital but cheap, while diamonds are relatively useless but expensive.
    c. fact that consumers have different preferences and utility schedules.
    d. law of demand.
    e. issue of why the consumer surplus from water equals the consumer surplus from diamonds.

© 2015 Pearson Education, Inc.

4. One reason why water is cheap compared to diamonds is because the
    a. marginal utility of water is enormous.
    b. marginal utility of water is small.
    c. total utility of water is enormous.
    d. total utility of water is small.
    e. total utility of water and diamonds must be equal but the marginal utility of water is much lower than the marginal utility of diamonds.

5. In the paradox of value between expensive diamonds and inexpensive water, we see that
    a. the consumer surpluses are very high for both goods.
    b. diamonds have a low consumer surplus while water has a high consumer surplus.
    c. diamonds have a high consumer surplus while water has a low consumer surplus.
    d. the consumer surpluses are very low for both goods.
    e. the consumer surpluses for the two goods cannot be compared.

Short Response Questions

■ FIGURE 13.4
Price (dollars per thousand gallons)

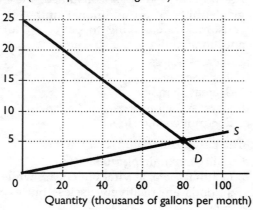

1. Figure 13.4 shows the market for water. Indicate the equilibrium price and then shade in the area of the consumer surplus.

■ FIGURE 13.5
Price (thousands of dollars per carat)

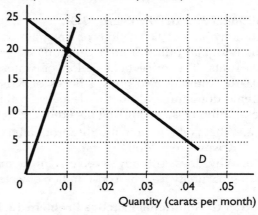

2. Figure 13.5 shows the market for rubies. Indicate the equilibrium price and then shade in the area of the consumer surplus.

3. Based on Figures 13.4 and 13.5, is there more consumer surplus for water or rubies? Which is larger: the marginal utility of a gallon of water or a carat of rubies?

Long Response Questions

1. Bobby consumes potato chips and Gatorade. He is maximizing his utility. His marginal utility from the last bag of chips he eats is 40 and his marginal utility from the last bottle of Gatorade he drinks is 60. The price of a bag of chips is $2. What must be the price of a bottle of Gatorade?

2. Does the price Bianca is willing to pay for another purse directly depend on her total utility from purses or her marginal utility from a purse? Explain your answer.

3. What is the paradox of value and what is its solution?

Additional Exercise (also in MyEconLab Test A)

1. Which good is more valuable to you: water or your economics text?

© 2015 Pearson Education, Inc.

SELF TEST ANSWERS

■ AP Self Test 13.1

True or false

1. True; page 316
2. True; page 317
3. True; page 319

Multiple choice

1. d; page 316
2. b; page 316
3. c; page 317
4. c; page 318
5. c; page 320

Short Response Question

■ FIGURE 13.6

Quantity (magazines per week)

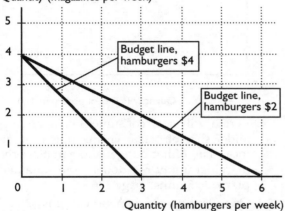

1. a. The budget line in Figure 13.6 labeled "hamburgers $4" is Jack's budget line; page 316.

   b. Jack can buy 2 magazines and 1 hamburger. Jack cannot buy 2 magazines and 3 hamburgers because that combination is outside his budget line; page 316.

Long Response Questions

1. A budget line is similar to the production possibilities frontier. Both curves show a limit to what is feasible. The *PPF* is a technological limit that does not depend on prices. But the budget line does depend on prices. Consumption possibilities change when prices or the available budget change; page 316.

Additional Exercises (also in MyEconLab Test A)

1. The affordable combinations of burgers and salad, all of which spend the $36 in Jenny's budget, are:
   - 0 burgers and 18 salads; page 316.
   - 2 burgers and 15 salads; page 316.
   - 4 burgers and 12 salads; page 316.
   - 6 burgers and 9 salads; page 316.
   - 8 burgers and 6 salads; page 316.
   - 10 burgers and 3 salads; page 316.
   - 12 burgers and 0 salads; page 316.

■ FIGURE 13.7

Quantity (burgers per week)

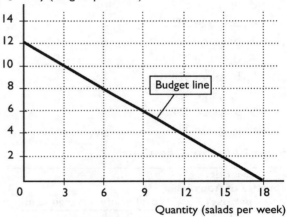

Quantity (salads per week)

2. Figure 13.7 shows Jenny's budget line.

   a. If the price of a salad rises, the budget line rotates inward and becomes steeper. The vertical intercept stays the same (12 burgers) but the horizontal intercept decreases.

   b. If Jenny's burger and salad budget decreases, the budget line shifts inward and its slope does not change; page 318.

3. The relative price of a salad is the opportunity cost of a salad—the number of burgers that Jenny must forgo to get 1 salad. The relative price of a salad equals the price of a salad divided by the price of a burger, which is $1 a salad ÷ $3 a burger = 1/3 of a burger

© 2015 Pearson Education, Inc.

for a salad. Hence the fall in the (money) price of a salad together with no change in the (money) price of a burger leads to a fall in the relative price of a salad; pages 319-320.

■ AP Self Test 13.2

True or false

1. True; page 322
2. False; page 322
3. False; page 324
4. True; pages 324-325
5. False; page 327

Multiple choice

1. c; page 322
2. a; page 322
3. e; page 322
4. d; page 322
5. b; page 324
6. d; page 324
7. b; page 324
8. c; page 326
9. a; page 327
10. e; page 327

Short Response Questions

Quantity (bottles of Aquafina per day)	Total utility	Marginal utility
0	0	
1	25	25
2	45	20
3	60	15
4	70	10
5	75	5
6	76	1

1. The completed table is above; page 322.

2. a. The completed table is at the top of the next column; page 322.

   b. Bertha will consume 2 cans of soda and 2 slices of pizza. This combination allocates all her budget and equalizes the marginal utility per dollar from soda and pizza at 20 units; page 326.

Pizza			Soda		
Quantity (slices per day)	Total utility, pizza	Marginal utility, pizza	Quantity (cans per day)	Total utility, soda	Marginal utility, soda
0	0		0	0	
1	45	45	1	25	25
2	85	40	2	45	20
3	120	35	3	60	15
4	150	30	4	70	10
5	175	25	5	75	5
6	195	20	6	76	1

■ FIGURE 13.8

Price (dollars per slice of pizza)

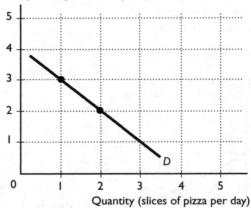

c. Bertha will now consume 3 cans of soda and 1 slice of pizza. This combination allocates all of her budget and equalizes the marginal utility per dollar from soda and pizza at 15 units; page 326.

d. One point on her demand curve is $2 and 2 slices of pizza; another point is $3 and 1 slice of pizza. Figure 13.8 shows Bertha's demand curve; page 327.

Long Response Questions

1. a. Lisa will buy 4 tacos and 2 hamburgers because this combination allocates her entire budget and sets the marginal utility per dollar from tacos equal to the marginal utility per dollar from hamburgers; page 326.

   b. Lisa will buy 2 tacos and 2 hamburgers because this combination allocates all her budget and equalizes the marginal utility per dollar from tacos and hamburgers at 20 units; page 326.

© 2015 Pearson Education, Inc.

c. When the price of a taco rises, the quantity of tacos demanded decreases; page 327.

2. To "allocate the entire available budget" means that we use the entire available budget. Using the entire budget doesn't mean not saving anything. The available budget is the amount available after choosing how much to save; page 324.

3. Marginal analysis compares the marginal gain from having more of one good with the marginal loss from having less of another good. The "equalize the marginal utility per dollar" rule is the result of marginal analysis. Suppose the marginal utility per dollar for a blouse exceeds that of a dollar for a purse. Marginal analysis indicates that the consumer can increase her total utility by spending a dollar less on purses and spending a dollar more on blouses because the gain in utility from the dollar spent on blouses exceeds the loss in utility from the dollar reduction on purses; page 326.

4. The income effect refers to the impact a price change has on consumers' real incomes, that is, on their purchasing power. If the price of a good falls, consumers are able to buy more of that good and/or more of other goods. In this case, consumers' real incomes have increased and so they wind up buying more normal goods. Hence a fall in the price of a normal good increases the quantity consumers purchase. The substitution effect refers to a change in the relative price of a good. If the price of a good falls, its relative price, that is, its price compared to the prices of other goods, falls. As a result, consumers increase their purchases of this good in place of other goods. By substituting more of the relatively cheaper good for other goods, consumers increase the quantity they purchase. Both the income and substitution effects lead to an increase in the quantity demanded of a good when its price falls, which means that the good's demand curve is downward sloping.

Additional Exercises (also in MyEconLab Test A)

1. The total utility of the third dish of pasta is 168 units and the total utility of the second dish of pasta is 120 units. The change in total utility equals the marginal utility, so the marginal utility is (168 units) − (120 units) = 48 units. The marginal utility per dollar from pasta when Wanda has 3 dishes of pasta a week is 48 units ÷ $4 = 12 units per dollar.

The total utility of the second can of juice is 40 units and the total utility of the first can of juice is 22 units. The change in total utility equals the marginal utility, so the marginal utility is (40 units) − (22 units) = 18 units. The marginal utility per dollar from juice when Wanda has 2 cans of juice a week 18 units ÷ $1 = 18 units per dollar on the 2nd can of juice; pages 322, 324.

2. Wanda is not maximizing her utility. She is not allocating all of her budget and the marginal utility per dollar from juice, 18 units per dollar, does not equal the marginal utility per dollar from pasta, 14 units per dollar. To maximize her utility, Wanda should buy 1 more can of juice so that she consumes 3 cans of juice and 2 dishes of pasta. This combination allocates all of her budget and sets the marginal utility per dollar from juice equal to the marginal utility per dollar from pasta—14 units per dollar; pages 324, 326.

■ AP Self Test 13.3

True or false

1. True; page 329
2. True; page 329
3. False; page 329
4. False; page 329
5. True; page 330

Multiple choice

1. e; page 329
2. a; page 329
3. b; page 329
4. b; page 329
5. b; page 330

© 2015 Pearson Education, Inc.

Short Response Questions

■ **FIGURE 13.9**

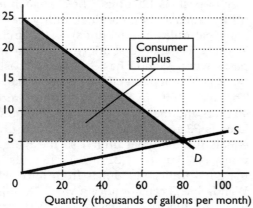

1. The equilibrium price is $5 per thousand gallons of water. The consumer surplus is the gray triangle in Figure 13.9; page 330.

■ **FIGURE 13.10**

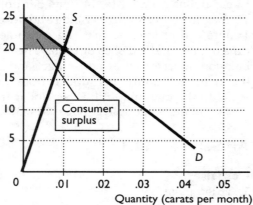

2. The equilibrium price is $20,000 a carat. Figure 13.10 shows the consumer surplus; page 330.

3. There is more consumer surplus for water than rubies. Because the price of a carat of rubies is much greater than the price of a gallon of water, it must be the case that the marginal utility of a carat of rubies is much greater than the marginal utility of a gallon of water; page 330.

Long Response Questions

1. Bobby maximizes his total utility by consuming the combination of chips and Gatorade such that the marginal utility per dollar for chips equals the marginal utility per dollar for Gatorade. The marginal utility from the last bag of chips is 40 and the price of a bag of chips is $2, so the marginal utility per dollar is 40 ÷ $2 = 20. Because the marginal utility of the Gatorade is 60, the price is $3 to make the marginal utility per dollar equal to 20; page 329.

2. The price Bianca is willing to pay for another purse depends on her marginal utility. Bianca maximizes her total utility by making her marginal utility per dollar equal for all goods. If her marginal utility from an additional purse is high, she is willing to pay a high price for the purse; page 329.

3. The paradox of value is that water, which is essential for life, is cheap while diamonds are relatively useless but expensive. The solution to the paradox is that people consume a lot of water, so the marginal utility of an additional gallon of water is very low. People consume only a few diamonds, so the marginal utility of an additional diamond is quite high. A household maximizes its total when the marginal utility per dollar is equal for all goods. So water has a low marginal utility and a low price, and diamonds have a high marginal utility and a high price; page 329.

Additional Exercise (also in MyEconLab Test A)

1. On the margin, the economics book is more valuable. The marginal utility from the economics book exceeds the marginal utility from another gallon of water. But, the total utility from the economics book is *much* less than the total utility from water. An economist can live without an economics book, but not even an economist can live without water!; page 329.

© 2015 Pearson Education, Inc.

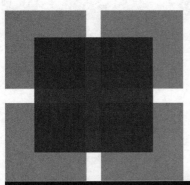

Production and Cost

Chapter 14

1 **Explain and distinguish between the economic and accounting measures of a firm's cost of production and profit.**

A firm's goal is to maximize its profit. The highest-valued alternative forgone is the opportunity cost of a firm's production. An explicit cost is paid in money. An implicit cost is incurred when a firm uses a factor of production but does not make a direct money payment for its use. The return to entrepreneurship is normal profit. A normal profit is part of the firm's costs because it compensates the entrepreneur for not running another business. Total cost is the sum of explicit costs and implicit costs, so it is the opportunity cost of production. A firm's economic profit equals total revenue minus total cost.

2 **Explain the relationship between a firm's output and labor employed in the short run.**

The short run is the time frame in which the quantities of some resources are fixed; the long run is the time frame in which the quantities of all resources can be varied. Marginal product is the change in total product that results from a one-unit increase in the quantity of labor employed. As firms hire labor, initially increasing marginal returns occur but eventually decreasing marginal returns set in. Average product is total product divided by the quantity of an input. When marginal product exceeds the average product, the average product curve slopes upward and average product increases as more labor is employed. And when marginal product is less than average product, the average product curve slopes downward and average product decreases as more labor is employed.

3 **Explain the relationship between a firm's output and costs in the short run.**

Fixed costs are paid to fixed factors of production; variable costs are paid to variable factors of production. Total cost is the sum of total fixed cost and total variable cost. Marginal cost is the change in total cost that results from a one-unit increase in total product. Average total cost is the sum of average fixed cost and average variable cost. The U-shape of the average total cost curve arises from the influence of two opposing forces: spreading total fixed cost over a larger output and decreasing marginal returns. The marginal cost curve intersects the average variable cost and average total cost curves at their minimum points. The average cost curve and the marginal cost curve shift when technology changes or when the price of a factor of production changes.

4 **Derive and explain a firm's long-run average cost curve.**

In the long run, all costs are variable. When a firm changes its plant size, it might experience economies of scale, diseconomies of scale, or constant returns to scale. The long-run average cost curve shows the lowest average total cost at which it is possible to produce each output when the firm has had sufficient time to change both its plant size and labor employed. The long-run average cost curve slopes downward with economies of scale and upward with diseconomies of scale.

© 2012 Pearson Education, Inc. Publishing as Addison Wesley

YOUR AP TEST HINTS

AP Topics

Topic on your AP test	What to Know	Corresponding textbook section
Economic and accounting measures of firms' costs	What are the differences?	Checkpoint 14.1
Short run output versus labor	What is the relationship for a firm?	Checkpoint 14.2
Short run costs versus output	What is the relationship for a firm?	Checkpoint 14.3
Long-run average cost curves	How do firms derive such curves?	Checkpoint 14.4

AP Vocabulary Covered

Terms	What to Know	Text Sections
Explicit cost	A cost paid in money	Checkpoint 14.1, p. 345
Implicit cost	A payment in opportunity costs for the use of a factor of production that doesn't include a direct money payment	Checkpoint 14.1, p. 345
Economic depreciation	An opportunity cost when a firm uses capital that it already owns. This is measured as the change in the market value of capital over time	Checkpoint 14.1, p. 345
Normal profit	Profit considering the opportunity cost for a firm based on the decision to operate the business and give up other options	Checkpoint 14.1, p. 345
Economic profit	Total revenues minus total costs	Checkpoint 14.1, p. 345
Short run (in economics)	The time when firms can't change quantities of resources to react to market changes	Checkpoint 14.2, p. 348
Long run (in economics)	The time when firms can change quantities of resources to react to market changes	Checkpoint 14.2, p. 348
Total product (TP)	Total quantity of a good produced in a stated time period	Checkpoint 14.2, p. 349
Marginal product (MP)	A one unit increase in the quantity of labor gives a MP change in the total product	Checkpoint 14.2, p. 350
Increasing marginal returns	MP of an additional worker exceeds the MP of the previous worker	Checkpoint 14.2, p. 350
Decreasing marginal returns	MP of an additional worker is less than the MP of the previous worker	Checkpoint 14.2, p. 350
Average product (AP)	The total product number divided by the quantity used of a factor of production, or *TP divided by Q of labor*	Checkpoint 14.2, p. 352
Total cost (TC)	All factors of production used by a firm in total, or *TFC plus TVC*	Checkpoint 14.3, p. 355
Total fixed cost (TFC)	The cost of the fixed factors of production for a firm such as land, capital, and entrepreneurship	Checkpoint 14.3, p. 355
Total variable cost (TVC)	The cost of the variable factor of production of labor	Checkpoint 14.3, p. 355
Marginal cost (MC)	The change in total cost that results in increasing output by one more unit	Checkpoint 14.3, p. 356

© 2012 Pearson Education, Inc. Publishing as Addison Wesley

Average fixed cost (*AFC*)	Total fixed cost per unit of production	Checkpoint 14.3, p. 357
Average variable cost (*AVC*)	Total variable cost per unit of output	Checkpoint 14.3, p. 357
Average total cost (*ATC*)	Total cost per unit or *AFC plus AVC*	Checkpoint 14.3, p. 357
Economy of scale	The firm's *ATC* falls as output is increased	Checkpoint 14.4, p. 363
Diseconomy of scale	The firm's *ATC* rises as output increases	Checkpoint 14.4, p. 364
Constant returns to scale	The firm's *ATC* is constant as output increases	Checkpoint 14.4, p. 364
Long-run average cost curve	A curve that shows lowest *ATC* range when the firm can change labor and plant sizes	Checkpoint 14.4, p. 364

Extra AP Materials

- *Normal profit* is a payment made to the entrepreneur to retain his or her services in the business. This is a minimum income that the entrepreneur will accept to stay in business and is a cost to the firm. *Economic profit* is the total revenue minus all of the opportunity costs, which includes the normal profits.

- Firms often have a choice of what combinations of inputs to use and the AP test sometimes asks about this. Firms use the cost-minimizing combination. This is the combination for which the marginal product of an input divided by its price (which equals the cost of producing another unit of output using this input) equals the marginal product divided by the price of all other inputs.

- Keep in mind that the word "marginal" means "change in. Therefore the term "marginal product" equals the *change in* the total product divided by the *change in* labor input.

CHECKPOINT 14.1

■ **Explain and distinguish between the economic and accounting measures of a firm's cost of production and profit.**

Quick Review

- *Explicit cost* A cost paid in money.
- *Implicit cost* A cost incurred by using a factor of production but for which no direct money payment is made.
- *Economic profit* Total revenue minus total opportunity cost. \

Additional Practice Problem 14.1

1. Gary manufactures toy gliders made of balsa wood. Each week, Gary pays $200 in wages, buys balsa wood for $400, pays $50 to lease saws, and pays $150 in rent for the workspace. To fund his operations, Gary withdrew his life's savings, $162,500, from his savings account at the bank, which paid interest of $250 a week. The normal profit for a glider company is $250. Gary sells $1,500 worth of gliders a week.
   a. How much are the weekly explicit costs?
   b. How much are the weekly implicit costs?
   c. What does an accountant compute for the weekly profit?
   d. What does an economist compute for the weekly economic profit?

© 2012 Pearson Education, Inc. Publishing as Addison Wesley

Solution to Additional Practice Problem 14.1

1a. The explicit costs are the wages, the balsa wood, the leased saws and sanders, and rent. The weekly explicit costs are $200 + $400 + $50 + $150, which equal $800.

1b. The implicit costs are the forgone interest and the normal profit. The weekly implicit costs are $250 + $250, which equal $500.

1c. Accountants calculate profit as total revenue minus explicit costs, which is $1,500 − $800 = $700.

1d. Economic profit is total revenue minus total cost. Total cost is the sum of explicit and implicit costs. So Gary's total cost is $800 + $500, which is $1,300. Gary's economic profit equals $1,500 − $1,300, which is $200.

■ AP Self Test 14.1

True or false

1. The firm's goal is to maximize profit.

2. An accountant measures profit as total revenue minus opportunity cost.

3. All of a firm's costs must be paid in money.

4. If a firm earns an economic profit, the return to the entrepreneur exceeds normal profit.

Multiple choice

1. The paramount goal of a firm is to
   a. maximize profit.
   b. maximize sales.
   c. maximize total revenue.
   d. minimize its costs.
   e. force its competitors into bankruptcy.

2. For a business, opportunity cost measures
   a. only the cost of labor and materials.
   b. only the implicit costs of the business.
   c. the cost of all the factors of production the firm employs.
   d. only the explicit costs the firm must pay.
   e. all of the firm's costs including its normal profit *and* its economic profit.

3. Costs paid in money to hire a resource is
   a. normal profit.
   b. an implicit cost.
   c. an explicit cost.
   d. an alternative-use cost.
   e. economic profit.

4. Which of the following is an example of an implicit cost?
   a. wages paid to employees
   b. interest paid to a bank on a building loan
   c. the cost of using capital an owner donates to the business
   d. dollars paid to a supplier for materials used in production
   e. liability insurance payments made only once a year

5. The opportunity cost of a firm using its own capital is
   a. economic depreciation.
   b. self ownership depreciation.
   c. economic loss.
   d. normal loss.
   e. capital loss.

6. The difference between a firm's total revenue and its total cost is its ____ profit.
   a. explicit
   b. normal
   c. economic
   d. accounting
   e. excess

Short Response Questions

1. What is likely to happen to a firm that does not maximize profit?

2. Why are wages a cost to a business? Why is a normal profit a cost to a business?

Long Response Question

1. Bobby quits his job as a veterinarian to open a model train store. Bobby made $80,000 a year as a veterinarian. The first year his train store is open, Bobby pays a helper $26,000. He also pays $24,000 in rent, $10,000 in utilities, and buys $200,000 of model trains. Bobby had a good year because he sold all of his

© 2015 Pearson Education, Inc.

model trains for $300,000. Bobby's normal profit is $30,000.

a. What would an accountant calculate as Bobby's profit?

b. What is Bobby's total opportunity cost? What is his economic profit?

Additional Exercises (also in MyEconLab Test A)

1. In 2009, Toni taught music and earned $20,000. She also earned $4,000 by renting out her basement. On January 1, 2010, she quit teaching, stopped renting out her basement, and began to use it as the office for her new Web site design business. She took $2,000 from her savings account to buy a computer. During 2010, she paid $1,500 for the lease of a Web server and $1,750 for high-speed Internet service. She received a total revenue from Web site designing of $45,000 and earned interest at 5 percent a year on her savings account balance. Normal profit is $55,000 a year. At the end of 2010 Toni could have sold her computer for $500. Calculate Toni's explicit costs, implicit costs, and economic profit in 2010.

CHECKPOINT 14.2

■ **Explain the relationship between a firm's output and labor employed in the short run.**

Quick Review

- *Marginal product* The change in total product that results from a one-unit increase in the quantity of labor employed.
- *Formula for the marginal product* The marginal product equals:

Change in total product÷change in quantity of labor

Additional Practice Problems 14.2

1. Bobby runs a cat grooming service. Bobby hires students to groom the cats. The table to the right shows how many cats Bobby's service can groom when Bobby changes the number of students he hires.

Labor (students per day)	Total product (cats groomed per day)
0	0
1	5
2	12
3	18
4	22
5	25

Labor (students per day)	Average product (cats groomed per day)	Marginal product (cats groomed per day)
1	____	____
2	____	____
3	____	____
4	____	____
5	____	____

a. Complete the table above.

b. Draw Bobby's average product curve and his marginal product curve. When does the marginal product equals the average product?

2. The first five members of the men's basketball squad are each 6 feet tall. A sixth player, whose height is 7 feet, is added. Has the average height increased or decreased with the addition of this player? A seventh player, whose height is 5 feet, is added. What happens to the team's average height? An eighth player, whose height is 6 feet, is added. What is the effect on the average height? What is the general rule about how the marginal player's height changes the average height of the team?

© 2015 Pearson Education, Inc.

Solutions to Additional Practice Problems 14.2

Labor (students per day)	Average product (cats groomed per day)	Marginal product (cats groomed per day)
1	5.0	
		5.0
2	6.0	
		7.0
3	6.0	
		6.0
4	5.5	
		4.0
5	5.0	
		3.0

1a. The completed table is above. The average product equals total product ÷ total labor and the marginal product equals change in total product ÷ change in quantity of labor.

1b. The figure is to the right. The marginal product equals the average product when the average product is at its maximum. Both equal 6 cats groomed per day.

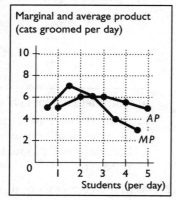

Marginal and average product (cats groomed per day)

2. The 7-foot player is above the average height, so adding him to the team increases the average height. The 5-foot player is below the average height, so adding him decreases the average height. When the 6-foot player is added, the team's average height equals 6 feet, so his addition has no effect on the average height. The general rule is that when a marginal value lies above the average, the average rises. When the marginal value is below the average, the average falls. And when the marginal value equals the average, the average does not change.

■ AP Self Test 14.2

True or false

1. In the short run, the firm's fixed inputs cannot be changed.

2. Points on and below the total product curve are efficient.

3. Most production processes initially have decreasing marginal returns followed eventually by increasing marginal returns.

4. When the marginal product of labor exceeds the average product of labor, the average product curve is downward sloping.

Multiple choice

1. The short run is a time period during which
   a. some of the firm's resources are fixed.
   b. all of the firm's resources are fixed.
   c. all of the firm's resources are variable.
   d. the fixed cost equals zero.
   e. the firm cannot increase its output.

2. In the short run, firms can increase output
   a. only by increasing the size of their plant.
   b. only by decreasing the size of their plant.
   c. only by increasing the amount of labor used.
   d. only by decreasing the amount of labor used.
   e. either increasing the amount of labor used or increasing the size of their plant.

3. Which of the following is correct?
   a. The short run for a firm can be longer than the long run for the same firm.
   b. The short run is the same for all firms.
   c. The long run is the time frame in which the quantities of all resources can be varied.
   d. The long run is the time frame in which all resources are fixed.
   e. The long run does not exist for some firms.

© 2015 Pearson Education, Inc.

4. Marginal product equals
   a. the total product produced by a certain amount of labor.
   b. the change in total product that results from a one-unit increase in the quantity of labor employed.
   c. total product divided by the total quantity of labor.
   d. the amount of labor needed to produce an increase in production.
   e. total product minus the quantity of labor.

5. If 5 workers can wash 30 cars a day and 6 workers can wash 33 cars a day, then the marginal product of the 6th worker equals
   a. 30 cars a day.
   b. 33 cars a day.
   c. 5 cars a day.
   d. 5.5 cars a day.
   e. 3 cars a day.

6. Increasing marginal returns occur when the
   a. average product of an additional worker is less than the average product of the previous worker.
   b. marginal product of an additional worker exceeds the marginal product of the previous worker.
   c. marginal product of labor is less than the average product of labor.
   d. total output of the firm is at its maximum.
   e. total product curve is horizontal.

7. If 25 workers can pick 100 flats of strawberries an hour, then average product is
   a. 100 flats an hour.
   b. 125 flats an hour.
   c. 75 flats an hour.
   d. 4 flats an hour.
   e. More information is needed about how many flats 24 workers can pick.

Short Response Questions
1. The table at the top of the next column gives the total product schedule at Al's Turkey Town Farm.
   a. Complete this table. (The marginal product is entered midway between rows to emphasize that it is the result of changing

Quantity of labor (workers)	Total product (turkeys per day)	Average product (turkeys per worker)	Marginal product (turkeys per worker)
0	0	xx	
			100
1	100	100	
			___
2	300	___	
			___
3	450	___	
			30
4	___	___	
			___
5	___	100	

■ **FIGURE 14.1**

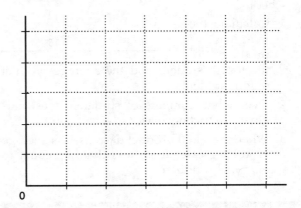

inputs, that is, moving from one row to the next.)
   b. In Figure 14.1 label the axes and plot the marginal product (*MP*) and average product (*AP*) curves. (Plot the *MP* curve midway between the quantities of labor.) Where do the two curves intersect?
   c. When the *MP* curve is above the *AP* curve, is the *AP* curve rising or falling? When the *MP* curve is below the *AP* curve, is the *AP* curve rising or falling?

2. If the marginal product of a new worker exceeds the average product, what happens to the average product?

© 2015 Pearson Education, Inc.

Long Response Questions

1. What is the difference between the short run and the long run?

2. Pizza Hut opens a new store nearby. As the owner adds workers, what happens to their marginal product? Why?

3. What is the law of decreasing returns?

Additional Exercises (also in MyEconLab Test A)

Lizzie hires students in the summer to paint houses. The table sets out her total product schedule.

Labor (students)	Total product (houses painted per week)
0	0
1	2
2	5
3	9
4	12
5	14
6	15

1. Calculate the marginal product of the fourth student and the average product of four students.

2. Over what numbers of students does marginal product decrease?

3. When marginal product decreases, is average product greater than, less than, or equal to marginal product?

CHECKPOINT 14.3

■ **Explain the relationship between a firm's output and costs in the short run.**

Quick Review

- *Total cost* The cost of all the factors of production used by a firm. Total cost equals the sum of total fixed cost and total variable cost.

- *Marginal cost* The cost that arises from a one-unit increase in output.

- *Average total cost* Total cost per unit of output, which equals average fixed cost plus average variable cost as well as total cost divided by output.

Additional Practice Problems 14.3

Labor	Output	TC	MC	TC	MC
0	0	___	___	___	___
1	1	___	___	___	___
2	5	___	___	___	___
3	9	___	___	___	___
4	12	___	___	___	___
5	14	___	___	___	___
6	15	___	___	___	___

1. Pearl owns a company that produces pools. Pearl has total fixed cost of $2,000 a month and pays each of her workers $2,500 a month. The table above shows the number of pools Pearl's company can produce in a month.

   a. Complete the left side of the table.

   b. Suppose that the wage Pearl pays her workers increases to $3,000 a month. Complete the right side of the table.

   c. What was the effect of the wage hike on Pearl's marginal cost?

2. In the figure to the right is an *ATC* curve. In this figure sketch an *AVC* curve and a *MC* curve. Tell what relationships these curves must obey so that they are drawn correctly.

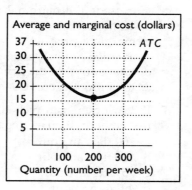

© 2015 Pearson Education, Inc.

Solutions to Additional Practice Problems 14.3

Labor	Output	TC	MC	TC	MC
0	0	2,000		2,000	
			2,500		3,000
1	1	4,500		5,000	
			625		750
2	5	7,000		8,000	
			625		750
3	9	9,500		11,000	
			833		1,000
4	12	12,000		14,000	
			1,250		1,500
5	14	14,500		17,000	
			2,500		3,000
6	15	17,000		20,000	

1a. The completed table is above. Total cost, *TC*, equals the sum of total fixed cost and total variable cost. For example, when Pearl hires 6 workers, total cost is ($2,000) + (6 × $2,500), which is $17,000. Marginal cost equals the change in the total cost divided by the change in output. For example, when output increases from 14 to 15 pools, marginal cost is ($17,000 − $14,500) ÷ (15 − 14), which is $2,500.

1b. The completed table is above.

1c. The increase in the wage rate increased Pearl's marginal cost at every level of output.

2. The completed figure is to the right. To be drawn correctly, there are three requirements: First, the *AVC* curve must reach its minimum at a lower level of output than does the *ATC* curve. Second, the vertical distance between the *ATC* and *AVC* curves must decrease as output increases. Finally the *MC* curve must go through the minimum points on both the *AVC* and *ATC* curves.

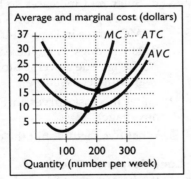

■ AP Self Test 14.3

True or false

1. In the short run, total fixed cost does not change when the firm changes its output.

2. Marginal cost is always less than average total cost.

3. The average total cost curve is U-shaped.

4. An increase in the wage rate shifts the marginal cost curve upward.

Multiple choice

1. Total cost is equal to the sum of
   a. total revenue and total cost.
   b. total variable cost and total product.
   c. total variable cost and total fixed cost.
   d. total fixed cost and total product.
   e. the marginal cost plus the total fixed cost plus the total variable cost.

2. Total fixed cost is the cost of
   a. labor.
   b. production.
   c. a firm's fixed factors of production.
   d. only implicit factors of production.
   e. only explicit factors of production.

3. Jay set up a hot dog stand near the business district. His total variable cost includes the
   a. annual insurance for the hot dog stand.
   b. cost of buying the hot dog stand.
   c. cost of the hot dogs and condiments.
   d. interest he pays on the funds he borrowed to pay for advertising.
   e. revenue he gets when he sells his first hot dog each day.

4. Marginal cost is equal to
   a. the total cost of a firm's production.
   b. total cost minus fixed cost.
   c. a cost that is not related to the quantity produced.
   d. the change in total cost that results from a one-unit increase in output.
   e. the change in fixed cost that results from a one-unit increase in output.

© 2015 Pearson Education, Inc.

5. To produce 10 shirts, the total cost is $80; to produce 11 shirts, the total cost is $99. The marginal cost of the 11th shirt is equal to
   a. $8.
   b. $9.
   c. $80.
   d. $99.
   e. $19.

6. Average total cost equals
   a. marginal cost divided by output.
   b. average fixed cost plus average variable cost.
   c. total fixed cost plus total variable cost.
   d. marginal cost plus opportunity cost.
   e. marginal cost multiplied by the quantity of output.

7. To produce 10 shirts, the total cost is $80; to produce 11 shirts, the total cost is $99. The average total cost of the 11th shirt is equal to
   a. $8.
   b. $9.
   c. $80.
   d. $99.
   e. $19.

8. One of the major reasons for the U-shaped average total cost curve is the fact that
   a. there are increasing returns to labor regardless of the number of workers employed.
   b. there eventually are decreasing returns to labor as more workers are employed.
   c. prices fall as output increases.
   d. the average fixed cost increases as more output is produced.
   e. the variable cost decreases as more output is produced.

Short Response Questions
1. Sue hires workers to produce subs at Sue's Super Supper Sub Shop. Sue pays her workers $10 an hour and has fixed costs of $30 an hour. The table in the next column shows Sue's total product schedule.
   a. Complete the table in the next column.
   b. Using the completed table, plot Sue's ATC and MC curves in Figure 14.2. (Plot the MCs midway between the quantities.)

Labor	Output	TC	ATC	MC
0	0	___	xx	
1	10	___	___	___
2	25	___	___	___
3	35	___	___	___
4	40	___	___	___
5	43	___	___	___
6	45	___	___	___

■ **FIGURE 14.2**

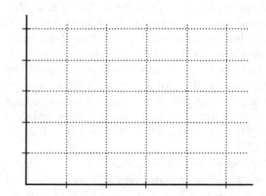

c. Sue's rent increases so her fixed cost rises to $75 an hour. Plot Sue's new ATC and MC curves in Figure 14.2.
d. How does the increase in fixed cost change Sue's average total cost curve? Her marginal cost curve?

2. Label the cost curves in Figure 14.3 (on the next page).
3. What two factors shift the cost curves?

Long Response Questions
1. If a firm closes and produces nothing, does it still have any costs?
2. What is the difference between marginal cost and average total cost?
3. Why is the average total cost curve U-shaped?
4. Where does the marginal cost curve intersect the average variable cost and average total cost curves?

© 2015 Pearson Education, Inc.

■ **FIGURE 14.3**

Total cost (dollars per unit)

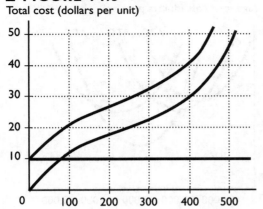

Output (units per hour)

Additional Exercises (also in MyEconLab Test A)

Lizzie hires students at $250 a week to paint houses. She leases equipment that costs her $500 a week. The table shows her total product schedule.

Labor (students)	Total product (houses painted per week)
0	0
1	2
2	5
3	9
4	12
5	14
6	15

1. What is Lizzie's total cost, average total cost, and marginal cost if she paints 12 houses?

2. At what output is Lizzie's average total cost a minimum?

3. Explain why the gap between total cost and total variable cost is the same at all output amounts.

CHECKPOINT 14.4

■ **Derive and explain a firm's long-run average cost curve.**

Quick Review

- *Long-run average cost curve* The long-run average cost curve shows the lowest average cost at which it is possible to produce each output when the firm has had sufficient time to adjust its labor force and its plant.

Additional Practice Problems 14.4

1. The figure shows three average total cost curves for A1 Sewing, a company that sells sewing machines. The company can use three different sized stores, which account for the different cost curves.

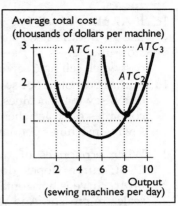

a. Which average cost curve occurs when A-1 uses the smallest store? The largest store?

b. Indicate A1's long-run average cost curve, *LRAC* in the figure.

c. If A1 plans to sell 6 sewing machines per day, what sized store will A1 use?

d. Over what range of output does A1 Sewing have economies of scale? Diseconomies of scale?

2. Describe economies of scale and diseconomies of scale along a long-run average total cost curve.

Solutions to Additional Practice Problems 14.4

1a. When A1 uses the smallest store, its plant size is the smallest and so its average total cost curve is ATC_1 in the figure. When A1 uses the largest store, its plant size is the largest and so its average total cost curve is ATC_2 in the figure.

1b. The long-run average cost curve is the curve that shows the lowest average total cost to produce each output. In the figure to the right, the *LRAC* curve is the

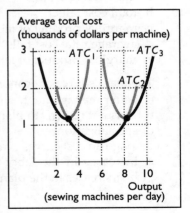

© 2015 Pearson Education, Inc.

darkened parts of the three average total cost curves.

1c. If A1 plans to sell 6 sewing machines, it will use the middle sized store because that is the store that gives it the lowest average total cost when selling 6 sewing machines a day.

1d. A1 has economies of scale when selling from 0 to 6 sewing machines per day. It has diseconomies of scale when it sells more than 6 sewing machines per day.

2. When economies of scale are present, the *LRAC* curve slopes downward. When the *LRAC* curve is horizontal, constant returns to scale are present. And when the *LRAC* curve slopes upward, diseconomies of scale are present.

■ AP Self Test 14.4

True or false

1. All costs are fixed in the long run.

2. When a firm increases its plant size and labor, greater specialization of capital and labor can lead to economies of scale.

3. Constant returns to scale occur when the firm increases its output and its average total cost remains the same.

Multiple choice

1. Economies of scale definitely occur whenever a firm's technology is such that when the firm increases its output, its
   a. marginal cost falls.
   b. total cost falls.
   c. marginal product of labor increases.
   d. average total cost falls.
   e. marginal product of labor decreases.

2. The main source of economies of scale is
   a. better management.
   b. constant returns to plant size.
   c. specialization.
   d. long-run cost curves eventually slope up.
   e. increases in the labor force not matched by increases in the plant size.

■ **FIGURE 14.4**

Average total cost (dollars per unit)

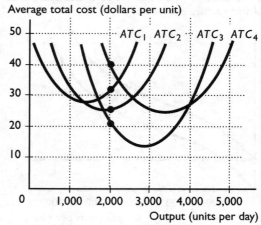

3. Figure 14.4 shows four of a firm's *ATC* curves. If the firm produces 2,000 units per day, it will use the plant size with
   a. *ATC₁*.
   b. *ATC₂*.
   c. *ATC₃*.
   d. *ATC₄*.
   e. either *ATC₁* or *ATC₄*.

4. Diseconomies of scale can occur as a result of which of the following?
   a. increasing marginal returns as the firm increases its size
   b. lower total fixed cost as the firm increases its size
   c. management difficulties as the firm increases its size
   d. greater specialization of labor and capital as the firm increases its size
   e. increases in the labor force not matched by increases in the plant

5. In the long run, constant returns to scale necessarily occur when the firm increases its production and the firm's
   a. total cost increases.
   b. total cost does not change.
   c. average total cost increases.
   d. average total cost does not change.
   e. production increases by more than does the firm's total cost.

© 2015 Pearson Education, Inc.

6. A firm's long-run average cost curve shows the ____ average cost at which it is possible to produce each output when the firm has had ____ time to change both its labor force and its plant.
   a. highest; sufficient
   b. lowest; sufficient
   c. lowest; insufficient
   d. highest insufficient
   e. average; sufficient

7. Economies of scale and diseconomies of scale explain
   a. cost behavior in the short run.
   b. profit maximization in the long run.
   c. the U-shape of the long-run cost curve.
   d. the U-shape of the short-run cost curves.
   e. the U-shape of the marginal cost curves.

Short Response Question

■ **FIGURE 14.5**

Average total cost (dollars per unit)

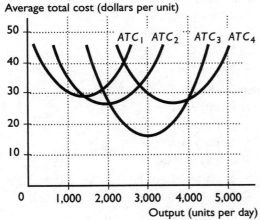

1. In Figure 14.5, darken the firm's long-run average total cost curve. Show over which range of output the firm has economies of scale and over which range of output the firm has diseconomies of scale.

Long Response Questions

1. Describe how a long-run average cost curve is constructed.

2. What are economies of scale? What leads to economies of scale?

Additional Exercises (also in MyEconLab Test A)

Lizzie hires students at $50 a day to paint houses. She leases equipment that costs her $100 a day. Suppose that Lizzie doubles the number of students she hires and doubles the amount of equipment that she leases. Lizzie experiences diseconomies of scale.

1. Explain how Lizzie's average total cost curve with one unit of equipment differs from that when she uses double the amount of equipment.

2. Explain what might be the source of Lizzie's diseconomies of scale.

© 2015 Pearson Education, Inc.

SELF TEST ANSWERS

■ AP Self Test 14.1

True or false
1. True; page 344
2. False; page 344
3. False; page 345
4. True; pages 345-346

Multiple choice
1. a; page 344
2. c; page 344
3. c; page 345
4. c; page 345
5. a; page 345
6. c; page 345

Short Response Questions
1. A firm that does not seek to maximize profit is either driven out of business or bought by firms that do seek that goal; page 344.
2. Wages are a cost because they are paid to hire a factor of production, labor. A normal profit is a cost because it is paid to obtain the use of another factor of production, entrepreneurship; page 345.

Long Response Question
1. a. An accountant calculates profit as total revenue minus explicit costs. Bobby's explicit costs are $26,000 + $24,000 + $10,000 + $200,000, which equals $260,000. The accountant calculates profit as $300,000 − $260,000, which is $40,000; page 344.
   b. Bobby's opportunity cost is the sum of his explicit costs and his implicit costs. Bobby's explicit costs are $260,000. His implicit costs are the sum of his income forgone as a veterinarian, $80,000, and normal profit, $30,000. So Bobby's implicit costs are $110,000. His total opportunity cost is $260,000 + $110,000, which is $370,000. Bobby's economic profit is his total revenue minus his opportunity cost, which is $300,000 − $370,000 = −$70,000. Bobby incurs an economic loss; pages 345-346.

Additional Exercise (also in MyEconLab Test A)
1. Explicit costs are the $1,500 for the lease of a Web server and $1,750 for high-speed Internet service. The total explicit costs are $3,250. Implicit costs are the $20,000 in wages forgone, $4,000 in rent forgone, $100 in forgone interest payments on the savings, $55,000 in normal profit, and $1,500 in economic depreciation for the computer. The total implicit costs are $80,600.

   The economic profit equals total revenue minus total opportunity costs, which is $45,000 − ($3,250 + $80,600) = −$38,850. Toni incurred an economic loss of $38,850 for the year; pages 345-346.

■ AP Self Test 14.2

True or false
1. True; page 348
2. False; page 350
3. False; page 350
4. False; pages 352-353

Multiple choice
1. a; page 348
2. c; page 348
3. c; page 348
4. b; pages 350-351
5. e; pages 350-351
6. b; page 350
7. d; page 352

Short Response Questions
1. a. The completed table is on the next page; pages 349-352.
   b. Figure 14.6 (on the next page) plots the *MP* and *AP* curves. The curves intersect where the *AP* curve is at its maximum; page 352.
   c. When the *MP* curve is above the *AP* curve, the *AP* curve is rising. When the *MP* curve is below the *AP* curve, the *AP* curve is falling; pages 352-353.

© 2015 Pearson Education, Inc.

Quantity of labor	Total product (turkeys per day)	Average product (turkeys per worker)	Marginal product (turkeys per worker)
0	0	xx	
			100
1	100	100	
			200
2	300	150	
			150
3	450	150	
			30
4	480	120	
			20
5	500	100	

■ **FIGURE 14.6**

Total product (turkeys per day)

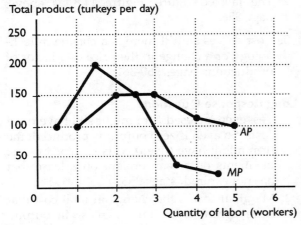

2. If the marginal product of a worker exceeds the average product, then hiring the worker will increase the average product; page 353.

Long Response Questions

1. The short run is the time frame in which the quantities of some resources (the plant) are fixed. The long run is the time frame in which the quantities of *all* resources can be changed; page 348.

2. As Pizza Hut initially adds workers, the marginal product of each additional worker exceeds the marginal product of the previous worker. The marginal product increases because the workers can specialize. Some workers can make the pizzas and others can deliver them. As more workers are added,

eventually the marginal product of each additional worker is less than the marginal product of the previous worker. The marginal product decreases because more workers are using the same equipment, so there is less productive work for each new worker; page 350.

3. The law of decreasing returns states that as a firm uses more of a variable input, with a given quantity of fixed inputs, the marginal product of the variable input eventually decreases; page 352.

Additional Exercises (also in MyEconLab Test A)

1. The marginal product of the fourth student is the change in total product that results from hiring the fourth student. The total product with 3 students is 9 houses painted a week and the total product with 4 students is 12 houses painted a week. The marginal product of the fourth student is 12 houses painted a week minus 9 houses painted a week, or 3 houses painted a week. The average product equals total product divided by the number of students. When 4 students are hired, the average product is 12 houses painted a week divided by 4 students, which equals 3 houses painted a week; pages 350-352.

2. The marginal product decreases between 4 and 6 students; pages 351-352.

3. When the marginal product, though decreasing, exceeds the average product the average product increases as more workers are hired. Eventually as the marginal product decreases it becomes less than the average product. When the marginal product is less than the average product, the average product decreases as more workers are hired; pages 352-353.

■ **AP Self Test 14.3**

True or false

1. True; page 355
2. False; page 358
3. True; page 358
4. True; page 361

© 2015 Pearson Education, Inc.

Multiple choice

1. c; page 355
2. c; page 355
3. c; page 355
4. d; page 356
5. e; page 356
6. b; page 357
7 b; page 357
8. b; page 359

Short Response Questions

Labor	Output	TC	ATC	MC
0	0	<u>30</u>	xx	
				<u>1.00</u>
1	10	<u>40</u>	<u>4.00</u>	
				<u>0.67</u>
2	25	<u>50</u>	<u>2.00</u>	
				<u>1.00</u>
3	35	<u>60</u>	<u>1.71</u>	
				<u>2.00</u>
4	40	<u>70</u>	<u>1.75</u>	
				<u>3.33</u>
5	43	<u>80</u>	<u>1.86</u>	
				<u>5.00</u>
6	45	<u>90</u>	<u>2.00</u>	

■ FIGURE 14.7

Average and marginal cost (dollars per sub)

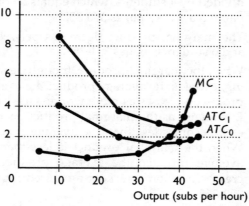

1. a. The completed table is above; page 355.
   b. Figure 14.7 plots the curves as ATC_0 and MC.
   c. Figure 14.7 plots the new curves as ATC_1 and MC; page 357.
   d. The average cost curve shifts upward; the marginal cost curve does not change; page 360.

■ FIGURE 14.8

Total cost (dollars per unit)

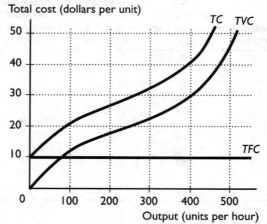

Output (units per hour)

2. The labeled figure, Figure 14.8, is above; page 356.

3. Cost curves shift if there is a change in technology or a change in the price of a factor of production; pages 360-361.

Long Response Questions

1. Yes, even a closed firm might still have fixed costs. So even if zero output is produced, the firm might have (fixed) costs such as interest payments on a loan or rent on a lease that has not expired; page 355

2. Marginal cost is the change in total cost that results from a one-unit increase in output. Average total cost is total cost per unit of output, which equals average fixed cost plus average variable cost; pages 356-357.

3. When output increases, the firm spreads its total fixed cost over a larger output and its average fixed cost decreases—its average fixed cost curve slopes downward.

   Decreasing marginal returns means that as output increases, ever larger amounts of labor are needed to produce an additional unit of output. So average variable cost eventually increases, and the AVC curve eventually slopes upward.

   Initially as output increases, both average fixed cost and average variable cost decrease, so average total cost decreases and the ATC curve slopes downward. But as output in-

© 2015 Pearson Education, Inc.

creases further and decreasing marginal returns set in, average variable cost begins to increase. Eventually, average variable cost increases more quickly than average fixed cost decreases, so average total cost increases and the *ATC* curve slopes upward; page 359.

4. The marginal cost curve intersects the average variable cost curve and the average total cost curve at the point where they are the minimum; page 358.

Additional Exercises (also in MyEconLab Test A)

1. When Lizzie paints 12 houses a week, she must hire 4 students. These 4 students create a variable cost of $1,000. Lizzie has fixed costs of $500, so her total cost for painting 12 houses a week is $1,500. Here average total cost is equal to $1,500 ÷ 12 houses, which is $125. Her marginal cost equals the change in total cost divided by the change in the number of houses painted. Going from 9 to 12 houses, the total cost when 9 houses are painted is $1,250 so the change in total cost is $250. The change in the number of houses painted is 3. So the marginal cost is $250 ÷ 3, which is $83.33. Going from 12 to 14, the total cost when 14 houses are painted is $1,750 so the change in total cost is $250. The change in the number of houses is painted is 2. So the marginal cost is $250 ÷ 2, which is $125.00. So averaging these two marginal costs numbers, Lizzie's marginal cost of painting the 12th house is $104.17; pages 355-357.

2. Lizzie's average total cost is at its minimum when she paints 12 or 14 houses a week. At these output levels, her average total cost is $125; page 355.

3. The difference between the total cost and total variable cost is equal to total fixed cost because total cost equals total variable cost plus total fixed cost. Since total fixed cost does not change as output changes, the gap is the same at all outputs; page 356.

■ AP Self Test 14.4

True or false

1. False; page 363
2. True; page 363
3. True; page 364

Multiple choice

1. d; page 363
2. c; page 363
3. c; pages 364-365
4. c; page 364
5. d; page 364
6. b page 364
7. c; pages 364-365

Short Response Question

■ FIGURE 14.9

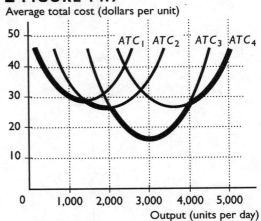
Average total cost (dollars per unit)

1. Figure 14.9 darkens the firm's long-run average total cost curve. The firm has economies of scale at all output levels less than 3,000 and has diseconomies of scale at all output levels greater than 3,000; pages 364-365.

Long Response Questions

1. A long-run average cost curve is a curve that shows the lowest average total cost at which it is possible to produce each output when the firm has had sufficient time to change both its plant size and labor employed. Suppose a newspaper publisher can operate with four different plant sizes. The segment of each of the four average total cost curves for

© 2015 Pearson Education, Inc.

which that plant has the lowest average total cost is the scallop-shaped curve that is the long-run average cost curve; page 364.

2. Economies of scale is a feature of the firm's technology so that in the long run when output increases the firm's average total cost falls. The main source of economies of scale is greater specialization of both labor and capital (specialization of capital is a source of economies of scale because in the long run the firm can change the amount it uses of both labor and capital); page 363.

Additional Exercises (also in MyEconLab Test A)

1. At low levels of production, Lizzie's average total cost curve with one unit of equipment lies below her average total cost curve with two units of equipment. At higher levels of production, however, Lizzie's average total cost curve with one unit of equipment lies above her average total cost curve with two units of equipment; pages 363-364.

2. The source of her diseconomies of scale could be management problems when she hires more students and leases more equipment. Trying to organize more equipment and more students across different houses in different areas of the town requires more communication and coordination. If she is unable to manage the larger firm as efficiently as she was able to manage the small firm, she has diseconomies of scale; page 364.

© 2015 Pearson Education, Inc.

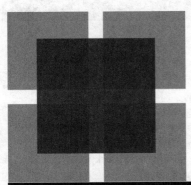

Chapter

15

Perfect Competition

In Chapter 15 we study perfect competition, the market in which firms face the maximum amount of competition.

1   Explain a perfectly competitive firm's profit-maximizing choices and derive its supply curve.

Perfect competition exists when: many firms sell an identical product to many buyers; there are no restrictions on entry into (or exit from) the market; established firms have no advantage over new firms; and sellers and buyers are well informed about prices. A firm in perfect competition is a price taker—it cannot influence the price of its product. The *market* demand curve is downward sloping. But a perfectly competitive firm faces a perfectly elastic demand so the *firm's* demand curve is horizontal. Marginal revenue, *MR*, is the change in total revenue that results from a one-unit increase in the quantity sold. In perfect competition, marginal revenue equals price. A firm maximizes its profit by producing the quantity of output at which total revenue exceeds total cost by the largest amount. Another way to find the profit-maximizing output is to use marginal analysis. A firm maximizes its profit by producing the quantity of output at which marginal revenue equals marginal cost. If a firm shuts down, it incurs a loss equal to its total fixed cost. The shutdown point is the price that equals the minimum average variable cost. A firm's supply curve is its marginal cost curve above minimum average variable cost.

2   Explain how output, price, and profit are determined in the short run.

The market supply curve in the short run shows the quantity supplied at each price by a fixed number of firms. Market demand and market supply determine the market price and quantity bought and sold. Each firm takes the price as given and produces its profit-maximizing output. When price equals the average total cost, a firm makes zero economic profit, that is, its owners earn a normal profit. The firm makes an economic profit when price exceeds average total cost and incurs an economic loss when price is less than average total cost.

3   Explain how output, price, and profit are determined in the long run and explain why perfect competition is efficient.

Economic profit is an incentive for new firms to enter a market, but as they do so, the price falls and the economic profit of each existing firm decreases. Economic loss is an incentive for firms to exit a market, and as they do so the price rises and the economic loss of each remaining firm decreases. In the long run, a firm makes zero economic profit and there is no entry or exit. In a market undergoing technological change, firms that adopt the new technology make an economic profit. Firms that stick with the old technology incur economic losses. They either exit the market or switch to the new technology. Competition eliminates economic profit in the long run. Perfect competition is efficient because in a perfectly competitive market the market demand curve is the same as the marginal benefit curve and the market supply curve is the same as the (market's) marginal cost curve.

© 2015 Pearson Education, Inc.

YOUR AP TEST HINTS

AP Topics

Topic on your AP test	What to Know	Corresponding textbook section
Market types	Characteristics of perfect competition, monopoly, monopolistic competition, and oligopoly	Checkpoint 15.1
Perfectly competitive firm	What defines the market and how supply curves are created	Checkpoint 15.1
Short-run outcomes	In the short run, perfectly competitive firms can earn an economic profit, zero economic profit, or incur an economic loss	Checkpoint 15.2
Long-run outcome	In the long run, entry and exit mean a perfectly competitive firm earns zero economic profit	Checkpoint 15.3

AP Vocabulary Covered

Terms	What to Know	Text Sections
Price taker	Firms in a perfect competition must set their price equal to the market price	Checkpoint 15.1, p. 373
Marginal revenue	The change in TR that results from a one unit increase in quantity sold	Checkpoint 15.1, p. 373
Profit-maximizing output	The output at which marginal revenue equals marginal cost, $MR = MC$	Checkpoint 15.1, p. 374
Shutdown point	The minimum point on the AVC curve	Checkpoint 15.1, p. 377
Short-run equilibrium	In the short run, perfectly competitive firms can make an economic profit ($P > ATC$), can make zero economic profit ($P = ATC$), or incur an economic loss ($P < ATC$).	Checkpoint 15.2, p. 382
Long-run equilibrium	If firms are making an economic profit, entry of new firms occurs; if they are incurring an economic loss, exit of some occurs. In the long run entry and exit lead to zero economic profit (the owners receive a normal profit).	Checkpoint 15.3, p. 387

Extra AP material

- The result that maximizing profit requires producing the quantity for which $MR = MC$ is one of the most important points in this chapter.
- If a firm closes, its loss equals its fixed costs. Remember that firms will operate at a loss as long as those losses are less than the firm's fixed costs. Operating at a temporary loss that is less than the fixed cost is not as bad as incurring a loss equal to the entire fixed costs.
- The amount of profit the firm makes depends on its price and average total cost. If $P = ATC$ (so that the ATC curve is tangent to the MR line) the firm earns zero economic profit. If $P > ATC$ (so that the ATC dips below the MR line) the firm makes an economic profit. Finally, if $P < ATC$ (so that the ATC curve lies above the MR line) the firm incurs an economic loss. Analysis of these graphs is central to any micro course and the AP exam materials.

© 2015 Pearson Education, Inc.

CHECKPOINT 15.1

■ **Explain a perfectly competitive firm's profit-maximizing choices and derive its supply curve.**

Quick Review

- *MC = MR* Profit is maximized when production is such that marginal cost equals marginal revenue.
- *A firm's short-run supply curve* At prices less than its minimum average variable cost, the firm shuts down. At prices above the minimum average variable cost, the firm's supply curve is the marginal cost curve.
- *Shutdown point* The price at which price equals the minimum average variable cost.

Additional Practice Problem 15.1

1. Patricia is a perfectly competitive wheat farmer. Her average variable cost curve and her marginal cost are shown in the figure.

   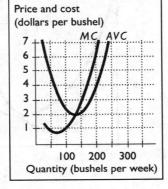

   a. If the price of a bushel of wheat is $6 per bushel, how much wheat will Patricia produce?

   b. If the price of a bushel of wheat falls to $4 per bushel, how much wheat will Patricia produce?

   c. What are two points on Patricia's supply curve?

   d. What is the lowest price for which Patricia will produce wheat rather than shut down?

   e. Suppose that when the price of a bushel of wheat is $6, Patricia produces a quantity of wheat such that her marginal revenue is greater than marginal cost. Explain why she is not maximizing her profit.

Solutions to Additional Practice Problem 15.1

1a. When the price of a bushel of wheat is $6 per bushel, Patricia's marginal revenue curve is shown in the figure as MR_1. To maximize her profit, Patricia produces 200 bushels of wheat, the quantity at which marginal revenue equals marginal cost.

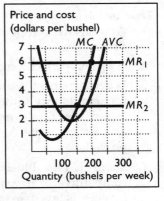

1b. If the price of wheat falls to $3 per bushel, Patricia's marginal revenue curve is shown in the figure as MR_2. She decreases the quantity of wheat she produces to 150 bushels per week because that is the quantity at which marginal revenue equals marginal cost.

1c. One point on Patricia's supply curve is a price of $6 and 200 bushels. Another point is a price of $3 and a quantity of 150 bushels.

1d. The lowest price for which Patricia produces rather than shuts down is the price equal to her minimum average variable cost. The figure shows that this price is equal to $2 per bushel.

1e. If marginal revenue exceeds marginal cost, then the extra revenue from selling one more bushel of wheat exceeds the extra cost incurred to produce it. So if Patricia produces one more bushel of wheat, the marginal revenue that she receives from selling that bushel is greater than the cost to produce that bushel and this bushel increases her profit. To maximize profit, Patricia must increase her output until she reaches the point where the marginal revenue equals the marginal cost.

© 2015 Pearson Education, Inc.

■ AP Self Test 15.1

True or false

1. A perfectly competitive market has many firms.

2. A firm in perfect competition is a price taker.

3. When a perfectly competitive firm is maximizing its profit, the vertical difference between the firm's marginal revenue curve and its marginal cost curve is as large as possible.

4. Stan's U-Pick blueberry farm, a perfectly competitive firm, will shut down if its total revenue is less than its total cost.

5. A perfectly competitive firm's short-run supply curve is its average total cost above minimum average variable cost.

Multiple choice

1. The four market types are
   a. perfect competition, imperfect competition, monopoly, and oligopoly.
   b. oligopoly, monopsony, monopoly, and imperfect competition.
   c. perfect competition, monopoly, monopolistic competition, and oligopoly.
   d. oligopoly, oligopolistic competition, monopoly, and perfect competition.
   e. perfect competition, imperfect competition, monopoly, and duopoly.

2. A perfectly competitive firm is a price taker because
   a. many other firms produce the same product.
   b. only one firm produces the product.
   c. many firms produce a slightly differentiated product.
   d. a few firms compete.
   e. it faces a vertical demand curve.

3. The demand curve faced by a perfectly competitive firm is
   a. horizontal.
   b. vertical.
   c. downward sloping.
   d. upward sloping.
   e. U-shaped.

4. For a perfectly competitive corn grower in Nebraska, the marginal revenue curve is
   a. downward sloping.
   b. the same as its demand curve.
   c. upward sloping.
   d. U-shaped.
   e. vertical at the profit maximizing quantity of production.

5. A perfectly competitive firm maximizes its profit by producing at the point where
   a. total revenue equals total cost.
   b. marginal revenue is equal to marginal cost.
   c. total revenue is equal to marginal revenue.
   d. total cost is at its minimum.
   e. total revenue is at its maximum.

■ FIGURE 15.1

Price and cost (dollars per shirt)

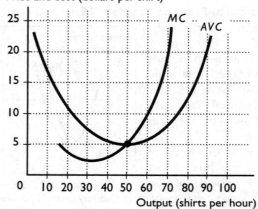

6. Figure 15.1 shows cost curves for Wring Around the Collar, a perfectly competitive dry cleaner. If the price of dry cleaning a shirt is $20 per shirt, the firm will dry clean _____ shirts per hour.
   a. 0
   b. between 1 and 49
   c. 50
   d. 60
   e. 61 or more.

© 2015 Pearson Education, Inc.

7. In Figure 15.1, if the price of dry cleaning a shirt is $10 per shirt, the firm will dry clear ____ shirts per hour.
   a. 0
   b. between 1 and 49
   c. 50
   d. 60
   e. 61 or more

8. Based on Figure 15.1, the lowest price for which the company might remain open is
   a. $25 per shirt.
   b. $20 per shirt.
   c. $15 per shirt.
   d. $10 per shirt.
   e. $5 per shirt.

9. If the market price is lower than a perfectly competitive firm's average total cost, the firm will
   a. immediately shut down.
   b. continue to produce if the price exceeds the average fixed cost.
   c. continue to produce if the price exceeds the average variable cost.
   d. shut down if the price exceeds the average fixed cost.
   e. shut down if the price is less than the average fixed cost.

10. One part of a perfectly competitive trout farm's supply curve is its
    a. marginal cost curve below the shutdown point.
    b. entire marginal cost curve.
    c. marginal cost curve above the shutdown point.
    d. average variable cost curve above the shutdown point.
    e. marginal revenue curve above the demand curve.

Short Response Questions

1. What are the conditions that define perfect competition?

2. What is a "price taker"? Why are perfectly competitive firms price takers?

3. Willy, a perfectly competitive wheat farmer, can sell 999 bushels of wheat for $3 per bushel or 1,000 bushels for $3 per bushel. What is Willy's marginal revenue and total revenue if he sells 1,000 bushels of wheat?

■ FIGURE 15.2

Price and cost (dollars per unit)

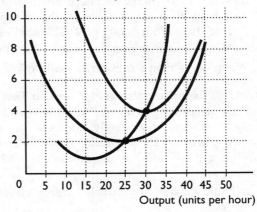

4. Figure 15.2 shows a perfectly competitive firm's cost curves.
   a. Label the curves.
   b. If the market price is $8, what is the firm's equilibrium output and price?
   c. If the market price is $4, what is the firm's equilibrium output and price?
   d. What is the firm's shutdown price?
   e. Darken the firm's supply curve.

Long Response Questions

1. What is the difference between a perfectly competitive firm's demand curve and the market demand curve?

Quantity (hogs)	Total cost (dollars)	Total revenue (dollars)	Economic profit (dollars)
0	300	___	___
1	350	___	___
2	425	___	___
3	575	___	___
4	825	___	___
5	1,200	___	___

2. Peter owns Peter's Porkers, a small hog farm. The above table gives Peter's total cost schedule. Peter is in a perfectly competitive market and can sell each hog for $200.
   a. Complete the table.

© 2015 Pearson Education, Inc.

b. What is Peter's profit-maximizing number of hogs and what price will Peter set?

c. When Peter increases his production from 2 hogs to 3 hogs, what is the marginal cost? Is the third hog profitable for Peter?

d. When Peter increases his production from 3 hogs to 4 hogs, what is the marginal cost? Is the fourth hog profitable for Peter?

e. What is the marginal cost of the third hog?

3. When will a firm temporarily shut down?

Additional Exercises (also in MyEconLab Test A)

Paula is an asparagus farmer, and the world asparagus market is perfectly competitive. The market price is $15 a bundle. Paula sells 800 bundles a week and her marginal cost is $18 a bundle.

1. Is Paula maximizing profit? Explain your answer.

2. The price falls to $12 a bundle, and Paula cuts her output to 500 bundles a week. Her average variable cost and marginal cost fall to $12 a bundle. Is Paula maximizing profit? Is she making an economic profit or a loss?

3. What is one point on Paula's supply curve?

CHECKPOINT 15.2

■ **Explain how output, price, and profit are determined in the short run.**

Quick Review

- *Economic profit* If the market price exceeds the average total cost, the firm makes an economic profit.

- *Economic loss* If the market price is less than the average total cost, the firm incurs an economic loss.

- *Zero economic profit* If the market price equals the average total cost ($P = ATC$), the firm makes zero economic profit and the owners receive a normal profit.

Additional Practice Problem 15.2

Quantity (roses per week)	Average total cost	Marginal cost
	(dollars per rose)	
100	2.00	1.50
200	1.50	1.50
300	1.67	2.50
400	2.00	5.00

1. Growing roses is a perfectly competitive industry. There are 100 rose growers and all have the same cost curves. The above table gives the costs of one of the growers, Rosita's Roses. The market demand schedule for roses is in the table to the right.

Price (dollars per rose)	Quantity (roses per week)
1.00	50,000
1.50	45,000
2.00	40,000
2.50	30,000
3.00	20,000

a. Plot the market supply curve and the market demand curve in the figure.

b. What is the equilibrium price of a rose?

c. How many roses does Rosita produce? What is her economic profit or loss?

Price and cost (dollars per rose)

6
5
4
3
2
1

10 20 30 40 50
Quantity
(thousands of roses per week)

Solution to Additional Practice Problem 15.2

1a. The market demand curve and market supply curve are plotted in the figure. The quantity supplied in the market at any price is the sum of the quantities supplied by each firm at that price. Because each firm is identical, the market quantity supplied is 100 times the quantity supplied by any one firm. The firm's supply curve is its marginal cost curve above the

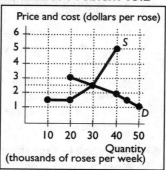

Price and cost (dollars per rose)

6
5
4
3
2
1

10 20 30 40 50
Quantity
(thousands of roses per week)

© 2015 Pearson Education, Inc.

minimum average variable cost. For instance, when the price is $2.50 a rose, Rosita's marginal cost schedule shows she will supply 300 roses a week. So the quantity supplied in the market equals 100 × (300 roses a week), which is 30,000 roses a week.

1b. The figure shows that the equilibrium market price of a rose is $2.50.

1c. In the short run, a firm can make an economic profit or incur an economic loss. A firm makes an economic profit when price exceeds average total cost and incurs an economic loss when price is less than average total cost. In the case at hand, Rosita produces 300 roses. Rosita makes an economic profit. Rosita's economic profit per rose equals the price of a rose minus the average total cost, which is $2.50 − $1.67 = $0.83. She produces 300 roses, a week so her total economic profit is (300 roses a week) × ($0.83) = $249 a week.

■ AP Self Test 15.2

True or false

1. The market supply curve in the short run shows the quantity supplied at each price by a fixed number of firms.

2. Market supply in a perfectly competitive market is perfectly elastic at all prices.

3. A perfectly competitive firm makes an economic profit if price equals average total cost.

4. In a perfectly competitive industry, a firm's economic profit is equal to price minus marginal revenue multiplied by quantity.

5. A perfectly competitive firm has an economic loss if price is less than the marginal cost.

Multiple choice

1. If the market supply curve and market demand curve for a good intersect at 600,000 units and there are 10,000 identical firms in the market, then each firm is producing
   a. 600,000 units.
   b. 60,000,000,000 units.
   c. 60,000 units.
   d. 60 units.
   e. 10,000 units.

2. In the short run, a perfectly competitive firm
   a. must make an economic profit.
   b. must incur an economic loss.
   c. must make zero economic profit.
   d. might make an economic profit, an economic loss, or zero economic profit.
   e. None of the above answers is correct.

3. A perfectly competitive firm definitely makes an economic profit in the short run if price is
   a. equal to marginal cost.
   b. equal to average total cost.
   c. greater than average total cost.
   d. greater than marginal cost.
   e. greater than average variable cost.

4. If a perfectly competitive firm is maximizing its profit and is making an economic profit, which of the following is correct?
   i.   price equals marginal revenue
   ii. marginal revenue equals marginal cost
   iii. price is greater than average total cost
   a. i only.
   b. i and ii only.
   c. ii and iii only.
   d. i and iii only.
   e. i, ii, and iii.

© 2015 Pearson Education, Inc.

■ **FIGURE 15.3**

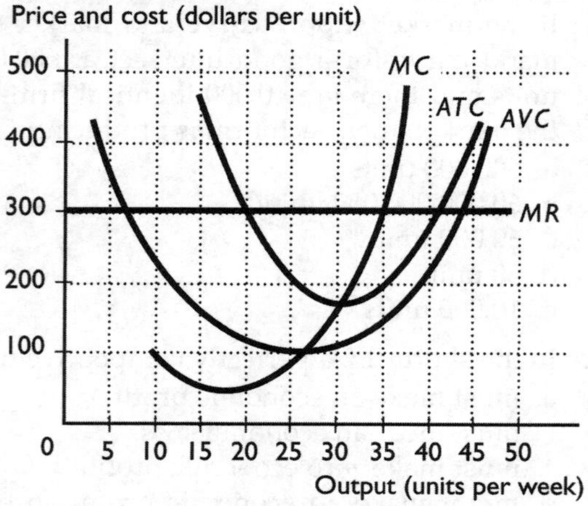

Price and cost (dollars per unit)

5. Figure 15.3 shows the marginal revenue and cost curves for a perfectly competitive firm. The firm
   a. is incurring an economic loss.
   b. will shut down and will incur an economic loss.
   c. will shut down and will make zero economic profit.
   d. is making zero economic profit.
   e. is making an economic profit.

6. The market for watermelons in Alabama is perfectly competitive. A watermelon producer making zero economic profit could make an economic profit if the
   a. average total cost of selling watermelons does not change.
   b. average total cost of selling watermelons falls.
   c. average total cost of selling watermelons rises.
   d. marginal cost of selling watermelons does not change.
   e. marginal cost of selling watermelons rises.

7. Juan's Software Service Company is in a perfectly competitive market. Juan's total fixed cost is $25,000, average variable cost for 1,000 service calls is $45, and marginal revenue is $75. Juan's makes 1,000 service calls a month. What is his economic profit?
   a. $5,000
   b. $25,000
   c. $45,000
   d. $75,000
   e. $50,000

8. If a perfectly competitive firm finds that price is less than its *ATC*, then the firm
   a. will raise its price to increase its economic profit.
   b. will lower its price to increase its economic profit.
   c. is making an economic profit.
   d. is incurring an economic loss.
   e. is making zero economic profit.

9. A perfectly competitive furniture-rental firm in Phoenix incurs an economic loss if the average total cost of each rental is
   a. greater than the price of each rental.
   b. less than the marginal cost of each rental.
   c. equal to the marginal revenue of each rental.
   d. equal to the price of each rental.
   e. greater than the average variable cost of each rental.

© 2015 Pearson Education, Inc.

Short Response Questions

■ FIGURE 15.4

Price and cost (dollars per lawn)

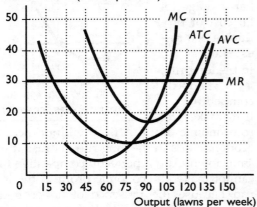

Output (lawns per week)

1. Moe's Mowers is a perfectly competitive lawn mowing company. Moe's costs and marginal revenue are illustrated in Figure 15.4.
   a. How many lawns does Moe's mow?
   b. Is Moe's making an economic profit or incurring an economic loss? Darken the area that shows the economic profit or loss. What is the amount of economic profit or loss?

■ FIGURE 15.5

Price and cost (dollars per lawn)

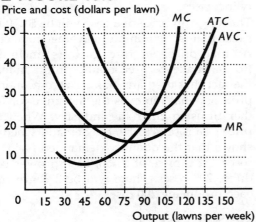

Output (lawns per week)

2. Larry's Lawns is (another) perfectly competitive lawn mowing company in another city. Larry's costs and marginal revenue are illustrated in Figure 15.5.
   a. How many lawns does Larry's mow?

b. Is Larry's making an economic profit or incurring an economic loss? Darken the area that shows the economic profit or loss. In the short run, will Larry's remain open or shut down?

Long Response Questions

1. In a perfectly competitive market, how is the market supply calculated?
2. If price is less than average total cost, is the firm making an economic profit or incurring an economic loss?

Additional Exercises (also in MyEconLab Test A)

Tom's Tattoos is a tattooing business in a perfectly competitive market in Miami. The price of a tattoo is $20. The table shows Tom's total costs.

Quantity (tattoos per hour)	Total cost (dollars per hour)
0	30
1	50
2	65
3	75
4	90
5	110
6	140

1. How many tattoos an hour does Tom's Tattoos sell? What is Tom's Tattoos' economic profit in the short run?
2. If the market price of a tattoo falls to $15, how many tattoos an hour does Tom's Tattoos sell? What is Tom's Tattoos' economic profit in the short run?
3. At what market price will Tom's Tattoos shut down? If Tom's Tattoos shuts down temporarily, what is its economic loss?

CHECKPOINT 15.3

■ **Explain how output, price, and profit are determined in the long run and explain why perfect competition is efficient.**

Quick Review

- *Entry* Economic profit is an incentive for new firms to enter a market, but as they do so, the price falls and the economic

© 2015 Pearson Education, Inc.

profit of each existing firm decreases.

- *Exit* Economic loss is an incentive for firms to exit a market, but as they do so, the price rises and the economic loss of each remaining firm decreases.

Additional Practice Problem 15.3

Quantity (roses per week)	Average total cost (dollars)	Marginal cost (dollars)
100	2.00	1.50
200	1.50	1.50
300	1.67	2.50
400	2.00	5.00

1. Growing roses is a perfectly competitive industry. Initially there are 100 rose growers and all have the same cost curves. The above table gives the costs of one of the growers, Rosita's Roses. The table to the right has the market demand schedule for roses. The price for a rose initially is $2.50.

Price (dollars per rose)	Quantity (roses per week)
1.00	50,000
1.50	45,000
2.00	40,000
2.50	30,000
3.00	20,000

a. Plot Rosita's marginal cost curve and her marginal revenue curve in the figure to the right. Is Rosita making an economic profit or is Rosita incurring an economic loss?

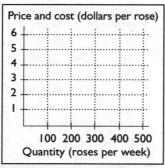

Price and cost (dollars per rose)

b. As time passes, what takes place in the market?

c. What will be the long-run price of a rose? What will be Rosita's profit in the long run? In the long run, how many growers will be in the market?

Solutions to Additional Practice Problem 15.3

1a. The figure shows Rosita's marginal cost curve and marginal revenue curve. The figure shows that she is producing 300 roses a week. Rosita is making an economic profit

because the price of a rose, $2.50, exceeds her average total cost of producing 300 roses, $1.67.

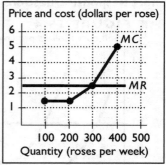

Price and cost (dollars per rose)

1b. In the long run, a perfectly competitive firm makes zero economic profit. A firm will not incur an economic loss in the long run because it will shut down. And a perfectly competitive firm cannot make an economic profit in the long run because the presence of an economic profit attracts entry, which drives down the price and eliminates economic profit. Competitive firms cannot prevent entry into their market and so they cannot protect any economic profit.

In the case of the rose growers, rose growers are making an economic profit, so more rose growers enter the market. The supply of roses increases and the market supply curve shifts rightward. The equilibrium price of a rose falls and the market equilibrium quantity increases.

1c. The long-run price of a rose will be $1.50 because that is the minimum average total cost. At that price, all rose growers, including Rosita, make zero economic profit. Indeed, the fact that they are making zero economic profit is what removes the incentive for further firms to enter the industry. When the price of a rose is $1.50, the demand schedule shows that the quantity demanded is 45,000 roses. At a price of $1.50, each grower produces 200 roses. There will be 225 growers, each producing 200 roses.

■ AP Self Test 15.3

True or false

1. When the price equals average total cost, the firm makes zero economic profit.

2. Entry into a perfectly competitive market lowers the price.

© 2015 Pearson Education, Inc.

3. In the long run, firms respond to an economic loss by exiting a perfectly competitive market.

4. New technology shifts a firm's cost curves upward and the market supply curve leftward.

5. Perfect competition is efficient because the efficient quantity is produced.

Multiple choice

1. In the long run, new firms enter a perfectly competitive market when
   a. normal profit is greater than zero.
   b. economic profit is equal to zero.
   c. normal profit is equal to zero.
   d. economic profit is greater than zero.
   e. the existing firms are weak because they are incurring economic losses.

2. If perfectly competitive firms are making an economic profit, the economic profit
   a. attracts entry by more firms, which lowers the price.
   b. can be made both in the short run and the long run.
   c. is greater than the price.
   d. leads to a decrease in market demand.
   e. generally leads firms to exit as they seek higher profit in other markets.

3. If perfectly competitive firms are making an economic profit, then
   a. the market is in its long-run equilibrium.
   b. new firms enter the market and the economic profit of the firms already in the market decreases.
   c. new firms enter the market and the economic profit of the firms already in the market increases.
   d. firms exit the market and the economic profit of the surviving firms in the market decreases.
   e. firms exit the market and the economic profit of the surviving firms in the market increases.

4. Firms exit a competitive market when they incur an economic loss. In the long run, this exit means that the economic losses of the surviving firms
   a. increase.
   b. decrease until they equal zero.
   c. decrease until economic profits are made.
   d. do not change.
   e. might change but more information is needed about what happens to the price of the good as the firms exit.

5. If firms in a perfectly competitive market incur economic losses, then as time passes firms ____ and the market ____.
   a. enter; demand curve shifts leftward
   b. enter; supply curve shifts rightward
   c. exit; demand curve shifts leftward
   d. exit; supply curve shifts rightward
   e. exit; supply curve shifts leftward

6. As a result of firms leaving the perfectly competitive frozen yogurt market in the early 2000s, the market
   a. supply curve shifted leftward.
   b. supply curve did not change.
   c. demand curve shifted rightward.
   d. supply curve shifted rightward.
   e. demand curve shifted rightward.

7. In the long run, a firm in a perfectly competitive market will
   a. make zero economic profit, so that its owners earn a normal profit.
   b. make zero normal profit but its owners will make an economic profit.
   c. remove all competitors and become a monopolistically competitive firm.
   d. incur a normal loss but will make a positive economic profit.
   e. remove all competitors and become a monopoly.

8. Technological change brings a ____ to firms that adopt the new technology.
   a. permanent economic profit
   b. temporary economic profit
   c. permanent economic loss
   d. temporary economic loss
   e. None of the above answers is correct.

© 2015 Pearson Education, Inc.

Short Response Questions

■ FIGURE 15.6

Price and cost (dollars per unit)

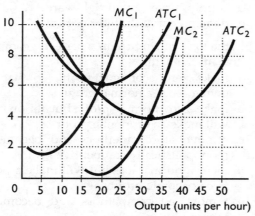

1. In Figure 15.6, suppose that the price of the good is $20. Show the long-run equilibrium for a perfectly competitive firm that produces 150 units per week.

■ FIGURE 15.7

Price and cost (dollars per unit)

2. Figure 15.7 shows cost curves for two firms in an industry undergoing technological change. Firm 1 uses the old technology and has an average total cost curve ATC_1 and marginal cost curve MC_1. Firm 2 uses the new technology and has an average total cost curve ATC_2 and marginal cost curve MC_2. Initially the price of the product was $6.

a. At the price of $6, do firm 1 and firm 2 make an economic profit, zero economic profit, or incur economic loss?

b. As more firms adopt the new technology, what happens to market supply and price? Do firms 1 and 2 make an economic profit, zero economic profit, or incur an economic loss?

c. In the long run, what will be the new price? Will firm 1 make an economic profit, zero economic profit, or incur an economic loss? Will firm 2 make an economic profit, zero economic profit, or incur an economic loss?

Long Response Questions

1. Why are perfectly competitive firms unable to make an economic profit in the long run? Why won't they incur an economic loss in the long run?

2. Is perfect competition efficient?

3. The Eye on Your Life discusses how competition benefits you by leading to the production of the vast array of goods and services you consume. Competition also benefits you by affecting the prices you pay for goods and services. The market for home delivered pizza is extremely competitive. How does this competition affect the price you pay for home delivered pizza?

Additional Exercises (also in MyEconLab Test A)

Tom's Tattoos is a tattooing business in a perfectly competitive market in Miami. The table shows Tom's total costs.

Quantity (tattoos per hour)	Total cost (dollars per hour)
0	30
1	50
2	65
3	75
4	90
5	110
6	140

1. If the market price is $20 a tattoo, what is Tom's economic profit in the short run? Do new firms enter or existing firms exit the industry in the long run?

© 2015 Pearson Education, Inc.

2. In the long run, what is the price of a tattoo, how many tattoos per hour does Tom sell, and what is Tom's economic profit?

3. If an advance in Tattoo technology lowers the fixed cost of tattooing to $10 an hour, how does the price and quantity change in the short run and in the long run? Does the number of firms producing tattoos increase, decrease, or remain the same?

© 2015 Pearson Education, Inc.

SELF TEST ANSWERS

■ AP Self Test 15.1

True or false

1. True; page 372
2. True; page 373
3. False; page 376
4. False; page 377
5. False; pages 378-379

Multiple choice

1. c; page 372
2. a; page 373
3. a; page 374
4. b; page 374
5. b; page 376
6. e; page 376
7. d; page 376
8. e; pages 377-378
9. c; pages 377-378
10. c; pages 378-379

Short Response Questions

1. Perfect competition exists when many firms sell an identical product to many buyers; there are no restrictions on entry into (or exit from) the market; established firms have no advantage over new firms; and sellers and buyers are well informed about prices; page 372.

2. A price taker is a firm that cannot influence the price of the good or service it produces. Perfectly competitive firms are price takers because there are many competing firms selling an identical product. Any individual firm is such a small part of the market that its actions cannot affect the price; page 373.

3. Willy's marginal revenue equals the price of a bushel of wheat, which is $3. His total revenue equals price multiplied by quantity, which is $3,000; page 375.

4. a. Figure 15.8 labels the curves; page 378.
   b. Output is 35 units and the price is $8; page 376.
   c. Output is 30 units and the price is $4; page 376.

■ FIGURE 15.8

Price and cost (dollars per unit)

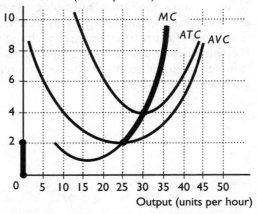

d. The shutdown price is $2; pages 377-378.
e. The firm's supply curve is darkened in Figure 15.8; page 379.

Long Response Questions

1. A perfectly competitive firm's demand is perfectly elastic because all sellers produce goods that are perfect substitutes. So the firm's demand curve is horizontal. The market demand curve is downward sloping; page 374.

Quantity (hogs)	Total cost (dollars)	Total revenue (dollars)	Economic profit (dollars)
0	300	0	−300
1	350	200	−150
2	425	400	−25
3	575	600	25
4	825	800	−25
5	1,200	1,000	−200

2. a. The completed table is above; page 375.
   b. The profit-maximizing number of hogs is 3. Peter charges $200 a hog; page 375.
   c. The marginal cost is the change in total cost that results from producing the third hog. So marginal cost is $150. This is a profitable hog because the marginal revenue from the hog exceeds its marginal cost; page 376.

© 2015 Pearson Education, Inc.

d. The marginal cost is $250. This hog is not profitable; page 376.

e. The marginal cost of the third hog is $200, which is the average of the marginal cost of increasing production from 2 to 3 hogs and of increasing production from 3 to 4 hogs. The marginal cost of the third hog equals the marginal revenue so 3 hogs is the profit-maximizing output; page 376.

3. If a firm shuts down, it incurs an economic loss equal to total fixed cost. If the firm produces some output, it incurs an economic loss equal to total fixed cost plus total variable cost minus total revenue. If total revenue exceeds total variable cost, the firm's economic loss is less than total fixed cost. It pays the firm to produce. But if total revenue is less than total variable cost, the firm's economic loss exceeds total fixed cost. The firm shuts down; pages 377-378.

Additional Exercises (also in MyEconLab Test A)

1. The market is perfectly competitive, so Paula's marginal revenue equals the price, $15 a box. Paula is not maximizing profit because marginal cost ($18) is greater than marginal revenue ($15). She should decrease her production until marginal cost falls to $15 because then her marginal cost equals her marginal revenue and she would maximize her profit; page 376.

2. If the price is $12 a box, Paula's marginal revenue is $12 a box. Paula is maximizing profit by selling 500 boxes a week because marginal cost equals the marginal revenue. Paula is incurring an economic loss if she has any fixed costs because in that case price is less than average total cost; pages 376-377.

3. One point on Paula's supply curve is a price of $12 and quantity of 500 boxes a week. The combination of a price of $15 and quantity of 800 boxes a week is *not* on Paula's supply curve because at that combination she is not maximizing her profit. So this combination is only temporary because Paula will change her production in order to maximize her profit; pages 378-379.

■ AP Self Test 15.2

True or false
1. True; page 381
2. False; page 381
3. False; page 382
4. False; page 383
5. False; page 384

Multiple choice
1. d; page 381
2. d; pages 382-384
3. c; page 383
4. e; page 383
5. e; page 383
6. c; page 383
7. a; page 383
8. d; page 384
9. a; page 384

Short Response Questions

■ FIGURE 15.9
Price and cost (dollars per lawn)

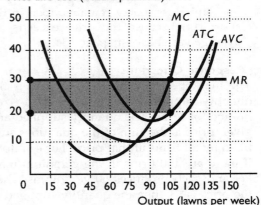

1. a. Moe mows 105 lawns per week because that is the quantity at which marginal revenue equals marginal cost; page 376.

   b. Moe makes an economic profit. Figure 15.9 illustrates the economic profit. The economic profit per lawn equals price minus average total cost, which is $30 − $20 = $10 per lawn. The quantity is 105 lawns, so the total economic profit equals ($10 per

© 2015 Pearson Education, Inc.

lawn) × (105 lawns), which is $1,050 a week; page 383.

■ **FIGURE 15.10**

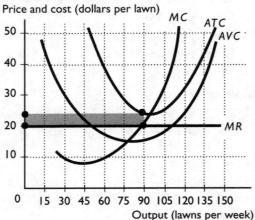

Price and cost (dollars per lawn)

2. a. Larry mows 90 lawns per day because that is the quantity at which marginal revenue equals marginal cost; page 386.

   b. Larry has an economic loss. Figure 15.10 illustrates the economic loss as the darkened rectangle. Even though he has an economic loss, Larry remains open in the short run because the price exceeds his average variable cost; page 384.

Long Response Questions

1. The market supply in the short run is the quantity supplied at each price by a fixed number of firms. The quantity supplied at a given price is the sum of the quantities supplied by all firms at that price. For example, if there are 100 firms in the geranium market and each produces 50 geraniums when the price is $3, then the quantity supplied in the market at $3 is 5,000 geraniums; page 381.

2. The firm incurs an economic loss. If the price is less than average total cost, the firm incurs an economic loss on each unit produced and so has an overall economic loss; page 384.

Additional Exercises (also in MyEconLab Test A)

1. If the market price is $20 a tattoo, the marginal revenue is $20 a tattoo. The marginal cost of the fifth tattoo is the total cost of 5 tattoos minus the total cost of 4 tattoos, which is $110 − $90 = $20. So, Tom sells 5 tattoos an hour because the marginal cost of the fifth tattoo, $20, equals the marginal revenue.

   The average total cost of a tattoo equals the total cost divided by the quantity of tattoos, or $110 ÷ 5 tattoos = $22 a tattoo. The price of a tattoo is $20 a tattoo, so Tom makes an economic "profit" of $20 minus $22, which is −$2 a tattoo. Tom sells 5 tattoos an hour, so his total economic "profit" equals −$2 × 5 tattoos, which is −$10. Tom incurs an economic loss of $10 an hour; pages 376, 384.

2. If the market price falls to $15 a tattoo, the marginal revenue is $15 a tattoo. If Tom remains open, the marginal cost of the fourth tattoo is the total cost of 4 tattoos minus the total cost of 3 tattoos, which is $90 − $75 = $15. So, Tom sells 4 tattoos an hour because the marginal cost of the fourth tattoo, $15, equals the marginal revenue. Alternatively, Tom might shut down and produce 0 because the price, $15, is the same as the minimum average variable cost.

   If Tom remains open, the average total cost of a tattoo equals the total cost divided by the quantity of tattoos, which is $90 ÷ 4 tattoos = $22.50 a tattoo. The price of a tattoo is $15, so Tom makes an economic "profit" of $15.00 minus $22.50, which is −$7.50 a tattoo. Tom sells 4 tattoos an hour, so his total economic "profit" equals −$7.50 × 4 tattoos, which is −$30. Tom incurs an economic loss of $30 an hour. Alternatively, if Tom shuts down, then Tom's economic loss equals his fixed cost, $30. Tom's loss is the same regardless of whether he remains open or shuts down; pages 376-377, 384.

3. The price at which Tom shuts down equals minimum average *variable* cost. Average variable cost equals total variable cost divided by the quantity produced. And, total

© 2015 Pearson Education, Inc.

variable cost equals total cost minus fixed cost. Tom's total fixed cost is $30, his total cost when zero tattoos are produced. When Tom produces 4 tattoos, his total variable cost is $90 − $30, which is $60 and so his average variable cost is $60 ÷ 4 = $15. This is the minimum average variable cost. As a result, Tom shuts down at any price less than $15 a tattoo.

When Tom shuts down, his loss equals his total fixed cost, which is $30; pages 377, 384.

■ AP Self Test 15.3

True or false
1. True; page 386
2. True; pages 387-388
3. True; pages 388-389
4. False; page 389
5. True; page 392

Multiple choice
1. d; page 387
2. a; pages 387-388
3. b; pages 387-388
4. b; pages 388-389
5. e; pages 388-389
6. a; page 388
7. a; pages 387-389
8. b; page 389

Short Response Questions
1. Figure 15.11 shows a perfectly competitive firm in long-run equilibrium. The marginal revenue curve is horizontal at the price of $20. The firm produces 150 units because that is the quantity at which marginal revenue equals marginal cost. The firm makes zero economic profit because the price, $20 per unit, equals the average total cost, also $20 per unit; page 386.

2. a. At the price of $6, the marginal revenue curve is MR_1 in Figure 15.12. Firm 1 produces 20 units and makes zero economic profit because the $6 price equals average

■ **FIGURE 15.11**

Price and cost (dollars per unit)

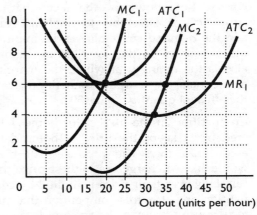

total cost. Firm 2 produces 35 units and makes an economic profit because the $6 price exceeds average total cost; pages 386, 389.

b. Market supply increases and the price falls. Firm 1 now incurs an economic loss and Firm 2 makes a smaller economic profit; page 390.

c. In the long run, the new price will be $4 because that is the minimum of the new average total cost. Firm 1 will either have adopted the new technology and be making zero economic profit or will have exited the industry. Firm 2 will make zero economic profit; page 390.

© 2015 Pearson Education, Inc.

Long Response Questions

1. Perfectly competitive firms cannot make an economic profit in the long run because the existence of an economic profit invites entry by new firms. As these new firms enter, the market supply increases, driving down the price and eventually eliminating the economic profit. If perfectly competitive firms incur an economic loss, they close because no firm will incur an economic loss in the long run. As some firms close, the price rises and the economic loss of the surviving firms decreases and is eventually eliminated when enough firms have closed; pages 387-389.

2. Perfect competition is efficient. In a perfectly competitive market, equilibrium occurs at the intersection of the supply and demand curves. Key, however, the facts that the supply curve also is the marginal cost curve and the demand curve also is the marginal benefit curve. So the equilibrium quantity also is the quantity at which the marginal cost equals the marginal benefit, which is the efficient quantity; page 392.

3. Competition in the market for home delivered pizza keeps the price of home delivered pizza low. The producers of pizza would like to charge the highest price they can. However their price is limited by competition and it is this competition that protects you by keeping the price of home delivered pizza low.

Additional Exercises (also in MyEconLab Test A)

1. If the market price is $20 a tattoo, marginal revenue equals $20 a tattoo. The marginal cost of the fifth tattoo is the total cost of 5 tattoos minus the total cost of 4 tattoos, which is $110 − $90 = $20. So, Tom sells 5 tattoos an hour because the marginal cost of the fifth tattoo, $20, equals the marginal revenue. The average total cost of a tattoo equals the total cost divided by the quantity of tattoos, which is $110 ÷ 5 tattoos = $22 a tattoo. The price of a tattoo is $20 a tattoo, so Tom makes an economic "profit" of $20 minus $22, which is −$2 a tattoo. Tom sells 5 tattoos an hour, so his total economic "profit" equals −$2 × 5 tattoos, which is −$10. Tom incurs an economic loss of $10. Because firms are incurring an economic loss, tattoo firms exit the industry; pages 386-387.

2. In the long run, the price is equal to minimum average total cost, which is $22 a tattoo. In the long run, Tom sells five tattoos an hour because at this quantity price equals minimum average total cost. In the long run, Tom makes zero economic profit; page 386.

3. The decrease in the fixed cost does not change Tom's marginal cost schedule, so in the short run there is no change in the price or quantity. In the long run, however, the number of firms producing tattoos increases because the existing firms make an economic profit as a result of the lower fixed costs. The new long-run price is $17.50 a tattoo, the minimum of the new, lower average total cost; page 390.

© 2015 Pearson Education, Inc.

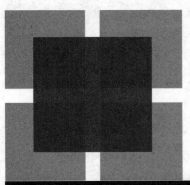

Monopoly

Chapter

16

CHAPTER CHECKLIST

In Chapter 16 we study how a monopoly chooses its price and quantity, discuss whether a monopoly is efficient or fair, and investigate how monopolies can be regulated.

1 Explain how monopoly arises and distinguish between single-price monopoly and price-discriminating monopoly.

A monopoly is a market with a single supplier of a good or service that has no close substitutes and in which natural, ownership, or legal barriers to entry prevent competition. A single-price monopoly is a monopoly that sells each unit of its output for the same price to all its customers. A price-discriminating monopoly is a monopoly that is able to sell different units of a good or service for different prices.

2 Explain how a single-price monopoly determines its output and price.

The demand curve for a monopoly is the downward sloping market demand curve. For a single-price monopoly, marginal revenue is less than price, so the marginal revenue curve lies below the demand curve. A monopoly maximizes profit by producing the quantity at which marginal revenue equals marginal cost and finding the highest price at which it can sell this output on the demand curve.

3 Compare the performance of a single-price monopoly with that of perfect competition.

Compared to perfect competition, a single-price monopoly produces a smaller output and charges a higher price. A monopoly is inefficient because it creates a deadweight loss. A monopoly redistributes consumer surplus so that the producer gains and the consumers lose. Rent seeking is the act of obtaining special treatment by the government to create an economic profit or divert consumer surplus or producer surplus away from others. Rent seeking aims to restrict competition and create a monopoly.

4 Explain how price discrimination increases profit.

To be able to price discriminate, a firm must be able to identify and separate different types of buyers and sell a product that cannot be resold. Price discrimination converts consumer surplus into economic profit, so price discrimination increases the firm's profit. Perfect price discrimination leaves no consumer surplus but is efficient.

5 Explain why natural monopoly is regulated and the effects of regulation.

Regulation sets the prices a regulated firm can charge. The social interest theory of regulation is that regulation seeks an efficient use of resources. The capture theory is that regulation helps producers maximize economic profit. Natural monopolies are usually regulated. A marginal cost pricing rule sets price equal to marginal cost and achieves an efficient level of output but the regulated firm incurs an economic loss. An average cost pricing rule sets price equal to average total cost. The firm makes zero economic profit, but there is a deadweight loss. Rate of return regulation sets the price so that the firm earns a target rate of return on its capital. Price cap regulation specifies the highest price the firm can set.

© 2015 Pearson Education, Inc.

YOUR AP TEST HINTS

AP Topics

Topic on your AP test	What to Know	Corresponding textbook section
Monopoly	How they arise and the two types	Checkpoint 16.1
Single-price monopoly	Profit-maximizing price and quantity produced	Checkpoint 16.2
Monopoly versus perfect competition	Output, price, efficiency, rent-seeking, and fairness	Checkpoint 16.3
Price discrimination	How profit is increased	Checkpoint 16.4
Monopoly regulation	Regulation schemes and efficiency	Checkpoint 16.5

AP Vocabulary Covered

Terms	What to Know	Text Sections
Barrier to entry	A constraint that protects the firm from entry by new competitors; barriers to entry can be legal barriers, ownership barriers, or natural barriers (cost-related)	Checkpoint 16.1, p. 400
Natural monopoly	One company meets market demand at a lower *ATC* than could two or more companies	Checkpoint 16.1, p. 400
Legal monopoly	Government legal limits are in place against competition	Checkpoint 16.1, p. 401
Single price monopoly	Each unit is sold at the same price to all customers	Checkpoint 16.1, p. 402
Price-discriminating monopoly	Different units are sold for different prices not related to cost differences	Checkpoint 16.1, p. 402
Monopoly profit maximization	To maximize profit, a monopoly produces the quantity at which $MR = MC$ and sets its price from its demand curve	Checkpoint 16.2, p. 407
Monopoly versus perfect competition	A monopoly sets a higher price, produces a smaller quantity, and creates a deadweight loss	Checkpoint 16.3, p. 410
Rent seeking	Lobbying to create economic profit or divert consumer and producer surpluses away from others	Checkpoint 16.3, p. 411
Perfect price discrimination	Charging the highest price consumers are willing to pay to gain the maximum consumer surplus	Checkpoint 16.4, p. 416

Extra AP material

- Students must give a great deal of attention to the basic figures (Figure 14.7 and Figure 15.4b in the text) to learn the differences, especially the difference in the marginal revenue curve.
- On the AP test, three factors are deemed necessary to price discriminate. The first factor is "ability to segment the market," which means the ability to identify and separate different types of buyers. The second condition is "no resale of the good or service." The "no resale" condition is sometimes called "no arbitrage." And the third condition is that there must be some market power, that is, the firm must be able to set the price it charges. This last requirement means that firms in perfect competition cannot price discriminate because they are price takers and have no influence over the price they charge. Discriminating among groups of buyers is related to the elasticity of demand: Buyers with an inelastic demand pay a higher price than buyers with an elastic demand.
- On the AP test, a marginal cost pricing rule can be termed as setting the "social optimum price." An average cost pricing can be called the "fair return price."

© 2015 Pearson Education, Inc.

CHECKPOINT 16.1

■ **Explain how monopoly arises and distinguish between single-price monopoly and price-discriminating monopoly.**

Quick Review

- *Barrier to entry* Any constraint that protects a firm from competitors.

Additional Practice Problem 16.1

1. What is the source of the monopoly for each of the following situations? What sort of barrier to entry protects these producers?
    a. The U.S. Postal Service has a monopoly on first class mail delivery.
    b. DeBeer's controls about 80 percent of the world's diamond sales.
    c. Tampa Electric is the only electric utility company supplying power to Tampa, Florida.

Solutions to Additional Practice Problem 16.1

1a. The U.S. Postal Service derives its monopoly status by a government franchise to deliver first class mail. So the U.S. Postal Service is protected by a legal barrier to entry. Though it retains its franchise on first class mail delivery, it faces competition from the overnight services provided by FedEx, United Parcel Service, and others.

1b. DeBeers gained its monopoly power in diamond sales by buying up supplies of diamonds from sources throughout the world. So DeBeers is protected by an ownership barrier to entry.

1c. Tampa Electric has been granted a public franchise to be the only distributor of electricity in Tampa. Although Tampa Electric might be a natural monopoly, the public franchise, a legal barrier to entry, is perhaps the most immediate source of monopoly.

■ **AP Self Test 16.1**

True or false

1. A legal barrier creates a natural monopoly.

2. A firm experiences economies of scale along a downward-sloping long-run average total cost curve.

3. A monopoly always charges all customers the same price.

Multiple choice

1. A monopoly market has
    a. a few firms.
    b. a single firm.
    c. two dominating firms in the market.
    d. only two firms in it.
    e. some unspecified number of firms in it.

2. A natural monopoly is one that arises from
    a. patent law.
    b. copyright law.
    c. a firm buying all of a natural resource.
    d. economies of scale.
    e. ownership of a natural resource.

3. A legal barrier is created when a firm
    a. has economies of scale, which allow it to produce at a lower cost than two or more firms.
    b. is granted a public franchise, government license, patent, or copyright.
    c. produces a unique product or service.
    d. produces a standardized product or service.
    e. has an ownership barrier to entry.

4. Pizza producers charge one price for a single pizza and almost give away a second one. This is an example of
    a. monopoly.
    b. a barrier to entry.
    c. behavior that is not profit-maximizing.
    d. price discrimination.
    e. rent seeking.

Short Response Questions

1. What conditions define monopoly?
2. What are the two types of barriers to entry?

Long Response Question

1. What are the two pricing strategies a monopoly can use? Why don't perfectly competitive firms have these same strategies?

© 2015 Pearson Education, Inc.

Additional Exercises (also in MyEconLab Test A)

The following list has five different firms:

- A department store in a large downtown Houston shopping mall
- Tiffany, the upscale jeweler
- Wal-Mart
- The only shoe-shine stand licensed to operate in St. Louis airport
- The U.S. Postal Service

1. Which of the five firms are monopolies?

2. Which of the firms are natural monopolies and which are legal monopolies? Which can price discriminate, which cannot, and why?

CHECKPOINT 16.2

■ **Explain how a single-price monopoly determines its output and price.**

Quick Review

- *Marginal revenue* The change in total revenue resulting from a one-unit increase in the quantity sold.
- *Maximize profit* A single-price monopoly maximizes its profit by producing where $MR = MC$ and then using the demand curve to determine the price for this quantity of output.

Additional Practice Problems 16.2

Quantity (pizzas per hour)	Total cost (dollars per pizza)	ATC (dollars per pizza)	MC (dollars per pizza)
0	1.00		
1	6.00	___	___
2	13.00	___	___
3	22.00	___	___
4	33.00	___	___

1. In a small town, Leonardo's Pizza is the sole restaurant. The table above gives Leonardo's total cost schedule. Complete the table.

Quantity demanded (pizzas per hour)	Price (dollars per pizza)	MR (dollars per pizza)
0	16.00	
1	14.00	___
2	12.00	___
3	10.00	___
4	8.00	___

2. The table above gives the demand schedule for Leonardo's pizzas. Complete the table.

3. In a figure, plot Leonardo's demand curve, average total cost curve, marginal cost curve, and marginal revenue curve.

   a. What is Leonardo's equilibrium quantity and price?

   b. What is Leonardo's economic profit or loss? In the figure show the economic profit or loss.

Solutions to Additional Practice Problems 16.2

Quantity (pizzas per hour)	Total cost (dollars per pizza)	ATC (dollars per pizza)	MC (dollars per pizza)
0	1.00		
			5.00
1	6.00	6.00	
			7.00
2	13.00	6.50	
			9.00
3	22.00	7.33	
			11.00
4	33.00	8.25	

1. The completed table is above.

Quantity demanded (pizzas per hour)	Price (dollars per pizza)	Marginal revenue (dollars per pizza)
0	16.00	
		14.00
1	14.00	
		10.00
2	12.00	
		6.00
3	10.00	
		2.00
4	8.00	

2. The completed table is above.

© 2015 Pearson Education, Inc.

3. The figure shows Leonardo's demand curve, average total cost curve, marginal cost curve, and marginal revenue curve.

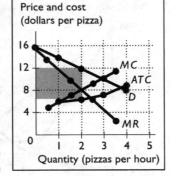

Price and cost (dollars per pizza)

3a. Both a monopoly and a perfectly competitive firm maximize their profit by producing the quantity at which marginal revenue equals marginal cost. So Leonardo's maximizes its profit by producing 2 pizzas per hour. The price, from the demand curve, is $12 per pizza.

3b. Leonardo's sells each pizza for $12.00. The average total cost for 2 pizzas is $6.50. So for each pizza Leonardo's makes an economic profit of $5.50 for a total economic profit of $5.50 per pizza × 2 pizzas, or $11.00. This economic profit is equal to the area of the darkened rectangle in the figure.

■ AP Self Test 16.2

True or false

1. For a single-price monopoly, marginal revenue exceeds price.

2. Marginal revenue is always positive for a monopoly.

3. A single-price monopoly maximizes profit by producing the quantity at which marginal revenue equals marginal cost.

Multiple choice

1. For a single-price monopoly, price is
   a. greater than marginal revenue.
   b. one half of marginal revenue.
   c. equal to marginal revenue.
   d. unrelated to marginal revenue.
   e. always less than average total cost when the firm maximizes its profit.

2. A single-price monopoly can sell 1 unit for $9.00. To sell 2 units, the price must be $8.50 per unit. The marginal revenue from selling the second unit is
   a. $17.50.
   b. $17.00.
   c. $8.50.
   d. $8.00.
   e. $9.00.

3. When demand is elastic, marginal revenue is
   a. positive.
   b. negative.
   c. zero.
   d. increasing as output increases.
   e. undefined.

4. To maximize its profit, a single-price monopoly produces the quantity at which
   a. the difference between marginal revenue and marginal cost is as large as possible.
   b. marginal revenue equals marginal cost.
   c. average total cost is at its minimum.
   d. the marginal cost curve intersects the demand curve.
   e. the marginal revenue curve intersects the horizontal axis.

5. Once a monopoly has determined how much it produces, it will charge a price that
   a. is determined by the intersection of the marginal cost and average total cost curves.
   b. minimizes marginal cost.
   c. is determined by its demand curve.
   d. is independent of the amount produced.
   e. is equal to its average total cost.

Short Response Questions

1. What is the relationship between the elasticity of demand and marginal revenue?

© 2015 Pearson Education, Inc.

Quantity (hamburgers per hour)	Price (dollars)	Marginal revenue (dollars)
1	8.00	
2	7.00	———
3	6.00	———
4	5.00	———
5	4.00	———

■ FIGURE 16.1

Price and marginal revenue (dollars per hamburger)

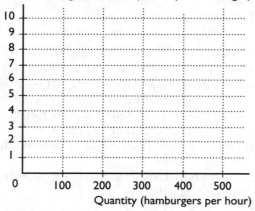

2. The table above gives the demand schedule for Bud's Burgers, a monopoly seller of hamburgers in a small town. Complete the table by calculating the marginal revenue.

a. In Figure 16.1 draw the demand curve and marginal revenue curve.

b. Suppose the marginal cost is $3 no matter how many hamburgers Bud's produces. Draw the marginal cost curve in the figure. To maximize his profit, how many burgers will Bud grill in an hour and what will be their price?

3. Figure 16.2 shows a monopoly's cost curves and its demand and marginal revenue curves. Label the curves. Identify the profit-maximizing quantity price. Is the monopoly making an economic profit or incurring an economic loss? Darken the area that shows the economic profit or economic loss.

■ FIGURE 16.2

Price and cost (dollars per unit)

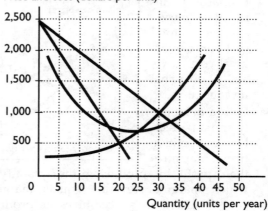

Long Response Questions

1. Both perfectly competitive and monopoly firms maximize their profit by producing where $MR = MC$. Why do both use the same rule?

2. Why can a monopoly make an economic profit in the long run?

Additional Exercises (also in MyEconLab Test A)

Price (thousands of dollars per ride)	Quantity (rides per month)	Total revenue (thousands of dollars per month)	Marginal revenue (thousands of dollars per ride)
220	0	0	
			200
200	1	200	
			160
180	2	360	
			120
160	3	480	
			80
140	4	560	
			40
120	5	600	

HotAir Balloon Rides is a single-price monopoly. The table shows the demand schedule for balloon rides (columns 1 and 2) and HotAir's total cost schedule (columns 2 and 3).

1. Calculate HotAir's total revenue and marginal revenue schedules.

2. Draw the demand curve and HotAir's marginal revenue curve.

© 2015 Pearson Education, Inc.

3. Calculate HotAir's profit-maximizing output, price, and economic profit.

4. If the government imposes a fixed tax of $60,000 a month on HotAir, what are the new profit-maximizing output, price, and economic profit?

5. If instead of imposing a fixed tax on HotAir, the government taxes HotAir by $30,000 per ride, what are the new profit-maximizing output, price, and economic profit?

CHECKPOINT 16.3

■ **Compare the performance of a single-price monopoly with that of perfect competition.**

Quick Review

* *Monopoly and competition compared* Compared to perfect competition, a single-price monopoly produces less output and charges a higher price.

Additional Practice Problems 16.3

1. In River Bend, Ohio, the owners of the Acme cab company have convinced the city government to grant it a public franchise so it is the only cab company in town. Prior to this, the cab market had been perfectly competitive. The figure shows the market demand and marginal revenue curves for cab rides as well as the marginal cost curve.

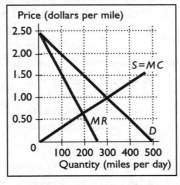

a. Before the government granted Acme its monopoly, how many miles of taxi rides were driven and what was the price?

b. As a monopoly, how many miles of taxi rides will Acme drive? What is the price Acme sets?

c. What is the efficient number of miles?

d. On the graph, show the deadweight loss that results from Acme's monopoly.

2. Suppose that Acme is put up for sale. Looking at the entire future, say Acme's total economic profit is $2 million. If the bidding for Acme is a competitive process, what do you expect will be the price for which the company is sold? What result are you illustrating?

Solutions to Additional Practice Problems 16.3

1a. Before the monopoly was granted, the equilibrium number of miles and price were determined by the demand and supply curves. As the figure shows, the number of miles was 300 miles per day and the price was $1.00 per mile.

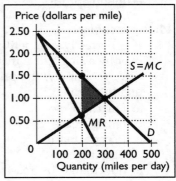

1b. To maximize its profit, the figure shows that Acme drives 200 miles per day because that is the quantity at which marginal revenue equals marginal cost. The price is set from the demand curve and is $1.50 per mile.

1c. The efficient quantity is the quantity at which marginal benefit equals marginal cost. The demand curve is the marginal benefit curve, so the figure shows that the efficient quantity is 300 miles a day.

1d. Single-price monopolies create a deadweight loss because a monopoly produces where $MR = MC$ but efficiency requires production where $MB = MC$. The figure illustrates the deadweight loss as the darkened triangle.

2. Bidders are willing to pay up to $2 million for Acme because if they can buy it for any price less than $2 million, they receive an economic profit. The bidding is competitive, so the price of Acme will be bid up to $2 million and the winning bidder makes zero economic profit. This result demonstrates a rent-seeking equilibrium in which the rent-seeking costs exhaust the economic profit.

© 2015 Pearson Education, Inc.

■ AP Self Test 16.3

True or false

1. A monopoly charges a higher price than a perfectly competitive industry.

2. A monopoly redistributes consumer surplus so that consumers gain and the producer loses.

3. The buyer of a monopoly always makes an economic profit.

Multiple choice

1. If a perfectly competitive industry is taken over by a single firm that operates as a single-price monopoly, the price will _____ and the quantity will _____.
   a. fall; decrease
   b. fall; increase
   c. rise; decrease
   d. rise; increase
   e. not change; decrease

■ FIGURE 16.3

Price and costs (dollars per gallon)

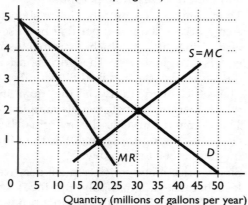

Quantity (millions of gallons per year)

2. Figure 16.3 shows the market for gasoline in a town. If the market is perfectly competitive, the price is _____ per gallon and if the market is taken over by a firm that operates as a single-price monopoly, the price is _____.
   a. $1; $2
   b. $1; $3
   c. $1; $1
   d. $2; $1
   e. $2; $3

3. Figure 16.3 shows the market for gasoline in a town. If the market is perfectly competitive, the quantity is _____ million gallons a year and if the market is taken over by a firm that operates as a single-price monopoly, the quantity is _____ million gallons a year.
   a. 50; 20
   b. 50; 30
   c. 30; 20
   d. 50; 10
   e. 20; 30

4. Comparing single-price monopoly to perfect competition, monopoly
   a. increases the amount of consumer surplus.
   b. has the same amount of consumer surplus.
   c. has no consumer surplus.
   d. decreases the amount of consumer surplus.
   e. decreases the amount of economic profit.

5. Is a single-price monopoly efficient?
   a. Yes, because it creates a deadweight loss.
   b. No, because it creates a deadweight loss.
   c. Yes, because consumers gain and producers lose some of their surpluses.
   d. Yes, because consumers lose and producers gain some of their surpluses.
   e. Yes, because it produces the quantity at which $MR=MC$.

6. Monopolies _____ fair and _____ efficient.
   a. are always; are not
   b. might be; are always
   c. might be; might be
   d. are always; are always
   e. are never; are always

7. In equilibrium, rent seeking eliminates the
   a. deadweight loss.
   b. economic profit.
   c. consumer surplus.
   d. demand for the product.
   e. opportunity to price discriminate.

© 2015 Pearson Education, Inc.

Short Response Questions

■ FIGURE 16.4
Price and costs (dollars per ostrich)

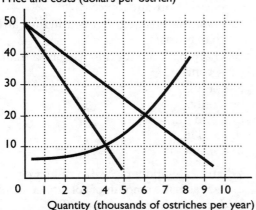

Quantity (thousands of ostriches per year)

1. Figure 16.4 shows the market for ostrich farming, an industry that is initially perfectly competitive. Then one farmer buys all the other farms and operates as a single-price monopoly. In the figure, label the curves. What was the competitive price and quantity? What is the monopoly price and quantity? Darken the deadweight loss area.

2. What happens to consumer surplus with a single-price monopoly?

Long Response Questions

1. How does the quantity produced and the price set by a single-price monopoly compare to those in a perfectly competitive market?

2. What is rent seeking? How does rent seeking affect society?

Additional Exercises (also in MyEconLab Test A)

Sandy Cove is the only beach resort on a small island and the only beach activity it offers is jet ski rides. Figure 16.5 shows the marginal cost of a ride and the market demand for rides. The resort is single-price monopoly.

1. How many rides an hour are taken and what is the price of a ride?

2. Is the equilibrium number of rides the efficient quantity? Explain your answer.

3. What are the consumer surplus redistributed to the resort and the deadweight loss created because the resort has no competitors?

■ FIGURE 16.5
Price and cost (dollars per ride)

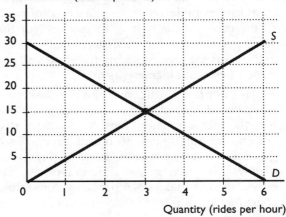

Quantity (rides per hour)

CHECKPOINT 16.4

■ Explain how price discrimination increases profit.

Quick Review

- *Price discrimination* Selling a good at a number of different prices.
- *Consumer surplus* The consumer surplus of a good is its marginal benefit, which equals the maximum price the consumer is willing to pay for the unit of the good, minus the price paid for it, summed over the quantity consumed.

Additional Practice Problems 16.4

1. Frequently the price of the first scoop of ice cream in a cone is less than the price of the second scoop. Why does the ice cream shop use this pricing strategy?

2. Why is the price to attend a movie less on a weekday afternoon than on a weekend evening?

3. How does price discrimination affect the amount of consumer surplus? The amount of the firm's economic profit?

Solutions to Additional Practice Problems 16.4

1. The ice cream store is price discriminating among units of the good by charging different

© 2015 Pearson Education, Inc.

prices for different scoops of ice cream. The store knows that consumers' marginal benefit from ice cream decreases as more is consumed, so the consumer is willing to pay less for the second scoop than for the first scoop. By charging less for the second scoop, the store will sell more scoops and increase its profit.

2. When the price to attend a movie is less on a weekday afternoon than on a weekend evening, the movie theater is practicing price discrimination among two groups of buyers. Each group has a different willingness to pay to see a movie. By setting two different prices, the movie theater maximizes profit by converting consumer surplus into economic profit.

3. Price discrimination decreases consumer surplus because it allows the business to set a price that is closer to the maximum the consumer is willing to pay. Price discrimination increases the firm's profit.

■ AP Self Test 16.4

True or false

1. Price discrimination lowers a firm's profit.

2. Price discrimination converts producer surplus into consumer surplus.

3. With perfect price discrimination, the firm produces the efficient quantity of output and has a larger profit than it would if it did not price discriminate.

Multiple choice

1. Which of the following must a firm be able to do to successfully price discriminate?
   i. divide buyers into different groups according to their willingness to pay
   ii. prevent resale of the good or service
   iii. identify into which group (high willingness to pay or low willingness to pay) a buyer belongs
   a. ii only.
   b. i and ii.
   c. i and iii.
   d. iii only.
   e. i, ii, and iii.

2. Which of the following is (are) price discrimination?
   i. charging different prices based on differences in production cost
   ii. charging business flyers a higher airfare than tourists
   iii. charging more for the first pizza than the second
   a. i only.
   b. ii only.
   c. ii and iii.
   d. i and iii.
   e. i, ii, and iii.

3. When a monopoly price discriminates, it
   a. increases the amount of consumer surplus.
   b. decreases its economic profit.
   c. converts consumer surplus into economic profit.
   d. converts economic profit into consumer surplus.
   e. has no effect on the deadweight loss.

4. If a monopoly is able to perfectly price discriminate, then consumer surplus is
   a. equal to zero.
   b. maximized.
   c. unchanged from what it is with a single-price monopoly.
   d. unchanged from what it is in a perfectly competitive market.
   e. not zero but is less than with a single-price monopoly.

5. With perfect price discrimination, the quantity of output produced by a monopoly is _____ the quantity produced by a perfectly competitive market.
   a. greater than but not equal to
   b. less than
   c. equal to but not greater than
   d. not comparable to
   e. either greater than or equal to

© 2015 Pearson Education, Inc.

Short Response Question

■ FIGURE 16.6

Price and cost (dollars per article of clothing)

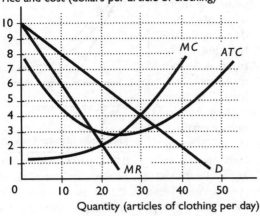

Quantity (articles of clothing per day)

1. Figure 16.6 shows the cost and demand curves for a dry-cleaner that has a monopoly in a small town.
   a. In the figure, lightly darken the area of the economic profit for a single-price monopoly. What is the amount of economic profit this firm makes?
   b. Suppose the firm can price discriminate and set one price for the first 10 articles of clothing and another price for the second 10 articles of clothing. What prices would it set? Darken the additional economic profit the firm makes. What is the amount of the firm's economic profit now?
   c. Suppose the firm is able to perfectly price discriminate. More heavily darken the additional economic profit the firm now makes. What is the amount of the firm's economic profit now?

Long Response Questions

1. Explain the effect of price discrimination on consumer surplus and economic profit.
2. When does a price discriminating monopoly produce the efficient quantity of output?

Additional Exercises (also in MyEconLab Test A)

Consider the following situations in California:

- The weekend price of a hotel room is less than the mid-week price.
- Stand-by passengers can fly at lower fares

than passengers who buy etickets.
- Colleges charge out-of-state students a higher tuition than those from California.
- A supermarket sells water for $2 a bottle or $18 for a box of 12 bottles.
- A bank charges a student a higher interest rate on a car loan than on a student loan.
- The price of water is higher for a car wash firm than it is for a farmer.
- A cell phone company offers free calls on the weekend.
- A museum offers discounts to students and senior citizens.

1. Which of the situations is *not* an example of price discrimination? Explain why not.
2. For the situations that *are* examples of price discrimination, explain how the discrimination is achieved.

CHECKPOINT 16.5

■ Explain why natural monopoly is regulated and the effects of regulation.

Quick Review

- *Marginal cost pricing rule* A price rule for a natural monopoly that sets price equal to marginal cost.
- *Average cost pricing rule* A price rule for a natural monopoly that sets price equal to average cost.

Additional Practice Problems 16.5

1. The figure shows the demand and cost curves for the local water distributing company. The company is a natural monopoly.
   a. If the company is unregulated, what price does it charge

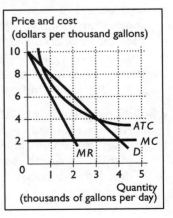

Price and cost (dollars per thousand gallons)

Quantity (thousands of gallons per day)

© 2015 Pearson Education, Inc.

for water and how much is distributed? Does the firm have an economic profit, zero economic profit, or an economic loss?

b. If the company is regulated using an average cost pricing rule, what price does it charge for water and how much is distributed? Does the firm have an economic profit, zero economic profit, or an economic loss?

c. If the company is regulated using a marginal cost pricing rule, what price does it charge for water and how much is distributed? Does the firm have an economic profit, zero economic profit, or an economic loss?

2. The Airmail Act of 1934 awarded airline routes on the basis of competitive bidding. The airlines bid for routes (the bids were the fares the airline would charge) and the low bidder won. The Interstate Commerce Commission regulated the fares. Frequently, after having won a route, an airline was allowed to raise its fare to a profitable level.

The Civil Aeronautics Act was passed in 1938 and served to regulate airlines for the next four decades. There was complete control over entry and exit, as well as fare and route structure. Over this period of time, virtually no new airlines were allowed to enter the market. For two decades after World War II, utilization continued to decline until less than half of seating capacity was being utilized.

In 1978, deregulation occurred. Airlines were free to enter or exit and were also free to determine the fare they would charge. Since deregulation in 1978, passenger airline miles have more than doubled, prices have fallen, and mergers have occurred.

Which theory, the social interest or capture theory, best describes each of these three periods of the airline industry history?

Solutions to Additional Practice Problems 16.5

1a. An unregulated monopoly produces the quantity where marginal revenue equals marginal cost and the price is determined by the demand curve. In the figure, marginal

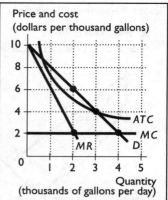

revenue equals marginal cost when 2 thousand gallons of water per day are distributed. The price is $6 per thousand gallons. The firm makes an economic profit.

1b. If an average cost pricing rule is used, price and quantity are determined by where the average total cost curve intersects the demand curve. From the figure, the price is $4 per thousand gallons and the quantity is 3 thousand gallons per day. The firm makes zero economic profit.

1c. If a marginal cost pricing rule is used, price and quantity are determined by where the marginal cost curve intersects the demand curve. From the figure, the price is $2 per thousand gallons and the quantity is 4 thousand gallons per day. The firm incurs an economic loss.

2. From 1934 to 1938, the competitive bidding suggests that social interest might have been more important than in the 1938 to 1978 period. But during the early four-year period, airlines were learning to expect a handout from government regulators.

During the era of the Civil Aeronautics Act, the industry is best described by the capture theory. Airlines were protected from competition by new entrants. They also faced little competition from existing airlines because fares were fixed. Competition took the form of frills, such as fancy dinners, champagne, and attractive accommodations and services.

Since 1978 airline behavior more typically resembles social interest theory and has as its legacy lower prices, higher capacity utilization, new low-fare entrants, bankruptcies, and mergers.

© 2015 Pearson Education, Inc.

■ AP Self Test 16.5

True or false

1. Social interest theory assumes that the political process introduces regulation that eliminates deadweight loss.

2. A regulated natural monopoly produces the efficient quantity of output when it is regulated to use a marginal cost pricing rule.

3. Price cap regulation is designed to give firms the incentive to raise the price of their output, provided competition in the market increases.

Multiple choice

1. The theory that regulation seeks an efficient use of resources is the
   a. social interest theory.
   b. producer surplus theory.
   c. consumer surplus theory.
   d. capture theory.
   e. deadweight loss theory.

2. Which of the following best describes the capture theory of regulation?
   i. Regulation seeks an efficient use of resources
   ii. Regulation is aimed at keeping prices as low as possible
   iii. Regulation helps firms maximize economic profit
   a. i only.
   b. ii only.
   c. iii only.
   d. i and ii.
   e. i, ii, and iii.

3. When regulators require a natural monopoly to set a price that is equal to its marginal cost, the firm
   a. makes zero economic profit.
   b. makes an economic profit.
   c. incurs an economic loss.
   d. sets $P = MC = ATC$.
   e. makes either zero economic profit or an economic profit, depending on whether the firm's average total cost equals or is less than its marginal cost.

4. If a natural monopoly is told to set price equal to its average cost, then the firm
   a. is not able to set marginal revenue equal to marginal cost.
   b. automatically also sets price equal to marginal cost.
   c. will make a substantial economic profit.
   d. will incur an economic loss
   e. sets a price that is lower than its marginal cost.

■ FIGURE 16.7

Price and cost (dollars per month)

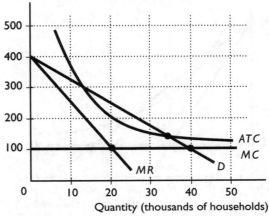

5. If the natural monopoly illustrated in Figure 16.7 was regulated using a marginal cost pricing rule, the price would be ____.
   a. $100
   b. between $100.01 and $200.00
   c. between $200.01 and $300.00
   d. between $300.01 and $400.00
   e. more than $400.01

6. If the natural monopoly illustrated in Figure 16.7 was regulated using an average total cost pricing rule, the price would be ____.
   a. $100
   b. between $100.01 and $200.00
   c. between $200.01 and $300.00
   d. between $300.01 and $400.00
   e. more than $400.01

© 2015 Pearson Education, Inc.

7. If the natural monopoly illustrated in Figure 16.7 was unregulated, the price would be ____.

   a. $100

   b. between $100.01 and $200.00

   c. between $200.01 and $300.00

   d. between $300.01 and $400.00

   e. more than $400.01

Short Response Questions

■ **FIGURE 16.8**

Price and cost (dollars per month)

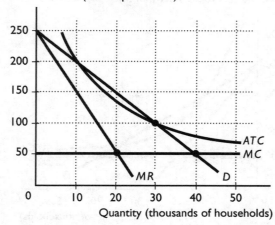

1. Figure 16.8 shows both the average total cost curves of a cable TV company that is a regulated monopoly. Also given are the demand curve and marginal revenue curve.

   a. What price would the regulator set using the marginal cost pricing rule?

   b. What price would the regulator set using the average cost pricing rule?

   c. What price would the firm set if it was unregulated?

2. What is the advantage of using a marginal cost pricing rule to regulate a natural monopoly? The disadvantage?

3. What is the goal of price cap regulation?

Long Response Questions

1. Why doesn't the government regulate all industries?

2. What is the social interest theory of regulation? The capture theory?

Additional Exercises (also in MyEconLab Test A)

■ **FIGURE 16.9**

Price (cents per can)

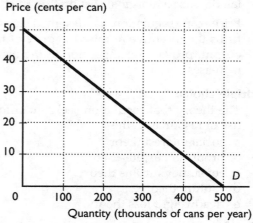

Quantity (thousands of cans per year)

An unregulated natural monopoly cans Mt. McKinley air, unique clean air that has no substitutes. The monopoly's total fixed cost is $30,000, and its marginal cost is 10 cents a can. Figure 16.9 illustrates the demand for Mt McKinley air.

1. How many cans of Mt. McKinley air does the monopoly sell and what is the price of a can of Mt. McKinley air?

2. If the monopoly captures the regulator, how might the monopoly be regulated?

3. If the regulator sets a price cap such that the monopoly breaks even, what is the quantity produced and price at which it is sold? Would the regulated monopoly produce efficiently?

© 2015 Pearson Education, Inc.

SELF TEST ANSWERS

■ AP Self Test 16.1

True or false
1. False; pages 400-401
2. True; page 401
3. False; page 402

Multiple choice
1. b; page 400
2. d; page 400
3. b; page 401
4. d; page 402

Short Response Questions
1. Monopoly occurs when there is a market with a single firm selling a good or service that has no close substitutes and in which the firm is protected by either a natural, ownership, or a legal barrier to entry; page 400.
2. Barriers to entry are anything that protects a firm from the entry of new competitors. Barriers to entry are either natural barriers, ownership barriers, or legal barriers; pages 400-401.

Long Response Question
1. A monopoly can sell each unit of its output for the same price to all its customers or it can price discriminate by selling different units of its good or service at different prices. A perfectly competitive firm cannot affect the price so it must charge a single price determined by market demand and market supply; page 402.

Additional Exercises (also in MyEconLab Test A)
1. A large shopping mall in downtown Houston is not a monopoly because there are many other similar stores and malls nearby. Tiffany is not a monopoly because there are many other upscale jewelers. Wal-Mart is not a monopoly because there are many other similar retailers. The only shoe-shine stand licensed to operate in an airport is a monopoly. The U.S. Postal Service is a monopoly when it comes to first class mail; page 400.

2. The shoe-shine stand and U.S. Postal Service are legal monopolies. The shoe-shine stand and the U.S. Postal service can price discriminate because the service they produce cannot be resold; pages 400-402.

■ AP Self Test 16.2

True or false
1. False; page 404
2. False; page 405
3. True; page 407

Multiple choice
1. a; page 404
2. d; page 404
3. a; page 405
4. b; page 407
5. c; page 407

Short Response Questions
1. If demand is elastic, marginal revenue is positive; if demand is unit elastic, marginal revenue is zero; and if demand is inelastic, marginal revenue is negative; page 405.

Quantity (hamburgers per hour)	Price (dollars)	Marginal revenue (dollars)
1	8.00	
		6.00
2	7.00	
		4.00
3	6.00	
		2.00
4	5.00	
		0.00
5	4.00	

2. The completed table is above.
   a. Figure 16.10 plots the demand and marginal revenue curves; page 407.
   b. Figure 16.10 (on the next page) shows the marginal cost curve. To maximize his profit, Bud produces the quantity at which marginal revenue equals marginal cost. So Bud prepares 300 hamburgers per hour. From the demand curve, the price of a hamburger is $6; pages 406-407.

© 2015 Pearson Education, Inc.

■ FIGURE 16.10

Price and marginal revenue (dollars per hamburger)

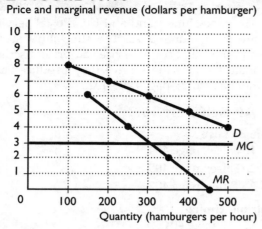

Quantity (hamburgers per hour)

■ FIGURE 16.11

Price and cost (dollars per unit)

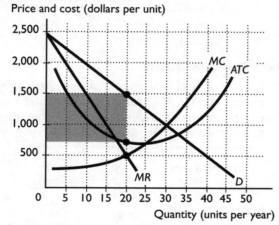

Quantity (units per year)

3. The curves are labeled in Figure 16.11. The profit-maximizing quantity is 20 units and the price is $1,500. The economic profit equals the area of the dark rectangle; page 407.

Long Response Questions

1. Both perfectly competitive and monopoly firms maximize profit by producing where $MR = MC$ because for *any* firm, a unit of output is produced if $MR > MC$ and is not produced if $MR < MC$. As long as $MR > MC$, *any* firm increases its total profit by continuing to produce additional output until it reaches the point at which $MR = MC$; pages 406-407.

2. A monopoly can make an economic profit in the long run because it is protected by a bar-

rier to entry. Other firms want to enter the market in order also to make some economic profit, but they cannot do so; page 407.

Additional Exercises (also in MyEconLab Test A)

Price (thousands of dollars per ride)	Quantity (rides per month)	Total revenue (thousands of dollars per month)	Marginal revenue (thousands of dollars per ride)
220	0	0	
			200
200	1	200	
			160
180	2	360	
			120
160	3	480	
			80
140	4	560	
			40
120	5	600	

1. The total revenue equals the price multiplied by the quantity and the marginal revenue equals the change in total revenue divided by the change in quantity. A table showing HotAir's total revenue and marginal revenue is above; pages 404-405.

■ FIGURE 16.12

Price and marginal revenue (thousands of dollars per ride)

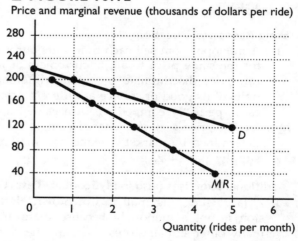

Quantity (rides per month)

2. Figure 16.12 illustrates HotAir's demand and marginal revenue curves; page 404.

3. HotAir's marginal cost equals marginal revenue at 2 1/2 rides a month, where both equal $120,000. From the demand curve, the price is $170,000 a ride. The total cost of 2 1/2

© 2015 Pearson Education, Inc.

rides a month is $320,000. HotAir's total revenue equals the number of rides multiplied by the price per ride, which is (2 1/2 rides per month) × ($170,000) = $425,000. So the total economic profit is total revenue minus total cost, which is $425,000 – $320,000 = $105,000; pages 406-407.

4. As a result of the tax, HotAir's fixed cost changes, but its marginal cost does not. The profit-maximizing level of output is still 2 1/2 rides a month and the price still equals $170,000. The tax decreases HotAir's economic profit by $60,000 so the new economic profit is $45,000; pages 406-407.

5. A $30,000 per ride tax increases HotAir's marginal cost by $30,000 at every level of output. With the increase in the marginal costs, HotAir now sells 2 rides a month because this is the level at which the new marginal cost equals the marginal revenue (both equal $140,000). From the demand curve, HotAir sets a price of $180,000 a ride. Total profit equals total revenue minus total cost. The total revenue is 2 rides × $180,000, which is $360,000. The total cost is $260,000 plus the tax of $60,000, which is $320,000. The new economic profit is $360,000 – $320,000 = $40,000; pages 406-407.

■ AP Self Test 16.3

True or false

1. True; page 409
2. False; page 410
3. False; page 411

Multiple choice

1. c; page 409
2. e; page 409
3. c; page 409
4. d; page 410
5. b; page 410
6. c; page 411
7. b; page 412

Short Response Questions

■ FIGURE 16.13

Price and cost (dollars per ostrich)

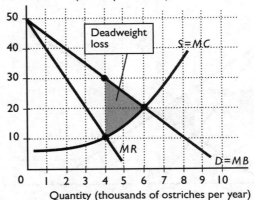

Quantity (thousands of ostriches per year)

1. Figure 16.13 shows that the perfectly competitive price is $20 an ostrich and the quantity is 3,000 ostriches. The monopoly price is $30 an ostrich and the quantity is 2,000 ostriches a year. The deadweight loss is the dark triangular area; page 410.

2. Consumer surplus decreases with a single-price monopoly. Consumer surplus decreases because the monopoly produces less output and charges a higher price; page 410.

Long Response Questions

1. The price set by a monopoly exceeds the price in a competitive market and the quantity produced by a monopoly is less than the quantity produced in a competitive market; page 410.

2. Rent seeking is the act of obtaining special treatment by the government to create economic profit or to divert consumer surplus or producer surplus away from others. Rent seeking harms society because in a competitive rent-seeking equilibrium, the amount of the deadweight loss increases; page 411.

© 2015 Pearson Education, Inc.

Additional Exercises (also in MyEconLab Test A)

■ **FIGURE 16.14**

Price and cost (dollars per ride)

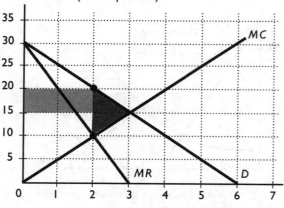

Quantity (rides per hour)

1. Figure 16.14 is helpful in answering this question. In Figure 16.14, the marginal revenue curve has been included. Marginal revenue equals marginal cost when 2 rides per hour are sold. The price per ride, from the demand is curve, is $20 per ride; page 409.

2. The number of rides is less than the efficient quantity. The efficient quantity is 3 rides per hour, where the marginal cost curve and marginal benefit curve (which is the same as the demand curve) intersect; page 410.

3. The consumer surplus when the market was perfectly competitive is the area of the triangle under the demand curve and above the equilibrium price, $15 per ride. The consumer surplus in this case equals 1/2 × 3 rides × $15, which is $22.50. The consumer surplus when the market is a monopoly is the area of the triangle under the demand curve and above the monopoly price, $20 per ride. The consumer surplus in this case equals 1/2 × 2 rides × $10, which is $10. Hence consumers lose a total $12.50 of consumer surplus. But not all of this amount is redistributed to the firm. Only $10—the area of the light grey rectangle in Figure 16.14—is redistributed to the firm. The remainder, $2.50, is lost as part of the deadweight loss.

The deadweight loss is equal to the area of the dark grey triangle in Figure 16.14. This area equals 1/2 × 1 ride × $10, which is $5; pages 410-411.

■ AP Self Test 16.4

True or false

1. False; pages 414-416
2. False; page 414
3. True; page 417

Multiple choice

1. e; page 414
2. c; page 414
3. c; pages 414-416
4. a; page 417
5. c; page 417

Short Response Question

■ **FIGURE 16.15**

Price and cost (dollars per article of clothing)

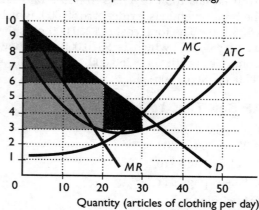

Quantity (articles of clothing per day)

1. a. The economic profit is the light gray rectangle in Figure 16.15. The economic profit equals the area of the rectangle, which is $60 a day; page 415.

   b. The firm will set a price of $8 for each of the first 10 articles and $6 for each of the second 10 articles. The added profit is the darker gray rectangle for the first 10 articles. The total economic profit the firm now makes is $80 a day; page 416.

© 2015 Pearson Education, Inc.

c. The economic profit is increased by the addition of the three very dark gray areas. The economic profit is now $120 a day; page 417.

Long Response Questions

1. Price discrimination decreases consumer surplus and increases economic profit. Price discrimination allows the firm to charge a price closer to the maximum the consumer is willing to pay, which is the marginal benefit of the good. Consumer surplus is converted into economic profit; page 414.

2. With perfect price discrimination, the monopoly increases output to the point at which price equals marginal cost. This output is identical to that of perfect competition. Deadweight loss with perfect price discrimination is zero. So perfect price discrimination produces the efficient quantity; page 417.

Additional Exercises (also in MyEconLab Test A)

1. All are examples of price discrimination *except* the bank loan. Different interest rates reflect borrowers' different risks, which is a possible cost. Charging different interest rates is not price discriminating; page 414.

2. For a firm to price discriminate it must be able to identify specific consumers' willingness to pay different prices and must be able to prevent the resale of the good or service. So if a firm can identify customers' willingness to pay different prices *and* if the firm can prevent resale of its good or service, then the firm can price discriminate.

For the hotel, weekend guests are likely vacation travelers with a lower willingness to pay than the mid-week guests, who are likely business travelers. The hotel can discriminate because it is not possible for the weekend guest to re-sell the room to a mid-week guest.

Stand-by passengers have a lower willingness to pay than passengers who buy the ticket in advance. The airline can discriminate because it is not possible for a stand-by traveler to re-sell the lower priced ticket to another traveler.

For the college, out-of-state students have a higher willingness to pay since they are willing to move far away from home to attend the college. The college can discriminate because it enforces residency requirements.

The supermarket is selling 12 bottles of water at an average price of $1.50 rather than the $2.00 price when it sells one bottle. The supermarket can discriminate because customers who purchase the 12 bottle box are highly unlikely to stand outside the supermarket reselling the water to customers who otherwise would buy only 1 bottle.

The water company is price discriminating by charging two different users different prices for the water. The water company can do so because it is not possible for a farmer to resell water to a car wash firm.

The cell phone company is price discriminating because it charges a lower fee for weekend calls, which are more likely pleasure calls with a lower willingness to pay, than it charges for weekday calls, which are more likely business calls, with a higher willingness to pay. The cell phone company can discriminate because it is not possible for a weekend call to be sold to a weekday caller.

The museum is price discriminating because it charges less to students and senior citizens, who likely have a lower willingness to pay, than to other visitors. The museum can discriminate because it is not possible for senior or student to resell the ticket to other visitors; page 414.

■ AP Self Test 16.5

True or false
1. True; page 421
2. True; page 422
3. False; page 425

Multiple choice
1. a; page 421
2. c; page 421

© 2015 Pearson Education, Inc.

3. c; page 422

4. a; page 423

5. a; page 422

6. b; page 423

7. c; page 407

Short Response Questions

1. a. Using marginal cost pricing, the regulator sets a price of $50 a month; page 421.

   b. Using average cost pricing, the regulator sets a price of $100 a month; page 423.

   c. The firm serves 20,000 households, where marginal revenue equals marginal cost, and sets the price at $150 a month; pages 406-407.

2. The advantage of using a marginal cost pricing rule is that the firm produces the efficient quantity of output. The disadvantage is that the firm incurs an economic loss; page 422.

3. Price cap regulation gives regulated firms the incentive to cut their costs and produce efficiently, without exaggerating their costs or wasting resources; page 425.

Long Response Questions

1. The government does not regulate all industries because not all industries need to be regulated. Competitive industries do not need regulation because competition produces an efficient outcome. But a natural monopoly is not a competitive industry and so government regulation might help move the monopoly toward efficiency; pages 420-425.

2. The social interest theory of regulation is that the regulators pursue the public's interest by devising regulation that achieves an efficient use of resources. The capture theory of regulation is that the producers have "captured the regulators" and, as a result, the regulation helps producers maximize their economic profit; page 421.

Additional Exercises (also in MyEconLab Test A)

1. The firm produces 100,000 cans, which is the quantity at which marginal cost equals marginal revenue. The firm sets a price of $0.40 a can, which, as the demand curve shows, is the maximum price at which consumers are willing to buy the 200,000 cans produced; page 407.

2. If the monopoly can capture the regulator, the firm gets the regulator to allow it to maximize its economic profits. This outcome occurs when 100,000 cans are produced; page 420.

3. The monopoly produces 300,000 cans. When it is producing 300,000 cans, its price is $0.20 a can. And when 300,000 cans are produced, the company's average fixed cost is $0.10 a can and its average variable cost is equal to its marginal cost, $0.10 a can. So average total cost is $0.20 a can, which is equal to its price. The company is not producing efficiently. Only if the regulated monopoly produces 400,000 cans (where the demand curve crosses the marginal cost curve) does it produce an efficient outcome; pages 424-425.

© 2015 Pearson Education, Inc.

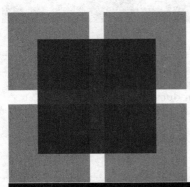

Monopolistic Competition

CHAPTER CHECKLIST

In Chapter 17 we study a market structure that lies between the extremes of perfect competition and monopoly: monopolistic competition.

1 Describe and identify monopolistic competition.

Monopolistic competition is a market structure in which a large number of firms compete; each firm produces a differentiated product; firms compete on product quality, price, and marketing; and firms are free to enter and exit. Product differentiation means making a product that is slightly different from the products of competing firms. Product differentiation allows the firm to compete on product quality, price, and marketing. There are no barriers to entry in monopolistic competition. The four-firm concentration ratio and the Herfindahl-Hirschman Index (HHI) measure the extent to which a market is dominated by a small number of firms. The four-firm concentration ratio is the percentage of the value of the sales accounted for by the four largest firms in the industry; the HHI is the square of the percentage market share of each firm summed over the 50 largest firms in the market. Small values of these indexes indicate competitive markets.

2 Explain how a firm in monopolistic competition determines its output and price in the short run and the long run.

A firm in monopolistic competition has a downward-sloping demand curve. The firm maximizes profit by producing the output at which marginal revenue equals marginal cost. Its price is determined from the demand curve and is the highest price for which the firm can sell the quantity it produces. In the short run, the firm might have an economic profit or an economic loss. Entry and exit result in zero economic profit in the long run. In the long run, a firm in monopolistic competition has excess capacity because it produces less than the efficient scale of output. In monopolistic competition price exceeds marginal cost, which indicates inefficiency, but the inefficiency arises from product variety, a gain for consumers.

3 Explain why advertising costs are high and why firms use brand names in monopolistic competition.

To try to make an economic profit, firms in monopolistic competition develop new products and incur huge costs to ensure that buyers appreciate the differences between their products and those of their competitors. Selling costs, such as advertising, increase a firm's *total* cost, but might lower *average* total cost if they increase the quantity sold by a large enough amount. Firms advertise to signal to the consumer the high quality of the product. Brand names also signal the consumer about the product's quality and give the firm the incentive to maintain the expected level of product quality. Advertising and brand names provide consumers with information, but the opportunity cost of the additional information must be weighed against the gain to the consumer, making the efficiency of monopolistic competition ambiguous.

© 2015 Pearson Education, Inc.

YOUR AP TEST HINTS

AP Topics

Topic on your AP test	What to Know	Corresponding textbook section
Monopolistic competition	Definition and the importance of differentiated products	Checkpoint 17.1
Output and price decisions	Profit maximization; long run zero economic profit, efficiency	Checkpoint 17.2
Advertising costs	Why they are high and brand names are used	Checkpoint 17.3

AP Vocabulary Covered

Terms	What to Know	Text Sections
Product differentiation	A product that is slightly different from the products of competing firms with close substitutes but not perfect substitutes	Checkpoint 17.1, p. 432
Four-firm concentration ratio	The percentage of total revenue of an industry accounted for by the four largest firms; the smaller (larger) the value the more (less) competitive the market	Checkpoint 17.1, p. 434
Herfindahl-Hirschman index	(HHI) The square percentage of market share of each firm summed over the 50 largest firms in the market; the smaller (larger) the value, the more (less) competitive the market	Checkpoint 17.1, p. 435
Monopolistic competition profit maximization	To maximize profit, a firm in monopolistic competition produces the quantity at which $MR = MC$ and sets its price from its demand curve	Checkpoint 17.2, p. 438
Monopolistic competition in the long run	In the long run, competition and adjustments will create zero economic profit for the balanced market	Checkpoint 17.2, p. 440
Efficient scale	The quantity at which average total cost is at its minimum	Checkpoint 17.2, p. 441
Excess capacity	The amount by which the efficient scale exceeds the quantity the firm produces	Checkpoint 17.2, p. 441
Markup	The amount a price exceeds the marginal cost	Checkpoint 17.2, p. 441
Signal	An action by the informed to the uninformed	Checkpoint 17.3, p. 448

Extra AP material

- As in the previous two chapters, be sure to understand the figures and the curves (demand curve, D, marginal revenue curve, MR, marginal cost curve, MC, and average total cost curve ATC).
- The demand curve for a monopolistically competitive firm is more elastic than the demand curve for a monopoly because there are more close substitutes for the product produced by a monopolistically competitive firm.
- In the long run, a monopolistically competitive firm is not allocatively efficient because price is greater than marginal cost: The marginal benefit of a unit of the good to the consumer, which equals the price, exceeds the marginal cost of producing the unit. But in exchange consumers receive product variety from this industry structure.
- The material in Checkpoint 17.3 about advertising costs, brand names, and innovation is not on the AP test.

© 2015 Pearson Education, Inc.

CHECKPOINT 17.1

■ Describe and identify monopolistic competition.

Quick Review

*   *Four-firm concentration ratio* The percentage of the value of sales accounted for by the four largest firms in the industry.

*   *Herfindahl-Hirschman Index (HHI)* The square of the percentage market share of each firm summed over the 50 largest firms (or summed over all the firms if there are fewer than 50) in a market.

Additional Practice Problem 17.1

Firm	Total revenue (millions of dollars)	Percent of total revenue (percent)
McDonald's	1,200	____
Burger King	600	____
Wendy's	600	____
Hardee's	300	____
Checker's	180	____
Other 20 smaller firms	720	____

1. The table gives some hypothetical data on sales in the fast-food hamburger market. Suppose that the total revenue of each of the 20 smallest firms is the same and each has total revenue of $36 million.
    a. Complete the table.
    b. Calculate the four-firm concentration ratio.
    c. Calculate the Herfindahl-Hirschman Index.
    d. Based on the hypothetical concentration ratios, in what market structure would you classify the fast-food hamburger market?

Solution to Additional Practice Problem 17.1

1a. The total revenue shares are in the table above. To calculate the total revenue shares, first determine the total revenue within the market, which is $3,600 million. A firm's total revenue equals its total revenue divided by $3,600 million and then multiplied by 100.

Firm	Total revenue (millions of dollars)	Percent of total revenue (percent)
McDonald's	1,200	33.3
Burger King	600	16.7
Wendy's	600	16.7
Hardee's	300	8.3
Checker's	180	5.0
Other 20 smaller firms	720	20.0

1b. The four-firm concentration ratio is the percentage of the total revenue accounted for by the four largest firms in the industry, which is 33.3 percent + 16.7 percent + 16.7 percent + 8.3 percent = 75.0 percent.

1c. To calculate the Herfindahl-Hirschman Index (HHI), we need to square and then sum the market shares of the firms. The market shares are equal to each firm's percentage of total revenue. Each of the 20 smaller firms has total revenue of $36 million, so each has a 1 percentage point market share. So the HHI = $(33.3)^2 + (16.7)^2 + (16.7)^2 + (8.3)^2 + (5.0)^2 + (1.0)^2 \times 20 = 1,108.89 + 278.89 + 278.89 + 68.89 + 25.00 + 20.00$, which is 1,780.56.

1d. Based on concentration ratios, the fast-food hamburger market is just on the borderline between monopolistic competition and oligopoly. To make a decision whether this industry is monopolistically competitive or an oligopoly, information about the presence or absence of barriers to entry is needed.

■ AP Self Test 17.1

True or false

1. Firms in monopolistic competition are free to enter or exit the market.

2. Each firm in monopolistic competition constantly tries to collude with its competitors.

3. The goods and services produced by firms in monopolistic competition all have virtually the same, if not identical, quality.

4. The larger the four-firm concentration ratio, the more competitive the industry.

5. Concentration ratios might overstate the degree of competition within an industry

© 2015 Pearson Education, Inc.

because concentration ratios take a national view of the market.

Multiple choice

1. In monopolistic competition there
   a. are a large number of firms.
   b. are several large firms.
   c. is one large firm.
   d. might be many, several, or one firm.
   e. are many firms but only a few buyers.

2. A firm in monopolistic competition has a ____ market share and ____ influence the price of its good or service.
   a. large; can
   b. large; cannot
   c. small; can
   d. small; cannot
   e. large; might be able to

3. Product differentiation means
   a. making a product that has perfect substitutes.
   b. making a product that is entirely unique.
   c. the inability to set your own price.
   d. making a product that is slightly different from products of competing firms.
   e. making your demand curve horizontal.

4. A firm in monopolistic competition has ____ demand curve.
   a. a downward-sloping
   b. an upward-sloping
   c. a vertical
   d. a horizontal
   e. a U-shaped

5. Firms in monopolistic competition compete on
   i. quality.
   ii. price.
   iii. marketing.
   a. i and ii.
   b. ii only.
   c. ii and iii.
   d. i and iii.
   e. i, ii, and iii.

6. The absence of barriers to entry in monopolistic competition means that in the long run firms
   a. make an economic profit.
   b. make zero economic profit.
   c. incur an economic loss.
   d. make either an economic profit or zero economic profit.
   e. make either zero economic profit or suffer an economic loss.

7. Each of the ten firms in an industry has 10 percent of the industry's total revenue. The four-firm concentration ratio is
   a. 80.
   b. 100.
   c. 1,000
   d. 40.
   e. 10.

8. Each of the four firms in an industry has a market share of 25 percent. The Herfindahl-Hirschman Index equals
   a. 3,600.
   b. 100.
   c. 625.
   d. 25.
   e. 2,500.

9. If the four-firm concentration ratio for the market for pizza is 28 percent, then this industry is best characterized as
   a. a monopoly.
   b. monopolistic competition.
   c. an oligopoly.
   d. perfect competition.
   e. oligoplistic competition.

10. The larger the four-firm concentration ratio, the ____ competition within an industry; the larger the Herfindahl-Hirschman Index, the ____ competition within an industry.
    a. more; more
    b. more; less
    c. less; more
    d. less; less
    e. The premise of the question is wrong because the four-firm concentration ratio applies only to markets with four firms in it and these markets are, by definition, not competitive.

© 2015 Pearson Education, Inc.

Short Response Questions

1. Industry A has 1 firm with a market share of 57 percent and 43 other firms, each with a market share of 1 percent. Industry B has 4 firms, each with a market share of 15 percent, and 40 other firms, each with a market share of 1 percent.
   a. Calculate the four-firm concentration ratio for the two industries.
   b. Calculate the Herfindahl-Hirschman Index for the two industries.

Firm	Total revenue (millions of dollars)	Percent of total revenue (percent)
Dell	1,000	____
HP	800	____
IBM	500	____
Toshiba	400	____
Other 46 smaller firms	2,300	____

2. The table gives some hypothetical data on sales in the desktop computer market. Suppose that the total revenue of each of the 46 smallest firms is the same and each has total revenue of $50 million.
   a. Complete the table.
   b. Calculate the four-firm concentration ratio.
   c. Calculate the Herfindahl-Hirschman Index.

Long Response Question

1. What conditions define monopolistic competition?

Additional Exercises (also in MyEconLab Test A)

The table shows the total revenue of the six U.S. firms that make fine chocolates. Use this information to answer exercises 1, 2, and 3.

Firm	Total revenue (dollars)
Mayfair	30
Bond	40
Magic	10
All Nature	30
Truffles	60
Gold	30
Industry	**200**

1. Calculate the four-firm concentration ratio and the HHI.

2. What is the market structure of the chocolate industry? What would be the market structure of the chocolate industry if U.S. firms in the chocolate industry faced fierce competition from foreign suppliers?

3. What additional information would you need about the chocolate industry to be sure that it is an example of monopolistic competition?

4. Suppose that a new chocolate-making technology enables anyone with a kitchen to produce outstanding chocolates. How might the market structure of the chocolate industry change?

CHECKPOINT 17.2

■ **Explain how a firm in monopolistic competition determines its output and price in the short run and the long run.**

Quick Review

- *Profit maximization* A firm produces where marginal revenue equals marginal cost and determines the price from the demand curve.
- *Economic profit and economic loss*: Economic profit brings entry into the market and economic loss brings exit from the market.

Additional Practice Problems 17.2

1. The figure shows the demand and costs for Bernie's Burger barn, a firm in monopolistic competition.
   a. To maximize its profit, how many burgers does Bernie produce in an hour? What is the price Bernie sets for one of his burgers?

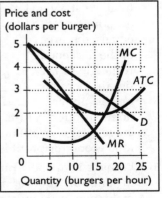

© 2015 Pearson Education, Inc.

b. Is the firm making an economic profit or economic loss and, if so, how much?

c. Does this figure show the firm in the short run or the long run? Explain your answer.

2. The Piece A' Pie company is a pizza restaurant in competition with many other pizza restaurants. Piece A' Pie produces 50 pizzas an hour.

a. If Piece A' Pie's average total cost is $10 a pizza and its price is $12 a pizza, what is its economic profit?

b. If Piece A' Pie's average total cost is $12 a pizza and its price is $12 a pizza, what is its economic profit?

c. If Piece A' Pie's average total cost is $15 a pizza and its price is $12 a pizza, what is its economic profit?

d. Which of the three situations outlined in parts (a), (b), and (c) can represent a short-run equilibrium? A long-run equilibrium?

Solutions to Additional Practice Problems 17.2

1a. To maximize its profit, Bernie's will produce where $MR = MC$. So Bernie's produces 15 burgers per hour. Bernie's demand curve shows that Bernie will set a price of $3 for a burger.

1b. Bernie's is making an economic profit because its price is greater than its average total cost. Its economic profit equals the area of the darkened rectangle in the figure. Bernie's makes an economic profit of $1 (its price, $3, minus its average total cost, $2) on each burger and so its total economic profit is $1 × 15 = $15.

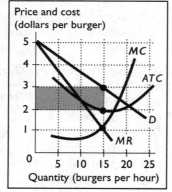

1c. Bernie's is in short-run equilibrium. It is not in long-run equilibrium because the firm is making an economic profit. Firms in monopolistic competition cannot make an economic

profit in the long run; they can make an economic profit only in the short run.

2a. Piece A' Pie's economic profit on a pizza is equal to price minus average total cost. So Piece A' Pie makes an economic profit of $12 a pizza minus $10 a pizza, which is $2 a pizza. Piece A' Pie produces 50 pizzas an hour, so its total economic profit is $2 a pizza × 50 pizzas an hour, which is $100 an hour.

2b. Piece A' Pie's economic profit on a pizza is equal to price minus average total cost. So Piece A' Pie makes an economic profit of $12 a pizza minus $12 a pizza, which is zero dollars a pizza. Piece A' Pie makes zero economic profit so its owners earn a normal profit.

2c. Piece A' Pie's economic profit on a pizza is equal to price minus average total cost. So Piece A' Pie makes an economic profit of $12 a pizza minus $15 a pizza, which is –$3 a pizza. Piece A' Pie produces 50 pizzas an hour, so its total economic profit is –$3 a pizza × 50 pizzas an hour, which is –$150 an hour. So Piece A' Pie incurs an economic loss of $150 an hour.

2d. In the short run, depending on market conditions, a firm in monopolistic competition can make an economic profit, can make zero economic profit, or can incur an economic loss. Only the situation in part (b) can represent a long-run equilibrium. In the long run, the absence of barriers to entry means that firms in monopolistic competition make zero economic profit.

■ AP Self Test 17.2

True or false

1. A firm in monopolistic competition makes its output decision just like a monopoly and produces the quantity where marginal revenue equals marginal cost.

2. A firm in monopolistic competition can make an economic profit in the short run.

© 2015 Pearson Education, Inc.

3. A firm in monopolistic competition can never incur an economic loss.

4. A firm in monopolistic competition has a positive markup.

5. In a broader view of efficiency, monopolistic competition brings gains for consumers.

Multiple choice

1. A firm in monopolistic competition maximizes profit by producing the quantity at which
   a. price and marginal revenue.
   b. price and marginal cost.
   c. demand and marginal cost.
   d. marginal revenue and marginal cost.
   e. price and average total cost.

2. Once a firm in monopolistic competition has determined how much to produce, the firm determines its price by referring to its
   a. demand curve.
   b. marginal cost curve.
   c. marginal revenue curve.
   d. average total cost curve.
   e. average variable cost curve.

■ **FIGURE 17.1**

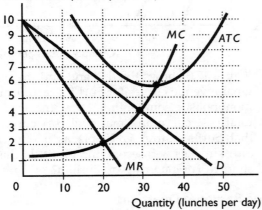

3. Figure 17.1 shows Louie's Lunches, a lunch counter in competition with many other res-

taurants. To maximize its profit, Louie's Lunches produces _____ lunches per day.
   a. 10
   b. 20
   c. 30
   d. between 31 and 40
   e. more than 40

4. Figure 17.1 shows Louie's Lunches, a lunch counter in competition with many other restaurants. To maximize its profit, Louie's Lunches sets a price of _____ per lunch.
   a. $2
   b. $4
   c. between $5.00 and $5.99
   d. $6
   e. more than $6.01

5. Figure 17.1 shows the costs and demand curves for Louie's Lunches. Louie's Lunches is in the _____ and is _____.
   a. short run; making an economic profit
   b. short run; making zero economic profit
   c. short run; incurring an economic loss
   d. long run; making an economic profit
   e. long run; making zero economic profit

6. A firm in monopolistic competition definitely incurs an economic loss if
   a. price equals marginal revenue.
   b. price is less than average total cost.
   c. marginal revenue equals marginal cost.
   d. marginal revenue is less than average total cost.
   e. price is greater than marginal cost.

7. In the long run, a firm in monopolistic competition
   a. makes zero economic profit.
   b. produces at a minimum average total cost.
   c. has deficient capacity.
   d. makes either zero economic profit or an economic profit.
   e. produces a quantity where its demand curve is upward sloping.

© 2015 Pearson Education, Inc.

8. A firm's efficient scale of production is the output at which its
   a. marginal cost is at a minimum.
   b. average total cost is at a minimum.
   c. profit is maximized.
   d. marginal revenue is at a maximum.
   e. marginal revenue equals marginal cost.

9. In the long run, a firm in monopolistic competition ____ excess capacity and a firm in perfect competition ____ excess capacity.
   a. has; has
   b. has; does not have
   c. does not have; has
   d. does not have; does not have
   e. might have; might have

10. In the long run, a firm in monopolistic competition ____ a markup of price over marginal cost and a firm in perfect competition ____ a markup of price over marginal cost.
    a. has; has
    b. has; does not have
    c. does not have; has
    d. does not have; does not have
    e. might have; might have

11. Monopolistic competition is efficient when compared to
    a. perfect competition.
    b. complete product uniformity.
    c. the short run.
    d. the long run.
    e. None of the above answers is correct.

Short Response Questions

1. What rule do firms in monopolistic competition follow to determine their profit-maximizing quantity of output? How does this rule compare to the rule followed by a monopoly? To the rule followed by a firm in perfect competition?

2. Figure 17.2 shows the demand and marginal revenue curves for Seaside Pizza, a firm in monopolistic competition. Draw the average total cost curve and marginal cost curve so that Seaside's output is 40 pizzas a day and its economic profit is $160. Is this a short-run or long-run equilibrium?

■ **FIGURE 17.2**
Price and cost (dollars per pizza)

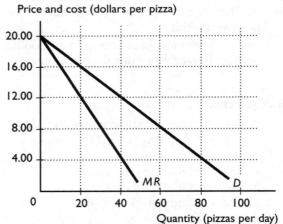

■ **FIGURE 17.3**
Price and cost (dollars per pizza)

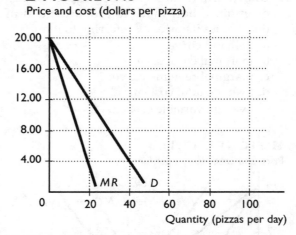

3. Figure 17.3 shows the demand and the marginal revenue curves for Surf Pizza, a firm in monopolistic competition. Draw the average total cost curve and marginal cost curve so that Surf's output is 20 pizzas a day and Surf's makes zero economic profit. Is this a short-run or long-run equilibrium?

Long Response Questions

1. Why do firms in monopolistic competition make zero economic profit in the long run?

2. Is monopolistic competition efficient?

© 2015 Pearson Education, Inc.

Additional Exercises (also in MyEconLab Test A)

Lorie restrings tennis racquets. Her fixed costs are $1,000 a month, and it costs her $15 of labor to string one racquet. The table shows the demand schedule for Lorie's restringing services.

Price (dollars per racquet)	Quantity (racquets per month)
25	0
20	10
15	20
10	30
5	40
0	50

1. Calculate Lorie's profit-maximizing output, price, and economic profit.

2. Do you expect other firms to enter the tennis racquet restringing business and compete with Lorie?

3. What happens to the demand for Lorie's restringing services in the long run? What happens to Lorie's economic profit in the long run?

CHECKPOINT 17.3

■ **Explain why advertising costs are high and why firms use brand names in monopolistic competition.**

Quick Review

- *Selling costs* Selling costs such as advertising expenditures might lower average total cost if they increase the quantity sold by a large enough amount.

Additional Practice Problems 17.3

1. The figure to the right shows a firm in monopolistic competition.

   a. What quantity does the firm produce and what price does it set?

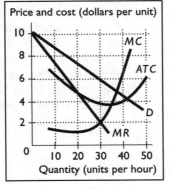

b. How much is the firm's markup?

2. Selling costs are high in monopolistic competition. The table gives the costs of producing a pair of Nikes.

   a. The cost of producing the shoe in Asia is $20. The remaining costs are selling costs. What percentage of the retail price is selling costs?

   b. When the shoes reach America, selling costs are the result of activity at Nike Headquarters and local retailing activity. What proportion of the $70 price is attributable to Nike and what proportion to local retailers?

Item	Cost (dollars)
Asia	
Materials	9.00
Labor	2.75
Capital	3.00
Profit	1.75
Shipping	0.50
Import duty	3.00
Nike	
Distribution	5.00
Advertising	4.00
R and D	0.25
Profit	6.25
Local	
Labor	9.50
Shop rent	9.00
Other costs	7.00
Profit	9.00

Solutions to Additional Practice Problems 17.3

1a. As the figure shows, the firm produces 30 units, because this is the quantity at which $MR = MC$, and sets its price from the demand curve at $6 per unit.

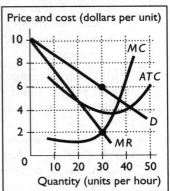

1b. The markup equals the difference between the price and the marginal cost. The price is $6 and the marginal cost is $2, so the markup is $4.

2a. Selling costs account for ($50 ÷ $70) × 100, which is 71.4 percent of the price.

2b. Nike accounts for ($15.50 ÷ $70) × 100, which is 22.1 percent of the price. Local retailers account for ($34.50 ÷ $70) × 100, which is 49.3 percent of the price.

© 2015 Pearson Education, Inc.

■ AP Self Test 17.3

True or false

1. Firms in monopolistic competition develop new products without regard to cost.

2. Firms in monopolistic competition often undertake extensive advertising.

3. Because advertising increases the demand for a firm's product, increasing the amount of advertising shifts the firm's cost curves downward.

4. Brand names give the firm an incentive to achieve a high and consistent standard of quality.

5. Whether monopolistic competition is efficient depends on the value people place on product variety.

Multiple choice

1. Because economic profits are eliminated in the long run in monopolistic competition, to make an economic profit in some markets firms continuously
   a. shut down.
   b. exit the industry.
   c. develop and market new products.
   d. declare bankruptcy.
   e. decrease their costs by decreasing their selling costs.

2. A firm in monopolistic competition that introduces a new and differentiated product will temporarily have a ____ demand for its product and be able to charge ____.
   a. less elastic, a lower price than before
   b. less elastic, a higher price than before
   c. more elastic, a lower price than before
   d. more elastic, a higher price than before
   e. less elastic, the same price as before

3. Developing a new version of a product
   a. depends on the marketing department.
   b. always benefits the firm's customers.
   c. is based on the marginal cost and the marginal revenue of the development.
   d. is impossible in monopolistic competition.
   e. None of the above answers is correct.

4. Advertising costs and other selling costs are
   a. efficient.
   b. fixed costs.
   c. variable costs.
   d. marginal costs.
   e. considered as part of demand because they affect the demand for the good.

5. For a firm in monopolistic competition, selling costs
   a. increase costs and reduce profits.
   b. always increase demand.
   c. can change the quantity produced and lower the average total cost.
   d. can lower total cost.
   e. has no effect on the quantity sold.

6. If advertising increases the number of firms in an industry, each firm's demand
   a. increases.
   b. does not change.
   c. decreases.
   d. might increase or decrease depending on whether the new firms produce exactly the same product or a product that is slightly differentiated.
   e. None of the above answers is correct.

7. One reason a company advertises is to
   a. signal consumers that its product is high quality.
   b. lower its total cost.
   c. produce more efficiently.
   d. lower its variable costs.
   e. lower its fixed costs.

8. The efficiency of monopolistic competition
   a. is as clear-cut as the efficiency of perfect competition.
   b. depends on whether the gain from extra product variety offsets the selling costs and the extra cost that arises from excess capacity.
   c. comes from its excess capacity.
   d. is eliminated in the long run.
   e. is equal to that of monopoly.

© 2015 Pearson Education, Inc.

Short Response Question

1. Why do firms in monopolistic competition engage in developing new products or new variations of existing products?

Long Response Question

1. How does advertising act as a signal?

Additional Exercises (also in MyEconLab Test A)

Bianca bakes delicious cookies. Her total fixed cost is $40 a day, her average variable cost is $1 a bag, and she maximizes profit by selling 10 bags a day for $5 a bag. Now Bianca changes her recipe (at no cost) and bakes an even more delicious cookie. People prefer Bianca's new cookies to those of other bakers.

1. How will Bianca's price, quantity produced, and economic profit change?

2. Bianca estimates that if she spends $50 a day on advertising, she will be able to sell 25 bags a day at $5 a bag. If Bianca decides to advertise, will she increase her economic profit?

© 2015 Pearson Education, Inc.

SELF TEST ANSWERS

■ AP Self Test 17.1

True or false

1. True; page 432
2. False; page 432
3. False; page 433
4. False; page 434
5. True; page 436

Multiple choice

1. a; page 432
2. c; page 432
3. d; page 432
4. a; page 433
5. e; page 433
6. b; page 433
7. d; page 434
8. e; page 435
9. b; page 435
10. d; pages 434-435

Short Response Questions

1. a. The four-firm concentration ratios are equal for both industries, 60 percent; page 434.
   b. The Herfindahl-Hirschman Index is 3,292 for Industry A and 940 for Industry B; page 435.

Firm	Total revenue (millions of dollars)	Percent of total revenue (percent)
Dell	1,000	20
HP	800	16
IBM	500	10
Toshiba	400	8
Other 46 smaller firms	2,300	46

2 a. The total revenue shares are in the table above. The total revenue within the market is $5,000 million. A firm's total revenue share equals its total revenue divided by $5,000 million and then multiplied by 100.

   b. The four-firm concentration ratio is the percentage of the total revenue accounted for by the four largest firms in the industry, which is 20 percent + 16 percent + 10 percent + 8 percent = 54 percent; page 434.

c. To calculate the Herfindahl-Hirschman Index (HHI), square and then sum the market shares of the firms. The market shares are equal to each firm's percentage of total revenue. Each of the 20 smaller firms has total revenue of $50 million, so each has a 1 percentage point market share. The HHI = $(20)^2 + (16)^2 + (10)^2 + (8)^2 + (1)^2 \times 50 = 400 + 256 + 100 + 64 + 50$, which is 870; page 435.

Long Response Question

1. Monopolistic competition occurs when a large number of firms compete; each firm produces a differentiated product, the firms compete on product quality; price, and marketing; and firms are free to enter and exit; page 432.

Additional Exercises (also in MyEconLab Test A)

1. The firms and the percentage of their total revenue shares are Truffles (30 percent), Bond (20 percent), Mayfair (15 percent), All Nature (15 percent), Gold (15 percent), and Magic (5 percent). The 4 largest are Truffles, Bond, and then any two of Mayfair, All Nature, and Gold. The four-firm concentration ratio is 30 + 20 + 15 + 15, which is 80. The HHI equals $30^2 + 20^2 + 15^2 + 15^2 + 15^2 + 5^2 = 2,000$; pages 434-435.

2. Based on the four-firm concentration ratio and the HHI alone, one would presume that the chocolate industry is an oligopoly. If chocolate firms face competition from foreign suppliers, the industry is more competitive than the four-firm concentration ratio and HHI suggest. In this case the industry might be monopolistic competition; page 436.

3. To be sure that the industry is monopolistic competition, we need to know the extent to which firms engage in product differentiation, whether firms are free to enter and exit, and the extent to which firms compete on product quality, price, and marketing; pages 432-433.

4. The new technology lowers the barriers to

© 2015 Pearson Education, Inc.

entry. Probably there would be entry of new firms, so there would be greater product differentiation and fiercer competition on product quality, price, and marketing; page 432.

■ AP Self Test 17.2

True or false
1. True; page 438
2. True; page 438
3. False; page 439
4. True; page 441
5. True; page 442

Multiple choice
1. d; page 438
2. a; page 438
3. b; page 438
4. d; page 438
5. c; page 439
6. b; page 439
7. a; page 440
8. b; page 441
9. b; page 441
10. b; page 441
11. b; page 442

Short Response Questions
1. Firms in monopolistic competition produce the quantity at which marginal revenue equals marginal cost. This rule is the same rule that a monopoly and perfectly competitive firm follow; page 438.

2. Figure 17.4 shows the average total cost curve and marginal cost curve so that Seaside Pizza's output is 40 pizzas a day and economic profit is $160. The figure shows a short-run equilibrium because Seaside is making an economic profit; page 438.

3. Figure 17.5 shows the average total cost curve and marginal cost curve so that Surf Pizza's output is 20 pizzas a day and it makes zero economic profit. The figure shows a long-run equilibrium because Surf is making zero economic profit; page 440.

■ FIGURE 17.4
Price and cost (dollars per pizza)

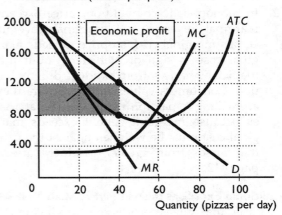

■ FIGURE 17.5
Price and cost (dollars per pizza)

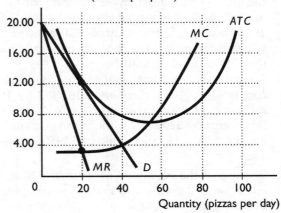

Long Response Questions
1. There is no restriction on entry in monopolistic competition, so if firms in an industry are making an economic profit, other firms have an incentive to enter the industry. The entry of new firms decreases the demand for each firm's product. The demand curve and marginal revenue curve shift leftward. When firms in the industry are making zero economic profit, there is no new incentive for new firms to enter and the industry is in long-run equilibrium. Similarly, if firms in an industry are incurring an economic loss, they have an incentive to exit the industry

© 2015 Pearson Education, Inc.

and in the long run the remaining firms make zero economic profit; page 440.

2. In monopolistic competition, price exceeds marginal revenue and marginal revenue equals marginal cost, so price exceeds marginal cost—a sign of inefficiency. But this inefficiency arises from product differentiation. Consumers value variety and are they are willing to pay for it. So the loss that arises because marginal benefit exceeds marginal cost must be weighed against the gain that arises from greater product variety; page 442.

Additional Exercises (also in MyEconLab Test A)

1. Lorie maximizes profits by producing 10 racquets. Her marginal cost is $15 a racquet. Her marginal revenue between zero and 10 racquets is $20 and between 10 and 20 racquets is $10, so marginal revenue equals $15 at 10 racquets. Lorie's charges $20 a racquet, which is the price from the demand curve for the 10th racquet a month.

   Lorie's fixed cost is $1,000 and her variable cost is $150 ($15 a racquet multiplied by 10 racquets). Her total cost is $1,150 and her total revenue is $200. Lorie incurs an economic loss of $200 − $1,150, which is $950; page 438.

2. Because of the economic loss, firms will not enter. Indeed, firms will *exit* the restringing business; pages 439-440.

3. In the long run, as other firms exit the market the demand for Lorie's restringing business will increase if she stays in the market. In the long run, Lorie's business will make zero economic profit. Lori will either leave the industry or if she remains open, the demand for her services increases as other firms leave and she earns a normal profit; page 440.

■ AP Self Test 17.3

True or false
1. False; page 444
2. True; page 445

3. False; page 446
4. True; page 447
5. True; page 449

Multiple choice
1. c; page 444
2. b; page 444
3. c; page 444
4. b; page 446
5. c; page 446
6. c; page 447
7. a; page 448
8. b; page 449

Short Response Question
1. Firms develop new products new versions of old products to increase the demand for their product and make an economic profit; page 444.

Long Response Question
1. Advertising sends a signal to the consumer that the product being advertised is high quality. Producers are willing to pay for expensive advertising only if they know that their product is of high enough quality that the consumer will buy it repeatedly; pages 448-449.

Additional Exercises (also in MyEconLab Test A)
1. The increase in demand will increase the number of cookies sold and increase the price she charges. Her economic profit will increase; page 444.

2. If additional advertising enables sales to increase so that total revenue increases more than total cost, she can increase economic profit. In the case at hand, her total revenue will increase by $125 and her total cost will increase by $50 plus whatever is the increase in her variable costs of producing the cookies. Because her *AVC* when she produces 10 bags is only $1, it is likely that her variable costs will increase by less than $75, which means that advertising will be profitable; pages 445-447.

© 2015 Pearson Education, Inc.

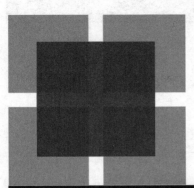

Chapter 18

Oligopoly

CHAPTER CHECKLIST

In Chapter 18 we study oligopoly, a market structure that lies between perfect competition and monopoly.

1 Describe and identify oligopoly and explain how it arises.

An oligopoly is a market structure in which a small number of firms compete because natural or legal barriers prevent the entry of new firms. A duopoly is a market with only two firms. Because there are a small number of firms in the market, the firms are interdependent: each firm's actions affect the other firms. Firms in oligopoly have a temptation to form a cartel and collude to limit output, raise price, and increase economic profit. The key feature to identifying an oligopoly is uncovering whether the firms are so few that they recognize the interdependence among them.

2 Explain the dilemma faced by firms in oligopoly.

Firms in oligopoly can make the same economic profit as a monopoly *if* they act together in a cartel to restrict output to the monopoly level. In the cartel, each firm can make a bigger economic profit for itself by increasing its production, but this action decreases the economic profit of the other firms. The dilemma faced by firms in an oligopoly cartel is that if each firm in the cartel increases output to maximize its profit, then every firm ends up making a smaller economic profit.

3 Use game theory to explain how price and quantity are determined in oligopoly.

Game theory is the tool economists use to analyze strategic behavior. Games have rules, strategies, and payoffs. Strategies are all the possible actions of each player in a game. The prisoners' dilemma is a game between two prisoners that shows why it is hard to cooperate, even when it would be beneficial to both players to do so. The Nash equilibrium of a game occurs when each player takes the best possible action given the action of the other player. The Nash equilibrium of the prisoners' dilemma game is each confesses, which is not the best outcome for the prisoners. The duopolists' dilemma is like the prisoners' dilemma: the firms reach a Nash equilibrium in which they produce more and have lower profit than if they restricted production. In a repeated game, a punishment strategy can produce a monopoly output, a monopoly price, and an economic profit.

4 Describe the antitrust laws that regulate oligopoly.

Antitrust law regulates and prohibits certain kinds of market behavior. The Sherman Act of 1890 was the first federal antitrust law in the United States. Section 1 outlaws "every contract, combination in the form of a trust or otherwise, or conspiracy in restraint of trade." Section 2 declares that "every person who shall monopolize, or attempt to monopolize, … shall be deemed guilty of a felony." The Clayton Act, Robinson-Patman Act, and Celler-Kefauver Act prohibit practices if they "substantially lessen competition or create monopoly." Price fixing is *always* illegal. But resale price maintenance and tying arrangements are more controversial because they *might* lead to efficiency.

© 2015 Pearson Education, Inc.

YOUR AP TEST HINTS

AP Topics

Topic on your AP test	What to Know	Corresponding textbook section
Oligopoly	Definition and how the market arises	Checkpoint 18.1
Oligopoly dilemmas	The duopolist's markets and issues	Checkpoint 18.2
Game theory	Definition in the oligopoly market	Checkpoint 18.3
Antitrust law	Sherman Act, Clayton Act, merger rules	Checkpoint 18.4

AP Vocabulary Covered

Terms	What to Know	Text Sections
Oligopoly	A market with a small number of firms; natural or legal barriers prevent the entry of new firms	Checkpoint 18.1, p. 456
Cartel	A group of firms in an oligopoly colluding together to decrease output, raise price, and increase economic profit	Checkpoint 18.1, p. 456
Duopoly	A market with only two firms	Checkpoint 18.1, p. 456
Game theory	An analysis of strategic behavior, behavior that recognizes mutual interdependence and expected behaviors of others	Checkpoint 18.3, p. 465
Prisoner's dilemma	A game between two prisoners that shows why they find it hard to cooperate even when cooperation would be beneficial to *both*	Checkpoint 18.3, p. 465
Strategies	All of a player's possible actions in a game	Checkpoint 18.3, p. 466
Payoff matrix	A matrix with all the possible payoffs for each player in a game	Checkpoint 18.3, p. 466
Nash equilibrium	Each player takes the best possible action given the action of the other player	Checkpoint 18.3, p. 466
Antitrust law	Laws that regulate oligopolies to prevent them from becoming monopolies or behaving like monopolies	Checkpoint 18.4, p. 473
Sherman Act and Clayton Act	The first and second federal U.S. antitrust laws; Sherman Act prohibits price fixing and "monopolization"; Clayton Act prohibits several specific business practices if they "substantially lessen competition or create monopoly."	Checkpoint 18.4, p. 473
Resale price maintenance	A manufacturer agrees with a distributor on the resale price of a product	Checkpoint 18.4, p. 473
Predatory pricing	Setting a low price with intent to drive competitors out of business and then set a higher, monopolistic price	Checkpoint 18.4, p. 475
Tying arrangement	An agreement to sell one product only if the buyer agrees to buy another, different product.	Checkpoint 18.4, p. 475

Extra AP material

- The AP test will require that students know these game theory concepts:
  - A *dominant strategy* is a strategy that always yields the highest payoff regardless of what choice the other player makes.
  - A *Nash equilibrium* is the equilibrium in which each player takes the best possible action given the action of the other player.
  - The *payoff matrix* for a duopoly.
  - There are conditions where there are no *dominant strategies* for companies.

© 2015 Pearson Education, Inc.

CHECKPOINT 18.1

■ Describe and identify oligopoly and explain how it arises.

Quick Review

*   *Oligopoly* An oligopoly is characterized by having a small number of firms competing with natural or legal barriers preventing the entry of new firms.

Additional Practice Problems 18.1

1. What is the key difference between oligopoly and monopolistic competition?

2. What does it mean for firms to be interdependent? Why are firms in oligopoly interdependent?

Solutions to Additional Practice Problems 18.1

1. The key difference between oligopoly and monopolistic competition is that oligopoly is characterized by having only a small number of interdependent firms. Monopolistic competition has a large number of competing firms. Because there are only a few firms in oligopoly and because they are interdependent, the firms in oligopoly face the temptation to collude, which is an incentive absent from monopolistic competition.

2. Firms are interdependent when one firm's actions have an impact on another firm's profit. Firms in oligopoly are interdependent because there are only a few firms. In this case, one firm's actions have a major effect on the profits of its (few) competitors.

■ AP Self Test 18.1

True or false

1. Oligopoly is a market in which a small number of firms compete.

2. The aim of a cartel is to lower price, increase output, and increase economic profit.

3. Only legal barriers to entry can create oligopoly.

4. Economies of scale can limit the number of firms that are in a market.

5. A market in which the HHI exceeds 1,800 is usually an oligopoly.

Multiple choice

1. Oligopoly is a market structure in which
   a. many firms each produce a slightly differentiated product.
   b. one firm produces a unique product.
   c. a small number of firms compete.
   d. many firms produce an identical product.
   e. the number of firms is so small that they do not compete with each other.

2. The fact that firms in oligopoly are interdependent means that
   a. there are barriers to entry.
   b. one firm's profits are affected by other firms' actions.
   c. they can produce either identical or differentiated goods.
   d. there are too many of them for any one firm to influence price.
   e. they definitely compete with each other so that the price is driven down to the monopoly level.

3. Collusion results when a group of firms
   i. act separately to limit output, lower price, and decrease economic profit.
   ii. act together to limit output, raise price, and increase economic profit.
   iii. in the United States legally fix prices.
   a. i only.
   b. ii only.
   c. iii only.
   d. i and iii.
   e. ii and iii.

4. A cartel is a group of firms
   a. acting separately to limit output, lower price, and decrease economic profit.
   b. acting together to limit output, raise price, and increase economic profit.
   c. legally fixing prices.
   d. acting together to erect barriers to entry.
   e. that compete primarily with each other rather than the other firms in the market.

© 2015 Pearson Education, Inc.

5. A market with only two firms is called a
   a. duopoly.
   b. two-firm monopolistic competition.
   c. two-firm monopoly.
   d. cartel.
   e. two-firm quasi-monopoly.

6. The efficient scale of one firm is 20 units and the average total cost at the efficient scale is $30. The quantity demanded in the market as a whole at $30 is 40 units. This market is
   a. a natural duopoly.
   b. a legal duopoly.
   c. a natural monopoly.
   d. a legal monopoly.
   e. monopolistically competitive.

7. Even though four firms can profitably sell hotdogs downtown, the government licenses only two firms. This market is a
   a. natural duopoly.
   b. legal duopoly.
   c. natural monopoly.
   d. legal monopoly.
   e. market-limited oligopoly.

8. To determine if a market is an oligopoly, we need to determine if
   a. the market's HHI is less than 900.
   b. there are many firms in the market.
   c. the firms are so few that they recognize their mutual interdependencies.
   d. the firms make identical or differentiated products.
   e. cartels are legal in their market.

Short Response Questions
1. What conditions define oligopoly?
2. What is a cartel?
3. How does the HHI for monopolistic competition compare to the HHI for oligopoly?

Long Response Question
1. Firms in oligopoly are interdependent. Firms in monopolistic competition are not. What accounts for the difference?

Additional Exercises (also in MyEconLab Test A)
1. Identify an oligopoly market in which you bought something recently.
2. Why are the firms that make boxes of chocolates on the borderline between oligopoly and monopolistic competition?

CHECKPOINT 18.2

■ **Explain the dilemma faced by firms in oligopoly.**

Quick Review
- *Duopoly* A market with only two firms.
- *Range of outcomes* The price and quantity in a duopoly can range from the competitive outcome to the monopoly outcome.

Additional Practice Problem 18.2
1. Isolated Island has two natural gas wells, one owned by Tom and the other owned by Jerry. Each well has a valve that controls the rate of flow of gas, and the marginal cost of producing gas is zero. The table gives the demand schedule for gas on this island. Suppose Tom and Jerry agree to operate as a monopoly. A

Price (dollars per unit)	Quantity demanded (units per day)
12	0
11	1
10	2
9	3
8	4
7	5
6	6
5	7
4	8
3	9
2	10
1	11
0	12

monopoly produces 6 units and charges $6 a unit. Tom and Jerry agree that each will produce 3 units and charge $6. There are no fixed costs.

a. If neither Tom nor Jerry cheat on the agreement what is Tom's profit? Jerry's profit? The combined profit?
b. Suppose Tom decides to cheat on the agreement by producing 4 units. Jerry sticks to the agreement. If 7 units are pro-

© 2015 Pearson Education, Inc.

duced, what is the price? What is Tom's profit? Jerry's profit? The combined profit?

c. Why would Tom ever consider cheating on the agreement he made with Jerry?

Solutions to Additional Practice Problem 18.2

1a. Profit is equal to total revenue because total cost is zero. Tom's profit is $18, Jerry's profit is $18, and the combined profit is $36.

1b. If 7 units are produced, the price is $5 a unit. Tom's profit on his 4 units is $20 and Jerry's profit on his 3 units is $15. The combined profit is $35.

1c. Tom considers cheating because cheating increases his profit. Tom realizes that if he alone cheats, his profit will be more, $20 versus $18. Jerry's profit falls more than Tom's rises but Tom is concerned only about his own profit.

■ AP Self Test 18.2

True or false

1. In a duopoly, the highest price that the firms might set is the perfectly competitive price.

2. The only possible outcome for a duopoly is the monopoly outcome.

3. Once a duopoly has achieved the monopoly outcome, neither firm can increase its total profit.

4. A duopoly is currently making, in total, the same economic profit as a monopoly. If one firm increases its output, the economic profit of the other firm increases.

5. A duopoly's total profit is the largest when it produces more than the monopoly level of output.

Multiple choice

■ FIGURE 18.1

Price and cost (dollars per bottle of shampoo)

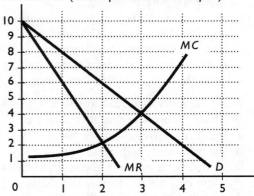

Quantity (millions of bottles of shampoo per day)

1. Suppose only two companies make shampoo. Figure 18.1 shows the market demand curve and associated marginal revenue curve. It also shows the combined marginal cost curve of the two companies. If these companies formed a cartel that operated as a monopoly, production is ____ million bottles of shampoo and the price is ____ per bottle of shampoo.
   a. 5; $4
   b. 2; $6
   c. 3; $6
   d. 2; $2
   e. 3; $4

2. Suppose the two companies that make shampoo illustrated in Figure 18.1 operate as perfect competitors. In this case, production is ____ million bottles of shampoo and the price is ____ per bottle of shampoo.
   a. 5; $4
   b. 2; $6
   c. 3; $6
   d. 2; $2
   e. 3; $4

© 2015 Pearson Education, Inc.

3. For a duopoly, the highest price is charged when the duopoly achieves
   a. the competitive outcome.
   b. the monopoly outcome.
   c. an outcome between the competitive outcome and the monopoly outcome.
   d. its noncooperative equilibrium.
   e. Both answers (a) and (d) are correct because both refer to the same price.

4. For a duopoly, the smallest *total* quantity is produced when the duopoly achieves
   a. the competitive outcome.
   b. the monopoly outcome.
   c. an outcome between the competitive outcome and the monopoly outcome.
   d. its noncooperative equilibrium.
   e. Both answers (a) and (d) are correct because both refer to the same quantity.

5. For a duopoly, the maximum *total* profit is reached when the duopoly produces
   a. the same amount of output as the competitive outcome.
   b. the same amount of output as the monopoly outcome.
   c. an amount of output that lies between the competitive outcome and the monopoly outcome.
   d. more output than the competitive outcome.
   e. less output than the monopoly outcome.

6. If a duopoly has reached the monopoly outcome, a firm can increase its profit if it and it alone ____ its price and ____ its production.
   a. raises; increases
   b. raises; decreases
   c. lowers; increases
   d. lowers; decreases
   e. raises; does not change

7. If a duopoly has reached the monopoly outcome and only one firm increases its production, that firm's profit ____ and the other firm's profit ____.
   a. increases; increases
   b. increases; decreases
   c. decreases; increases
   d. decreases; decreases
   e. increases; does not change

8. Suppose a duopoly had reached the monopoly outcome and then the first firm increased its production. If the second firm next increases its production, the second firm's profit ____ and the first firm's profit ____.
   a. increases; increases
   b. increases; decreases
   c. decreases; increases
   d. decreases; decreases
   e. increases; does not change

9. If both firms in a duopoly increase their production by one unit beyond the monopoly output, each firm's profit ____ and the *total* profit of the duopoly ____.
   a. increases; increases
   b. does not change; does not change
   c. decreases; decreases
   d. does not change; increases
   e. decreases; does not change

10. The very best outcome possible for the firms in a duopoly is to produce the
    a. monopoly level of output.
    b. perfectly competitive level of output.
    c. amount of output that maximizes total revenue.
    d. amount of output that minimizes total cost.
    e. equilibrium level of output if the game is not repeated.

Short Response Questions
1. Why do firms in an oligopoly have an incentive to form a cartel that boosts the price and decreases the output?

© 2015 Pearson Education, Inc.

2. Why does a firm have the incentive to cheat on a collusive agreement to limit production and raise the price?

Quantity (thousands of newspapers per day)	Price (cents)	Marginal revenue (cents)
0	60	60
2	50	40
4	40	20
6	30	0
8	20	−20

3. Anytown, USA has two newspapers that have a duopoly in the local market. The table contains information on the market demand and marginal revenue for newspapers. Marginal cost of a newspaper is 20 cents.

   a. Graph the demand curve, marginal revenue curve, and marginal cost curve in Figure 18.2.

   ■ **FIGURE 18.2**

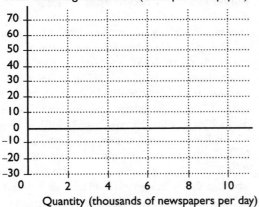

Price and marginal revenue (cents per newspaper)

Quantity (thousands of newspapers per day)

   b. What price and quantity represent the competitive outcome?

   c. What price and quantity represent the monopoly outcome?

   d. What range of price and quantity represent the potential duopoly outcomes?

Long Response Question

1. In oligopoly, one firm's profit-maximizing actions might decrease its competitors' profits. Why is this fact a problem for firms in oligopoly?

Additional Exercises (also in MyEconLab Test A)

Isolated Island has three natural gas wells, one owned by Tom, one owned by Jerry, and one owned by Joey. The table gives the demand schedule for gas on this island. The marginal cost of producing gas is zero. Use this information to answer Exercises 1 and 2.

Price (dollars per unit)	Quantity demanded (units per day)
12	0
11	1
10	2
9	3
8	4
7	5
6	6
5	7
4	8
3	9
2	10
1	11
0	12

1. What is the price of gas and the quantity produced if Tom, Jerry, and Joey form a cartel and maximize their joint profit?

2. If Tom, Jerry, and Joey are forced to sell at the perfectly competitive price, what will be the price of gas and the quantity produced?

Duracell and Energizer are the only major producers of batteries. Each company has developed a long-lasting battery and aggressively advertises it. The two firms are locked in a duopolists' dilemma.

3. Describe the dilemma facing Duracell and Energizer.

4. Suppose that Duracell and Energizer secretly were to form a cartel. What do you predict would happen to the price of a battery? How would the two firms change their advertising and research and development budgets?

© 2015 Pearson Education, Inc.

CHECKPOINT 18.3

■ **Use game theory to explain how price and quantity are determined in oligopoly.**

Quick Review

- *Game theory* The tool that economists use to analyze strategic behavior—behavior that recognizes mutual interdependence and takes account of the expected behavior of others.

- *Nash equilibrium* An equilibrium in which each player takes the best possible action given the action of the other player.

Additional Practice Problem 18.3

1. Coke and Pepsi are engaged in an advertising game. They each know that if they both limit their advertising, they will make the maximum attainable joint economic profit of $400 million, divided so that each has an economic profit of $200 million. They also know that if either of them advertises while the other does not, the one advertising makes an economic profit of $300 million and the one that not advertising incurs an economic loss of $100 million dollars. And they also know that if they both advertise, they both make zero economic profit.

    a. Construct a payoff matrix for the game that Coke and Pepsi must play.

    b. Find the Nash equilibrium. How is this game similar to the prisoners' dilemma?

    c. What is the equilibrium if this game is played repeatedly?

    d. Suppose that Coke and Pepsi are both playing a tit-for-tat strategy and that last time both did not advertise. Today, however, Coke really needs some extra income. So Coke advertises. What takes place today and in the future?

Solution to Additional Practice Problem 18.3

1a. A payoff matrix is a table that shows payoffs for every possible action by each player, Coke and Pepsi, given every possible action by the other player. The payoff matrix is given

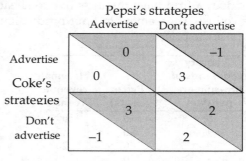

above. The number in each square is the economic profit in millions of dollars.

1b. To find the Nash equilibrium of a game, place yourself in the position of the first player. Ask yourself "what if" your opponent takes one action: what will you do? Then ask "what if" the opponent takes the other action: now what will you do? This analysis allows you to determine the first player's action. Then place yourself in the position of the second player and repeat the "what if" analysis to determine the second player's action. So, to find Coke's strategy, ask what Coke will do for each of Pepsi's choices. If Pepsi advertises (the first column of the payoff matrix), Coke advertises because that gives Coke a larger profit ($0 versus a loss of $1 million). If Pepsi does not advertise (the second column of the payoff matrix), Coke advertises gallons because that gives Coke a larger profit ($3 million versus $2 million). Regardless of Pepsi's action, Coke advertises. Similar reasoning shows that Pepsi also advertises. So the Nash equilibrium is for each to advertise and make zero economic profit. The game is similar to a prisoners' dilemma game because there is a conflict between each player's incentives to do what is best for the player versus what is best for both of them taken together. In the prisoners' dilemma game, both prisoners confess, leading to the worst joint outcome. In this game, both players advertise, again leading to the worst joint outcome.

1c. In a repeated game, Coke and Pepsi both do not advertise and make the maximum joint

© 2015 Pearson Education, Inc.

economic profit. This outcome occurs if they use a tit-for-tat strategy.

1d. Today, Coke makes an economic profit of $3 million and Pepsi incurs an economic loss of $1 million. But in the second year, Pepsi will advertise. Coke might go back to not advertising to induce Pepsi to not advertise in the third year. So in the second year, Pepsi makes an economic profit of $3 million and Coke incurs an economic loss of $1 million. Over the two years, Coke makes a total economic profit of $2 million (and Pepsi also makes a total economic profit of $2 million.) But if Coke had not "cheated" on the agreement and advertised in the first year, then over the two years Coke's total economic profit would have been $4 million, not just $2 million. So, by cheating on the agreement Coke makes more profit immediately but over the longer haul makes less profit.

■ AP Self Test 18.3

True or false

1. Game theory is used to analyze strategic behavior.
2. A prisoners' dilemma has no equilibrium.
3. A Nash equilibrium is the best outcome for all players in a prisoners' dilemma game.
4. The monopoly outcome is more likely in a repeated game than in a one-play game.
5. If firms in oligopoly play a repeated game and end up restricting their output, then oligopoly is efficient.

Multiple choice

1. One of the main tools economists use to analyze strategic behavior is
   a. the Herfindahl-Hirschman Index.
   b. game theory.
   c. cartel theory.
   d. the collusion index.
   e. dual theory, which is used to study duopolies.

2. A Nash equilibrium occurs
   a. when each player acts without considering the actions of the other player.
   b. when each player takes the best possible action given the action of the other player.
   c. only when players use the tit-for-tat strategy.
   d. only if the game is played in Nashville, TN.
   e. when each player takes the action that makes the combined payoff for all players as large as possible.

3. Game theory reveals that
   a. the equilibrium might not be the best solution for the parties involved.
   b. firms in oligopoly are not interdependent.
   c. each player looks after what is best for the industry.
   d. if all firms in an oligopoly take the action that maximizes their profit, then the equilibrium will have the largest possible combined profit of all the firms.
   e. firms in an oligopoly choose their actions without regard for what the other firms might do.

4. The prisoners' dilemma game
   a. shows that prisoners are better off if they cooperate.
   b. shows it is easy to cooperate.
   c. has an equilibrium in which both prisoners are made as well off as possible.
   d. would have the same outcome even if the prisoners can communicate and cooperate.
   e. has an equilibrium in which one prisoner is made as well off as possible and the other prisoner is made as worse off as possible.

© 2015 Pearson Education, Inc.

Katie's strategies

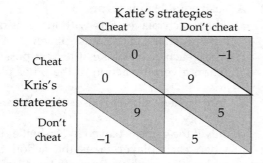

5. Katie and Kris are duopolists who formed a collusive agreement to boost prices and decrease production. Their payoff matrix is above and the entries are millions of dollars of economic profit. They now have the choice of cheating on the agreement or not cheating. If Kris cheats, then
   a. Kris definitely makes an economic profit of $9 million.
   b. Kris definitely makes $0.
   c. Kris definitely incurs an economic loss of $1 million.
   d. Kris definitely makes an economic profit of $5 million.
   e. Kris might make an economic profit of $9 million or might make $0 depending on what Katie does.

6. Based on the payoff matrix above, the Nash equilibrium is for
   a. Kris to cheat and Katie to cheat.
   b. Kris to not cheat and Katie to not cheat.
   c. Kris to cheat and Katie to not cheat.
   d. Kris to not cheat and Katie to cheat.
   e. Kris and Katie to invite a third person to determine what each of them should do.

7. Based on the payoff matrix above, in the Nash equilibrium the total economic profit that Katie and Kris make together is _____ million.
   a. $8
   b. $9
   c. $10
   d. $0
   e. −$1

8. A collusive agreement to form a cartel is difficult to maintain because
   a. each firm can increase its own profits by cutting its price and selling more.
   b. forming a cartel is legal but frowned upon throughout the world.
   c. supply will decrease because of the high cartel price.
   d. demanders will rebel once they realize a cartel has been formed.
   e. each firm can increase its profit if it decreases its production even more than the decrease set by the cartel.

9. Firms in oligopoly can achieve an economic profit
   a. always in the long run.
   b. if they cooperate.
   c. only if the demand for their products is inelastic.
   d. only if the demand for their products is elastic.
   e. if they reach the non-cooperative equilibrium.

10. When duopoly games are repeated and a "tit-for-tat" strategy is used,
    a. the competitive outcome is more likely to be reached than when the game is played once.
    b. the monopoly outcome is more likely to be reached than when the game is played once.
    c. both firms begin to incur economic losses.
    d. one firm goes out of business.
    e. because the game is repeated it is impossible to predict whether the competitive or the monopoly outcome is more likely.

11. Oligopoly is
    a. always efficient.
    b. efficient only if the firms cooperate.
    c. efficient only if the firms play non-repeated games.
    d. generally not efficient.
    e. efficient only if the firms innovate.

© 2015 Pearson Education, Inc.

Short Response Questions

Cameron's strategies

Art's strategies

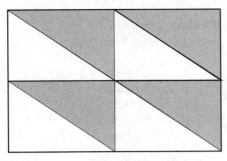

1. Art and Cameron own the only two movie theaters in a town. They have recently (illegally) agreed to boost their ticket prices. If they both comply with the agreement, both make $1 million of economic profit. If one cheats by lowering his price, the cheater makes $1.5 million of economic profit and the other incurs an economic loss if $0.5 million. If they both cheat by lowering their prices, each makes zero economic profit.

a. Complete the payoff matrix above.

b. What is the Nash equilibrium?

Intel's strategies

AMD's strategies

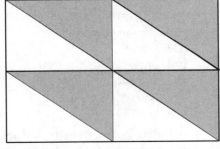

2. Intel and AMD are involved in a game to determine the amount they will spend on research and development. If they each spend $2 billion, each has an economic profit of zero. If they each spend $1 billion, each has an economic profit of $500 million. And if one spends $2 billion and the other spends $1 billion, the one spending $2 billion has an eco-

nomic profit of $1,500 million and the other has an economic loss of $100 million.

a. Complete the payoff matrix above.

b. What is the Nash equilibrium of this game?

3. How does the number of players in a game affect its outcome?

Long Response Questions

1. What are "strategies" in game theory?

2. In a prisoners' dilemma, why don't the players cooperate?

3. In the duopolists' dilemma, why don't the players cooperate?

Additional Exercises (also in MyEconLab Test A)

Bud and Wise are racing to develop a new brand of coconut milk that they both believe will be the next big soft drink. Bud and Wise know that if they both develop the new product, they will both make zero economic profit; if only one of them develops the new product, that firm will make an economic profit of $2 million a week and the other will incur an economic loss of $1 million a week; and if neither of them develops the new product, both will make zero economic profit.

1. Construct a payoff matrix for this game.

2. Find the Nash equilibrium.

3. Is there any chance of cooperation in this research and development game?

CHECKPOINT 18.4

■ **Describe the antitrust laws that regulate oligopoly.**

Quick Review

- *Sherman Act* The first U.S. antitrust law, Section 1 of the Sherman Act prohibits conspiring with others to restrict competition and Section 2 outlaws attempts to monopolize.

- *Clayton Act* The second antitrust law, the Clayton Act prohibits certain business

© 2015 Pearson Education, Inc.

practices if they substantially lessen competition or create monopoly.

Additional Practice Problem 18.4

1. Cooperative agreements among firms such as the New York Yankees and the Chicago White Sox that limit the number of games played and that restrict the number of teams for which an athlete can play show cartel-like behavior. Except for professional sports teams, cartels are generally illegal in the United States. For instance, Microsoft and Hewlett Packard do not draft college graduates and so they cannot agree that a particular college graduate will work for Microsoft and not Hewlett Packard. Why do you think the Supreme Court made a decision in the case of professional sporting teams to permit cartel-like behavior?

Solution to Additional Practice Problem 18.4

1. Under competitive conditions, rich teams such as the New York Yankees, with plenty of fans and lucrative media contracts, would be able to purchase all the best players. Putting all the best players on a single team would prevent another team from winning. The teams unable to win would be unable to entice fans to their stadiums. The entire sports industry would die if only one team were profitable and dominant. This situation is unlike the case with Microsoft and Hewlett Packard because if one of these firms becomes dominant, its absolute dominance would not spell the end of the industry. The sports leagues, in an exception to general American policy, are allowed to have league rules that seek to apportion talent equally to preserve the competitive nature of the sport.

■ AP Self Test 18.4

True or false

1. The Sherman Act outlaws contracts and conspiracies in restraint of trade.

2. The Clayton Act outlaws all price discrimination.

3. Price fixing is *always* illegal.

4. Resale price maintenance always leads to efficiency.

5. The Federal Trade Commission uses the four-firm concentration ratio as the guideline to determine which mergers it will examine and possibly block.

Multiple choice

1. The first antitrust act was____ passed in ____.
   a. the Clayton Act; 1890
   b. the Sherman Act; 1890
   c. the Clinton Act; 1999
   d. the Rockefeller Act; 1890
   e. the Clayton Act; 1914

2. The Clayton Act
   a. replaced the Sherman Act.
   b. along with its amendments, outlawed several business practices if they substantially lessened competition or created monopoly.
   c. along with its amendments, prohibited all business practices that substantially lessen competition or create monopoly.
   d. was the first anti-trust law in the United States.
   e. was repealed in 1985.

3. Which of the following is (are) prohibited if it substantially lessens competition or creates a monopoly?
   i.   price discrimination
   ii. tying arrangements
   iii. exclusive dealing
   a. i only.
   b. ii only.
   c. ii and iii.
   d. iii only.
   e. i, ii, and iii.

4. If Polka Cola agrees to sell its cola to a retailer only if the retailer also buys a lemon-lime drink, Polka Up, then Polka Cola is engaged in
   a. a tying arrangement.
   b. a requirement contract.
   c. an exclusive deal.
   d. territorial confinement.
   e. price discrimination.

© 2015 Pearson Education, Inc.

5. Which of the following is *always* illegal?
   a. possessing a very large market share
   b. selling at a price below other producers because of efficiency
   c. price fixing
   d. attempting to merge with a competitor
   e. price discrimination

6. Resale price maintenance
   a. can lead to efficiency by preventing low-price shops from being free riders.
   b. can lead to inefficiency by preventing low-price shops from being free riders.
   c. is always legal.
   d. is a clear example of predatory pricing.
   e. is an example of a tying arrangement.

7. Predatory pricing occurs when a firm sets a ____ price to drive competitors out of business with the intention of then setting a ____ price.
   a. monopoly; high
   b. monopoly; low
   c. low; monopoly
   d. low; low
   e. high; monopoly

8. In the case against Microsoft, it was claimed that combining Internet Explorer and Windows was
   a. predatory pricing.
   b. an illegal tying agreement.
   c. creating one product that is convenient for the consumers.
   d. illegal territorial confinement.
   e. an inefficient resale maintenance agreement.

9. In a concentrated industry with a Herfindahl-Hirschman Index that exceeds 2,500, the Federal Trade Commission will challenge any merger that increases the Herfindahl-Hirschman index by a minimum of
   a. 50 points.
   b. 100 points.
   c. 1,000 points.
   d. 1,800 points.
   e. 10,000 points.

Short Response Questions

1. Airlines routinely price discriminate, charging pleasure travelers a significantly lower price than business travelers. The Clayton Act, however, mentioned price discrimination as one of the business practices it covers and prohibits. Why can airlines routinely price discriminate?

2. What is the law about price fixing?

Long Response Questions

1. General Motors is a huge company, with total revenue exceeding $150 billion a year. Why doesn't the government challenge General Motors and take it to court for antitrust violations?

Company	Market share (percent)
Acme	27
ABC	18
Banks	10
Cooper	8
37 individual firms	1 each

2. The table above has a list of companies that make up the market for steel, along with each companies' share of the market.
   a. What is the Herfindahl-Hirschman Index for this market? How would you describe the competitiveness of this market?
   b. If Acme acquires Banks, what is the new Herfindahl-Hirschman Index? Would the Department of Justice challenge this acquisition? Why or why not? How would you describe the competitiveness of this market if the merger occurs?

Additional Exercise (also in MyEconLab Test A)

1. In 1911, Standard Oil Company was found guilty under the Sherman Act and was ordered to divest itself. Some of the oil companies that were created as a result of the 1911 order have now merged to form large companies. Why do you think Standard Oil Company was found guilty under the Sherman Act while recent oil company mergers have been approved?

© 2015 Pearson Education, Inc.

SELF TEST ANSWERS

■ AP Self Test 18.1

True or false

1. True; page 456
2. False; page 456
3. False; page 456
4. True; page 457
5. True; page 458

Multiple choice

1. c; page 456
2. b; page 456
3. b; page 456
4. b; page 456
5. a; page 456
6. a; page 457
7. b; page 458
8. c; page 458

Short Response Questions

1. Oligopoly occurs when a small number of firms compete and natural or legal barriers prevent the entry of new firms; page 456.

2. A cartel is a group of firms acting together to limit output, raise price, and increase economic profit; page 456.

3. The HHI for monopolistic competition is less than that for oligopoly. For monopolistic competition, the HHI usually lies between 1,000 and 1,800. For oligopoly, the HHI usually lies above 1,800; page 458.

Long Response Question

1. The difference is because there are only a small number of firms in oligopoly. Because there are only a small number of firms, one firm's actions affect the profits of all its (few) competitors; page 456.

Additional Exercises (also in MyEconLab Test A)

1. Some common oligopoly markets are CPUs for computers, long-distance telephone service, cellular telephone service, automobiles, and cigarettes; page 456.

2. The HHI is relatively high for the chocolate industry, but there are a large number of chocolate producers. So based on the HHI, the industry seems oligopoly but based on the large number of firms (and the point that often the relevant market is local rather than national) the industry might be monopolistic competition; page 459.

■ AP Self Test 18.2

True or false

1. False; page 461
2. False; page 461
3. False; page 461
4. False; page 461
5. False; pages 460-461

Multiple choice

1. b; page 460
2. e; page 460
3. b; page 461
4. b; page 461
5. b; page 461
6. c; page 461
7. b; page 461
8. b; page 462
9. c; page 462
10. a; page 462

Short Response Questions

1. If the firms can form and maintain a cartel that boosts the price and decreases the output, all the firms' profits can increase; page 461.

2. Every firm has the incentive to cheat on an output-limiting agreement because if it and it alone cheats by boosting its output and cutting its price, its economic profit will increase; page 461.

© 2015 Pearson Education, Inc.

■ **FIGURE 18.3**

Price and marginal revenue (cents per newspaper)

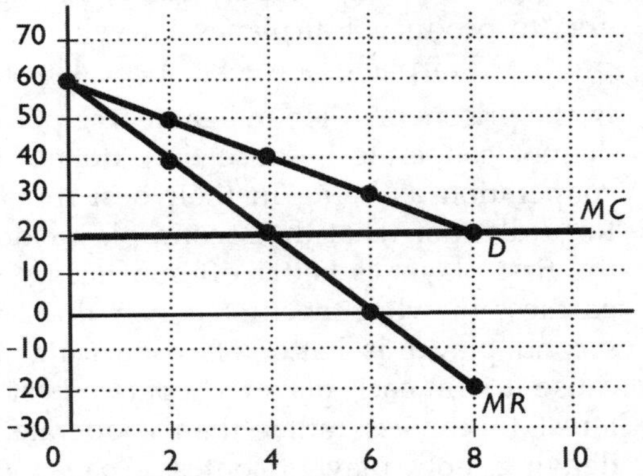

3. a. The curves are graphed in Figure 18.3.

   b. The competitive equilibrium is 8,000 newspapers a day and a price of 20¢ a newspaper; page 460.

   c. The monopoly equilibrium is 4,000 newspapers a day and a price of 40¢ a newspaper; pages 460-461.

   d. The exact price and quantity can't be predicted, but it will be somewhere between the competitive and monopoly outcomes. The price will be between 40¢ and 20¢ a newspaper and the output will be between 4,000 and 8,000 newspapers a day; pages 460-462.

Long Response Question

1. The point that one firm's actions can decrease another firm's profits is what makes competition difficult in an oligopoly. While the firms might be better off cooperating, each firm trying to increase its profit takes actions that lead the profits of its competitors to decrease, so that all the firms wind up worse off; pages 460-462.

Additional Exercises (also in MyEconLab Test A)

1. The price equals $6. The profit-maximizing price does not depend on the number of firms in the cartel, though the more firms in the cartel, the lower is each firm's production quota; page 460.

2. The price equals zero and the quantity produced is 12 units a day; pages 460-461.

3. The dilemma is that if *both* firms reduced their advertising, *both* firms' profit would increase. But if only *one* firm cut its advertising, its profit would plunge while its competitor would make a fortune. Because neither firm can trust the other to follow through on an agreement to cut advertising, both advertise heavily even though there is a better outcome possible for both firms; page 462.

4. If Duracell and Energizer adhere to the cartel agreement to restrict output, the price of a battery will rise. To the extent that one or both firms cheat on the agreement, the price of a battery will be less than when both firms comply. If the firms comply with the cartel agreement, advertising expenditure as well as research and development expenditure will be cut. To the extent that one or both firms cheat on the agreement, advertising expenditure and research and development expenditure will be greater than when both firms comply; pages 461-462.

■ **AP Self Test 18.3**

True or false

1. True; page 465
2. False; pages 466-467
3. False; page 467
4. True; page 468
5. False; page 468

Multiple choice

1. b; page 465
2. b; page 466
3. a; page 467
4. a; page 467
5. e; page 466
6. a; page 468
7. d; page 468
8. a; page 468
9. b; page 468
10. b; page 470
11. d; page 470

© 2015 Pearson Education, Inc.

Short Response Questions

Cameron's strategies

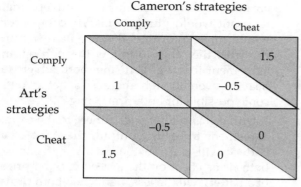

1. a. The completed payoff matrix is above. The payoffs are in millions of dollars; page 466.

   b. The Nash equilibrium is for both Cameron and Art to cheat on the collusive agreement and each make zero economic profit; page 468.

Intel's strategies

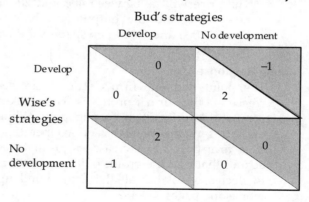

2. a. The completed payoff matrix is above. The payoffs are in millions of dollars; page 466.

   b. The Nash equilibrium is for both Intel and AMD to spend $2 billion on research and development and each make zero economic profit; page 468.

3. The more players in a game, the harder it is to maintain the monopoly outcome; page 468.

Long Response Questions

1. Strategies are all the possible actions of each player. In the prisoners' dilemma game, strategies are "to confess" or "to deny;" in the Airbus/Boeing duopoly game, strategies are "to produce 4 airplanes a week" or "to produce 3 airplanes a week;" page 466.

2. In the prisoners' dilemma game, the players do not cooperate because they do not see cooperation as being in their best interest. Regardless of what the second player does, the first player is better off confessing. Regardless of what the first player does, the second player is better off confessing. Because it is in each player's separate best interest to confess rather than cooperate by denying, both players confess; pages 465-467.

3. In the duopolists' dilemma game, the players do not cooperate for precisely the same reason they do not cooperate in the prisoners' dilemma game: the players do not see cooperation as being in their best interest. As a result, because each player's profit-maximizing actions harm the other player, the equilibrium can be the worst outcome for both; page 468.

Additional Exercises (also in MyEconLab Test A)

Bud's strategies

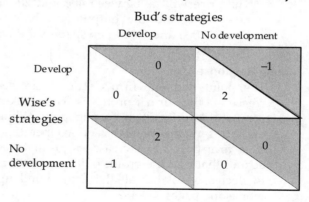

1. The payoff matrix is above with the entries in millions of dollars. If Bud and Wise both develop the drink, each makes zero economic profit. If neither develops, both make zero economic profit, while if one develops and the other does not, the developer makes $2 million economic profit and the non-

© 2015 Pearson Education, Inc.

developer incurs an economic loss of $1 million; page 466.

2. The game has a Nash equilibrium in which both develop the drink. For instance, if Wise develops, Bud wants to develop the drink because otherwise he loses $1 million. And if Wise does not develop the drink, Bud wants to develop the drink so that he can make an economic profit of $2 million. No matter what Wise does, Bud will develop the drink. Similar reasoning shows that Wise, too, will develop the drink; pages 466-467.

3. There is a chance of cooperation in this research and development game if the game is played repeatedly and cheating on the agreement is punished using a tit for tat strategy; page 470.

■ AP Self Test 18.4

True or false
1. True; page 474
2. False; page 474
3. True; page 473
4. False; pages 473-474
5. False; page 477

Multiple choice
1. b; page 473
2. b; page 474
3. e; page 474
4. a; page 474
5. c; page 473
6. a; pages 473-474
7. c; page 475
8. b; page 476
9. b; page 477

Short Response Questions
1. The Clayton Act prohibited several businesses practices *only if* they "substantially lessen competition or create monopoly." Price discrimination by the airlines does not substantially lessen competition or create a monopoly. Price discrimination by the airlines is legal; page 474.

2. The law about price fixing is clear: It is *always* illegal. If price fixing can be proven, the firms are automatically guilty because there can be no acceptable excuse; page 473.

Long Response Questions
1. General Motors is, indeed, a huge company. But it competes with other huge companies in a gigantic market, the new car market. Ford has total revenue over $140 billion a year; Toyota's total revenue is comparable. In fact, in 2008 General Motors was bailed out by the government and, even so, in 2009 General Motors was forced to declare bankruptcy. General Motors suffered this fate because its other huge competitors were better at meeting consumer demand at lower cost than could GM. Antitrust laws deal with markets where there is little competition, not with markets where the many competitors are large; pages 473, 477.

2. a. HHI = $27^2 + 18^2 + 10^2 + 8^2 + 37 = 1,254$. Because this falls below 1,500, the market is considered competitive; page 477.

   b. HHI = $37^2 + 18^2 + 8^2 + 37 = 1,794$. The Federal Trade Commission would not challenge this acquisition the initial HHI is less than 1,500. After this merger, the market is moderately concentrated; page 477.

Additional Exercise (also in MyEconLab Test A)
1. The Standard Oil Company was broken up years ago because the courts believed that it was restraining trade to an unreasonable level. In recent years, some of these individual firms have merged. These actions are a result of the market changing. This outcome would be analogous to the government allowing fragmented portions of the old AT&T to merge. The communications market has changed and new types of competitors have developed. In the petroleum industry, the government has decided that the merged firms now represent a *more* efficient operation and that they face sufficient competition to restrain their behavior; page 477.

© 2015 Pearson Education, Inc.

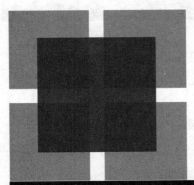

Markets for Factors of Production

Chapter 19

CHAPTER CHECKLIST

In this chapter we study demand, supply, and equilibrium in factor markets.

1 Explain how the value of marginal product determines the demand for a factor of production.

The four factors of production are labor, capital, land (natural resources), and entrepreneurship. Natural resources are either renewable or nonrenewable. The wage rate is the price of labor services, the (capital) rental rate is the price of capital services, and the (land) rental rent is the price of the services of land. The demand for a factor of production is derived from the demand for the goods and services it is used to produce. The value of marginal product is the value to a firm of hiring one more unit of a factor of production and equals the price of a unit of output multiplied by the factor's marginal product. To maximize its profit, a firm hires labor up to the point at which the value of marginal product of labor equals the wage rate. A firm's demand for labor curve is its value of marginal product curve. The demand for labor changes and the demand for labor curve shifts when the price of the firm's output changes, the prices of other factors of production change, or technology changes.

2 Explain how wage rates and employment are determined and how labor unions influence labor markets.

An individual's labor supply curve can be backward bending at higher wage rates so that an increase in the wage rate decreases the quantity of labor supplied. The key factors that change the supply of labor are the adult population, preferences, and time spent in school and training. In a competitive labor market, the equilibrium between the demand for labor and the supply of labor determines the wage rate and employment. A labor union is an organized group of workers that aims to increase the wages of its members. Labor unions try to increase the demand for their members' labor (by increasing the value of marginal product of union members and by supporting minimum wage laws, immigration restrictions, and import restrictions). Unions also try to restrict the supply of non-union labor.

3 Explain how capital and land rental rates and natural resource prices are determined.

The demand for capital is based on the value of marginal product of capital. Equilibrium in the capital market determines the capital rental rate and quantity of capital. The quantity of land is fixed, so the supply of each particular block of land is perfectly inelastic. Equilibrium in the land market determines the land rental rate. The proven reserves of a nonrenewable resource increase over time because advances in technology enable ever less accessible sources to be discovered. The supply of a nonrenewable resource in any given time period is perfectly elastic at the price that gives the owners the same expected profit as selling it in the next time period. The Hotelling Principle is the proposition that the price of a nonrenewable natural resource is expected to rise at a rate equal to the interest rate.

© 2015 Pearson Education, Inc.

YOUR AP TEST HINTS

AP Topics

Topic on your AP test	What to Know	Corresponding textbook section
Marginal product and demand for a factor	How demand is determined in factor markets	Checkpoint 19.1
Labor markets	Supply of labor, market equilibrium, unions in labor markets	Checkpoint 19.2
Price determination	Capital, land rental rates, natural resource prices	Checkpoint 19.3

AP Vocabulary Covered

Terms	What to Know	Text Sections
Factor markets	The services of factors of production are traded here	Checkpoint 19.1, p. 484
Factor prices	Service prices for the factors of production	Checkpoint 19.1, p. 484
Nonrenewable natural resources	Natural resources that can be used only once	Checkpoint 19.1, p. 484
Derived demand	The demand for a factor of production, derived from the demand for the goods and services it is used to produce	Checkpoint 19.1, p. 485
Labor union	Worker organization that bargains for wages and work conditions on behalf of members.	Checkpoint 19.2, p. 494

Extra AP material

- The AP test uses the term "Marginal Revenue Product (MRP)" rather than "Value of the Marginal Product." The value of the marginal product equals $P \times MP$ and the marginal revenue product equals $MR \times MP$. For a firm in perfect competition, $P = MR$ and the two concepts are the same. On the AP test, the wage rate can be referred to as the "marginal resource cost." The point is that the wage rate is the *cost* to the firm of hiring one more (a *marginal*) worker (which is a labor *resource*). With the two vocabulary definitions above, the profit-maximizing quantity of a resource to hire is the amount that sets the marginal revenue product (MRP) equal to the marginal resource cost (MRC).

- The AP test refers to three factors that change the demand for a resource: changes in the demand for the product being produced (which change the price of the product); changes in productivity (which can be the result of changes in technology, changes in the quantities of other resources, or changes in the quality of other resources); and changes in the prices of other resources.

- The elasticity of demand for a resource measures the sensitivity of producers to a change in the resource's price. The elasticity of demand for a resource is larger: the greater the rate of decline of the marginal product; the more easily resources can be substituted for each other; the larger the elasticity of demand for the product being produced; and, the larger the proportion of total cost paid for the resource.

- Firms can use different combinations of resources to produce goods and services. The issue of the optimum combination of resources deals the question: What is the least costly combination of resources? The Least Cost rule states that the cost of any output is minimized when the marginal product per dollar cost of each resource is the same. For instance, if the marginal product of labor is 20 units per hour and the wage rate is $10 per hour, then the marginal product per dollar is 20 units per hour ÷ $10 per hour, or $2 per unit.

© 2015 Pearson Education, Inc.

CHECKPOINT 19.1

■ **Explain how the value of marginal product determines the demand for a factor of production.**

Quick Review

- *Factors of production* The four factors of production are labor, capital, land, and entrepreneurship.

- *Value of marginal product* The value to a firm of hiring one more unit of a factor of production, which equals the price of a unit of output multiplied by the marginal product of the factor of production.

Additional Practice Problems 19.1

1. Tell whether each of the following are land, labor, capital, or entrepreneurship.

   a. oil
   b. an oil worker
   c. an oil platform in the Gulf of Mexico
   d. the Chief Executive Officer of Exxon
   e. a professor
   f. a beach in Florida

2. Casey's lawn service, The Other Side of the Fence, hires workers to mow lawns. The market for lawn mowing is perfectly competitive, and the price of mowing a lawn is $20.00. The labor market is competitive, and the wage rate is $40 a day. The table shows the workers' total product, *TP*:

Workers	Lawns per day
1	3
2	7
3	14
4	18
5	20
6	21

   a. Calculate the marginal product of hiring the third worker.
   b. Calculate the value of marginal product of the third worker.
   c. Complete the table to the right showing the value of marginal product.

Workers	Value of the MP
1	___
2	___
3	___
4	___
5	___
6	___

   d. How many workers will Casey hire to maximize his profit?
   e. How many lawns a day will Casey mow to maximize its profit?
   f. What is Casey's total revenue if he hires 4 workers? What is Casey's total revenue if he hires 5 workers? What is the change in total revenue if Casey hires 5 workers?
   g. How does the increase in Casey's total revenue from hiring the 5th worker compare to the value of marginal product of the 5th worker?

Solutions to Additional Practice Problems 19.1

1a. Oil is a gift of nature and therefore is land.

1b. An oil well worker is labor.

1c. The oil platform is capital.

1d. The Chief Executive Officer is in charge of running Exxon and so is entrepreneurship.

1e. The professor is labor.

1f. The beach is a gift of nature and is land.

2a. The marginal product of hiring the third worker equals the total product of hiring three workers, which is 14 lawns, minus the total product of hiring two workers, which is 7 lawns. So the marginal product of hiring the third worker is 7 lawns.

2b. To calculate the value of marginal product, multiply the marginal product of the third worker by the price of mowing a lawn. The value of marginal product of the third worker is 7 lawns a day × $20.00, which is $140 a day.

2c. The completed table is to the right.

Workers	Value of the MP
1	$60
2	$80
3	$140
4	$80
5	$40
6	$20

2d. To answer this practice problem, recall that to maximize profit, a firm hires labor up to the point at which the value of marginal product equals the wage rate. So, to maximize his profit, Casey hires up to the point at which the value of marginal product equals the wage rate. The wage rate is $40 a day and the answer to part (c) shows that the value of marginal product of the fifth worker is also $40 a day. So Casey hires 5 workers.

© 2015 Pearson Education, Inc.

2e. To maximize its profit, Casey hires 5 workers and the 5 workers mow 20 lawns.

2f. When Casey hires 4 workers, Casey's company mows 18 lawns. Total revenue is 18 lawns a day × $20, which is $360 a day. When Casey hires 5 workers, Casey's company mows 20 lawns a day. Total revenue is 20 lawns a day × $20, which is $400 a day. Casey's total revenue increases by $40 when Casey hires the fifth worker.

2g. The change in Casey's total revenue equals the value of marginal product of the fifth worker.

■ AP Self Test 19.1

True or false

1. As a factor of production, coal is considered to be land.

2. The demand for labor is derived from the demand for the goods and services that the labor is hired to produce.

3. A firm's demand for labor curve is also its value of marginal product curve.

4. A rise in the wage rate decreases the quantity of labor demanded.

Multiple choice

1. The four factors of production that produce goods and services are
   a. labor, capital, profits, and entrepreneurship.
   b. money, labor, rent, and profit.
   c. labor, capital, land, and entrepreneurship.
   d. wages, interest, rent, and profit.
   e. wages, prices, quantities, and employment.

2. The wage rate paid to labor is
   a. a factor output.
   b. a factor price.
   c. a factor input.
   d. an input of the workforce.
   e. part of the firm's normal profit.

3. The demand for labor is derived from the
   a. supply of labor.
   b. wage rate.
   c. supply of the good the labor is used to produce.
   d. demand for the goods and services the labor helps produce.
   e. supply of all the other factors of production that can be substituted for labor.

4. The value of marginal product of labor is equal to the marginal product of labor ____ the price of a unit of output.
   a. divided by
   b. multiplied by
   c. minus
   d. plus
   e. squared and then multiplied by

5. The rule for maximizing profit is to hire labor up to the point at which the value of marginal product of labor
   a. equals the wage rate.
   b. is greater than the wage rate.
   c. is less than the wage rate.
   d. is a mirror image of the wage rate.
   e. equals the price of the product produced.

6. Which of the following is true?
   a. The value to a firm of hiring another worker is the worker's value of marginal product.
   b. A firm will hire more workers if the wage rate is greater than the value of marginal product.
   c. The value of marginal product is the cost of hiring a worker.
   d. The value of marginal product increases as more workers are hired.
   e. The value of marginal product equals the price of the good produced divided by the marginal product.

© 2015 Pearson Education, Inc.

7. An increase in the price of a firm's output leads to a
   a. movement up along the demand for labor curve.
   b. movement down along the demand for labor curve.
   c. rightward shift of the demand for labor curve.
   d. leftward shift of the demand for labor curve
   e. rightward shift of the supply of labor curve.

Short Response Questions

1. For what are factors of production used?

2. Petroleum is categorized as what type of factor of production?

Quantity of labor (workers)	Marginal product (lawns per week)	Value of marginal product 1 (dollars)	Value of marginal product 2 (dollars)
1	13	___	___
2	12	___	___
3	11	___	___
4	10	___	___
5	9	___	___

3. Gene's Lawn Service hires workers to mow lawns. The market for lawns is perfectly competitive and Gene charges $25 a lawn. The table above shows the workers' marginal product schedule.
   a. Calculate the value of marginal product for each quantity of workers and record your answers in the "Value of marginal product 1" column. In Figure 19.1, plot Gene's demand for labor curve. Label it LD_1.
   b. Suppose the price of mowing a lawn rises to $30 per lawn. Calculate the new value of marginal products and record them in the "Value of marginal product 2" column. In Figure 19.1, plot Gene's new demand for labor curve and label it LD_2. How did the increase in the price of mowing a lawn change Gene's demand for labor curve?

4. Figure 19.2 shows the labor demand curves for two groups of labor.
   a. Which group of labor, group 1 or group 2, has a larger value of its marginal product?

b. What does the difference in the value of marginal product between the two groups equal?

■ FIGURE 19.1

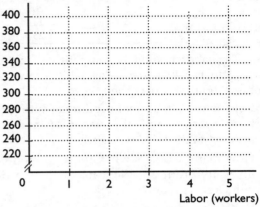

Wage rate (dollars per week)

■ FIGURE 19.2

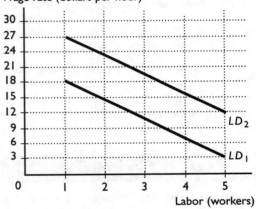

Wage rate (dollars per hour)

b. What does the difference in the value of marginal product between the two groups equal?

Long Response Questions

1. Why does the value of marginal product decrease as more workers are employed?

2. What is the relationship between the demand for labor curve and the value of marginal product curve?

3. What factors change the demand for labor and shift the demand for labor curve?

© 2015 Pearson Education, Inc.

Additional Exercises (also in MyEconLab Test A)

Greg's Grooming hires workers to groom dogs. The market for dog grooming is perfectly competitive, and the price is $20 a dog. The labor market is competitive, and the wage rate is $40 a day. The table shows the workers' total product schedule.

Workers	Groomings per day
1	4
2	7
3	11
4	16
5	20
6	23
7	25

1. Calculate the marginal product of hiring the third worker and the value of marginal product of the third worker.

2. How many workers will Greg's hire to maximize its profit and how many dogs a day will Greg's groom?

3. If the wage rate rises to $60 a day, how many workers will Greg's hire?

4. Greg installs a machine that doubles the workers' productivity. If the price of a grooming falls to $10, how many workers will Greg's hire at $40 a day?

5. More and more people shop on the Internet. What are three types of labor for which the demand will continue to increase and three types for which the demand will continue to decrease? Explain your answer.

CHECKPOINT 19.2

■ **Explain how wage rates and employment are determined and how labor unions influence labor markets.**

Quick Review

• *Changes in the demand for labor* The demand for labor depends on the price of the firm's output, the prices of other factors of production, and technology.

• *Changes in the supply of labor* The key factors that change the supply of labor are the adult population, preferences, and time spent in school and training.

Additional Practice Problems 19.2

1. Why does an individual labor supply curve bend backward?

2. Tell how each of the events given below affects the labor market. Draw a labor supply and labor demand diagram to determine the effect on the equilibrium wage rate and employment.

   a. More workers reach retirement age and retire.

   b. New technology increases workers' productivity.

   c. Suppose that the price of clothing falls. What is the impact of this change in the labor market for textile workers.

Solutions to Additional Practice Problems 19.2

1. To see how the wage rate influences the quantity of labor supplied, think about Emma's labor supply decision. Emma enjoys leisure time but, if her boss offers her $12 an hour, Emma chooses to work 30 hours a week. This wage rate is high enough to make Emma regard this use of her time as the best available to her. If Emma were offered a higher wage rate, she would want to work even longer hours, but only up to a point. If Emma is offered $25 an hour, she would be willing to work a 40-hour week. But if the wage rate is increased above $25 an hour, Emma would cut back on her work hours and take more leisure. Emma's labor supply curve eventually bends backward.

2a. When more workers reach retirement age and then retire, the supply of labor decreases. The labor supply curve shifts leftward, shown in the figure by the shift from LS_0 to LS_1. As a result, the equi-

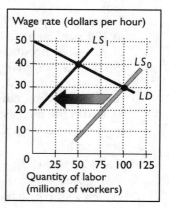

© 2015 Pearson Education, Inc.

librium wage rate rises and the equilibrium quantity of employment decreases.

2b. By making workers more productive, the new technology, increases the demand for labor. The labor demand curve shifts rightward, in the figure from LD_0 to LD_1. The equilibrium wage rate rises

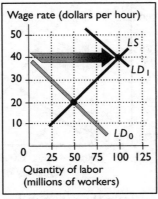

and the equilibrium amount of employment increases.

2c. A fall in the price of clothing decreases the value of marginal pro-duct of textile workers. As a result, the demand for labor decreases and the labor demand curve shifts leftward, from LD_0 to LD_1

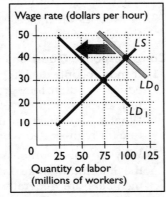

in the figure. The equilibrium wage rate falls and the equilibrium amount of employment decreases.

■ AP Self Test 19.2

True or false

1. An individual's supply of labor curve shows that the quantity of labor supplied always increases when the wage rate rises.

2. An increase in college enrollment decreases the supply of low-skilled labor.

3. If the wage rate is less than the equilibrium wage rate, the wage rate will rise to eliminate the surplus of labor.

4. Compared to a competitive labor market, unions boost their members' wages.

5. Unions are likely to support import restrictions.

Multiple choice

1. An individual's labor supply curve eventually bends backward because at a high enough wage rate,
   a. people are willing to work more hours.
   b. employers are willing to hire more workers.
   c. people desire more leisure time.
   d. very few workers are hired.
   e. more people enter the labor market to search for jobs.

2. How does an increase in the adult population affect the labor market?
   a. The demand for labor will become more inelastic.
   b. The supply of labor will decrease.
   c. The supply of labor will increase.
   d. The demand for labor will decrease.
   e. The demand for labor will increase.

3. The supply of labor curve shifts leftward if
   a. the population increases.
   b. the demand for labor curve shifts leftward.
   c. the supply of labor increases.
   d. the wage rate falls.
   e. the supply of labor decreases.

4. If the wage rate is above the equilibrium wage rate, the quantity of labor demanded is ____ the quantity of labor supplied.
   a. greater than
   b. less than
   c. equal to
   d. the negative of
   e. not comparable to

5. The more people who remain in school for full-time education and training, the ____ is the ____ low-skilled labor.
   a. smaller; demand for
   b. smaller; supply of
   c. larger; supply of
   d. larger; demand for
   e. less elastic; demand for

© 2015 Pearson Education, Inc.

6. If the supply of labor decreases, then the equilibrium wage rate _____ and equilibrium employment _____.
   a. does not change; decreases
   b. rises; increases
   c. rises; decreases
   d. falls; increases
   e. falls; decreases

7. Of the following, a union is *least* likely to support
   a. an increase in the minimum wage rate.
   b. laws that restrict immigration into the country.
   c. on-the-job training that makes their members more productive.
   d. laws that increase the quantity of the nation's imports.
   e. programs that boost the demand for the goods and services their members produce.

Short Response Questions

■ FIGURE 19.3

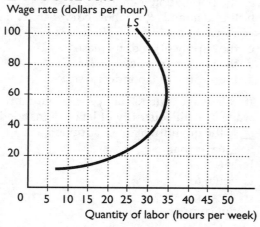

Wage rate (dollars per hour)

1. Figure 19.3 shows Hank's supply of labor curve. At what wage rate does an increase in the wage rate decrease the quantity of labor Hank supplies?

2. Figure 19.4 shows the labor market for Internet security programmers. Suppose that more companies start conducting more of their business on the Internet and so need more Internet security. In Figure 19.4, illus-

■ FIGURE 19.4

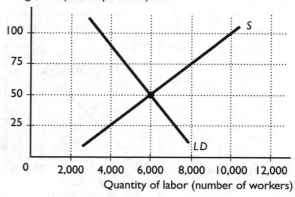

Wage rate (dollars per hour)

trate the effect in the market for these programmers. What happens to the equilibrium wage rate and number of programmers?

3. How does an increase in the adult population change the supply of labor?

Long Response Questions

1. If more people decide to obtain an advanced education, after they graduate what is the effect on the supply of high-skilled labor? What is the effect on the equilibrium wage rate for high-skilled workers?

2. Why do labor unions support increases in the minimum wage rate even though their members are generally paid more than the minimum wage?

Additional Exercises (also in MyEconLab Test A)

1. Ski instructors are skilled workers. Consider the market for ski instructors in the greater Salt Lake City region and explain how that market would change if ski holidays became more popular.

2. What do you think the effect of Internet commerce has been on the markets for truck drivers, couriers, and sales clerks?

3. Why does the United Farm Workers union want the government to limit the immigration of farm workers from Mexico?

© 2015 Pearson Education, Inc.

CHECKPOINT 19.3

■ **Explain how capital and land rental rates and natural resource prices are determined.**

Quick Review

- *Renewable natural resources* Natural resources that can be used repeatedly.
- *Nonrenewable natural resources* Natural resources that can be used only once and that cannot be replaced once they have been used.

Additional Practice Problem 19.3

1. Petroleum is a nonrenewable natural resource and is constantly being used. Additionally, there are new technologies being developed that allow petroleum to be discovered in new locations and also new technologies being developed that make more efficient use of petroleum. What effects do these changes have on the known reserves of petroleum, the demand for petroleum, and the price of petroleum?

Solution to Additional Practice Problem 19.3

1. Using a natural resource such as petroleum decreases its known reserves, which, by itself, raises the price. But new technologies that lead to the discovery of previously unknown reserves increase the known reserves, which, by itself, lowers the price. And the new technologies that enable a more efficient use of a nonrenewable natural resource decrease the demand for the resource, which, by itself, lowers the price. So whether the known reserves increase or decrease and whether the price rises or falls depends on which of the effects is larger.

■ AP Self Test 19.3

True or false

1. If the supply of capital increases, the rental rate of capital rises.

2. The demand for land is perfectly elastic, and the supply of land is perfectly inelastic.

3. Because new natural gas deposits are always being discovered, natural gas is a renewable natural resource.

4. The price of a natural resource can only rise over time.

Multiple choice

1. The supply of each particular block of land is
   a. perfectly elastic.
   b. unit elastic.
   c. elastic but not perfectly elastic.
   d. perfectly inelastic.
   e. inelastic but not perfectly inelastic.

2. The equilibrium quantity of capital is
   a. determined by only the supply of capital because the supply is perfectly inelastic.
   b. determined by only the supply of capital because the supply is perfectly elastic.
   c. expected to increase at the same rate as the interest rate.
   d. determined by the supply of capital and the demand for capital.
   e. the only factor of production whose quantity is not determined in a market.

3. A natural resource is nonrenewable if it
   a. never has to rest.
   b. can be used repeatedly.
   c. cannot be replaced once it has been used.
   d. is available at a price of zero.
   e. has a perfectly elastic supply.

4. Oil is an example of
   a. a nonrenewable natural resource.
   b. a renewable natural resource.
   c. physical capital.
   d. a resource for which the true value cannot be measured.
   e. a resource with a perfectly inelastic demand.

5. The demand for a nonrenewable resource is
   a. determined by the value of its marginal product.
   b. fixed and cannot change.
   c. perfectly inelastic.
   d. perfectly elastic.
   e. not defined because the resource can be used only once.

© 2015 Pearson Education, Inc.

6. A producer's supply of a nonrenewable natural resource is
   a. always decreasing because the resource is always being used.
   b. perfectly inelastic.
   c. perfectly elastic.
   d. not relevant because nonrenewable resources are used only once.
   e. is determined by the value of the resource's marginal product.

Short Response Questions

Rent (dollars per acre per month)	Land demanded (thousands of acres)
400	10
350	20
300	30
250	40
200	50

1. The table above shows the demand schedule for land. The supply of land is fixed at 20,000 square acres.
   a. In Figure 19.5, label the axes and graph the demand and the supply curve of land.

■ **FIGURE 19.5**

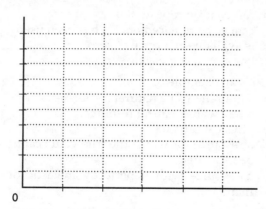

   b. What is the equilibrium rent and quantity?
   c. Suppose the demand decreases so that the quantity of land demanded decreases by 10 thousand acres at each rent. What is the new equilibrium rent and quantity? Comment on the change in the rent and the change in the quantity.

2. There are billions of barrels of petroleum still in the ground. Why, then, is petroleum considered a nonrenewable natural resource?

Long Response Questions

Capital rental rate (dollars)	Demand for capital (billions of dollars)	Supply of capital (billions of dollars)
400	150	90
500	130	100
600	110	110
700	90	120
800	70	130

1. The table above gives the demand and supply schedules for capital.
   a. What is the equilibrium rental rate and quantity of capital?
   b. Suppose that population growth increases the quantity of capital demanded by $20 billion at each rental rate and also increases the quantity of capital supplied by $20 billion at each rental rate. Now what is the equilibrium rental rate and quantity of capital?

2. Explain the role played by the interest rate play in how the price of a nonrenewable natural resource changes over time.

3. The Eye on Your Life discussed salaries of different professions. When you are thinking about a major and a possible career, probably salary implications ought to play some role. And you can use the demand and supply model to help make informal predictions about the future prospects of different career paths. For instance, the U.S. population is aging and older people tend to use more hospital care. How will this fact affect the future job prospects and salary of a person going into nursing?

Additional Exercises (also in MyEconLab Test A)

1. New technology has allowed oil to be pumped from much deeper offshore oil fields than before. For example, 28 deep ocean rigs operate in the deep waters of the Gulf of Mexico. What effect do you think

© 2015 Pearson Education, Inc.

deep ocean sources have had on the world oil price? Who will benefit from drilling for oil in the Gulf of Mexico? Explain your answer.

2. Water is a natural resource that is plentiful in Canada but not plentiful in Arizona and southern California. If Canadians start to export bulk water to Arizona and southern California, what do you predict will be the effect on the price of bulk water? Will Canada eventually run out of water?

3. In the 1970s, few people drank bottled spring water and the major producers of bottled spring water were in Europe. Today, lots of people drink bottled spring water. How has this increase in the demand for spring water been satisfied? Will this increase in demand lead to some springs running dry?

4. As cities grow, good farmland is being replaced by urban sprawl. Why do farmers sell their land to urban developers?

© 2015 Pearson Education, Inc.

SELF TEST ANSWERS

■ AP Self Test 19.1

True or false

1. True; page 484
2. True; page 485
3. True; pages 486-487
4. True; pages 486-487

Multiple choice

1. c; page 484
2. b; page 484
3. d; page 485
4. b; page 485
5. a; pages 486-487
6. a; page 486
7. c; page 488

Short Response Questions

1. Factors of production are used to produce goods and services; page 484.
2. Petroleum is a gift of nature, so as a factor of production it is included as land; page 484.

Quantity of labor (workers)	Marginal product (lawns per week)	Value of marginal product 1 (dollars)	Value of marginal product 2 (dollars)
1	13	325	390
2	12	300	360
3	11	275	330
4	10	250	300
5	9	225	270

3. a. The completed table is above. Figure 19.6 plots the demand for labor curve LD_1; pages 485-487.

   b. The completed table is above. Figure 19.6 plots the demand for labor curve LD_2. The increase in the price of mowing a lawn increases Gene's demand for labor and his demand for labor curve shifts rightward; page 488.

4. a. Group 2's value of marginal product is higher because its demand curve lies to the right of group 1's demand curve; page 486.

   b. Because the demand curve is the same as the value of marginal product curve, the

■ FIGURE 19.6

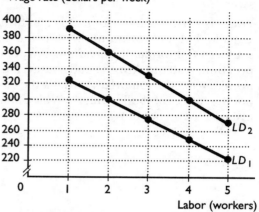
Wage rate (dollars per week)

vertical distance between the two demand curves equals the difference in the value of marginal product. So group 2's value of marginal product is $7.50 more per hour than group 1's value of marginal product; pages 486-487

Long Response Questions

1. The value of marginal product equals the price of a unit of the output multiplied by the marginal product of the factor of production. As more of the factor of production is employed, marginal product decreases, and as a result, the value of marginal product also decreases; pages 485-486.

2. The demand for labor curve and the value of marginal product curve are the same; pages 486-487.

3. Three factors change the demand for labor and shift the demand for labor curve: changes in the price of the firm's output, changes in the prices of other factors of production, and changes in technology; page 488.

Additional Exercises (also in MyEconLab Test A)

1. The marginal product of the third worker is 4 groomings a day. The value of marginal product of the third worker is (4 groomings a day) × ($20 a grooming), which is $80 a day; page 485.

© 2015 Pearson Education, Inc.

2. Greg will hire 7 workers because the value of marginal product of the seventh worker is $40 a day, (2 groomings a day × $20 a grooming) which equals the wage rate. When Greg hires 7 workers, 25 dogs are groomed a day; pages 487–488.

3. If the wage rate rises to $60, Greg hires 6 workers. The value of marginal product of the sixth worker is $60, which equals the new wage rate; page 488.

4. With the increase in productivity and the fall in the price of a dog grooming, Greg hires 7 workers. The value of marginal product of the seventh worker equals the marginal product, which is now 4 groomings a day, multiplied by the price of a grooming, which is now $10. So the value of marginal product of the seventh worker is (4 groomings a day) × ($10 a grooming) = $40, which is equal to the wage rate; pages 485–486 .

5. As more people use the Internet, computer sales increase. These computers will break and need repair. The demand for PC producers and repair people increases. As more firms enter the Internet market, they hire Web-page designers. The demand for Web-page designers also increases. The demand for other types of workers decreases. As more people use the Internet for news, the demand for newspapers decreases so newspapers lay off people. If more sales are transacted via the Internet, fewer sales clerks are needed. Fewer customer service representatives are needed as people use the Internet to get product information; page 488.

■ AP Self Test 19.2

True or false
1. False; page 490
2. True; page 492
3. False; pages 492–493
4. True; page 494
5. True; page 495

Multiple choice
1. c; page 490

2. c; page 492
3. e; page 492
4. b; pages 492–493
5. b; page 492
6. c; page 493
7. d; page 495

Short Response Questions

■ FIGURE 19.7

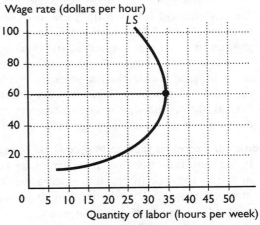
Wage rate (dollars per hour)

1. Figure 19.7 shows that for wage rates exceeding $60 an hour, Hank decreases the quantity of labor he supplies as the wage rate rises; page 490.

■ FIGURE 19.8

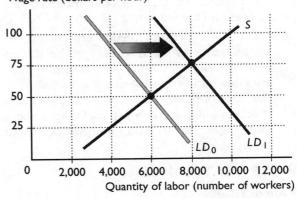
Wage rate (dollars per hour)

2. In Figure 19.8 the demand for Internet security programmers increases. The demand for labor curve shifts rightward from LD_0 to LD_1. The equilibrium wage rate rises and the

© 2015 Pearson Education, Inc.

quantity of these programmers employed increases; pages 492-493.

3. An increase in the adult population increases the supply of labor; page 492.

Long Response Questions

1. As more people obtain advanced degrees the supply of high-skilled labor increases. The equilibrium wage rate for high-skilled labor falls; pages 492-493.

2. Unions support hikes in the minimum wage because lower-skilled workers, who are paid the minimum wage, are substitutes for higher-skilled union labor. If the wage rate that must be paid lower skilled workers increases, some firms will hire instead higher-skilled union labor, thereby increasing the demand for union labor; page 495.

Additional Exercises (also in MyEconLab Test A)

1. If ski holidays become more popular, the demand for ski instructors increases. The number of ski instructors employed increases and the wage rate rises; page 492.

2. The demand for truck drivers and couriers increases. As a result, the number of truck drivers and couriers employed increases and the wage rate rises. The demand for sales clerks in stores decreases as more transactions take place via the Internet. As a result, the number of sales clerks employed decreases and the wage rate falls; page 492.

3. Farm workers from Mexico are substitutes for the labor of the members of the United Farm Workers union. If fewer immigrants are allowed in from Mexico, the demand for the labor of the members of the United Farm Workers union increases so that employment and wages paid to the union members both rise; page 495.

■ AP Self Test 19.3

True or false

1. False; page 497
2. False; page 498
3. False; page 499
4. False; page 500

Multiple choice

1. d; page 498
2. d; page 497
3. c; page 499
4. a; page 499
5. a; page 499
6. c; page 500

Short Response Questions

■ FIGURE 19.9

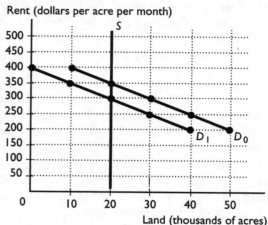

Rent (dollars per acre per month)

1. a. Figure 19.9 shows the completed figure; page 498.

   b. The equilibrium rent is $350 an acre per month and the equilibrium quantity is 20,000 acres; page 498.

   c. The decrease in demand lowers the equilibrium rent to $300 per acre and the equilibrium quantity remains 20,000 acres. The change in demand changed *only* the rent; the quantity is unchanged. Because the supply is perfectly inelastic, changes in demand change only the rent and do not affect the quantity; page 498.

2. Petroleum is a nonrenewable natural resource because once any particular barrel is used, that barrel cannot be used again; page 499.

Long Response Questions

1. a. The equilibrium rental rate is $600 because this is the rental rate at which the quantity of capital demanded equals the quantity

© 2015 Pearson Education, Inc.

of capital supplied. The equilibrium quantity of capital is $110 billion; page 497.

  b. In this question, both the demand and supply of capital have increased by the same amount. So the equilibrium rental rate remains the same, $600, and the equilibrium quantity of capital increases to $130 billion; page 497.

2. The Hotelling Principle is the result that the price of a nonrenewable resource is expected to rise at a rate that equals the interest rate. The explanation for this result lies in the behavior of the owners of the resource: They can either sell the resource and invest the proceeds in an interest bearing asset or else hold the resource and sell it next period. If the price is expected to rise at a rate that is less than the interest rate, the owners will increase their supply today in order to use the proceeds to buy an interest bearing asset. The supply will continue to increase, which lowers the resource's price, until today's price falls enough so that its rate of increase from today to the next period is equal to the interest rate. At this point, the owners will no longer increase the supply. Similarly, if the price is expected to rise at a rate greater than the interest rate, the owners will decrease their supply in order to hold the resource and enjoy the high return. The supply will continue to decrease, which raises the resource's price, until today's price rises enough so that its rate of increase from today to the next period is equal to the interest rate. At this point, the owners will no longer decrease the supply. So the equilibrium, which occurs when the owners are neither increasing nor decreasing the supply (that is, the supply curve is not shifting) occurs only when the price of the resource is expected to rise at a rate that equals the interest rate; page 501.

3. A large fraction of nurses are hired by hospitals. As the nation ages and more individuals require hospital care, the demand for nurses is likely to increase. The increase in the demand for nurses will raise the salary paid nurses and increase the quantity employed. So by using the supply and demand model, it is possible to make an informed prediction that the career possibilities of nurses are fairly bright; page 499.

Additional Exercises (also in MyEconLab Test A)

1. The deep ocean oil fields increased the supply of oil and have kept oil prices from rising higher than they have. The people benefiting from the new technology are the owners of the oil rigs and the firms selling this oil. Consumers also benefit because the price of oil is lower. If oil is drilled from the Gulf of Mexico, the owners and producers of this oil will benefit as will consumers of oil; pages 500-501.

2. With the increased supply, the price of water will fall in Arizona and California. Water is a renewable resource in Canada so it will not run out; pages 484, 499.

3. The increased demand for bottled water has encouraged land owners to sell the spring water produced on their land. Springs are renewable resources and will not run dry; pages 484, 499.

4. Farmers sell their land to urban developers because they believe their return from selling the land is greater than they will receive from farming. The price offered for the land is high because the demand for land to use for development is high; page 498.

© 2015 Pearson Education, Inc.

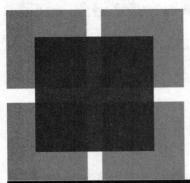

Economic Inequality

CHAPTER CHECKLIST

1 Describe the economic inequality in the United States.

Market income is a household's wages, interest, rent, and profit earned in factor markets before paying taxes. Money income is market income plus cash payments from the government. Income and wealth are distributed unequally. The extent of inequality is measured using a Lorenz curve. A Lorenz curve graphs the cumulative percentage of income (or wealth) against the cumulative percentage of households. The farther the Lorenz curve is from the 45° line of equality, the more unequally income (or wealth) is distributed. In the United States, inequality has increased over the past few decades and economic mobility, moving up or down 1 quintile in the distribution of income, has decreased. Education, household size, and martial status are important factors affecting a household's income. Poverty is a state in which a household's income is too low to buy the quantities of food, shelter, and clothing that are deemed necessary. Poverty rates for blacks and Hispanics exceed those for white households. The longer poverty lasts, the larger the problem for the household. For more than 20 percent of poor households poverty lasts for more than a year.

2 Explain how economic inequality arises.

Human capital is people's accumulated skill and knowledge. Differences in skills lead to differences in earnings. High-skilled labor has a greater value of marginal product than low-skilled labor, so at a given wage rate, the quantity of high-skilled labor demanded exceeds that of low-skilled labor. Skills are costly to acquire, so at a given wage rate, the quantity of high-skilled labor supplied is less than that of low-skilled labor. The equilibrium wage rate of high-skilled labor is higher than that of low-skilled labor. Discrimination according to race or sex is another possible source of inequality. High income people typically own large amounts of physical and financial capital while some have great entrepreneurial ability. Personal and family characteristics also affect an individual's income.

3 Explain how governments redistribute income and describe the effects of redistribution on economic inequality.

The government redistributes income using income taxes, income maintenance programs, and subsidized services. Income maintenance programs include Social Security, unemployment compensation, and welfare programs. The distribution of disposable income (income after taxes and benefits) is more equal than the market distribution. Utilitarianism suggests that more equality is fairer. But government redistribution weakens work incentives both for the recipient and the wage earner, which create the big tradeoff between equity and efficiency. A major challenge is to ensure that welfare programs do not weaken the incentives to acquire human capital; the current approach attempts to avoid weakening these incentives. The negative income tax is a redistribution scheme that provides every household with a guaranteed minimum annual income and taxes all earned income above the minimum at a fixed rate.

© 2015 Pearson Education, Inc.

YOUR AP TEST HINTS

AP Topics

Topic on your AP test	What to Know	Corresponding textbook section
Income inequality	How income inequality is measured	Checkpoint 20.1
How income inequality arises	How labor market outcomes lead to income inequality; factors that affect labor market outcomes	Checkpoint 20.2
Income redistribution	Government policies; reasons for redistribution	Checkpoint 20.3

AP Vocabulary Covered

Terms	What to Know	Text Sections
Market income	Wages, interest, rent, and profit earned in a factor market *before* paying taxes	Checkpoint 20.1, p. 508
Money income	Market income *plus* cash payments to households by the government	Checkpoint 20.1, p. 508
Lorenz curve	A graph of the cumulative percent of incomes (or wealth) against the cumulative percent of households; used to measure income (or wealth) inequality	Checkpoint 20.1, p. 509
Poverty	When a household's income is too low to buy basic food, clothing, and shelter needs	Checkpoint 20.1, p. 513
Human capital	The accumulated skill and knowledge of human beings	Checkpoint 20.2, p. 516
Progressive tax	Tax rates increase with levels of income	Checkpoint 20.3, p. 522
Income maintenance programs	Redistribution programs like social security, unemployment compensation, and welfare programs	Checkpoint 20.3, p. 522
Disposable income	Market income plus cash benefits paid by the government minus taxes paid to the government	Checkpoint 20.3, p. 524
Utilitarianism	Theory that supports the redistribution of income based on the idea of equality	Checkpoint 20.3, p. 525
Median voter theory	Theory that governments pursue policies that make the median voter as well off as possible	Checkpoint 20.3, p. 526
TANF	Temporary Assistance for Needy Families ; current government welfare program; sets five-year limit for a family to receive assistance	Checkpoint 20.3, p. 526
Negative income tax	A theory where minimum annual income is guaranteed to all households with a fixed rate of income taxes	Checkpoint 20.3, p. 527

Extra AP material

- The different approaches to fairness of taxation, the benefit approach and the ability to pay approach, can be related to the fairness of redistributing income more equally.

© 2015 Pearson Education, Inc.

CHECKPOINT 20.1

■ **Describe the economic inequality in the United States.**

Quick Review

- *Lorenz curve* A curve that graphs the cumulative percentage of income (or wealth) against the cumulative percentage of households. The farther the Lorenz curve is from the line of equality, the greater is the inequality.

Additional Practice Problems 20.1

1978	
Households	**Income (percentage)**
Lowest 20 percent	4.3
Second 20 percent	10.3
Third 20 percent	16.9
Fourth 20 percent	24.7
Highest 20 percent	43.8

1. The table above shows the distribution of money income in the United States in 1978:
   a. Draw the Lorenz curve for the United States in 1978.
   b. Was the distribution of income in the United States more or less equal than in recent years?

2. In the figure are the Lorenz curves for three nations, *A, B,* and *C.* In which nation is income distributed the most unequally? The most equally? In which nation is average income the highest?

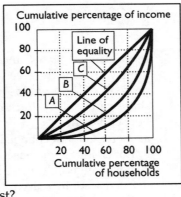

Solutions to Additional Practice Problems 20.1

1a. When drawing a Lorenz curve, the key is that it plots the *cumulative* percentage of income against the *cumulative* percentage of households. To create a Lorenz curve calculate cumulative percentages, which is done

1978	
Households (cumulative percent)	**Income (cumulative percent)**
20 percent of households	4.3
40 percent of households	14.6
60 percent of households	31.5
80 percent of households	56.2
100 percent of households	100.0

by adding the income owned by *all* the people who fall in the income group in and below the percentage being considered. So, to draw the Lorenz curve, we first need to calculate the cumulative percentage of households and the cumulative percentage of income. The table above has these percentages. The Lorenz curve in the figure plots the cumulative percentage of income and cumulative percentage of households in the above table.

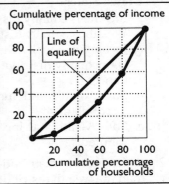

1b. The distribution of income in the United States in recent years has become less equal that what it was in 1978.

2. Income is distributed the most unequally in nation *A* because its Lorenz curve is farthest from the line of equality. Income is distributed the most equally in nation *C* because its Lorenz curve is the closest to the line of equality. Based on the Lorenz curves it is impossible to determine in which nation average income is the highest. Lorenz curves give information about the distribution of income, *not* about its amount.

■ AP Self Test 20.1

True or false

1. The Lorenz curve always lies above the line of equality.

© 2015 Pearson Education, Inc.

2. Since 1970, the percentage of the money income received by the richest 20 percent of households decreased.

3. Inequality of annual income overstates the degree of lifetime inequality.

4. When it comes to determining household income, education is a more important characteristic than is race.

5. In the United States, poverty is distributed equally across the races, with approximately 15 percent of households of each race living in poverty.

Multiple choice

1. Which of the following is correct about the United States?
   a. Income is equally distributed.
   b. Wealth is equally distributed.
   c. Income is equally distributed but wealth is unequally distributed because of inheritances.
   d. Both wealth and income are unequally distributed.
   e. Both wealth and income are equally distributed.

2. If the income distribution is more unequal than the wealth distribution, then the
   a. Lorenz curve for income will be farther away from the line of equality than the Lorenz curve for wealth.
   b. government has imposed a higher tax rate on income.
   c. Lorenz curve for wealth will be farther away from the line of equality than the Lorenz curve for income.
   d. Lorenz curve for wealth will lie above the Lorenz curve for income.
   e. It is not possible to draw the Lorenz curve for wealth on the same figure with the Lorenz curve for income.

■ **FIGURE 20.1**

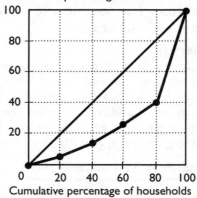

Cumulative percentage of income

3. In Figure 20.1, the richest 20 percent of households receive ____ percent of total income.
   a. 20
   b. 100
   c. 80
   d. 40
   e. 60

4. In the United States in 2004, the wealthiest 1 percent of households owned approximately ____ percent of all wealth.
   a. 1
   b. 13
   c. 27
   d. 34
   e. 88

5. In the United States since 1970, the share of money income received by the richest 20 percent of households has ____ and the share received by the lowest 20 percent of households has ____.
   a. increased; not changed
   b. not changed; increased
   c. not changed; decreased
   d. decreased; increased
   e. increased; decreased

© 2015 Pearson Education, Inc.

6. The inequality of annual income
   a. overstates the degree of lifetime inequality.
   b. understates the degree of lifetime inequality.
   c. cannot change from one year to the next.
   d. is about the same as the amount of lifetime inequality.
   e. cannot be compared to the amount of lifetime inequality.

7. Of all the characteristics that lead to income inequality, the factor with the largest impact is
   a. race.
   b. sex.
   c. age.
   d. education.
   e. location.

8. Which of the following statements about poverty is (are) correct?
   i. Blacks and Hispanics have higher poverty rates than whites.
   ii. Over the last 40 years, poverty rates for all groups have generally increased.
   iii. Most household spells of poverty last much longer than 1 year.
   a. i only.
   b. ii only.
   c. iii only.
   d. ii and iii.
   e. i, ii, and iii.

Short Response Question
1. What does the distance between a Lorenz curve for income and the line of equality tell about the distribution of income?

Long Response Questions
1. Can a Lorenz curve ever lie above the line of equality? Why or why not?

2. The table above has data for the nation of Beta. Complete the table by calculating the cumulative percentages for the last column. In Figure 20.2, plot the Lorenz curve for Beta.

3. How has the distribution of income and the amount of economic mobility changed in the United States over the past few decades?

Household percentage	Percentage of income	Cumulative percentage of income
Lowest 20 percent	5.0	____
Second 20 percent	9.0	____
Third 20 percent	20.0	____
Fourth 20 percent	26.0	____
Highest 20 percent	40.0	____

■ FIGURE 20.2

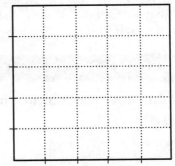

4. What is poverty? How many Americans live in poverty? How have poverty rates changed over the last few decades?

Additional Exercises (also in MyEconLab Test A)

Distribution of income in Canada

Households	Income (percentage)
Lowest 20 percent	7.4
Second 20 percent	13.2
Third 20 percent	18.1
Fourth 20 percent	24.9
Highest 20 percent	36.4

Distribution of income in the United Kingdom

Households	Income (percentage)
Lowest 20 percent	3
Second 20 percent	5
Third 20 percent	14
Fourth 20 percent	25
Highest 20 percent	53

Table 20.1(a) on page 508 of the textbook shows the distribution of income in the United States. The top table above shows the distribution of income in Canada and the bottom table shows the distribution of income in the United Kingdom.

1. Create a table that shows the cumulative

© 2015 Pearson Education, Inc.

percentages of households and income in the United Kingdom.

2. Draw the Lorenz curves for the United Kingdom and the United States. Compare the distribution of income in the United Kingdom with that in the United States. Which distribution is more unequal?

3. Draw the Lorenz curves for the United Kingdom and Canada. Compare the distribution of income in the United Kingdom with that in Canada. Which distribution is more unequal?

CHECKPOINT 20.2

■ **Explain how economic inequality arises.**

Quick Review

- *Demand for high-skilled labor and low-skilled labor* The vertical distance between the demand curve for low-skilled labor and the demand curve for high-skilled labor is equal to the value of marginal product of skill.

- *Supply of high-skilled labor and low-skilled labor* The vertical distance between the supply curve of low-skilled labor and the supply curve of high-skilled labor is equal to the compensation that high-skilled workers require for the cost of acquiring the skill.

Additional Practice Problems 20.2

1. What is the opportunity cost of acquiring a skill?

2. The figure shows the demand and supply curves for high-skilled and low-skilled labor at the beginning of the 1990s. Since then, new technology has increased the value of marginal product of

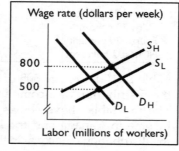

skill. In the figure, show the effect of this change. Is the income difference between high-skilled labor and low-skilled labor greater now or in 1990?

Solutions to Additional Practice Problems 20.2

1. The opportunity cost of acquiring a skill includes actual expenditures on tuition and books, as well as costs in the form of lost or reduced earnings while the skill is being acquired. When a person goes to school full time, that cost is the total earnings forgone. When a person receives on-the-job training, he or she is paid a lower wage than one who is doing a comparable job but not undergoing training. In this case, the cost of acquiring the skill is equal to the wage paid to a person not being trained minus the wage paid to a person being trained.

2. High-skilled labor has a higher value of marginal product than low-skilled labor. The technology changes increased the

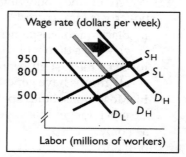

value of marginal product even more. The demand for high-skilled labor increased and the demand curve shifted rightward. As the figure shows, the wage rate paid high skilled-workers increased. So the income difference between high-skilled labor and low-skilled labor is greater now than in 1990.

■ **AP Self Test 20.2**

True or false

1. At a given wage rate, the quantity of high-skilled labor demanded exceeds the quantity of low-skilled labor demanded.

2. The horizontal distance between the demand curve for high-skilled labor and the demand curve for low-skilled labor

© 2015 Pearson Education, Inc.

measures the value of marginal product of skill.

3. The greater the cost of acquiring a skill, the greater is the vertical distance between the supply curve of high-skilled labor and the supply curve of low-skilled labor.

4. The wage rate paid high-skilled workers exceeds that paid low-skilled workers.

5. Discriminating against some group of workers has no cost to a prejudiced employer.

Multiple choice

1. Differences in skills
   i. can arise from differences in education and/or from differences in on-the-job training.
   ii. can lead to large differences in earnings.
   iii. result in different demand curves for high-skilled and low-skilled labor.
   a. i only.
   b. ii only.
   c. ii and iii.
   d. i and iii.
   e. i, ii, and iii.

2. The cost of acquiring a skill accounts for why the
   a. demand for high-skilled workers is different than the demand for low-skilled workers.
   b. supply of high-skilled workers is different than the supply of low-skilled workers.
   c. demand for high-skilled workers is different from the supply of high-skilled workers.
   d. demand for high-skilled workers is different from the supply of low-skilled workers.
   e. supply curves of high-skilled and low-skilled workers cross.

3. If decreased student aid increases the cost of acquiring skills, the equilibrium wage rate paid high-skilled workers ____ and the employment of high-skilled workers ____.
   a. rises; decreases
   b. rises; does not change
   c. falls; decreases
   d. rises; increases
   e. falls; does not change

4. If the value of marginal product of skill increases, the wage rate paid high-skilled workers ____ and the employment of high-skilled workers ____.
   a. might rise, fall, or not change; decreases
   b. falls; decreases
   c. rises; decreases
   d. rises; increases
   e. does not change; increases

■ **FIGURE 20.3**

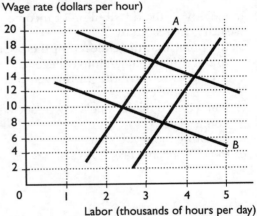

5. Figure 20.3 shows supply and demand curves for high-skilled and low-skilled labor. The curve labeled A is the supply curve for ____ workers and the curve labeled B is the demand curve for ____ workers.
   a. both high-skilled and low-skilled; both high-skilled and low-skilled
   b. high-skilled; high-skilled
   c. high-skilled; low-skilled
   d. low-skilled; high-skilled
   e. low-skilled; low-skilled

© 2015 Pearson Education, Inc.

6. Figure 20.3 shows supply and demand curves for high-skilled and low-skilled labor. The wage rate paid high-skilled workers is ____ per hour and the wage rate paid low-skilled workers is ____ per hour.
   a. $14; $10
   b. $16; $14
   c. $14; $10
   d. $16; 10
   e. $16; $8

7. If discrimination against women decreases their value of marginal product, then women will have ____ wage rate than men and there will be ____ high-paying jobs for women.
   a. a lower; more
   b. a higher; fewer
   c. a lower; fewer
   d. a higher; more
   e. the same; fewer

8. Inequality in the distribution of income and wealth is increased by
   a. the point that the children of the poorest find it difficult to get into college.
   b. saving to redistribute an uneven income over the life cycle.
   c. marrying outside one's own socioeconomic class.
   d. donating money to charities.
   e. the U.S. income tax.

Short Response Questions

■ **FIGURE 20.4**

Wage rate (dollars per hour)

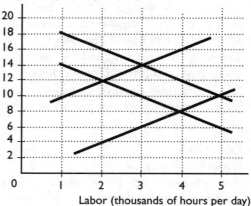

Labor (thousands of hours per day)

1. Figure 20.4 shows demand and supply curves for high-skilled and low-skilled workers.
   a. Label the demand curve for the high-skilled workers D_H and the demand curve for low-skilled workers D_L. Label the supply curves similarly, using S_H and S_L.
   b. What is the value of marginal product of skill?
   c. What is the compensation required for the cost of acquiring the skill?
   d. What is the equilibrium wage rate for high-skilled workers and low-skilled workers?

■ **FIGURE 20.5**

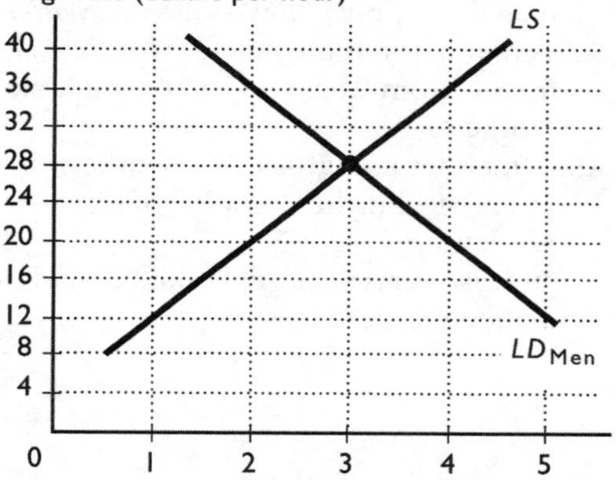

Wage rate (dollars per hour)

LS

LD Men

Labor (thousands of hours per day)

2. Suppose that the supply of labor for men and

© 2015 Pearson Education, Inc.

women is identical and Figure 20.5 shows this supply curve, labeled *LS*. It also shows the demand curve for men, labeled *LD*Men.

a. If that men and women have equal values of marginal products but employers are prejudiced against women. As a result, at any wage rate employers demand 2,000 fewer hours of female labor. Draw the demand curve for women in Figure 20.5.

b. What is the wage rate paid men? Paid women?

c. How do these wage rates make it costly for employers to discriminate against women?

Long Response Questions

1. a. How does the demand for high-skilled workers compare to the demand for low-skilled workers? How does the supply of high-skilled workers compare to the supply of low-skilled workers?

b. How does the wage rate of high-skilled workers compare to the wage rate of low-skilled workers?

c. How does the quantity of high-skilled workers employed compare to the quantity of low-skilled workers employed?

2. Why is discrimination costly for a prejudiced employer?

Additional Exercises (also in MyEconLab Test A)

In the United States in 2000, 2 million people worked full-time in protective services and were paid an average of $600 a week. At the same time, 7 million people worked as full-time machine operators and were paid an average of $450 a week. Use this information to answer Exercises 1 and 2.

1. Explain why people who are employed in protective services are paid more than machine operators.

2. Explain why fewer people are employed in protective services than as machine operators.

3. In Canada and Australia, the manager of a manufacturing plant earns 20 times what the factory floor worker earns. In Hong Kong and Malaysia, such a manager earns 40 times

what the factory floor worker earns. Can you explain this difference?

CHECKPOINT 20.3

■ **Explain how governments redistribute income and describe the effects of redistribution on economic inequality.**

Quick Review

- *Market income* Market income equals income earned from factors of production with no government redistribution.

- *Disposable income* Disposable income is market income plus cash benefits from the government minus taxes.

- *Median voter theory* The theory that governments pursue policies that make the median voter as well off as possible.

Additional Practice Problem 20.3

Households	Income (millions of dollars per year)	Income (percentage of total income)
Lowest 20 percent	5	2.5
Second 20 percent	15	7.5
Third 20 percent	35	17.5
Fourth 20 percent	55	27.5
Highest 20 percent	90	45.0

1. The table above shows the distribution of market income in an economy.

a. Suppose the government imposes a proportional income tax of 10 percent upon everyone. It then distributes the funds it collects by paying benefits to the bottom two percentile income groups. The lowest 20 percent group receives one half of the funds collected and the second lowest receives the other half. Calculate the income shares of each 20 percent of households after the tax and the benefits are paid.

b. Draw the Lorenz curves for this economy before and after taxes and benefits. Have the government's taxes and benefits made the distribution more or less equal?

© 2015 Pearson Education, Inc.

Solution to Additional Practice Problem 20.3

Household percentage	Tax paid (millions of dollars)	Income after tax and benefits (millions of dollars)	Income (percentage of total income)
Lowest 20 percent	0.5	14.5	7.25
Second 20 percent	1.5	23.5	11.75
Third 20 percent	3.5	31.5	15.75
Fourth 20 percent	5.5	49.5	24.75
Highest 20 percent	9.0	81.0	40.50

1a. To solve this practice problem, subtract the amount paid as income tax and add the income received as benefits to obtain the new amount of income of each group. Then construct the Lorenz curve for the new income shares. In the above table, the second column shows the tax paid by each group. Total taxes collected are $20 million. The lowest and second lowest 20 percentile groups each receive half of this amount, so each receives $10 million in benefits. The third column adds benefits to the market income and subtracts the tax. The last column has the income shares. To find a group's income share divide income after tax and benefits by total income, which is $200 million, and multiply by 100.

Household percentage	Cumulative percentage (before)	Cumulative percentage (after)
Lowest 20 percent	2.50	7.25
Second 20 percent	10.00	19.00
Third 20 percent	27.50	34.75
Fourth 20 percent	55.00	59.50
Highest 20 percent	100.00	100.00

1b. The table above has the cumulative percentage of income before tax and benefits and after tax and benefits. The cumulative percentages are

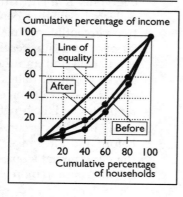

plotted in the Lorenz curve in the figure. The Lorenz curve after the taxes and benefits is closer to the line of equality so the government's taxes and benefits have made the distribution of income more equal.

■ AP Self Test 20.3

True or false

1. In general, U.S. federal and state taxes are progressive.

2. Subsidized services from the government go to only households with below-average incomes.

3. The distribution of income after taxes and benefits is more equal than the market distribution of income.

4. The redistribution of income creates the big tradeoff between earning an income and losing welfare benefits.

5. Under a negative income tax, some households would receive more money from the government than they would pay in taxes.

Multiple choice

1. Which of the following is a way income is redistributed in the United States?
   i. subsidizing services
   ii. income taxes
   iii. income maintenance programs
   a. i only.
   b. ii only.
   c. ii and iii.
   d. ii and iii.
   e. i, ii, and iii.

2. A ____ tax is one that taxes income at an average rate that increases with the level of income.
   a. regressive
   b. progressive
   c. flat
   d. consumption
   e. proportional

3. Of the following types of income tax systems, the one that provides the greatest

© 2015 Pearson Education, Inc.

amount of redistribution from the rich to the poor is a

a. progressive income tax.
b. proportional income tax.
c. regressive income tax.
d. flat-rate income tax.
e. money-income tax.

4. The three major types of income maintenance programs are
   a. Social Security programs, unemployment compensation, and welfare programs.
   b. food stamps, unemployment compensation, and agricultural price supports.
   c. student loans, rent control, and welfare programs.
   d. corporate welfare, minimum wages, and affirmative action laws.
   e. minimum wages, food stamps, and student loans.

5. A household's income earned from the markets for factors of production and with no government redistribution is its
   a. money income.
   b. welfare.
   c. market income.
   d. exploitative income.
   e. factored income.

6. The median voter theorem says government
   a. must redistribute income.
   b. does not face the big tradeoff.
   c. ought to use progressive taxes.
   d. cannot affect the distribution of income.
   e. policies aim to make the median voter as well off as possible.

7. When government redistributes income, one dollar collected from a rich person translates into ____ received by a poor person.
   a. one dollar
   b. less than one dollar
   c. more than one dollar
   d. zero dollars
   e. either exactly one dollar or, with some programs, more than one dollar

8. With a negative income tax that has a $10,000 guaranteed minimum income and a

25 percent tax rate, a household that has earned income of $16,000 has a total income of

a. $16,000.
b. $22,000.
c. $26,000.
d. $24,000.
e. $10,000.

Short Response Questions

1. Define a "progressive" tax and a "regressive" tax.

2. What are the nation's three main types of income maintenance programs?

Long Response Questions

1. Would progressive or regressive income taxes redistribute more money from the rich to the poor? Why?

2. Currently the government more heavily taxes high-income households and transfers money to low-income households. What are the likely reactions of the recipients of the money? Of the taxpayers? How do these reactions reflect the big tradeoff?

3. Suppose a negative income tax plan is passed so that a household is guaranteed an income of $20,000 and market income is taxed at a rate of 25 percent.
   a. What is the total income of a household that has a market income of $20,000?
   b. What is the total income of a household that has a market income of $60,000?

© 2015 Pearson Education, Inc.

Additional Exercises (also in MyEconLab Test A)

Households	Income (millions of dollars per year)
Lowest 20 percent	5
Second 20 percent	10
Third 20 percent	18
Fourth 20 percent	28
Highest 20 percent	39

Households	Income tax (percent)	Benefits (millions of dollars)
Lowest 20 percent	0	10
Second 20 percent	10	8
Third 20 percent	18	3
Fourth 20 percent	28	0
Highest 20 percent	39	0

1. Data about an economy are given in the tables above. The top table shows the distribution of market income in an economy. The government initially redistributes income by collecting income taxes and paying benefits shown in the second table. The government lowers the tax rate on the third 20 percent to 15 percent, on the fourth 20 percent to 25 percent, and on the highest 20 percent to 30 percent but benefits are unchanged.

   a. Calculate the income shares of each 20 percent of households after tax and redistribution.

   b. Draw this economy's Lorenz curve before and after taxes and benefits.

2. Suppose the government increases the benefits paid to the lowest 20 percent to $12 million, to the second 20 percent to $10 million, and to the third 20 percent to $5 million but keeps the tax rates unchanged. Calculate the income shares of each 20 percent of households after tax and redistribution.

© 2015 Pearson Education, Inc.

SELF TEST ANSWERS

■ AP Self Test 20.1

True or false
1. False; page 509
2. False; page 510
3. True; page 511
4. True; page 512
5. False; page 513

Multiple choice
1. d; page 509
2. a; page 509
3. e; page 509
4. d; page 508
5. e; page 510
6. a; page 511
7. d; page 512
8. a; page 513

Short Response Question
1. The farther the Lorenz curve from the line of equality, the less equal the distribution of income; page 509.

Long Response Questions
1. The table and Lorenz curve (in Figure 20.6) are in the next column. In the table, the cumulative percentage of income for any income group equals its percentage of income plus the percentages of income of all groups lower than it. The Lorenz curve plots these cumulative percentages of income against the cumulative percentage of households; pages 508-509.

2. A Lorenz curve can never lie above the line of equality. The Lorenz curve plots the cumulative percentage of income against the cumulative percentage of households. Because the households are arranged by order of income, the cumulative percentage of income must always be less than the cumulative percentage of households; pages 508-509.

3. The distribution of income has become less equal in the United States over the last few decades. The distribution of income changed

Household percentage	Percentage of income	Cumulative percentage of income
Lowest 20 percent	5.0	5.0
Second 20 percent	9.0	14.0
Third 20 percent	20.0	34.0
Fourth 20 percent	26.0	60.0
Highest 20 percent	40.0	100.0

■ FIGURE 20.6

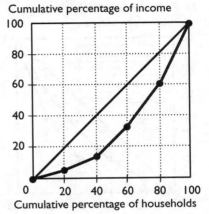

because higher income groups have gained more income than the lower income groups. Economic mobility has decreased over the same years. Fewer families are now moving up or down 1 or more quintile in the distribution of income and more families are remaining in the same quintile; page 510.

4. Poverty is a state in which a household's income is too low to buy the quantities of food, shelter, and clothing that are deemed necessary. In 2010 46 million Americans lived in poverty. Over the last several decades, poverty rates for whites and blacks have generally decreased, while poverty rates for Hispanics at first rose and then decreased, strikingly, during the 1990s; pages 513-514.

© 2015 Pearson Education, Inc.

Additional Exercises (also in MyEconLab Test A)

Households	Income (cumulative percentage)
Lowest 20 percent	3
Second 20 percent	8
Third 20 percent	22
Fourth 20 percent	47
Highest 20 percent	100

1. The cumulative distribution of income for the United Kingdom is in the table above.

■ FIGURE 20.7

Cumulative percentage of income

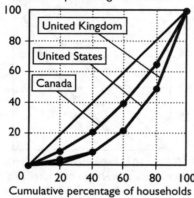

Cumulative percentage of households

2. The Lorenz curves are in Figure 20.7. Income is distributed *slightly* more equally in the United States than in the United Kingdom. The only real differences are in the second and fourth quintiles but the Lorenz curves are otherwise virtually identical; page 509.

3. The Lorenz curves are in Figure 20.7. The distribution of income is more unequal in the United Kingdom than in Canada. The U.K. Lorenz curve is farther from the line of equality than is the Canadian Lorenz curve so the distribution of income in the U.K. is less equally distributed than in Canada; page 509.

■ AP Self Test 20.2

True or false
1. True; pages 516-517
2. False; page 517
3. True; pages 516-517
4. True; pages 516-517
5. False; page 519

Multiple choice
1. e; pages 516-517
2. b; pages 516-517
3. a; pages 517-518
4. d; pages 517-518
5. c; page 517
6. e; page 517
7. c; page 519
8. a; page 520

Short Response Questions

■ FIGURE 20.8

Wage rate (dollars per hour)

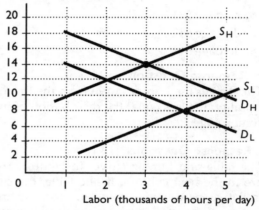

Labor (thousands of hours per day)

1. a. Figure 20.8 on the next page labels the curves; page 517.
   b. The value of marginal product of skill is $4 an hour because that is the vertical distance between the demand curve for high-skilled workers and the demand curve for low-skilled workers; page 517.
   c. The compensation required for the cost of acquiring the skill is $8 an hour because that is the vertical distance between the supply curve for high-skilled workers and the supply curve for low-skilled workers; page 517.
   d. The equilibrium wage rate for high-skilled workers is $14 an hour and the equilibrium wage rate for low-skilled workers is $8 an hour; page 517.

© 2015 Pearson Education, Inc.

■ FIGURE 20.9

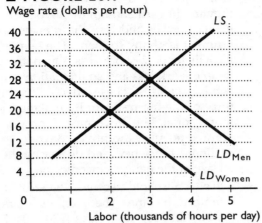

Wage rate (dollars per hour)

2. a. Figure 20.9 has the demand curve for women. It lies to the left of the demand curve by men by 2,000 hours of labor at every wage rate; page 519.

   b. Men are paid a wage of $28 an hour and women are paid a wage of $20 an hour; page 519.

   c. If a firm discriminates against women, it costs the firm $28 an hour to hire a man when it could get the same output if it hired a woman for $20. A discriminating firm's costs are higher as a result of its discrimination; page 519.

Long Response Questions

1. a. Because the value of marginal product of high-skilled workers exceeds that of low-skilled workers, the demand for high-skilled workers exceeds the demand for low-skilled workers. Because skills are costly to attain, the supply of high-skilled workers is less than the supply of low-skilled workers; pages 516-517.

   b. The demand for high-skilled workers exceeds the demand for low-skilled workers and the supply of high-skilled workers is less than the supply of low-skilled workers. So the wage rate received by high-skilled workers exceeds the wage rate received by low-skilled workers; page 517.

   c. The quantity of high-skilled workers employed compared to the quantity of low-

skilled workers employed depends on the positions of the demand and supply curves of both types of labor. The demand curve for high-skilled labor lies to the right of the demand curve for low-skilled labor. The supply curve of high-skilled labor lies to the left of the supply curve of low-skilled labor. Because the positions of these curves determine the quantity of labor employed, we cannot say with certainty how the quantity of high-skilled workers employed compares that the quantity of low-skilled workers employed; page 518.

2. Discrimination is costly for employers. Discrimination means that they hire the high-wage, favored group of workers rather than the low-wage, not favored group of workers. The firm's costs are higher than necessary and hence its profit is less than it could be. The reduced profit is the opportunity cost a prejudiced employer must pay; page 519.

Additional Exercises (also in MyEconLab Test A)

1. The value of marginal product for protective services and therefore the demand for labor for protective services exceeds that of machine operators. Likely the supply of labor for protective services is less than that for machine operators. As a result of the higher demand and lower supply, people working in protective services are paid more than people working as machine operators; page 517.

2. If the demand for labor for protective services is only slightly greater than the demand for machine operators and the supply of labor for protective services is much less than the supply of labor for machine operators, then the equilibrium quantity of machine operators exceeds the equilibrium quantity of people working in protective services; page 517.

3. The difference in pay is a result of the fact that managerial skills are in much smaller supply in Hong Kong and Malaysia. There are many low-skilled factory floor workers in

© 2015 Pearson Education, Inc.

Hong Kong and Malaysia. There are few high-skilled managers. As a result, the equilibrium wage rate paid to the few high-skilled managers in Hong Kong and Malaysia is many times greater than the wage rate paid to the many low-skilled factory floor workers; page 517.

■ **AP Self Test 20.3**

True or false

1. True; page 522
2. False; page 523
3. True; page 524
4. True; page 525
5. True; page 527

Multiple choice

1. e; page 522
2. b; page 522
3. a; page 522
4. a; page 522
5. c; page 523
6. e; page 526
7. b; page 525
8. b; page 527

Short Response Questions

1. A progressive tax is a tax for which the average tax rate rises with income. A regressive tax is a tax for which the average tax rate falls with income; page 522.

2. The three types of income maintenance programs are Social Security programs, unemployment compensation, and welfare programs; page 522.

Long Response Questions

1. A progressive income tax will redistribute more income away from the rich to the poor. A progressive income tax has a higher average tax rate as income rises. As a result, the rich pay a greater amount of taxes than do the poor because the rich have more income and because the average tax rate on that income is higher; page 522.

2. The recipients of the money payments likely will work less. If they were to work more, they might earn enough to move into a higher tax bracket and lose the money the government is giving to them. The taxpayers also will tend to work less. On both counts, people work less and so the nation's total income decreases. These effects illustrate the force of the big tradeoff: By making incomes more equal, the government program has blunted people's incentives to work, lessened economic efficiency, and decreased the overall size of the nation's income; page 525.

3. a. The household receives its $20,000 guaranteed income. Then, on its market income of $20,000, it pays ($20,000 × 25 percent) = $5,000 in taxes, leaving $15,000 in income after taxes. Its total income is $20,000 + $15,000 = $35,000. This household receives a "negative income tax" payment of $15,000; page 527.

   b. The household receives its $20,000 guaranteed income. Then, on its market income of $60,000, it pays ($60,000 × 25 percent) = $15,000 in taxes, leaving $45,000 in income after taxes. Its total income is $20,000 + $45,000 = $65,000. This household receives a "negative income tax" payment of $5,000; page 527.

Additional Exercises (also in MyEconLab Test A)

Households	Market income (millions of dollars)	Tax paid (millions of dollars)	Benefits received (millions of dollars)
Lowest 20 percent	5.0	0.0	10
Second 20 percent	10.0	1.0	8
Third 20 percent	18.0	2.7	3
Fourth 20 percent	28.0	7.0	0
Highest 20 percent	39.0	11.7	0

Households	Income after tax and benefits (millions of dollars)	Income (percentage)
Lowest 20 percent	15.0	15.2
Second 20 percent	17.0	17.2
Third 20 percent	18.3	18.6
Fourth 20 percent	21.0	21.3
Highest 20 percent	27.3	27.7

1. a. The top table shows the market income,

© 2015 Pearson Education, Inc.

taxes paid, and benefits received by the 5 percentile groups. The second table then shows the income after the tax is subtracted and the benefits added. It also shows the percentage of this adjusted income that each group receives; page 508.

■ FIGURE 20.10

Cumulative percentage of income

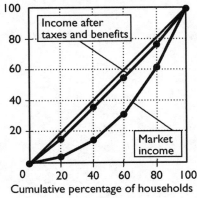

Cumulative percentage of households

b. Figure 20.10 shows the Lorenz curves before and after taxes and benefits. To draw these Lorenz curves, calculate the cumulative percentage shares. For instance, after taxes and benefits, the lowest 20 percent have 15.2 percent of total income and the

lowest 40 percent have 32.4 percent (15.2 + 17.2). The remaining the cumulative percentages are calculated similarly.

Households	Market income (millions of dollars)	Tax paid (millions of dollars)	Benefits received (millions of dollars)
Lowest 20 percent	5.0	0.0	12
Second 20 percent	10.0	1.0	10
Third 20 percent	18.0	3.2	5
Fourth 20 percent	28.0	7.8	0
Highest 20 percent	39.0	15.2	0

Households	Income after tax and benefits (millions of dollars)	Income (percentage)
Lowest 20 percent	17.0	17.0
Second 20 percent	19.0	19.0
Third 20 percent	19.8	19.8
Fourth 20 percent	20.2	20.2
Highest 20 percent	23.8	23.8

2. The top table shows the market income, taxes paid, and benefits received by the 5 percentile groups. The second table then shows the income after the tax is subtracted and the benefits added. It also shows the percentage of this adjusted income that each group receives.

© 2015 Pearson Education, Inc.

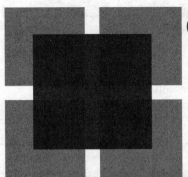

GDP: A Measure of Total Production and Income

Chapter 21

CHAPTER CHECKLIST

1 **Define GDP and explain why the value of production, income, and expenditure are the same for an economy.**

Gross Domestic Product, GDP, is the market value of all the final goods and services produced within a country in a given time period. Only final goods and services are included in GDP; intermediate goods and services are not included. Expenditures are consumption expenditure (C), investment (I), government expenditure on goods and services (G), and net exports of goods and services (NX). Investment is the purchase of new capital goods and additions to inventories. Total expenditure is equal to $C + I + G + NX$. Firms pay out the revenue they receive to households as payment for labor, capital, land, and entrepreneurship. These payments are households' income. We call total income Y. The circular flow shows that total expenditure equals total income so that $Y = C + I + G + NX$.

2 **Describe how economic statisticians measure GDP and distinguish between nominal GDP and real GDP.**

GDP is measured using the expenditure approach and the income approach. The expenditure approach adds the four sources of expenditure: consumption expenditure, investment, government expenditure on goods and services, and net exports of goods and services. Expenditures on used goods and financial assets are not in GDP. The income approach adds two categories of income (wage income plus interest, rent, and profit income). This sum is net domestic product at factor cost. To get to GDP, subsidies are subtracted, and indirect taxes and depreciation are added. A statistical discrepancy is added or subtracted to the income approach GDP so that GDP using the income approach equals GDP using the expenditure approach. Disposable personal income is income received by households minus personal income taxes paid. Real GDP is the value of final goods and services produced in a given year expressed in the prices of a base year; nominal GDP is the value of final goods and services produced in a given year using prices of that year.

3 **Describe the uses of real GDP and explain its limitations as a measure of the standard of living.**

The standard of living is the level of the consumption of the goods and services that people enjoy. Average income per person determines the standard of living so real GDP per person is used to compare the standard of living over time or across nations. Real GDP fluctuates around potential GDP in a business cycle, going from an expansion to a peak to a recession to a trough. Potential GDP is the value of real GDP when all factors of production are fully employed. A recession is commonly defined as a time when real GDP decreases for at least two successive quarters. Real GDP per person is an imperfect measure of the standard of living because it excludes household production, underground production, the value of leisure time, environmental quality, health and life expectancy, and political freedom and justice.

© 2015 Pearson Education, Inc.

YOUR AP TEST HINTS

AP Topics

Topic on your AP test	What to Know	Corresponding textbook section
GDP	The definition and values of production, income, expenditures	Checkpoint 21.1
Measuring GDP	What is included and differences between nominal and real	Checkpoint 21.2
Uses of real GDP	Limitations on measuring the standard of living	Checkpoint 21.3

AP Vocabulary Covered

Terms	What to Know	Text Sections
Gross domestic product (GDP) (Y)	The market value of all final goods and services produced within a country during a given time period	Checkpoint 21.1, p. 534
Final goods and services	Produced for a final user and not a component of another good or service	Checkpoint 21.1, p. 534
Expenditure approach to GDP (C+I+G+NX)	GDP equals the sum of consumption expenditures, investments, government expenditures, and net exports	Checkpoint 21.1, p. 536
Net taxes	Taxes minus cash benefits received from government	Checkpoint 21.1, p. 536
Saving	Income not paid in net taxes or spent on consumption	Checkpoint 21.1, p. 536
Income approach to GDP	GDP equals the sum of wage income, interest, rent, and profit income, equal to the expenditure approach	Checkpoint 21.2, p. 541
Depreciation	A decrease in the value of capital resulting from its use	Checkpoint 21.2, p. 542
Real GDP	The value of goods and services produced in a given year expressed in terms of the prices in a reference year	Checkpoint 21.2, p. 544
Nominal GDP	The value of goods and services produced in a given year expressed in terms of that same year	Checkpoint 21.2, p. 544
Standard of living	The value of goods and services that a country's people enjoy, on average; measured by real GDP per person	Checkpoint 21.3, p. 547
Potential GDP	The potential GDP level when all the economy's factors of production are fully employed	Checkpoint 21.3, p. 547
Business cycle	A periodic but irregular up and down movement of total production: expansion-peak-recession-trough	Checkpoint 21.3, p. 548
Recession	Commonly defined as when real GDP decreases for at least two consecutive quarters (6 months)	Checkpoint 21.3, p. 548
Expansion	Real GDP increases	Checkpoint 21.3, p. 548
Peak	The highest point in the cycle where an expansion ends	Checkpoint 21.3, p. 548
Trough	The lowest point in the cycle where a recession ends	Checkpoint 21.3, p. 548

Extra AP material

- On the AP test, *depreciation* can be called "consumption of fixed capital." Also on the AP test, the *underground economy* can be known as the "black market."
- The *expenditure approach* to GDP is a central macroeconomic concept; you *must* know it. The formula is written as GDP = $C + I + G + NX$. C is consumption expenditure, I is (gross) investment, G is government expenditure, and NX is net exports, the value of exports minus the value of imports.
- For the business cycle, the term *contraction* is sometimes used in place of the term *recession*.

© 2015 Pearson Education, Inc.

CHECKPOINT 21.1

■ **Define GDP and explain why the value of production, income, and expenditure are the same for an economy.**

Quick Review

- *Total expenditure* The total amount received by producers of final goods and services and equals $C + I + G + NX$.

- *Total income* The income paid to all factors of production and equals total expenditure.

Additional Practice Problems 21.1

1. Last year in a small country to the south, consumption expenditure was $70 billion, investment was $16 billion, government purchases of goods and services were $12 billion, exports were $4 billion, and imports were $3 billion.
   a. What did GDP last year equal?
   b. This year imports increased to $5 billion. If all the other types of expenditure stay the same, what does GDP this year equal?

2. Suppose that GDP equals $12 trillion, consumption expenditure equals $7 trillion, investment equals $3.5 trillion, and government expenditure on goods and services equals $2.5 trillion. What does net exports equal?

3. One of the four expenditure categories is net exports. How can net exports be negative?

Solutions to Additional Practice Problems 21.1

1a. To solve this problem use the equality between GDP and expenditure, GDP = $C + I + G + NX$. Last year's GDP = $70 billion + $16 billion + $12 billion + ($4 billion − $3 billion) = $99 billion.

1b. This year, imports increased from $3 billion to $5 billion, so replace the $3 billion in the calculation with $5 billion and GDP for this year is $97 billion. The $2 billion increase in imports results in a $2 billion decrease in GDP.

2. GDP = $C + I + G + NX$. So NX = GDP − C − I − G. In this case, NX = $12 trillion − $7 trillion − $3.5 trillion − $2.5 trillion, which equals −$1 trillion.

3. Net exports equals the value of exports of goods and services minus the value of imports of goods and services. If, as is the case in the United States, the value of imports exceeds the value of exports, net exports is negative.

■ **AP Self Test 21.1**

True or false

1. The computer chip that Dell Corp. buys from Intel Corp. is a final good.

2. Expenditure on a bulldozer is consumption expenditure.

3. The value of net exports of goods and services can be negative.

4. The value of production equals income, which equals expenditure.

Multiple choice

1. The abbreviation "GDP" stands for
   a. Gross Domestic Product.
   b. Gross Domestic Prices.
   c. General Domestic Prices.
   d. Great Domestic Prices.
   e. Government's Domestic Politics.

2. GDP is equal to the _____ value of all the final goods and services produced within a country in a given period of time.
   a. production
   b. market
   c. wholesale
   d. retail
   e. typical

3. The following are all *final* goods except
   a. flour used by the baker to make cupcakes.
   b. bread eaten by a family for lunch.
   c. pencils used by a 6th grader in class.
   d. Nike shoes used by a basketball player.
   e. a computer used by Intel to design new computer chips.

© 2015 Pearson Education, Inc.

4. Investment is defined as
   a. the purchase of a stock or bond.
   b. financial capital.
   c. what consumers do with their savings.
   d. the purchase of new capital goods by firms.
   e. spending on capital goods by governments.

5. In one year, a firm increases its production by $9 million and increases sales by $8 million. All other things in the economy remaining the same, which of the following is true?
   a. GDP increases by $8 million and inventory investment decreases by $1 million.
   b. GDP increases by $9 million and inventory investment increases by $1 million.
   c. Inventory investment decreases by $1 million.
   d. GDP increases by $8 million and investment increases by $1 million.
   e. GDP increases by $17 million.

6. Total expenditure equals
   a. $C + I + G + NX$.
   b. $C + I + G - NX$.
   c. $C + I - G + NX$.
   d. $C - I + G + NX$.
   e. $C - I - G - NX$.

Short Response Questions

1. Classify each of the following into the components of U.S. GDP: consumption expenditure, investment, government purchases of goods and services, exports, or imports.
   a. The purchase in Portland of a Sony DVD player made in Japan.
   b. A family's purchase of a birthday cake at the local Safeway grocery store.
   c. Microsoft's purchase of 100 Dell servers.
   d. The purchase of a new pizza oven by a Pizza Hut in Houston.
   e. The U.S. government's purchase of 15 stealth fighters.

2. Additions to inventories are counted in what component of GDP?

Long Response Questions

1. Why aren't intermediate goods or services counted in GDP?

2. Why does total expenditure equal total income?

Additional Exercises (also in MyEconLab Test A)

1. Classify the following items as a final good or an intermediate good and expenditure on final goods as consumption expenditure or investment:
   a. The fertilizer bought by a Florida tomato grower.
   b. The ringtone you bought today.
   c. New computers bought by PepsiCo.
   d. The aircraft bought by Southwest Airlines.

■ **FIGURE 21.1**

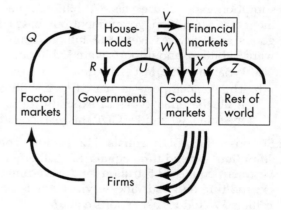

2. Figure 21.1 shows the flows of expenditure and income on Big Foot Island. In 2007, W was $60 million; V was $20 million; U was $15 million; X was $25 million; and Z was zero. Calculate total income and net taxes.

© 2015 Pearson Education, Inc.

CHECKPOINT 21.2

■ **Describe how economic statisticians measure GDP and distinguish between nominal GDP and real GDP.**

Quick Review

- *Expenditure approach* GDP equals the sum of consumption expenditure, investment, government expenditure on goods and services and net exports of goods and services.

- *Income approach* GDP equals the sum of wage income plus interest, rent, and profit income minus subsidies plus indirect taxes and depreciation plus or minus any statistical discrepancy.

Additional Practice Problem 21.2

Item	Amount (billions of dollars)
Wages	8,273
Consumption expenditure	10,667
Indirect taxes less subsidies	1,039
Interest, rent, and profit	3,818
Depreciation	1,940
Investment	1,896
Statistical discrepancy	− 73
Net exports	−604

1. The table above gives some of the items in the U.S. National Income and Product Accounts in 2011.

   a. Calculate U.S. GDP in 2011.

   b. Did you use the expenditure approach or the income approach for this calculation?

   c. What was the government's expenditure on goods and services in 2011?

Solutions to Additional Practice Problem 21.2

1a. This question focuses on calculating GDP. To solve problems such as this, you need to know how to use the expenditure approach and the income approach. The expenditure approach adds four categories of expenditure while the income approach adds the two income categories and then makes a few additional adjustments.

To calculate GDP using the expenditure approach the four categories of expenditure you need to know are: consumption, investment, government expenditure on goods and services, and net exports. The table does not give the value of government expenditures on goods and services, so you cannot find GDP using the expenditure approach.

To calculate GDP using the income approach you need to know the values of wage income and of interest, rent, and profit income. Adding these two income streams together yields net domestic income at factor cost. To adjust to GDP, you also need indirect taxes less subsidies, depreciation, and any statistical discrepancy. All these items are listed in the table, so GDP can be calculated using the income approach. In this case, GDP = $10,667 billion + $3,818 + $1,039 billion + $1,940 billion − $73, which is $14,997 billion.

1b The only way GDP can be calculated in part (a) is by the income approach, which is the approach used.

1c. GDP was calculated in part (a) using the income approach. The expenditure approach notes that GDP = $C + I + G + NX$. Subtract C, I, and NX from both sides of the equation to show that $G = \text{GDP} − C − I − NX$. Using the values of GDP, C, I, and NX yields $G =$ $14,997 billion − $10,667 billion − $1,896 billion + $604 billion = $3,038 billion. (The net exports were negative, so −(−$604 billion) equals + $604 billion).

■ **AP Self Test 21.2**

True or false

1. The expenditure approach measures GDP by using data on consumption expenditure, investment, government expenditures on goods and services, and net exports of goods and services.

2. In the United States, expenditure on used goods is becoming an increasingly large fraction of GDP.

© 2015 Pearson Education, Inc.

3. The income approach uses data on consumption expenditure, investment, government purchases of goods and services, and net exports of goods and services to calculate GDP.

4. Disposable personal income is usually larger than GDP.

Multiple choice

1. In calculating GDP, economists
   a. use only total expenditure.
   b. can use either total expenditure or total income.
   c. use only total income.
   d. measure total income minus total expenditure.
   e. measure total income plus total expenditure.

2. The expenditure approach to measuring GDP is based on summing
   a. wages, interest, rent, and profit.
   b. each industry's production.
   c. the values of final goods, intermediate goods, used goods, and financial assets.
   d. consumption expenditure, investment, government expenditure on goods and services, and net exports of goods and services.
   e. consumption expenditure, investment, government expenditure on goods and services, and net exports minus wages, interest, rent, and profit.

3. Suppose GDP is $10 billion, consumption expenditure is $7 billion, investment is $2 billion, and government expenditure on goods and services is $2 billion. Net exports of goods and services must be
   a. $1 billion.
   b. −$1 billion.
   c. $2 billion.
   d. −$2 billion.
   e. $10 billion.

4. According to the expenditure approach to measuring GDP, in the United States the largest component of GDP is
   a. consumption expenditure.
   b. investment.
   c. government expenditure.
   d. net exports of goods and services.
   e. wages.

5. Which of the following is <u>NOT</u> one of the income categories used in the income approach to measuring GDP?
   a. wages
   b. rent
   c. interest
   d. taxes paid by persons
   e. profit

6. Nominal GDP can change
   a. only if prices change.
   b. only if the quantities of goods and services change.
   c. only if prices increase.
   d. if either prices *or* the quantities of goods and services change.
   e. only if prices *and* the quantities of the goods and services change.

7. The difference between nominal GDP and real GDP is
   a. the indirect taxes used in their calculations.
   b. the prices used in their calculations.
   c. that nominal GDP includes the depreciation of capital and real GDP does not.
   d. that nominal GDP includes net exports and real GDP includes net imports.
   e. that real GDP includes the depreciation of capital and nominal GDP does not.

© 2015 Pearson Education, Inc.

Short Response Question

Item	Amount (dollars)
Wages	3,900
Consumption expenditure	4,000
Indirect taxes minus subsidies	400
Interest, rent, and profit	1,400
Government expenditure	1,000
Investment	1,100
Net exports	300
Statistical discrepancy	300

1. The table above gives data for a small nation:
   a. What is the nation's GDP? Did you use the expenditure or income approach to calculate GDP?
   b. What is the net domestic product at factor cost?
   c. What does depreciation equal?

Long Response Questions

1. What adjustments must be made to net domestic product at factor cost to convert it to GDP? Why must these adjustments be made?

2. What adjustments must be made to GDP to calculate GNP? To calculate disposable personal income?

3. What is the difference between real GDP and nominal GDP? Are the two ever equal?

4. To measure changes in production, why do we use real GDP rather than nominal GDP?

Additional Exercises (also in MyEconLab Test A)

Item	Amount (trillions of dollars)
Wages	6.0
Government expenditure	2.0
Interest, rent, and profit	2.4
Consumption expenditure	7.4
Investment	1.6
Net exports	0
Indirect taxes minus subsidies	0.7
Retained profits	1.6
Transfer payments	1.3
Personal income taxes	1.1
GNP	10.5
Depreciation	1.3

The table above shows some of the items in the

U.S. National Income and Product Accounts in 2005. Use the table to answer Exercises 1, 2, and 3.

1. Use the income approach to calculate net domestic product at factor cost and the statistical discrepancy.

2. Calculate the differences between GDP, GNP, and U.S. national income.

3. Calculate disposable personal income. What percentage of total income is disposable personal income and what percentage of disposable personal income is consumption expenditure?

GDP data for 2010		
Item	Quantity	Price
Apples	60	$0.50
Oranges	80	$0.25

GDP data for 2012		
Item	Quantity	Price
Apples	160	$1.00
Oranges	220	$2.00

4. The two tables show some data for an economy. If the base year is 2012, calculate the economy's nominal GDP and real GDP in 2010.

CHECKPOINT 21.3

■ **Describe the uses of real GDP and explain its limitations as a measure of the standard of living.**

Quick Review

- *Potential GDP* The value of real GDP when all factors of production—labor, capital, land, and entrepreneurial ability—are fully employed.

- *Standard of living* The standard of living among different nations or over a period of time can be compared using real GDP per person.

- *Goods and services omitted from GDP* Household production, underground

© 2015 Pearson Education, Inc.

production, leisure time, and environmental quality are omitted from GDP.

Additional Practice Problems 21.3

1. How has real GDP per person changed in the United States since 1961?

2. How do you think the standard of living in the United States today compares with the standard of living 150 years ago?

Solutions to Additional Practice Problems 21.3

1. Real GDP per person has increased substantially since 1961. In fact, real GDP per person has more than doubled since 1961. In the United States for the past 100 years real GDP per person has doubled about every 30 years.

2. The standard of living now is dramatically higher than it was 150 years ago. First, even though totally accurate data for real GDP per person from 150 years ago is not available, it is certain that real GDP per person is much higher today even after taking account of the fact that household production was more common 150 years ago when many more people grew their own food. People today enjoy significantly more leisure time, which significantly boosts today's standard of living. Perhaps the edge on environment quality goes to the past or perhaps not because solid waste pollution (from horses) was a major issue 150 years ago. Considering health and life expectancy, and political freedom and social justice, people today are much better off than people 150 years ago.

■ AP Self Test 21.3

True or false

1. A recession follows a business cycle peak.

2. As currently measured, real GDP does not include the value of household production.

3. Production in the underground economy is part of the "investment" component of GDP.

4. The production of anti-pollution devices installed by electric utilities is not counted in GDP because the devices are designed only to eliminate pollution.

5. A country's real GDP does not take into account the extent of political freedom in the country.

Multiple choice

1. In the years after 1998, the most severe recession occurred during
   a. 1998.
   b. 2000-2001.
   c. 2008-2009.
   d. 1999-2001.
   e. 2007 to 2009.

2. Which of the following is <u>NOT</u> part of the business cycle?
   a. recession
   b. peak
   c. inflation
   d. trough
   e. expansion

3. In the business cycle, what immediately precedes the time when real GDP is falling?
   a. recession
   b. peak
   c. depression
   d. trough
   e. expansion

4. GDP handles household production by
   a. estimating a dollar value of the goods purchased to do housework.
   b. estimating a dollar value of the services provided.
   c. ignoring it.
   d. including it in exactly the same way that all other production is included.
   e. including it in real GDP but not in nominal GDP because there are no prices paid for the work.

© 2015 Pearson Education, Inc.

5. You hire some of your friends to help you move to a new house. You pay them $200 and buy them dinner at Pizza Hut. Which of the following is true?
   a. The $200 should be counted as part of GDP but not the dinner at Pizza Hut.
   b. If your friends do not report the $200 on their tax forms, it becomes part of the underground economy.
   c. The dinner at Pizza Hut should be counted as part of GDP but not the $200.
   d. Hiring your friends is an illegal activity and should not be counted in GDP.
   e. Neither the $200 nor the dinner should be counted in GDP because both are household production.

6. The value of leisure time is
   a. included in GDP and, in recent years, has become an increasing large part of GDP.
   b. excluded from GDP.
   c. zero.
   d. directly included in GDP but, in recent years, has become a decreasing large part of GDP.
   e. directly included in GDP and, in recent years, has not changed much as a fraction of GDP.

7. A new technology is discovered that results in all new cars producing 50 percent less pollution. The technology costs nothing to produce and cars do not change in price. As a result of the technology, there is a reduction in the number of visits people make to the doctor to complain of breathing difficulties. Which of the following is true?
   a. Real GDP decreases as a result of fewer doctor services being provided.
   b. Real GDP is not affected.
   c. Nominal GDP increases to reflect the improvement in the health of the population.
   d. Real GDP decreases to reflect the decrease in pollution.
   e. Nominal GDP does not change and real GDP increases.

Short Response Questions

1. What is the relationship between real GDP and potential GDP?
2. If you cook a hamburger at home, what happens to GDP? If you go to Burger King and purchase a hamburger, what happens to GDP?

Long Response Questions

1. What are the parts of a business cycle? What is their order?
2. What general categories of goods and services are omitted from GDP? Why is each omitted?

Additional Exercise (also in MyEconLab Test A)

1. The United Nations Human Development Report gives the following data for real GDP per person in 2002: China, $4,580; Russia, $8,230; Canada, $29,480; United States, $35,750. Life expectancy at birth is 79.3 in Canada, 77.0 in the United States, 70.5 in China, and 66.7 in Russia. Freedom House rates political freedom as follows: Canada and the United States, 1.1 (1.0 is the most free); Russia, 4.5; and China, 7.6 (ratings in the 7+ range are the least free). How do life expectancy at birth and political freedom change the relative ranking of living standards that real GDP per person indicate?

© 2015 Pearson Education, Inc.

SELF TEST ANSWERS

■ AP Self Test 21.1

True or false

1. False; page 534
2. False; page 535
3. True; page 536
4. True; page 537

Multiple choice

1. a; page 534
2. b; page 534
3. a; page 534
4. d; page 535
5. b; page 535
6. a; page 536

Short Response Questions

1. a. Import; page 536.
   b. Consumption expenditure; page 535.
   c. Investment; page 535.
   d. Investment; page 535.
   e. Government expenditure on goods and services; page 536.
2. Additions to inventory are included as part of investment; page 535.

Long Response Questions

1. Intermediate goods or services are not counted in GDP because if they were, they would be double counted. A computer produced by Dell Corp. is included in GDP. But if the Intel chip that is part of the computer is also included in GDP, then the Intel chip is counted twice: once when it is produced by Intel, and again when it is included in the computer produced by Dell; page 534.

2. Total expenditure is the amount received by producers of final goods and services from the sales of these goods and services Because firms pay all the revenue they receive to households in payment for the factors of production, total expenditure equals total income. From the viewpoint of firms, the value of production is the cost of production, and the cost of produc-

tion is equal to income. From the viewpoint of consumers of goods and services, the value of production is the cost of buying the production, which equals expenditure; pages 536-537.

Additional Exercises (also in MyEconLab Test A)

1. a. The fertilizer is an intermediate good because it will be used to grow tomatoes; page 534.
   b. The ringtone is a final good because you are the final user. It is part of consumption expenditure; pages 534-535.
   c. The computers are a final good. Because they are purchased by Pepsi, they are investment; pages 534-535.
   d. The aircraft bought by Southwest Airlines are a final good. Because they are purchased by Southwest Airlines, they are investment; pages 534-535.

■ FIGURE 21.2

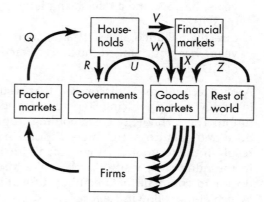

2. Total income equals total expenditure and total expenditure equals the sum of consumption expenditure, investment, government expenditure on goods and services, and net exports of goods and services. In Figure 21.2, consumption expenditure is flow W and is $60 million; investment is X and is $25 million; government expenditure on goods and services is U and is $15 million; and, net exports of goods and services is Z and is $0. Total expenditure equals the sum of these flows, $100 million. Total income equals total

© 2015 Pearson Education, Inc.

expenditure, so total income equals $100 million. To calculate net taxes, subtract from households' total income their consumption expenditure and their saving. Total income equals total expenditure, so total income equals $100 million. Consumption expenditure is $60 million and saving, V, is $20 million, so net taxes equals $20 million; pages 536-537.

■ AP Self Test 21.2

True or false
1. True; page 539
2. False; page 540
3. False; page 541
4. False; page 543

Multiple choice
1. b; page 539
2. d; page 539
3. b; page 539
4. a; page 539
5. d; page 541
6. d; page 544
7. b; page 544

Short Response Question
1. a. GDP = $6,400, which is the sum of consumption expenditure, investment, government expenditures on goods and services, and net exports of goods and services. The expenditure approach was used; page 539.
   b. Net domestic product at factor cost equals $5,300, the sum of wage income plus interest, rent, and profit income; page 541.
   c. The difference between GDP and net domestic product at factor cost, which is $1,100, equals indirect taxes minus subsidies plus depreciation plus any statistical discrepancy. The statistical discrepancy equals zero. Indirect taxes minus subsidies equals $400, so depreciation equals $700; pages 541-542.

Long Response Questions
1. To change net domestic product at factor cost to GDP, three sets of adjustments must be made. First, net domestic product at factor cost is measured at firms' costs; to convert costs to equal the market prices paid, taxes must be added and subsidies subtracted. Second, net domestic product does not include depreciation but GDP does. So, depreciation must be added. Finally, any statistical discrepancy must be added or subtracted; pages 541-542.

2. To calculate GNP, net factor income from abroad must be added (or subtracted, if it is negative) from GDP. Then, to calculate disposable personal income, from GNP depreciation and retained profits must be subtracted, transfer payments must be added, and then any statistical discrepancy must be either added or subtracted; page 543.

3. The difference between real GDP and nominal GDP lies in the prices used to value the final goods and services. Real GDP uses prices from a fixed base year. Nominal GDP uses prices from the current year for which GDP is being calculated. Real GDP equals nominal GDP in the base year; page 544.

4. Nominal GDP is computed using prices and quantities from the given year. From one year to the next, both prices and quantities can change, so nominal GDP will change if either the prices change or the quantities change. Real GDP uses prices from a base year. So from one year to the next changes in real GDP reflect changes in the quantities, that is, changes in production; page 544.

Additional Exercises (also in MyEconLab Test A)
1. Using the income approach, net domestic product at factor cost = Wages + Interest, rent, and profit = $6.0 trillion + $2.4 trillion = $8.4 trillion.
   The statistical discrepancy equals the GDP expenditure total minus the GDP income total. GDP calculated using the expenditure approach is $11.0 trillion. To calculate GDP using the income approach, add net domestic product at factor cost, indirect taxes less subsidies, and depreciation. So GDP using the income approach equals $8.4 trillion + $0.7

© 2015 Pearson Education, Inc.

trillion + $1.3 trillion = $10.4 trillion. So the statistical discrepancy equals $11.0 trillion − $10.4 trillion = $600 billion; pages 531-532.

2. GNP equals GDP plus net factor income from other countries, so the difference between the two is net factor income from other countries. Net factor income from other countries = GNP − GDP, so using the data in the problem, net factor income from other countries = $11.0 trillion − $10.5 trillion = $500 billion.

   U.S. national income = GNP − depreciation − statistical discrepancy = $10.5 trillion − $1.3 trillion − $600 billion = $7.6 trillion; page 543.

3. Disposable personal income = national income − retained profits plus transfer payments − personal income taxes = $7.6 trillion − $1.6 trillion + $1.3 trillion − $1.1 trillion = $6.2 trillion.

   As a percentage of U.S. national income, disposable personal income is ($6.2 trillion ÷ $7.6 trillion) × 100 = 81.6 percent. As a percentage of disposable personal income, consumption is ($7.4 trillion ÷ $6.2 trillion) × 100 = 119 percent; page 543.

4. Nominal GDP is (60 apples × $0.50 per apple) + (80 oranges × $0.25 per orange) = $50. Real GDP in 2010 is uses the 2010 quantities and the 2012 prices. Real GDP equals (60 apples × $1.00 per apple) + (80 oranges × $2.00 per orange) = $220; pages 544-545.

■ AP Self Test 21.3

True or false

1. True; pages 548-549
2. True; page 551
3. False; page 551
4. False; page 551
5. True; page 552

Multiple choice

1. e; page 548
2. c; pages 549-550
3. b; pages 549-550
4. c; page 551
5. b; page 551
6. b; page 551
7. a; page 551

Short Response Questions

1. Potential GDP is the value of real GDP when all factors of production are fully employed. Over time potential GDP grows. Real GDP fluctuates around the growth path of potential GDP. These fluctuations reflect the business cycle; pages 547-548.

2. If you cook a hamburger at home, the meat you purchased is included in GDP but the production of the hamburger is not included in GDP because it is household production. If you buy a hamburger at Burger King, the production of the hamburger is included in GDP; page 551.

Long Response Questions

1. The business cycle is made up of the expansion phase, when real GDP is growing; the peak, when real GDP reaches its highest level; the recession phase, when real GDP is falling for at least 6 months; and the trough, when real GDP is at its lowest level. The order of the business cycle is from expansion to peak to recession to trough, and then back to expansion; pages 548-549.

2. Goods and services omitted from GDP are household production, underground production, leisure time, and environmental quality. GDP measures the value of goods and services that are bought in markets. Because household production, leisure time, and environmental quality are not purchased in markets, they are excluded from GDP. Even though underground production frequently is bought in markets, the activity is unreported and is not included in GDP; page 551.

Additional Exercise (also in MyEconLab Test A)

1. The relatively high life expectancy and political freedom means Canada's and the United States' relative rankings rise. The low life expectancy and political freedom decrease China's and Russia's rankings; page 553.

© 2015 Pearson Education, Inc.

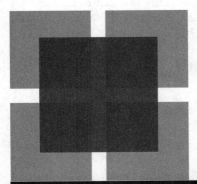

Chapter 21

Appendix: Measuring Real GDP

The appendix shows how the Bureau of Economic Analysis calculates real GDP.

▮ Measuring Real GDP

Real GDP depends on the prices used to value the production of goods and services. The Bureau of Economic Analysis (BEA) uses prices from adjacent years to value the production and thereby creates a chained-dollar real GDP. For instance, between 2013 and 2014, first, prices from 2013 are used to value the goods and services produced in 2013 and the goods and services produced in 2014. Then the growth rate between these two years is calculated. Second, prices from 2014 are used to value the production in 2013 and the production in 2014. Then the (second) growth rate between these two years is calculated. These two growth rates are averaged to give the final growth rate between these two years. This growth rate is applied to real GDP for 2013 to calculate real GDP for 2014. The real GDPs for all the years are chained back to the base year real GDP by the growth rates between years.

YOUR AP TEST HINTS

AP Topics

Topic on your AP test	What to Know	Corresponding textbook section
Real GDP calculations	How the Bureau of Economic Analysis measures real GDP	Appendix

AP Vocabulary Covered

Terms	What to Know	Text Sections
Chained dollar real GDP	Chaining method used to calculate real GDP; values GDP using prices from two adjacent years, then uses the averages the growth rates as the growth rate of real GDP	Appendix, p. 559

Extra AP material

- The AP test does not allow the use of calculators. Therefore, any math computations are simple and in easily manipulated numbers and percentages such as 5 percent, 10 percent, etc. Students will probably not be required calculate *chained GDP* but should be prepared to understand the conversion concept.

- A common economic concept for measuring the difference between nominal and real GDP is the *GDP Deflator*. The GDP deflator is another price index, similar to the CPI but based on the prices of the goods and services in GDP.

© 2015 Pearson Education, Inc.

CHECKPOINT I

■ Measuring Real GDP

Quick Review

- *Real GDP* The value of the final goods and services produced in a given year valued at the prices of a base year.

- *Nominal GDP* The value of the final goods and services produced in a given year valued at the prices that prevailed in that year.

Additional Practice Problem I

1. In a small, tropical nation suppose real GDP in 2013 is $5 billion and nominal GDP in 2013 is $10 billion. In 2014, nominal GDP is $12 billion. If GDP in 2014, measured using 2013 prices is $11.5 billion and GDP in 2013, measured using 2014 prices, is $11 billion, what does real GDP in 2014 equal?

Solution to Additional Practice Problem I

1. This question gives you practice you need in how real GDP is calculated. Take each part step-by-step:

   First we need the growth rate of GDP from 2013 to 2014 measured using 2013 prices. Nominal GDP in 2013 (which is GDP in 2013 measured using 2013 prices) is $10 billion and GDP in 2014 measured using 2013 prices is $11.5 billion. So the growth rate of GDP using 2013 prices is [($11.5 billion − $10.0 billion) ÷ $10 billion] × 100, which is 11.5 percent.

   Next we need the growth rate of GDP from 2013 to 2014 measured using 2014 prices. GDP in 2013 measured with 2014 prices is $11 billion and nominal GDP in 2014 (which is GDP in 2014 measured using 2014 prices) is $12 billion. So the growth rate of GDP using 2014 prices is [($12 billion − $11 billion) ÷ $11 billion] × 100, which is 9.1 percent.

   Finally, we average the two growth rates to give a growth rate of 10.3 percent between 2013 and 2014. This percentage change is applied to real GDP in 2013, $5 billion, to give

real GDP in 2014. This procedure means that real GDP in 2014 equals $5 billion × 1.103, which is $5.52 billion.

■ AP Self Test I

True or false

1. Real GDP is just a more precise name for GDP.

2. Real GDP equals nominal GDP in the base year.

3. The base year for real GDP changes each year.

Multiple choice

1. Real GDP measures the value of goods and services produced in a given year valued using
   a. base year prices.
   b. prices of that same year.
   c. no prices.
   d. future prices.
   e. government approved prices.

2. In a small country, using prices of 2013, GDP in 2013 was $100 and GDP in 2014 was $110. Using prices of 2014, GDP in 2013 was $200 and GDP in 2014 was $210. The country's BEA will calculate ____ percent as the growth in real GDP between those years.
   a. 10
   b. 5
   c. 15
   d. 7.5
   e. None of the above answers is correct.

3. Using prices from 2013, GDP grew 10 percent between 2013 and 2014; using prices from 2014, GDP grew 8 percent between 2013 and 2014. For its link back to the base year, the BEA will use ____ percent as the growth in real GDP between 2013 and 2014.
   a. 10
   b. 8
   c. 2
   d. 18
   e. 9

© 2015 Pearson Education, Inc.

Short Response Question

Item	Data for 2013 Quantity	Price	Data for 2014 Quantity	Price
Pizza	100	$10.00	150	$20.00
Soda	50	$2.00	75	$4.00

1. An economy produces only pizza and soda. The table above gives the quantities produced and prices in 2013 and 2014. The base year is 2013.

   a. What is nominal GDP in 2013?
   b. What is real GDP in 2013?
   c. What is nominal GDP in 2014?
   d. What is real GDP in 2014?

Long Response Question

1. How does the chained-dollar method of calculating real GDP link the current year's real GDP to the base year's real GDP?

© 2015 Pearson Education, Inc.

SELF TEST ANSWERS

■ AP Self Test I

True or false
1. False; page 559
2. True; page 559
3. False; page 561

Multiple choice
1. a; page 559
2. d; pages 560-561
3. e; page 561

Short Response Question
1. a. Nominal GDP = (100 pizzas × $10 per pizza) + (50 sodas × $2 per soda) = $1,100, the sum of expenditure on pizza and expenditure on soda; pages 559-560.
   b. Because 2013 is the base year, real GDP = nominal GDP, so real GDP = $1,100; pages 559-561.
   c. Nominal GDP = (150 pizzas × $20 per pizza) + (75 sodas × $4 per soda) = $3,300, the sum of expenditure on pizza and expenditure on soda; pages 559-560.
   d. Using 2013 prices, GDP grew from $1,100 in 2013 to $1,650 in 2014, a percentage increase of 50 percent. Using 2014 prices, GDP grew 50 percent between 2013 and 2014. The average growth is 50 percent, so real GDP in 2014 is 50 percent higher than in 2013, which means that real GDP in 2014 is $1,650; pages 560-561.

Long Response Question
1. From one year to the next, real GDP is scaled by the growth rate (which is the percentage change) from the first year to the next. For instance, real GDP in 2013 is linked to real GDP in 2012 using the growth rate from 2012. Next in turn, real GDP in 2014 is linked to real GDP in 2013 using the growth rate from 2013, and so on. These links are like the links in a chain. They link real GDP in the current year back to the base year and the base year prices; page 561.

© 2015 Pearson Education, Inc.

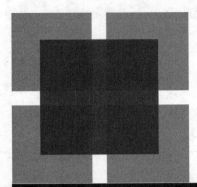

Jobs and Unemployment

CHAPTER CHECKLIST

1 Define the unemployment rate and other labor market indicators.

The Current Population Survey is a monthly survey of 60,000 households across the country that is the basis for the nation's labor market statistics. The working-age population is non-institutionalized people aged 16 and over who are not in the U.S. Armed Forces. The labor force is the sum of the number of people employed and the number unemployed. To be unemployed, a person must have no employment, be available for work, and either have made an effort to find a job during the previous four weeks or be waiting to be recalled to a job from which he or she was laid off. The unemployment rate is the percentage of people in the labor force who are unemployed. The labor force participation rate is the percentage of the working-age population who are members of the labor force. A marginally attached worker is a person who is available and willing to work but has not made specific efforts to find a job within the previous four weeks but has looked for work sometime in the recent past. A discouraged worker is a marginally attached worker who is not searching for work because previous attempts to find a job within the past four weeks were unsuccessful. Full-time workers are those who usually work 35 hours or more a week. Some part-time workers are looking for full-time work but cannot find it because of unfavorable economic conditions and are called "part time for economic reasons".

2 Describe the trends and fluctuations in the indicators of labor market performance in the United States.

Since 1948, the average U.S. unemployment rate has been 5.8 percent. In the Great Depression of the 1930s, the U.S. unemployment rate reached 25 percent. From 1960 to 2013, the labor force participation rate increased. Over these years the labor force participation rate for men decreased and for women increased. A broad measure of the unemployment rate, called U-6, includes discouraged workers, marginally attached workers, and part time for economic reason workers. The number of workers who are part time for economic reasons rises during recessions and falls during expansions.

3 Describe the types of unemployment, define full employment, and explain the link between unemployment and real GDP.

Unemployment is classified into three types: frictional (normal labor turnover), structural (changes in necessary job skills or job locations), or cyclical (changes in the business cycle). The duration of unemployment increases in recessions. Full employment occurs when there is no cyclical unemployment. At full employment, the unemployment rate is the natural unemployment rate and GDP equals potential GDP. The natural unemployment rate increases when: the number of young workers increases; there is a rapid pace of technological change; the real wage exceeds the equilibrium real wage; and, unemployment benefits increase. The output gap is real GDP minus potential GDP expressed as a percentage of potential GDP. In recessions, the GDP gap becomes negative and unemployment rises.

© 2015 Pearson Education, Inc.

YOUR AP TEST HINTS

AP Topics

Topic on your AP test	What to Know	Corresponding textbook section
Unemployment rate and labor market indicators	Definitions of labor force, unemployment, discouraged workers, full and part time workers	Checkpoint 22.1
Trends and changes in labor markets	Definitions and links to real GDP	Checkpoint 22.3

AP Vocabulary Covered

Terms	What to Know	Text Sections
Working-age population	Total of people 16 and over, not in jail, hospitals, or some other institution, not in the Armed Forces	Checkpoint 22.1, p. 564
Labor force	Number of people employed plus the unemployed	Checkpoint 22.1, p. 564
Unemployed	People without employment who are seeking employment and are available for employment	Checkpoint 22.1, p. 564
Unemployment rate	Number of unemployed workers divided by the labor force then multiplied by 100 (to make it a percentage)	Checkpoint 22.1, p. 565
Labor force participation rate	Percentage of the working age population who are in the labor force	Checkpoint 22.1, p. 566
Marginally attached worker	People who do not have a job, are available and willing to work, but made no effort to find a job; not counted as unemployed	Checkpoint 22.1, p. 566
Part-time worker	Those who work less than 35 hours a week	Checkpoint 22.1, p. 567
Frictional unemployment	Unemployment from normal labor market turnover	Checkpoint 22.3, p. 575
Structural unemployment	Unemployment from mismatches between the needs of employers and the skills and talents of workers	Checkpoint 22.3, p. 575
Cyclical unemployment	Unemployment from changes in the business cycle	Checkpoint 22.3, p. 576
Full employment	Employment when there is no cyclical unemployment	Checkpoint 22.3, p. 576
Natural unemployment rate	The unemployment rate when no cyclical unemployment is present	Checkpoint 22.3, p. 576
Potential GDP	GDP produced when the economy is at full employment	Checkpoint 22.3, p. 578
Output gap	Real GDP minus potential GDP; negative in recessions, positive in expansions	Checkpoint 22.3, p. 578

Extra AP material

- On the AP test, the term *working-age population* might be described as the *civilian non-institutional population, aged 16 years and over.*
- The AP test will not ask how the unemployment rate, labor force participation rate, or aggregate hours have changed over time. Newer Bureau of Labor Statistics measures of unemployment, U-1 through U-6, are not part of the AP curriculum.
- *Marginally attached workers* are people who have looked for work but have now quit looking. Students must know that this group is *not* counted as unemployed in the official measure of unemployment. However students must know that part-time workers *are* counted as employed.

© 2015 Pearson Education, Inc.

CHECKPOINT 22.1

■ **Define the unemployment rate and other labor market indicators.**

Quick Review

- *Unemployment rate* The percentage of the people in the labor force who are unemployed. That is,

$$\text{Unemployment rate} = \frac{\text{(Unemployed people)}}{\text{(Labor force)}} \times 100$$

- *Labor force participation rate* The percentage of the working-age population who are members of the labor force. It equals

$$\text{Participation rate} = \frac{\text{(Labor force)}}{\text{(Working - age people)}} \times 100$$

Additional Practice Problems 22.1

1. Determine the labor market status of each of the following people:
   a. Don is 21 and a full-time college student.
   b. Shirley works for 20 hours a week as an administrative assistant and is looking for a full-time job.
   c. Clarence was laid off from his job selling keyboards to computer manufacturers and is actively seeking a new job.
   d. Pat quit her job as an account executive 6 months ago but, unable to find a new position, has stopped actively searching.

2. The Bureau of Labor Statistics reported that in June 2005, the labor force was 149.1 million, employment was 141.6 million, and the working-age population was 225.9 million. Calculate for that month the:
   a. Unemployment rate.
   b. Labor force participation rate.

Solutions to Additional Practice Problems 22.1

1a. Don is neither working nor looking for work, so he is not in the labor force.

1b. Shirley is working for pay for more than 1 hour a week, so she is employed and part of the labor force. She is working less than 35 hours a week, so she is a part-time worker. Because she is looking for a full-time job, Shirley is an involuntary part-time worker.

1c. Clarence is actively seeking a new job, so he is unemployed. Clarence is part of the labor force.

1d. Pat is neither working nor actively looking for work, so she is not in the labor force. Pat is a discouraged worker.

2a. The labor force equals the sum of the number of people employed and the number of people unemployed. Subtracting the number employed from the labor force gives the number of unemployed. The labor force is 149.1 million and the number of employed is 141.6 million, so the number unemployed is 149.1 million − 141.6 million, which is 7.5 million. To calculate the unemployment rate, divide the number of unemployed by the labor force and multiply by 100. The unemployment rate equals (7.5 million ÷ 149.1 million) × 100, which is 5.0 percent.

2b. The labor force participation rate is the percentage of the working-age population who are members of the labor force. The labor force participation rate equals the labor force divided by the working-age population all multiplied by 100, which is (149.1 million ÷ 225.9 million) × 100 = 66.0 percent.

■ **AP Self Test 22.1**

True or false

1. If Bob has been laid off by Ford, but expects to be recalled within the next three weeks, he is part of the labor force.

2. People are counted as unemployed if they work less than 40 hours per week.

3. The unemployment rate decreases when unemployed workers find jobs.

4. The labor force participation rate measures the percentage of the labor force that is employed.

5. Marginally attached workers have jobs.

© 2015 Pearson Education, Inc.

Multiple choice

1. Assume the U.S. population is 300 million. If the working age population is 240 million, 150 million are employed, and 6 million are unemployed, what is the labor force?
   a. 300 million
   b. 240 million
   c. 156 million
   d. 150 million
   e. 144 million

2. To be counted as employed by the BLS, in the week before the survey the person must have worked for pay for _____.
   a. at least 1 hour
   b. at least 5 hours
   c. more than 20 hours
   d. 40 hours
   e. None of the above are right because the BLS counts as employed anyone who works volunteer hours at a non-profit institution.

3. Bo is available and willing to work but has not actively looked for work in the past month. Bo is _____ of the labor force and is _____.
   a. part; counted as being unemployed
   b. part; not counted as being unemployed
   c. not part; not counted as being unemployed
   d. not part; counted as being unemployed only if he has had a job within the last 12 months
   e. not part; counted as being unemployed regardless of whether or not he has had a job within the last 12 months

4. Which of the following statements about the United States is (are) correct?
   i. The labor force is larger than the number of employed people.
   ii. The labor force is larger than the number of unemployed people.
   iii. The number of unemployed people is larger than the number of employed people.
   a. ii only.
   b. iii only.
   c. ii and iii.
   d. i and ii.
   e. i, ii, and iii.

5. The unemployment rate equals
   a. (number of people without a job ÷ population) × 100.
   b. (number of people unemployed ÷ labor force) × 100.
   c. (number of people without a job ÷ working-age population) × 100.
   d. (number of people unemployed ÷ population) × 100.
   e. [(working-age population − number of people employed) ÷ labor force] × 100.

6. If the working age population is 200 million, 150 million are employed, and 6 million are unemployed, the unemployment rate is _____.
   a. 3.0 percent
   b. 25.0 percent
   c. 4.0 percent
   d. 12.0 percent
   e. 3.8 percent

7. Discouraged workers and marginally attached workers are
   a. counted as being employed by the BLS but are not part of the labor force.
   b. counted as being employed by the BLS and are part of the labor force.
   c. counted as being unemployed by the BLS and are part of the labor force.
   d. not part of the labor force.
   e. counted as being unemployed by the BLS but are not part of the labor force.

8. While in school, Kiki spends 20 hours a week as a computer programmer for Microsoft and studies 30 hours a week.
   a. Kiki is classified as a full-time worker, working 50 hours a week.
   b. Kiki is classified as a part-time worker, working 30 hours a week.
   c. Kiki is classified as a part-time worker, working 20 hours a week.
   d. Because Kiki is a student, she is not classified as working.
   e. Because Kiki is a student, she is classified as a full-time worker, working 20 hours a week at a paid job.

© 2015 Pearson Education, Inc.

9. Part-time workers for noneconomic reasons are people who
   a. work less than 35 hours a week but would like to work more than 35 hours a week.
   b. work more than 35 hours a week but would like to work less than 35 hours a week.
   c. have lost their jobs within the last four weeks and are seeking another job.
   d. do not want to work full time.
   e. are discouraged workers.

Short Response Questions

Category	Number of people
Total population	2,600
Working-age population	2,000
Not in the labor force	500
Employed	1,300

1. The table above gives the status of the population of a (small!) nation.
   a. What is the size of the labor force?
   b. What is the number of unemployed workers?
   c. What is the unemployment rate?
   d. What is the labor force participation rate?

Category	Number of people
Working-age population	3,000
Unemployed	100
Employed	1,900

2. The table above gives the status of the population of another (small!) nation.
   a. What is the size of the labor force?
   b. What is the unemployment rate?
   c. What is the labor force participation rate?

3. Are part-time workers who are part time for economic reasons counted as being employed, underemployed, or unemployed?

Long Response Questions

1. What criteria must a person meet to be counted as being unemployed?

2. How does a discouraged worker relate to a marginally attached worker? Explain why a discouraged worker is not counted as part of the labor force.

Additional Exercises (also in MyEconLab Test A)

1. The Bureau of Labor Statistics reported that in June 2005, the labor force was 151.1 million, employment was 143.3 million, and the working-age population was 226.2 million. Calculate the unemployment rate and the labor force participation rate in June 2005.

2. Statistics Canada reported that in June 2005, the Canadian labor force was 17.1 million, employment was 15.7 million, and the working-age population was 25.1 million. Calculate the Canadian unemployment rate and the labor force participation rate in June 2005.

3. In June 2005, the U.S. labor force was 151.1 million, U.S. employment was 143.3 million, and the U.S. working-age population was 226.2 million In June 2005, in Canada, the labor force was 17.1 million, employment was 15.7 million, and the working-age population was 25.1 million. Do you think jobs are harder to find in Canada or in the United States? Why?

Item	MA	U.S.
	(thousands)	
Working-age population	5,000	226,000
Labor force	3,400	149,300
Employment	3,200	141,700
Unemployment	200	7,600

4. The table above sets out data on the labor force in Massachusetts (MA) and in the United States in 2005. Calculate the unemployment rate and the labor force participation rate in Massachusetts. Compare these two labor market indicators in Massachusetts with the U.S. averages.

© 2015 Pearson Education, Inc.

CHECKPOINT 22.2

■ **Describe the trends and fluctuations in the indicators of labor market performance in the United States.**

Quick Review

- *Labor force participation rate* The percentage of the working-age population who are members of the labor force.

- *U-6* An alternative measure of the unemployment rate which counts discouraged workers, marginally attached workers, and people employed part time for economic reasons as unemployed members of the labor force.

Additional Practice Problems 22.2

1. How does the unemployment rate change in a recession? Since 1929, in what time period was the unemployment rate the highest and what did it equal?

2. Are workers employed part time for economic reasons counted as unemployed when calculating the official U-3 unemployment rate? If they are, how do they affect the unemployment rate; if they are not, how would their inclusion affect the unemployment rate?

Solutions to Additional Practice Problems 22.2

1. The unemployment rate rises during recessions. Since 1929, the unemployment rate reached its peak of approximately 25 percent in 1932 during the Great Depression.

2. Workers employed part time for economic reasons are *not* counted as unemployed in the official U-3 unemployment rate. Indeed, they are counted as employed when computing that unemployment rate. If they were counted as unemployed, the unemployment rate would increase. As Figure 22.5 in the textbook shows, the increase would be larger during recessions because the number of workers employed part time for economic reasons increases during recessions.

■ AP Self Test 22.2

True or false

1. The unemployment rate during the 2008-2009 recession was lower than the unemployment rate during the Great Depression.

2. Although the female labor force participation rate increased over the last 40 years, it is still less than the male labor force participation rate.

3. During the 2008-2009 recession, the unemployment rate that included marginally attached workers and discouraged workers as unemployed was double the unemployment rate that did not include these workers.

4. The number of workers employed part-time for economic reasons rises during recessions.

Multiple choice

1. From 1948 to 2013, the average unemployment rate in the United States was approximately
   a. 3.1 percent.
   b. 5.8 percent.
   c. 12.0 percent.
   d. 24.4 percent.
   d. 9.6 percent.

2. From 1981 to 2013, the unemployment rate in the United States
   a. was always lower than the unemployment rate in Japan.
   b. almost always equaled the unemployment rate in Canada.
   c. generally rose while the unemployment rate in the Eurozone fell.
   d. was usually lower than the unemployment rate in the Eurozone.
   e. was usually higher than the unemployment rate in Canada.

© 2015 Pearson Education, Inc.

3. The women's labor force participation rate is
   a. higher in Japan than in the United States.
   b. higher in the United States than in France.
   c. higher in Italy than in the United States.
   d. higher in Spain than in Iceland.
   e. higher in the United States than in Iceland or Norway.

4. In a recession, which unemployment rate is the highest?
   a. The U-1 unemployment rate.
   b. The U-6 unemployment rate.
   c. The U-2 unemployment rate.
   d. The U-3 unemployment rate.
   e. None of the above answers are correct because the highest unemployment rate changes from one recession to the next.

5. In 2013, part-time workers for noneconomic reasons were about ____ of total employment and part-time workers for economic reasons were about ____ of total employment.
   a. 3 percent; 25 percent
   b. 17 percent; 17 percent
   c. 2 percent; 12 percent
   d. 13 percent; 20 percent
   e. 13 percent; 6 percent

6. The number of part-time workers for economic reasons ____ during recessions and the number of part-time workers for noneconomic reasons ____ during recessions.
   a. increases; increases
   b. increases; decreases
   c. increases; does not change
   d. does not change; does not change
   e. decreases; increases

Short Response Question

1. During a recession, what happens to:
   a. the unemployment rate?
   b. the number of part-time workers for economic reasons?
   c. the number of part-time workers for noneconomic reasons?

Long Response Questions

1. How does the unemployment rate during the Great Depression compare with more recent unemployment rates?

2. How do the U-3, U-5, and U-6 measures of the unemployment rate differ? What happens to them when the economy enters a recession?

Additional Exercise (also in MyEconLab Test A)

1. During which decade—the 1970s, 1980s, or 1990s—did the labor force participation rate of women increase most? Suggest some reasons why this rapid increase occurred during that decade.

CHECKPOINT 22.3

■ **Describe the types of unemployment, define full employment, and explain the link between unemployment and real GDP.**

Quick Review

- *Frictional unemployment* Unemployment that arises from normal labor market turnover.
- *Structural unemployment* Unemployment that arises when changes in technology or international competition change the skills needed to perform jobs or change the location of jobs.
- *Cyclical unemployment* Unemployment that fluctuates over the business cycle, rising during a recession and falling during an expansion.
- *Full employment* When there is no cyclical unemployment.
- *Natural unemployment rate* The unemployment rate at full employment.
- *Potential GDP* The value of real GDP when all the economy's factors of production are employed.
- *Output gap* Real GDP minus potential GDP, expressed as a percentage of potential GDP.

© 2015 Pearson Education, Inc.

Additional Practice Problems 22.3

1. Each of the following people is actively seeking work. Classify each as either frictionally, structurally, or cyclically unemployed:

   a. Perry lost his job when foreign competition bankrupted his company.

   b. Sam did not like his boss and so he quit his job.

   c. Sherry just graduated from college.

   d. Jose was fired when his company downsized in response to a recession.

   e. Pat was laid off from her job at the Gap because customers liked the fashions at JCPenney better.

2. In a recession, what happens to the output gap?

Solutions to Additional Practice Problems 22.3

1a. Perry is structurally unemployed.

1b. Sam is frictionally unemployed.

1c. Sherry is frictionally unemployed.

1d. Jose is cyclically unemployed.

1e. Pat is frictionally unemployed.

2. In a recession, real GDP is less than potential GDP, so the output gap is negative.

■ AP Self Test 22.3

True or false

1. There can easily be times when there is no unemployment.

2. The unemployment that arises when technology changes is termed technological unemployment.

3. When the U.S. economy is at full employment, the unemployment rate is zero.

4. Increasing unemployment benefits increase the natural unemployment rate.

5. Potential GDP is the amount of real GDP when the economy is at full employment.

Multiple choice

1. Bobby graduates from college and starts to look for a job. Bobby is

   a. frictionally unemployed.

   b. structurally unemployed.

   c. cyclically unemployed.

   d. unnecessarily unemployed.

   e. employed because he is looking for work.

2. If an entire industry relocates to a foreign country, the relocation leads to a higher rate of ____ unemployment.

   a. frictional

   b. structural

   c. structural and cyclical

   d. cyclical

   e. None of the above answers is correct because there is no unemployment created.

3. Who is cyclically unemployed?

   a. Casey, who lost his job because the technology changed so that he was no longer needed.

   b. Katrina, an office manager who quit her job to search for a better job closer to home.

   c. Kathy, a steelworker who was laid off but has stopped looking for a new job because she can't find one.

   d. David, a new car salesman who lost his job because of a recession.

   e. Samantha, who quit her job to return to college to earn her MBA.

4. An increase in unemployment benefits ____ unemployment and an increase in international competition that changes the location of jobs ____ unemployment.

   a. increases structural; decreases frictional

   b. decreases structural; decreases cyclical

   c. decreases cyclical; decreases cyclical

   d. increases frictional; increases structural

   e. decreases cyclical; increases cyclical

© 2015 Pearson Education, Inc.

5. Which of the following *lowers* frictional unemployment?
   a. more young people in the economy.
   b. decreasing unemployment benefits.
   c. increasing the pace of technological change.
   d. increasing the minimum wage.
   e. None of the above answers is correct because all of the answers raise frictional unemployment.

6. When the economy is at full employment,
   a. the natural unemployment rate equals zero.
   b. the amount of cyclical unemployment equals zero.
   c. the amount of structural unemployment equals zero.
   d. there is no unemployment.
   e. the amount of frictional unemployment equals zero.

7. When the unemployment rate is less than the natural unemployment rate, real GDP is _____ potential GDP.
   a. greater than
   b. less than
   c. unrelated to
   d. equal to
   e. not comparable to

Short Response Questions

1. What are the three types of unemployment?
2. How does the average time a worker spends as unemployed change during a recession?

Long Response Questions

1. What is the relationship between full employment, the natural unemployment rate, and potential GDP?
2. If the unemployment rate exceeds the natural unemployment rate, what is the relationship between real GDP and potential GDP? Is the output gap at this time positive or negative?

© 2015 Pearson Education, Inc.

SELF TEST ANSWERS

■ AP Self Test 22.1

True or false
1. True; page 564
2. False; page 564
3. True; page 565
4. False; page 566
5. False; page 566

Multiple choice
1. c; page 564
2. a; page 564
3. c; page 564
4. d; page 564
5. b; page 565
6. e; page 565
7. d; page 566
8. c; page 567
9. d; page 567

Short Response Questions
1. a. 1,500; page 564.
   b. 200; page 564.
   c. 13.3 percent; page 565.
   d. 75.0 percent; page 566.

2. a. 2,000; page 564.
   b. 5.0 percent; page 565.
   c. 66.7 percent; page 566.

3. Underemployed; page 567.

Long Response Questions
1. The person must be without employment, available for work, and actively searching or waiting to be recalled to a job from which he or she was laid off; page 564.

2. A marginally attached worker is a person without a job, who is not looking for work at the present but has looked for work in the recent past. A discouraged worker is marginally attached worker who is not looking for work because previous job searches were unsuccessful.. A discouraged worker is not counted as unemployed because the worker is not actively seeking a job; page 566.

Additional Exercises (also in MyEconLab Test A)
1. Unemployment rate = (151.1 million − 143.3 million) ÷ 151.1 million × 100 = 5.2 percent. Labor force participation rate = (151.1 million ÷ 226.2 million) × 100 = 66.8 percent; pages 565-566.

2. Unemployment rate = (17.1 million − 15.7 million) ÷ 17.1 million × 100 = 8.2 percent. Labor force participation rate = (17.1 million ÷ 25.1 million) × 100 = 68.1 percent; pages 565-566.

3. Probably it is more difficult to find a job in the nation with the higher unemployment rate. In that case, jobs were harder to find in Canada because Canada's unemployment at that time exceeded the U.S. unemployment rate; page 565.

4. In Massachusetts the unemployment rate equals 200 thousand ÷ 3,400 thousand × 100 = 5.9 percent and the labor force participation rate equals (3,400 thousand ÷ 5,000 thousand) × 100 = 68.0 percent. In the United States, the unemployment rate equals 7,600 thousand ÷ 149,300 thousand × 100 = 5.1 percent and the labor force participation rate equals (149,300 thousand ÷ 226,000 thousand) × 100 = 66.1 percent. The unemployment rate is higher in Massachusetts and so is the labor force participation rate; pages 565-566.

■ AP Self Test 22.2

True or false
1. True; page 569
2. True; pages 570-571
3. False; page 572
4. True; page 573

Multiple choice
1. b; page 569
2. d; page 570
3. b; page 571
4. b; page 572

© 2015 Pearson Education, Inc.

5. e; page 573

6. c; page 573

Short Response Questions

1. a. The unemployment rate rises; pages 569-570.

   b. The number of part-time workers for economic reasons increases; page 573.

   c. The number of part-time workers for non-economic reasons does not change; page 573.

Long Response Questions

1. The unemployment rate during the Great Depression was *much* higher, reaching near 25 percent, than recent unemployment rates, which reached approximately 10 percent in 1982 and 2009; pages 569-570.

2. The U-3 measure of the unemployment rate is the "official measure;" it counts as unemployed only unemployed workers. The U-5 measure of the unemployment rate counts discouraged workers and marginally attached workers as unemployed members of the labor force. The U-6 measure of the unemployment modifies the U-5 measure by also counting part-time workers for economic reasons as unemployed. All three measures rise when the economy enters a recession; page 572.

Additional Exercise (also in MyEconLab Test A)

1. The 1970s was the decade in which the labor force participation rate of women increased the most. Women generally increased their labor force participation rate throughout the last 50 years for four reasons: They pursued a college education and so increased their earning power; technological change created a large number of white-collar jobs with flexible work hours that a large number of women found attractive; technological change in the home increased time available for paid employment; and more families wanted two income earners. Because the 1970s had relatively high unemployment rates, the major

reason for the large increase in women's participation rate during the 1970s was the last of the four reasons—specifically more families wanted two income earners to help with their budgets; pages 570-571.

■ AP Self Test 22.3

True or false

1. False; page 575

2. False; page 575

3. False; page 577

4. True; page 577

5. True; page 578

Multiple choice

1. a; page 575

2. b; page 575

3. d; page 576

4. d; pages 575-576

5. b; page 577

6. b; page 576

7. a; pages 577-578

Short Response Questions

1. Unemployment is either frictional, structural, or cyclical; page 575.

2. The average duration of unemployment (the length of time a person is unemployed) rises in a recession; page 576.

Long Response Questions

1. When the economy is at full employment, the unemployment rate is the natural unemployment rate. When the economy is at full employment, the amount of GDP produced is potential GDP; pages 576-578.

2. If the unemployment rate exceeds the natural unemployment rate, real GDP is less than potential GDP. The output gap is negative; pages 577-578.

© 2015 Pearson Education, Inc.

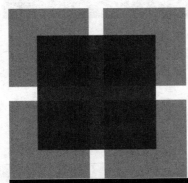

The CPI and the Cost of Living

Chapter 23

Chapter 23 explores how the CPI and other price level indices are measured.

1 Explain what the Consumer Price Index (CPI) is and how it is calculated.

The Consumer Price Index (CPI) measures the average of the prices paid by urban consumers for a fixed market basket of consumer goods and services. The CPI compares the cost of the fixed market basket of goods and services at one time with the cost of the fixed market basket in the reference base period, currently 1982–1984. The CPI in the base period is 100. If the CPI is now 150, it costs 50 percent more to buy the same goods and services than it cost in the base period. To construct the CPI market basket, households are surveyed on what they buy. Then each month the Bureau of Labor Statistics checks the prices of the 80,000 goods and services in the basket. To calculate the CPI, the cost of the market basket using current prices is divided by the cost of the basket using base period prices and the result is multiplied by 100. The inflation rate is the percentage change in the price level from one year to the next and is equal to [(CPI in current year − CPI in previous year) ÷ (CPI in previous year)] × 100.

2 Explain the limitations of the CPI and describe other measures of the price level.

The CPI has four sources of bias that lead to an inaccurate measure of the cost of living. These biases are the new goods bias (new goods replace old goods), the quality change bias (goods and services increase in quality), the commodity substitution bias (changes in relative prices lead consumers to change the items they buy), and the outlet substitution bias (consumers switch to shopping more often in discount stores). The overall CPI bias has been estimated to overstate inflation by 1.1 percentage points per year. The CPI bias distorts private contracts, increases government outlays and decreases government tax revenues. The GDP price index is an average of current prices of all the goods and services included in GDP expressed as a percentage of base-year prices. The GDP price index uses the prices of all goods and services in GDP and weights each item using information about current quantities. The PCE (Personal Consumption Expenditure) price index is an average of the current prices of the goods and services included in the consumption expenditure component of GDP expressed as a percentage of base year prices. The core inflation rate is the percentage change in the PCE index excluding the prices of food and energy. The CPI inflation rate generally exceeds the PCE inflation rate.

3 Adjust money values for inflation and calculate real wage rates and real interest rates.

To compare values measured in dollars in different years, the nominal values must be converted to real values. Real GDP equals nominal GDP divided by the price level and multiplied by 100. The real wage rate measures the quantity of goods and services that an hour's work can buy. It equals the nominal wage rate divided by the CPI and multiplied by 100. The real interest rate equals the nominal interest rate minus the inflation rate.

© 2015 Pearson Education, Inc.

YOUR AP TEST HINTS

AP Topics

Topic on your AP test	What to Know	Corresponding textbook section
Consumer Price Index (*CPI*)	The market basket, base years, inflation rate	Checkpoint 23.1
CPI limitations	New goods, quality changes, commodity substitution, etc.	Checkpoint 23.2
Adjusting for inflation	Calculating real wages and real interest rates	Checkpoint 23.3

AP Vocabulary Covered

Terms	What to Know	Text Sections
Consumer Price Index, (*CPI*)	Measures average prices paid by urban consumers for a fixed market basket of consumption goods and services; the CPI equals the cost of the basket at current prices divided by cost of the basket in the base year x 100	Checkpoint 23.1, p. 586
Reference base period	The period used as the point of comparison for later values of the CPI; the CPI in the base period equals 100. In many federal references this is the time of 1982 to 1984	Checkpoint 23.1, p. 586
CPI market basket	The goods and services whose prices are used for the CPI	Checkpoint 23.1, p. 586
Inflation rate	CPI in current year minus CPI in previous year divided by CPI in previous year then multiplied by 100	Checkpoint 23.1, p. 589
Deflation	The price level is falling and inflation is negative	Checkpoint 23.1, p. 589
Cost of living index	Money people need to spend for a standard of living	Checkpoint 23.2, p. 592
GDP Price Index, (also called GDP deflator)	An average of the current prices of all goods and services included in GDP expressed as a percentage of the base-year period	Checkpoint 23.2, p. 595
Personal Consumption Expenditures price index, (*PCE*)	An average of the current prices of goods and services included in the consumption expenditure component of GDP expressed as a percentage of base-year prices	Checkpoint 23.2., p. 595
Core inflation rate	The PCE inflation rate excluding the prices of food and energy	Checkpoint 23.2, p. 595
Nominal wage rate	The average hourly wage in current dollars	Checkpoint 23.3, p. 600
Real wage rate	The average hourly wage rate in dollars of a given base year; it equals the nominal wage rate divided by the CPI then multiplied by 100	Checkpoint 23.3, p. 600
Nominal interest rate	The interest rate in terms of dollars	Checkpoint 23.3, p. 602
Real interest rate	The interest rate in terms of goods and services; it equals the nominal interest rate minus the inflation rate	Checkpoint 23.3, p. 602

Extra AP material

- The formula for calculating inflation rates, the later year minus the earlier year divided by the earlier year then multiplied by 100 is used often on the AP test.
- The CPI and the GDP Price Index (GDP deflator) are the two most common price indices. The AP test also refers to the Producer Price Index (PPI), which measures the average prices paid by producers (firms) for the raw material or semi-finished goods and services they buy to produce their output.

© 2015 Pearson Education, Inc.

CHECKPOINT 23.1

■ **Explain what the Consumer Price Index (CPI) is and how it is calculated.**

Quick Review

- *CPI market basket* The goods and services in the CPI and the relative importance attached to each of them.
- *CPI formula* The CPI equals:

$$\frac{\text{Cost of CPI basket at current period prices}}{\text{Cost of CPI basket at base period prices}} \times 100.$$

- *Inflation rate* The inflation rate equals:

$$\frac{(\text{CPI in current year} - \text{CPI in previous year})}{\text{CPI in previous year}} \times 100.$$

Additional Practice Problem 23.1

Item	Quantity (2013)	Price (2013)	Quantity (2014)	Price (2014)
Limes	20	$1.00	15	$1.00
Biscuits	30	$1.00	45	$0.75
Rum	10	$10.00	8	$11.00

1. A Consumer Expenditure Survey in Scurvy shows that people consume only limes, biscuits, and rum. The Consumer Expenditure Survey for both 2013 and 2014 are in the table above. The base year is 2013.

    a. What and how much is in the CPI market basket?

    b. What did the CPI market basket cost in 2013? What was the CPI in 2013?

    c. What did the CPI market basket cost in 2014? What was the CPI in 2014?

    d. What was the inflation rate between 2013 and 2014?

Solution to Additional Practice Problem 23.1

1a. The market basket is 20 limes, 30 biscuits, and 10 rums, the quantities consumed in the base year of 2013.

1b. In 2013 the market basket cost (20 × $1.00) + (30 × $1.00) + (10 × $10.00) = $150. Because 2009 is the base year, the CPI = 100.0.

1c. In 2014 the market basket cost (20 × $1.00) + (30 × $0.75) + (10 × $11.00) = $152.50. The CPI in 2014 is equal to ($152.50) ÷ ($150.00) × 100, which is 101.7.

1d. The inflation rate equals [(101.7 − 100.0) ÷ 100] × 100 = 1.7 percent.

■ AP Self Test 23.1

True or false

1. In the reference base period, the CPI equals 1.0.

2. The CPI market basket is changed from one month to the next.

3. If the cost of the CPI basket at current period prices equals $320, then the CPI equals 320.

4. If the cost of the CPI market basket at current period prices exceeds the cost of the CPI market basket at base period prices, the inflation rate between these two periods is positive.

5. If the CPI increases from 110 to 121, the inflation rate is 11 percent.

Multiple choice

1. The CPI is reported once every
    a. year.
    b. quarter.
    c. month.
    d. week.
    e. other year.

2. The Consumer Price Index (CPI) measures
    a. the prices of a few consumer goods and services.
    b. the prices of those consumer goods and services that increased in price.
    c. the average of the prices paid by urban consumers for a fixed market basket of goods and services.
    d. consumer confidence in the economy.
    e. the average of the costs paid by businesses to produce a fixed market basket of consumer goods and services.

© 2015 Pearson Education, Inc.

3. If a country had a CPI of 105.0 last year and a CPI of 102.0 this year, then
   a. the average prices of goods and services increased between last year and this year.
   b. the average prices of goods and services decreased between last year and this year.
   c. the average quality of goods and services decreased between last year and this year.
   d. there was an error when calculating the CPI this year.
   e. the quantity of consumer goods and services produced decreased between last year and this year.

4. The period for which the Consumer Price Index is defined to equal 100 is called the
   a. reference base period.
   b. base year.
   c. starting point.
   d. zero period.
   e. beginning period.

5. In the United States, the good or service given the most weight in the CPI basket when calculating the CPI is
   a. food and beverages.
   b. taxes.
   c. housing.
   d. medical care.
   e. recreation.

6. Suppose the market basket of consumer goods and services costs $180 using the base period prices, and the same market basket of goods and services costs $300 using the current period prices. The CPI for the current period equals
   a. 166.7.
   b. 66.7.
   c. 160.0.
   d. 60.0.
   e. 300.0.

7. Suppose the CPI last year was 82.3 and this year is 90.9. Based on this information, we can calculate that the inflation rate between these years is
   a. 10.4 percent.
   b. 8.6 percent.
   c. 90.9 percent.
   d. 82.3 percent.
   e. 9.09 percent.

8. In the United States, the inflation rate since 1999 generally was
   a. higher than between 1979 to 1981.
   b. much higher than in the 1980s.
   c. lower than between 1979 to 1981.
   d. much higher than between 1989 to 1999.
   e. negative.

Short Response Questions

Item	Quantity (2013)	Price (2013)	Quantity (2014)	Price (2014)
Pizza	10	$10.00	15	$10.00
Burritos	20	$1.00	25	$0.75
Rice	30	$0.50	20	$1.00

1. The table above gives the expenditures of households in the small nation of Studenvia. 2013 is the reference base period.
   a. What is the cost of the CPI market basket in 2013?
   b. What is the cost of the CPI market basket in 2014?
   c. What is the CPI in 2013?
   d. What is the CPI in 2014?
   e. What is the inflation rate in 2014?

2. Suppose the CPI was 100.0 in 2013, 110.0 in 2014, 121.0 in 2015, and 133.1 in 2016. What is the inflation rate in 2014, 2015, and 2016?

3. When is the inflation rate larger: when the price level rises from 105 to 115 or when the price rises from 180 to 195?

Long Response Question

1. If the price level rises slowly, is the inflation rate positive or negative? Why?

Additional Exercises (also in MyEconLab Test A)

The people of Firestorm City buy only firecrackers and bandages. A Consumer Expendi-

© 2015 Pearson Education, Inc.

ture Survey in 2011 shows that the average household spent $150 on firecrackers and $15 on bandages. In 2011, the reference base year, the price of a firecracker was $2, and the price of bandages was $1 a pack. In the current year, 2012, firecrackers are $3 each and bandages are $1.25 a pack.

1. Calculate the CPI market basket and the percentage of a household's budget spent on firecrackers in the base year.

2. Calculate the CPI in 2012 and the inflation rate in 2012.

CHECKPOINT 23.2

■ **Explain the limitations of the CPI and describe other measures of the price level.**

Quick Review

- *Commodity substitution bias* People cut back on their purchases of items that become relatively more costly and increase their consumption of items that become relatively less costly.

Additional Practice Problems 23.2

1. When households buy broccoli, they discard some of it because it is bruised. Say 20 percent is discarded. Now suppose that new, genetically engineered broccoli is developed that does not bruise so that all the broccoli that is purchased can be used. People prefer the new broccoli, so they switch to buying the new broccoli. If the price of the new broccoli is 10 percent higher than the old, what actually happens to the CPI and what should happen to the CPI?

2. When the price of textbook is $105 a book, Anthony buys his books at the bookstore closest to him. When textbooks rise in price to $145 a book at that store, Anthony drives several miles away to a store where the books are sold for only $125. How does Anthony's decision affect the CPI?

Solutions to Additional Practice Problems 23.2

1. With the introduction of the new broccoli, the CPI rises because the new broccoli's price is higher (10 percent) than the old broccoli. But, the CPI should actually decrease because people pay only 10 percent more for 20 percent more (useable) broccoli. This problem illustrates how the quality change bias can bias the CPI upwards.

2. Anthony's decision reflects outlet substitution. When the price of a good rises, consumers, such as Anthony, switch the stores from which they buy goods and services to less expensive outlets. But the CPI, as constructed, does not take into account this point. The CPI will record that the price of textbooks rose by $40, from $105 to $145. This outlet substitution bias means that the CPI overstates the true rise in the cost of living.

■ **AP Self Test 23.2**

True or false

1. The CPI is a biased measure of the cost of living.

2. Commodity substitution bias refers to the ongoing replacement of old goods by new goods.

3. The bias in the CPI is estimated to overstate inflation by approximately 1.1 percentage points a year.

4. The CPI bias can distort private contracts.

5. The GDP price index is influenced by the prices of investment goods as well as the prices of exported goods and services.

6. The core inflation rate is the inflation rate of energy and food prices.

7. Inflation measured using the GDP price index is generally lower than inflation measured using the CPI.

© 2015 Pearson Education, Inc.

Multiple choice

1. All of the following are a bias in the CPI EX-CEPT the
   a. new goods bias.
   b. outlet substitution bias.
   c. commodity substitution bias.
   d. GDP price index bias.
   e. quality change bias.

2. An example of the new goods bias in the calculation of the CPI is a price increase in
   a. butter relative to margarine.
   b. an HD LCD (liquid crystal display) TV relative to CRT (cathode ray tube) TV.
   c. a 2014 Honda Civic Si Coupe relative to a 2014 Honda Civic Si Sedan.
   d. textbooks bought through a bookstore relative to textbooks bought through Amazon.com.
   e. a Caribbean cruise for a couple who has never been on a cruise before.

3. The price of dishwashers has remained constant while the quality of dishwashers has improved. The CPI
   a. is adjusted monthly to reflect the improvement in quality.
   b. is increased monthly to reflect the increased quality of dishwashers.
   c. has an upward bias if it is not adjusted to take account of the higher quality.
   d. has an upward bias because it does reflects the increased production of dishwashers.
   e. does not take account of any quality changes because it is a price index not a quality index.

4. Joe buys chicken and beef. If the price of beef rises and the price of chicken does not change, Joe will buy _____ for the CPI.
   a. more beef and create a new goods bias
   b. more chicken and create a commodity substitution bias
   c. the same quantity of beef and chicken and create a commodity substitution bias
   d. less chicken and beef and create a quality change bias
   e. more chicken and eliminate the commodity substitution bias

5. The CPI bias was estimated by the Congressional Advisory Commission on the Consumer Price Index as
   a. understating the actual inflation rate by about 5 percentage points a year.
   b. understating the actual inflation rate by more than 5 percentage points a year.
   c. overstating the actual inflation rate by about 1 percentage point a year.
   d. overstating the actual inflation rate by more than 5 percentage points a year.
   e. understating the actual inflation rate by about 1 percentage point a year.

6. A consequence of the CPI bias is that it
   a. decreases government outlays.
   b. increases international trade.
   c. reduces outlet substitution bias.
   d. distorts private contracts.
   e. means that it is impossible to measure the inflation rate.

7. Because the CPI is a biased measure of the inflation rate, government outlays will
   a. increase at a faster rate than the actual inflation rate.
   b. increase at the same rate as the actual inflation rate.
   c. increase at a slower rate than the actual inflation rate.
   d. sometimes increase faster and sometimes increase slower than the actual inflation rate depending on whether the actual inflation rate exceeds 1.1 percent per year or is less than 1.1 percent per year.
   e. None of the above because the bias in the CPI does not affect government outlays.

Short Response Question

1. How is the core inflation rate calculated?

Long Response Questions

1. What are the sources of bias in the CPI? Briefly explain each.

2. Once you graduate, you move to a new town and sign a long-term lease on a townhouse. You agree to pay $1,000 a month rent and to change the monthly rent annually by the

© 2015 Pearson Education, Inc.

percentage change in the CPI. For the next 4 years, the CPI increases 5 percent each year. What will you pay in monthly rent for the second, third, and fourth years of your lease? Suppose the CPI overstates the inflation rate by 1 percentage point a year. If the CPI bias was eliminated, what would you pay in rent for the second, third, and fourth years?

Additional Exercise (also in MyEconLab Test A)

Item	3005		3006	
	Quantity	Price	Quantity	Price
Games	20	$60	10	$70
Time travel	0	--	20	$8,000

1. In Virtual Reality, time travel became possible only in 3006. Economists in the Statistics Bureau decided to conduct a Consumer Expenditure Survey in both 3005 and 3006 to check the substitution bias of the CPI. The table shows the results of the survey. It shows the items that consumers buy and their prices. The Statistics Bureau fixes the reference base year as 3005. Calculate the CPI in 3006 and the inflation rate measured by the CPI in 3006.

CHECKPOINT 23.3

■ **Adjust money values for inflation and calculate real wage rates and real interest rates.**

Quick Review

- *Real wage rate* The real wage rate equals the nominal wage rate divided by the CPI and multiplied by 100.
- *Real interest rate* The real interest rate equals the nominal interest rate minus the inflation rate.

Additional Practice Problems 23.3

Year	Minimum wage (dollars per hour)	CPI
1955	0.75	26.7
1965	1.25	31.6
1975	2.10	56.7
1985	3.35	107.5
1995	4.25	152.4
2005	5.15	194.1

1. The table above shows the minimum wage and the CPI for six different years. The reference base period is 1982–1984.
   a. Calculate the real minimum wage in each year in 1982–1984 dollars.
   b. In which year was the minimum wage the highest in real terms?
   c. In which year was the minimum wage the lowest in real terms?

2. Nominal GDP = $10 trillion, real GDP = $9 trillion. What is the GDP price index?

3. Suppose Sally has saved $1,000 dollars. Sally wants a 3 percent real interest rate on her savings. What nominal interest rate would she need to receive if the inflation rate is 7 percent?

Solutions to Additional Practice Problems 23.3

Year	Real minimum wage (1982-1984 dollars per hour)
1955	2.81
1965	3.96
1975	3.70
1985	3.12
1995	2.79
2005	2.65

1a. Using the CPI to adjust nominal values to real values is a key use of the CPI. Keep in mind that to convert a nominal price (such as the nominal wage rate) into a real price (such as the real wage rate), you divide by the CPI and multiply by 100, but to convert the nominal interest rate into the real interest rate, you subtract the inflation rate. To convert the nominal minimum wages in the table to real prices, divide the price by the CPI in that year and then multiply by 100. In 1955, the nominal minimum wage gas was $0.75 an

© 2015 Pearson Education, Inc.

hour and the CPI was 26.7, so the real minimum wage is ($0.75 ÷ 26.7) × 100 = $2.81. The rest of the real minimum wages in the table above are calculated similarly.

1b. In real terms, the minimum wage was highest in 1965 when it equaled $3.96.

1c. In real terms, the minimum wage was the lowest in 2005 when it equaled $2.65.

2. GDP price index = (Nominal GDP ÷ Real GDP) × 100 = ($10 trillion ÷ $9 trillion) × 100 = 111.1.

3. The real interest rate equals the nominal interest rate minus the inflation rate. Rearranging this formula shows that the nominal interest rate equals the real interest rate plus the inflation rate. To get a 3 percent real interest rate with a 7 percent inflation rate, Sally needs the nominal interest rate to be equal to 3 percent plus 7 percent, or 10 percent.

■ AP Self Test 23.3

True or false

1. Real prices and nominal prices are unrelated.

2. Real GDP equals nominal GDP divided by the CPI, multiplied by 100.

3. A change in the real wage rate measures the change in the goods and services that an hour's work can buy.

4. The nominal interest rate is the percentage return on a loan expressed in dollars; the real interest rate is the percentage return on a loan expressed in purchasing power.

5. If the nominal interest rate is 8 percent a year and the inflation rate is 5 percent a year, then the real interest rate is 3 percent a year.

Multiple choice

1. In 2013 apples cost $1.49 a pound. The CPI was 120 in 2013 and 140 in 2014. If there is no change in the real price of an apple in 2014, what is the price of a pound of apples in 2014?
   a. $2.74
   b. $1.69
   c. $1.66
   d. $1.74
   e. $1.28

2. In 1970, the CPI was 39 and in 2000 it was 172. A local phone call cost $0.10 in 1970. What is the price of this phone call in 2000 dollars?
   a. $1.42
   b. $0.39
   c. $1.72
   d. $0.44
   e. $0.23

3. Nominal GDP is $12.1 trillion and real GDP is $11.0 trillion. The GDP price index is
   a. 90.1.
   b. 121.0.
   c. 1.10.
   d. 91.0.
   e. 110.0

4. The nominal wage rate is the
   a. minimum hourly wage that a company can legally pay a worker.
   b. average hourly wage rate measured in the dollars of a given base year.
   c. minimum hourly wage rate measured in the dollars of a given reference base year.
   d. average hourly wage rate measured in current dollars.
   e. wage rate after inflation has been adjusted out of it.

5. The average starting salary for a history major is $29,500. If the CPI is 147.5, the real salary is
   a. $200.00 an hour.
   b. $20,000.
   c. $35,000.
   d. $43,513.
   e. $14,750.

6. Since 1982, the
   a. real wage rate increased steadily.
   b. nominal wage rate increased and the real wage rate did not change by very much.
   c. real wage rate increased more than the nominal wage rate.
   d. nominal wage rate increased at an uneven pace whereas the increase in the real wage rate was steady and constant.
   e. nominal wage rate and real wage rate both decreased.

© 2015 Pearson Education, Inc.

7. The real interest rate is equal to the
   a. nominal interest rate plus the inflation rate.
   b. nominal interest rate minus the inflation rate.
   c. nominal interest rate times the inflation rate.
   d. nominal interest rate divided by the inflation rate.
   e. inflation rate minus the nominal interest rate.

8. You borrow at a nominal interest rate of 10 percent. If the inflation rate is 4 percent, then the real interest rate is
   a. the $10 in interest you have to pay.
   b. 16 percent.
   c. 2.5 percent.
   d. 6 percent.
   e. 14 percent.

9. In the United States for the last 40 years, the nominal interest rate
   a. and the real interest rate both decreased in almost every year.
   b. and the real interest rate were both constant in almost every year.
   c. was constant in most years and the real interest rate fluctuated.
   d. exceeded the real interest rate in virtually all the years.
   e. exceeded the real interest rate in about half of the years and the real interest rate was greater than the nominal interest rate in the other half of the years.

Short Response Questions

1. For each of the following pairs of real GDP and nominal GDP, calculate the price level.
   a. Nominal GDP = $12 trillion, real GDP = $10 trillion.
   b. Nominal GDP = $12 trillion, real GDP $16 trillion.
   c. Nominal GDP = $8 trillion, real GDP = $4 trillion.

Job	Salary (dollars per year)	CPI
Job A	20,000	105
Job B	25,000	120
Job C	34,000	170

2. Often the cost of living varies from state to state or from large city to small city. After you graduate, suppose you have job offers in 3 locales. The nominal salary and the CPI for each job is given in the table above.
   a. Which job offers the highest real salary?
   b. Which job offers the lowest real salary?
   c. In determining which job to accept, what is more important: the real salary or the nominal salary? Why?

Year	Real interest rate (percent per year)	Nominal interest rate (percent per year)	Inflation rate (percent per year)
2012	____	10	5
2013	____	6	1
2014	4	6	____
2015	5	____	3

3. The table above gives the real interest rate, nominal interest rate, and inflation rate for various years in a foreign country. Complete the table.

Long Response Question

1. In 1980, the nominal interest rate was 12 percent. In 2013, the nominal interest rate was 4 percent. From this information, can you determine if you would rather have saved $1,000 in 1980 or 2013? Explain your answer.

Additional Exercises (also in MyEconLab Test A)

1. In 2005, the GDP price index was 105 and real GDP was $4 trillion (2000 dollars). In 2006, nominal GDP was $5.4 trillion and real GDP was $4.5 trillion (2000 dollars). Calculate the increase in nominal GDP and the increase in the GDP price index in 2006.

© 2015 Pearson Education, Inc.

Year	Nominal interest rate	Inflation rate
	(percent per year)	
1992	4.6	1.7
1993	3.0	1.2
1994	2.1	0.7
1995	1.2	−0.1
1996	0.4	0.1

2. The table shows the nominal interest rate and inflation rate in Japan for several years. In which year was the real interest rate the highest and in which year was the real interest rate the lowest?

3. In 1986, 1996, and 2006, average weekly earnings in the United States were $310, $413, and $567 respectively. The CPI was 110, 157, and 202 respectively. In which of these three years was the real average weekly earnings highest and in which year was it lowest?

© 2015 Pearson Education, Inc.

SELF TEST ANSWERS

■ AP Self Test 23.1

True or false

1. False; page 586
2. False; page 586
3. False; page 589
4. True; page 589
5. False; page 589

Multiple choice

1. c; page 586
2. c; page 586
3. b; page 586
4. a; page 586
5. c; page 587
6. a; page 589
7. a; page 589
8. c; page 590

Short Response Questions

1. a. The cost is $135; page 588.
   b. The cost is $145. The quantities used to calculate this cost are the base period, 2013, quantities; page 588.
   c. The CPI is 100; page 589.
   d. The CPI is 107.4; page 589.
   e. The inflation rate is 7.4 percent; page 589.

2. The inflation rate for each year is 10 percent; page 589.

3. The inflation rate is larger when the price level rises from 105 to 115 because the inflation rate equals $\dfrac{(115-105)}{105}\times100$ which is 9.5 percent. When the price level rises from 180 to 195, the inflation rate is equal to $\dfrac{(195-180)}{180}\times100$ which is 8.3 percent; page 589.

Long Response Question

1. Whenever the price level rises, the inflation rate is positive. If the price level rises slowly, the inflation rate is small; if the price level rises rapidly, the inflation rate is large; page 589.

Additional Exercises (also in MyEconLab Test A)

1. The CPI market basket is the quantities bought during the Expenditure Survey year, 2011. Households spend $150 on firecrackers at $2 a firecracker so the quantity of firecrackers bought was 75. Households spend $15 on bandages at $1 a pack so the quantity of bandages bought was 15 packs. The CPI market basket is 75 firecrackers and 15 packs of bandages.

   In the base year, expenditure on firecrackers was $150 and expenditure on bandages was $15, so the household budget was $165. Expenditure on firecrackers was ($150 ÷ $165) × 100, which is 90.9 percent of the household budget; pages 588-589.

2. To calculate the CPI in 2012, find the cost of the CPI market basket in 2012 and 2011. In 2011, the CPI market basket costs $165 ($150 for firecrackers and $15 for bandages). In 2012, the CPI basket costs $225 for firecrackers (75 × $3 a firecracker) plus $18.75 (15 packs of bandages × $1.25 a pack), which sums to $243.75. The CPI in 2012 equals ($243.75 ÷ $165) × 100 = 147.7.

   The inflation rate in 2012 is [(147.7 − 100.0) ÷ 100.0] × 100, which is 47.7 percent; pages 588-589.

■ AP Self Test 23.2

True or false

1. True; page 592
2. False; page 593
3. True; page 593
4. True; page 594
5. True; page 595
6. False; page 595
7. True; page 596

© 2015 Pearson Education, Inc.

Multiple choice

1. d; page 592
2. b; page 592
3. c; page 593
4. b; page 593
5. c; page 593
6. d; page 594
7. a; page 594

Short Response Question

1. The core inflation rate is the inflation rate calculated using the PCE price level excluding the prices of energy and food; page 595.

Long Response Questions

1. There are four sources of bias in the CPI: the new goods bias, the quality change bias, the commodity substitution bias, and the outlet substitution bias. The new goods bias refers to the fact that new goods replace old goods. The quality change bias occurs because at times price increases in existing goods are the result of increased quality. The commodity substitution bias occurs because consumers buy fewer goods and services when their prices rise compared to other, comparable products. Finally, the outlet substitution bias refers to the fact that when prices rise, people shop more frequently at discount stores to take advantage of the lower prices in these stores; pages 592-593.

2. The monthly rent increases by 5 percent each year. For the second year the monthly rent equals $1,000 × 1.05, which is $1,050. For the third year the monthly rent equals $1,050 × 1.05, which is $1,102.50. And for the fourth year the monthly rent equals $1,102.50 × 1.05, which is $1,157.63. If the CPI bias was eliminated, the monthly rent would increase by 4 percent each year. The monthly rent would be $1,040 for the second year, $1,081.60 for the third year, and $1,124.86 for the third year; page 594.

Additional Exercise (also in MyEconLab Test A)

1. Using the 3005 CPI market basket, the cost of the basket in 3005 is $1,200 and the cost of the basket in 3006 is $1,400. (Note that time travel does not enter into the cost in 3006 because it is not in the CPI market basket.) So the CPI in 3006 is ($1,400 ÷ $1,200) × 100, which is 116.7. The change in the CPI from 3005 to 3006 is 16.7. The initial CPI in 3005 is 100.0 (since it is a base year). So the inflation rate is equal to (16.7 ÷ 100) × 100, or 16.7 percent; pages 588-589, 592.

■ AP Self Test 23.3

True or false

1. False; page 598
2. False; page 600
3. True; pages 600-601
4. True; page 602
5. True; page 602

Multiple choice

1. d; page 598
2. d; page 598
3. e; page 600
4. d; page 600
5. b; page 600
6. b; pages 600-601
7. b; page 602
8. d; page 602
9. d; page 603

Short Response Questions

1. a. GDP price index = ($12 trillion ÷ $10 trillion) × 100 = 120; page 600.

   b. GDP price index = ($12 trillion ÷ $16 trillion) × 100 = 75; page 600.

   c. GDP price index = ($8 trillion ÷ $4 trillion) × 100 = 200; page 600.

2. a. The real salary equals (nominal salary ÷ CPI) × 100. The real salary is $19,048 for Job A, $20,833 for Job B, and $20,000 for Job C. The real salary is highest for Job B; page 600.

© 2015 Pearson Education, Inc.

b. The real salary is lowest for Job A; page 600.

c. The real salary is more important than the nominal salary because the real salary measures the quantity of goods and services you can buy; pages 600-601.

Year	Real interest rate (percent per year)	Nominal interest rate (percent per year)	Inflation rate (percent per year)
2012	5	10	5
2013	5	6	1
2014	4	6	2
2015	5	8	3

3. The completed table is above; page 602.

Long Response Question

1. You cannot determine when you would rather have been a saver. Savers are interested in the real interest rate because the real interest rate is the percentage return expressed in purchasing power. Without knowing the inflation rate, there are not enough data given to compute the real interest rate; page 602.

Additional Exercises (also in MyEconLab Test A)

1. Nominal GDP = real GDP × P ÷ 100, where P is the GDP price index. So in 2005 nominal GDP equals $4 trillion × 105 ÷ 100, which is $4.2 trillion. Between 2005 and 2006, nominal GDP has increased by $1.2 trillion, which is 28.6 percent.

The equality Nominal GDP = real GDP × P ÷ 100 can be rearranged to give P = nominal GDP ÷ real GDP × 100. So in 2006, the GDP price index equals $5.4 trillion ÷ $4.5 trillion × 100, which is 120. Between 2005 and 2006, the GDP price index has increased by 15, which is 14.3 percent; pages 599-600.

2. The real interest rate for each year is equal to the nominal interest rate minus the inflation rate. Using this formula yields:

1992   4.6 percent – 1.7 percent = 2.9 percent
1993   3.0 percent – 1.2 percent = 1.8 percent
1994   2.1 percent – 0.7 percent = 1.4 percent
1995   1.2 percent – (–0.1) percent = 1.3 percent
1996   0.4 percent – 0.1 percent = 0.3 percent

The real interest rate was the highest in 1992 and lowest in 1996; page 602.

3. The real wage rate is equal to the nominal wage rate divided by the CPI and then multiplied by 100. So the 1986 real wage rate equals $310 ÷ 110 × 100, or $281.82. The 1996 real wage rate equals $413 ÷ 157 × 100, or $263.06. And the 2006 real wage rate equals $567 ÷ 202 × 100, or $280.69. The real wage rate was the highest in 1986 and was the lowest in 1996; page 600.

© 2015 Pearson Education, Inc.

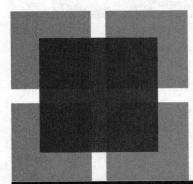

Potential GDP and the Natural Unemployment Rate

Chapter 24

Chapter 24 begins by introducing different macroeconomic schools of thought. The three main schools of thought are classical macroeconomics, Keynesian macroeconomics, and monetarist macroeconomics. Classical macroeconomics asserts that markets work well and, although the economy will fluctuate, no government intervention is needed. But classical macroeconomics couldn't explain why the Great Depression lasted so long. Keynesian economics was borne during the Great Depression and asserted that depressions were the result of too little spending. Keynesian economics calls for government intervention to assist the economy. Monetarist macroeconomics says that the classical approach is generally correct but that fluctuations in the quantity of money also create business cycles. The consensus view is that classical economics explains the economy when it is at or close to full employment and Keynesian economics applies in recessions and depressions. Monetarist economics explains inflation and also adds to the Keynesian view by suggesting other causes of recessions. The consensus view emphasizes that maintaining economic growth is more important than eliminating business cycle fluctuations because the Lucas wedge (the cost of slower economic growth) is much larger than Okun gaps (the cost of business cycle recessions).

1 Explain what determines potential GDP.

Potential GDP is the value of real GDP when all the economy's factors of production—labor, capital, land, and entrepreneurial ability—are fully employed. The production function shows the maximum quantity of real GDP that can be produced as the quantity of labor employed changes and all other influences on production remain the same. Its shape reflects diminishing returns, so that each additional hour of labor employed produces a successively smaller addition of real GDP. The quantity of labor employed is determined in the labor market. The quantity of labor demanded increases when the real wage rate falls and decreases when the real wage rate rises. The quantity of labor supplied increases when the real wage rate rises and decreases when the real wage rate falls. Labor market equilibrium occurs at the intersection of the labor supply curve and the labor demand curve. When the labor market is in equilibrium, the economy is at full employment. At this point real GDP, which is determined using equilibrium employment and the production function, equals potential GDP.

2 Explain what determines the natural unemployment rate.

The natural unemployment rate is the unemployment rate at full employment and consists of frictional and structural unemployment. The two fundamental causes of unemployment at full employment are job search, which is the activity of looking for an acceptable job, and job rationing, which occurs when the real wage rate exceeds the equilibrium wage rate creating a surplus of labor. The amount of job search depends on demographic change, unemployment benefits, and structural change. Job rationing occurs when there is an efficiency wage, a minimum wage, or a union wage because all of these factors force the real wage above the equilibrium real wage.

© 2015 Pearson Education, Inc.

YOUR AP TEST HINTS

AP Topics

Topic on your AP test	What to Know	Corresponding textbook section
Historic Schools of Economics	Classical, Keynesian, Monetarist schools	Chapter Introduction
Gross Domestic Product (*GDP*) and potential GDP	Definition; how determined; role of production function and labor market	Checkpoint 23.1
Natural unemployment rate	Definition; job search; job rationing	Checkpoint 23.2

AP Vocabulary Covered

Terms	What to Know	Text Sections
Classical macroeconomics	Markets work well and deliver the best macroeconomic performance	Chapter intro. p. 610
Keynesian macroeconomics	Markets are inherently unstable and require active government intervention	Chapter intro. p. 610
Monetarist macroeconomics	Market economies work well and fluctuations in the quantity of money create the business cycle	Chapter intro. p. 611
Potential GDP	Real GDP when all the factors of production are fully employed	Checkpoint 24.1, p. 613
Production function	Maximum real GDP as quantity of labor changes but other factors remain the same	Checkpoint 24.1, p. 614
Diminishing returns	Each additional amount of labor employed will produce smaller amounts of real GDP	Checkpoint 24.1, p. 614
Natural unemployment rate	The unemployment rate when unemployment is only frictional, structural, seasonal (no cyclical unemployment; the result of job search and job rationing)	Checkpoint 24.2, p. 622
Job search	Looking for an acceptable job	Checkpoint 24.2, p. 623
Job rationing	The situation when the real wage rate is above the full employment level so there is a surplus of labor	Checkpoint 24.2, p. 624
Efficiency wage	A real wage rate above the equilibrium wage rate to encourage greater effort by the workers	Checkpoint 24.2, p. 625
Minimum wage	The lowest wage for which labor can legally be hired	Checkpoint 24.2, p. 625
Union wage	A wage set by collective bargaining between a firm and a union	Checkpoint 24.2, p. 625

Extra AP material

- The different schools of economics are important for understanding policy options, discussed in later chapters. The AP test includes many references to Keynesian fiscal policy decisions. Also, the AP test uses the term *monetary policy* to describe central bank/Federal Reserve Board policies. Students must know that *monetarist theories* and *monetary policy* are separate concepts.

- On the AP test, the "GDP gap" equals the difference between potential GDP (full employment GDP) and the GDP that is actually produced. In a recession, the GDP gap is positive.

- On the AP test, the *natural unemployment rate* is the same as the *natural rate of unemployment (NRU)*.

© 2015 Pearson Education, Inc.

CHECKPOINT 24.1

■ **Explain what determines potential GDP.**

Quick Review

- *Production function* The production function shows the maximum quantity of real GDP that can be produced as the quantity of labor employed changes and all other influences on production remain constant.
- *Equilibrium in a market* The equilibrium in a market occurs at the intersection of the demand and supply curves.

Additional Practice Problem 24.1

Quantity of labor demanded (billions of hours per year)	Real GDP (hundreds of billions of 2009 dollars)	Real wage rate (2009 dollars per hour)
0	0	50
10	5	40
20	9	30
30	12	20
40	14	10

1. The table above describes a small economy's production function and its demand for labor. The table below describes the supply of labor in this economy.

Quantity of labor supplied (billions of hours per year)	Real wage rate (2009 dollars per hour)
0	10
10	20
20	30
30	40
40	50

a. Make graphs of the production function and the labor market.
b. Does the production function show diminishing returns?
c. What is the equilibrium employment, real wage rate, and potential GDP?
d. Suppose that the population grows so that the quantity of labor supplied increases by 20 billion hours at every real wage rate.

What is the effect on the real wage rate and on potential GDP?

Solutions to Additional Practice Problem 24.1

1a. The production function is a graph of the first two columns of the first table. The figure to the right shows the relationship between labor and real GDP.

The second figure to the right shows the labor market. The labor demand curve is the first and third columns in the first table. It shows the relationship between the real wage rate and the quantity of labor demanded. The labor supply curve is from the second table and shows the relationship between the real wage rate and the quantity of labor supplied.

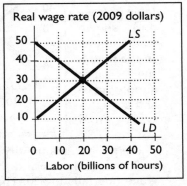

1b. The production function shows diminishing returns because every additional 10 billion hours of labor employed increases real GDP by less.

1c. Find the equilibrium in the labor market. Then use the production function to determine how much GDP this full-employment quantity of labor produces, which is the potential GDP. Equilibrium employment is where the labor demand curve and the labor supply curve intersect. The second figure in part (a) shows that the equilibrium real wage rate is $30 an hour and the equilibrium em-

© 2015 Pearson Education, Inc.

ployment is 20 billion hours per year. The production function, in the first figure in part (a), shows that when 20 billion hours of labor are employed, GDP is $900 billion, so potential GDP equals $900 billion.

Quantity of labor supplied (billions of hours per year)	Real wage rate (2009 dollars per hour)
20	10
30	20
40	30
50	40
60	50

1d. The new labor supply schedule is given in the table above and shown in the figure. In the figure, the labor supply curve shifts rightward from LS_1 to LS_2.

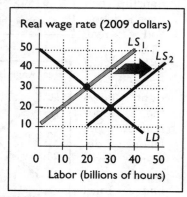

The equilibrium quantity of labor increases to 30 billion hours and the equilibrium real wage rate falls to $20. The production function in the first table in the practice problem shows that when employment is 30 billion hours, real GDP is $1,200 billion. So, the increase in the population increases potential GDP to $1,200 billion.

■ AP Self Test 24.1

True or false

1. Classical macroeconomics says that markets work well and government intervention cannot improve on the performance of markets.

2. The consensus view asserts that the problem of business cycle fluctuations is much more important than the problem of sustaining economic growth.

3. Real GDP can exceed potential GDP permanently.

4. The production function shows how the quantity of labor hired depends on the real wage rate.

5. The nominal wage rate influences the quantity of labor demanded because what matters to firms is the number of dollars they pay for an hour of labor.

6. At the labor market equilibrium the real wage rate sets the quantity of labor demanded equal to the quantity of labor supplied.

7. When the labor market is in equilibrium, the economy is at full employment and real GDP equals potential GDP.

Multiple choice

1. ____ adopts the view that aggregate fluctuations are a natural consequence of an expanding economy.
   a. Classical macroeconomics
   b. Keynesian economics
   c. Monetarist macroeconomics
   d. The Lucas wedge
   e. The Okun gap

2. Potential GDP
   a. is the quantity of GDP produced when the economy is at full employment of all resources.
   b. can never be exceeded.
   c. can never be attained.
   d. is another name for real GDP.
   e. is another name for nominal GDP.

3. With fixed quantities of capital, land, and entrepreneurship and fixed technology, the amount of real GDP produced increases when ____ increases.
   i. the quantity of labor employed
   ii. the inflation rate
   iii. the price level
   a. i only.
   b. ii only.
   c. iii only.
   d. ii and iii.
   e. i, ii, and iii.

© 2015 Pearson Education, Inc.

4. The production function graphs the relationship between
   a. nominal GDP and real GDP.
   b. real GDP and the quantity of labor employed.
   c. real GDP and capital.
   d. nominal GDP and the quantity of labor employed.
   e. real GDP and the supply of labor.

5. The quantity of labor demanded definitely increases if the
   a. real wage rate rises.
   b. real wage rate falls.
   c. nominal wage rate rises.
   d. nominal wage rate falls.
   e. supply of labor decreases.

6. The labor supply curve has a ____ slope because as the real wage rate rises, ____.
   a. negative; firms hire fewer workers
   b. positive; the opportunity cost of leisure rises
   c. positive; the opportunity cost of leisure falls
   d. negative; households work more hours
   e. positive; firms offer more jobs

■ **FIGURE 24.1**

Real wage rate (2009 dollars per hour)

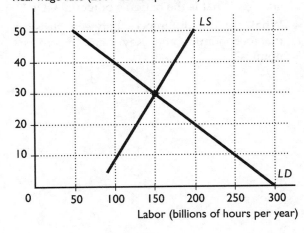

7. In Figure 24.1, the equilibrium real wage rate is ____ per hour and equilibrium employment is ____ billions of hours per year.
   a. $50; 200
   b. $10; 100
   c. $30; more than 300
   d. $20; 125
   e. $30; 150

8. In Figure 24.1, full employment is reached when employment is ____ billions of hours a year.
   a. 150
   b. 200
   c. 250
   d. more than 300
   e. More information is needed about the nation's production function to answer the question.

9. When the labor market is in equilibrium, real GDP ____ potential GDP.
   a. is greater than
   b. is equal to
   c. is less than
   d. might be greater than, less than, or equal to
   e. is not comparable to

10. Compared to the U.S. production function, the European production function is
    a. higher.
    b. lower.
    c. the same.
    d. lower than the U.S. production function at low levels of employment and higher than the U.S. production function at high levels of employment.
    e. higher than the U.S. production function at low levels of employment and lower than the U.S. production function at high levels of employment.

© 2015 Pearson Education, Inc.

Short Response Questions

1. What is the relationship between equilibrium in the labor market and potential GDP? Be sure to explain the role played by the production function.

2. Suppose a nation's production function shifts upward. If the equilibrium quantity of labor does not change, what is the effect on the nation's potential GDP?

3. Suppose a nation's production function shifts upward and the equilibrium quantity of labor increases. What is the effect on the nation's potential GDP?

Long Response Questions

Quantity of labor (billions of hours per year)	Real GDP (billions of 2009 dollars)
0	0
10	400
20	725
30	900
40	960
50	1,000

■ FIGURE 24.2

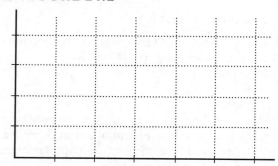

1. The above table gives data for a nation's production function. In Figure 24.2, draw the production function. Label the axes. How are diminishing returns reflected?

■ FIGURE 24.3

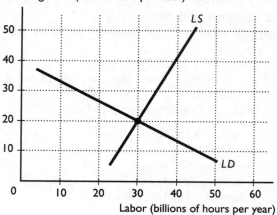

2. Figure 24.3 illustrates the labor market for the nation with the production function given in the previous problem. In the figure, identify the equilibrium real wage rate and employment. Using the production function in Figure 24.2, what is the nation's potential GDP?

3. Using the data in Questions 1 and 2, suppose that both the labor supply and labor demand curves shift rightward by 10 billion labor hours and the production function does not change. What is the nation's potential GDP?

4. What are the differences between classical macroeconomics and Keynesian macroeconomics?

© 2015 Pearson Education, Inc.

Additional Exercise (also in MyEconLab Test A)

Quantity of labor demanded (billions of hours per year)	Real GDP (billions of 2009 dollars)	Real wage (2009 dollars per hour)
0	0	
1	5	5
2	9	4
3	12	3
4	14	2
5	15	1

Quantity of labor supplied (billions of hours per year)	Real wage (2009 dollars per hour)
0	1.50
1	2.00
2	2.50
3	3.00
4	3.50
5	4.00

1. This first table above describes an economy's production function and demand for labor. The second table above describes the supply of labor in this economy.

   Use the data in the tables to make graphs of the labor market and production function. What are equilibrium employment, real wage rate, and potential GDP?

CHECKPOINT 24.2

■ **Explain what determines the natural unemployment rate.**

Quick Review

- *Job search* The activity of looking for an acceptable vacant job. Job search is influenced by demographic changes, unemployment benefits, and structural change.

- *Job rationing* The situation that arises when the real wage rate is above the full-employment equilibrium level. An efficiency wage, a minimum wage, or a union wage can lead to job rationing.

Additional Practice Problems 24.2

1. Why do demographic changes affect the amount of job search?
2. What factors can keep the real wage rate above the full-employment level? How do these factors affect the amount of employment?
3. Since 1969, how has the real minimum wage generally changed in the United States? What effect would this trend have on the natural unemployment rate?

Solutions to Additional Practice Problems 24.2

1. Demographic changes affect the amount of job search because younger workers conduct more job search than do older workers. In particular, older workers generally have already settled into a career, whereas younger workers are often entering the labor market for the first time. As new entrants, younger workers must search for a job. In addition, younger workers often switch between jobs before settling upon their career and while they are switching, they are searching for a new job.

2. Job rationing, when the real wage rate is above the full-employment equilibrium level, is the result of efficiency wages, the minimum wage, and union wages. An efficiency wage is a real wage that a firm sets above the full-employment equilibrium level in order to motivate its workers to work harder. A minimum wage is a government regulation that sets the lowest wage legal to pay. A union wage is a wage rate negotiated between a labor union and a firm. Because these wage rates are above the full-employment level, the quantity of labor employed is less than it otherwise would be.

3. Since 1969 there has been a general downward trend in the real minimum wage. The drop was most prolonged between 1979 and 1989, after which the real minimum wage has generally hovered near $6 an hour. The general downward trend in the real minimum wage reduces the amount of job rationing, thereby decreasing the natural unemployment rate.

© 2015 Pearson Education, Inc.

■ AP Self Test 24.2

True or false

1. The amount of job search depends on a number of factors including demographic change.

2. An increase in unemployment benefits, other things remaining the same, will increase the amount of time spent on job search.

3. Job rationing has no effect on the natural unemployment rate.

4. Job rationing results in a shortage of labor.

5. Teenage labor is not affected by the minimum wage.

Multiple choice

1. In the United States since 1960, the average unemployment rate was highest during the decade of the
   a. 1960s.
   b. 1970s.
   c. 1980s.
   d. 1990s.
   e. 2000s.

2. The two fundamental causes of unemployment at full employment are
   a. seasonal jobs and technological change.
   b. foreign competition and financial bankruptcies.
   c. job search and job rationing.
   d. decreases in labor productivity and more generous retirement benefits.
   e. demographic change and decreases in the demand for labor.

3. Job search is defined as
   a. the activity of looking for an acceptable, vacant job.
   b. saying you are looking for a job when you are actually not looking.
   c. attending school to increase your employability.
   d. equivalent to job rationing.
   e. being paid an efficiency wage.

4. The more generous the amount of unemployment benefits, the
   a. higher the opportunity cost of job search.
   b. lower the opportunity cost of job search.
   c. shorter the time spent searching until accepting a suitable job.
   d. shorter the time spent searching for a suitable job and the higher the opportunity cost of being unemployed.
   e. lower the natural unemployment rate.

5. Job rationing occurs if
   a. the minimum wage is set below the equilibrium wage rate.
   b. an efficiency wage is set below the equilibrium wage rate.
   c. a union wage is set below the equilibrium wage rate.
   d. the real wage rate is pushed above the equilibrium wage rate.
   e. the Lucas wedge is positive.

6. Intel wants to attract the most productive and knowledgeable workers. To achieve this goal it could pay ____ wage.
   a. an efficiency
   b. a minimum
   c. a nominal
   d. an equilibrium
   e. a Lucas wedge

7. Collective bargaining by unions can result in a union wage rate that is ____ the equilibrium real wage rate and creates a ____ of labor.
   a. above; surplus
   b. above; shortage
   c. below; surplus
   d. below; shortage
   e. equal to; surplus

© 2015 Pearson Education, Inc.

■ FIGURE 24.4

Real wage rate (2009 dollars per hour)

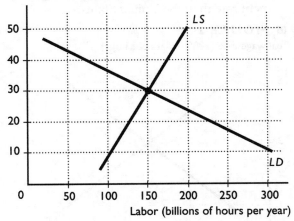

8. In Figure 24.4, of the wages listed below, there is the most job rationing and unemployment if the real wage rate equals
   a. $10 per hour.
   b. $20 per hour.
   c. $30 per hour.
   d. $40 per hour.
   e. None of the above is correct because at any real wage rate there is never any job rationing.

9. In Figure 24.4, if there is any job rationing, the real wage rate must be ____ per hour and employment is ____ billion hours.
   a. less than $30; more than 150
   b. equal to $30; equal to 150
   c. less than $30; less than 150
   d. more than $30; less than 150
   e. less than $20; less than 150

Short Response Questions

1. What types of unemployment are included in the natural unemployment rate? What types are not included?

2. The demographics of the United States are such that there will be an increase in young people entering the labor force between 2009 and 2014. What do you predict will be the effect on the U.S. unemployment rate?

3. Why do unemployment benefits affect the natural unemployment rate?

4. An efficiency wage is a wage that exceeds the equilibrium wage rate. Why would a firm pay an efficiency wage?

Long Response Questions

■ FIGURE 24.5

Real wage rate (2009 dollars per hour)

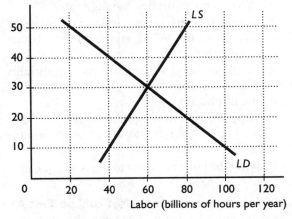

1. Figure 24.5 illustrates the labor market.
   a. What is the equilibrium wage rate? Equilibrium employment?
   b. What must a firm do to set an efficiency wage?
   c. Suppose the government imposes a minimum wage that creates a surplus of 60 billion hours of labor a year. What is the minimum wage?
   d. If a union negotiates on behalf of its members, what can you say about the range of wage rates the union will try to obtain?
   e. In your answers to (b), (c), and (d), is there any unemployment? Compare your answers to parts (b), (c), and (d). How does the employment that results in these situations compare with that in part (a)?

© 2015 Pearson Education, Inc.

Real wage rate (2009 dollars per hour)	Quantity of labor demanded (billions of hours per year)	Quantity of labor supplied (billions of hours per year)
10	180	150
20	160	160
30	140	170
40	120	180

2. The above table gives the labor demand and labor supply schedules for a nation.

   a. What is the equilibrium wage rate?

   b. Suppose firms set an efficiency wage of $30 an hour. What is the effect of this wage rate?

   c. Suppose the government sets a minimum wage of $30 an hour. What is the effect of the minimum wage?

   d. Suppose unions negotiate a wage of $30 an hour. What is the effect of the union wage?

   e. How do your answers to parts (b), (c), and (d) compare?

Additional Exercises (also in MyEconLab Test A)

The economy of Sweden has seen changes during the past 50 years, but the change has been steady and population growth has been modest. Sweden has high unemployment benefits, a high minimum wage, and strong labor unions. Use this information to answer Exercises 1 and 2.

1. Does the unemployment that Sweden experiences arise primarily from job search or job rationing?

2. Which of the factors listed suggest that Sweden has a higher natural unemployment rate than the United States and which suggest that Sweden has a lower natural unemployment rate than the United States?

■ FIGURE 24.6

Real wage rate (2009 dollars per hour)

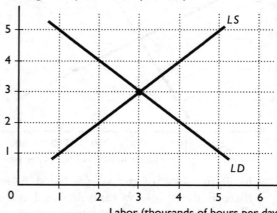

Labor (thousands of hours per day)

Figure 24.6 illustrates the labor market on Sandy Island. In addition (not shown in the figure), a survey tells us that when Sandy Island is at full employment, people spend 1,000 hours a day in job search. Use this information to answer Exercises 3 and 4.

3. Find the full-employment equilibrium real wage rate and quantity of labor employed and calculate the natural unemployment rate.

4. If the government introduces a minimum wage of $4 an hour, how much unemployment is created?

© 2015 Pearson Education, Inc.

SELF TEST ANSWERS

■ AP Self Test 24.1

True or false

1. True; page 610
2. False; pages 611-612
3. False; page 612
4. False; page 614
5. False; page 615
6. True; pages 618-619
7. True; page 619

Multiple choice

1. a; page 610
2. a; page 613
3. a; pages 613-614
4. b; page 614
5. b; pages 615-616
6. b; pages 617-618
7. e; pages 618-619
8. a; page 619
9. b; page 619
10. b; page 620

Short Response Questions

1. The equilibrium quantity of labor is the amount of full employment. The production function shows how much GDP this full-employment quantity of labor produces and this quantity of GDP is potential GDP; page 619.

2. If the production function shifts upward, the amount of real GDP produced by every quantity of labor increases. The nation's potential GDP increases; pages 614, 619.

3. On both counts, the upward shift of the production function and the increase in employment, potential GDP increases; pages 614, 619.

Long Response Questions

1. Figure 24.7 illustrates the production function. In the table, diminishing returns are demonstrated by the fact that each additional 10 billion hours of labor increases real GDP

■ FIGURE 24.7

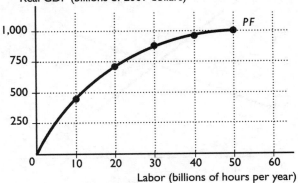

Real GDP (billions of 2009 dollars)

by a smaller amount. In the figure, diminishing returns are illustrated by the slope of the production function, which becomes less steep as the quantity of labor increases; pages 614-615.

2. The equilibrium real wage rate is $20 an hour and the equilibrium employment is 30 billion hours. Potential GDP is $900 billion; page 619.

3. If both the labor demand and labor supply curves shift rightward by 10 billion labor hours, then equilibrium employment increases by 10 billion hours to 40 billion hours. Potential GDP increases to $960 billion; page 619.

4. Classical macroeconomics believes that markets work well and government intervention cannot improve the economy. Keynesian economics believes that a market economy is unstable and needs government intervention to help it reach full employment and sustained economic growth; pages 610-611.

Additional Exercise (also in MyEconLab Test A)

1. The demand for labor curve and supply of labor curve are illustrated in Figure 24.8 (on the next page). The production function is illustrated in Figure 24.9.

The equilibrium wage rate and employment is determined in the labor market, illustrated in Figure 24.8. The equilibrium quantity of labor is 3 billion hours and the equilibrium

© 2015 Pearson Education, Inc.

■ **FIGURE 24.8**

Real wage rate (2009 dollars per hour)

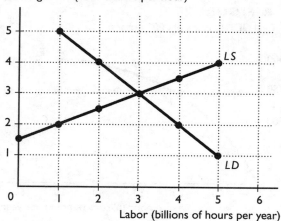

■ **FIGURE 24.9**

Real GDP (billions of 2009 dollars per year)

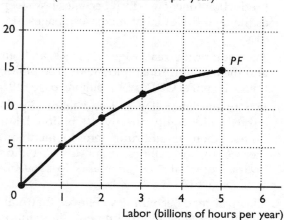

real wage rate is $3 an hour. This is the real wage rate at which the quantity of labor demanded equals the quantity of labor supplied.

Potential GDP is the real GDP produced by the equilibrium quantity of labor. The production function in Figure 24.9 shows that 3 billion hours of labor produces potential GDP of $12 billion; pages 618-619.

■ **AP Self Test 24.2**

True or false

1. True; page 623
2. True; page 623

3. False; pages 624-625
4. False; pages 625-626
5. False; page 625

Multiple choice

1. c; page 622
2. c; page 623
3. a; page 623
4. b; page 623
5. d; pages 624-625
6. a; page 625
7. a; page 625
8. d; page 626
9. d; pages 624-626

Short Response Questions

1. The natural unemployment rate includes frictional, structural, and seasonal unemployment. It does *not* include cyclical unemployment; page 625.

2. The natural unemployment rate increases as more young people enter the labor force and search for jobs. The natural unemployment rate in the United States likely will increase between 2009 and 2014; page 623.

3. If unemployment benefits increase, the opportunity cost of job search decreases. Workers spend more time unemployed, searching for jobs and so the natural unemployment rate increases; page 623.

4. A firm pays an efficiency wage rate to motivate its employees to work hard. The employees work hard to avoid being let go because they know that if they have to take another job, they would probably be paid the lower equilibrium wage rate; page 625.

Long Response Questions

1. a. The equilibrium wage rate is $30 and employment is 60 billion hours; page 619.

   b. An efficiency wage is set higher than the equilibrium wage rate, so the firm must set the wage rate above $30; page 625.

   c. A minimum wage of $50 an hour creates a labor surplus of 60 billion hours a year; pages 625-626.

© 2015 Pearson Education, Inc.

d. The union will strive to set a wage rate that is higher than the competitive wage, so the union will try to set a wage that is higher than $30; pages 625-626.

e. In each of the answers to parts (a), (b), and (c), unemployment occurs. And in each of the answers, employment is less than 60 billion hours; page 626.

2. a. The equilibrium wage rate is $20 an hour because that is the wage rate at which the quantity of labor demanded equals the quantity supplied. Employment is 60 billion hours; page 619.

b. If firms set an efficiency wage of $30 an hour, there is a labor surplus of 30 billion hours a year (170 billion hours supplied minus 140 billion hours demanded); pages 625-626.

c. If the government sets a minimum wage of $30 an hour, there is a labor surplus of 30 billion hour a year; pages 625-626.

d. If unions negotiate a wage of $30 an hour, there is a labor surplus of 30 billion hours a year; pages 625-626.

e. In each of the answers to parts (b), (c), and (d) there is a labor surplus of 30 billion hours a year. All three of the events raise the wage rate above its equilibrium and create unemployment. All three of the events lower employment; page 626.

Additional Exercises (also in MyEconLab Test A)

1. Of the factors mentioned, high unemployment benefits lead to increased job search. But a high minimum wage and strong labor unions lead to job rationing. So it is not possible to determine if Sweden's unemployment arises primarily from job rationing or job search; pages 623-625.

2. Of the factors mentioned, the only one that points toward Sweden having a lower natural unemployment rate than the United States is the modest population growth. All of the other factors—high unemployment benefits, high minimum wage, and strong labor force unions—point toward Sweden having a higher natural unemployment rate than the United States; pages 623-625.

3. The full-employment equilibrium real wage rate is $3 per hour and the full-employment quantity of labor is 3,000 hours per day.
There are 1,000 hours per day of unemployed people searching for jobs, so the total labor force is 3,000 hours + 1,000 hours, which is 4,000 hours per day. The unemployment rate is (1,000 hours) ÷ (4,000 hours) × 100, or 25 percent; page 626.

4. If the government introduces a minimum wage of $4.00 an hour, 4,000 hours of labor are supplied by households but only 2,000 hours of labor are demanded by firms. So the resulting unemployment is 4,000 hours − 2,000 hours, or 2,000 hours per day; pages 625-626.

© 2015 Pearson Education, Inc.

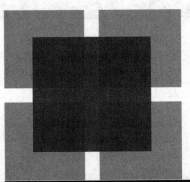

Economic Growth

CHAPTER CHECKLIST

Chapter 25 discusses the factors that determine economic growth, studies different theories that explain economic growth, and examines possible government polices to speed economic growth.

1 Define and calculate the economic growth rate, and explain the implications of sustained growth.

Economic growth is a sustained expansion of production possibilities and is measured as the increase in real GDP over a given time period. The economic growth rate is the annual percentage change of real GDP. The standard of living depends on real GDP per person, which equals real GDP divided by the population. The Rule of 70 says that the number of years it takes for the level of a variable to double approximately equals 70 divided by the annual percentage growth rate of the variable.

2 Explain the sources of labor productivity growth.

Labor productivity is the quantity of real GDP produced by one hour of labor. When labor productivity grows, real GDP per person grows. Growth of labor productivity depends on saving and investment in more physical capital, and expansion of human capital and discovery of better technologies. Capital is subject to the law of diminishing returns. The productivity curve is the relationship that shows how real GDP per hour of labor changes as the quantity of capital per hour of labor changes. As the quantity of capital per hour of labor increases, additional capital raises labor productivity by less. Expansion of human capital and discovery of better technologies shift the productivity curve upward, increasing labor productivity. Real GDP equals labor productivity multiplied by aggregate hours of labor.

3 Review the theories of economic growth.

Old growth theory, called the classical theory, predicts that labor productivity growth is temporary. If real GDP rises above the subsistence level, a population explosion occurs. Labor productivity falls and real GDP per person returns to the subsistence level. New growth theory predicts that our unlimited wants will lead us to ever greater labor productivity and perpetual economic growth. It emphasizes that human capital growth and discoveries are the result of choices. It also says that technological discoveries bring profit and competition destroys profit, thereby creating the incentive for more technological discoveries. Additionally as capital increases, although a *firm* experiences diminishing returns, the *economy* does not which means that labor productivity can grow indefinitely.

4 Describe policies that speed economic growth.

The preconditions for economic growth are economic freedom, property rights, and markets. Economic freedom occurs when people are able to make personal choices, their private property is protected by rule of law, and they are free to buy and sell in markets. Governments can increase economic growth by creating incentives to save, invest, and innovate; by encouraging saving; by encouraging research and development; by encouraging international trade; and by improving the quality of education.

© 2015 Pearson Education, Inc.

YOUR AP TEST HINTS

AP Topics

Topic on your AP test	What to Know	Corresponding textbook section
Economic growth rate	Formula for calculating economic growth rate; Rule of 70	Checkpoint 25.1
Sources of labor productivity growth	Expansion of capital; new technologies	Checkpoint 25.2
Theories of economic growth	Classical; neoclassical; new growth	Checkpoint 25.3
Policies for faster growth	Preconditions; government policies	Checkpoint 25.4

AP Vocabulary Covered

Terms	What to Know	Text Sections
Economic growth rate	The annual growth rate of real GDP; equals current year real GDP minus previous year real GDP divided by previous year real GDP then multiplied by 100	Checkpoint 25.1, p. 634
Real GDP per person	A measure of the standard of living; equals real GDP divided by the population	Checkpoint 25.1, p. 634
Rule of 70	The approximate number of years that it takes for the level of any variable to double; equals 70 divided by the annual percentage growth rate	Checkpoint 25.1, p. 635
Labor productivity	The quantity of real GDP produced by one hour of labor; equals real GDP divided by aggregate labor hours	Checkpoint 25.2, p. 638
Productivity curve	How real *GDP* per hour of labor changes as the *Q* of capital per labor hour changes	Checkpoint 25.2, p. 639
Classical growth theory	Theory concludes that economic growth creates rapid population growth so wages return to subsistence level; also called Malthusian theory after Thomas Malthus	Checkpoint 25.3, p. 646
New growth theory	Theory concludes that unlimited wants will lead to ever greater productivity and perpetual economic growth	Checkpoint 25.3, p. 646
Economic freedom	A necessary precondition for economic growth; exists when people are able to make personal choices, private property is protected by rule of law, people can buy and sell in free markets, and an efficient legal system exists and insures the ability to enforce contracts	Checkpoint 25.4, p. 650
Property rights	Economic freedom requires property rights, which are the social arrangements that govern the protection of private property	Checkpoint 25.4, p. 650

Extra AP material

- The AP test does not test growth theories by names. The *Rule of 70* is tested however.

- When illustrating economic growth, the AP test uses the *production possibilities frontier* (also called on the AP test the *production possibilities curve*) rather than a production function. Economic growth results in the production possibilities curve shifting outward. More rapid growth means more rapid outward shifts.

© 2015 Pearson Education, Inc.

CHECKPOINT 25.1

■ **Define and calculate the economic growth rate, and explain the implications of sustained growth.**

Quick Review

- *Growth rate* The growth rate of real GDP equals

$$\frac{\left(\begin{array}{c}\text{Real GDP in}\\\text{current year}\end{array}\right)-\left(\begin{array}{c}\text{Real GDP in}\\\text{previous year}\end{array}\right)}{\left(\text{Real GDP in previous year}\right)}\times100$$

- *Growth rate of real GDP per person* The growth rate of real GDP per person equals (growth rate of real GDP)–(growth rate of population).

- *Rule of 70* The number of years it takes for the level of any variable to double is approximately 70 divided by the annual percentage growth rate of the variable.

Additional Practice Problem 25.1

1. In the nation of Transylvania in 2013, real GDP was $3.0 million and the population was 1,000. In 2014, real GDP was $3.3 million and the population was 1,050.
   - a. What is Transylvania's economic growth rate in 2014?
   - b. What is the population growth rate?
   - c. What is Transylvania's growth rate of real GDP per person?
   - d. Did Transylvania's standard of living rise?
   - e. Approximately how long will it take for real GDP per person to double?

Solution to Additional Practice Problem 25.1

1. This question uses three growth rate formulas. The first is the formula that calculates the economic growth rate; the second is the formula that calculates the growth rate of real GDP per person; the third is the Rule of 70.
   - 1a. The economic growth rate is the growth rate of real GDP. Transylvania's economic growth rate equals [($3.3 million – $3.0 million) ÷ $3.0 million] × 100 = 10 percent.

1b. Transylvania's population growth rate equals [(1,050 – 1,000) ÷ 1,000] × 100 = 5 percent.

1c. Transylvania's real GDP per person growth rate equals the growth rate of real GDP minus the growth rate of the population, or 10 percent – 5 percent = 5 percent.

1d. Transylvania's real GDP per person rose, so Transylvania's standard of living increased.

1e. The number of years it takes for real GDP per person to double is given by the Rule of 70. Transylvania's real GDP per person is growing at 5 percent per year, so it will take approximately 70 ÷ 5 or 14 years for Transylvania's real GDP per person to double.

■ AP Self Test 25.1

True or false

1. If real GDP last year was $1.00 trillion and real GDP this year is $1.05 trillion, the growth rate of real GDP is 5 percent.
2. Real GDP per person equals real GDP divided by the population.
3. If a nation's population grows at 2 percent and its real GDP grows at 4 percent, then the growth rate of real GDP per person is 2 percent.
4. If real GDP is growing at 2 percent a year, it will take 50 years for real GDP to double.

Multiple choice

1. The economic growth rate is measured as the
   - a. annual percentage change of real GDP.
   - b. annual percentage change of employment.
   - c. level of real GDP.
   - d. annual percentage change of the population.
   - e. amount of population.

2. Real GDP is $9 trillion in the current year and $8.6 trillion in the previous year. The economic growth rate between these years is
   - a. 10.31 percent.
   - b. 4.65 percent.
   - c. 5.67 percent.
   - d. 7.67 percent.
   - e. $0.4 trillion.

© 2015 Pearson Education, Inc.

3. The standard of living is measured by
   a. real GDP.
   b. employment.
   c. employment per person.
   d. real GDP per person.
   e. the population.

4. If the population growth rate is greater than the growth rate of real GDP, then real GDP per person
   a. falls.
   b. rises.
   c. does not change.
   d. might rise or fall.
   e. cannot be measured.

5. If real GDP increases by 6 percent and at the same time the population increases by 2 percent, then real GDP per person grows by
   a. 6 percent.
   b. 4 percent.
   c. 2 percent.
   d. 8 percent.
   e. 3 percent.

6. If a country's real GDP is growing at 4 percent a year, its real GDP will double in
   a. 14 years.
   b. 17.5 years.
   c. 23.3 years.
   d. 35 years.
   e. 25 years.

Short Response Questions

Year	Real GDP (billions of 2005 dollars)
2010	100.0
2011	110.0
2012	121.0
2013	133.1

1. The above table gives a nation's real GDP. What is the growth rate of real GDP in 2011? In 2012? In 2013?

2. If a nation's real GDP grows at 3 percent a year, how long does it take for real GDP to double? If the growth rate is 4 percent, how long does it take for real GDP to double? If the growth rate is 5 percent, how long does it take real GDP to double?

Year	Real GDP growth rate (percent)	Population growth rate (percent)
2010	3	2
2011	4	2
2012	1	2
2013	4	4

3. The table above has a nation's real GDP growth rate and its population growth rate.
   a. What is the growth rate of real GDP per person for each year?
   b. In what years did the standard of living improve?

Additional Exercises (also in MyEconLab Test A)

1. In Canada, real GDP was $1,012 billion in 2000 and $1,028 billion in 2001. The population was 30.8 million in 2000 and 31.1 million in 2001. Calculate Canada's economic growth rate in 2001, the growth rate of real GDP per person in Canada in 2001, and the approximate number of years it will take for real GDP per person in Canada to double if the 2001 economic growth and population growth rates are maintained.

2. Calculate the change in the number of years it will take for real GDP per person in China to double if its economic growth rate increases from 10.6 percent to 12 percent a year and its population growth rate rises from 1 percent to 2 percent a year.

CHECKPOINT 25.2

■ **Explain the sources of labor productivity growth.**

Quick Review

- *Labor productivity* Labor productivity equals real GDP divided by aggregate hours. When labor productivity grows, real GDP per person grows.

Additional Practice Problem 25.2

Item	2003	2004
Aggregate hours (billions)	232.2	234.5
Real GDP (trillions of 2009 dollars)	13.27	13.77

1. The table above provides some data for the

© 2015 Pearson Education, Inc.

U.S. economy in 2003 and 2004.

    a. What is the growth rate of real GDP in 2004?

    b. What is labor productivity in 2003 and 2004?

    c. Calculate the growth rate of labor productivity in 2004.

    d. How does the growth rate of labor productivity you calculated compare with the typical growth in the United States since 1960?

Solution to Additional Practice Problem 25.2

1a. The growth rate of real GDP in 2004 is [($13.77 trillion − $13.27 trillion) ÷ $13.27 trillion] × 100, which is 3.8 percent.

1b. Labor productivity is real GDP divided by aggregate hours. So labor productivity in 2003 is $13.27 trillion ÷ 232.2 billion hours, which is $57.15 per hour of labor. In 2004 labor productivity is $13.77 trillion ÷ 234.5 billion hours, which is $58.72 per hour of labor.

1c. The growth rate of labor productivity is labor productivity in 2004 minus the labor productivity in 2003, divided by labor productivity in 2003, all multiplied by 100. The growth rate of labor productivity equals [($58.72 per hour − $57.15 per hour) ÷ $57.15 per hour] × 100, which is 2.75 percent.

1d. The increase in labor productivity in 2004 was lower than in the early 1960s but was higher than the average since then.

■ AP Self Test 25.2

True or false

1. Real GDP increases if aggregate hours increase or labor productivity increases.

2. If labor productivity increases and aggregate hours do not change, then real GDP per person increases.

3. Capital is not subject to the law of diminishing returns.

4. The productivity curve shows that an increase in capital decreases labor productivity.

5. The discovery and applications of new technology has increased labor productivity.

Multiple choice

1. If real GDP is $1,200 billion, the population is 60 million, and aggregate hours are 80 billion, labor productivity is
   a. $5.00 an hour.
   b. $6.67 an hour.
   c. $15.00 an hour.
   d. $20,000.
   e. $150 an hour.

2. If aggregate hours are 100 billion hours and labor productivity is $40 an hour, than real GDP equals
   a. $100 billion.
   b. $40 billion.
   c. $100 trillion.
   d. $2.5 trillion.
   e. $4 trillion.

3. Which of the following lists gives factors that increase labor productivity?
   a. saving and investment in physical capital, and wage increases
   b. expansion of human capital, labor force increases, and discovery of new technologies
   c. expansion of human capital, population growth, and discovery of new technologies
   d. saving and investment in physical capital, expansion of human capital, and discovery of new technologies
   e. labor force increases and wage increases

4. Growth in physical capital depends most directly upon the
   a. amount of saving and investment.
   b. number of firms in the nation.
   c. rate of population growth.
   d. amount of government expenditures.
   e. level of human capital.

5. The productivity curve shifts upward when
   a. physical capital increases.
   b. human capital decreases.
   c. hours of labor increase.
   d. hours of labor decrease.
   e. technology advances.

© 2015 Pearson Education, Inc.

6. Human capital is
   a. the same as labor productivity.
   b. a measure of the number of labor hours available.
   c. the accumulated skills and knowledge of workers.
   d. the average number of years of schooling of the labor force.
   e. is what people are born with and cannot be changed.

Short Response Questions

Year	Real GDP (trillion of 2009 dollars)	Aggregate hours (billions)
1964	3.73	133.6
1974	5.39	158.7
1984	7.28	185.3
1994	9.89	211.5
2004	13.77	234.5

1. The table above has data from the United States. For each year, calculate labor productivity.

2. Real GDP is $9 trillion and aggregate hours are 200 billion. What is labor productivity?

3. Aggregate hours are 200 billion and labor productivity is $45 an hour. What is real GDP?

Long Response Questions

■ FIGURE 25.1

Real GDP per hour of labor (2009 dollars)

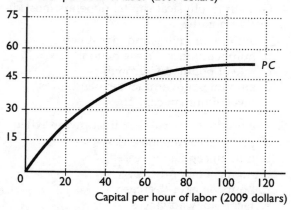

Capital per hour of labor (2009 dollars)

1. Figure 25.1 shows a productivity curve.
   a. How does this figure show diminishing

marginal returns?
   b. In the figure, show the effect of an increase in human capital.
   c. In the figure, show the effect of an advance in technology

2. What three factors increase labor productivity?

Additional Exercises (also in MyEconLab Test A)

Year	Aggregate hours (billions)	Real GDP (billions of 2009 dollars)	Capital per hour of labor (2009 dollars)
2012	240.0	14,833	105.0
2013	249.6	14,418	107.1

The table provides some data on an economy in 2012 and 2013.

1. Calculate the growth rate of real GDP in 2013.

2. Calculate labor productivity in 2012 and 2013.

3. Calculate the growth rate of labor productivity in 2013.

4. Compare the growth rate of labor productivity and the growth rate of capital per hour of labor in 2013. Why might they differ?

CHECKPOINT 25.3

■ **Review the theories of economic growth.**

Quick Review

- *Old growth theory* The clash between an exploding population and limited resources will eventually bring economic growth to an end. Income is driven to the subsistence level. Old growth theory is called the "classical growth theory" or "Malthusian theory" or the "Doomsday theory."

- *New growth theory* Unlimited wants will lead us to ever greater productivity and perpetual economic growth.

Additional Practice Problems 25.3

1. In the classical theory, why is an increase in labor productivity only temporary?

© 2015 Pearson Education, Inc.

2. Some economic advisors urge less developed nations to restrict their birth rate. These economists claim that a high birth rate impoverishes a nation.
   a. What growth theory are these advisors following?
   b. What would a new growth theory proponent say about this recommendation?

Solutions to Additional Practice Problems 25.3

1. An increase in labor productivity lifts real GDP per person above the subsistence level, the minimum amount necessary to sustain life. People respond by increasing the birth rate so a population explosion occurs. The population grows so large that capital per worker and hence labor productivity falls. The fall in labor productivity forces real GDP per person back to the subsistence level, after which population growth ends.

2a. These advisors are following the classical theory of economic growth. They believe that if real GDP per person rises in these nations, then the birth rate will increase and drive real GDP per person back to the subsistence level. They identify the low real GDP per person in these nations with a high birth rate and resulting high population growth rate.

2b. A new growth theory proponent likely would disagree with the suggestion to limit the birth rate. According to this theory, the pace at which new discoveries are made and at which technology advances depends on how many people are looking for a new technology and how intensively they are looking. In this case, limiting the population leads to a reduction in the discovery of new technologies and a decrease in the growth rate of real GDP per person.

■ AP Self Test 25.3

True or false

1. The classical growth theory concludes that eventually real GDP per person returns to the subsistence level.

2. Malthusian theory is another name for the new growth theory.

3. The new growth theory emphasizes that people make choices about how long to remain in school, developing their human capital.

4. The new growth theory points out that because production activities can be replicated, the economy does not experience diminishing returns.

5. The new growth theory predicts that economic growth can persist indefinitely.

Multiple choice

1. If real GDP per person is above the subsistence level, the according to classical growth theory,
   a. the population will increase.
   b. the population will decrease.
   c. the standard of living continues to improve.
   d. labor productivity will increase.
   e. more technological advances occur.

2. Classical growth theory predicts that increases in
   a. real GDP per person are permanent and sustainable.
   b. real GDP per person are temporary and not sustainable.
   c. resources permanently increase labor productivity.
   d. resources permanently increase real GDP per person.
   e. competition increase economic growth.

3. The theory that suggests that our unlimited wants will lead to perpetual economic growth is the
   a. classical growth theory.
   b. sustained growth theory.
   c. old growth theory.
   d. new growth theory.
   e. Malthusian growth theory.

© 2015 Pearson Education, Inc.

4. The new growth theory states that
   a. technological advances are the result of random chance.
   b. technological advances result from choices.
   c. technological advances are the responsibility of the government.
   d. the subsistence income level leads to technological advances.
   e. it is impossible to replicate production activities.

5. According to the new growth theory ___ is the factor that motivates technological change.
   a. random chance
   b. profit
   c. diminishing returns
   d. the replication of activities
   e. decisions about how much human capital to acquire

Long Response Questions

1. What role do technological advances play in each of the three growth theories?

2. In which of the two growth theories does population growth play a critical role and what is its role?

3. What role do diminishing returns play in the new growth theory?

4. Which growth theory is most pessimistic about the prospects for persistent economic growth? Which is most optimistic?

Additional Exercises (also in MyEconLab Test A)

1. What are the three facts about market economies that new growth theory emphasizes and how do those facts influence the economic growth rate? Provide examples.

2. Why don't diminishing returns limit growth in new growth theory?

3. Families in China are permitted to have only one child. Predict the effects of this policy on economic growth according to classical, neoclassical, and new growth theories.

CHECKPOINT 25.4

■ **Describe policies that speed economic growth.**

Quick Review

- *Preconditions for economic growth* The three preconditions are economic freedom, property rights, and markets.
- *Policies to achieve growth* Five policies are to create incentive mechanisms, encourage saving, encourage research and development, encourage international trade, and improve the quality of education.

Additional Practice Problem 25.4

1. In 1949 East and West Germany had about the same real GDP per person. By 1989, when East Germany collapsed, West Germany had a real GDP per person more than twice the level of East Germany's. Why did East Germany grow so much more slowly than West Germany over those 40 years?

Solution to Additional Practice Problem 25.4

1. In 1949, East Germany was formed with state ownership of capital and land, and virtually no economic freedom. West Germany was formed with private ownership of most capital and land, and significant economic freedom.
   West Germany had the preconditions for economic growth; East Germany did not. When East Germany collapsed in 1989, West Germany had more human capital, more capital per hour of labor, and better technology. The different incentives had given West German workers the incentive to acquire human capital, West German investors the incentive to acquire physical capital, and West German entrepreneurs the incentive to innovate new and better technology.

■ **AP Self Test 25.4**

True or false

1. To achieve economic growth, economic freedom must be coupled with a democratic political system.

© 2015 Pearson Education, Inc.

2. Markets slow specialization and hence slow economic growth.

3. Encouraging saving can increase the growth of capital and stimulate economic growth.

4. Limiting international trade will increase economic growth.

Multiple choice

1. Economic freedom means that
   a. firms are regulated by the government.
   b. some goods and services are free.
   c. people are able to make personal choices and their property is protected.
   d. the rule of law does not apply.
   e. the nation's government is a democracy.

2. Property rights protect
   a. only the rights to physical property.
   b. only the rights to financial property.
   c. all rights except rights to intellectual property.
   d. rights to physical property, financial property, and intellectual property.
   e. the government's right to impose taxes.

3. Which of the following statements is FALSE?
   a. Saving helps create economic growth.
   b. Improvements in the quality of education are important for economic growth.
   c. Free international trade helps create economic growth.
   d. Faster population growth is the key to growth in real GDP per person.
   e. Economic freedom requires property rights.

4. Saving
   a. slows growth because it decreases consumption.
   b. finances investment which brings capital accumulation.
   c. has no impact on economic growth.
   d. is very low in most East Asian nations.
   e. is important for a country to gain the benefits of international trade.

5. The fastest growing nations today are those with
   a. barriers that significantly limit international trade.
   b. the fastest growing exports and imports.
   c. government intervention in markets to ensure high prices.
   d. few funds spent on research and development.
   e. the least saving.

Long Response Questions

1. Does persistent economic growth necessarily occur when a nation meets all the preconditions for growth?

2. What role do specialization and trade play in determining economic growth?

3. Is it possible for the government to create a large increase in the economic growth rate, say from 3 percent to 10 percent in a year?

4. The Eye on Your Life discussed the roles played by economic growth in your life. How important do you think the technological advances that have lead to economic growth are in determining the quality of your life?

Additional Exercises (also in MyEconLab Test A)

1. What is the key reason why economic growth is either absent or slow in some societies?

2. Is economic freedom the same as democracy? Can you think of a country that enjoys economic freedom and achieves rapid economic growth but does not have democracy?

3. Why are markets a necessary precondition for economic growth?

4. Explain why, other things remaining the same, a country or region that adopts free international trade (for example, Hong Kong) has a faster economic growth rate than a country that restricts international trade (for example, Myanmar).

© 2015 Pearson Education, Inc.

SELF TEST ANSWERS

■ AP Self Test 25.1

True or false
1. True; page 634
2. True; page 634
3. True; page 635
4. False; page 635

Multiple choice
1. a; page 634
2. b; page 634
3. d; page 634
4. a; page 635
5. b; page 635
6. b; page 635

Short Response Questions
1. 10 percent; 10 percent; 10 percent; page 634.
2. a. 1 percent; 2 percent; –1 percent; 0 percent; page 635.
   b. 2005 and 2006; page 634.
3. Use the Rule of 70. So, 70 ÷ 3 = 23.3 years; 70 ÷ 4 = 17.5 years; 70 ÷ 5 = 14 years; page 635.

Additional Exercises (also in MyEconLab Test A)
1. Canada's economic growth rate = [($1,028 billion – $1,012 billion) ÷ $1,012] billion × 100 = 1.6 percent. The growth rate of Canada's population is [(31.1 million – 30.8 million) ÷ 30.8 million] × 100, which is 1.0 percent. Canada's growth rate of real GDP per person = 1.6 percent – 1.0 percent = 0.6 percent. Real GDP per person doubles in approximately 70 ÷ 0.6 = 116.7 years; pages 634-635.

2. Before the changes, real GDP per person is growing at 10.6 percent – 1 percent = 9.6 percent per year. At this rate, real GDP per person will double in approximately 70 ÷ 9.6 = 7.3 years. After the changes, real GDP per person is growing at 12.0 percent – 2 percent = 10.0 percent per year. At this rate, real GDP per person will double in approximately 70 ÷ 10.0 = 7.0 years. So these changes shave 0.3 of a year off of the time it takes for real GDP to double; page 635.

■ AP Self Test 25.2

True or false
1. True; pages 638, 643
2. True; page 638
3. False; page 639
4. False; page 640
5. True; pages 641-642

Multiple choice
1. c; page 638
2. e; page 638
3. d; page 638
4. a; page 638
5. e; page 642
6. c; page 640

Short Response Questions
1. Labor productivity equals real GDP ÷ aggregate hours. So labor productivity in 1964 was $27.92 an hour; in 1974 was $33.96 an hour; in 1984 was $39.29 an hour; in 1994 was $46.76 an hour; and in 2004 was $58.72 an hour; page 638.
2. Labor productivity is $45 an hour; page 638.
3. Real GDP is $9 trillion; page 638.

Long Response Questions

■ FIGURE 25.2

Real GDP per hour of labor (2009 dollars)

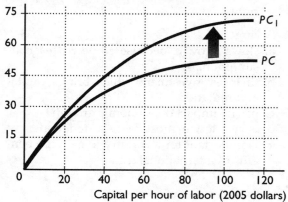

Capital per hour of labor (2005 dollars)

1. a. Diminishing marginal returns mean that

© 2015 Pearson Education, Inc.

when capital per hour of labor is small, an increase brings a larger increase in real GDP per hour of labor than when capital per hour of labor is large. This law is shown by the shape of the productivity curve. In the figure, along productivity curve *PC* an increase in capital per hour of labor from $20 to $40 raises real GDP per hour of labor by $15 while an increase from $60 to $80 increases real GDP per hour of labor by only $5; page 640.

b. An increase in human capital shifts the productivity curve upward, in Figure 25.2 to a curve such as *PC*₁; page 642.

c. Similar to an increase in human capital, an advance in technology shifts the productivity curve upward, in Figure 25.2 again to a curve such as *PC*₁; page 642.

2. Three factors increase labor productivity. First, increasing saving and investment in physical capital gives workers more capital with which to work, which increases labor productivity. Second, increasing the amount of human capital makes workers more productive and increases labor productivity. Human capital can increase either through formal schooling or on-the-job experience. Finally, discovering new technologies makes workers more productive and increases labor productivity. Often these new technologies are embedded in new capital equipment; pages 638-642.

Additional Exercises (also in MyEconLab Test A)

1. Growth rate of real GDP in 2013 = [($14,418 billion − $14,833 billion) ÷ $14,833 billion]× 100 = −2.8 percent; page 634.

2. Labor productivity in 2012 = $14,833 billion ÷ 240 billion hours = $61.80 an hour. Labor productivity in 2013 = $14,418 billion ÷ 249.6 billion hours = $57.76 an hour; page 638.

3. The growth rate of labor productivity equals the change in labor productivity divided by the initial level and then multiplied by 100, which is [($57.76 − $61.80) ÷ $61.80] × 100 = −6.5 percent; page 634.

4. The growth rate of capital per hour of labor equals the change in capital per hour of labor divided by the initial level and then multiplied by 100, which equals [($107.1 − $105.0) ÷ $105.0] × 100 = 2.00 percent. The growth of labor productivity was negative and consequently much slower than the growth rate of capital per hour of labor. The negative growth rate of labor productivity reflects the fact that growth in labor productivity was slow because of the recession in the late 2000s. Additionally, there is no necessary reason why growth in capital per hour of labor should translate one-to-one into growth in labor productivity; pages 638-642.

■ AP Self Test 25.3

True or false
1. True; page 646
2. False; page 646
3. True; page 647
4. True; page 647
5. True; page 647

Multiple choice
1. a; page 646
2. b; page 646
3. d; page 646
4. b; pages 646-647
5. b; pages 646-647

Long Response Questions
1. In the classical growth theory, advances in technology start a temporary period of economic growth. Ultimately, however, economic growth stops. In the new growth theory, economic growth continues indefinitely, in part because technology grows indefinitely; page 646.

2. Population growth plays a crucial role only in the classical growth theory. In the classical, or "Malthusian theory," population growth after a technological advance forces the economy back to a subsistence real income; page 646.

© 2015 Pearson Education, Inc.

3. The new growth theory assumes that although a *firm* is subject to diminishing returns, the *economy* is not subject to diminishing returns. So as capital accumulates, economy-wide labor productivity grows indefinitely; page 647.

4. The most optimistic theory is the new growth theory, which concludes that economic growth can continue forever. The most pessimistic theory is the old growth theory, which concludes that the economy will return to a subsistence level of real income; pages 646-647.

Additional Exercises (also in MyEconLab Test A)

1. First, human capital grows because of choices. Second, discoveries result from choices. Lastly, discoveries bring profit and competition destroys profit. With respect to the first factor, human capital growth depends, in part, on how long people remain in school, what they study, and how hard they study. Discoveries result from choices, which depend on how many people are looking for new technology and how intensively they are looking, not mere luck. And, competition serves to squeeze profits. People are constantly seeking lower-cost methods of production or new and better products, which leads to economic growth; pages 646-647.

2. New growth theory suggests that diminishing returns are not growth limiting. According to the new growth theory, as capital accumulates, labor productivity grows indefinitely as long as people devote resources to expanding human capital and introducing new technologies. In addition, new growth theory points out that even though there might be diminishing returns to a *firm*, there are not necessarily diminishing returns to the *economy* as a whole because activities can be replicated. In other words, it is possible for the economy as a whole to add another, say, computer chip factory identical to a first factory. Because the second factory is identical to the first, the output should be identical to the first and so the economy as whole does

not experience diminishing returns; page 647.

3. According to the old growth theory, that is the classical theory of growth, an effort by China to slow population growth by limiting the number of children in each family initially would have the effect of increasing the amount of capital per hour of labor. So, labor productivity and real GDP per person increase. As GDP per person rises, real GDP per person rises above the subsistence level and population should increase yet again. The overall effect is unclear: If China can successfully limit population growth in face of the tendency for it to increase when real GDP per person rises, then real GDP per person can remain above the subsistence level. However, if China's best efforts are insufficient, then the rise in GDP per person serves to increase population growth and real GDP per person returns to the subsistence level.

According to new growth theory, the pace at which new discoveries are made and at which technology advances depends on how many people are looking for a new technology and how intensively they are looking. This assumption leads to the conclusion that efforts to limit population through regulating the number of children that people are allowed to have will lead to a reduction in the discovery of new technologies and a decrease in the rate of labor productivity growth. So, China's growth policy slows the growth in real GDP per person; pages 646-647.

■ AP Self Test 25.4

True or false
1. False; page 650
2. False; page 650
3. True; page 651
4. False; page 652

Multiple choice
1. c; page 650
2. d; page 650

© 2015 Pearson Education, Inc.

3. d; pages 650-651

4. b; pages 650-651

5. b; page 652

Long Response Questions

1. No, economic growth does not necessarily occur when all preconditions for growth are satisfied. Without the preconditions, economic growth will not occur but simply having them is not enough to guarantee economic growth. For growth to occur and be persistent, people must have incentives that encourage saving and investment, expansion of human capital, and the discovery and application of new technologies. With these incentives and the preconditions, economic persisting growth will occur; pages 650-651.

2. Growth begins when people can specialize in the activities in which they have a comparative advantage and trade with each other. As an economy reaps the benefits from specialization and trade, production and consumption grow, real GDP per person increases, and the standard of living rises; page 651.

3. No, the government cannot create a huge increase in the economic growth rate. The government can pursue policies that will nudge the growth rate upward. And, over time, policies that create even small increases in the economic growth rate will have large benefits; page 652.

4. The importance of these technological advances is hard to overstate. For instance, the next time you watch a movie from the 1930s, the 1940s, the 1950s, the 1960s, 1970s, or even the 1980s look carefully at what is *not* present. Do you see portable computers? Smart phones? iPads? Elaborate life-saving equipment in hospitals? Cars with enhanced safety features and incredible durability? GPS? The answers are, of course, no. All of these technological advances came in response to people's insatiable desire for a higher standard of living and other people's equally insatiable pursuit of profit.

Additional Exercises (also in MyEconLab Test A)

1. The key reason why economic growth is either absent or slow is that some societies lack the incentive system that encourages growth-producing activities. And economic freedom is the fundamental precondition for creating the incentives that lead to economic growth; page 650.

2. Economic freedom is not the same as democracy. The rule of law is the key requirement to economic freedom, not democracy. Several non-democratic countries enjoy economic freedom and achieve rapid economic growth. China is an example of a non-democratic but rapidly growing nation; page 650.

3. Markets enable people to trade and to save and invest. Markets are where buyers and sellers get information and do business with each other; pages 650-651.

4. Free trade stimulates growth by extracting all the available gains from specialization and exchange. Countries that have substantial trade barriers often have slower economic growth because the restrictions they impose on their countries promote inefficient industries and punish potentially efficient industries that could find markets beyond their borders; page 652.

© 2015 Pearson Education, Inc.

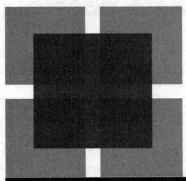

Finance, Saving, and Investment

CHAPTER CHECKLIST

1 Describe the financial markets and the key financial institutions.

Finance is the lending and borrowing that moves funds from savers to spenders. Physical capital is the tools, machines, buildings, and other items that have been produced in the past and are used to produce additional goods and services. Financial capital is the funds firms use to buy and operate physical capital. Gross investment is the total amount spent on new capital goods; net investment equals gross investment minus depreciation. Net investment is the change in the quantity of capital. Saving is the amount of income that is not paid in taxes or spent on consumption. Saving is the source of financial capital. Borrowers and savers interact in the markets for financial capital: the loan markets, the bond markets, and the stock markets. Financial institutions, such as investment banks, commercial banks, government-sponsored mortgage lenders, pension funds, and insurance companies, are firms that operate on both sides of the markets for financial capital. A financial institution's net worth is the market value of what it has lent minus the market value of what it has borrowed. If net worth is negative, the firm is insolvent; if a firm is faced with a sudden demand to repay more of what it has borrowed than the amount of cash it has on hand, the firm is illiquid. There is an inverse relationship between the interest rate and the price of an asset; if the asset price rises, the interest rate falls.

2 Explain how borrowing and lending decisions are made and how these decisions interact in the loanable funds market.

The main source of the demand for loanable funds is firms demand for loanable funds to finance investment. Other things remaining the same, the higher the real interest rate, the smaller the quantity of loanable funds demanded, so the demand for loanable funds curve slopes downward. The demand for loanable funds changes when the expected profit changes; if the expected profit increases, the demand for loanable funds increases. The main source of the supply of loanable funds is households supply of savings. Other things remaining the same, the higher the real interest rate, the greater the quantity of loanable funds supplied so that the supply of loanable funds curve slopes upward. Factors that change the supply of loanable funds are: disposable income, wealth, expected future income, and default risk. The loanable funds market equilibrium occurs at the real interest rate at which the quantity of loanable funds demanded equals the quantity supplied.

3 Explain how a government budget surplus or deficit influences the real interest rate, investment, and saving.

A government budget surplus adds to the supply of loanable funds, thereby lowering the real interest rate and increasing the quantity of investment. A government budget deficit adds to the demand for loanable funds, raising the real interest rate and decreasing (crowding out) investment. The Ricardo-Barro effect says that private saving increases to offset a government budget deficit so no crowding out occurs.

© 2015 Pearson Education, Inc.

YOUR AP TEST HINTS

AP Topics

Topic on your AP test	What to Know	Corresponding textbook section
Financial markets	Money versus capital; markets for financial capital and key financial institutions	Checkpoint 26.1
Loanable funds (private savings market)	Market for loanable funds; supply, demand, and equilibrium; borrowing and lending	Checkpoint 26.2
Impact of government in loanable funds market	Budget surplus and deficit; crowding out effect	Checkpoint 26.3

AP Vocabulary Covered

Terms	What to Know	Text Sections
Capital (physical capital)	The tools, instruments, machines, and buildings that have been produced in the past and used to produce goods and services	Checkpoint 26.1, p. 660
Gross investment	The total spent on new capital, usually per year	Checkpoint 26.1, p. 660
Net investment	The change in the quantity of capital; equals gross investment minus depreciation	Checkpoint 26.1, p. 660
Wealth	The total value of all things people own	Checkpoint 26.1, p. 660
Bond	A loan promising to make specified payments on specific dates	Checkpoint 26.1, p. 662
Stock	Represents ownership of part of a corporation and a claim to the firm's profits	Checkpoint 26.1, p. 662
Financial institution	Firms that operate as both lenders and borrowers; banks, mortgage lenders, and insurance companies are examples	Checkpoint 26.1, p. 663
Net worth	A financial institution's total market value based on what is lent minus what has been borrowed	Checkpoint 26.1, p. 664
Demand for loanable funds	The quantity of loanable funds demanded by businesses, government budget deficits, and international lending; inversely related to the real interest rate	Checkpoint 26.2, p. 666
Supply of loanable funds	The quantity of loanable funds supplied by private savings, government budget surpluses, and international borrowing; positively related to the real interest rate	Checkpoint 26.2, p. 669
Equilibrium in loanable funds market	Equilibrium real interest rate sets the quantity of loanable funds demanded equal to the quantity of loanable funds supplied	Checkpoint 26.2, p. 672
Government budget surplus	Government outlays are less than tax revenues; increasing the supply of loanable funds	Checkpoint 26.3, p. 676
Government budget deficit	Government outlays exceed tax revenue; budget deficits increase the demand for loanable funds	Checkpoint 26.3, p. 677
Crowding-out effect	An increase in the budget deficit increases the demand for loanable funds. The real interest rises and reduces investment	Checkpoint 26.3, p. 678

Extra AP material

- On the AP test, *private saving* is called *loanable funds*. The *loanable funds market* is called the *private savings market*.
- The Ricardo-Barro Effect is a theory that disputes "crowding out" but is not on the AP test.

© 2015 Pearson Education, Inc.

CHECKPOINT 26.1

■ **Describe the financial markets and the key financial institutions.**

Quick Review

- *Net investment* Net investment is the change in the quantity of capital and equals gross investment minus depreciation.
- *Interest rates and asset prices* The interest rate on an asset is a percentage of the asset's price. So if the asset's price rises, then the interest rate on the asset falls, and if the asset's price falls, then the interest rate on the asset rises.

Additional Practice Problems 26.1

1. On December 31, 2013 CSX railroad had capital of $19.5 billion dollars. During 2014 CSX made investments of $1.0 billion and had $0.4 billion of capital depreciate.
   a. What was CSX's gross investment?
   b. What was CSX's net investment?
   c. What was the amount of CSX's capital stock on December 31, 2014? By how much did the capital stock change? How does this answer compare to the answer to part (b)?

2. Nvidia, a graphics card company, wanted to raise $200 million to build a new headquarters building and buy other physical capital. What methods could Nvidia have used to obtain the financial capital to purchase the physical capital it needed?

3. For a financial institution, what is the relationship between net wealth, solvency, and insolvency?

Solutions to Additional Practice Problems 26.1

1a. CSX's gross investment is equal to their total investment, $1.0 billion.

1b. CSX's net investment is equal to its gross investment minus its depreciation, or $1.0 billion minus $0.4 billion, which is $0.6 billion.

1c. CSX's capital stock on December 31, 2014 equals its capital stock on December 31, 2013 plus its (gross) investment minus its depreciation, or $19.5 billion + $1.0 billion – $0.4 billion, which is $20.1 billion. CSX's capital increased by $0.6 billion, which is the same as CSX's net investment. It is the case that the change in the capital stock equals net investment.

2. Nvidia had a number of choices in the markets for financial capital. It could have sold new shares of stock, so the current stockholders would share future profits with new stockholders. It could have sold bonds, which means it would be borrowing the funds from the buyers of the bonds. Or it could have arranged a bank loan. If Nvidia sold bonds or borrowed from a bank, Nvidia would have increased its debt and would be required at some time to repay whoever loaned it the funds. As it happens, Nvidia actually financed its new capital by selling bonds.

3. A financial institution's net worth is the market value of what it has lent (which are its assets) minus the market value of what it has borrowed (which are its liabilities). If the net worth is positive, the firm is solvent but if the net worth is negative, then the firm is insolvent.

■ AP Self Test 26.1

True or false

1. Financial capital and physical capital are two different names for the same thing.

2. Net investment equals gross investment minus depreciation.

3. The loan market is one of the nation's financial capital markets.

4. A bond issued by a firm is a certificate of ownership and claim to the profits that the firm makes.

5. Investment banks and commercial banks are both examples of financial institutions.

6. A firm that is insolvent must also be illiquid.

© 2015 Pearson Education, Inc.

Multiple choice

1. Which of the following is *not* an example of physical capital?
   a. a building
   b. a bond
   c. a dump truck
   d. a lawn mower
   e. a computer

2. The decrease in the value of capital that results from its use and obsolescence is
   a. appreciation.
   b. deconstruction.
   c. depreciation.
   d. gross investment.
   e. net investment.

3. Which of the following formulas is correct?
   a. Net investment = gross investment + depreciation
   b. Net investment = gross investment + capital
   c. Net investment = gross investment − depreciation
   d Net investment = gross investment − saving
   e. Net investment = gross investment − wealth

4. Intel's capital at the end of the year equals Intel's capital at the beginning of the year
   a. minus its stock dividends.
   b. plus net investment.
   c. minus depreciation.
   d. plus gross investment.
   e. plus depreciation.

5. When a student uses a credit card to buy an iPad, the student is
   a. borrowing in the bond market.
   b. lending in the bond market.
   c. lending in the loan market.
   d. borrowing in the loan market.
   e. lending in the stock market.

6. Which of the following is *not* a financial institution?
   a. an insurance company
   b. a pension fund
   c. Freddie Mac
   d. a commercial bank
   e. None of the above is correct because they are all financial institutions.

7. If the market value of what it has lent is less than the market value of it has borrowed, a financial institution's net worth is ____ and it is ____.
   a. negative; illiquid but not necessarily insolvent
   b. negative; insolvent but not necessarily illiquid
   c. positive; illiquid and insolvent
   d. negative; illiquid and insolvent
   e. positive; insolvent but not necessarily illiquid

8. A bond's price is $80 and the bond pays $8 in interest every year. The bond's interest rate is ____.
   a. 8 percent
   b. 10 percent
   c. 4 percent
   d. 80 percent
   e. None of the above is correct.

Short Response Questions

1. What is the relationship between physical capital and financial capital?

2. In 2014, Regis Hair purchased 10 hair dryers for $3,300 each. During the year, depreciation was $13,000. What was the amount of Regis' gross investment and net investment?

3. What are Fannie Mae and Freddie Mac? How do they operate on both sides of the financial markets?

4. Suppose a bond pays interest of $40 per year and its price is $600. What is the interest rate on the bond? If the price rises to $800, what now is the bond's interest rate?

© 2015 Pearson Education, Inc.

Long Response Question

1. What is the difference between gross investment and capital?

Additional Exercises (also in MyEconLab Test A)

1. Annie runs a fitness center. On December 31, 2013, she bought an existing business with exercise equipment and a building worth $300,000. During 2014, business was poor, so she sold some of her equipment for $100,000. What was Annie's gross investment, depreciation, and net investment during 2014? What was the value of Annie's capital at the end of 2014?

2. Karrie is a golf pro, and after she paid taxes, her income from golf and from stocks and bonds was $1,500,000 in 2014. At the beginning of 2014, she owned $900,000 worth of stocks and bonds. At the end of 2014, Karrie's stocks and bonds were worth $1,900,000. How much did Karrie save during 2014 and how much did she spend on consumption goods and services?

CHECKPOINT 26.2

■ **Explain how borrowing and lending decisions are made and how these decisions interact in the loanable funds market.**

Quick Review

- *Demand for loanable funds* The relationship between the quantity of loanable funds demanded and the real interest rate, other things remaining the same.
- *Supply of loanable funds* The relationship between the quantity of loanable funds supplied and the real interest rate, other things remaining the same.

Additional Practice Problems 26.2

1. Over the past decade or so, the development of ever more powerful computers has increased the profit from investing in new personal computers. This effect has affected all firms in the economy. The initial demand for loanable funds is shown in the figure. Use the figure to show the effect the higher expected profit has on the demand for loanable funds.

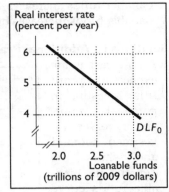

2. In 2015, in the United States at a real interest rate of 4 percent a year, the quantity of loanable funds supplied is $2.0 trillion; at a real interest rate of 6 percent a year, the quantity of loanable funds supplied is $2.5 trillion; and at a real interest rate of 8 percent a year, the quantity of loanable funds supplied is $3.0 trillion.

   a. In the figure, draw a graph of the U.S. supply of loanable funds curve.

   b. In 2015 a large number of households start to believe that their future disposable income

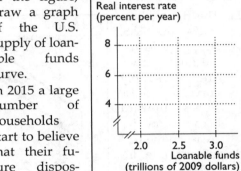

   will be higher than they had previously thought. Explain how this belief influences the supply of loanable funds. Illustrate the effect of this change on the supply of loanable funds curve.

   c. In 2015, the housing market recovers so that house prices soar and U.S. households' wealth increases. If other things remain the same, explain how this change influences the supply of loanable funds. What is the effect on the supply of loanable funds curve?

3. Draw a graph illustrating the effect on the equilibrium real interest rate and equilibrium saving and investment when the supply of

© 2015 Pearson Education, Inc.

loanable funds increases and the demand for loanable funds increases by more.

Solutions to Additional Practice Problems 26.2

1. An increase in the expected profit from investing in personal computers increases investment demand and shifts the demand for loanable funds curve rightward. In the figure, the demand for loanable funds curve

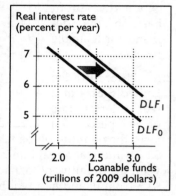

shifts rightward from DLF_0 to DLF_1. At any real interest rate firms have increased the quantity of investment they demand.

2a. The figure illustrates the U.S. supply of loanable funds curve. The supply curve, SLF_0, slopes upward because an increase in the real interest rate increases saving, which increases the quantity of loanable funds supplied.

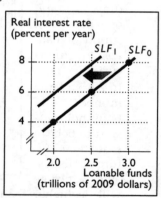

2b. An increase in expected future income decreases the amount people's saving and thereby decreases the supply of loanable funds. The U.S. supply of loanable funds curve decreases and the supply of loanable funds curve shifts leftward. In the above figure, the supply of loanable funds curve shifts leftward from SLF_0 to SLF_1. At any real interest rate, households have decreased the quantity of loanable funds they supply.

2c. The increase in people's wealth decreases the amount they save at each real interest rate. Saving decreases so the supply of loanable

funds decreases and the supply of loanable funds curve shifts leftward. In the above figure, the supply of loanable funds curve shifts leftward from SLF_0 to SLF_1.

3. The figure that shows the demand for loanable funds curve and the supply of loanable funds curve illustrates how the real interest rate is determined. Use this diagram the same way you use the supply and demand figures you studied in Chapter 4. Equilibrium occurs where the demand for loanable funds curve intersects the supply of loanable funds curve and a shift in either curve changes the equilibrium real interest rate and the equilibrium quantity of loanable funds.

In this case, the increase in the supply of loanable funds shifts the supply of loanable funds curve rightward. The increase in the demand for loanable funds shifts the demand for loanable funds curve rightward.

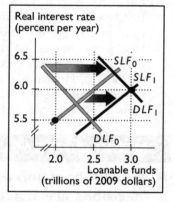

The shift of the demand for loanable funds curve exceeds the shift of the supply of loanable funds curve, so, as illustrated in the figure, the real interest rate rises, from 5.5 percent to 6.0 percent, and the quantity of loanable funds increases, from $2 trillion to $3 trillion.

■ AP Self Test 26.2

True or false

1. Other things remaining the same, the higher the real interest rate, the smaller the quantity of loanable funds demanded.

2. When the expected profit changes, there is a movement along the demand for loanable funds curve.

3. The real interest rate is the opportunity cost of consumption expenditure.

© 2015 Pearson Education, Inc.

4. An increase in wealth leads to a decrease in saving.

5. If the real interest rate is greater than the equilibrium real interest rate, there is a shortage of loanable funds in the financial market.

Multiple choice

1. If the real interest rate falls, other things being the same, the quantity of loanable funds demanded ____ and the quantity of loanable funds supplied ____.
   a. increases; decreases
   b. increases; increases
   c. decreases; does not change
   d. does not change; decreases
   e. decreases; decreases

2. The demand for loanable funds
   a. increases in a recession.
   b. decreases in an expansion.
   c. increases when firms are optimistic about the profit from investing in capital.
   d. increases when wealth increases.
   e. decreases when wealth increases.

■ **FIGURE 26.1**

Real interest rate (percent per year)

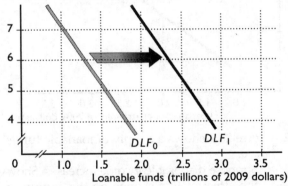

Loanable funds (trillions of 2009 dollars)

3. The shift of the demand for loanable funds curve in Figure 26.1 could reflect ____ in investment and might be the result of ____.
   a. an increase; an increase in households' wealth
   b. an increase; a decrease in households' wealth
   c. a decrease; a fall in expected profit
   d. a decrease; a fall in the default risk
   e. an increase; a rise in expected profit

4. Other things remaining the same, a ____ in the real interest rate ____ the quantity of saving and ____ the quantity of loanable funds supplied.
   a. fall; increases; increases
   b. rise; increases; increases
   c. fall; increases; decreases
   d. fall; decreases; increases
   e. rise; increases; decreases

5. If the real interest rate falls, there is
   a. an upward movement along the supply of loanable funds curve.
   b. a downward movement along the supply of loanable funds curve.
   c. a rightward shift of the supply of loanable funds curve and no shift in the demand for loanable funds curve.
   d. a leftward shift of the supply of loanable funds curve and no shift in the demand for loanable funds curve.
   e. a leftward shift of the supply of loanable funds curve and a rightward shift in the demand for loanable funds curve.

6. An increase in wealth leads to ____ loanable funds.
   a. an increase in the supply of
   b. an increase in the demand for
   c. a decrease in the supply of
   d. a decrease in the demand for
   e. no change in either the supply of loanable funds or the demand for

© 2015 Pearson Education, Inc.

7. If, at the current interest rate, the quantity of loanable funds supplied is less than the quantity of loanable funds demanded, then
   a. the supply of loanable funds curve shifts rightward and the real interest rate rises.
   b. the supply of loanable funds curve shifts leftward and the real interest rate falls.
   c. the real interest rate falls.
   d. the real interest rate rises.
   e. the supply of loanable funds curve shifts leftward and the real interest rate rises.

8. If expected profit falls, the demand for loanable funds curve shifts ____ and the real interest rate ____.
   a. rightward; rises
   b. rightward; falls
   c. leftward; rises
   d. leftward; falls
   e. leftward; does not change

■ **FIGURE 26.2**
Real interest rate (percent per year)

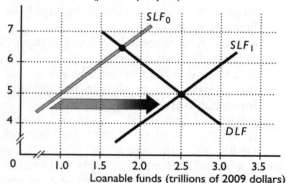

9. In Figure 26.2, ____ has increased and the equilibrium quantity of loanable funds ____.
   a. wealth; increases
   b. default risk; increases
   c. expected profit; decreases
   d. expected future income; decreases
   e. disposable income; increases

Short Response Questions

■ **FIGURE 26.3**
Real interest rate (percent per year)

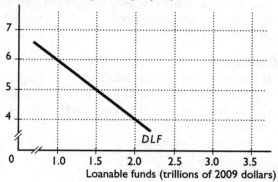

1. Figure 26.3 shows a demand for loanable funds curve. Because the economy enters an expansion, the expected profit increases. Show the effect of this change on the demand for loanable funds curve in Figure 26.3.

■ **FIGURE 26.4**
Real interest rate (percent per year)

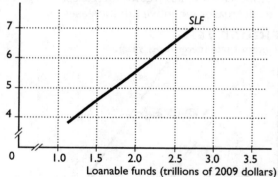

2. Figure 26.4 shows a supply of loanable funds curve.
   a. Suppose disposable income increases. Show the effect of this change on the supply of loanable funds curve in Figure 26.4.
   b. Suppose wealth increases. Show the effect of this change on the supply of loanable funds curve in Figure 26.4.

© 2015 Pearson Education, Inc.

Real interest rate (percent per year)	Demand for loanable funds (trillions of 2009 dollars)	Supply of loanable funds (trillions of 2009 dollars)
4	2.5	1.5
5	2.0	2.0
6	1.5	2.5
7	1.0	3.0

■ **FIGURE 26.5**

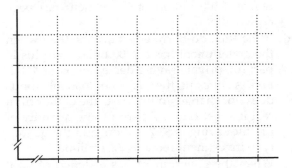

3. The table above gives a supply of loanable funds schedule and a demand for loanable funds schedule.
   a. Label the axes and draw the supply of loanable funds curve and the demand for loanable funds curve in Figure 26.5.
   b. What is the equilibrium real interest rate? What is the equilibrium quantity of loanable funds?
   c. Suppose that firms become more optimistic about their expected profit. In Figure 26.5, show this change. What is the effect on the real interest rate and quantity of loanable funds and investment?

Long Response Questions
1. What is the relationship between investment and the demand for loanable funds?
2. Why does an increase in the real interest rate decrease the quantity of loanable funds demanded?
3. What factors shift the demand for loanable funds curve? The supply of loanable funds curve?
4. If the real interest rate is less than its equilibrium value, what drives it to its equilibrium?

Additional Exercises (also in MyEconLab Test A)
In 2015, the Lee family had a disposable income of $80,000, wealth of $140,000, and an expected future income of $80,000 a year. At a real interest rate of 4 percent a year, the Lee family saves $15,000 a year; at a real interest rate of 6 percent a year, they save $20,000 a year; and at a real interest rate of 8 percent, they save $25,000 a year. Use this information to answer Exercises 1 and 2.
1. Draw a graph of the Lee family's supply of loanable funds curve.
2. In 2016, suppose that the stock market crashes and the Lee family's wealth decreases by 50 percent. Explain how this decrease in wealth influences the Lee family's supply of loanable funds curve.
3. Draw graphs that illustrate the effect of an increase in the demand for loanable funds and an even larger increase in the supply of loanable funds on the real interest rate and the equilibrium quantity of loanable funds.

CHECKPOINT 26.3

■ **Explain how a government budget surplus or deficit influences the real interest rate, investment, and saving.**

Quick Review
• *Crowding-out effect* The tendency for a government budget deficit to raise the real interest rate and decrease investment.

Additional Practice Problems 26.3
1. The table has the demand for loanable funds schedule and the private supply of loanable funds schedule.
   a. If the government's budget is balanced (so there is no budget deficit nor budget surplus),

Real interest rate (percent per year)	Demand for loanable funds	Supply of loanable funds
	(trillions of 2009 dollars per year)	
4	2.7	2.1
5	2.6	2.2
6	2.5	2.3
7	2.4	2.4
8	2.3	2.5
9	2.2	2.6
10	2.1	2.7

© 2015 Pearson Education, Inc.

what is the equilibrium real interest rate, the equilibrium the quantity of loanable funds, and the quantity of investment?

b. If the government budget surplus is $200 billion, and there is no Ricardo-Barro effect, what are the equilibrium real interest rate, the quantity of private saving, and the quantity of investment?

c. If the government budget deficit is $200 billion, and there is no Ricardo-Barro effect, what are the equilibrium real interest rate, the quantity of private saving, and the quantity of investment? Is there any crowding out?

d. If the Ricardo-Barro effect occurs, how do your answers to part (b) and part (c) change? How does the equilibrium real interest rate and quantity of investment in these two cases compare to your answer to part (a)?

2. With a Ricardo-Barro effect, what is the impact of a government budget deficit or surplus? Does the size of the deficit or surplus matter?

Solutions to Additional Practice Problems 26.3

1a. With no budget deficit or surplus, private saving is the total supply of loanable funds and private investment is the total demand for loanable funds. The equilibrium real interest rate is 7 percent a year. The equilibrium quantity of loanable funds is $2.4 trillion. Investment also is $2.4 trillion.

1b. When the government has a $200 billion budget surplus, it is adding that amount to private saving. At the initial real interest rate of 7 percent, there is a surplus of loanable funds. The real interest rate falls. When the real interest rate falls to 6 percent, the quantity of private saving is $2.3 trillion and the total quantity of loanable funds is $2.5 trillion. The quantity of loanable funds demanded is also $2.5 trillion so this real interest is the equilibrium. The equilibrium real interest rate is 6 percent, the equilibrium quantity of private saving is $2.3 trillion, and the equilibrium quantity of investment is $2.5 trillion.

1c. If the government has a $200 billion deficit, the demand for loanable funds at every real interest rate is $200 billion more than the private demand for loanable funds shown in the table. The equilibrium real interest rate is 8 percent because at this interest rate, the total quantity of loanable funds supplied, $2.5 trillion, equals the total quantity of loanable funds demanded. Private saving is $2.5 trillion and investment is $2.3 trillion. In comparison to the situation with no government deficit, $100 billion of investment has been crowded out.

1d. If the Ricardo-Barro effect occurs, then when the government has a $200 billion surplus in part (b), private saving decreases by $200 billion. As a result, the supply of loanable funds does not change. In this case, the equilibrium real interest rate is 7 percent, the quantity of private saving is $2.2 trillion, and the quantity of investment remains $2.4 trillion.

When the government has a deficit of $200 billion in part (c), private saving increases by $200 billion so the supply of loanable funds increases. The equilibrium real interest rate is 7 percent, the quantity of private saving is $2.6 trillion, and the quantity of investment remains $2.4 trillion.

2. The Ricardo-Barro effect says that government deficits and surpluses do not matter. Private saving changes to offset the budget deficit or surplus. Whether a deficit or surplus is large or small is inconsequential because it does not change the real interest rate or the quantity of investment.

■ AP Self Test 26.3

True or false

1. Governments do not participate in the loanable funds market.

2. With no Barro-Ricardo effect, an increase in government saving leads to a fall in the real interest rate.

3. With no Barro-Ricardo effect, an increase in government saving leads to an increase in the quantity of investment.

© 2015 Pearson Education, Inc.

4. The crowding-out effect is the tendency of a government budget surplus to crowd out private saving.

5. The Ricardo-Barro effect holds that the government budget deficit has no effect on the real interest rate or investment.

Multiple choice

1. With no Ricardo-Barro effect, a government budget surplus
   a. increases the supply of loanable funds.
   b. increases the demand for loanable funds.
   c. decreases the supply of loanable funds.
   d. decreases the demand for loanable funds.
   e. has no effect on either the supply or the demand for loanable funds.

2. Suppose the government has a budget surplus. Then
   a. private saving is equal to investment.
   b. private saving is greater than investment and government saving is positive.
   c. private saving is less than investment and government saving is positive.
   d. private saving is greater than investment and government saving is positive.
   e. private saving is greater than investment and government saving is negative.

3. With no Ricardo-Barro effect, a government budget surplus ____ the real interest rate because the ____ loanable funds increases.
   a. raises; demand for
   b. lowers; demand for
   c. raises; supply of
   d. lowers; supply of
   e. None of the above answers is correct because the real interest rate does not change.

4. If there is no Ricardo-Barro effect, a government budget deficit will ____ the real interest rate and ____ the quantity of investment.
   a. raise; increase
   b. raise; decrease
   c. lower; increase
   d. lower; decrease
   e. not change; not change

5. The "crowding-out effect" refers to how a government budget deficit
   a. shifts only the supply of loanable funds curve leftward.
   b. shifts only the demand for loanable funds curve leftward.
   c. shifts both the demand for and the supply of loanable funds curves leftward.
   d. decreases the equilibrium quantity of investment.
   e. increases the equilibrium quantity of investment.

6. The Ricardo-Barro effect says that a government budget deficit leads to
   a. a higher real interest rate.
   b. a lower real interest rate.
   c. no change in the real interest rate.
   d. an increase in demand for loanable funds.
   e. an increase in the quantity of investment.

Long Response Questions

Real interest rate (percent per year)	Demand for loanable funds (trillions of 2009 dollars)	Supply of loanable funds (trillions of 2009 dollars)
4	2.5	1.5
5	2.0	2.0
6	1.5	2.5
7	1.0	3.0

1. The above table has a supply of loanable funds schedule and a demand for loanable funds schedule.
   a. In Figure 26.6 label the axes. Assuming there is no government saving, draw the supply of loanable funds curve and the demand for loanable funds curve.
   b. If the government has no budget deficit or surplus, what is the equilibrium real interest rate and quantity of investment?
   c. If the government has a $1.0 trillion deficit, and there is no Ricardo-Barro effect, draw the demand for loanable funds curve in Figure 26.6. What is the equilibrium real interest rate and quantity of investment?
   d. If the government has a $1.0 trillion defi-

© 2015 Pearson Education, Inc.

■ **FIGURE 26.6**

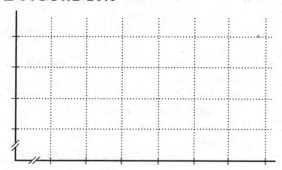

cit, and there is a Ricardo-Barro effect, draw the demand for loanable funds curve in Figure 26.6. What is the equilibrium real interest rate and quantity of investment?

2. What is the crowding-out effect?

3. How does the Ricardo-Barro effect modify the conclusion of the crowding-out effect?

4. The Eye on Your Life discussed some of the many transactions you will make in the loanable funds markets. Many students are financing part or all of their college educations by using student loans. How does the decision to finance a college education using student loans compare to a firm's decision to finance a new piece of capital equipment by using loans?

Additional Exercises (also in MyEconLab Test A)

Real interest rate (percent per year)	Loanable funds demanded	Loanable funds supplied
	(trillions of 2009 dollars per year)	
4	8.5	5.5
5	8.0	6.0
6	7.5	6.5
7	7.0	7.0
8	6.5	7.5
9	6.0	8.0
10	5.5	8.5

In the loanable funds market set out in the table above, the demand for loanable funds increases by $1 trillion at each real interest rate and the supply of loanable funds increases by $2 trillion at each interest rate. Suppose there is no Ricardo-Barro effect.

1. If the government budget is balanced, what are the real interest rate, the quantity of loanable funds, investment, and private saving? Is there any crowding out in this situation?

2. If the government budget deficit is $1 trillion, what are the real interest rate, the quantity of loanable funds, investment, and private saving? (Recall that there is no Ricardo-Barro effect.) Is there any crowding out in this situation?

3. If the government wants to stimulate the quantity of investment and increase it to $9 trillion, what must it do?

© 2015 Pearson Education, Inc.

SELF TEST ANSWERS

■ AP Self Test 26.1

True or false
1. False; page 660
2. True; page 660
3. True; page 661
4. False; page 662
5. True; page 663
6. False; page 664

Multiple choice
1. b; page 660
2. c; page 660
3. c; page 660
4. b; page 660
5. d; page 661
6. e; page 663
7. b; page 664
8. b; page 664

Short Response Questions
1. Physical capital is the tools, machines, buildings, and other items that have been produced in the past and are used to produce additional goods and services. Financial capital is the funds firms use to buy and operate physical capital. Hence a firm needs financial capital in order to buy a piece of physical capital; page 660.
2. Regis' gross investment was $33,000, and net investment, which equals gross investment minus depreciation, was $20,000; page 660.
3. Fannie Mae and Freddie Mac are government-sponsored enterprises. They both buy and sell in financial markets. On the buying side, they buy mortgages from banks. They then package these mortgages into mortgage-backed securities and sell them to others, such as pension funds; page 663.
4. The interest rate equals the (amount paid) ÷ (price of the asset) × 100. In the first case in the problem, the interest rate is ($40) ÷ ($600) × 100, which is 6.67 percent. When the price rises to $800, the interest rate falls to ($40) ÷ ($800) × 100, or 5.00 percent.; page 664.

Long Response Question
1. Capital is the tools, machines, buildings, and other items that have been produced in the past and are used to produce additional goods and services. Investment is the purchase of new capital, so investment *adds* to the total amount of capital. Gross investment is the total amount of investment spent on new capital goods; page 660.

Additional Exercises (also in MyEconLab Test A)
1. Annie's gross investment during 2014 was –$100,000 because she sold some of her capital. Annie's depreciation during 2014 was $0. Annie's net investment during 2014 was –$100,000, which equals gross investment (–$100,000) minus depreciation ($0). Anne's capital equals her capital at the beginning of 2014, $300,000, plus her net investment in 2014, –$100,000, so her capital at the end of 2014 was $200,000; pages 660-661.
2. Karrie's wealth increased by $1,000,000 in 2014. So her saving in 2014 was $1,000,000. (This point assumes no capital gains or losses on her stocks and bonds.) Her income after taxes was $1,500,000. Her consumption equals her income minus her saving, which is $1,500,000 – $1,000,000 = $500,000; pages 660-661.

■ AP Self Test 26.2

True or false
1. True; page 667
2. False; page 668
3. True; page 669
4. True; page 670
5. False; page 672

Multiple choice
1. a; pages 667, 669
2. c; page 668
3. e; page 668
4. b; page 669

© 2015 Pearson Education, Inc.

5. b; pages 669-670

6. c; page 670

7. d; page 672

8. d; pages 668, 673

9. e; pages 670, 673

Short Response Questions

■ **FIGURE 26.7**

Real interest rate (percent per year)

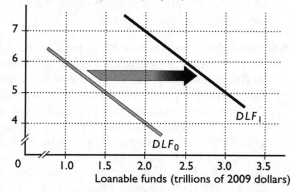

1. The increase in expected profit increases investment and thereby increases the demand for loanable funds. The demand for loanable funds curve shifts rightward, from DLF_0 to DLF_1 in Figure 26.7; page 668.

■ **FIGURE 26.8**

Real interest rate (percent per year)

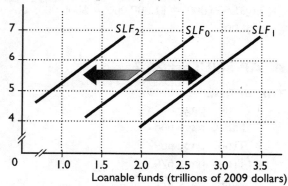

Loanable funds (trillions of 2009 dollars)

2. a. An increase in disposable income increases saving and the supply of loanable funds curve shifts rightward, from SLF_0 to SLF_1 in Figure 26.8; pages 670-671.

b. An increase in wealth decreases saving and thereby decreases the supply of loan

able funds. The supply of loanable funds curve shifts leftward, in Figure 26.8 from SLF_0 to SLF_2; pages 670-671.

■ **FIGURE 26.9**

Real interest rate (percent per year)

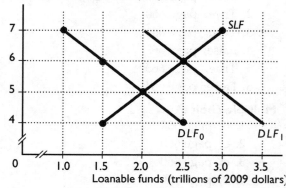

Loanable funds (trillions of 2009 dollars)

3. a. The axes are labeled and the curves are drawn in Figure 26.9. The supply of loanable funds curve is SLF and the demand for loanable funds curve is DLF_0; pages 667, 670.

b. The equilibrium real interest rate is 5 percent a year. The equilibrium quantity of loanable funds is $2.0 trillion; page 672.

c. The increase in the expected profit increases investment and shifts the demand for loanable funds curve rightward from DLF_0 to DLF_1. The real interest rate rises and the quantity of investment and loanable funds increase; page 673.

Long Response Questions

1. The demand for loanable funds comes from business investment, a government budget deficit, and international investment or lending. Of these three sources of demand, the largest is business investment, so it is the largest part of the demand for loanable funds; page 666.

2. The real interest rate is the opportunity cost of the funds used for investment. These funds might be borrowed or they might be the financial resources of the firm's owners. The opportunity cost of *both* sources is the real interest rate. In the case of borrowed funds, the real interest rate is the opportunity

© 2015 Pearson Education, Inc.

cost because it is what is really paid to the lender. In the case of the owners' funds, the real interest rate is the opportunity cost because the funds could be loaned and earn the real interest rate. An increase in the real interest rate increases the opportunity cost of financing investment so the quantity of loanable funds demanded decreases; page 667.

3. The demand for loanable funds curve shifts when the expected profit changes. Technological change, changes in the phase of the business cycle, population growth, and subjective influences, that is, swings of optimism and pessimism, all change the expected profit and shift the demand for loanable funds curve. The supply of loanable funds curve shifts when disposable income, wealth, expected future disposable income; and default risk change; pages 668-669.

4. If the real interest rate is less than the equilibrium real interest rate, the quantity of loanable funds demanded exceeds the quantity of loanable funds supplied. Borrowers can't find all the loans they want, but lenders are able to lend all the funds they have available. So the real interest rate rises and the quantity of loanable funds demanded decreases, while the quantity of loanable funds supplied increases. The equilibrium occurs when the interest rate is such that quantity of loanable funds demanded equals the quantity of loanable funds supplied; page 672.

Additional Exercises (also in MyEconLab Test A)

1. The graph showing the Lee family's supply of loanable funds curve is in Figure 26.10; page 670.

2. A stock market crash decreases the Lee family's wealth, so the Lee family increases its saving. The Lee family's supply of loanable funds increases and its supply of loanable funds curve shifts rightward; page 671.

3. The increase in the demand for loanable funds raises the real interest rate and increases the equilibrium quantity of loanable funds. The increase in the supply of loanable funds lowers the real interest rate and in-

■ FIGURE 26.10
Real interest rate (percent per year)

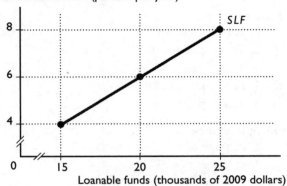

creases the equilibrium quantity of loanable funds. If the change in the supply of loanable funds exceeds the change in the demand for loanable funds, the real interest rate falls. Both changes increase the equilibrium quantity of loanable funds, so the equilibrium quantity of loanable funds increases.

■ FIGURE 26.11
Real interest rate (percent per year)

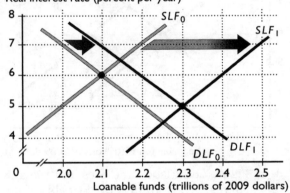

Figure 26.11 illustrates this situation. The increase in the demand for loanable funds shifts the demand for loanable funds curve rightward from DLF_0 to DLF_1. The increase in the supply of loanable funds shifts the supply of loanable funds curve rightward from SLF_0 to SLF_1. As Figure 26.11 shows, the real interest rate falls, from 6 percent a year to 5 percent a year. The equilibrium quantity of loanable funds increases, from $2.1 trillion to $2.3 trillion; page 673.

© 2015 Pearson Education, Inc.

■ AP Self Test 26.3

True or false

1. False; page 676
2. True; pages 676-677
3. True; pages 676-677
4. False; page 678
5. True; page 678

Multiple choice

1. a; page 676
2. c; pages 676-677
3. d; pages 676-677
4. b; pages 677-678
5. d; page 678
6. c; page 678

Long Response Questions

■ FIGURE 26.12

Real interest rate (percent per year)

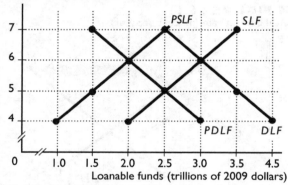

Loanable funds (trillions of 2009 dollars)

1. a. Figure 26.12 labels the axes and plots the curves. The supply of loanable funds curve is labeled *PSLF*. With no government budget surplus, this curve is the same as the overall supply of loanable funds curve. The demand for loanable funds curve is labeled *PDLF*. With no government budget deficit, this curve is the same as the overall demand for loanable funds curve; page 677.

   b. If the government has no budget deficit or surplus, then in Figure 26.12 the supply of loanable funds curve is the same as the supply of loanable funds curve labeled

PSLF and the demand for loanable funds curve is the same as the demand for loanable funds curve labeled *PDLF*. The equilibrium real interest rate is 6 percent a year and the equilibrium quantity of loanable funds, which is the equilibrium quantity of investment, is $2.0 trillion; page 677.

c. With the government budget deficit and no Ricardo-Barro effect, the total quantity of loanable funds demanded equals the quantity of investment plus the government budget deficit of $1.0 trillion. Using this result, the total demand for loanable funds is labeled *DLF* in Figure 26.12. This curve equals the private demand for loanable funds curve plus an additional $1.0 trillion at every real interest rate. The equilibrium real interest rate is 7 percent, the equilibrium quantity of loanable funds is $2.5 trillion, and the quantity of investment decreases to $1.5 trillion; pages 677-678.

d. With a $1.0 trillion government deficit, the Ricardo-Barro effect asserts that private saving increases by the amount of the deficit. So at every interest rate, the quantity of loanable funds is $1 trillion more than the amount given in the table. The total supply of loanable funds curve with the Ricardo-Barro effect is *SLF* in Figure 26.12. The equilibrium real interest rate is 5 percent, the equilibrium quantity of loanable funds is $3.0 trillion, and investment is $2.0 trillion. This amount of investment is the same as in part (a); page 678.

2. The crowding-out effect is the tendency for a government budget deficit to decrease private investment. It occurs because a government deficit increases the demand for loanable funds, thereby raising the real interest rate and decreasing investment; pages 677-678.

3. The Ricardo-Barro effect says that private savers increase their saving in response to a government budget deficit. Private saving offsets any change in government saving. In

© 2015 Pearson Education, Inc.

this case, a government budget deficit has no effect on the equilibrium quantity of loanable funds, investment, or the equilibrium real interest rate; page 678.

4. The decision to finance a college education using loans is very similar to a firm's decision to finance a piece of capital equipment using loans. In both cases, the payoff from the purchase occurs throughout the future and the payments for the purchase are also made throughout the future. A business, of course, looks at the expected future profit from the capital before the business buys it. Similarly, one of the benefits from a college education is higher future income. These are reasons why a college education is said to help develop a person's "human capital."

Additional Exercises (also in MyEconLab Test A)

1. The real interest rate is 6 percent, and the quantity of loanable funds, private saving, and investment are all $8.5 trillion. There is no crowding out; page 672.

2. The equilibrium real interest rate becomes 7 percent. The equilibrium quantity of loanable funds is $9.0 trillion, the equilibrium quantity of investment is $8.0 trillion, and the equilibrium quantity of private saving is $9.0 trillion. There is crowding out of $500 billion of investment; pages 677-678.

3. Assuming no Ricardo-Barro effect, the government needs to have a budget surplus of $1 trillion. In this case, the new equilibrium real interest rate is 5 percent, the quantity of investment is $9 trillion, and the quantity of private saving is $8 trillion; pages 676-677.

© 2015 Pearson Education, Inc.

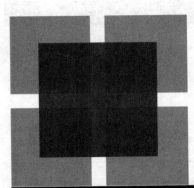

The Monetary System

Chapter

27

CHAPTER CHECKLIST

1 Define money and describe its functions.

Money is any commodity or token that is generally accepted as a means of payment. Money serves as a medium of exchange, a unit of account, and a store of value. Money consists of currency (dollar bills and coins outside of banks) and deposits at banks and other financial institutions. Currency in a bank, credit cards, debit cards, and electronic checks are not money. M1 (currency, traveler's checks, and checkable deposits owned by individuals and businesses) and M2 (M1 plus savings and small time deposits, money market funds and other deposits) are two measures of money.

2 Describe the functions of banks.

Banks (and other financial institutions) accept deposits and provide services that enable payments to be made and received. Banks profit by making loans at a higher interest rate than the interest rate paid on deposits. A bank's reserves are the currency in its vault and the balance in its reserve account at a Federal Reserve Bank. The Fed sets the required reserve ratio, the minimum percentage of deposits that must be held as reserves. The federal funds rate is the interest rate on interbank loans.

3 Describe the functions of the Federal Reserve System (the Fed).

The Federal Reserve System is the U.S. central bank. The Federal Open Market Committee is the Fed's main policy-making committee. The Fed has four policy tools: required reserve ratios, discount rate (the interest rate at which the Fed stands ready to lend reserves to commercial banks), open market operations (purchase or sale of government securities by the Fed in the open market), and extraordinary crisis measures (quantitative easing, credit easing [the Fed buys private securities], and operation twist). The monetary base is the sum of coins, Federal Reserve notes, and banks' reserves held at the Fed.

4 Explain how the banking system creates money and how the Fed controls the quantity of money.

When a bank makes a loan, it deposits the loan in the borrower's checkable deposit, thereby creating money. To spend the loan, the borrower writes a check. The loaning bank loses deposits and reserves when the check clears. The bank in which the check is deposited gains the reserves and deposits. It now has excess reserves, which it lends. This process eventually concludes because at each round the change in excess reserves shrinks. Open market operations change the quantity of money. If the Fed buys government securities, banks' excess reserves increase, banks lend the excess reserves, new deposits are created, and the quantity of money increases. If the Fed sells government securities, the reverse occurs. The monetary base changes by the amount of the open market operation. The money multiplier is the number by which a change in the monetary base is multiplied to find the change in the quantity of money; it equals $(1 + C/D) \div (R/D + C/D)$ where C is currency, D is deposits and R is reserves so C/D is the currency drain ratio and R/D is the desired reserve ratio.

© 2015 Pearson Education, Inc.

YOUR AP TEST HINTS

AP Topics

Topic on your AP test	What to Know	Corresponding textbook section
Money	What it is; functions of money; measures	Checkpoint 27.1
Banking system	The functions of the banking system	Checkpoint 27.2
Federal Reserve System	Organization; open market operations; policy tools	Checkpoint 27.3
Money creation	Process by which banks create money; required reserves and excess reserves; money multiplier	Checkpoint 27.4

AP Vocabulary Covered

Terms	What to Know	Text Sections
Money	Any commodity or token that is generally accepted as a means of payment (a method of settling a debt)	Checkpoint 27.1, p. 686
Medium of payment	A method of settling a debt	Checkpoint 27.1, p. 686
Medium of exchange	An object accepted in return for goods or services	Checkpoint 27.1, p. 687
Barter	Direct exchanges of goods and services for other goods and services without the use of money	Checkpoint 27.1, p. 687
Fiat money	Money set in value by government decree	Checkpoint 27.1, p. 688
Currency	Money as notes of bills and coins	Checkpoint 27.1, p. 688
M1	Currency, traveler's checks, and checkable deposits owned by individuals and businesses	Checkpoint 27.1, p. 688
M2	M1 plus savings deposits and small time deposits, money market funds, and other deposits	Checkpoint 27.1, p. 688
Commercial bank	A firm chartered to make loans and accept deposits	Checkpoint 27.2, p. 692
Reserves	A bank's reserves are the currency held in its vaults and its balance held with the Federal Reserve	Checkpoint 27.2, p. 693
Federal funds rate	The interest rate banks charge each other for overnight loans; targeted by the Federal Reserve	Checkpoint 27.2, p. 694
The Federal Reserve System, (the Fed)	The central bank of the U.S.; consists of 12 regional Federal Reserve banks; conducts the nation's monetary policy	Checkpoint 27.3, p. 697
Federal Open Market Committee (FOMC)	The Fed's monetary policy making committee; consists of 5 (of 12) Presidents of Federal Reserve banks and the 7 members of the Board of Governors	Checkpoint 27.3, p. 698
Discount rate	The interest rate at which the Fed lends reserves to banks	Checkpoint 27.3, p. 699
Open market operations	The purchase or sale of securities by the Fed on the open market; run by the New York Fed Bank	Checkpoint 27.3, p. 699
Monetary base	The sum of coins, Federal Reserve notes, and banks' reserves held at the Fed	Checkpoint 27.3, p. 699
Excess reserve	Actual reserves minus desired reserves; if desired reserves equal actual reserves, then excess reserves equal actual reserves minus required reserves	Checkpoint 27.4, p. 702
Money multiplier	Number by which a change in the monetary base is multiplied to calculate the change in money	Checkpoint 27.4, p. 707

© 2015 Pearson Education, Inc.

Extra AP Materials

- The AP test does not use the concept of *desired reserves*. Students can assume that banks *desired reserves* will equal the *required reserves* and the remaining reserves will all be *excess reserves*.
- The *money multiplier* is used often on the test. Students must know that the calculation is (1/required reserve ratio). Take the excess reserves to be used for loans, multiply by the *money multiplier* and "new" demand deposit amounts are created for the banking system.
- Students must know that deposits into a checking account become a bank's "demand deposits" and are a bank liability. The new deposits equal the bank's new total reserves and are a bank asset. Total reserves are divided into required reserves and excess reserves.

CHECKPOINT 27.1

■ **Define money and describe its functions.**

Quick Review

- *M1* M1 consists of currency held by individuals and businesses, traveler's checks, and checkable deposits owned by individuals and businesses. Currency inside banks is not counted as part of M1.
- *M2* M2 consists of M1 plus savings deposits and small time deposits, money market funds, and other deposits.

Additional Practice Problems 27.1

1. You go to the bank and withdraw $200 from your checking account. You keep $100 in cash and deposit the other $100 in your savings account. What is the change in M1? What is the change in M2?

2. Janice goes to her bank's website and transfers $300 from her checking account to her savings account. What is the change in M1? What is the change in M2

3. In September 2009, currency held by individuals and businesses and traveler's checks were $863 billion; checkable deposits owned by individuals and businesses were $787 billion; savings deposits were $4,531 billion; small time deposits were $1,218 billion; and money market funds and other deposits were $899 billion.
   a. What was M1 in September 2009?
   b. What was M2 in September 2009?

Solutions to Additional Practice Problems 27.1

1. Your checking account decreased by $200, your currency increased by $100, and your savings account increased by $100. M1, which includes your currency and your checkable deposit, is changed by the decrease in the checking account and the increase in currency. The net effect on M1 is −$200 + $100 = −$100, that is, M1 decreases by $100. M2, which includes your currency, your checkable deposits, and your savings account, does not change. The change in your checkable deposits, −$200, is balanced by the change in your currency, +$100, and the change in your savings account, +100. There was no change in M2.

2. M1 decreases by $300. While the funds were in Janice's checking account, they were part of M1. But once they are transferred to her savings account, they are no longer part of M1. M2 does not change. The $300 was part of M2 when it was in Janice's checking account because funds in checking accounts are part of M1 and all of M1 is in M2. And, funds in savings accounts are also part of M2. So switching funds from a checking account to a savings account does not change M2.

3a. M1 is the sum of currency, traveler's checks, and checkable deposits owned by individuals and businesses. So, M1 equals $863 billion + $787 billion, which is $1,650 billion.

3b. M2 equals M1 plus savings deposits, small time deposits, and money market funds and other deposits. So M2 equals $1,650 billion + $4,531 billion + $1,218 billion + $899 billion, which is $8,298 billion.

© 2015 Pearson Education, Inc.

■ AP Self Test 27.1

True or false

1. Using money as a medium of exchange is called barter.

2. Prices in terms of money reflect money's role as a unit of account.

3. Currency is money but checkable deposits at banks are not money.

4. M1 and M2 are official measures of money.

5. A debit card is not money.

Multiple choice

1. Which of the following best defines what money is now and what it has been in the past?
   a. currency
   b. currency plus checking deposits
   c. currency plus credit cards
   d. anything accepted as a means of payment
   e. anything used as a store of value

2. Which of the following is not a function of money?
   i. unit of account
   ii. store of value
   iii. unit of debt
   a. i only.
   b. ii only.
   c. iii only.
   d. Both ii and iii.
   e. Both i and ii.

3. Barter is
   a. the exchange of goods and services for money.
   b. the pricing of goods and services with one agreed upon standard.
   c. the exchange of goods and services directly for other goods and services.
   d. a generally accepted means of payment.
   e. storing money for use at a later date.

4. If someone buries money in a tin can beneath a tree, the money is functioning as a
   a. medium of exchange.
   b. unit of account.
   c. means of payment.
   d. store of value.
   e. bartering tool.

5. Which of the following counts as part of M1?
   a. $5,000 worth of gold
   b. $5,000 worth of government bonds
   c. $5,000 in a checking account
   d. $5,000 credit line on a credit card
   e. $5,000 of real estate

6. M2 equals
   a. M1 and is just another name for currency outside of banks.
   b. M1 plus savings deposits, small time deposits, and money market fund deposits.
   c. M1 minus traveler's checks because they are not really money.
   d. currency plus savings deposits, all time deposits, and money market funds and other deposits.
   e. M1 plus savings deposits and small time deposits minus money market fund deposits.

7. If currency outside of banks is $800 billion; traveler's checks are $10 billion; checkable deposits owned by individuals and businesses are $700 billion; savings deposits are $4,000 billion; small time deposits are $1,000 billion; and money market funds and other deposits are $800 billion, then M1 equals _____ billion.
   a. $7,310
   b. $5,800
   c. $2,510
   d. $1,510
   e. $710

© 2015 Pearson Education, Inc.

8. Credit cards, debit cards, and e-checks are
   a. always counted as money.
   b. not money.
   c. sometimes counted as money, depending on how they are used.
   d. sometimes counted as money, depending on what is purchased.
   e. sometimes counted as money, depending on what measure of money is being used.

Short Response Questions

1. Why was it possible at one time to use whale's teeth as money?

2. Why is currency money?

3. Why are e-checks not money?

Long Response Questions

1. What are the functions of money?

2. In January 2005, currency held by individuals and businesses was $699.6 billion; traveler's checks were $7.5 billion; checkable deposits owned by individuals and businesses were $649.2 billion; savings deposits were $3,544.7 billion; small time deposits were $824.5 billion; and money market funds and other deposits were $711.4 billion.
   a. What was M1 in January 2005?
   b. What was M2 in January 2005?

3. Some parts of M2 are not money. Why are these parts included in M2?

Additional Exercises (also in MyEconLab Test A)

1. Which of the following items are money in the United States today?
   a. Checkable deposits at First Boston Bank
   b. General Motors stock held by individuals
   c. A Sacagawea dollar coin
   d. U.S. government securities
   e. Money market funds

2. Sara withdraws $2,000 from her time deposit account at Bank of America, keeps $100 in cash, and deposits the balance in her checking account at Citibank. What are the immediate changes in M1 and M2?

3. In March 2004, currency outside of banks was $666.8 billion; traveler's checks in circulation were $7.8 billion; checkable deposits owned by individuals and businesses were $651.1 billion; savings deposits were $3,279.1 billion; time deposits were $802.7 billion; and money market funds and other deposits were $760.5 billion. Calculate M1 and M2 in March 2004.

CHECKPOINT 27.2

■ Describe the functions of banks.

Quick Review

- *Reserves* A bank's reserves consist of the currency in its vault plus the balance on its reserve account at a Federal Reserve Bank.

Additional Practice Problems 27.2

1. The Acme Bank just sold $100 in securities in exchange for a $100 bill. It made a $50 loan, and the borrower left with the cash. It also accepted a $60 cash deposit.
   a. How have the bank's reserves changed as a result of all these actions?
   b. How have its deposits changed?

2. A bank has the following deposits and assets: $300 in checkable deposits, $800 in savings deposits, $900 in small time deposits, $1,000 in loans to businesses, $950 in government securities, $20 in currency, and $30 in its reserve account at the Fed. Calculate the bank's:
   a. Total deposits
   b. Deposits that are part of M1
   c. Deposits that are part of M2
   d. Reserves
   e. What is the ratio of the bank's reserves to its deposits?

Solutions to Additional Practice Problems 27.2

1a. The $100 sale of securities adds $100 to reserves. The $50 loan which the borrower then withdrew as cash removes $50 from the bank and out of its reserves, and the $60 deposit adds to reserves. The net result is +$100 − $50 + $60, which is +$110. Acme has $110 more in reserves.

© 2015 Pearson Education, Inc.

1b. The $60 deposit is the only transaction that affects its deposits, so deposits rise by $60.

2a. Total deposits are the sum of checkable deposits, $300, savings deposits, $800, and small time deposits, $900, which equals a total of $2,000.

2b. The only deposits that are part of M1 are checkable deposits, $300.

2c. All of the bank's deposits are part of M2, so deposits that are part of M2 are $2,000.

2d. Reserves are the currency in the bank's vault plus the balance on its reserve account at a Federal Reserve Bank. Reserves are $20 + $30, which equals $50.

2e. The ratio of reserves to deposits is $50 ÷ $2,000, which equals 2.5 percent.

■ AP Self Test 27.2

True or false

1. A commercial bank accepts checkable deposits, savings deposits, and time deposits.

2. A commercial bank maximizes its stockholders' wealth by refusing to make any risky loans.

3. When a credit union has excess reserves, it makes loans to its members at an interest rate called the federal funds rate.

Multiple choice

1. A commercial bank's main goal is to
   a. provide loans to its customers.
   b. maximize the wealth of its stockholders.
   c. help the government when it needs money.
   d. lend money to the Federal Reserve banks.
   e. open checking and savings accounts.

2. A commercial bank's reserves are
   a. bonds issued by the U.S. government that are very safe.
   b. the provision of funds to businesses and individuals.
   c. currency in its vault plus the balance on its reserve account at a Federal Reserve Bank.
   d. savings and time deposits.
   e. its loans.

3. Which of the following lists includes only banks' assets?
   a. liquid assets, loans, securities, and reserves.
   b. reserves, savings deposits, securities, and loans.
   c. reserves, securities, and savings deposits
   d. securities, reserves, checkable deposits, and liquid assets.
   e. reserves, checkable deposits, and loans.

4. A bank has $400 in checkable deposits, $800 in savings deposits, $700 in time deposits, $900 in loans to businesses, $300 in outstanding credit card balances, $500 in government securities, $10 in currency in its vault, and $20 in deposits at the Fed. The bank's deposits that are part of M1 equal
   a. $1,900.
   b. $400.
   c. $1,210.
   d. $530.
   e. $410.

5. Which of the following accepts deposits from and/or sell shares to the general public?
   i. money market funds
   ii. thrift institutions
   iii. commercial banks
   a. i only.
   b. ii only.
   c. iii only.
   d. ii and iii.
   e. i, ii, and iii.

© 2015 Pearson Education, Inc.

6. Which of the following is a thrift institution?
   a. a savings and loan association
   b. a money market fund
   c. a commercial bank
   d. a loan institution
   e. the Federal Reserve

Short Response Question

1. What is the federal funds rate? Why is it important?

Long Response Question

1. What are a bank's reserves? How does a bank use its account at the Federal Reserve Bank?

Additional Exercises (also in MyEconLab Test A)

1. Explain how a bank makes a profit.

A savings and loan association (S&L) has $550 in checkable deposits, $1,600 in home loans, $900 in savings deposits, $600 in government securities, $800 in time deposits, $50 in currency, and no deposit at the Fed. Use this information to answer Exercises 2, 3, and 4.

2. Calculate the S&L's total deposits, deposits that are part of M1, and deposits that are part of M2.

3. Calculate the S&L's loans and reserves.

4. On which items does the S&L pay interest and on which items does it receive interest?

CHECKPOINT 27.3

■ Describe the functions of the Federal Reserve System (the Fed).

Quick Review

- *Federal Reserve System* The Federal Reserve System is the central bank of the United States.

Additional Practice Problems 27.3

1. What are required reserve ratios?

2. What is the discount rate?

3. In August, 2005 Federal Reserve notes and coins were $785 billion, and banks' reserves at the Fed were $9 billion, the gold stock was $11 billion, and the Fed owned $742 billion of government securities. What did the monetary base equal?

Solutions to Additional Practice Problems 27.3

1. Banks are required by law to hold a certain fraction of their deposits as reserves. The Federal Reserve determines what fraction banks must hold as reserves. These fractions are called the banks' required reserve ratios.

2. Banks can borrow reserves from the Federal Reserve. The interest rate they pay on these loans is the discount rate.

3. The monetary base is the sum of the coins and Federal Reserve notes plus banks' reserves at the Fed. In this case the monetary base equals $785 billion + $9 billion, which is $794 billion.

■ AP Self Test 27.3

True or false

1. The Federal Reserve System is the central bank of the United States.

2. An open market operation is the purchase or sale of government securities by the Federal Reserve from the U.S. government.

3. If banks use $1 million of reserves to buy $1 million worth of newly printed bank notes from the Fed, the monetary base does not change.

Multiple choice

1. Regulating the amount of money in the United States is one of the most important responsibilities of the
   a. State Department.
   b. state governments.
   c. Treasury Department.
   d. Federal Reserve.
   e. U.S. Mint.

2. The Fed's Board of Governors has
   a. 12 members appointed by the president of the United States.
   b. 12 members elected by the public.
   c. seven members appointed by the president of the United States.
   d. seven members elected by the public.
   e. seven members appointed to life terms.

© 2015 Pearson Education, Inc.

3. The Fed's policy tools include
   a. required reserve ratios, the discount rate, open market operations, and extraordinary crisis measures.
   b. holding deposits for the U.S. government, reserve requirements, and the discount rate.
   c. setting regulations for lending standards and extraordinary crisis measures.
   d. supervision of the banking system and buying and selling commercial banks.
   e. required reserve ratios, income tax rates, and open market operations.

4. The Fed's policy is determined by the
   a. Federal Open Market Committee.
   b. Executive Council to the Governor.
   c. Regional Federal Reserve Banks.
   d. Board of Governors.
   e. Federal Monetary Policy Committee.

5. The minimum percent of deposits that banks must hold is determined by the
   a. interest rate.
   b. discount rate.
   c. required reserve ratio.
   d. federal funds rate.
   e. ratio of M2 to M1.

6. The discount rate is the interest rate that
   a. commercial banks charge their customers.
   b. commercial banks charge each other for the loan of reserves.
   c. the Fed charges the government for loans.
   d. the Fed charges commercial banks when it loans reserves to the banks.
   e. the Fed pays commercial banks on their reserves held at the Fed.

7. The monetary base is the
   a. minimum reserves banks must hold to cover any losses from unpaid loans.
   b. sum of coins, Federal Reserve notes, and banks' reserves at the Fed.
   c. sum of gold and foreign exchange held by the Fed.
   d. sum of government securities and loans to banks held by the Fed.
   e. sum of coins, required reserves, and bank loans.

8. If Federal Reserve notes and coins are $765 billion, and banks' reserves at the Fed are $8 billion, the gold stock is $11 billion, and the Fed owns $725 billion of government securities, what does the monetary base equal?
   a. $765 billion
   b. $773 billion
   c. $776 billion
   d. $744 billion
   e. $1,509 billion

9. If the Federal Reserve ____ the required reserve ratio, the interest rate ____.
   a. lowers; rises
   b. lowers; falls
   c. raises; does not change
   d. raises; falls
   e. Not enough information is given because the effect depends also on the size of the monetary base.

Short Response Questions

1. How many people are on the Board of Governors of the Federal Reserve System? How are they selected?

2. What is the monetary base?

Long Response Questions

1. What is the FOMC and who are its members?

2. Suppose that banks' deposits are $600 billion and that the required reserve ratio is 10 percent.
   a. What is the minimum amount of reserves banks must hold?
   b. Suppose the Federal Reserve lowers the required reserve ratio to 8 percent. Now what is the minimum amount of reserves banks must hold?
   c. Suppose the Federal Reserve raises the required reserve ratio to 12 percent. Now what is the minimum amount of reserves banks must hold?

3. What is the difference between open market operations and quantitative easing?

© 2015 Pearson Education, Inc.

Additional Exercises (also in MyEconLab Test A)

1. What is a central bank and what is the central bank in the United States?

2. Suppose that in September 2019, the monetary base in the United States was $750 billion, Federal Reserve notes were $630 billion, and the quantity of coins was $40 billion. What were the commercial banks' deposits at the Fed?

3. Suppose that in December 2019, the monetary base in Canada was $85 billion, Bank of Canada notes were $75 billion, and the quantity of coins was $3 billion. What were the reserve deposits of the Canadian banks at the Bank of Canada?

CHECKPOINT 27.4

■ **Explain how the banking system creates money and how the Fed controls the quantity of money.**

Quick Review

- *Excess reserves* Excess reserves equal actual reserves minus desired reserves.
- *Money multiplier* The number by which a change in the monetary base is multiplied to find the resulting change in the quantity of money.

Additional Practice Problems 27.4

1. The desired reserve ratio is 0.05 and banks have no excess reserves. Katie deposits $500 in currency in her bank. Calculate:
   a. The change in the bank's reserves as soon as Katie makes the deposit.
   b. The bank's excess reserves as soon as Katie makes the deposit.
   c. The maximum amount that Katie's bank can loan.

2. If the desired reserve ratio is 10 percent and the currency drain ratio is 30 percent of deposits, what is the size of the money multiplier? By how much will a $10 billion increase in the monetary base change the quantity of money?

3. If the desired reserve ratio is 20 percent and the currency drain ratio is 30 percent of deposits, what is the size of the money multiplier? By how much will a $10 billion increase in the monetary base change the quantity of money?

4. Using Problems 2 and 3, what is the effect on the money multiplier when the desired reserve ratio rises?

Solutions to Additional Practice Problems 27.4

1a. The new deposit of $500 increases the bank's actual reserves by $500.

1b. The bank wants to keep 5 percent of deposits as reserves. So desired reserves increase by 5 percent of the deposit, or ($500) × (0.05), which is $25. As a result, excess reserves, which are actual reserves minus desired reserves, increase by $500 − $25, which is $475.

1c. The crucial point to keep in mind is that banks can loan their excess reserves in order to boost their revenue and profit. So Katie's bank can loan a maximum of $475.

2. The money multiplier = $(1 + C/D) \div (R/D + C/D)$ where C/D is the currency drain ratio and R/D is the desired reserve ratio. So the money multiplier equals $(1 + 0.3) \div (0.1 + 0.3)$, which is 3.25. With this money multiplier, a $10 billion increase in the monetary base increases the quantity of money by 3.25 × $10 billion, or $32.5 billion.

3. The money multiplier = $(1 + C/D) \div (R/D + C/D)$ where C/D is the currency drain ratio and R/D is the desired reserve ratio. The money multiplier equals $(1 + 0.3) \div (0.2 + 0.3)$, which is 2.6. A $10 billion increase in the monetary base increases the quantity of money by 2.6 × $10 billion, or $26 billion.

4. An increase in the desired reserve ratio shrinks the size of the money multiplier.

■ **AP Self Test 27.4**

True or false

1. When a bank increases its loans, it creates money.

© 2015 Pearson Education, Inc.

2. The desired reserve ratio has no effect on the amount of money banks can create.

3. When the Fed buys securities in an open market operation, it pays for them with newly created bank reserves.

4. When the Fed buys government securities, the effect on the money supply depends on whether the Fed buys the securities from a bank or the general public.

5. When the Fed sells government securities, it decreases the quantity of banks' reserves.

6. If the Fed increases the monetary base by $1 billion, the ultimate increase in the quantity of money will be less than $1 billion.

7. The larger the currency drain ratio, the larger the money multiplier.

8. If the currency drain ratio is 20 percent and the desired reserve ratio is 10 percent, the money multiplier is 1.675.

Multiple choice

1. Excess reserves are the
   a. same as the required reserves.
   b. amount of reserves the Fed requires banks to hold.
   c. amount of reserves held above what is desired.
   d. amount of reserves a bank holds at the Fed.
   e. amount of reserves banks keep in their vaults.

2. Banks can make loans up to an amount equal to their
   a. total deposits.
   b. total reserves.
   c. required reserves.
   d. excess reserves.
   e. total government securities.

3. If the Fed buys government securities, then
   a. the quantity of money is not changed, just its composition.
   b. new bank reserves are created.
   c. the quantity of money decreases.
   d. bank reserves are destroyed.
   e. banks' excess reserves decrease.

4. The Citizens First Bank sells $100,000 of government securities to the Fed. This sale immediately
   a. decreases the quantity of money.
   b. decreases the bank's checkable deposits.
   c. increases the bank's reserves.
   d. decreases the bank's assets.
   e. increases the bank's required reserves.

5. When the Fed sells securities in an open market operation
   a. the monetary base increases and the quantity of money increases.
   b. the monetary base does not change.
   c. only commercial banks can be buyers.
   d. the monetary base does not change.
   e. buyers pay for the securities with money and bank reserves.

6. When the Fed conducts an open market purchase, the first round changes in the money creation process are that excess reserves ____, bank deposits ____, and the quantity of money ____.
   a. decreases; decreases; decrease
   b. increases; do not change; increase
   c. decreases; increases; does not change
   d. do not change; increases; increase
   e. increase; increase; increases

7. The money multiplier is used to determine how much the
   a. monetary base increases when the Fed purchases government securities.
   b. quantity of money increases when the monetary base increases.
   c. monetary base increases when the quantity of money increases.
   d. quantity of money increases when the required reserve ratio increases.
   e. monetary base increases when the Fed sells government securities.

8. A currency drain is cash ____ and has ____ effect on the money multiplier.
   a. draining into the banks; no
   b. draining into the banks; an
   c. held outside the banks; an
   d. held at the Fed; an
   e. held as reserves; no

© 2015 Pearson Education, Inc.

Short Response Questions

Round	Increase in deposits (dollars)	Increase in currency (dollars)	Increase in reserves (dollars)	Increase in excess reserves (dollars)
A			1,000	1,000
B	___	___	___	___
C	___	___	___	___
D	___	___	___	___

1. Suppose the Fed buys $1,000 of government securities from Hayward National Bank. The desired reserve ratio is 10 percent and the currency drain ratio is 25 percent of deposits. Suppose that all banks loan all of their excess reserves. Complete the above table. Calculate the total increase in deposits and currency following the first four rounds of the multiplier process.

Round	Increase in deposits (dollars)	Increase in currency (dollars)	Increase in reserves (dollars)	Increase in excess reserves (dollars)
A			1,000	1,000
B	___	___	___	___
C	___	___	___	___
D	___	___	___	___

2. Suppose the Fed buys $1,000 of government securities from Fremont National Bank. The desired reserve ratio is 10 percent and the currency drain ratio is 100 percent of deposits. Suppose that all banks loan all of their excess reserves. Complete the above table. Calculate the total increase in deposits and currency following the first four rounds of the multiplier process.

3. In which question, 1 or 2, was the increase in the quantity of money largest after four rounds?

Long Response Questions

1. Calculate the money multiplier when the desired reserve ratio is 10 percent and the currency drain ratio is 20 percent of deposits. Calculate the money multiplier when the desired reserve ratio is 10 percent and the currency drain ratio is 60 percent of deposits. As the currency drain ratio increases, what happens to the magnitude of the money multiplier?

2. Calculate the money multiplier when the desired reserve ratio is 10 percent and the currency drain ratio is 20 percent of deposits. Calculate the money multiplier when the desired reserve ratio is 20 percent and the currency drain ratio is 20 percent of deposits. As the desired reserve ratio increases, what happens to the magnitude of the money multiplier?

3. Why does an increase in the desired reserve ratio or in the currency drain ratio decrease the magnitude of the money multiplier?

4. The Eye on Your Life talks about your role in creating money. Money also will play a role in your life if you travel because nations often have different moneys. But the U.S. dollar is often accepted, especially in less developed nations. If you take some dollars with you when you travel and then spend a U.S. dollar bill in another nation, how does that affect the amount of U.S. M1?

Additional Exercises (also in MyEconLab Test A)

1. Your bank manager tells you that she doesn't create money, she just lends what is deposited. Explain why she is wrong and how she creates money.

2. If the Fed makes an open market sale of $1 million of securities, what initial changes occur in the economy and what is the process by which the quantity of money in the economy changes?

3. If the Fed makes an open market sale of $1 million of securities, by how much does the quantity of money change and what is the magnitude of the money multiplier?

© 2015 Pearson Education, Inc.

SELF TEST ANSWERS

■ AP Self Test 27.1

True or false
1. False; page 687
2. True; page 687
3. False; page 688
4. True; page 688
5. True; page 690

Multiple choice
1. d; page 686
2. c; page 686
3. c; page 687
4. d; page 687
5. c; page 688
6. b; page 688
7. d; page 689
8. b; pages 689-690

Short Response Questions
1. It was possible to use whale's teeth as money because whale's teeth were generally accepted as a means of payment. At one time, most people were willing to trade goods and services in exchange for whale's teeth; pages 686-687.
2. Currency is money because it is generally accepted as a means of payment. It is generally accepted because the government has declared that currency is money, so that currency is fiat money; page 688.
3. E-checks are not money because they are instructions to transfer money from one person's deposit account to another person's deposit account; page 690.

Long Response Questions
1. Money has three functions. It is a medium of exchange, an object that is generally accepted in return for goods and services. It is a unit of account, an agreed-upon measure for stating the prices of goods and services. And it is a store of value, a commodity or token that can be held and exchanged at a later date for goods and services; pages 686-687.

2. a. M1 is the sum of currency, traveler's checks, and checkable deposits owned by individuals and businesses. So, M1 equals $699.6 billion + $7.5 billion + $649.2 billion, which is $1,356.3 billion; pages 688-689.
   b. M2 equals M1 plus savings deposits, small time deposits, and money market funds and other deposits. So M2 equals $1,356.3 billion + $3,544.7 billion + $824.5 billion + $711.4 billion, which is $6,436.9 billion; pages 688-689.
3. Time deposits, money market funds, and some of the savings deposits included in M2 are not money. They are not money because they are not a means of payment. They are included in M2 because they are very easily converted into money; page 689.

Additional Exercises (also in MyEconLab Test A)
1. a. Checkable deposits are money; page 688.
   b. General Motors stock is not money because it is not a medium of exchange; page 687.
   c. The Sacagawea dollar coin is money; page 688.
   d. U.S. government securities are not money because they are not a medium of exchange; page 687.
   e. Money market funds are not money. They are not a means of payment; page 687.
2. M1 immediately rises by the full amount of the $2,000 withdrawal. The reason is that before, this $2,000 was only a part of M2 not M1. Now because both cash and checkable accounts are part of M1, M1 rises by $2,000. However, because M2 includes everything that is a part of M1, M2 is left unchanged; page 688.
3. M1 = currency + traveler's checks + checkable deposits = $666.8 billion + $7.8 billion + $651.1 billion = $1,325.7 billion; page 688.
   M2 = M1 + saving deposits + time deposits + money market funds = $1,325.7 billion + $3,279.1 billion + $802.7 billion + $760.5 billion = $6,168.0 billion; page 688.

© 2015 Pearson Education, Inc.

■ AP Self Test 27.2

True or false

1. True; page 692
2. False; page 693
3. False; page 694

Multiple choice

1. b; page 693
2. c; page 693
3. a; page 694
4. b; page 694
5. e; pages 692, 695
6. a; page 695

Short Response Question

1. The federal funds rate is the interest rate on one bank's loans to another. It is important because the Federal Reserve targets it; page 692.

Long Response Question

1. A bank's reserves are the currency in its vault plus the balance on its reserve account at a Federal Reserve Bank. A bank uses its account at the Fed to receive and make payments to other banks and to obtain currency; page 693.

Additional Exercises (also in MyEconLab Test A)

1. A bank makes a profit by making loans at a higher interest rate than the interest rate it pays on its deposits; page 693.

2. Total deposits = checkable deposits + savings deposits + time deposits = $550 + $900 + $800 = $2,250. The only deposits that are part of M1 are the checking deposits of $550. The entire $2,250 of deposits are part of M2; page 688.

3. Total loans are $1,600. Reserves are deposits at the Fed plus currency. Because there are no reserves at the Fed, the reserves equal currency, which is $50; page 693.

4. The S&L pays interest on checking deposits, on savings deposits, and on time deposits. It receives interest on the home loans and government securities; pages 694-695.

■ AP Self Test 27.3

True or false

1. True; page 697
2. False; page 699
3. True; page 699

Multiple choice

1. d; page 697
2. c; page 698
3. a; page 698
4. a; page 698
5. c; page 698
6. d; page 699
7. b; page 699
8. b; page 699
9. b; page 699

Short Response Questions

1. There are seven members on the Board of Governors of the Federal Reserve System. They are appointed by the president of the United States and confirmed by the U.S. Senate; page 698.

2. The monetary base is the sum of coins, Federal Reserve notes, and banks' reserves at the Federal Reserve; page 699.

Long Response Questions

1. The FOMC is the Federal Open Market Committee and it is the main policy-making committee of the Federal Reserve. The members are the seven members of the Board of Governors, the president of the Federal Reserve Bank of New York, and, on an annual rotating basis, four presidents of the other regional Federal Reserve banks; page 698.

2. a. If the required reserve ratio is 10 percent, banks must keep ($600 billion × 0.10) = $60 billion as reserves; page 698.

   b. If the required reserve ratio is lowered to 8 percent, banks must keep ($600 billion × 0.08) = $48 billion as reserves. A decrease in the required reserve ratio decreases the total amount of reserves banks must keep; page 698.

© 2015 Pearson Education, Inc.

c. If the required reserve ratio is raised to 12 percent, banks must keep ($600 billion × 0.12) = $72 billion as reserves. An increase in the required reserve ratio increases the total amount of reserves banks must keep page 698.

3. The difference between open market operations and quantitative easing is mainly one of degree. An open market operation is the purchase or sale of U.S. government securities by the Federal Reserve in the open market. When the Fed buys securities, it creates reserves. Quantitative easing refers to times when the Fed conducts large-scale open market operations, at very low federal funds rates. When the Fed uses quantitative easing it might also buy private securities as well as government securities; page 699.

Additional Exercises (also in MyEconLab Test A)

1. A central bank is a public authority that provides banking services to banks and regulates financial institutions and markets. The central bank of the United States is the Federal Reserve System; page 697.

2. The monetary base is the sum of coins, Federal Reserve notes, and banks' reserves at the Federal Reserve. In the question, the monetary base is $750 billion, Federal Reserve notes are $630 billion, and coins are $40 billion. Banks' deposits at the Fed equal $80 billion, which is the monetary base minus Federal Reserve notes and coins; page 699.

3. Similar to the previous exercise, reserves of the Canadian banks at the Bank of Canada equal $7 billion, the monetary base minus Bank of Canada notes and coins; page 699.

■ AP Self Test 27.4

True or false

1. True; page 701
2. False; page 702
3. True; pages 703-706
4. False; pages 704-705
5. True; page 706
6. False; pages 706-707

7. False; page 709
8. False; page 709

Multiple choice

1. c; page 702
2. d; page 702
3. b; page 704
4. c; page 704
5. e; page 706
6. e; page 706
7. b; page 707
8. c; pages 707-709

Short Response Questions

Round	Increase in deposits (dollars)	Increase in currency (dollars)	Increase in reserves (dollars)	Increase in excess reserves (dollars)
A			1,000.00	1,000.00
B	800.00	200.00	800.00	720.00
C	576.00	144.00	576.00	518.40
D	414.72	103.68	414.72	373.25

1. The completed table is above. After four rounds, currency increases by $447.68, deposits increase by $1,790.72, and the quantity of money increases by the sum of the increase in currency and the increase in deposits, which is $2,238.40; page 706.

Round	Increase in deposits (dollars)	Increase in currency (dollars)	Increase in reserves (dollars)	Increase in excess reserves (dollars)
A			1,000	1,000
B	500.00	500.00	500.00	450.00
C	225.00	225.00	225.00	202.50
D	101.25	101.25	101.25	91.13

2. The completed table is above. After four rounds, currency increases by $826.25, deposits increase by $826.25, and the quantity of money increases by the sum of the increase in currency and the increase in deposits, which is $1,652.50; page 706.

3. The increase in the quantity of money is greater when the currency drain is smaller, in question 1; page 709.

© 2015 Pearson Education, Inc.

Long Response Questions

1. The money multiplier = $(1 + C/D) \div (R/D + C/D)$ where C/D is the currency drain ratio and R/D is the desired reserve ratio. The money multiplier for the first part of the question equals $(1 + 0.20) \div (0.20 + 0.10)$, or $(1.20) \div (0.30)$ which is 4.00. The money multiplier for the second part of the question is $(1 + 0.60) \div (0.60 + 0.10)$, or $(1.60) \div (0.70)$, which is 2.29. As the currency drain ratio increases, the magnitude of the money multiplier decreases; pages 708-709.

2. The money multiplier = $(1 + C/D) \div (R/D + C/D)$ where C/D is the currency drain ratio and R/D is the desired reserve ratio. The money multiplier for the first part of the question equals $(1 + 0.20) \div (0.20 + 0.10)$, or $(1.20) \div (0.30)$ which is 4.00. The money multiplier for the second part of the question is $(1 + 0.20) \div (0.20 + 0.20)$, or $(1.20) \div (0.40)$, which is 3.00. As the desired reserve ratio increases, the magnitude of the money multiplier decreases; pages 708-709.

3. The money multiplier exists because of the repeating process of loaning, depositing the proceeds in another bank, and then making another loan. The more each bank loans, the greater the final increase in the quantity of money and the larger the money multiplier. If the desired reserve ratio increases in size, banks will be able to loan less of any additional deposit they receive. And if the currency drain ratio increases, less is deposited in a bank and the bank will be able to loan less. Because an increase in the desired reserve ratio and an increase in the currency drain ratio decrease the amount that can be loaned, both decrease the size of the money multiplier; pages 706-707.

4. If you spend a U.S. dollar bill in another country, there is no effect on the amount of U.S. M1. Indeed, there are estimates that upwards of one half of all U.S. currency is abroad, being used by foreign residents. But the precise amount of U.S. currency abroad is very difficult to measure because often the currency is used for illegal purposes and hence the users are not terribly eager to line up to have their holdings counted by their government!

Additional Exercises (also in MyEconLab Test A)

1. Explain to the bank manager that when the bank makes a loan, it creates a checkable deposit that previously did not exist. Because checkable deposits are part of M1, then we can safely say that making a loan is the equivalent of creating money; page 701.

2. When the Fed sells securities to banks, the Fed receives payment for the securities. If banks directly buy the securities, the payment will be by decreasing the reserves of the banks from to which it sells the securities. If members of the non-bank buy the securities, the Fed will receive payment in the form of a check drawn on the purchaser's bank and the Fed will "cash" the check by decreasing that bank's reserves. In either case, banks have fewer reserves to loan. Banks' excess reserves fall, so banks call in loans, refuse to renew loans, and make fewer new loans. Bank deposits decrease so that the quantity of money decreases. The initial decrease in the quantity of money spreads as people cut back on their purchases so that firms receive less money in exchange. These firms' banks then have fewer reserves, so they must cut loans, and the process circles into another round; page 706.

3. If the Fed makes an open market sale of $1 million of securities, the quantity of money will decrease by more than $1 million. The quantity of money decreases by an amount equal to the initial decrease in reserves ($1 million) multiplied by the money multiplier. The magnitude of the money multiplier is inversely related to the size of the desired reserve ratio and to the currency drain ratio; that is, an increase in either the desired reserve ratio or the currency drain ratio decreases the magnitude of the money multiplier; pages 706, 708.

© 2015 Pearson Education, Inc.

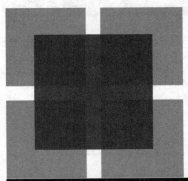

Money, Interest, and Inflation

Chapter 28

Chapter 28 discusses how the quantity of money determines the equilibrium nominal interest rate and then studies the relationship between money and the price level. The effects of money on the economy differ in the short run and the long run. This chapter looks at the short run and long run but not at how the long run is reached—examining these ripple effects is the task of the next two chapters.

1 Explain what determines the demand for money and how the demand for money and the supply of money determine the *nominal* interest rate.

The amount of money that households and firms choose to hold is the quantity of money demanded. The nominal interest rate is the opportunity cost of holding money. The demand for money curve shows the quantity of money demanded at each nominal interest rate. The supply of money is a fixed quantity. Equilibrium in the money market determines the nominal interest rate. In the short run, the Fed changes the nominal interest rate by changing the quantity of money. When the Fed increases the quantity of money, the nominal interest rate falls

2 Explain how in the long run, the quantity of money determines the price level and money growth brings inflation.

In the long run, the value of money adjusts to make the quantity of money demanded equal to the quantity supplied. The price level equals the GDP price index divided by 100, so the value of money is the inverse of the price level, $1/P$. If the price level rises, the value of money falls. The long-run demand for money curve shows the quantity of money demanded at each value of money. In the long run, a change in the quantity of money brings an equal percentage change in the price level. The quantity theory of money is the proposition that when real GDP equals potential GDP, an increase in the quantity of money brings an equal percentage increase in the price level. The equation of exchange shows that the quantity of money multiplied by the velocity of circulation equals nominal GDP. In rates of change, the equation of exchange is money growth + velocity growth equals inflation + real GDP growth. In the long run, other things remaining the same, a change in the growth rate of the quantity of money brings an equal change in the inflation rate. A hyperinflation is inflation at a rate that exceeds 50 percent a month.

3 Identify the costs of inflation and the benefits of a stable value of money.

The four costs of inflation are tax costs, shoe-leather costs, confusion costs, and uncertainty costs. Inflation is a tax. With inflation, households and business lose purchasing power, which is the tax on holding money. Inflation interacts with the income tax to lower saving and investment. Shoe-leather costs are costs that arise from an increase in the amount of running around that people do to try to avoid the losses from the falling value of money. Confusion costs are costs of making errors because of rapidly changing prices. Uncertainty costs arise because long-term planning is difficult, so people have a shorter-term focus. Investment falls and the growth rate slows.

© 2015 Pearson Education, Inc.

YOUR AP TEST HINTS

AP Topics

Topic on your AP test	What to Know	Corresponding textbook section
Demand for money	Demand for money; supply of money; determination of equilibrium *nominal* interest rate	Checkpoint 28.1
Quantity of money	Long run determination of price levels and money growth with inflation	Checkpoint 28.2
Inflation	The cost of inflation and benefits of stable money values	Checkpoint 28.3

AP Vocabulary Covered

Terms	What to Know	Text Sections
Quantity of money demanded	Amount of money held by households and firms	Checkpoint 28.1, p. 717
Nominal to real money	Nominal minus inflation = real, or nominal = real + inflation	Checkpoint 28.1, p. 718
Demand for money	The relationship between the quantity of money demanded and the nominal interest rate	Checkpoint 28.1, p. 718
Supply of money	The quantity of money in the economy; determined by the Fed; a vertical line in the money market figure	Checkpoint 28.1, p. 720
Money market	Equilibrium nominal interest rate sets the quantity of money demanded equal to the quantity supplied; interest rate changes when the Fed changes the quantity of money	Checkpoint 28.2, p. 725
Quantity theory of money	Predicts that when real GDP equals potential GDP an increase in the quantity of money brings an equal percentage increase in the price level	Checkpoint 28.2, p. 728
Velocity of circulation	The average number of times in a year that each dollar of money is used to buy goods and services	Checkpoint 28.2, p. 728
Equation of exchange	The quantity of money multiplied by the velocity of circulation equals the price level multiplied by real GDP; in a formula, $M \times V = P \times Y$	Checkpoint 28.2, p. 729
Hyperinflation	Inflation above 50% per month (over 12,000% per year)	Checkpoint 28.2, p. 732

Extra AP material

- The *demand for money* can be divided into two parts: *transactions demand* and *asset demand*. The transaction demand results from use of money as a medium of exchange. An increase in the real GDP means more transactions are undertaken and so the demand for money increases. The asset demand for money results from using money as a store of value and is influenced by the (nominal) interest rate. A higher interest rate increases the opportunity cost of holding money and thereby decreases the quantity of money demanded.

- The money market figure appears often on the AP test. The key is to show the money supply curve as vertical, and then shift it in response to monetary policy actions of the Federal Reserve. The money demand curve shifts due to changes by consumers and changes in fiscal policy.

- The AP test often uses "Q" instead of "Y" for real GDP in the equation of exchange. Hence the equation of exchange is written on the AP test as $M \times V = P \times Q$ rather than $M \times V = P \times Y$.

- The AP test might ask how the cost of anticipated inflation can be less than the cost of unanticipated inflation. The AP test also frequently focuses on the difference between anticipated infla-

© 2015 Pearson Education, Inc.

tion and unanticipated inflation. Some groups are harmed (or helped) by unanticipated inflation but not by anticipated inflation. For instance, if there is unanticipated inflation, lenders are harmed (because the real interest rate they actually receive is less than what they expected to receive) and borrowers are helped because the real interest rate they actually pay is less than what they expected to pay). But if the inflation is anticipated, the nominal interest rate rises so that lenders are not harmed and borrowers are not helped. Frequently this difference is quite important on the AP test.

- The AP test might ask about types of inflation. Inflation that starts from an increase in aggregate demand is called *demand-pull inflation*; inflation that starts from a decrease in aggregate supply is called *cost-push inflation*. Both types of inflation require increases in the quantity of money to continue.

CHECKPOINT 28.1

■ **Explain what determines the demand for money and how the demand for money and the supply of money determine the *nominal* interest rate.**

Quick Review

- *Shifts in the demand for money curve* When real GDP, the price level, or financial technology change, the demand for money curve shifts.
- *Equilibrium nominal interest rate* The equilibrium nominal interest rate occurs where the demand for money curve intersects the supply curve because at this interest rate the quantity of money demanded equals the quantity supplied.

Additional Practice Problems 28.1

1. The figure shows the money market.
   a. What is the equilibrium nominal interest rate and quantity of money?
   b. Use the figure to show what happens to the interest rate

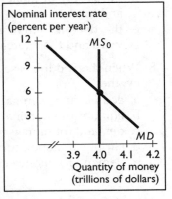

if the Fed increases the quantity of money from $4.0 trillion to $4.1 trillion.

2. Tomorrow all stores will install retinal scanner identification machines, which allow people to make a purchase without having to carry a credit card. What effect will this technological advance have on the demand for money and on the nominal interest rate?

Solutions to Additional Practice Problems 28.1

1a. This problem shows how the nominal interest rate is determined in the money market. As the figure shows, the equilibrium interest rate is 6 percent because this is the interest rate at which the quantity of money demanded equals the quantity of money supplied. The equilibrium quantity of money is $4.0 trillion.

1b. The increase in the quantity of money shifts the supply of money curve rightward, from MS_0 to MS_1. The equilibrium nominal interest rate falls from 6 percent to 3 percent.

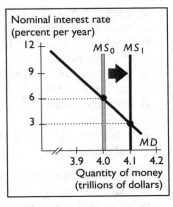

2. This change in technology makes credit purchases more attractive for consumers and merchants. There is an increase in credit purchases and a decrease in the purchases made with money. The demand for money decreases. People want to hold less money than they are actually holding. They buy bonds. The price of a bond rises and the nominal interest rate falls.

© 2015 Pearson Education, Inc.

■ AP Self Test 28.1

True or false

1. The real interest rate is the opportunity cost of holding money.

2. An increase in real GDP decreases the demand for money.

3. If the price of a government bond rises, the interest rate on the bond rises.

4. When the interest rate is above its equilibrium level, people buy bonds and the interest rate falls.

5. An increase in the quantity of money lowers the interest rate.

Multiple choice

1. The quantity of money demanded
   a. is infinite.
   b. has no opportunity cost.
   c. is the quantity that balances the benefit of holding an additional dollar of money against the opportunity cost of doing so.
   d. is directly controlled by the Fed.
   e. changes very infrequently.

2. Which of the following statements is correct?
   a. Real interest rate − Inflation rate = Nominal interest rate
   b. Real interest rate + Inflation rate = Nominal interest rate
   c. Inflation rate − Real interest rate = Nominal interest rate
   d. Inflation rate + Price index = Nominal interest rate
   e. Inflation rate ÷ Real interest rate = Nominal interest rate

3. The opportunity cost of holding money is the
   a. real interest rate.
   b. nominal interest rate.
   c. inflation rate.
   d. time it takes to go to the ATM or bank.
   e. growth rate of real GDP.

4. The demand for money curve shows the relationship between the quantity of money demanded and
   a. the nominal interest rate.
   b. the real interest rate.
   c. the inflation rate.
   d. real GDP.
   e. nominal GDP.

5. The demand for money ____ when the ____.
   a. increases; price level rises
   b. decreases; price level rises
   c. remains constant; price level rises
   d. increases; nominal interest rate rises
   e. increases; supply of money decreases

6. Every day ____ adjusts to make the quantity of money demanded equal the quantity of money supplied.
   a. the inflation rate
   b. the nominal interest rate
   c. the quantity of money
   d. potential GDP
   e. real GDP

7. If the nominal interest rate is above its equilibrium level, then
   a. people sell financial assets and the interest rate falls.
   b. people buy financial assets and the interest rate falls.
   c. the demand for money curve shifts rightward and the interest rate rises.
   d. the supply of money curve shifts leftward and the interest rate rises.
   e. the demand curve for money shifts leftward and the interest rate falls.

8. When the Fed increases the quantity of money, the
   a. equilibrium nominal interest rate falls.
   b. equilibrium nominal interest rate rises.
   c. demand for money curve shifts rightward.
   d. supply of money curve shifts leftward.
   e. demand for money curve shifts leftward.

© 2015 Pearson Education, Inc.

Nominal interest rate (percent per year)	Quantity of money, (trillions dollars)
5	3.1
6	3.0
7	2.9
8	2.8
9	2.7
10	2.6

9. The table above gives the demand for money schedule. When the Fed increases the quantity of money from $2.7 trillion to $2.9 trillion, the nominal interest rate ____ from ____.
   a. falls; 9 percent to 5 percent
   b. falls; 7 percent to 6 percent
   c. rises; 5 percent to 8 percent
   d. rises; 6 percent to 8 percent
   e. falls; 9 percent to 7 percent

■ **FIGURE 28.1**

Nominal interest rate (percent per year)

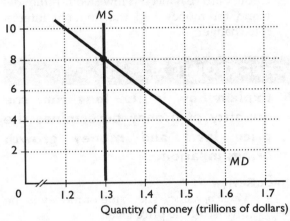

10. The figure above shows the money market. If the Fed increases the quantity of money from $1.3 trillion to $1.4 trillion, the nominal interest rate ____ from ____.
    a. falls; 9 percent to 7 percent
    b. falls; 8 percent to 6 percent
    c. rises; 5 percent to 8 percent
    d. rises; 6 percent to 8 percent
    e. falls; 12 percent to 7 percent

Short Response Questions

1. What are the benefits from holding money?

2. What effect does an increase in real GDP have on the demand for money?

Nominal interest rate (percent per year)	Quantity of money, (trillions dollars)
5	1.2
6	1.0
7	0.8
8	0.6
9	0.4
10	0.2

3. The table above has data on the nominal interest rate and the quantity of money demanded.
   a. Using the data, label the axes and plot the demand for money curve in Figure 28.2.
   b. Suppose the Fed sets the quantity of money at $0.6 trillion. Plot this quantity in Figure 28.2. What is the equilibrium nominal interest rate?
   c. Suppose the Fed wants to change the nominal interest rate to 6 percent a year. What action must the Fed take?

■ **FIGURE 28.2**

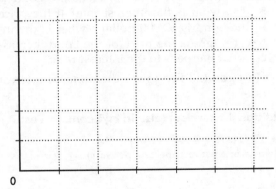

4. Figure 28.3 (on the next page) shows a demand for money curve and a supply of money curve.
   a. What is the equilibrium nominal interest rate?
   b. Suppose the price level rises so that the demand for money changes by $0.2 trillion at every interest rate. Which direction does the demand for money curve shift? Draw the new demand for money curve in the figure. What is the equilibrium nominal interest rate?

© 2015 Pearson Education, Inc.

■ **FIGURE 28.3**

Nominal interest rate (percent per year)

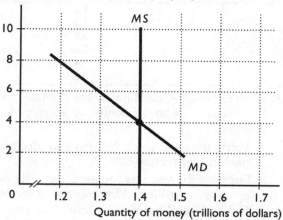

Quantity of money (trillions of dollars)

Long Response Questions

1. What is the opportunity cost of holding money and why is this the opportunity cost?

2. Suppose a government bond pays $100 in interest each year. If the price of the bond is $1,000, what is the interest rate? If the price of the bond is $2,000 dollars, what is the interest rate? As the price of the bond increases, what happens to the interest rate?

3. How can the Fed lower the nominal interest rate?

Additional Exercises (also in MyEconLab Test A)

■ **FIGURE 28.4**

Nominal interest rate (percent per year)

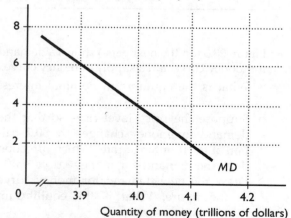

Quantity of money (trillions of dollars)

1. Figure 28.4 shows the demand for money curve. The quantity of money supplied is $3.9 trillion. What is the nominal interest rate?

2. Figure 28.4 shows the demand for money curve. If real GDP decreases, how will the interest rate change? Explain what happens in the market for bonds as the money market returns to equilibrium.

3. Figure 28.4 shows the demand for money curve. If the Fed increases the quantity of money from $3.9 trillion to $4.0 trillion, what is the change in the nominal interest rate? What happens to the price of bonds?

4. Suppose that banks launch an aggressive marketing campaign to get everyone to use credit cards for every conceivable transaction. They offer prizes to new cardholders and slash the interest rate on outstanding credit card balances. How would the demand for money and the nominal interest rate change?

CHECKPOINT 28.2

■ **Explain how in the long run, the quantity of money determines the price level and money growth brings inflation.**

Quick Review

- *Value of money* The value of money is the inverse of the price level.

- *Inflation rate in the long run* In the long run and other things remaining the same, a given percentage change in the quantity of money brings an equal percentage change in the price level.

- *Quantity theory of money* The proposition that when real GDP equals potential GDP, an increase in the quantity of money brings an equal percentage increase in the price level.

- *Equation of exchange* States that the quantity of money multiplied by the velocity of circulation equals the price level multiplied by real GDP, that is $M \times V = P \times Y$.

© 2015 Pearson Education, Inc.

Additional Practice Problems 28.2

1. How does an increase in the price level affect the value of money?

2. In the long run, how does an increase in the quantity of money affect the price level?

3. In the long run, according to the quantity theory of money, how does an increase in the growth rate of the quantity of money affect the inflation rate?

4. The quantity of money is $90 billion, real GDP is $900 billion, and the price level is 110. What is the velocity of circulation?

Solutions to Additional Practice Problems 28.2

1. An increase in the price level decreases the value of money because with the higher price level a given quantity of money can buyer fewer goods and services.

2. In the long run, the price level rises by the same proportion as the increase in the quantity of money.

3. In the long run, an increase in the growth rate of the quantity of money raises the inflation rate by the same percentage. For instance, if the growth rate of the quantity of money increases by 3 percentage points, in the long run the inflation rate increases by 3 percentage points.

4. The velocity of circulation is the number of times in a year that the average dollar of money gets used to buy final goods and services. The velocity of circulation is calculated using the formula $V = (P \times Y) \div M$. Nominal GDP, which equals $P \times Y$, is $990 billion. So velocity equals ($990 billion) ÷ $90 billion = 11.

■ AP Self Test 28.2

True or false

1. The value of money is the inverse of the nominal interest rate.

2. The long-run demand for money curve is a vertical line.

3. In the long run, an increase in the quantity of money raises the price level.

4. $M \times P = V \times Y$ is the formula for the equation of exchange.

5. According to the quantity theory of money, in the long run with other things remaining the same, a 5 percent increase in the quantity of money brings a 5 percent increase in the price level.

6. According to the quantity theory of money, if the quantity of money grows 2 percent a year faster than before, the inflation rate falls 2 percentage points from what it had been before the increase in the growth rate of the quantity of money.

Multiple choice

1. In the long run, the price level adjusts
   a. so that the real interest rate equals the nominal interest rate.
   b. so that the inflation rate equals zero.
   c. to achieve money market equilibrium.
   d. so that the inflation rate equals the growth rate of real GDP.
   e. so that the inflation rate is moderate.

2. In the long run, an increase in the quantity of money _____ the value of money and _____ the price level.
   a. raises; raises
   b. does not change; raises
   c. raises; lowers
   d. lowers; raises
   e. lowers; lowers

3. Other things remaining the same, if the quantity of money increases by a given percentage, then in the long run the _____ by the same percentage.
   a. price level rises
   b. price level falls
   c. real interest rate rises
   d. real interest rate falls
   e. nominal interest rate falls

4. Suppose that $P \times Y$ is $5,000 million a year and the quantity of money is $500 million. Then the velocity of circulation is
   a. 50.
   b. 500.
   c. 10.
   d. 20.
   e. 2,500,000.

© 2015 Pearson Education, Inc.

5. The quantity theory of money is a proposition about
   a. the Fed's methods used to change the quantity of money.
   b. nominal and real interest rate.
   c. the relationship between a change in the quantity of money and the price level.
   d. the relationship between financial assets and currency demanded.
   e. the nominal interest rate and the quantity of money demanded.

6. If the quantity of money grows at 3 percent a year, velocity does not grow, and real GDP grows at 2 percent a year, then the inflation rate equals
   a. 6 percent.
   b. 5 percent.
   c. 1 percent.
   d. –1 percent.
   e. 12 percent.

7. If the quantity of money grows at 4 percent a year, velocity grows at 2 percent, and real GDP grows at 2 percent a year, then the inflation rate equals
   a. 6 percent.
   b. 2 percent.
   c. 0 percent.
   d. 8 percent.
   e. 4 percent.

8. Hyperinflation is
   a. inflation caused by negative growth in the quantity of money.
   b. inflation at a rate that exceeds 50 percent a month.
   c. inflation caused by excessive growth in the demand for money.
   d. inflation at a rate that exceeds 5 percent a month.
   e. only theoretical and has never occurred in the real world.

Short Response Questions

1. In the long run, what is the effect of a 5 percent increase in the quantity of money, other things remaining the same?

Year	Quantity of money (billions of dollars)	Velocity of circulation	Price level (2005 = 100)	Real GDP (billions of 2005 dollars)
2013	100	11	____	1,000
2014	110	11	____	1,000
2015	121	11	____	1,000

2. The table above gives data for the nation of Quantoland, a small nation to the south. In 2013, 2014, and 2015, real GDP equals potential GDP.
   a. Complete the table.
   b. Calculate the percentage change in the quantity of money in 2013 and 2014. Then calculate the percentage change in the price level in 2014 and 2015.
   c. What key proposition is illustrated in your answer to part (b)?

Year	Growth in quantity of money (percent)	Growth in velocity of circulation (percent)	Inflation rate (percent)	Growth in Real GDP (percent)
2013	4	2	____	3
2014	7	2	____	3
2015	____	1	4	3

3. The table above gives data for the nation of Velocoland, a small nation to the north. In 2013, 2014, and 2015, real GDP equals potential GDP.
   a. Complete the table.
   b. Between 2013 and 2014, by how much does the growth rate of the quantity of money change? By how much does the inflation rate change?

Long Response Questions

1. Why is $1/P$ equal to the value of money?

2. In the long run, if real GDP grows at 3 percent a year, velocity does not change, and the quantity of money grows at 5 percent a year, what is the inflation rate?

3. What is a hyperinflation? What leads to hyperinflation?

Additional Exercises (also in MyEconLab Test A)

1. In 2002, the United Kingdom was at full employment. Nominal GDP was £850 billion,

© 2015 Pearson Education, Inc.

the real interest rate was 5 percent per year, the inflation rate was 6 percent a year, and the price level was 120. Calculate the nominal interest rate. If the real interest rate remains unchanged when the inflation rate in the long run decreases to 3 percent a year, explain how the nominal interest rate changes.

2. In 2003, the United Kingdom was at full employment. Nominal GDP was £900 billion, the nominal interest rate was 8 percent per year, the price level was 130, and the velocity of circulation was constant at 2. What was the quantity of money in the United Kingdom?

3. In exercise 2, if the velocity of circulation remains at 2, money grows at 8 percent a year, and real GDP grows at 5 percent a year in the long run, what is the inflation rate in the long run?

CHECKPOINT 28.3

■ **Identify the costs of inflation and the benefits of a stable value of money.**

Quick Review

- *The inflation rate and income tax* Inflation increases the nominal interest rate, and because income taxes are paid on nominal interest income, the true income tax rate rises with inflation.

Additional Practice Problem 28.3

1. In the island of Atlantis where you live, the inflation rate has been varying between 3 percent a year and 10 percent a year in recent years. You are willing to lend money if you are guaranteed a real interest rate of at least 2 percent a year. There are potential borrowers, but they will borrow only if they are guaranteed a real interest rate of not more than 5 percent a year.

   a. Can you successfully make a loan if everyone can accurately predict the inflation rate?

   b. Can you successfully make a loan if neither you nor the borrowers can accurately predict the inflation rate?

   c. What bearing does your answer to part (b) have on the cost of inflation?

Solution to Additional Practice Problem 28.3

1a. If you and potential borrowers can accurately predict the inflation rate, it is possible to make a loan. If everyone knows the inflation rate is 10 percent a year, you are willing to lend as long as you receive a nominal interest rate of at least 12 percent a year. Borrowers are willing to pay a real interest rate of no more than 5 percent a year, so borrowers are willing to agree to a loan as long as the nominal interest rate is no more than 15 percent a year. Because they are willing to pay up to 15 percent a year and you are willing to take as little as 12 percent a year, it is possible to make a loan with a nominal interest rate between 12 percent a year and 15 percent a year. Similarly, if everyone knows the inflation rate is 3 percent a year, a loan can be made with a nominal interest rate between 5 percent a year and 8 percent a year.

1b. To receive a real interest rate of at least 2 percent a year you must receive a nominal interest rate of at least 12 percent a year in case inflation is 10 percent a year. If borrowers pay a nominal interest rate of 12 percent a year and inflation is 3 percent a year, they are paying a real interest rate of 9 percent a year, well above their maximum real interest rate of 5 percent a year. Because of the uncertainty about the inflation rate, you don't make the loan.

1c. When inflation is uncertain, the loan is not made. Presumably the loan would benefit both the lender and the borrower. The fact it is not made means that both are worse off and reflects the uncertainty costs of inflation.

© 2015 Pearson Education, Inc.

■ AP Self Test 28.3

True or false

1. Inflation is a tax.

2. The "shoe-leather costs" of inflation are the result of the increase in the velocity of circulation when inflation increases.

3. One of the benefits of inflation is that it makes the value of money change, which benefits both borrowers and lenders.

4. When there is a high inflation rate, the growth rate slows.

Multiple choice

1. Which of the following is <u>NOT</u> a cost of inflation?
   a. tax costs
   b. confusion costs
   c. uncertainty costs
   d. government spending costs
   e. shoe-leather costs

2. Becky holds $30,000 as money. After a year during which inflation was 5 percent a year, the inflation tax over that year was
   a. $500.
   b. $1,000.
   c. $1,500.
   d. $3,000.
   e. $5.

3. Suppose a country has a real interest rate of 4 percent and an inflation rate of 3 percent. If the income tax rate is 20 percent, then the after-tax real interest rate is
   a. 2.6 percent a year.
   b. 4.0 percent a year.
   c. 5.6 percent a year.
   d. 7.0 percent a year.
   e. 1.4 percent a year.

4. Shoe-leather costs arise from inflation because the velocity of circulation of money ____ as the inflation rate ____.
   a. increases; falls
   b. decreases; rises
   c. increases; rises
   d. does not change; rises
   e. does not change; falls

5. A consequence of hyperinflation is that people
   a. who make fixed-payment loans to others receive higher payments as inflation increases.
   b. spend time trying to keep their money holdings near zero.
   c. receive higher real wage hikes, which increases their purchasing power for goods and services.
   d. want to lend funds because interest rates are so high.
   e. increase the quantity of money demanded.

6. The uncertainty costs of inflation cause people to
   a. increase their demand for money.
   b. increase investment causing growth to decrease.
   c. focus on the short run, which decreases investment and slows growth.
   d. focus on the long run, which increases investment and speeds growth.
   e. incur more shoe leather costs.

7. The costs of inflation ____ when inflation is more rapid and ____ when inflation is more unpredictable.
   a. increase; increase
   b. increase; decrease
   c. decrease; increase
   d. increase; do not change
   e. do not change; increase

© 2015 Pearson Education, Inc.

8. It is estimated that if the inflation rate is lowered from 3 percent a year to 0 percent a year, the growth rate of real GDP will rise by _____ percentage points a year.
   a. 0.06 to 0.09
   b. 1 to 3
   c. 2.3
   d. 3.2
   e. 0

Short Response Questions

1. Jose holds $600 of money. If the inflation rate is 5 percent a year, what is Jose's inflation tax?

2. On what factors does the cost of inflation depend?

Long Response Questions

1. The real interest rate is 2 percent a year and the inflation rate is zero percent a year. If the income tax rate is 25 percent, what is the real after-tax interest rate? If the inflation rate rises to 6 percent a year, what is the real after-tax interest rate? If the inflation rate rises to 10 percent a year, what is the real after-tax interest rate?

2. Why does the velocity of circulation increase in a hyperinflation?

3. The Eye on "What Causes Inflation?" on page 733 shows how the quantity theory can be used to predict inflation trends. How might this help you make decisions on your job?

Additional Exercises (also in MyEconLab Test A)

Sally has a credit card balance of $4,000. The credit card company charges a nominal interest rate of 18 percent a year on unpaid balances. The inflation rate is 3 percent a year.

1. Calculate the real interest rate that Sally pays the credit card company.

2. If the inflation rate falls to 2 percent a year and the nominal interest rate remains the same, calculate the real interest rate that Sally pays

© 2015 Pearson Education, Inc.

SELF TEST ANSWERS

■ AP Self Test 28.1

True or false

1. False; pages 717-718
2. False; page 719
3. False; page 721
4. True; page 721
5. True; pages 722-723

Multiple choice

1. c; page 717
2. b; page 718
3. b; page 718
4. a; pages 718-719
5. a; page 719
6. b; page 720
7. b; page 721
8. a; pages 722-723
9. e; pages 722-723
10. b; pages 722-723

Short Response Questions

1. The benefit from holding money is that a person can use the money to make payments and do transactions; page 717.

2. An increase in real GDP increases the demand for money; page 719.

■ FIGURE 28.5

Nominal interest rate (percent per year)

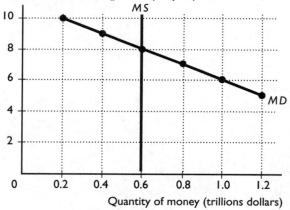

3. a. Figure 28.5 plots the demand for money curve; page 719.

b. Figure 28.5 shows the supply of money curve when the Fed sets the quantity of money at $0.6 trillion. The equilibrium nominal interest rate is 8 percent a year at the intersection of the *MD* and *MS* curves; pages 720-721.

c. To lower the nominal interest rate to 6 percent a year, the Fed increases the quantity of money to $1.0 trillion; page 723.

■ FIGURE 28.6

Nominal interest rate (percent per year)

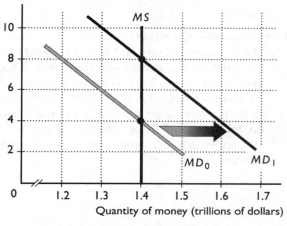

4. a. The equilibrium nominal interest rate is 4 percent; pages 720-721.

b. The demand for money increases and the demand for money curve shifts rightward. Figure 28.6 shows the new equilibrium interest rate is 8 percent; pages 719, 722-723.

Long Response Questions

1. The opportunity cost of holding money is the nominal interest rate. By holding money rather than a financial asset, the nominal interest rate is forgone. If Seemi can earn 5 percent a year on a bond, then holding $1,000 in money costs her $50 a year; pages 717-718.

2. When the price of the bond is $1,000, the interest rate equals ($100 ÷ $1,000) × 100, which is 10 percent. When the price of the bond is $2,000, the interest rate equals ($100 ÷ $2,000)

© 2015 Pearson Education, Inc.

× 100, which is 5 percent. When the price of the bond increases, the interest rate falls; page 721.

3. To lower the interest rate, the Fed increases the quantity of money; pages 722-723.

Additional Exercises (also in MyEconLab Test A)

1. The nominal interest rate is 6 percent a year because that is the nominal interest rate at which the quantity of money demanded equals the quantity of money supplied; pages 720-721.

2. If real GDP decreases, the nominal interest rate falls. When real GDP decreases, the demand for money curve shifts leftward. At the original nominal interest rate, people want to hold less money than they are actually holding. So they spend the money by buying other financial assets such as bonds. The demand for financial assets increases, the prices of these assets rise, and the nominal interest rate falls. The nominal interest rate keeps falling until the quantity of money that people want to hold increases to equal the quantity of money supplied; pages 719, 721.

3. If the Fed increases the quantity of money to $4.0 trillion, the nominal interest rate falls to 4 percent a year. At the original interest rate, people would like to hold less money then they are actually holding. So they try to get rid of money by buying other financial assets such as bonds. The demand for financial assets increases, the prices of these assets rise, and the nominal interest rate falls. The nominal interest rate keeps falling until the quantity of money that people want to hold increases to equal the quantity of money supplied; pages 720-721 .

4. The demand for money decreases as people use their credit cards more often and use money less often for transactions.
   Because the demand for money decreases, the nominal interest rate falls; pages 720-721.

■ AP Self Test 28.2

True or false

1. False; pages 725-726
2. False; page 726
3. True; page 727
4. False; page 729
5. True; pages 729-730
6. False; page 731

Multiple choice

1. c; page 725
2. d; page 727
3. a; page 727
4. c; pages 728-729
5. c; page 728
6. c; pages 730-731
7. e; pages 730-731
8. b; page 732

Short Response Questions

1. Other things remaining the same, in the long run a 5 percent increase in the quantity of money leads to a 5 percent increase in the price level; pages 727, 730.

Year	Quantity of money (billions of dollars)	Velocity of circulation	Price level (2005 = 100)	Real GDP (billions of 2005 dollars)
2013	100	11	110.0	1,000
2014	110	11	121.0	1,000
2015	121	11	133.1	1,000

2. a. The completed table is above. Use the equation of exchange to solve for the price level; pages 729-730.

   b. In 2014, the percentage change in the quantity of money is [($110 billion − $100 billion) ÷ $100 billion] × 100, which is 10 percent.
   In 2015, the percentage change in the quantity of money is [($121 billion − $110 billion) ÷ $110 billion] × 100, which also is 10 percent.

© 2015 Pearson Education, Inc.

In 2014, the percentage change in the price level is $[(121.0 - 110.0) \div 110.0] \times 100$, which is 10 percent.

In 2015, the percentage change in the price level is $[(133.1 - 121.0) \div 121.0] \times 100$, which also is 10 percent.

c. The answer to part (b) illustrates the quantity theory of money, the proposition that, when real GDP equals potential GDP, an increase in the quantity of money brings an equal percentage increase in the price level; pages 727, 730.

Year	Growth in quantity of money (percent)	Growth in velocity of circulation (percent)	Inflation rate (percent)	Growth in Real GDP (percent)
2013	4	2	<u>3</u>	3
2014	7	2	<u>6</u>	3
2015	<u>6</u>	1	4	3

3. a. The completed table is above. Use the equation of exchange in growth rates to solve for the unknowns; page 730.

b. Between 2013 and 2014, the growth rate of the quantity of money increased by 3 percentage points. Between these two years the inflation rate also increased by 3 percentage points; page 730.

Long Response Questions

1. The value of money equals $1/P$ (where P is the price level, which equals the price index divided by 100) because $1/P$ tells how many goods and services can be purchased with one dollar. If this number falls, then the dollar has lost value because a dollar buys fewer goods and services; pages 725- 726.

2. The inflation rate equals money growth plus velocity growth minus real GDP growth. Velocity does not grow, so the inflation rate equals 5 percent a year minus 3 percent a year, which is 2 percent a year; page 730.

3. A hyperinflation is inflation at a rate that exceeds 50 percent a month. A hyperinflation is the result of extraordinarily rapid growth in the quantity of money; page 732.

Additional Exercises (also in MyEconLab Test A)

1. The nominal interest rate equals the real interest rate plus the inflation rate. So the nominal interest rate equals the real interest rate, 5 percent a year, plus the inflation rate, 6 percent a year, which is 11 percent a year.

When the inflation rate decreases by 3 percentage points, the nominal interest rate falls by 3 percentage points, in this case from 11 percent a year to 8 percent a year; pages 718, 730.

2. The equation of exchange is $M \times V = P \times Y$. Rearranging this equation to solve for M gives $M = (P \times Y) \div V$. $P \times Y$ equals nominal GDP, which is given in the problem as £900 billion. Velocity was given as 2. So the quantity of money, M, is (£900 billion) $\div$ 2, which is £450 billion; page 729.

3. In growth rates, the equation of exchange is (Money growth) + (Velocity growth) = (Inflation) + (Real GDP growth). Rearranging this equation gives Inflation = (Money growth) + (Velocity growth) − (Real GDP growth). The velocity of circulation is constant (at 2) so its growth equals 0 percent. Real GDP grows at 5 percent a year and money grows at 8 percent a year, so inflation equals (8 percent a year) + (0 percent a year) − (5 percent a year), which is 3 percent a year; page 730.

■ AP Self Test 28.3

True or false
1. True; page 735
2. True; page 736
3. False; page 737
4. True; pages 737-738

Multiple choice
1. d; page 735
2. c; page 735
3. a; page 736
4. c; page 736
5. b; page 737
6. c; page 737
7. a; page 737
8. a; pages 737-738

© 2015 Pearson Education, Inc.

Short Response Questions

1. With an inflation rate of 5 percent a year, Jose losses ($600 × 0.05) = $30 in purchasing power. His money will buy only $570 worth of goods and services. Jose is paying an inflation tax of $30; page 735.

2. The costs of an inflation depend on its rate and its predictability. The higher the rate, the greater is the cost and the more unpredictable the rate, the greater is the cost; page 737.

Long Response Questions

1. The real after-tax interest rate equals the nominal after-tax interest rate minus the inflation rate. When inflation is zero percent a year, the nominal interest rate equals the real interest rate, which is 2 percent a year. With a 25 percent income tax, the nominal after-tax interest rate equals 1.5 percent a year, so the real after-tax interest rate is 1.5 percent a year. When the inflation rate is 6 percent a year, the nominal interest rate equals the real interest rate, 2 percent a year, plus the inflation rate, 6 percent, or 8 percent a year. The tax rate of 25 percent means that the nominal after-tax interest rate is 6 percent a year. In this case the real after-tax interest rate equals 6 percent a year minus the inflation rate, 6 percent a year, which is zero percent a year. When the inflation rate equals 10 percent a year, the nominal interest rate is 12 percent a year so the nominal after-tax interest rate is 9 percent a year. As a result, the real after-tax interest rate is 9 percent a year − 10 percent a year, which is −1 percent a year. In this case, the real after-tax interest rate is negative; page 736.

2. The velocity of circulation increases because people try to spend their money as rapidly as possible to avoid incurring losses from the falling value of money. When people spend their money more rapidly, the velocity of circulation increases, thereby creating more shoe-leather costs; page 736.

3. The use of the quantity theory illustrated in the Eye on the Cause of Inflation might help you on your job if you are sometimes required to predict or surmise what the inflation rate will be over the next few years. For instance, if you have a job in which you must help your company determine whether to make an investment in a new factory, predicting the inflation rate might be useful information in helping to determine the profitability of the new factory. You could then use the procedure outlined in the Eye on the Cause of Inflation to guide your prediction by focusing on the predicted growth rate of the quantity of money and the growth rate of real GDP. While the quantity theory won't precisely predict each year's inflation rate, nonetheless it does give a good indicator of what the inflation rate will tend to be over several years.

Additional Exercises (also in MyEconLab Test A)

1. The real interest rate is the nominal interest rate minus the inflation rate, which is 18 percent a year minus 3 percent a year = 15 percent; pages 718, 736.

2. The real interest rate rises to 16 percent a year (18 percent a year minus 2 percent a year); pages 718, 736.

© 2015 Pearson Education, Inc.

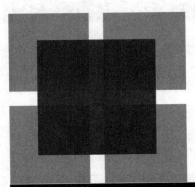

Aggregate Supply and Aggregate Demand

Chapter 29

1 Define and explain the influences on aggregate supply.

Aggregate supply is the output from all firms. Other things remaining the same, the higher the price level, the greater is the quantity of real GDP supplied and the lower the price level, the smaller is the quantity of real GDP supplied. The aggregate supply curve is upward sloping and the potential GDP line is vertical. Moving along the aggregate supply curve, the only influence on production plans that changes is the price level. All other influences on production plans, such as the money wage rate and the money prices of other resources, remain constant. Moving along the potential GDP line, when the price level changes, the money wage rate and the money prices of other resources change by the same percentage as the price level. Aggregate supply changes and the aggregate supply curve shifts when potential GDP changes, the money wage rate changes, or the money prices of other resources change. When the money wage rate or the money prices of other resources rise, aggregate supply decreases.

2 Define and explain the influences on aggregate demand.

Aggregate demand is the relationship between the quantity of real GDP demanded and the price level. Other things the same, the higher the price level, the smaller is the quantity of real GDP demanded and the lower the price level, the greater the quantity of real GDP demanded. A change in the price level changes in the buying power of money, the real interest rate, and the real prices of exports and imports, all of which influence the quantity of real GDP demanded. Factors that change aggregate demand and shift the aggregate demand curve are: expectations about the future; fiscal policy and monetary policy; and the state of the world economy. The aggregate demand multiplier is an effect that magnifies changes in expenditure plans and brings potentially large fluctuations in aggregate demand.

3 Explain how trends and fluctuations in aggregate demand and aggregate supply bring economic growth, inflation, and the business cycle.

Macroeconomic equilibrium occurs at the intersection of the aggregate supply and aggregate demand curves. The macroeconomic equilibrium can be a full-employment equilibrium (real GDP equals potential GDP), an equilibrium with an inflationary gap (real GDP exceeds potential GDP), or an equilibrium with a recessionary gap (real GDP is less than potential GDP). In a recessionary gap, the money wage rate falls so aggregate supply increases and the economy adjusts back to full employment. In an inflationary gap, the money wage rate rises so aggregate supply decreases and the economy adjusts back to full employment. Economic growth is the result of growth in potential GDP; inflation is the result of more rapid growth in aggregate demand than in potential GDP. Fluctuations in aggregate demand and aggregate supply lead to the business cycle. Demand pull inflation starts with an increase in aggregate demand, followed by persisting increases in the quantity of money. Cost-push inflation starts with a decrease in aggregate supply, followed by persisting increases in the quantity of money.

© 2015 Pearson Education, Inc.

YOUR AP TEST HINTS

AP Topics

Topic on your AP test	What to Know	Corresponding textbook section
Aggregate supply	Difference between *AS* curve and potential GDP curve; factors that shift both curves	Checkpoint 29.1
Aggregate demand	Components; factors that shift *AD* curve	Checkpoint 29.2
Macroeconomic equilibrium	Determination of macroeconomic equilibrium; effects from changes in aggregate demand and aggregate supply; inflationary gap and recessionary gap	Checkpoint 29.3

AP Vocabulary Covered

Terms	What to Know	Text Sections
Aggregate supply, *AS* (SRAS)	The relationship between the quantity of real GDP supplied and the price level; slopes upward in an *AS/AD* figure	Checkpoint 29.1, p. 744
Potential GDP line (LRAS)	Does not depend on the price level; vertical line in an *AS/AD* figure; *also known as the long run aggregate supply line*	Checkpoint 29.1, p. 745
Factors shifting *AS* and potential GDP curves	Changes in potential GDP shift *both* curves; changes in money wage rate or money prices of other resources shift *only* the *AS* curve	Checkpoint 29.1, p. 747
Aggregate demand, *AD*	The relationship between the quantity of real GDP demanded and the price level; equals $C + I + G + NX$; slopes downward in an *AS/AD* figure	Checkpoint 29.2, p. 750
Fiscal policy	Changes aggregate demand and shifts the *AD* curve; cut in taxes, increase in transfer payments, and increase in government expenditure increase aggregate demand	Checkpoint 29.2, p. 753
Monetary policy	Changes aggregate demand and shifts the *AD* curve; cut in interest rate increases aggregate demand	Checkpoint 29.2, p. 753
Macroeconomic equilibrium	The point of intersection of the *AD* curve and the *AS* curve; not necessarily equal to potential GDP	Checkpoint 29.3, p. 756
Full-employment equilibrium	When equilibrium real GDP equals potential GDP	Checkpoint 29.3, p. 757
Inflationary gap	When equilibrium real GDP exceeds potential GDP	Checkpoint 29.3, p. 757
Recessionary gap	When equilibrium real GDP is less than potential GDP	Checkpoint 29.3, p. 757
Stagflation	A time with rising unemployment and rising inflation rates	Checkpoint 29.3, p. 761

Extra AP material

- The aggregate demand/aggregate supply model and the figure showing the *AD/AS (AD/SRAS)* curves are the most commonly tested concepts on the macroeconomics AP test, so be certain you understand them.
- On the AP test, the *AS* curve is called the *Short-Run Aggregate Supply (SRAS)* curve and the vertical line showing potential GDP is called the *Long-Run Aggregate Supply (LRAS)* curve. The *LRAS* curve is the same concept as the Production Possibilities Curve and changes that affect the *PPF* affect the *LRAS*.
- *Disinflation* is the term for inflation rates *falling; deflation* means the inflation rate is negative.

© 2015 Pearson Education, Inc.

CHECKPOINT 29.1

■ Define and explain the influences on aggregate supply.

Quick Review

- *Aggregate supply* The relationship between the quantity of real GDP supplied and the price level when all other influences on production plans remain the same.
- *Factors that change aggregate supply* Aggregate supply decreases and the aggregate supply curve shifts leftward when potential GDP decreases, when the money wage rate rises, and when the money prices of other resources rise.

Additional Practice Problem 29.1

1. The table shows the aggregate supply schedule for the United Kingdom.

Price level (GDP price index)	Real GDP supplied (billions of 2009 pounds)
90	650
100	700
110	750
120	800
130	850

   a. Plot the aggregate supply curve in the figure.

   b. In the figure, show the effect on the aggregate supply curve of an increase in the U.K. money wage rate. Is there a movement along the curve or a shift of the curve?

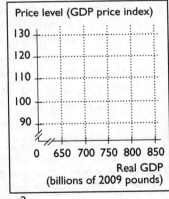

Price level (GDP price index)

Real GDP (billions of 2009 pounds)

Solution to Additional Practice Problem 29.1

1a. The aggregate supply curve is plotted in the figure in the next column above as AS_0. The aggregate supply curve has a positive slope, so as the price level rises, the quantity of real GDP supplied increases.

1b. Changes in the price level change in the aggregate quantity supplied and result in movements along the aggregate supply curve. Aggregate supply changes and the aggregate supply curve shifts when any influence on production plans other than the price level changes. An increase in the money wage rate decreases aggregate supply and shifts the aggregate supply curve leftward, as illustrated by the shift to AS_1. A change in the money wage rate shifts the aggregate supply curve.

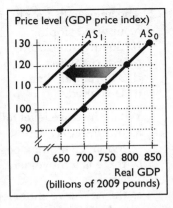

Price level (GDP price index)

Real GDP (billions of 2009 pounds)

■ AP Self Test 29.1

True or false

1. Along the aggregate supply curve, a rise in the price level decreases the quantity of real GDP supplied.

2. A rise in the price level decreases potential GDP.

3. Anything that changes potential GDP shifts the aggregate supply curve.

4. An increase in potential GDP shifts the aggregate supply curve rightward.

Multiple choice

1. Moving along the potential GDP line, the money wage rate changes by the same percentage as the change in the price level so that the real wage rate
   a. increases.
   b. decreases.
   c. stays at the full-employment equilibrium level.
   d. might either increase or decrease.
   e. stays the same, though not necessarily at the full-employment equilibrium level.

© 2015 Pearson Education, Inc.

2. The aggregate supply curve is
   a. upward sloping.
   b. downward sloping.
   c. a vertical line.
   d. a horizontal line.
   e. U-shaped.

3. When the price level falls,
   a. the *AS* curve shifts rightward but the potential GDP line does not shift.
   b. there is a movement upward along the *AS* curve.
   c. the *AS* curve shifts leftward but the potential GDP line does not shift.
   d. there is a movement downward along the *AS* curve.
   e. both the potential GDP line and the *AS* curve shift leftward.

4. As the price level rises relative to costs and the real wage rate falls, profits _____ and the number of firms in business _____.
   a. increase; increases
   b. increase; decreases
   c. decrease; increases
   d. decrease; decreases
   e. do not change; do not change

5. When potential GDP increases,
   a. the *AS* curve shifts rightward.
   b. there is a movement up along the *AS* curve.
   c. the *AS* curve shifts leftward.
   d. there is a movement down along the *AS* curve.
   e. there is neither a movement along or a shift in the *AS* curve.

6. If the money wage rate rises,
   a. the *AS* curve shifts rightward.
   b. there is a movement up along the *AS* curve.
   c. the *AS* curve shifts leftward.
   d. there is a movement down along the *AS* curve.
   e. there is neither a movement along nor a shift in the *AS* curve.

■ **FIGURE 29.1**

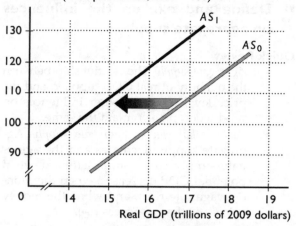

7. In Figure 29.1, which of the following might be the reason for the shift of the aggregate supply curve from AS_0 to AS_1?
   a. a fall in the money wage rate
   b. an increase in potential GDP
   c. an increase in investment
   d. a fall in the price of oil
   e. a rise in the money wage rate

Short Response Questions

1. Which of the following increase aggregate supply and shift the *AS* rightward? Which of the following decrease aggregate supply and shift the *AS* curve leftward? Which of the following do not shift the *AS* curve?
   a. A fall in the money wage rate
   b. An increase in government expenditure
   c. An increase in quantity of money
   d. A rise in the price of oil
   e. An increase in productivity

Price level (GDP price index 2009 = 100)	Quantity of real GDP supplied (trillions of 2009 dollars)	Potential GDP (trillions of 2009 dollars)
140	20	16
130	18	16
120	16	16
110	14	16
100	12	16

2. The table above gives the aggregate supply schedule and potential GDP schedule for a

© 2015 Pearson Education, Inc.

nation.

a. Label the axes and then plot the *AS* curve and potential GDP line in Figure 29.2.

b. Suppose the money wage rate falls. Show the effect of this change on aggregate supply and potential GDP in Figure 29.2.

c. Use the data in the table to again plot the *AS* curve and potential GDP line in Figure 29.3. Be sure to label the axes.

d. Potential GDP increases by $2 trillion. Show the effect of this change on aggregate supply and potential GDP in Figure 29.3.

■ **FIGURE 29.2**

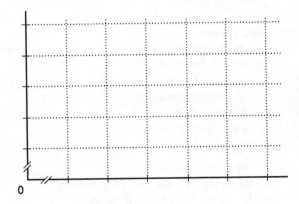

■ **FIGURE 29.3**

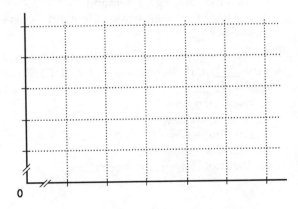

Long Response Questions

1. Why does the *AS* curve slope upward?

2. Why does the aggregate supply curve shift when the money wage rate rises? Why doesn't the potential GDP line also shift?

3. What is the effect on aggregate supply if the money price of oil rises?

Additional Exercise (also in MyEconLab Test A)

1. Many events have followed the ending of apartheid in South Africa. Explain the effect of each of the following events on South Africa's aggregate supply.

a. U.S. businesses have established branches in South Africa.

b. The price level has increased.

c. Unemployment decreased.

d. Money wage rates have increased.

e. Tourism increased, and many new hotels were built.

f. AIDS became more prevalent.

CHECKPOINT 29.2

■ **Define and explain the influences on aggregate demand.**

Quick Review

- *Factors that change aggregate demand* Aggregate demand changes and the aggregate demand curve shifts if expected future income, expected future inflation, or expected future profit change; if the government or the Federal Reserve take steps that change expenditure plans, such as changes in taxes or in the quantity of money; or the state of the world economy changes.

Additional Practice Problem 29.2

1. Draw aggregate demand curves and illustrate the effects of each event listed below either by a movement along the aggregate demand curve or a shift in the aggregate demand curve. These events are:

a. The price level falls.

b. Firms increase their investment because the expected profit increases.

c. The government cuts its taxes.

© 2015 Pearson Education, Inc.

Solution to Additional Practice Problem 29.2

1a. To answer this Practice Problem, remember that a change in any factor that influences expenditure plans other than the price level brings a change in aggregate demand and a shift in the *AD* curve. In this part, it *is* the price level that changes, so there is a change in the quantity of real GDP demanded and a movement

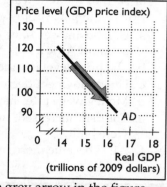

along the aggregate demand curve. Because the price level falls, there is a downward movement along the aggregate demand curve, as illustrated by the grey arrow in the figure.

1b. An increase in firms' investment increases aggregate demand. The aggregate demand curve shifts rightward, as shown in the figure by the shift from AD_0 to AD_1.

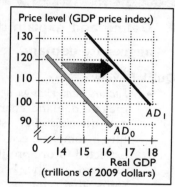

1c. When the government cuts its taxes, households' incomes rise and so they increase their consumption expenditure. Aggregate demand increases and the aggregate demand curve shifts rightward, as illustrated in the previous answer.

■ AP Self Test 29.2

True or false

1. As the price level falls, other things remaining the same, the quantity of real GDP demanded increases.

2. An increase in expected future income will not increase aggregate demand until the income actually increases.

3. A decrease in government expenditure shifts the aggregate demand curve rightward.

4. An increase in Mexican income decreases aggregate demand in the United States because Mexicans will buy more Mexican-produced goods.

Multiple choice

1. When the price level rises there is a ____ the aggregate demand curve.
   a. rightward shift of
   b. movement down along
   c. leftward shift of
   d. movement up along
   e. rotation of

2. A rise in the price level
   a. raises the buying power of money.
   b. decreases the prices of exports.
   c. lowers the buying power of money.
   d. increases aggregate demand.
   e. makes the aggregate demand curve steeper.

3. When the price level rises, the real interest rate ____ and the quantity of real GDP demanded ____.
   a. rises; increases
   b. rises; decreases
   c. falls; increases
   d. falls; decreases
   e. does not change; does not change

© 2015 Pearson Education, Inc.

■ **FIGURE 29.4**

Price level (GDP price index, 2009 = 100)

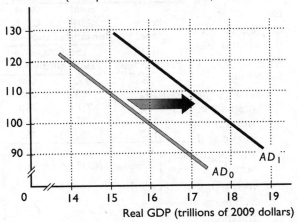

4. In Figure 29.4, the shift in the aggregate demand curve could be the result of
   a. an increase in the quantity of money
   b. a decrease in foreign incomes.
   c. a tax hike.
   d. a fall in the price level.
   e. a decrease in the expected future rate of profit.

5. A change in any of the following factors, <u>EXCEPT</u> ____, shifts the aggregate demand curve.
   a. expectations about the future
   b. the money wage rate
   c. monetary and fiscal policy
   d. foreign income
   e. the foreign exchange rate

6. Which of the following shifts the aggregate demand curve leftward?
   a. a decrease in government expenditure on goods and services
   b. an increase in the price level
   c. a tax cut
   d. an increase in foreign income
   e. a decrease in the price level

7. When investment increases, the ____ in aggregate demand is ____ the change in investment.
   a. increase; greater than
   b. increase; smaller than
   c. increase; the same as
   d. decrease; the same as
   e. decrease; greater than

Short Response Questions

1. Which of the following increase aggregate demand and shift the *AD* rightward? Which decrease aggregate demand and shift the *AD* curve leftward? Which do not shift the *AD* curve?
   a. A fall in the money wage rate
   b. An increase in government expenditure
   c. An increase in quantity of money
   d. A rise in the price of oil
   e. An increase in productivity
   f. An increase in taxes

■ **FIGURE 29.5**

Price level (GDP price index, 2009 = 100)

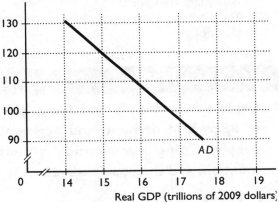

2. Figure 29.5 shows an aggregate demand curve.
   a. Suppose that government expenditure on goods and services increase. In Figure 29.5, illustrate the effect of this fiscal policy.
   b. Suppose the Federal Reserve decreases the quantity of money. In Figure 29.5, illustrate the effect of this monetary policy.

© 2015 Pearson Education, Inc.

Long Response Questions

1. Why does an increase in the price level decrease the quantity of real GDP demanded?
2. Expected future profit increases. Explain the effect on aggregate demand.
3. The government increases its taxes. What is the effect on aggregate demand?
4. What is the aggregate demand multiplier?

Additional Exercises (also in MyEconLab Test A)

1. Explain the effect on Japan's aggregate demand of each of the following events, one at a time.
   a. The price level in Japan rises.
   b. The Asian economies experience very strong growth.
   c. Japan adopts an expansionary fiscal policy and cuts taxes.
2. Explain the effect on China's aggregate demand of each of the following events, one at a time.
   a. The United States goes into recession.
   b. Japanese and European firms establish new plants in China.
   c. The Chinese yuan strengthens against the U.S. dollar.

CHECKPOINT 29.3

■ **Explain how trends and fluctuations in aggregate demand and aggregate supply bring economic growth, inflation, and the business cycle.**

Quick Review

- *Recessionary gap* A gap that exists when potential GDP exceeds real GDP. To restore full employment, the money wage rate falls and aggregate supply increases.
- *Inflationary gap* A gap that exists when real GDP exceeds potential GDP. To restore full employment, the money wage rate rises and aggregate supply decreases.

Additional Practice Problem 29.3

1. The table has the U.K. aggregate demand and aggregate supply schedules.

Price level (GDP price index)	Real GDP demanded	Real GDP supplied
	(billions of 2009 pounds)	
90	800	650
100	775	700
110	750	750
120	725	800
130	700	850

a. Plot the aggregate demand curve and the aggregate supply curve in the figure.

b. What is the macroeconomic equilibrium?

c. If U.K. potential GDP is £800 billion, what is the type of macroeconomic equilibrium?

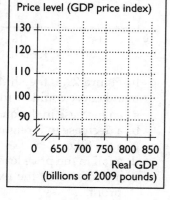

d. If the government increases its expenditure on goods and services, what is the effect on the British economy?

Solution to Additional Practice Problem 29.3

1a. The aggregate demand curve is in the figure. It has a negative slope, so as the price level falls, the quantity of real GDP demanded increases. The aggregate supply curve also is plotted in the figure.

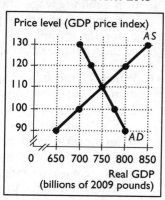

It has a positive slope, so as the price level rises, the quantity of real GDP supplied increases.

© 2015 Pearson Education, Inc.

1b. The macroeconomic equilibrium is at a price level of 110 and real GDP of £750 billion. The macroeconomic equilibrium is at the intersection of the aggregate supply curve and the aggregate demand curve.

1c. Potential GDP is £800 billion and the macroeconomic equilibrium real GDP is £750 billion, so as the figure shows, the economy is in a below full-employment equilibrium. Real GDP is less than potential GDP.

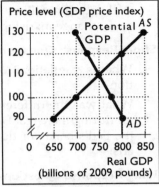

1d. If the government increases its expenditure on goods and services, aggregate demand increases and the aggregate demand curve shifts rightward. The price level rises and real GDP increases, moving the nation closer to a full-employment equilibrium.

■ AP Self Test 29.3

True or false

1. A recessionary gap has a shortage of labor.

2. In the *AS-AD* model, economic growth is demonstrated by persisting rightward movements of the *AD* curve.

3. Aggregate demand fluctuations are the main source of the business cycle.

4. Demand-pull inflation starts with an increase in aggregate demand that leads to an inflationary gap.

5. To persist, cost-push inflation does not need persisting increases in aggregate demand.

6. In the financial crisis of 2008, the Fed took action to bail out financial institutions and doubled the monetary base.

Multiple choice

■ FIGURE 29.6

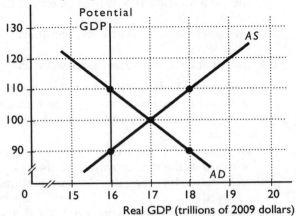

1. In Figure 29.6, the equilibrium price level is ____ and the equilibrium real GDP is ____ trillion.
   a. 110; $16
   b. 110; $18
   c. 100; $17
   d. 90; $16
   e. 90; $18

2. Figure 29.6 shows
   a. a full-employment equilibrium.
   b. an above full-employment equilibrium with an inflationary gap.
   c. an above full-employment equilibrium with a recessionary gap.
   d. a below full-employment equilibrium with an inflationary gap.
   e. a below full-employment equilibrium with a recessionary gap.

3. If the quantity of real GDP supplied equals the quantity of real GDP demanded, then
   a. nominal GDP must equal real GDP.
   b. real GDP must equal potential GDP.
   c. real GDP must be greater than potential GDP.
   d. real GDP might be greater than, equal to, or less than potential GDP.
   e. real GDP must be less than potential GDP.

© 2015 Pearson Education, Inc.

4. An inflationary gap is created when
   a. real GDP is greater than potential GDP.
   b. real GDP equal to potential GDP.
   c. the inflation rate is less than potential inflation.
   d. the price level exceeds the equilibrium price level.
   e. potential GDP is greater than real GDP.

5. The economy is at full employment. Aggregate demand increases, so ____ is created and the adjustment to full employment occurs because ____.
   a. an inflationary gap; the *AS* curve shifts leftward as the money wage rate rises
   b. an inflationary gap; the *AD* curve shifts leftward
   c. an inflationary gap; potential GDP increases to close the gap
   d. a recessionary gap; the *AS* curve shifts leftward as the money wage rate falls
   e. a recessionary gap; the *AS* curve shifts leftward as the money wage rate rises

6. The adjustment from a recessionary gap to full employment requires the money wage rate to ____, which then ____.
   a. rise; decreases aggregate supply
   b. rise; increases aggregate demand
   c. fall; decreases aggregate demand
   d. fall; increases potential GDP
   e. fall; increases aggregate supply

7. The main source of business cycle fluctuations is
   a. fluctuations in aggregate demand.
   b. persisting growth in aggregate demand.
   c. persisting growth in potential GDP
   d. fluctuations in aggregate supply.
   e. persisting growth in aggregate supply.

8. A cost-push inflation can be started by ____.
   a. an increase in the quantity of money
   b. a fall in the money price of oil
   c. an increase in potential GDP
   d. a rise in the money price of oil
   e. an increase in U.S. exports

9. Stagflation is a combination of ____ real GDP and a ____ price level.
   a. increasing; rising
   b. increasing; falling
   c. decreasing; rising
   d. decreasing; falling
   e. no change in; rising

Short Response Questions

1. What is stagflation? What can create stagflation?

2. What was the difference in the Fed's behavior during the Great Depression contrasted to the Fed's behavior during the 2008 financial crisis?

Long Response Questions

■ **FIGURE 29.7**

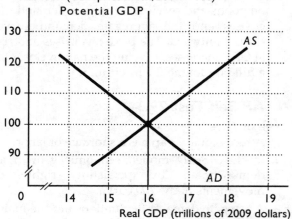

1. Use Figure 29.7 to show the effect of an increase in expected future profit on the price level and real GDP. Does this change create an inflationary gap or a recessionary gap? In the figure, show how the economy returns to potential GDP.

2. What is an inflationary gap and how is it eliminated?

© 2015 Pearson Education, Inc.

■ FIGURE 29.8

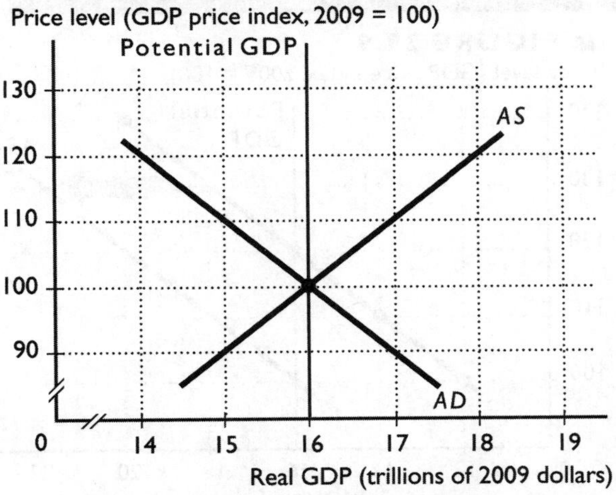

Price level (GDP price index, 2009 = 100)

Real GDP (trillions of 2009 dollars)

3. Use Figure 29.8 to show the effect a rise in the price of oil has on the price level and real GDP. Does this change create an inflationary gap or a recessionary gap?

4. Why is growth in the quantity of money necessary to sustain a demand-pull inflation?

5. What is the difference between a demand-pull inflation and a cost-push inflation? How are they similar?

6. The Eye on Your Life on discussed some of the uses you can make of the *AS-AD* model. Another use lies in the political arena. For instance, if a politician is running a campaign in which he or she suggests raising taxes, using the *AS-AD* model, what do you expect will happen to real GDP if this campaign promise is carried out?

Additional Exercises (also in MyEconLab Test A)
The Canadian economy is at full employment when the following events occur:
   a. The world economy goes into a strong expansion.
   b. Canadian businesses expect future profits to rise.

1. Explain the effect of each event separately on real GDP, the price level, and unemployment in Canada in the short run.

2. If the events occur separately, explain the adjustment that occurs in each case in the long run.

3. Explain the combined effect of these events on Canadian real GDP and price level.

© 2015 Pearson Education, Inc.

SELF TEST ANSWERS

■ AP Self Test 29.1

True or false
1. False; pages 744-745
2. False; pages 744-745
3. True; page 747
4. True; page 747

Multiple choice
1. c; pages 744-745
2. a; page 745
3. d; pages 744-745
4. a; page 746
5. a; page 747
6. c; page 748
7. e; page 748

Short Response Questions
1. Parts (a) and (e) increase aggregate supply and shift the *AS* curve rightward. Part (d) decreases aggregate supply and shift the *AS* curve leftward. Parts (b) and (c) do not shift the *AS* curve; pages 744-745.
2. a. Figure 29.9 labels the axes. The aggregate supply curve is labeled *AS*; page 745.
   b. The fall in the money wage rate has no effect on potential GDP, so the potential GDP line does not change. Aggregate supply, however, increases so the *AS* curve shifts rightward, to an *AS* curve such as *AS1*; page 748.
   c. Figure 29.10 labels the axes. The aggregate supply curve is labeled *AS*; page 745.
   d. The potential GDP line shifts rightward by $2 trillion, as indicated by the shift to Potential GDP1. The aggregate supply curve also shifts rightward by $2 trillion, as shown by the shift to *AS1*; page 747.

Long Response Questions
1. A movement along the *AS* curve brings a change in the real wage rate (and changes in the real cost of other resources whose money prices are fixed).

   If the price level rises and the money wage

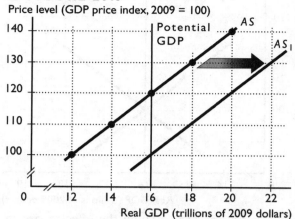

■ FIGURE 29.9

■ FIGURE 29.10

rate does not change, an extra hour of labor that was previously unprofitable becomes profitable. So, the quantity of labor demanded increases and production increases

In addition, if the price level rises and the money wage rate does not change, the real wage rate falls. A fall in the real wage rate boosts firms' profits. With the increase in profit, the number of firms in business increases. Finally fewer firms will shut down and more firms will open. All these changes increase the quantity of real GDP supplied. So as the price level rises, the quantity of real GDP supplied increases; pages 744-746.

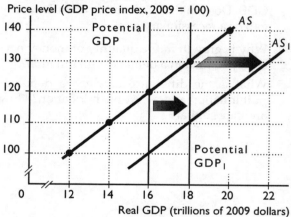

© 2015 Pearson Education, Inc.

2. An increase in the money wage rate increases firms' costs. The higher are firms' costs, the smaller is the quantity that firms are willing to supply at each price level. Aggregate supply decreases and the *AS* curve shifts leftward. A change in the money wage rate does not change potential GDP. Potential GDP depends only on the economy's real ability to produce and on the full-employment quantity of labor, which occurs at the equilibrium real wage rate. The equilibrium real wage rate can occur at any money wage rate; pages 747-748.

3. If the money price of oil rises, firm's costs increase. The higher firms' costs, the smaller the quantity of goods and services that firms will supply at each price level. Aggregate supply decreases and the aggregate supply curve shifts leftward; page 748.

Additional Exercise (also in MyEconLab Test A)

1. a. Establishing more branches of businesses within South Africa increases the number of business and increases aggregate supply; page 746.

   b. In the short run, the increase in the price level increases the aggregate quantity supplied; page 744.

   c. As unemployment decreases and employment increases, production increases and aggregate supply increases; page 744.

   d. An increase in money wage rates decreases aggregate supply; pages 747-748 .

   e. As tourism increases and new hotels are built, the quantity capital increases so that potential GDP increases and thereby aggregate supply increases; pages 744, 747.

   f. The spread of AIDS decreases the quantity of labor. As a result, potential GDP decreases so that aggregate supply decreases; page 744.

■ AP Self Test 29.2

True or false

1. True; page 750
2. False; page 752

3. False; page 753
4. False; page 754

Multiple choice

1. d; page 750
2. c; pages 750-751
3. b; pages 751-752
4. a; page 753
5. b; pages 752-754
6. a; pages 752-754
7. a; page 754

Short Response Questions

1. Parts (a) and (e) increase aggregate supply and shift the *AS* curve rightward. Part (d) decreases aggregate supply and shift the *AS* curve leftward. Parts (b), (c), and (f) do not shift the *AS* curve; pages 751-753.

■ FIGURE 29.11

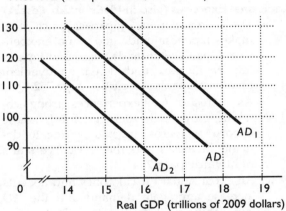

Price level (GDP price index, 2009 = 100)

2. a. An increase in government expenditure on goods and services increases aggregate demand and shifts the *AD* curve rightward, in Figure 29.11 from *AD* to *AD*₁; page 753.

   b. A decrease in the quantity of money decreases aggregate demand and shifts the *AD* curve leftward, in Figure 29.11 from *AD* to *AD*₂; page 753.

Long Response Questions

1. An increase in the price level decreases the quantity of real GDP demanded because an

© 2015 Pearson Education, Inc.

increase in the price level lowers the buying power of money, raises the real interest rate, raises the real prices of exports, and lowers the real price of imports; pages 750-752.

2. An increase in expected future profit increases the firms' investment and thereby increases aggregate demand; page 752.

3. The government can influence aggregate demand by changing taxes. When the government increases taxes, aggregate demand decreases; page 753.

4. The aggregate demand multiplier is an effect that magnifies changes in expenditure and increases fluctuations in aggregate demand. For example, an increase in investment increases aggregate demand and increases income. The increase in income induces an increase in consumption expenditure so aggregate demand increases by more than the initial increase in investment; page 754.

Additional Exercises (also in MyEconLab Test A)

1. a. The increase in the Japanese price level makes Japanese-made goods more expensive. Japan's exports decrease and Japan's imports increase, and there is a movement up along Japan's *AD* curve; page 752.

   b. As the rest of Asia experiences strong economic growth, the demand for Japanese exports increases. Japan's aggregate demand increases and the *AD* curve shifts rightward; page 754.

   c. An expansionary fiscal policy and tax cuts increase aggregate demand and the *AD* curve shifts rightward; page 753.

2. a. As the United States goes into recession, the demand for Chinese exports decreases. China's aggregate demand decreases and the *AD* curve shifts leftward; page 754.

   b. The new plants will have the first order effect of increasing China's potential GDP and its aggregate supply; pages 744-745.

   c. A stronger yuan makes China's exports more expensive and imports from the United States cheaper to residents of China. Chinese exports decrease and imports increase, which decreases China's aggre-

gate demand and shifts the *AD* curve leftward; page 753.

■ AP Self Test 29.3

True or false

1. False; page 757
2. False; page 758
3. True; page 759
4. True; page 760
5. False; page 761
6. True; page 762

Multiple choice

1. c; page 757
2. b; page 757
3. d; page 757
4. a; page 757
5. a; page 757
6. e; page 757
7. a; page 759
8. d; page 761
9. c; page 761

Short Response Questions

1. Stagflation is a combination of recession (falling real GDP) and inflation (rising price level). Stagflation can be created by a decrease in aggregate supply, that is, a leftward shift of the aggregate supply curve; page 761.

2. During the Great Depression, the Fed did little or nothing. The quantity of money contracted by a huge amount and aggregate demand collapsed. The result was that real GDP plummeted. During the financial crisis of 2008, the Fed actively bailed out financial institutions and doubled the monetary base so that the quantity of money continued to grow. Aggregate demand decreased but did not collapse; page 762.

© 2015 Pearson Education, Inc.

Long Response Questions

■ FIGURE 29.12

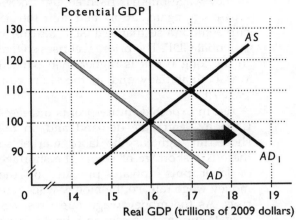

Price level (GDP price index, 2009 = 100)

■ FIGURE 29.13

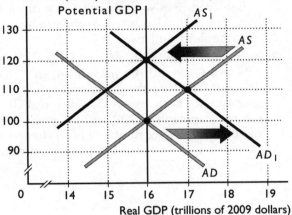

Price level (GDP price index, 2009 = 100)

1. An increase in expected profit increases firms' investment. Investment is part of aggregate demand, so the increase in investment increases aggregate demand. The aggregate demand curve shifts rightward, from *AD* to *AD*1 in Figure 29.12. Aggregate supply does not change, so in the figure the equilibrium price level rises to 110 and equilibrium real GDP increases to $17 trillion. An inflationary gap now exists because there is an above-full employment equilibrium. The money wage rate rises and aggregate supply decreases. This change is illustrated

in Figure 29.13, in which the *AS* curve shifts leftward. Eventually the *AS* curve shifts to *AS*1. Real GDP returns to potential GDP, $16 trillion, and the price level rises to 120; pages 752, 757.

2. An inflationary gap exists when real GDP exceeds potential GDP. Employment in the labor market exceeds full employment, so the money wage rate starts to rise. As the money wage rate rises, aggregate supply decreases and the aggregate supply curve shifts leftward. Eventually, real GDP returns to potential GDP and the inflationary gap is eliminated; page 757.

■ FIGURE 29.14

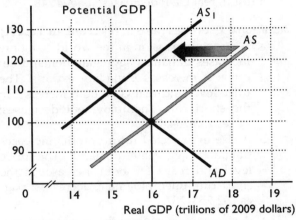

Price level (GDP price index, 2009 = 100)

3. Figure 29.14 shows the effect of a rise in the price of oil. Aggregate supply decreases and the *AS* curve shifts leftward from *AS* to *AS*1. Real GDP decreases to $15 trillion and the price level rises to 110. A recessionary gap is created because real GDP is less than potential GDP; pages 748, 757.

4. Demand-pull inflation starts with an increase in aggregate demand which raises the price level. In order for an inflation to occur, the price level must persistently continue to rise. The only factor that can create an on-going increase in the price level is (persisting) increases in the quantity of money because they create (persisting) increases in aggregate

© 2015 Pearson Education, Inc.

demand and thereby (persisting) increases in the price level; page 760

5. The difference between demand-pull and cost-push inflation can be traced to what starts the inflationary process. In a demand-pull inflation, the inflation starts with an event that increases aggregate demand. In a cost-push inflation, the inflation starts with an event that decreases aggregate supply. A demand-pull inflation and cost-push inflation are similar because both need constant increases in the quantity of money to create a persisting inflation; pages 760-761.

6. If the politician is elected and, as a result, taxes are raised, then aggregate demand decreases and the *AD* curve shifts leftward. As a result, real GDP decreases; pages 748, 757.

Additional Exercises (also in MyEconLab Test A)

1. a. A strong expansion in the world economy increases Canada's aggregate demand because it increases Canadian exports. The price level and real GDP both increase. In the short run, unemployment decreases; pages 753-754, 757.

   b. A rise in expected future profits increases Canada's aggregate demand. The price level and real GDP both increase. In the short run, unemployment decreases; pages 752-753, 757.

2. a. A strong expansion in the world economy increases Canada's aggregate demand and, in the short run, tightens the labor market so there is a shortage of labor. As time passes, the money wage rate rises, raising the real wage rate and decreasing aggregate supply. In the long run the money wage rate has risen enough to decrease aggregate supply and shift the *AS* curve enough so that real GDP returns to potential GDP. The price level rises so that in the long run it is higher than what it was both initially and in the short run; page 757.

   b. A rise in expected future profits increases Canada's aggregate demand and, in the short run, tightens the labor market so there is a shortage of labor. The shortage of labor puts upward pressure on the money wage rate, so the money wage rate rises. As the money wage rate rises, aggregate supply decreases and the *AS* curve shifts leftward. In the long run, real GDP returns to potential GDP. The price level, however, rises so that in the long run it is higher than what it was both initially and in the short run; page 757.

3. In the short run, both events increase Canada's real GDP and the price level, so Canada's real GDP and the price level rise. In the long run, for both events Canada's real GDP returns to potential GDP and the price level rises, so in the long run there is no change in Canada's real GDP but the price level rises; pages 752-754, 757.

© 2015 Pearson Education, Inc.

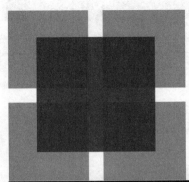

Aggregate Expenditure Multiplier

Chapter 30

CHAPTER CHECKLIST

1 Explain how real GDP influences expenditure plans.

Aggregate planned expenditure is planned consumption expenditure plus planned investment plus planned government expenditures plus planned net exports. The consumption function is the relationship between consumption expenditure and disposable income; when disposable income increases, consumption expenditure increases. The marginal propensity to consume, *MPC*, is the fraction of a change in disposable income that is spent on consumption. The slope of the consumption function equals the *MPC*. When real GDP increases, imports increase. The marginal propensity to import is the fraction of an increase in real GDP spent on imports.

2 Explain how real GDP adjusts to achieve equilibrium expenditure.

Autonomous expenditure are the components of aggregate planned expenditure that do not change when real GDP changes; induced expenditure are the components of aggregate planned expenditure that change when real GDP changes. Equilibrium expenditure occurs when aggregate *planned* expenditure equals real GDP which is at the point where the *AE* curve intersects the 45° line. If aggregate planned expenditure exceeds real GDP, an unplanned decrease in inventories occurs. Firms increase production and real GDP increases until equilibrium expenditure is reached. If aggregate planned expenditure is less than real GDP, an unplanned increase in inventories occurs. Firms decrease production and real GDP decreases until equilibrium expenditure is reached.

3 Explain the expenditure multiplier.

The expenditure multiplier is the amount by which a change in any component of autonomous expenditure is multiplied to determine the change that it generates in equilibrium expenditure and real GDP. The multiplier is greater than 1 because an increase in autonomous expenditure induces further changes in aggregate expenditure. Ignoring income taxes and imports, the multiplier equals $1/(1 - MPC)$. The multiplier is larger if the *MPC* is larger. Imports and income taxes reduce the size of the multiplier. In general, the multiplier equals $1/(1 - \text{slope of } AE \text{ curve})$. A business cycle expansion is triggered by an increase in autonomous expenditure that increases aggregate planned expenditure and real GDP; a business cycle recession is triggered by a decrease in autonomous expenditure.

4 Derive the *AD* curve from equilibrium expenditure.

The *AE* curve is the relationship between aggregate planned expenditure and real GDP. The *AD* curve is the relationship between the quantity of real GDP demanded and the price level. When the price level rises, aggregate planned expenditure decreases, the *AE* curve shifts downward, and equilibrium expenditure decreases. When the price level rises, aggregate planned expenditure increases, the *AE* curve shifts upward, and equilibrium expenditure increases. Each point of equilibrium expenditure corresponds to a point on the *AD* curve.

© 2015 Pearson Education, Inc.

YOUR AP TEST HINTS

AP Topics

Topic on your AP test	What to Know	Corresponding textbook section
Expenditure plans	How real GDP influences expenditures	Checkpoint 30.1
Equilibrium expenditure	How real GDP adjustments achieve the equilibrium	Checkpoint 30.2
Expenditure multiplier	Reason why multiplier exists; multiplier formulas	Checkpoint 30.3
Equilibrium and the *AD* curve	How the *AD* curve is derived	Checkpoint 30.4

AP Vocabulary Covered

Terms	What to Know	Text Sections
Aggregate demand	The expenditures of consumption + planned investment + planned government expenditures + planned exports minus planned imports	Checkpoint 30.1, p. 770
Consumption function	The relationship between consumption expenditure and disposable income	Checkpoint 30.1, p. 770
Marginal propensity to consume, *MPC*	The fraction of change in disposable income spent on consumption; equal to the change in consumption divided by the change in disposable income	Checkpoint 30.1, p. 772
Marginal propensity to import	The fraction increase in real GDP that is spent purchasing imports	Checkpoint 30.1, p. 774
Equilibrium expenditure	The level of aggregate expenditure that occurs when aggregate planned expenditures will equal real GDP	Checkpoint 30.2, p. 778
Multiplier	The amount by which changes in the component of aggregate expenditure is multiplied to determine the change in equilibrium expenditures and the real GDP generated	Checkpoint 30.3, p. 782
Marginal tax rate	The fractional change in real GDP that is paid in income taxes	Checkpoint 30.3, p. 784

Extra AP material

- The *Aggregate Expenditure (AE) model* is not included on the macroeconomic AP test, nor is the connection between the *AE* curve and the *AD* curve.

- On the AP test, the *marginal propensity to save* (*MPS*) is sometimes used. The marginal propensity to save is related to the *marginal propensity to consume* (*MPC*). The marginal propensity to consume is the additional consumption expenditure that results from an additional dollar of disposable income. The marginal propensity to save is the additional saving that results from an additional dollar of disposable income. Because an additional dollar of disposable income must be either spent or saved, it is the case that $MPC + MPS = 1$. This result can be rearranged to show that $MPS = 1 - MPC$. As a result, the formula for the *expenditure multiplier*, $1/(1 - MPC)$, can be rewritten as $1/(MPS)$.

- On the AP test, the multiplier using the marginal propensity to consume *(MPC)* is sometimes called the *consumption multiplier*. The AP test frequently uses the multiplier formula of $1/(1 - MPC)$.

© 2015 Pearson Education, Inc.

CHECKPOINT 30.1

■ Explain how real GDP influences expenditure plans.

Quick Review

- *Autonomous expenditure* The components of aggregate expenditure that do not change when real GDP changes.
- *Induced expenditure* The components of aggregate expenditure that change when real GDP changes
- *Consumption function* The relationship between consumption expenditure and disposable income, other things remaining the same.
- *Marginal propensity to consume, MPC* The fraction of a change in disposable income that is spent on consumption, which equals the change in consumption expenditure divided by the change in disposable income that brought it about.

Additional Practice Problems 30.1

1. Suppose disposable income increases by $1.5 trillion.
   a. If the marginal propensity to consume (*MPC*) is 0.8, what is the change in consumption expenditure?
   b. If the *MPC* equals 0.6, what is the change in consumption expenditure?
   c. What is the relationship between the *MPC* and the change in consumption expenditure for a given change in disposable income?

2. The figure shows the consumption function for a small nation. Use the figure to calculate the marginal propensity to consume and autonomous consumption in the nation.

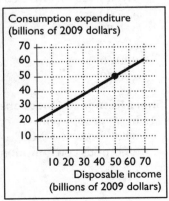

Consumption expenditure (billions of 2009 dollars)

Disposable income (billions of 2009 dollars)

Solutions to Additional Practice Problems 30.1

1a. The change in consumption expenditure equals the *MPC* multiplied by the change in disposable income. When the *MPC* is 0.8, the change in consumption expenditure equals ($1.5 trillion) × (0.8), which is $1.2 trillion.

1b. When the *MPC* is 0.6, the change in consumption expenditure is ($1.5 trillion) × (0.6), which is $0.9 trillion.

1c. The larger the *MPC*, the greater the change in consumption expenditure for a given change in disposable income.

2. The *MPC* is the slope of the consumption function and equals the change in consumption expenditure divided by the change in disposable income that brought it about. The figure shows that when disposable income increases from $0 to $50 billion, consumption expenditure increases from $20 billion to $50 billion. The *MPC* equals ($30 billion) ÷ ($50 billion), which is 0.60. Autonomous consumption is the amount of consumption when income equals zero and equals the *y*-axis intercept, $20 billion.

■ AP Self Test 30.1

True or false

1. Induced expenditure increases as real GDP increases.

2. The marginal propensity to consume equals total consumption expenditure divided by total disposable income.

Multiple choice

1. The components of aggregate expenditure are consumption expenditure,
   a. interest, gross spending, and net spending.
   b. investment, government expenditure on goods and services, and net income.
   c. interest, government expenditure on goods and services, and net exports.
   d. investment, government expenditure on goods and services, and net exports.
   e. investment, government expenditure on goods and services, and net taxes.

© 2015 Pearson Education, Inc.

2. Autonomous expenditure is the component of
   a. aggregate expenditure that changes when real GDP changes.
   b. induced expenditure that changes when real GDP changes.
   c. aggregate planned expenditure that changes only when government expenditure on goods and services change.
   d. aggregate expenditure that does not change when real GDP changes.
   e. aggregate expenditure that does not change when the interest rate changes.

3. The components of aggregate expenditure that change when real GDP changes are
   a. unplanned expenditure.
   b. induced expenditure.
   c. planned expenditure.
   d. autonomous expenditure.
   e. changeable expenditure.

4. The consumption function is the relationship between ____, other things remaining the same.
   a. consumption expenditure and saving
   b. consumption expenditure and the price level
   c. consumption expenditure and disposable income
   d. net taxes and disposable income
   e. consumption expenditure and net taxes

5. When disposable income increases from $9 trillion to $10 trillion, consumption expenditure increases from $6 trillion to $6.8 trillion. The *MPC* is
   a. 1.00.
   b. 0.80.
   c. 0.60.
   d. 0.68.
   e. $6.8 trillion.

■ **FIGURE 30.1**

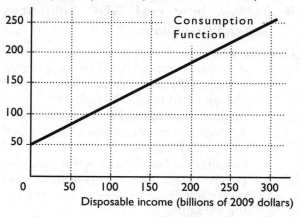

6. Figure 30.1 shows a consumption function. What is the amount of autonomous consumption?
   a. $0
   b. $50 billion
   c. $100 billion
   d. $150 billion
   e. $200 billion

7. Figure 30.1 shows a consumption function. What is the amount of induced consumption when disposable income equals $150 billion?
   a. $0
   b. $50 billion
   c. $100 billion
   d. $150 billion
   e. $200 billion

8. Figure 30.1 shows a consumption function. What does the *MPC* equal?
   a. 1.00
   b. 0.80
   c. 0.67
   d. 0.60
   e. 0.50

Short Response Questions

1. In a graph with a consumption function, what does the MPC equal? What does autonomous consumption equal?

© 2015 Pearson Education, Inc.

Disposable income (trillions of 2009 dollars)	Consumption expenditure, (trillions of 2009 dollars)
0.0	0.4
1.0	1.2
2.0	2.0
3.0	2.8
4.0	3.6
5.0	4.4

■ **FIGURE 30.2**

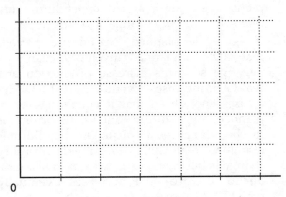

2. The table above has data on consumption expenditure and disposable income.
   a. Using the data, label the axes and plot the consumption function in Figure 30.2.
   b. Indicate the amount of autonomous consumption expenditure in Figure 30.2.
   c. What is the amount of saving if disposable income equals $1.0 trillion? $4.0 trillion?
   d. Calculate the marginal propensity to consume.
   e. Suppose the real interest rate falls and consumers increase their consumption by $0.6 trillion at every level of disposable income. Draw the new consumption function in Figure 30.2. What is the amount of autonomous consumption now?

Long Response Questions
1. What does aggregate planned expenditure equal?
2. What is the difference between autonomous expenditure and induced expenditure?

Change in disposable income (trillions of 2009 dollars)	Change in consumption expenditure (trillions of 2009 dollars)	Marginal propensity to consume, MPC
2	1.8	____
1	0.9	____
4	3.0	____

3. The table above shows the change in consumption expenditure when a change in disposable income occurs. Complete the table by calculating the marginal propensities to consume.

Additional Exercises (also in MyEconLab Test A)
1. The marginal propensity to consume in Japan is less than that in the United States, and for any amount of real GDP, Americans spend more on consumption than do the Japanese. Compare the consumption functions in Japan and the United States.
2. As China becomes richer, the marginal propensity to consume in China will decrease. Explain how the consumption function in China will change.
3. Autonomous consumption in the United Kingdom was £150 billion and the marginal propensity to consume was 0.9. Plot the U.K. consumption function and explain how a rise in the real interest rate will influence it.
4. The marginal propensity to import is higher in Singapore than it is in the United States. The growth rate of real GDP in Singapore exceeds that in the United States. Which country's imports grow more quickly and why?

CHECKPOINT 30.2

■ **Explain how real GDP adjusts to achieve equilibrium expenditure.**

Quick Review
- *Equilibrium expenditure* The level of aggregate expenditure that occurs when aggregate planned expenditure equals real GDP.

© 2015 Pearson Education, Inc.

Additional Practice Problem 30.2

GDP	C	I	G	X	M
50	50	20	25	25	10
100	85	20	25	25	15
150	120	20	25	25	20
200	155	20	25	25	25
250	190	20	25	25	30
300	225	20	25	25	35

1. The table gives the components of real GDP in billions of dollars.
   a. Draw the aggregate expenditure curve.
   b. What is equilibrium expenditure?
   c. At what levels of GDP does aggregate planned expenditure exceed real GDP? At what levels does real GDP exceed aggregate planned expenditure?
   d. At what levels of GDP is unplanned inventory change negative? At what levels is unplanned inventory change positive?
   e. What is the relationship between your answers to parts (c) and (d)?
   f. By what process is the equilibrium expenditure reached?

Solution to Additional Practice Problem 30.2

1a. Aggregate planned expenditure is equal to $C + I + G + X - M$. To construct the AE curve, use the formula for each level of real GDP. The AE curve is illustrated in the figure along with a 45° line.

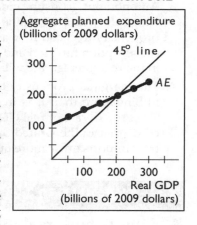

1b. Equilibrium expenditure occurs at the level of real GDP where the AE curve intersects the 45° line. The equilibrium expenditure is $200 billion.

1c. For all GDP less than $200 billion, aggregate planned expenditure exceeds real GDP. For all GDP greater than $200 billion, aggregate planned expenditure exceeds real GDP.

1d. For all GDP less than $200 billion, unplanned inventory change is negative. For all GDP greater than $200 billion, unplanned inventory change is positive.

1e. For all levels of GDP for which aggregate planned expenditure exceeds real GDP, unplanned inventory change is negative. And for all levels of GDP for which real GDP exceeds aggregate planned expenditure, unplanned inventory change is positive.

1f. If aggregate planned expenditure exceeds real GDP, unplanned inventory change is negative so firms increase production and real GDP increases. Eventually real GDP increases enough so that it equals aggregate planned expenditure and equilibrium is reached. If aggregate planned expenditure is less than real GDP, unplanned inventory change is positive and so firms decrease production and real GDP decreases. Eventually real GDP decreases by enough so that it equals aggregate planned expenditure and equilibrium is reached. When real GDP reaches $200 billion, aggregate planned expenditure equals real GDP. The economy is at equilibrium expenditure. The unplanned inventory change is zero and firms have no reason to change production.

■ AP Self Test 30.2

True or false

1. Equilibrium expenditure occurs at the intersection of the aggregate expenditure curve and the 45° line.

2. If aggregate planned expenditure is less than real GDP, unplanned inventories increase.

3. If aggregate planned expenditure exceeds real GDP, inventories decrease and firms decrease production.

4. If unplanned investment occurs, then the aggregate expenditure is not at its equilibrium level.

© 2015 Pearson Education, Inc.

Multiple choice

1. When aggregate planned expenditure exceeds real GDP, there is
   a. a planned decrease in inventories.
   b. a planned increase in inventories.
   c. an unplanned decrease in inventories.
   d. an unplanned increase in inventory.
   e. an unplanned decrease in the price level.

■ **FIGURE 30.3**

Aggregate planned expenditure (trillions of 2009 dollars)

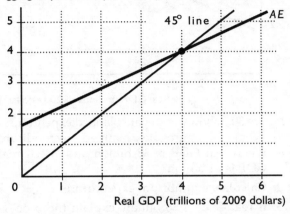

Real GDP (trillions of 2009 dollars)

2. In Figure 30.3, equilibrium expenditure equals ____ trillion.
   a. $1
   b. $2
   c. $3
   d. $4
   e. $5

3. In Figure 30.3, if real GDP is $5 trillion, then
   a. the economy is at its equilibrium.
   b. inventories are above their target.
   c. inventories are below their target
   d. the price level will rise to restore equilibrium.
   e. the price level will fall to restore equilibrium.

4. If aggregate planned expenditure is greater than real GDP,
   a. an unplanned decrease in inventories leads to an increase in production.
   b. an unplanned increase in inventories leads to a decrease in production.
   c. a planned decrease in inventories leads to an decrease in production.
   d. a planned increase in inventories leads to an increase in production.
   e. an unplanned decrease in inventories leads to an increase in the price level.

5. If real GDP equals aggregate planned expenditure, then inventories are
   a. above their target levels.
   b. below their target levels.
   c. equal their target levels.
   d. are either above or below their target levels but more information is needed to determine which.
   e. None of the above answers is necessarily correct because there is no relationship between inventories and aggregate planned expenditure.

6. Equilibrium expenditure is the level of expenditure at which
   a. firms' inventories are zero.
   b. firms' inventories are at the desired level.
   c. firms produce more output than they sell.
   d. aggregate planned expenditure minus planned changes in inventories equals real GDP.
   e. aggregate planned expenditure plus planned changes in inventories equals real GDP.

Long Response Questions

1. What is the relationship between aggregate planned expenditure and real GDP? Explain the relationship.

2. In a diagram with an *AE* curve, what does the 45° line represent? Why is equilibrium expenditure determined by the intersection of the aggregate expenditure curve and the 45° line?

© 2015 Pearson Education, Inc.

3. If aggregate planned expenditure is less than real GDP, what forces drive the economy to equilibrium expenditure?

GDP	C	I	G	X	M	AE
0.0	0.6	0.4	0.2	0.2	0.2	___
1.0	1.2	0.4	0.2	0.2	0.4	___
2.0	1.8	0.4	0.2	0.2	0.6	___
3.0	2.4	0.4	0.2	0.2	0.8	___
4.0	3.0	0.4	0.2	0.2	1.0	___
5.0	3.6	0.4	0.2	0.2	1.2	___

■ **FIGURE 30.4**

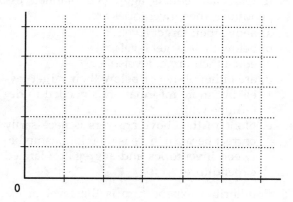

4. The table above gives the components of aggregate planned expenditure in trillions of 2009 dollars.
   a. Complete the table.
   b. Label the axes in Figure 30.4 (at the top of the next column) and plot the *AE* curve.
   c. In Figure 30.4, show the equilibrium expenditure.
   d. Over what range of GDP is there an unplanned increase in inventories? Over what range of GDP is there an unplanned decrease in inventories?
   e. What is the amount of planned and actual investment when GDP equals $3.0 trillion?

Additional Exercises (also in MyEconLab Test A)

■ **FIGURE 30.5**

Aggregate planned expenditure (trillions of 2009 dollars)

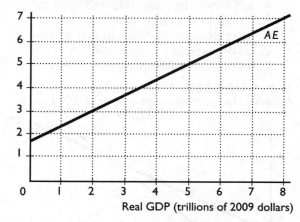

Real GDP (trillions of 2009 dollars)

Figure 30.5 shows aggregate planned expenditure.
1. What is aggregate planned expenditure when real GDP is $8 billion and when real GDP is $2 billion?
2. Calculate equilibrium expenditure.
3. If real GDP is $8 billion, explain the process that moves the economy toward equilibrium expenditure.
4. If real GDP is $2 billion, explain the process that moves the economy toward equilibrium expenditure.

CHECKPOINT 30.3

■ **Explain the expenditure multiplier.**

Quick Review
- *Multiplier* The expenditure multiplier is the amount by which a change in any component of autonomous expenditure is magnified or multiplied to determine the change that it generates in equilibrium expenditure and real GDP.
- *Basic multiplier formula* The defining multiplier formula is:

$$\text{Multiplier} = \frac{\text{Change in equilibrium expenditure}}{\text{Change in autonomous expenditure}}.$$

© 2015 Pearson Education, Inc.

- *Multiplier and the MPC* With no imports or income taxes, the multiplier is:

$$\text{Multiplier} = \frac{1}{(1 - MPC)}.$$

- *Multiplier, imports and income taxes* With imports and income taxes, the multiplier is:

$$\text{Multiplier} = \frac{1}{(1 - \text{slope of the } AE \text{ curve})}.$$

Additional Practice Problems 30.3

1. An economy has no imports or taxes, the *MPC* is 0.90, and real GDP is $12 trillion. If businesses increase investment by $0.1 trillion:

   a. Calculate the multiplier.

   b. Calculate the change in real GDP.

   c. Calculate the new level of real GDP.

2. An increase in autonomous expenditure of $2 trillion increases equilibrium expenditure by $4 trillion:

   a. Calculate the multiplier.

   b. Calculate the slope of the *AE* curve.

3. Suppose there are no income taxes or imports. How would the following events affect equilibrium expenditure and real GDP?

   a. Investment increases by $40 billion and the *MPC* equals 0.6.

   b. The president and Congress agree to increase military spending by $100 billion and the *MPC* is 0.8.

Solutions to Additional Practice Problems 30.3

1a. With no taxes or imports, the multiplier equals 1/(1 − *MPC*). The *MPC* is 0.9, so the multiplier equals 1/(1 - 0.9), which equals 10.0.

1b. The change in real GDP is equal to the multiplier times the change in investment, which is 10 × $0.1 trillion = $1 trillion.

1c. Real GDP increases by $1 trillion from $12 trillion to $13 trillion.

2a. The multiplier equals the change in equilibrium expenditure divided by the change in autonomous expenditure. The multiplier equals $4 trillion ÷ $2 trillion, which is 2.

2b. The expenditure multiplier equals 1/(1 − slope of the *AE* curve). The multiplier is 2, so 2 = 1/(1 − slope of the *AE* curve). Multiply both sides by (1 − slope of the *AE* curve) to get 2 × (1 − slope of the *AE* curve) = 1. Solve for the slope of the *AE* curve, which is that the slope of the *AE* curve is 0.50.

3a. The increase in investment is an increase in autonomous expenditure. The change in equilibrium expenditure and real GDP equals the multiplier times the change in autonomous expenditure. The multiplier equals 1/(1 − *MPC*) = 1/(1 − 0.6) = 2.5. The change in equilibrium expenditure and real GDP equals (2.5 × $40 billion), which is $100 billion. Equilibrium expenditure and real GDP increase by $100 billion.

3b. The increase in military spending is an increase in government purchases and is an increase in autonomous expenditure. The change in equilibrium expenditure and real GDP equals the multiplier times the change in autonomous expenditure. The multiplier equals 1/(1 − *MPC*). Because the *MPC* equals 0.8, the multiplier is 5.0. The change in equilibrium expenditure and real GDP equals (5.0 × $100 billion), which is $500 billion.

■ AP Self Test 30.3

True or false

1. The multiplier is greater than 1.

2. If the multiplier equals 4, then a $0.25 trillion increase in investment increases real GDP by $1.0 trillion.

3. The smaller the marginal propensity to consume, the larger is the multiplier.

4. A country that has a high marginal tax rate has a larger multiplier than a country with a low marginal tax rate, other things being the same.

© 2015 Pearson Education, Inc.

Multiple choice

1. The multiplier is equal to the change in _____ divided by the change in _____.
   a. autonomous expenditure; equilibrium expenditure
   b. dependent expenditure; autonomous expenditure
   c. real GDP; equilibrium expenditure
   d. equilibrium expenditure; autonomous expenditure
   e. the price level; real GDP

2. The multiplier is larger than one because
   a. an increase in autonomous expenditure induces further increases in aggregate expenditure.
   b. additional expenditure induces lower incomes.
   c. an increase in autonomous expenditure brings about a reduction in the real interest rate.
   d. an increase in autonomous expenditure induces further decreases in aggregate expenditure.
   e. the price level rises, thereby reinforcing the initial effect.

3. The multiplier equals 5 and there is a $3 million increase in investment. Equilibrium expenditure
   a. decreases by $15 million.
   b. increases by $3 million.
   c. increases by $5 million.
   d. increases by $15 million.
   e. increases by $0.60 million.

4. In an economy with no income taxes or imports, the marginal propensity to consume is 0.80. The multiplier is
   a. 0.20.
   b. 0.80.
   c. 1.25.
   d. 5.00.
   e. 10.00.

5. An increase in the marginal tax rate
   a. increases the multiplier.
   b. decreases the multiplier but cannot make it negative.
   c. has no effect on the multiplier.
   d. can either increase or decrease the multiplier.
   e. decreases the multiplier and can make it negative.

6. Which of the following increases the size of the multiplier?
   a. a decrease in the marginal propensity to consume
   b. an increase in autonomous spending
   c. an increase in the marginal income tax rate
   d. a decrease in the marginal propensity to import
   e. an increase in investment

7. If the slope of the *AE* curve is 0.5, then the expenditure multiplier equals
   a. 5.
   b. 4.
   c. 3.
   d. 2.
   e. 0.5.

8. At the beginning of a recession, the multiplier
   a. offsets the initial cut in autonomous expenditure and slows the recession.
   b. reinforces the initial cut in autonomous expenditure and adds force to the recession.
   c. offsets the initial cut in autonomous expenditure and reverses the recession.
   d. reinforces the initial cut in autonomous expenditure and reverses the recession.
   e. has no effect on the recession.

© 2015 Pearson Education, Inc.

Short Response Questions

■ **FIGURE 30.6**
Aggregate planned expenditure (trillions of 2009 dollars)

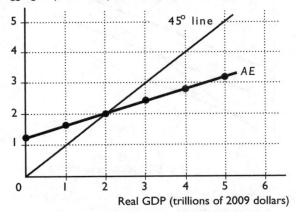

Real GDP (trillions of 2009 dollars)

1. Figure 30.6 has the aggregate planned expenditure curve for a nation. (This curve is the same curve you plotted in the "Complete the Graph" problem in Checkpoint 30.2.) Suppose that government expenditure on goods and services increases by $1.2 trillion.
   a. In Figure 30.6 plot the new aggregate expenditure curve.
   b. What is the new equilibrium expenditure? By how much did equilibrium expenditure change?
   c. What is the slope of the *AE* curve?
   d. What is the multiplier? Use the multiplier to find the change in equilibrium expenditure.

Marginal propensity to consume, MPC	Multiplier
0.9	——
0.8	——
0.7	——
0.6	——
0.5	——
0.4	——

2. The table gives various values for the marginal propensity to consume. Suppose there are no income taxes or imports. Complete the table by calculating the values of the multiplier. What is the relationship between the *MPC* and the multiplier?

Long Response Questions
1. Why is the multiplier greater than 1?
2. How does the multiplier affect business cycle turning points?

Additional Exercises (also in MyEconLab Test A)
An economy has no imports and no income taxes. The marginal propensity to consume is 0.60, and real GDP is $100 billion. Businesses decrease investment by $10 billion. Use this information to answer Exercises 1 and 2.
1. Calculate the multiplier and the change in real GDP.
2. Calculate the new level of real GDP and explain why real GDP decreases by more than $10 billion.

An economy has no imports and no income taxes. Autonomous expenditure increases by $2 trillion and the multiplier is 1.25. Use this information to answer Exercises 3 and 4.
3. Calculate the change in real GDP and the marginal propensity to consume.
4. If the government opens the country to international trade, explain how international trade influences the multiplier.

CHECKPOINT 30.4

■ **Derive the *AD* curve from equilibrium expenditure.**

Quick Review
- *Equilibrium expenditure* The level of aggregate expenditure that occurs when aggregate planned expenditure equals real GDP.
- *Aggregate demand* The aggregate demand schedule is real GDP at equilibrium expenditure and the associated price level.

Additional Practice Problem 30.4
1. Figure 30.7 (on the next page) shows the *AE* curve, AE_0, when the price level is 100.
   a. In the figure, show what occurs when the price level rises to 110 and aggregate

© 2015 Pearson Education, Inc.

■ **FIGURE 30.7**

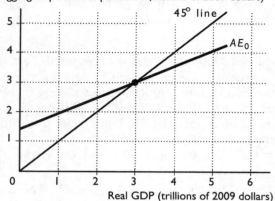

■ **FIGURE 30.9**

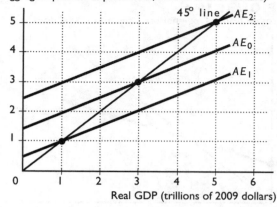

planned expenditure decreases by $1 trillion at every level of real GDP. What is the new equilibrium expenditure?

b. In the figure, show what occurs when the price level falls to 90 and aggregate planned expenditure increases by $1 trillion at every level of real GDP. What is the new equilibrium expenditure?

c. Use the results from parts (a) and (b) to draw an aggregate demand curve in Figure 30.8.

■ **FIGURE 30.8**

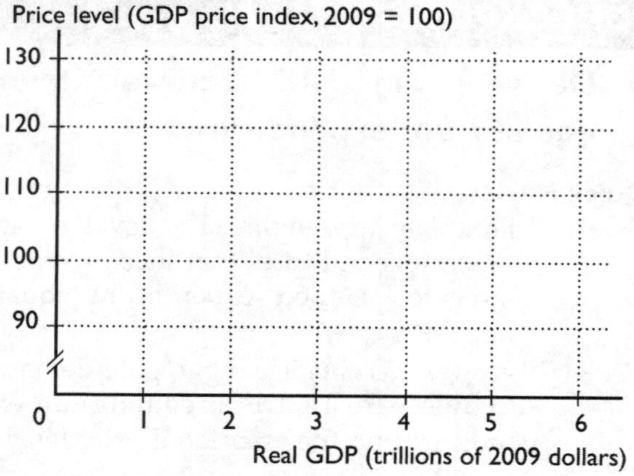

Price level (GDP price index, 2009 = 100)

Solution to Additional Practice Problem 30.4

1a. Figure 30.9 shows the new aggregate expenditure curve, labeled AE_1. The new equilibrium expenditure is $1 trillion, where the AE_1 curve intersects the 45° line.

1b. Figure 30.9 shows the new aggregate expenditure curve, labeled AE_2. The new equilibrium expenditure is $5 trillion.

■ **FIGURE 30.10**

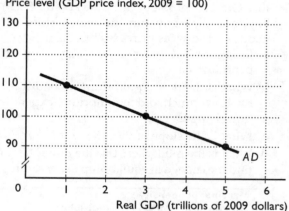

1c. Points on the aggregate demand schedule are the points of equilibrium expenditure. So each point of equilibrium expenditure corresponds to a point on the AD curve. When the price level is 110, real GDP is $1 trillion. When the price level is 100, real GDP is $3 trillion. And when the price level is 90, real GDP is $5 trillion. These points and the aggregate demand curve are shown Figure 30.10. The aggregate demand curve has been derived from the equilibrium expenditure model.

© 2015 Pearson Education, Inc.

■ AP Self Test 30.4

True or false

1. There is no relationship between equilibrium expenditure and the *AD* curve.

2. A change in the price level results in a movement along the *AD* curve.

3. A change in the price level results in a movement along the *AE* curve.

4. Each point of equilibrium expenditure on the *AE* curve corresponds to a point on the *AD* curve.

Multiple choice

1. A movement along the *AE* curve arises from a change in ____ and a movement along the *AD* curve arises from a change in ____.
   a. real GDP; the price level
   b. real GDP; investment
   c. the price level; the price level
   d. the price level; investment
   e. investment; the price level

2. A change in the price level
   a. shifts the *AE* curve and creates a movement along the *AD* curve.
   b. creates a movement along the *AE* curve and shifts the *AD* curve.
   c. shifts the *AE* curve and the *AD* curve in the same direction.
   d. shifts the *AE* curve and the *AD* curve in opposite directions.
   e. creates a movement along both the *AE* curve and the *AD* curve.

3. The *AD* curve is the relationship between
   a. aggregate planned expenditure and the price level.
   b. aggregate planned expenditure and the quantity of real GDP demanded.
   c. the quantity of real GDP demanded and the quantity of real GDP supplied.
   d. the quantity of real GDP demanded and the unemployment rate.
   e. aggregate planned expenditure and real GDP when the price level is fixed.

Short Response Question

1. What is the relationship between the *AE* curve and the *AD* curve?

Long Response Questions

■ FIGURE 30.11

Aggregate planned expenditure (trillions of 2009 dollars)

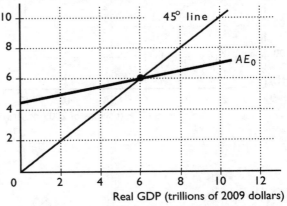

1. Figure 30.11 has the aggregate planned expenditure curve for a nation when the price level is 100. Autonomous expenditure equals $4.25 trillion.

   a. Suppose the price level rises to 120 and aggregate planned expenditure decreases by $0.75 trillion at every level of real GDP. In the figure, show the new aggregate expenditure line. What does equilibrium expenditure now equal?

   b. Suppose that the price level falls to 100 and, compared to the situation when the price level equaled 110, aggregate planned expenditure increases by $0.75 trillion at every level of real GDP. In the figure, show the new aggregate expenditure line. What does equilibrium expenditure now equal?

   c. Use the results from parts (a) and (b) to draw an aggregate demand curve in Figure 30.12 (on the next page).

2. What is the effect on the *AE* curve when the price level rises? What is the effect on the *AD* curve when the price level rises?

© 2015 Pearson Education, Inc.

■ **FIGURE 30.12**

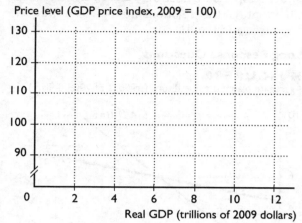

Price level (GDP price index, 2009 = 100)

Additional Exercises (also in MyEconLab Test A)

Real GDP (trillions of 2009 dollars)	Aggregate planned expenditure when the price level is (trillions of 2009 dollars)		
	110	100	90
0	1.0	1.5	2.0
1	1.5	2.0	2.5
2	2.0	2.5	3.0
3	2.5	3.0	3.5
4	3.0	3.5	4.0
5	3.5	4.0	4.5
6	4.0	4.5	5.0

In the economy described in the table above, autonomous expenditure increases by $0.5 trillion.

1. Make a graph to show three new *AE* curves. On the graph, mark equilibrium expenditure at each price level.

2. Construct the aggregate demand schedule and plot the *AD* curve.

3. Calculate the magnitude of the multiplier.

© 2015 Pearson Education, Inc.

SELF TEST ANSWERS

■ AP Self Test 30.1

True or false

1. True; page 770
2. False; page 772

Multiple choice

1. d; page 770
2. d; page 770
3. b; page 770
4. c; page 770
5. b; page 772
6. b; pages 770-771
7. c; pages 770-771
8. c; page 772

Short Response Questions

1. The MPC equals the slope of the consumption function. Autonomous consumption equals the y-axis intercept; pages 770, 772.

■ FIGURE 30.13

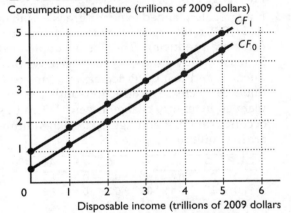
Consumption expenditure (trillions of 2009 dollars)

Disposable income (trillions of 2009 dollars)

2. a. Figure 30.13 plots the consumption function, labeled CF_0; page 771.

   b. Autonomous consumption is $0.4 trillion, the y-intercept of curve CF_0 in Figure 30.13; page 770.

   c. If disposable income is $1.0 trillion, consumption expenditure is $1.2 trillion, so saving is −$0.2 trillion. If disposable income is $4.0 trillion consumption expendi-

ture is $3.6 trillion, so saving is $0.4 trillion; page 771.

   d. The marginal propensity to consume is 0.80; page 772.

   e. The new consumption function is labeled CF_1 in Figure 30.13. Autonomous consumption is $1 trillion; pages 770-771.

Long Response Questions

1. Aggregate planned expenditure equals planned consumption expenditure plus planned investment plus planned government expenditures plus planned exports minus planned imports; page 770.

2. Autonomous expenditures are the components of aggregate expenditure that do not change when real GDP changes. Induced expenditures are the components of aggregate expenditure that change when real GDP changes; page 770.

Change in disposable income (trillions of 2009 dollars)	Change in consumption expenditure (trillions of 2009 dollars)	Marginal propensity to consume, MPC
2	1.8	0.90
1	0.9	0.90
4	3.0	0.75

3. The completed table is above. The marginal propensity to consume is equal to the change in consumption expenditure divided by the change in disposable income that brought it about; page 772.

Additional Exercises (also in MyEconLab Test A)

1. The U.S. consumption function and the Japanese consumption function differ in two aspects. First, because the marginal propensity to consume is less in Japan, the U.S. consumption function is steeper than the Japanese consumption function. Second, because for any level of real GDP, Americans spend more on consumption than do the Japanese, U.S. autonomous consumption exceeds Japanese autonomous consumption. So, the U.S.

© 2015 Pearson Education, Inc.

consumption function lies above the Japanese consumption function; page 772.

2. The decrease in the Chinese marginal propensity to consume makes the Chinese consumption function become less steep; page 772.

■ FIGURE 30.14

Consumption expenditure (billions of 2009 pounds)

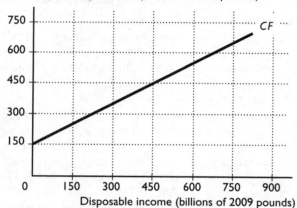

Disposable income (billions of 2009 pounds)

3. The U.K. consumption function is in Figure 30.14. The intercept on the *y*-axis is £150 billion, which is the amount of autonomous consumption expenditure. The slope is 0.90, which is the U.K. marginal propensity to consume. If the real interest rate rises, the consumption function shifts downward; pages 770-773.

4. Imports are related to a nation's real GDP via the marginal propensity to import. The higher the marginal propensity to import, the greater the amount of imports from any given real GDP. The growth rate of real GDP in Singapore exceeds that in the United States, so the growth of imports in Singapore will exceed the growth of imports in the United States; page 774.

■ AP Self Test 30.2

True or false

1. True; page 778
2. True; page 779
3. False; page 779
4. True; page 779

Multiple choice

1. c; page 779
2. d; page 778
3. b; page 779
4. a; page 779
5. c; pages 778-779
6. b; page 779

Long Response Questions

1. As real GDP increases, aggregate planned expenditure increases, so there is a positive relationship between real GDP and aggregate planned expenditure. Aggregate planned expenditure increases when real GDP increases because, as real GDP increases, induced expenditure increases; pages 776-777.

2. Along the 45° line real GDP equals aggregate planned expenditure. Equilibrium expenditure occurs when aggregate planned expenditure equals real GDP, which is the point where the *AE* curve intersects the 45° line; page 778.

3. If aggregate planned expenditure is less than real GDP, total expenditure is less than what firms are producing. There is an unplanned increase in inventories. Firms decrease production, and real GDP decreases. Firms continue to decrease production until the unplanned inventory change is zero. When this occurs, real GDP and aggregate expenditure are in equilibrium; page 779.

GDP	C	I	G	X	M	AE
0.0	0.6	0.4	0.2	0.2	0.2	<u>1.2</u>
1.0	1.2	0.4	0.2	0.2	0.4	<u>1.6</u>
2.0	1.8	0.4	0.2	0.2	0.6	<u>2.0</u>
3.0	2.4	0.4	0.2	0.2	0.8	<u>2.4</u>
4.0	3.0	0.4	0.2	0.2	1.0	<u>2.8</u>
5.0	3.6	0.4	0.2	0.2	1.2	<u>3.2</u>

4. a. Aggregate planned expenditure equals $C + I + G + X - M$. The completed table is above; pages 776-777.

© 2015 Pearson Education, Inc.

■ **FIGURE 30.15**

Aggregate planned expenditure (trillions of 2009 dollars)

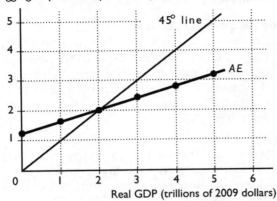

Real GDP (trillions of 2009 dollars)

b. Figure 30.15 shows the aggregate expenditure curve; page 777.

c. A 45° line has been added to Figure 30.15. Equilibrium expenditure is where the 45° line intersects the aggregate expenditure curve, so equilibrium expenditure is $2 trillion; page 778.

d. An unplanned increase in inventories occurs when real GDP exceeds aggregate planned expenditure. In Figure 30.15, real GDP exceeds planned expenditure when real GDP is greater than $2 trillion; page 778.

An unplanned decrease in inventories occurs when real GDP is less than aggregate planned expenditure. In Figure 30.15, real GDP is less than planned expenditure when real GDP is less than $2 trillion; page 778.

e. When GDP is $3 trillion, planned investment is $0.4 trillion. When GDP is $3 trillion, aggregate planned expenditure is $2.4 trillion, so there is an unplanned increase in inventories of $0.6 trillion. The actual investment is $1 trillion, the sum of planned investment plus the unplanned change in inventories; page 779.

Additional Exercises (also in MyEconLab Test A)

1. Aggregate planned expenditure when real GDP is $8 billion is $7 billion. Aggregate planned expenditure when real GDP is $2 billion is $3 billion; page 778.

2. Equilibrium expenditure occurs where aggregate planned expenditure equals real GDP. (Equivalently, equilibrium expenditure occurs where the *AE* curve intersects the 45° line.) Aggregate planned expenditure equals real GDP at $5 billion, so $5 billion is equilibrium expenditure; page 778.

3. If real GDP equals $8 billion, real GDP exceeds aggregate planned expenditure. Firms find that they are not selling all that they produce and inventories are climbing above their target levels. The unplanned inventory accumulation leads firms to decrease their production, so that real GDP decreases and the economy converges toward its equilibrium of $5 billion; page 779.

4. If real GDP equals $2 billion, aggregate planned expenditure exceeds real GDP. Firms find their inventories falling below the target levels. In response, firms increase production to restore their inventories to their target levels. Real GDP increases and the economy moves toward its equilibrium expenditure of $5 billion; page 779.

■ **AP Self Test 30.3**

True or false

1. True; pages 782-783
2. True; page 783
3. False; pages 783-784
4. False; page 784

Multiple choice

1. d; page 783
2. a; page 783
3. d; page 783
4. d; page 784
5. b; page 784
6. d; page 784
7. d; page 784
8. b; page 786

© 2015 Pearson Education, Inc.

Short Response Questions

■ **FIGURE 30.16**

Aggregate planned expenditure (trillions of 2009 dollars)

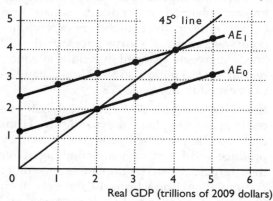

Real GDP (trillions of 2009 dollars)

1. a. Figure 30.16 has the new AE curve, labeled AE_1 and the initial curve labeled AE_0; page 782.

   b. Equilibrium expenditure increases by $2 trillion to $4 trillion; page 782.

   c. The slope of the AE curve equals ($0.4 trillion) ÷ ($1.0 trillion), which is 0.40; page 783.

   d. The formula for the multiplier is given by $\dfrac{1}{(1 - \text{slope of the } AE \text{ curve})}$. Thus the multiplier is $\dfrac{1}{(1 - 0.4)}$ = 1.67. The change is equal to the multiplier multiplied by the change in autonomous expenditure, which is (1.67) × ($1.2 trillion). The change in equilibrium expenditure is $2.0 trillion; pages 782, 784.

Marginal propensity to consume, MPC	Multiplier
0.9	10.0
0.8	5.0
0.7	3.3
0.6	2.5
0.5	2.0
0.4	1.7

2. The multiplier equals $1 \div (1 - MPC)$. The completed table is above. As the MPC in-

creases in size, the multiplier increases in size; pages 783-784.

Long Response Questions

1. The multiplier exceeds 1 because an initial change in autonomous expenditure leads to changes in induced expenditure. As a result, the change in aggregate expenditure exceeds the initial change in autonomous expenditure; page 783.

2. The forces that bring business-cycle turning points are the swings in autonomous expenditure such as investment and exports. The multiplier gives momentum to the economy's new direction; page 786.

Additional Exercises (also in MyEconLab Test A)

1. Because the economy has no imports or taxes, the multiplier equals $\dfrac{1}{(1 - MPC)}$, which is $\dfrac{1}{(1 - 0.6)} = \dfrac{1}{0.4} = 2.5$. The change in real GDP = change in investment × multiplier = –$10 billion × 2.5 = –$25 billion. Real GDP decreases by $25 billion; pages 783-784.

2. The new level of real GDP is $100 billion –$25 billion, which is $75 billion. Real GDP decreases by more than the $10 billion because the initial decrease in investment decreases real GDP. And the decrease in real GDP decreases induced expenditure, which decreases real GDP even more; page 783.

3. The change in real GDP equals the multiplier × the change in autonomous expenditure. Therefore the change in real GDP= 1.25 × $2 trillion = $2.5 trillion.

   Because there are no taxes or imports, the multiplier = $\dfrac{1}{(1 - MPC)}$. We know that the multiplier equals 1.25, so 1.25 = $\dfrac{1}{(1 - MPC)}$.

   Solve this formula for the MPC. Multiplying both sides by (1 − MPC) gives 1.25 × (1 − MPC) = 1. Multiplying both sides of the

© 2015 Pearson Education, Inc.

equation by 1.25 gives $1.25 - 1.25 \times MPC = 1$. Subtracting 1.25 from both sides gives $-1.25 \times MPC = -.25$. Dividing both sides by -1.25 gives $MPC = 0.2$; pages 783-784.

4. Opening the economy to trade decreases the magnitude of the multiplier; page 784.

■ AP Self Test 30.4

True or false

1. False; pages 788-789
2. True; pages 788-789
3. False; pages 788-789
4. True; pages 788-789

Multiple choice

1. a; page 788
2. a; pages 788-789
3. c; page 788

Short Response Question

1. The AE curve is used to derive the AD curve. Each point of equilibrium expenditure on the AE curve corresponds to a point on the AD curve; page 788.

Long Response Questions

1. a. Figure 30.17 has the new AE curve, labeled AE_1 and the initial curve labeled AE_0 Equilibrium expenditure decreases by $2 trillion to $4 trillion; pages 788-789.

b. Figure 30.17 has the new AE curve, labeled AE_2 Equilibrium expenditure increases by $2 trillion to $8 trillion; pages 788-789.

c. Figure 30.18 shows the aggregate demand curve. The three points identified have been derived from Figure 30.17 and equilibrium expenditure. When the price level is 120, equilibrium expenditure and real GDP is $4 trillion. When the price level is 110, equilibrium expenditure and real GDP is $6 trillion. And when the price level is 100, equilibrium expenditure and real GDP is $8 trillion; page 789

■ **FIGURE 30.17**

Aggregate planned expenditure (trillions of 2009 dollars)

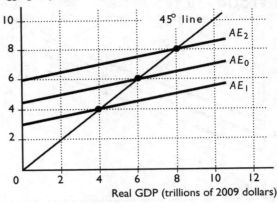

■ **FIGURE 30.18**

Price level (GDP price index, 2009 = 100)

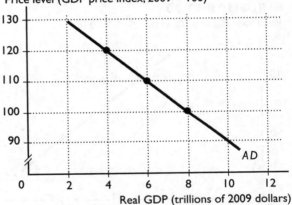

2. When the price level rises, the AE curve shifts downward and there is a movement up along the AD curve. When the price level falls, the AE curve shifts upward and there is a movement down along the AD curve; pages 788-789.

© 2015 Pearson Education, Inc.

Additional Exercises (also in MyEconLab Test A)

■ **FIGURE 30.19**

Aggregate planned expenditure (trillions of 2009 dollars)

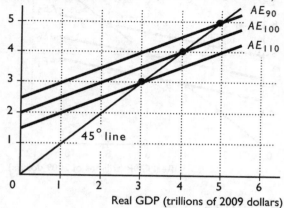

■ **FIGURE 30.20**

Price level (GDP price index, 2009 = 100)

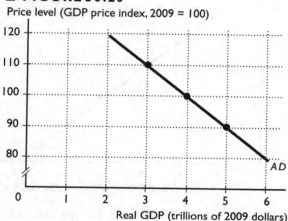

1. Figure 30.19 illustrates the three new *AE* curves. Figure 30.19 also shows the equilibrium expenditures. The equilibrium expenditure when the price level is 90 is $5 trillion. The equilibrium expenditure when the price level is 100 is $4 trillion. The equilibrium expenditure when the price level is 110 is $3 trillion; pages 788-789.

Price level	Quantity of real GDP demanded (trillions of 2009 dollars)
90	5
100	4
110	3

2. A table with the aggregate demand schedule is above. It shows the aggregate quantity demanded, which equals aggregate expenditure, at each price level. Figure 30.20 (on the previous page) plots the aggregate demand curve; pages 788-789.

3. Each $0.5 trillion increase in autonomous expenditure increased equilibrium GDP by $1 trillion. So, for each *AE* curve, the multiplier is 2.0; pages 788-789.

© 2015 Pearson Education, Inc.

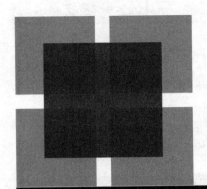

The Short-Run Policy Tradeoff

Chapter

31

1 Describe the short-run tradeoff between inflation and unemployment.

The short-run Phillips curve shows the relationship between the inflation rate and the unemployment rate when the natural unemployment rate and the expected inflation rate remain constant. The downward-sloping short-run Phillips curve indicates a tradeoff between inflation and unemployment: lower unemployment can be attained, but at the cost of higher inflation. The short-run Phillips curve is another way of looking at the upward-sloping aggregate supply curve, because a change in aggregate demand, which leads to a movement along the aggregate supply curve, changes real GDP so that the unemployment rate changes and changes the price level so that the inflation rate changes. For instance, moving up the aggregate supply curve, larger real GDP corresponds to lower unemployment and the higher price level corresponds to higher inflation. The relationship between output and unemployment is called Okun's Law. Okun's Law states that for each percentage point that the unemployment rate is above the natural unemployment rate, real GDP is two percentage points below potential GDP.

2 Distinguish between the short-run and the long-run Phillips curves and describe the shifting tradeoff between inflation and unemployment.

The long-run Phillips curve is a vertical line that shows the relationship between inflation and unemployment when the economy is at full employment. At full employment, the unemployment rate is the natural unemployment rate, but the inflation rate can take on any value. Along the long-run Phillips curve, there is no long-run tradeoff between inflation and unemployment. The short-run Phillips curve intersects the long-run Phillips at the expected inflation rate. If the expected inflation rate changes, the short-run Phillips curve shifts upward or downward to intersect the long-run Phillips curve at the new expected inflation rate. The natural rate hypothesis is the proposition that when the inflation rate changes, the unemployment rate changes temporarily and eventually returns to the natural unemployment rate. If the natural unemployment rate increases, both the long-run Phillips curve and the short-run Phillips curve shift rightward; if it decreases, both curves shift leftward.

3 Explain how the Fed can influence the inflation rate and the unemployment rate.

The expected inflation rate helps set the money wage rate and other money prices. To forecast inflation, people use data about past inflation and other relevant variables, as well as economic science. If the Fed tries to lower unemployment to less than the natural rate, the expected inflation rate rises. Eventually the unemployment rate will return to the natural unemployment rate but the inflation rate is permanently higher. If the Fed then lowers the inflation rate, unemployment temporarily rises above the natural rate as the economy moves into a recession. Ultimately the unemployment rate will return to the natural unemployment rate and the inflation rate will be lower.

© 2015 Pearson Education, Inc.

YOUR AP TEST HINTS

AP Topics

Topic on your AP test	What to Know	Corresponding textbook section
Inflation versus unemployment	Descriptions of the short-run tradeoff	Checkpoint 31.1
Short-run Phillips Curve, *SRPC* and the Long-run Phillips Curve, *LRPC*	What distinguishes the two curves and descriptions of the shifting tradeoffs between inflation and unemployment	Checkpoint 31.2
The role of the Fed in economic changes	How the Fed influences the rates of inflation and unemployment	Checkpoint 31.3

AP Vocabulary Covered

Terms	What to Know	Text Sections
Short-run Phillips Curve, *SRPC*	The curve showing the inverse relationship between the inflation rate (measured on the *y*-axis) and the unemployment rate (measured on the *x*-axis); higher inflation results in lower unemployment	Checkpoint 31.1, p. 796
Long-run Phillips Curve, *LRPC*	Vertical line showing the relationship between inflation and unemployment when the economy is at full employment; demonstrates that in the long run, the economy is at the natural unemployment rate (*NRU*) no matter the inflation rate	Checkpoint 31.2, p. 802
Natural rate hypothesis	The theory that inflation rate changes only temporarily change the natural rate of unemployment for a nation	Checkpoint 31.2, p. 804
Factors that shift the Phillips curves	Change in the natural unemployment rate shifts *both* the *SRPC* and *LRPC*; change in the expected inflation rate shifts *only* the *SRPC*	Checkpoint 31.2, p. 806

Extra AP material

- The AP test is moving in the direction of having students understand and graph the connection between the *AD/AS* diagram and the Phillips Curve diagram. In particular:
  - A change in aggregate demand, which shifts the *AD* curve and changes real GDP, the price level, and employment, corresponds to a movement <u>along</u> the *SRPC*, showing the resulting inflation rate and unemployment rate. An increase in aggregate demand (rightward shift of the *AD* curve) increases employment and the price level, thereby corresponding to an upward movement <u>along</u> the *SRPC*.
  - A change in aggregate supply, which shifts the *AS* (*SRAS*) curve and changes real GDP, the price level, and employment, corresponds to a *shift* in the *SRPC*. A decrease in aggregate supply (leftward shift of the *AS* curve) decreases employment and raises the price level, thereby corresponding to a rightward *shift* of the *SRPC*
- The AP test has included the result that government assistance to the unemployed *increases* the natural rate of unemployment because more assistance gives the unemployed more time to be selective about returning to work until the assistance ends. Removal of governmental assistance *reduces* the natural rate of unemployment because those who lose jobs will quickly accept any other job offer if there is no other assistance available.

CHECKPOINT 31.1

■ **Describe the short-run tradeoff between inflation and unemployment.**

Quick Review

- *Short-run Phillips curve* A curve that shows the relationship between the inflation rate and the unemployment rate when the natural unemployment rate and the expected inflation rate remain constant.

- *Okun's Law* For each percentage point that the unemployment rate is above (below) the natural unemployment rate, real GDP is two percentage points below (above) potential GDP.

Additional Practice Problems 31.1

1. For a nation, the table describes five possible situations that might arise in 2015, depending on the level of aggregate demand in that year. In this nation potential GDP is $7 trillion, and the natural unemployment rate is 5 percent.

	Price level (2009 = 100)	Unemployment rate (percentage)
A	101.5	9
B	104.0	6
C	105.0	5
D	106.5	4
E	109.0	3

   a. Calculate the inflation rate for each possible outcome.
   b. Use Okun's Law to find the real GDP associated with each unemployment rate in the table.
   c. Plot the short-run Phillips curve for 2015.
   d. Plot the aggregate supply curve for 2015.
   e. Mark the points *A, B, C, D,* and *E* on each curve that correspond to the data provided in the table and the data that you have calculated.

2. In the Practice Problem, what is the role played the aggregate demand curve? In the figure you have drawn with the aggregate supply curve, show an aggregate demand curve that would create an inflation rate of 5 percent. To what point on the Phillips curve does this aggregate demand/aggregate supply equilibrium correspond?

Solutions to Additional Practice Problems 31.1

1a. The inflation rate equals the change in the price level divided by the initial price level, all multiplied by 100. So, for row *A*, the inflation rate equals $\dfrac{101.5 - 100.0}{100.0} \times 100$, or 1.5

	Inflation rate (percent per year)
A	1.5
B	4.0
C	5.0
D	6.5
E	9.0

percent. The rest of the inflation rates are calculated similarly.

1b. Okun's Law states that for each percentage point the unemployment rate is above the natural unemployment rate, there is a 2 percent gap between real GDP and potential GDP. In row *A* of the table, the unemployment rate is 9 percent. The natural unemployment rate is 5 percent, so the unemployment rate is 4 percentage points above the natural unemployment rate. Based on Okun's law, real GDP is (2) × (4 percent) = 8 percent below potential GDP. Potential GDP is $7 trillion, so real GDP is (8 percent) × ($7 trillion) = $0.56 trillion dollars below potential GDP. In this case, real GDP equals $7 trillion minus $0.56 trillion, $6.44 trillion, as in the table to the right. The rest of the calculations of real GDP are similar.

	Real GDP (trillions of 2009 dollars)
A	6.44
B	6.86
C	7.00
D	7.14
E	7.28

1c. The figure plots the Phillips curve. The short-run Phillips curve shows the relationship between the inflation rate and the unemployment rate.

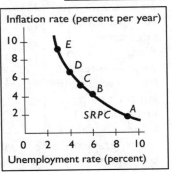

The unemployment rates are given in the table in the problem and the associated inflation rates are given in the answer to part (a).

© 2015 Pearson Education, Inc.

1d. The aggregate supply curve for 2015 is plotted in the figure. The price levels are given in the problem and the corresponding real GDPs are calculated from Okun's Law in part (b).

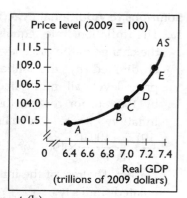

1e. The figures in part (c) and part (d) have the points labeled.

2. When aggregate demand increases, everything else remaining the same, there is a movement up along the aggregate supply curve. Real GDP increases and the price level rises. At the same time, the unemployment rate decreases and the inflation rate rises. There is a movement up along the short-run Phillips curve.

When aggregate demand decreases, everything else remaining the same, there is a movement down along the aggregate supply curve. Real GDP decreases and the price level falls. At the same time, the unemployment rate increases and the inflation rate falls. There is a movement down along the short-run Phillips curve.

Because the current price level is 100, to create an inflation rate of 5 percent, the aggregate demand curve must intersect the aggregate supply at a price level of 105. The figure shows

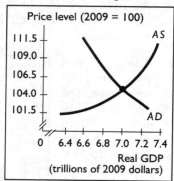

this aggregate demand curve. This price level corresponds to point *C*, so this aggregate demand/aggregate supply equilibrium corresponds to point *C* on the short-run Phillips curve

■ AP Self Test 31.1

True or false

1. The short-run Phillips curve shows the tradeoff between the natural unemployment rate and the expected inflation rate.

2. Moving along a short-run Phillips curve, the cost of a lower unemployment rate is a higher inflation rate.

3. Okun's Law states that for each percentage point that real GDP is less than potential GDP, the unemployment rate is 2 percentage points above the natural unemployment rate.

4. Points on the short-run Phillips curve correspond to points on the aggregate supply curve.

5. Aggregate demand fluctuations bring movements along the aggregate supply curve and along the short-run Phillips curve.

Multiple choice

1. The short-run Phillips curve shows the relationship between the
   a. inflation rate and the interest rate.
   b. inflation rate and real GDP.
   c. unemployment rate and the interest rate.
   d. inflation rate and the unemployment rate.
   e. price level and real GDP.

2. The short-run Phillips curve is
   a. vertical at the natural unemployment rate.
   b. upward sloping.
   c. downward sloping.
   d. horizontal at the expected inflation rate.
   e. U-shaped.

3. Moving along the short-run Phillips curve, as the unemployment rate increases the inflation rate
   a. decreases.
   b. increases.
   c. remains unchanged.
   d. initially decreases and then increases.
   e. initially increases and then decreases.

4. If real GDP exceeds potential GDP, then employment is ____ full employment and the

© 2015 Pearson Education, Inc.

unemployment rate is ____ the natural unemployment rate.

a. below; above

b. equal to; below

c. above; below

d. above; above

e. equal to; equal to

5. According to Okun's Law, if the natural unemployment rate is 5 percent, the actual unemployment rate is 4 percent, and potential GDP is $15 trillion, then actual real GDP is

a. $12.0 trillion.

b. $15.0 trillion.

c. $14.7 trillion.

d. $15.4 trillion.

e. $15.3 trillion.

6. When a movement up along the aggregate supply curve occurs, there is also

a. a movement down along the short-run Phillips curve.

b. a movement up along the short-run Phillips curve.

c. a rightward shift of the short-run Phillips curve.

d. a leftward shift of the short-run Phillips curve.

e. neither a movement along nor a shift in the short-run Phillips curve.

7. When aggregate demand increases, there is a movement ____ along the *AS* curve and ____.

a. up; a movement up along the short-run Phillips curve

b. up; a movement down along the short-run Phillips curve

c. up; an upward shift of the short-run Phillips curve

d. down; a downward shift of the short-run Phillips curve

e. down; a movement down along the short-run Phillips curve

Short Response Questions

1. What does the slope of the short-run Phillips curve indicate about the tradeoff between inflation and unemployment?

Inflation rate (percent per year)	Unemployment rate (percentage)
2	12
3	8
4	5
5	3
6	2

■ **FIGURE 31.1**

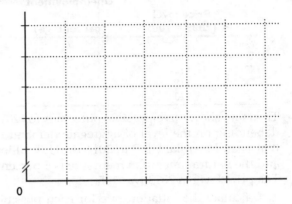

2. The table above has data on the inflation rate and the unemployment rate.

a. Using the data, label the axes and plot the short-run Phillips curve in Figure 31.1. Label the curve *SRPC*.

b. What is the effect of a decrease in the unemployment rate from 8 percent to 5 percent? Show the effect in Figure 31.1.

c. How does your answer to part (b) indicate the presence of a tradeoff?

Long Response Questions

Unemployment rate (percentage)	Real GDP (trillions of 2009 dollars)
4	____
5	____
6	____
7	____

1. The table above gives data for an economy. Suppose that for this economy the natural unemployment rate is 5 percent and potential GDP is $8 trillion.

a. What is Okun's Law?

© 2015 Pearson Education, Inc.

b. Using Okun's Law, complete the table by calculating real GDP for each unemployment rate.

2. What is the effect on the aggregate supply curve and on the short-run Phillips curve of an increase in aggregate demand?

Additional Exercises (also in MyEconLab Test A)

	Price level (2009 = 100)	Unemployment rate (percentage)
A	108	9
B	113	6
C	115	5
D	118	4
E	123	3

The table shows five possible outcomes for 2014 depending on the level of aggregate demand in that year. Potential GDP in 2014 is $11.0 trillion and the natural unemployment rate is 6 percent. The price level in 2013 was 105.

1. Calculate the inflation rate for each possible outcome.

2. Use Okun's Law to find the real GDP at each unemployment rate in the table.

3. What are the expected inflation rate and the expected price level in 2014?

4. Plot the short-run Phillips curve for 2014. Mark the points A, B, C, D, and E that correspond to the data in the table and that you have calculated.

5. Plot the aggregate supply curve for 2014. Mark the points A, B, C, D, and E that correspond to the data in the table.

CHECKPOINT 31.2

■ **Distinguish between the short-run and the long-run Phillips curves and describe the shifting tradeoff between inflation and unemployment.**

Quick Review

• *Long-run Phillips curve* The vertical line that shows the relationship between inflation and unemployment when the economy is at full employment.

• *Factor that shifts the long-run Phillips curve* An increase (decrease) in the natural unemployment rate shifts the long-run and short-run Phillips curve rightward (leftward).

• *Natural rate hypothesis* When the inflation rate changes, the unemployment rate changes temporarily and eventually returns to the natural unemployment rate.

Additional Practice Problems 31.2

1. The figure shows a short-run Phillips curve and a long-run Phillips curve.

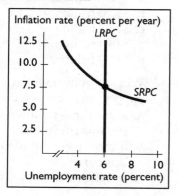

a. What is the expected inflation rate?

b. What is the natural unemployment rate?

c. If the expected inflation rate falls to 2.5 percent a year, show the new short-run and long-run Phillips curves.

d. If the natural unemployment rate decreases to 4 percent but the expected inflation rate does not change from what it is in the figure above, show the new short-run and long-run Phillips curves.

2. Explain how the inflation rate and unemployment rate might simultaneously increase.

Solutions to Additional Practice Problems 31.2

1a. The expected inflation rate is the inflation rate where the short-run Phillips curve and the long-run Phillips curve intersect. The expected inflation rate is 7.5 percent a year.

1b. The long-run Phillips curve is vertical at the natural unemployment rate. The natural unemployment rate is 6 percent.

© 2015 Pearson Education, Inc.

1c. When the ex-
pected inflation
rate decreases
to 2.5 percent a
year, the short-
run Phillips
curve shifts
downward but
the long-run
Phillips curve
does not shift.
The figure

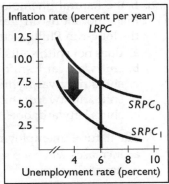

shows that the short-run Phillips curve shifts
downward from SRPC0 to SRPC1. The new
short-run Phillips curve intersects the long-
run Phillips curve at the new expected inflation rate, 2.5 percent.

1d. A decrease in
the natural un-
employment
rate shifts *both*
the short-run
Phillips curve
and the long-
run Phillips
curve leftward.
In the figure
the long-run
Phillips curve

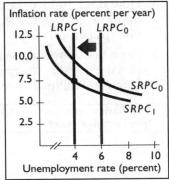

shifts leftward from LRPC0 to LRPC1 and the
short-run Phillips curve shifts leftward from
SRPC0 to SRPC1. The new short-run Phillips
curve intersects the new long-run Phillips
curve at the expected inflation rate.

2. If the natural
unemployment
rate increases,
the short-run
Phillips curves
shifts right-
ward. If simul-
taneously the
inflation rate
rises, it is possi-
ble to move
from a point on
its old short-

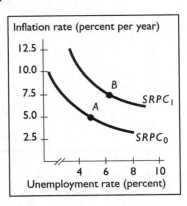

run Phillips curve to a point on the new short-
run Phillips curve such that both the inflation
rate and the unemployment rate increase. For
instance, in the figure the short-run Phillips
curve shifts and the inflation rate rises from 5.0
percent to 7.5 percent. The movement from
point A on the initial short-run Phillips curve
SRPC0 to point B on the new short-run Phillips
curve SRPC1 shows how both the unemployment rate and inflation rate can simultaneously
increase.

■ AP Self Test 31.2

True or false

1. The long-run Phillips curve is horizontal because it shows that at the expected inflation
rate, any unemployment rate might occur.

2. An increase in the expected inflation rate
shifts the long-run Phillips curve.

3. An increase in the expected inflation rate
shifts the short-run Phillips curve.

4. The natural rate hypothesis states that an increase in the inflation rate temporarily decreases the unemployment rate but does not
permanently change the unemployment rate.

5. A change in the natural unemployment rate
shifts both the short-run and long-run Phillips curves.

Multiple choice

1. The long-run Phillips curve is the relationship between
   a. unemployment and the price level at full
      employment.
   b. unemployment and the inflation rate at
      the expected price level.
   c. inflation and real GDP at full employment.
   d. inflation and unemployment when the
      economy is at full employment.
   e. inflation and the expected inflation rate.

2. The long-run Phillips curve is
   a. upward sloping.
   b. downward sloping.
   c. horizontal.
   d. vertical.
   e. upside-down U-shaped.

© 2015 Pearson Education, Inc.

3. When the expected inflation rate ____, the short-run Phillips curve ____.
   a. falls; shifts upward
   b. rises; shifts upward
   c. rises; shifts downward
   d. falls; does not shift
   e. rises; might shift upward or downward depending on how the long-run Phillips curve shifts

■ **FIGURE 31.2**

Inflation rate (percent per year)

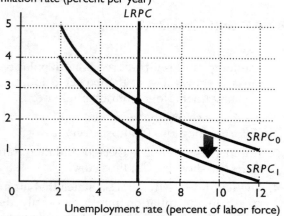

Unemployment rate (percent of labor force)

4. The shift in Figure 31.2 is the result of
   a. an increase in the expected inflation rate.
   b. a decrease in the expected inflation rate.
   c. an increase in the natural unemployment rate.
   d. a decrease in the natural unemployment rate.
   e. an increase in the inflation rate.

5. The natural rate hypothesis states that
   a. only natural economic policies can bring a permanent reduction in the unemployment rate.
   b. changes in the inflation rate temporarily change the unemployment rate.
   c. it is natural for the unemployment rate to exceed the inflation rate.
   d. it is natural for the unemployment rate to be less than the natural unemployment rate.
   e. changes in the inflation rate temporarily change the natural unemployment rate.

6. If the natural unemployment rate decreases, then the short-run Phillips curve ____ and the long-run Phillips curve ____.
   a. does not shift; shifts leftward
   b. shifts leftward; shifts leftward
   c. shifts rightward; shifts leftward
   d. shifts rightward; shifts rightward
   e. shifts leftward; does not shift

7. The natural unemployment rate
   a. increases when job search increases.
   b. never changes.
   c. always increases.
   d. decreases when the inflation rate rises.
   e. increases when the expected inflation rate rises.

Short Response Questions

1. How does an increase in the expected inflation rate change the short-run and long-run Phillips curves?

2. How does an increase in the natural unemployment rate change the short-run and long-run Phillips curves?

Inflation rate (percent per year)	Unemployment rate (percentage)
2	12
3	8
4	5
5	3
6	2

■ **FIGURE 31.3**

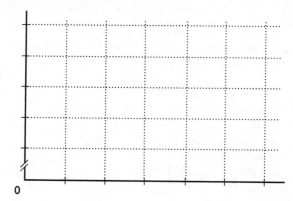

3. The table above has data on a nation's short-run Phillips curve. In this nation, the natural

© 2015 Pearson Education, Inc.

unemployment rate equals 5 percent.

a. Label the axes and then draw both the short-run Phillips curve and long-run Phillips curve in Figure 31.3.

b. What is the expected inflation rate?

c. Suppose the expected inflation rate falls by 1 percentage point. Show the effect of this change on the short-run Phillips curve and long-run Phillips curve in Figure 31.3.

■ FIGURE 31.4

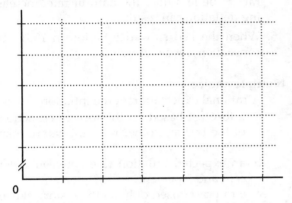

4. In Figure 31.4, redraw your initial short-run and long-run Phillips curves from Figure 31.3. Suppose that the natural unemployment rate falls to 3 percent and the expected inflation rate does not change. In Figure 31.4, show the effect of this change.

Long Response Questions

1. In the *AS-AD* model, does the aggregate demand curve, the aggregate supply curve, or the potential GDP line best correspond to the long-run Phillips curve?

2. What are the key points about the long-run Phillips curve and the relationship between the long-run Phillips curve and the short-run Phillips curve?

3. What is the natural rate hypothesis?

Additional Exercises (also in MyEconLab Test A)

In an economy, the natural unemployment rate is 7 percent and the expected inflation rate is 4 percent a year.

1. Draw a graph of the short-run Phillips curve and long-run Phillips curve.

2. If the expected inflation rate changes to 3 percent a year, show the new short-run and long-run Phillips curves.

3. If the natural unemployment rate becomes 6 percent, show the new short-run and long-run Phillips curves.

4. Aggregate demand growth slows and eventually the inflation rate falls to 2 percent a year. Explain how unemployment and inflation change.

CHECKPOINT 31.3

■ Explain how the Fed can influence the inflation rate and the unemployment rate.

Quick Review

• *Expected inflation rate* The inflation rate people forecast and use to set the money wage rate and other money prices.

Additional Practice Problem 31.3

1. The figure shows the short-run and long-run Phillips curves. The current inflation rate is 7.5 percent a year and the current unemployment rate is the natural unemployment rate, 5 percent. Suppose

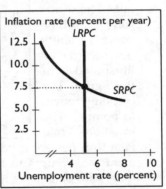

that the Fed believes that this inflation is too high and wants to lower it to 5 percent.

a. What policy will the Fed undertake to lower the inflation rate?

b. What will be the effect of the Fed's policy in the short run?

c. What will be the effect of the Fed's policy in the long run?

© 2015 Pearson Education, Inc.

Solutions to Additional Practice Problem 31.3

1a. To lower the inflation rate, the Fed must slow the growth of aggregate demand by slowing the money growth rate and raising the interest rate.

1b. In the short run, the Fed's action does not change the expected inflation rate, so the short-run Phillips curve does not shift. The economy moves along its short-run Phillips curve from point A to point B. The inflation rate falls to 5 percent and, as the economy moves into a recession, the unemployment rate rises to 8 percent.

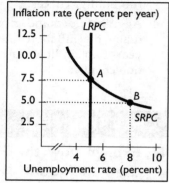

1c. In the long run, the expected inflation rate falls. The short-run Phillips curve shifts downward as illustrated in the figure. The economy moves to point C. The inflation rate falls to 5 percent a year and the unemployment rate returns to the natural unemployment rate of 5 percent. The reduction in the inflation rate had no lasting effect on the unemployment rate but there was a temporary recession with an increase in unemployment.

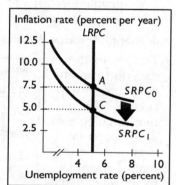

■ AP Self Test 31.3

True or false

1. The expected inflation rate never changes.

2. One factor that can be used to predict inflation is the Fed's monetary policy.

3. To lower the unemployment rate in the short run, the Fed will speed up the growth rate of money.

4. If the Fed tries to lower the unemployment rate to be less than the natural rate, increasing deflation can result.

5. When the Fed slowed inflation in 1981, the consequence was recession.

Multiple choice

1. A rational expectation of the inflation rate is
   a. a forecast based on the forecasted actions of the Fed and other relevant determinant factors.
   b. an expected inflation rate between 1 percent and 5 percent.
   c. a forecast based only on the historical evolution of inflation over the last 100 years.
   d. an expected inflation rate between 5 percent and 10 percent.
   e. always correct.

2. Because money growth is a major component determining the inflation rate, in order to forecast inflation we should forecast actions by the
   a. Office of the Treasury.
   b. president.
   c. Congress.
   d. Fed.
   e. U.S. Mint.

3. If the Fed tries to lower the unemployment rate so it is lower than the natural unemployment rate, before the expected inflation rate changes, the inflation rate _____ and the unemployment rate _____.
   a. does not change; falls
   b. falls; falls
   c. rises; falls
   d. rises; does not change
   e. falls; rises

© 2015 Pearson Education, Inc.

4. If the Fed tries to lower the unemployment rate so it is less than the natural unemployment rate, in the short run before the expected inflation rate changes, the *SRPC* ____ and the *LRPC* ____.
    a. does not change; does not change
    b. shifts downward; shifts leftward
    c. shifts upward; does not change
    d. shifts downward; does not change
    e. does not change; shifts rightward

5. If the Fed tries to lower the unemployment rate so it is less than the natural unemployment rate, in the long run the *SRPC* ____ and the *LRPC* ____.
    a. does not change; does not change
    b. shifts downward; shifts leftward
    c. shifts upward; does not change
    d. shifts downward; does not change
    e. does not change; shifts rightward

6. In 1981, the Fed
    a. created an expected inflation reduction policy and created an expansion.
    b. created an unexpected inflation reduction policy and created a recession.
    c. publicly announced an inflation reduction policy and created a recession.
    d. publicly announced an inflation reduction policy and created an expansion.
    e. took no action so that the inflation rate skyrocketed.

Long Response Questions

1. Figure 31.5 shows a nation's short-run and long-run Phillips curves. In this nation, the natural unemployment rate equals 6 percent and the actual and expected inflation rate is 20 percent. The nation's government decides to take actions to lower the inflation rate to 10 percent.
    a. In the figure, show what happens in the short run when the expected inflation rate does not change from 20 percent. Indicate the combination of the inflation rate and unemployment rate by labeling it point *A*.
    b. In the figure, show what happens in the short run when the expected inflation rate

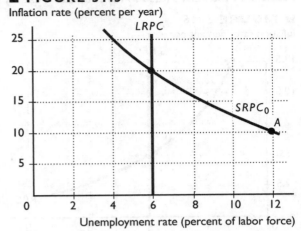

■ FIGURE 31.5

falls to 10 percent. Draw any new Phillips curve you need and indicate the new inflation rate and unemployment rate combination by labeling it *B*.

2. Suppose the Fed tries to lower the unemployment rate to be less than the natural rate. What are short-run effects of this policy on the short-run and long-run Phillips curve if there is no change in the expected inflation rate? What are the short-run effects on the inflation rate and the unemployment rate? What long-run effects does the policy have?

3. Why can the short-run effects of an increase in the inflation rate be different from the long-run effects?

4. The Eye on Your Life discusses how the short-run tradeoff between inflation and unemployment can affect your life. Another impact it can have might be more immediate. Would you rather look for a job when the Fed had just slowed the inflation rate? Based on your answer, what sort of policy would you prefer the Fed follow: One in which it keeps the inflation rate low and this fact is widely known or one in which the Fed occasionally slows the inflation rate when the slowing is unexpected by the public?

© 2015 Pearson Education, Inc.

Additional Exercises (also in MyEconLab Test A)

■ **FIGURE 31.6**

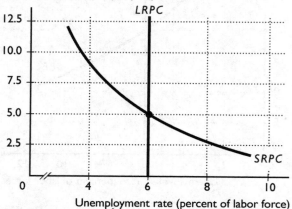

Inflation rate (percent per year)

In Figure 31.6, the current and expected inflation rate is 5 percent a year. The Fed decides it wants to lower the unemployment rate to 4 percent.

1. What are the short-run effects of the Fed's policy on inflation and unemployment?

2. What are the long-run effects of the Fed's policy on inflation and unemployment?

3. Comment on the temporary versus permanent nature of the changes in unemployment and inflation.

© 2015 Pearson Education, Inc.

SELF TEST ANSWERS

■ AP Self Test 31.1

True or false

1. False; page 796
2. True; page 796
3. False; page 797
4. True; pages 797-798
5. True; page 797

Multiple choice

1. d; page 796
2. c; page 796
3. a; page 796
4. c; page 797
5. e; page 797
6. b; pages 797-798
7. a; page 799

Short Response Questions

1. The slope of the short-run Phillips curve is negative, so when the unemployment rate falls, the inflation rate increases; page 796.

■ FIGURE 31.7

Inflation rate (percent per year)

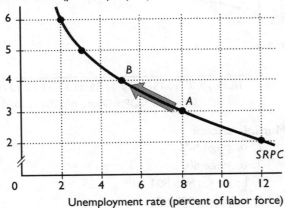

2. a. Figure 31.7 plots the short-run Phillips curve, labeled *SRPC*; page 796.

   b. The decrease in the unemployment rate brings a rise in the inflation rate. There is a movement along the short-run Phillips curve, as indicated by the movement from point *A* to point *B*; page 796.

c. The movement indicates a tradeoff because a decrease in the unemployment rate trades off a higher inflation rate; page 796.

Long Response Questions

1. a. Okun's Law states that for each percentage point that the unemployment rate is above the natural unemployment rate, there is a 2 percent gap between real GDP and potential GDP; page 797.

Unemployment rate (percentage)	Real GDP (trillions of 2009 dollars)
4	8.16
5	8.00
6	7.84
7	7.68

   b. The completed table is above. When the unemployment rate is 7 percent, it is 2 percentage points more than natural unemployment rate. According to Okun's Law, real GDP is (2) × (2 percent) or 4 percent below potential GDP. Real GDP is (4 percent) × ($8 trillion) or $0.32 trillion below potential GDP. Real GDP is $8 trillion minus $0.32 trillion = $7.68 trillion; page 797.

2. When aggregate demand increases, the aggregate demand curve shifts rightward and there is a movement up along the aggregate supply curve. The price level rises and real GDP increases. As the price level rises the inflation rate rises and as real GDP increases the unemployment rate decreases. There is a movement up along the short-run Phillips curve; page 799.

Additional Exercises (also in MyEconLab Test A)

	Inflation rate (percent per year)	Unemployment rate (percentage)	Price level	Real GDP (trillions of 2009 dollars)
A	2.9	9	108	10.34
B	7.6	6	113	11.00
C	9.5	5	115	11.22
D	12.4	4	118	11.44
E	17.1	3	123	11.66

1. The table gives the inflation rates for the dif-

ferent possible price levels. The inflation rates have been calculated starting with an initial price level of 105, which was the price level in 2013. So the inflation rate for possibility A is $[(108 - 105) \div 105] \times 100$, which is 2.9 percent; page 797.

2. The real GDP associated with each unemployment rate is in the above table. Okun's Law states that for each percentage point that the unemployment rate is above the natural unemployment rate, real GDP is 2 percentage points below potential GDP. In row A of the table, when the unemployment rate is 9 percent, the unemployment rate is 3 percent above the natural unemployment rate. So real GDP is $(2 \times 3$ percent$) = 6$ percent below potential GDP. As a result, real GDP is $(6$ percent $\times \$11$ trillion$) = \$0.66$ trillion below potential GDP, so that real GDP = $(\$11$ trillion $- \$0.66$ trillion$) = \$10.34$ trillion. The rest of the answers are calculated similarly; page 797.

3. The expected inflation rate is 7.6 percent a year because that is the inflation rate that corresponds with the price level at potential GDP, which is full employment and the natural unemployment rate. The corresponding price level is 113; page 798.

4. The Phillips curve in Figure 31.8 plots these inflation rates and unemployment rates; pages 797-798.

5. To plot the aggregate supply curve, real GDP is needed. These data are in the table above. The aggregate supply curve is then plotted in Figure 31.9 using the data from the table; pages 797-798.

■ AP Self Test 31.2

True or false
1. False; page 802
2. False; pages 803-804
3. True; pages 803-804
4. True; page 804
5. True; pages 805-806

■ **FIGURE 31.8**

Inflation rate (percent per year)

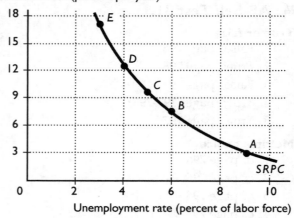

Unemployment rate (percent of labor force)

■ **FIGURE 31.9**

Price level (GDP price index, 2009 = 100)

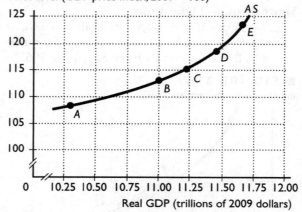

Real GDP (trillions of 2009 dollars)

Multiple choice
1. d; page 802
2. d; page 802
3. b; pages 803-804
4. b; pages 803-804
5. b; page 804
6. b; pages 805-806
7. a; page 806

Short Response Questions
1. An increase in the expected inflation rate shifts the short-run Phillips curve upward

© 2015 Pearson Education, Inc.

but does not change the long-run Phillips curve; pages 803-804.

2. An increase in the natural unemployment rate shifts *both* the long-run and short-run Phillips curves rightward; pages 805-806.

3. a. Figure 31.10 plots the short-run Phillips curve, labeled $SRPC_0$ and the long-run Phillips curve, labeled $LRPC$; page 803.

   b. The expected inflation rate is 4 percent a year because that is the inflation rate at which the short-run Phillips curve intersects the long-run Phillips curve; page 803.

   c. The new short-run Phillips curve is illustrated as $SRPC_1$; pages 803-804.

4. The initial short-run Phillips curve is labeled $SRPC_0$ and the initial long-run Phillips curve is labeled $LRPC_0$ in Figure 31.11. The decrease in the natural unemployment rate by 2 percentage points shifts both the long-run Phillips curve leftward from $LRPC_0$ to $LRPC_1$ and the short-run Phillips curve leftward from $SRPC_0$ to $SRPC_1$. The new short-run Phillips curve and the new long-run Phillips curve intersect at the expected inflation rate; pages 805-806.

Long Response Questions

1. The potential GDP line best corresponds to the long-run Phillips curve. The potential GDP line shows that a change in the price level does not change potential GDP and has no effect on the natural unemployment rate. The long-run Phillips curve shows that a change in the inflation rate does not change the natural unemployment rate; page 802.

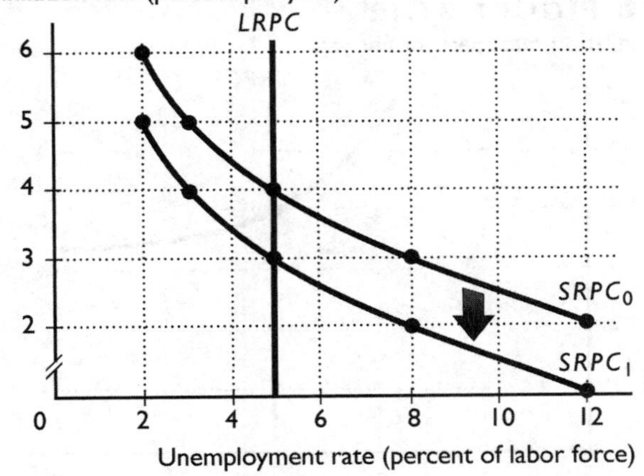

2. There are several key points: First, the long-run Phillips curve is vertical at the natural unemployment rate. Next, the short-run Phillips curve intersects the long-run Phillips curve at the expected inflation rate. Finally, changes in the expected inflation rate shift only the short-run Phillips curve, while changes in the natural unemployment rate shift both the short-run and long-run Phillips curves; pages 802-805.

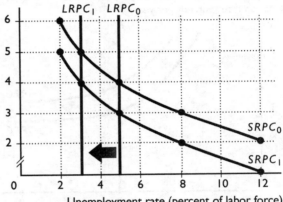

■ **FIGURE 31.10**

Inflation rate (percent per year)

■ **FIGURE 31.11**

Inflation rate (percent per year)

Unemployment rate (percent of labor force)

3. The natural rate hypothesis is the proposition that when the inflation rate changes, the unemployment rate changes temporarily and eventually returns to the natural unemployment rate. An increase in the inflation rate temporarily lowers the unemployment rate but eventually the unemployment rate returns to the natural unemployment rate. The fall in the unemployment rate was only temporary. Similarly, a decrease in the inflation rate temporarily raises the unemployment rate but eventually the unemployment rate returns to the natural unemployment rate. The rise in the unemployment rate was only temporary; page 804.

© 2015 Pearson Education, Inc.

Additional Exercises (also in MyEconLab Test A)

■ **FIGURE 31.12**

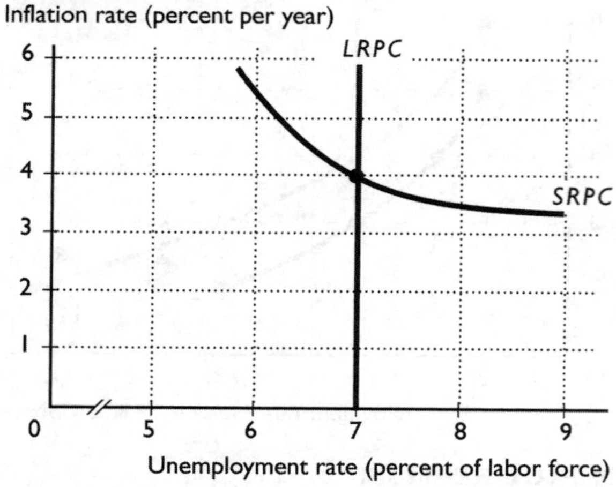

Inflation rate (percent per year)

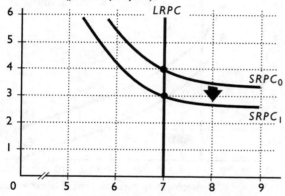

■ **FIGURE 31.13**

Inflation rate (percent per year)

1. Figure 31.12 shows the short-run and long-run Phillips curves. The long-run Phillips curve, *LRPC*, is vertical at the natural unemployment rate, 7 percent. The short-run Phillips curve, *SRPC*, intersects the long-run Phillips curve at the expected inflation rate, 4 percent a year; page 803.

2. When the expected inflation rate falls, the short-run Phillips curve shifts downward, as shown in Figure 31.13. In Figure 31.13, the new short-run Phillips curve, $SRPC_1$, intersects the long-run Phillips curve at the new expected inflation rate, 3 percent a year; page 803.

■ **FIGURE 31.14**

Inflation rate (percent per year)

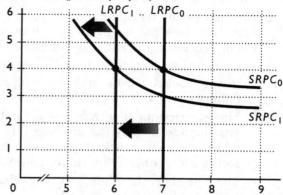

Unemployment rate (percent of labor force)

3. When the natural unemployment rate changes, both the long-run and the short-run Phillips curves shift. In Figure 31.14 (on the next page) the decrease in the natural unemployment rate to 6 percent shifts the long-run and short-run Phillips curves leftward by an equal amount. The new short-run Phillips curve, $SRPC_1$, intersects the new long-run Phillips curve, $LRPC_1$, where the inflation rate equals 4 percent a year because the expected inflation rate has not changed; pages 805-806.

4. When aggregate demand begins to grow more slowly, the inflation rate starts to drop. However, people will not immediately change their expected inflation rate so unemployment rises. Eventually, as the inflation rate reaches and then remains at 2 percent, the expected inflation rate is revised downward and the short-run Phillips curve (gradually) shifts downward. In the long run, the inflation rate falls to 2 percent and the unemployment rate returns to the natural unemployment rate; pages 804-805.

■ **AP Self Test 31.3**

True or false

1. False; page 809
2. True; page 809
3. True; page 810

© 2015 Pearson Education, Inc.

4. False; page 810

5. True; page 811

Multiple choice

1. a; page 809

2. d; page 809

3. c; page 810

4. a; page 810

5. c; page 810

6. b; page 811

Long Response Questions

■ **FIGURE 31.15**

Inflation rate (percent per year)

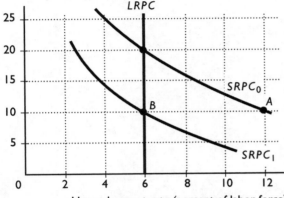

Unemployment rate (percent of labor force)

1. a. In the short run, because the expected inflation rate does not change, the short-run Phillips curve does not change. The economy moves along its short-run Phillips curve $SRPC_0$ to point A in Figure 31.15. The inflation rate is 10 percent and the unemployment rate is 12 percent; page 810.

   b. In the long run, the expected rate falls to 10 percent. With the fall in the expected inflation rate, the short-run Phillips curve shifts downward, in the figure to $SRPC_1$. It intersects the long-run Phillips curve at the new expected inflation rate. The economy moves to point B. The inflation rate is 10 percent and the unemployment rate is the natural rate of 6 percent; page 810.

2. In the short run, the Fed's policy increases the inflation rate and does not change the short-run or long-run Phillips curve. The economy moves up along the short-run Phillips curve. The inflation rate rises and the unemployment rate falls. In the long run, the increase in the inflation rate is matched by an increase in the expected inflation rate. The short-run Phillips curve shifts upward. The long-run Phillips curve does not change. The inflation rate permanently rises and the unemployment rate returns to the natural unemployment rate; page 810.

3. In the short run, the expected inflation rate might well not change. With people expected lower inflation than is actually the case, the money wage will not rise as much. Workers' real wage rates will fall and, in response, firms will boost employment so the unemployment rate falls to be less than the natural rate. But in the long run the expected inflation rate rises to equal the actual inflation rate. Once this occurs, the rise in the money wage matches the inflation rate. The real wage rate is no longer lower, so firms slash employment and the unemployment rate rises back to equal the natural rate; page 810.

4. If the Fed slows the inflation rate and the expected inflation rate does not change, then, the economy moves along its short-run Phillips curve and the unemployment rate rises. Looking for a job when the unemployment is high is not a pleasant experience! Based on this consideration, you might prefer that the Fed concentrate on keeping the inflation rate low so that the Fed does not need to unexpectedly lower the inflation rate when the Fed fears that inflation is getting out of hand.

Additional Exercises (also in MyEconLab Test A)

1. If the expected inflation rate does not change, then the short-run Phillips curve does not shift and the economy moves upward along $SRPC$ to a lower unemployment rate, 4 percent, and a higher inflation rate, 9 percent. The Fed has successfully lowered the unemployment rate. However, the inflation rate has risen; page 810.

2. In the long run, the expected inflation rate rises to match the actual inflation rate. When

© 2015 Pearson Education, Inc.

this occurs, the short-run Phillips curve shifts upward. In the long run, the unemployment rate returns to its natural rate, 6 percent, but the inflation rate remains permanently higher, 9 percent; page 810.

3. The result in Exercise 2 demonstrates that the Fed's lowering of the unemployment rate is only temporary but the increase in the inflation rate is permanent; page 810.

© 2015 Pearson Education, Inc.

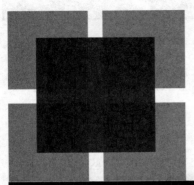

Fiscal Policy

Chapter 32

CHAPTER CHECKLIST

1 Describe the federal budget process and the recent history of tax revenues, outlays, deficits, and debts.

If tax revenues exceed outlays, the government has a budget surplus and if outlays exceed tax revenues, the government has a budget deficit. A budget deficit adds to the national debt, which is the total amount of government debt outstanding from past budget deficits. The government's Social Security and Medicare obligations are estimated at $91 trillion, much larger than the national debt of $12 trillion.

2 Explain how fiscal stimulus is used to fight a recession.

The Keynesian view is that fiscal stimulus (an increase in government outlays or a decrease in tax revenues) has a multiplier effect and boosts real GDP and employment. The mainstream view is that the multiplier from fiscal stimulus is lower than Keynesians believe and that the long-run effects from a fiscal stimulus are lower potential GDP and a slower real GDP growth rate. Fiscal policy can be discretionary, policy initiated by an act of Congress, or automatic, policy that is triggered by the state of the economy. Automatic stabilizers are features of fiscal policy, such as induced taxes and needs-tested spending, that stabilize real GDP without explicit action. Discretionary policy can be changes in government outlays or tax revenues. The government expenditure multiplier, tax multiplier, and transfer payments multiplier conclude that aggregate demand changes by more than an initiating change in government expenditures, taxes, or transfer payments. The balanced budget multiplier shows that an increase in government expenditure balanced by an equal sized increase in taxes still increases aggregate demand. If real GDP is less than potential GDP, fiscal stimulus can move the economy to potential GDP. The use of discretionary fiscal policy is hampered by law-making time lags, by the shrinking area of law-maker discretion, by difficulties in estimating potential GDP, and by economic forecasting.

3 Explain the supply-side effects of fiscal policy on employment, potential GDP, and the economic growth rate.

The effects of fiscal policy on potential GDP and the real GDP growth rate are the supply-side effects. A tax cut or an increase in government expenditure on productive services have supply-side effects that increase potential GDP and aggregate supply. An increase in the income tax on labor income increases the tax wedge between the before-tax and the after-tax wage rate and decreases the supply of labor, thereby decreasing employment and potential GDP. An increase in the income tax on interest income increases the interest rate tax wedge. The real-after tax real interest rate falls, thereby decreasing the quantity of saving and investment and slowing the growth rate of real GDP. The combined demand-side and supply-side effects of fiscal policy show that both the aggregate demand and aggregate supply curves shift in response to fiscal policy. Fiscal stimulus has large long-run negative effects if investment is crowded out by budget deficits.

YOUR AP TEST HINTS

AP Topics

Topic on your AP test	What to Know	Corresponding textbook section
The federal budget	Relationship to fiscal policy; budget surpluses and deficits	Checkpoint 32.1
Fiscal stimulus	How stimulus actions right recessions	Checkpoint 32.2
Supply-side effects	Fiscal policy's effects on aggregate supply	Checkpoint 32.3

AP Vocabulary Covered

Terms	What to Know	Text Sections
Fiscal policy	Use of the federal budget (taxes, transfer payments, expenditure on goods and services) to achieve economic growth and full employment	Checkpoint 32.1, p. 818
Budget deficit	Federal outlays exceed tax revenues	Checkpoint 32.1, p. 818
National debt	The *total* amount of government debt (from all past deficits)	Checkpoint 32.1, p. 819
Transfer payments	Social Security benefits, Medicare, Medicaid, unemployment benefits and other cash benefits to citizens	Checkpoint 32.1, p. 819
Automatic fiscal policy	An action that is triggered by certain changes in the economy	Checkpoint 32.2, p. 824
Discretionary fiscal policy	Policy actions only created by actions of Congress	Checkpoint 32.2, p. 824
Automatic stabilizers	Policies that occur automatically as tax revenues and outlays fluctuate with the business cycle	Checkpoint 32.2, p. 824
Structural surplus or debt	The budget balance that would occur if the economy were at full employment	Checkpoint 32.2, p. 825
Cyclical surplus or debt	The budget balance that arises because tax revenues and outlays are not at full employment levels	Checkpoint 32.2, p. 825
Government expenditure multiplier	The effect of a change in government expenditure on goods and services on aggregate demand	Checkpoint 32.2, p. 826
Tax multiplier	How tax changes affect the aggregate demand	Checkpoint 32.2, p. 826
Balanced budget multiplier	When simultaneous changes in taxes and government expenditures affect *AD* but leave the budget balanced	Checkpoint 32.2, p. 826
Supply-side effects	The effects of fiscal policy on potential GDP and the growth rate of the economy	Checkpoint 32.3, p. 830

Extra AP material

- *Fiscal policy* should be connected to the actions of Congress and changes in the federal budget. Fiscal policy is emphasized in the general theories of John Keynes, or *Keynesian economics*.
- *Transfer payments* to firms are also known as *business subsidy payments*.
- *Fiscal stimulus* is also called *expansionary fiscal policy* and occurs to fight recessions.
- The AP test expects students to understand that the *government expenditure multiplier* exceeds the *tax multiplier* because *all* of a change in government expenditure directly affects aggregate demand while only a fraction of the change in taxes affects aggregate demand. Some of the tax changes are not spent but are saved, reducing the *AD* effectiveness of the policy.

© 2015 Pearson Education, Inc.

CHECKPOINT 32.1

■ **Describe the federal budget process and the recent history of tax revenues, outlays, deficits, and debts.**

Quick Review

- *Budget surplus* When tax revenues exceed outlays.
- *Budget deficit* When outlays exceed tax revenues.
- *National debt* The amount of government debt outstanding that has arisen from past budget deficits.

Additional Practice Problems 32.1

1. What is the relationship between the budget deficit or surplus and the national debt?
2. Can the national debt rise when the government is running a budget surplus?

Solutions to Additional Practice Problems 32.1

1. The budget deficit or surplus shows the government's budget situation for that year. The national debt is the total accumulated amount of debt the government owes from all past budget deficits. If the government has a budget deficit, so that its expenditures exceed its tax revenues, then the national debt rises. If it has a budget surplus, so that tax revenues exceed expenditures, then the national debt decreases.

2. The national debt cannot rise when the government has a budget surplus. The national debt increases when the government has a budget deficit and decreases when the government has a budget surplus.

■ AP Self Test 32.1

True or false

1. The national debt and budget deficit are different names for the same thing.

2. If government outlays and taxes revenues increase by the same amount, the government's budget balance does not change.

3. Social Security and Medicare obligations are less than U.S. GDP.

4. For the past decade, the U.S. federal government has had a budget deficit.

Multiple choice

1. The annual statement of the outlays, tax revenues, and surplus or deficit of the government of the United States is the federal
   a. surplus record.
   b. deficit record.
   c. budget.
   d. spending.
   e. debt to the public.

2. When government outlays are less than tax revenues, the government has
   a. a budget with a positive balance.
   b. a budget deficit.
   c. a budget surplus.
   d. a budget with a negative debt.
   e. an illegal budget because outlays must exceed tax revenues.

3. National debt decreases in a given year when a country has
   a. a budget deficit.
   b. a balanced budget.
   c. a budget supplement.
   d. a budget surplus.
   e. no government budget.

Short Response Questions

1. What happens to the national debt if the government has a $1,400 billion budget deficit?

2. As a percent of GDP, how does the U.S. budget deficit compare to the budget deficits of other nations?

3. What is the amount of the U.S. Social Security and Medicare obligations? What actions might the government take to pay this debt?

Additional Exercise (also in MyEconLab Test A)

1. What is fiscal policy? What roles do the President and Congress play in making it? What is the time line for U.S. fiscal policy and is the federal budget in deficit or surplus?

© 2015 Pearson Education, Inc.

CHECKPOINT 32.2

■ **Explain how fiscal stimulus is used to fight a recession.**

Quick Review

- *Fiscal stimulus* An increase in government outlays or a decrease in tax revenue designed to boost real GDP.
- *Automatic fiscal policy* Fiscal policy that is triggered by the state of the economy.
- *Discretionary fiscal policy* Fiscal policy initiated by an act of Congress.
- *Government expenditure multiplier* The magnification effect of a change in government expenditure on aggregate demand.
- *Tax multiplier* The magnification effect of a change in taxes on aggregate demand.

Additional Practice Problems 32.2

1. The figure shows the U.S. economy in 2015.

   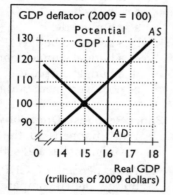

   a. What is the equilibrium price level and real GDP?

   b. What sorts of fiscal policies might be used to move the economy to potential GDP?

   c. In the figure, show the effect of these policies after real GDP equals potential GDP. What is the new equilibrium price level and real GDP?

2. What is the balanced budget multiplier and why is it greater than zero?

Solutions to Additional Practice Problems 32.2

1a. The equilibrium price level and real GDP are determined by the intersection of the aggregate demand, *AD*, curve and the aggregate supply, *AS*, curve. The figure shows that the equilibrium price is 100 and the equilibrium quantity of real GDP is $15 trillion.

1b. To move the economy to potential GDP, the government can use fiscal stimulus. Potential policy includes a decrease in taxes and/or an increase in government expenditures.

1c. The figure shows the effect of the fiscal stimulus. A decrease in taxes and an increase in government expenditure both increase aggregate demand. The aggregate demand curve shifts rightward,

   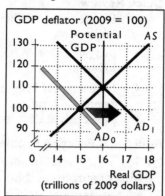

   from AD_0 to AD_1 in the figure. As a result, the price level rises from 100 to 110 and real GDP increases from $15 trillion back to potential GDP of $16 trillion.

2. The balanced budget multiplier is the magnification effect on aggregate demand of *simultaneous* changes in government expenditures and taxes that leave the budget balance unchanged. The balanced budget multiplier is not zero—it is positive—because the size of the government expenditure multiplier is larger than the size of the tax multiplier. That is, a $1 increase in government expenditures increases aggregate demand by more than a $1 increase in taxes decreases aggregate demand. So when both government expenditures and taxes increase by $1, aggregate demand still increases.

■ **AP Self Test 32.2**

True or false

1. Automatic stabilizers are features of fiscal policy that work to stabilize real GDP without explicit action by the government.

2. The cyclical deficit is larger when the economy is in a recession.

© 2015 Pearson Education, Inc.

3. The government expenditure multiplier is the magnification effect that a change in aggregate demand has on government expenditures on goods and services.

4. A tax cut is a possible fiscal stimulus designed to increase GDP.

5. Estimating potential GDP is a limitation of automatic fiscal policy.

Multiple choice

1. The ____ view says that fiscal stimulus has a multiplier effect that makes it a ____ tool to fight a deep recession.
   a. mainstream; powerful
   b. "free lunch"; powerful
   c. Keynesian; powerful
   d. Keynesian; weak
   e. None of the above answers is correct.

2. An example of automatic fiscal policy is
   a. an interest rate cut, initiated by an act of Congress.
   b. an increase in the quantity of money.
   c. a tax cut, initiated by an act of Congress.
   d. a decrease in tax revenues, triggered by the state of the economy.
   e. any change tax revenues, regardless of the cause.

3. If the structural deficit is $800 billion and the cyclical deficit is $600 billion, the actual budget deficit is ____.
   a. $200 billion
   b. $600 billion
   c. $800 billion
   d. $1,400 billion
   e. None of the above answers is correct.

4. The government expenditure multiplier reflects the magnification effect on ____ from a change in government expenditure on goods and services.
   a. aggregate demand
   b. the budget deficit
   c. tax revenues
   d. aggregate supply
   e. potential GDP

5. The magnitude of the tax multiplier is ____ the magnitude of the government expenditure multiplier.
   a. equal to
   b. greater than
   c. smaller than
   d. the inverse of
   e. exactly one half

6. An example of a discretionary fiscal stimulus policy is
   a. the automatic increase in needs-tested spending in a recession.
   b. induced taxes.
   c. decreasing government expenditure.
   d. decreasing needs-tested spending.
   e. cutting taxes.

■ FIGURE 32.1

Price level (GDP price index, 2009 = 100)

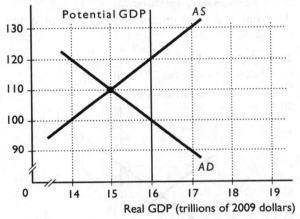

7. In Figure 32.1, a fiscal stimulus designed to restore GDP to potential GDP could be ____, which shifts the ____ curve ____.
   a. an increase in government expenditure; *AS*; leftward
   b. a tax hike; *AD*; leftward
   c. an increase in government expenditure; *AS*; rightward
   d. a tax hike; *AS*; rightward
   e. an increase in government expenditure; *AD*; rightward

© 2015 Pearson Education, Inc.

8. A fiscal stimulus works to close a recessionary gap by shifting the
   a. *AD* curve leftward.
   b. *AS* curve leftward.
   c. *AD* curve leftward and the *AS* curve leftward.
   d. *AD* curve rightward.
   e. potential GDP line leftward.

9. Discretionary fiscal policy is handicapped by
   a. induced taxes and automatic stabilizers.
   b. law-making time lags, estimation of potential GDP, and economic forecasting.
   c. economic forecasting, law-making time lags, and induced taxes.
   d. automatic stabilizers, law-making time lags, and potential GDP estimation.
   e. automatic stabilizers and induced taxes.

Short Response Questions

1. What are the demand-side effects of a tax cut?

■ FIGURE 32.2

Price level (GDP price index, 2009 = 100)

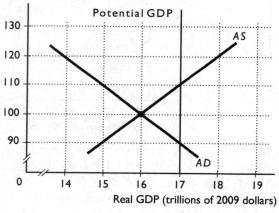

2. Figure 32.2 illustrates the situation in the United States in 2016. What type of fiscal stimulus might be used to restore this economy to full employment? In Figure 32.2, illustrate the effect of the policy you suggested.

Long Response Questions

1. What are automatic stabilizers? Can they eliminate a recession?

2. What is the relationship between the actual budget deficit, structural deficit, and cyclical deficit?

3. Why does government expenditure have a multiplier effect?

4. How can the government use fiscal stimulus to eliminate a recessionary gap?

5. It is not easy to determine potential GDP. Why does this fact hamper the use of discretionary fiscal policy?

Additional Exercises (also in MyEconLab Test A)

1. Classify each of the following items as discretionary fiscal policy or automatic fiscal policy or neither.
   a. The imposition of huge fines on tobacco companies
   b. A cut in the gas tax
   c. A cut in cross-border (custom) taxes
   d. An increase in payments to unemployed people

2. Explain the effects of a $100 billion decrease in government expenditure on aggregate demand.

3. Use an *AS-AD* graph to show the effects of a $100 billion decrease in taxes.

4. Use an *AS-AD* graph to show the effects of a simultaneous decrease in government expenditure and taxes of $100 billion.

CHECKPOINT 32.3

■ **Explain the supply-side effects of fiscal policy on employment and potential GDP.**

Quick Review

- *Supply-side effects* The effects of fiscal policy on potential GDP.

- *Tax wedge* The gap created by taxes between what a buyer pays and a seller receives.

© 2015 Pearson Education, Inc.

Additional Practice Problem 32.3

1. The figure shows the U.S. labor market when there is no income tax.

   a. What is the equilibrium real wage rate and amount of employment?

   b. Suppose the government imposes an income tax rate on labor income of $2 per hour. Show the effect in the figure.

   c. With the income tax, what is the before-tax real wage rate and what is the after-tax real wage rate? What is the amount of the tax wedge?

   d. With the income tax, what is equilibrium employment? How does the income tax affect potential GDP?

Solutions to Additional Practice Problem 32.3

1a. The equilibrium real wage rate is $22 an hour and the equilibrium level of employment is 200 billion hours.

1b. The figure shows the effect of the tax. The supply of labor decreases and the labor supply curve shifts to *LS*tax. The new labor supply curve lies above the initial labor supply curve by the amount of the tax, in this case, by $2.

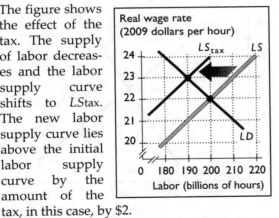

1c. The before-tax real wage rate is $23 per hour, determined by the intersection of the labor supply curve with the tax, *LS*tax, and the labor demand curve, *LD*. From this wage rate $2 must be sent to the government as the tax,

so the after-tax real wage rate is $21 per hour. The tax wedge equals the difference in the wage rates, which is $2.

1d. Equilibrium employment is 190 billion hours. Because the equilibrium employment decreases with the tax, potential GDP also decreases.

■ AP Self Test 32.3

True or false

1. Income taxes create a wedge between the wage rate paid by firms and the wage rate workers take home.

2. An income tax hike decreases the supply of labor but has no effect on employment or potential GDP.

3. An income tax cut increases potential GDP by shifting the nation's production function upward.

4. Taxes on interest income can drive a wedge between the interest rate borrowers pay and the interest rate lenders receive.

5. An increase in the budget deficit can raise the real interest rate and crowd out private investment.

6. A tax cut increases aggregate demand and decreases aggregate supply.

Multiple choice

1. The quantity of employment is determined in the ____ and that quantity, along with the ____, determines potential GDP.

   a. loanable funds market; production function

   b. goods and services market; labor market

   c. labor market; tax rate

   d. labor market; production function

   e. labor market; tax wedge

2. If the income tax rate is 20 percent and the tax rate on consumption expenditure is 15 percent, then the tax wedge is
   a. 2 percent.
   b. 5 percent.
   c. 35 percent.
   d. 300 percent.
   e. None of the above answers is correct.

3. Increasing the income tax rate ____ the ____.
   a. decreases; demand for labor
   b. increases; supply of labor
   c. decreases; supply of labor
   d. does not change; supply of labor
   e. increases; demand for labor

4. Increasing the income tax rate ____ the before-tax real wage rate and ____ the after-tax real wage rate.
   a. raises; raises
   b. does not change; raises
   c. lowers; lowers
   d. lowers; raises
   e. raises; lowers

5. The supply-side effects of an income tax cut ____ potential GDP and ____ aggregate supply.
   a. increase; increase
   b. increase; decrease
   c. decrease; increase
   d. decrease; decrease
   e. increases; do not change

6. An income tax on labor income decreases the ____ of potential GDP and a tax on interest income decreases the ____ of potential GDP.
   a. level; growth rate
   b. growth rate; level
   c. level; level
   d. growth rate; growth rate
   e. None of the above answers is correct.

7. If the nominal interest rate is 10 percent, the inflation rate is 6 percent, and the tax rate on interest income is 25 percent, what is the after-tax real interest rate?
   a. 4.0 percent
   b. 6.0 percent
   c. 3.0 percent
   d. 1.5 percent
   e. 3.5 percent

8. An income tax cut ____ aggregate demand and ____ aggregate supply.
   a. increases; increases
   b. increases; decreases
   c. decreases; increases
   d. decreases; decreases
   e. does not change; increases

9. If fiscal stimulus creates a large budget ____, then in the long run economic growth ____.
   a. surplus; increases
   b. surplus; decreases
   c. deficit; increases
   d. deficit; decreases
   e. None of the above answers is correct.

Short Response Questions

■ **FIGURE 32.3**

Real wage rate (2009 dollars per hour)

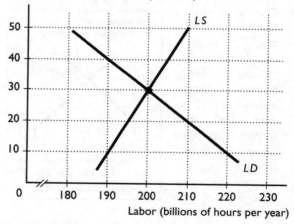

1. Figure 32.3 illustrates the labor market. Suppose that the government cuts taxes so that the supply of labor changes by 15 billion hours at each wage rate. Show the effects from the tax cut in the figure.

© 2015 Pearson Education, Inc.

■ **FIGURE 32.4**

Real GDP (trillions of 2009 dollars)

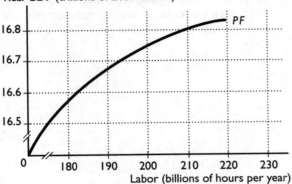

2. Figure 32.4 shows the nation's production function. Employment is initially 200 billion hours. If employment increases by 10 billion hours, show the effect on potential GDP.

3. Based on the previous two questions, how will a tax cut affect the aggregate supply curve?

■ **FIGURE 32.5**

Price level (GDP price index, 2009 = 100)

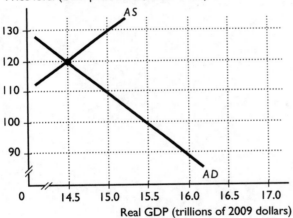

4. Figure 32.5 illustrates the economy. Potential GDP is $16 trillion. Suppose that the government cuts its taxes and that the supply-side effects are larger than the demand-side effects. If the economy moves back to potential GDP, in Figure 32.5, illustrate the effect of this government policy.

Long Response Questions

1. What are the supply-side effects of a tax cut? Why does a tax cut have supply-side effects?

2. What is the tax wedge on labor income? How does the tax wedge affect potential GDP? Why does the tax wedge affect potential GDP?

3. Suppose the tax rate on interest income is 25 percent.
   a. If the real interest rate is 4 percent and the inflation rate is zero percent, what is the nominal interest rate and the after-tax real interest rate? What is the true tax rate on interest income?
   b. If the real interest rate is 4 percent and the inflation rate is 4 percent, what is the nominal interest rate and the after-tax real interest rate? What is the true tax rate on interest income?
   c. How has higher inflation affected the true tax rate on interest income?

4. What is the effect on aggregate demand and aggregate supply of a tax cut? What is the effect on real GDP and the price level of a tax cut?

5. What can be the long-run adverse effects from a fiscal stimulus that increases the budget deficit?

6. The Eye on Your Life discusses how you can think about how fiscal policy relates to your values and opinions. You can also use this thought to make predictions about the future. For instance, if you think the election of a Presidential candidate who supports tax hikes for the rich is likely, how do you think that would affect the cruise industry? High-end clothing retailers? Expensive jewelers?

Additional Exercises (also in MyEconLab Test A)

1. The government raises the income tax rate. Explain the effects of this action on the supply of labor, the demand for labor, the equilibrium level of employment, the real wage rate, and potential GDP.

2. The government raises the income tax rate. Explain the effects of this action on saving,

© 2015 Pearson Education, Inc.

investment, the real interest rate, and the growth rate of real GDP.

3. Explain why inflation increases the true tax rate on interest income. What is the true income tax rate on interest income if the real interest rate is 3 percent, the inflation rate is 2 percent, and the tax rate on nominal interest is 25 percent?

4. The government increases its outlays but keeps tax revenue unchanged. Explain the effects of this action on saving, investment, the real interest rate, and the growth rate of real GDP.

© 2015 Pearson Education, Inc.

SELF TEST ANSWERS

■ AP Self Test 32.1

True or false

1. False; pages 818-819
2. True; page 818
3. False; page 820
4. True; page 821

Multiple choice

1. c; page 818
2. c; page 818
3. d; page 819

Short Response Questions

1. If the government has a $1,400 billion budget deficit, the national debt increases by $1,400 billion; page 819.

2. The United States has a government deficit that, as percent of GDP, is large compared to other countries. The U.S. budget deficit is about 6 percent of GDP. Only Japan (10 percent) and the U.K. (7 percent) have larger deficits. But the budget deficits of Australia, New Zealand, the Euro area, and Canada are much less than that in the United States; page 822.

3. Social Security and Medicare obligations are huge: $91 trillion. To pay the debt, the government must either raise income taxes, raise Social Security taxes, cut Social Security spending, and/or cut other federal government spending; page 820.

Additional Exercise (also in MyEconLab Test A)

1. Fiscal policy is using the federal budget, expenditures and taxes, to achieve sustained economic growth and full employment. The President proposes a budget to Congress each February. The Congress then passes budget acts in September. The President then either signs or vetoes the acts. The President's role is to propose potential fiscal policy while the Congress then enacts legislation that incorporates fiscal policy. The President can approve or disapprove of Congress's actions. The federal budget today is in deficit; pages 818-819.

■ AP Self Test 32.2

True or false

1. True; page 824
2. True; page 825
3. False; page 826
4. True; page 827
5. False; page 828

Multiple choice

1. c; page 823
2. d; page 824
3. d; page 825
4. a; page 826
5. c; page 826
6. e; page 826
7. e; page 827
8. d; page 827
9. b; page 828

Short Response Questions

1. A tax cut increases disposable income, which increases consumption expenditure and aggregate demand; page 827.

■ FIGURE 32.6

Price level (GDP price index, 2009 = 100)

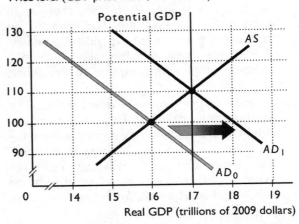

2. There is a recessionary gap because real GDP is less than potential GDP. An expansionary fiscal stimulus, such as increasing government expenditure on goods and services,

© 2015 Pearson Education, Inc.

increasing transfer payments, and/or cutting taxes, could be applied to return the economy to potential GDP. Aggregate demand increases and, as Figure 32.6 shows, the *AD* curve shifts rightward from AD_0 to AD_1. Real GDP increases from $16 trillion to $17 trillion and the price level rises from 100 to 110; page 827.

Long Response Questions

1. Automatic stabilizers are features of fiscal policy that stabilize real GDP without explicit action by the government. Automatic stabilizers include induced taxes and needs-tested spending. Induced taxes and needs-tested spending decrease the multiplier effect of a change in autonomous expenditure. Because they decrease the multiplier, they moderate both expansions and recessions and make real GDP more stable but they cannot eliminate a recession; page 824.

2. The actual budget deficit is equal to the sum of the structural deficit (the budget deficit that would occur if the economy was at full employment) plus the cyclical deficit (the budget deficit that arises because revenues and outlays are not at their full-employment levels); page 825.

3. Government expenditure has a multiplier effect because it induces further changes in consumption expenditure. For instance, an increase in government expenditure increases people's disposable income, which then increases their consumption expenditure; page 826.

4. A recessionary gap exists when real GDP is less than potential GDP. The government can eliminate the recessionary gap by using a fiscal stimulus to increase aggregate demand. The government can increase aggregate demand by increasing its expenditures on goods and services and/or by cutting taxes; page 827.

5. Because it is not easy to tell whether real GDP is below, above, or at potential GDP a discretionary fiscal action might move real GDP *away* from potential GDP instead of toward it; page 828.

Additional Exercises (also in MyEconLab Test A)

1. a. Huge fines on tobacco companies are not a fiscal policy because they are the judgment of a court; page 822.

   b. A cut in the gas tax is a discretionary fiscal policy because the cut requires an act of Congress; page 824.

   c. A cut in the cross-border (custom) taxes would be classified as a discretionary fiscal policy because the tax cut requires an act of Congress; page 824.

   d. An increase in payments to unemployed people is an automatic fiscal policy; page 823.

■ **FIGURE 32.7**

Price level (GDP price index, 2009 = 100)

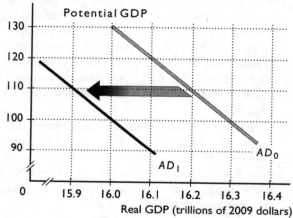

2. Figure 32.7 illustrates the effect of a $100 billion decrease in government expenditure. The decrease in government expenditure decreases aggregate demand and shifts the *AD* curve leftward from AD_0 to AD_1. The magnitude of the shift of the *AD* curve, $300 billion, exceeds the initial $100 billion decrease in government expenditure because of the multiplier effect; pages 826-827.

© 2015 Pearson Education, Inc.

■ FIGURE 32.8

Price level (GDP price index, 2009 = 100)

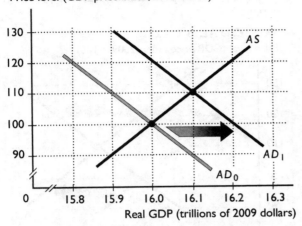

Real GDP (trillions of 2009 dollars)

3. Figure 32.8 illustrates the effect of a $100 billion decrease in taxes. The decrease in taxes increases aggregate demand and shifts the AD curve rightward from AD_0 to AD_1. The magnitude of the shift in the AD curve, $200 billion, exceeds $100 billion because of the multiplier effect. The AS curve might also shift rightward as a result of the lower taxes, but once again because the conventional view is that the shift is small, the AS curve is not changed in Figure 32.8. The tax cut increases real GDP and raises the price level; page 827.

■ FIGURE 32.9

Price level (GDP price index, 2009 = 100)

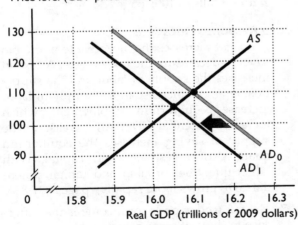

Real GDP (trillions of 2009 dollars)

4. When the government decreases its expendi-

ture *and* cuts its taxes by $100 billion, the effect on aggregate demand from the decrease in government expenditure exceeds the effect from the cut in taxes. Therefore, as shown in Figure 32.9, in accord with the balanced budget multiplier aggregate demand decreases and the aggregate demand curve shifts leftward, though the shift is not as large as in Exercise 2. The AS curve might shift in this case, but the direction of the shift is likely to be small and also is ambiguous. So once again the AS curve in Figure 32.9 is not changed. As the figure illustrates, the aggregate demand curve shifts leftward so the price level falls and real GDP decreases; pages 826-827.

■ AP Self Test 32.3

True or false

1. True; page 832
2. False; pages 832-833
3. False; pages 832-833
4. True; page 834
5. True; page 834
6. False; page 836

Multiple choice

1. d; page 830
2. c; page 831
3. c; pages 832-833
4. e; page 832
5. a; page 833
6. a; pages 833-834
7. d; page 834
8. a; page 836
9. d; page 837

© 2015 Pearson Education, Inc.

Short Response Questions

■ **FIGURE 32.10**

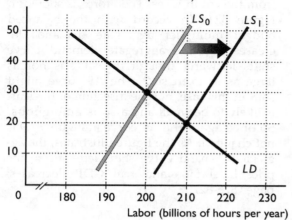

1. The cut in taxes increase the supply of labor so, as Figure 32.10 shows, the supply of labor curve shifts rightward by 15 billion hours of labor from LS_0 to LS_1. Equilibrium employment increases from 200 billion hours of labor to 210 billion hours and the real wage rate falls from $30 per hour to $20 per hour; pages 832-833.

■ **FIGURE 32.11**

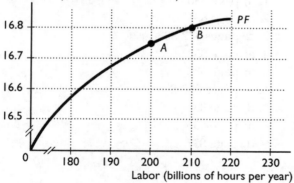

2. Figure 32.11 shows the results of the increase in employment. Potential GDP increases from $16.75 trillion at point A on the production function to $16.8 trillion at point B on the production function; page 833.

3. The tax cut increases potential GDP so the

tax cut also increases aggregate supply. The aggregate supply curve shifts rightward; page 833.

■ **FIGURE 32.12**

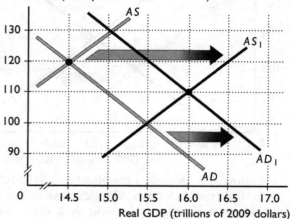

4. The tax cut increases both aggregate demand and aggregate supply, so in Figure 32.12, the aggregate demand curve shifts rightward from AD to AD_1 and the aggregate supply curve shifts rightward from AS to AS_1. Because the effect on aggregate supply exceeds the effect on aggregate demand, the shift of the AS curve is larger than the shift of the AD curve. Real GDP increases and the price level falls. The exact fall of the price level depends on the precise sizes of the shifts but in the figure it falls to 100; page 836.

Long Response Questions

1. A tax cut increases the incentive to work and save by decreasing the tax wedges. A tax cut increases the supply of labor and the supply of saving. An increase in the supply of labor increases equilibrium employment, which increases potential GDP. An increase in the supply of saving increases the equilibrium quantity of investment and capital. With larger quantities of labor and capital, potential GDP grows more rapidly; pages 831-834.

2. The tax wedge on labor income is the difference in the real wage rate paid by employers and the real wage rate received by employ-

© 2015 Pearson Education, Inc.

ees. It equals the sum of the income tax rate on labor income plus the tax rate on consumption expenditure.

The tax wedge decreases potential GDP because it decreases the supply of labor, which decreases equilibrium employment; pages 831-832.

3. a. The nominal interest rate is 4 percent (since the inflation rate is 0 percent) and the after-tax real interest rate is 3 percent. The true tax rate on interest income is 25 percent; page 834.

   b. The nominal interest rate is 10 percent (it equals the sum of the inflation rate plus the real interest rate). The after-tax real interest rate is 1.5 percent because the tax (which equals the 25 percent tax rate multiplied by the 10 percent nominal interest rate, or 2.5 percent) must be subtracted from the real interest rate. The tax has lowered the real interest rate by 1.5 percent (from 4 percent to 2.5 percent) so the true tax rate is (1.5 percent ÷ 4 percent) × 100, which is 37.5 percent; page 834.

   c. The increase in the inflation rate raised the true tax rate paid on interest income; page 834.

4. A tax cut increases both aggregate demand and aggregate supply. As a result, real GDP unambiguously increases but the effect on the price level is uncertain. If the increase in aggregate demand exceeds the increase in aggregate supply, the price level rate rises; if the increase in aggregate demand equals the increase in aggregate supply, the price level does not change; and, if the increase in aggregate demand is less than the increase in aggregate supply, the price level falls; pages 836-837.

5. If the budget deficit crowds out investment, the long-run negative consequences from the fiscal stimulus can be severe. With less investment, the economy will have less capital and so its economic growth rate slows. If the large budget deficit persists, the government might be tempted to instruct the central bank to make open market purchases of the debt, in which case inflation could soar; page 837.

6. The cruise industry, high-end clothing retailers, and expensive jewelry stores would all be harmed by taxes being increased on the rich. If you were thinking of making an investment in any of these endeavors—or other similar areas—you might well want to delay until you have more information about the extent of the tax increases. On the other hand, investment in a "dollar store" sort of opportunity ought not to be affected by the proposed taxes on the rich.

Additional Exercises (also in MyEconLab Test A)

1. The higher income tax rate decreases the supply of labor. The demand for labor does not change. As a result, the equilibrium level of employment falls so that potential GDP decreases. The before-tax real wage rate rises but the after-tax real wage rate falls; pages 832-833.

2. The higher income tax rate decreases the quantity of saving and investment. The after-tax real interest rate, which is the interest rate that is relevant to saving and investment, falls. Because there is less investment, the growth rate of real GDP decreases; page 834.

3. The tax on interest income is applied to the nominal interest rate. So the after-tax real interest rate equals the nominal interest rate minus the inflation rate (which equals the before-tax real interest rate) minus the tax paid on the interest income. When the inflation rate rises, the nominal interest rate rises. The higher nominal interest rate increases the tax paid on the interest rate, which decreases the after-tax real interest rate and thereby increases the true tax rate on interest income.

   If the real interest rate is 3 percent and the inflation rate is 2 percent, then the nominal interest rate is 5 percent. If the tax rate on nominal interest income is 25 percent, then of the 5 percent nominal interest rate, 1.25 percent is paid as taxes. The after-tax real interest rate equals the real interest rate minus the amount paid as taxes, which is 3 percent −

© 2015 Pearson Education, Inc.

1.25 percent, or 1.75 percent. The tax lowers the real interest rate from 3 percentage points to 1.75 percentage points, which is a fall of 1.25 percentage points for a true tax rate on interest income of 42 percent; page 834.

4. By increasing its outlays and keeping its tax revenue unchanged, the government budget deficit rises. This action decreases the supply of loanable funds to firms, which raises the real interest rate. The quantity of saving increases but the quantity of investment decreases—crowded out by the higher budget deficit. With less investment, the growth rate of real GDP slows; page 834.

© 2015 Pearson Education, Inc.

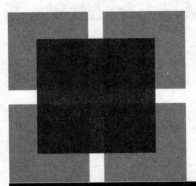

Monetary Policy

Chapter 33

1 **Describe the objectives of U.S. monetary policy, the framework for achieving those objectives, and the Fed's monetary policy actions.**

The goals of monetary policy are "maximum employment, stable prices, and moderate long-term interest rates." Financial stability is a necessary prerequisite for obtaining the Fed's goals which is why the Fed pursued that goal intensively in Fall 2008. The Fed uses the output gap, which is the percentage deviation of real GDP from potential GDP, as its "maximum employment" goal. It uses the core inflation rate, which is the annual inflation rate calculated using the PCE deflator *excluding* the prices of food and fuel, as its "stable prices" goal. The Fed's monetary policy instrument is the federal funds rate. The Fed uses a targeting strategy in which it sets the federal funds rate at a level that makes the Fed's forecast of its ultimate policy goals, the core inflation rate and the GDP gap, equal to their targeted goals. The Fed changes the federal funds rate using open market operations to change banks' reserves. During the global financial crisis the demand for reserves skyrocketed so to keep the federal funds rate from rising, the Fed responded with quantitative easing, a massive increase in reserves.

2 **Explain the transmission channels through which the Fed influences real GDP and the inflation rate.**

The transmission channel tells how monetary policy affects real GDP and the inflation rate. For instance, when the Fed lowers the federal funds rate, other short term interest rates fall and the exchange rate also falls. The quantity of money and the supply of loanable funds increase. The increase in the supply of loanable funds lowers the long-term real interest rate, which boosts consumption expenditure and investment. The lower exchange rate increases net exports. The increases in these three components of aggregate expenditure increase aggregate demand so that real GDP growth and the inflation rate rise. The effect of an increase in the federal funds rate is the opposite of what was just outlined. When the Fed fights a recession, it lowers the federal funds rate in order to boost aggregate demand and raise real GDP; when the Fed fights inflation, it raises the federal funds rate in order to decrease aggregate demand and lower the inflation rate. The links along the transmission channel can take a lengthy and variable time until they affect real GDP and the inflation rate.

3 **Explain and compare alternative monetary policy strategies.**

Using rules rather than discretion enable the Fed to keep inflation expectations anchored close to the inflation rate target. The Fed could have chosen to use an inflation targeting rule, which is similar to the Fed's current procedure but requires the Fed to make public its inflation target. Or the Fed could opt for a monetary targeting rule such as the k-percent rule, but if the demand for money is unstable money targeting is unreliable. The Fed could also use a nominal GDP targeting rule, under which the Fed would attempt to hit a target for nominal GDP growth (which is a variety of inflation targeting).

© 2015 Pearson Education, Inc.

YOUR AP TEST HINTS

AP Topics

Topic on your AP test	What to Know	Corresponding textbook section
Monetary policy	Goals of Fed actions	Checkpoint 33.1
Monetary policy transmission	Transmission mechanism; ultimate effect in *AD/AS* figure, real GDP, and inflation rates	Checkpoint 33.2
Alternative monetary policy strategies	Discretionary monetary policy; inflation targeting	Checkpoint 33.3

AP Vocabulary Covered

Terms	What to Know	Text Sections
Monetary policy	Fed's efforts to achieve its goals of "maximum employment, stable prices, and moderate long-term interest rates"	Checkpoint 33.1, p. 844
Financial stability	Financial markets and institutions functioning normally	Checkpoint 33.1, p. 845
Monetary policy instrument	Variables that the Fed can control or target in order to influence the economy	Checkpoint 33.1, p. 846
Federal Fund Rate	Banks charge each other interest on loans within the Federal Fund Market. The Fed "targets" this rate.	Checkpoint 33.1, p. 846
Instrument rule	A decision rule for policy actions using formulas based on the current state of the economy	Checkpoint 33.1, p. 848
Targeting rule	A monetary policy is set at a level so that a forecast will equal the policy's goals	Checkpoint 33.1, p. 848
Expansionary and contractionary policy	The Fed lowers the federal funds rate for expansionary monetary policy to fight recession; the Fed raises the federal funds rate for contractionary policy to fight inflation	Checkpoint 33.2, p. 856
Discretionary monetary policy	Policy decisions are based on Fed assessments of the current economic situation	Checkpoint 33.3, p. 862
Inflation targeting	A monetary policy strategy in which the Fed announces a specific inflation rate target and its policies for achieving that target	Checkpoint 33.3, p. 862
"k-percent" rule	A monetary policy strategy (from the economist Milton Friedman) that the quantity of money should grow at a constant rate ("k" percent) each year	Checkpoint 33.3, p. 863
Nominal GDP targeting	Adjusting the interest rates to achieve targeted growth rates for the nominal GDP	Checkpoint 33.3, p. 865

Extra AP material

- The "ripple effect" of Fed policies (see Figure 33.4) is an important summary that is important for preparation for the AP exam. Know these domestic and international links.
- It is important to bear in mind for the AP test that fiscal policy and monetary policy are independent of each other. Fiscal policy is under the control of the legislative branch and monetary policy is the Federal Reserve's responsibility. Students must be able to illustrate the effects of fiscal and monetary policy in aggregate demand/aggregate supply diagrams.

CHECKPOINT 33.1

- **Describe the objectives of U.S. monetary policy, the framework for achieving those objectives, and the Fed's monetary policy actions.**

Quick Review

- *Core inflation rate* The annual inflation rate calculated using the PCE deflator excluding the prices of food and fuel.
- *Monetary policy instrument* A variable that the Fed can directly control or closely target and that influences the economy in desirable ways.
- *Federal funds rate* The interest rate at which banks can borrow and lend reserves in the federal funds market.

Additional Practice Problems 33.1

1. Why does the Fed focus on the core inflation rate rather than the overall inflation rate?
2. What is the role of the President and the Congress in making monetary policy decisions?

Solutions to Additional Practice Problems 33.1

1 The Fed focuses on the core inflation rate because the Fed believes that this inflation rate is a better indicator of whether price stability is being achieved. The price of fuel is heavily influenced by oil prices and the price of food is heavily influenced by harvest conditions. Both of these events are outside of the economy's control, so the Fed uses the core inflation rate to better measure the stability of the prices that it can influence.

2. Neither the President nor the Congress has a direct role in making monetary policy decisions. These decisions are left to the Federal Reserve. But some U.S. Presidents have tried to influence the Fed and the Fed is required to report twice a year to Congress.

- **AP Self Test 33.1**

True or false

1. By law, the Fed is required to keep inflation equal to or less than 2 percent per year.

2. The core inflation rate excludes the cost of housing and medical care.

3. The Fed's monetary policy instrument is the federal funds rate.

4. The Fed uses a targeting rule in which it sets the federal funds at the level that makes the forecast of its policy goals equal to their targets.

5. To change the federal funds rate, the Fed uses open market operations.

Multiple choice

1. Maximum employment and moderate long-term interest rates are best achieved with
   a. high and stable inflation rates.
   b. high and variable inflation rates.
   c. high real interest rates.
   d. high short-term interest rates.
   e. price stability.

2. The operational goals the Fed uses for its monetary policy objectives are the
   a. federal funds rate and the supply of reserves.
   b. the demand for reserves and the supply of reserves.
   c. supply of reserves and the output gap.
   d. core inflation rate and the output gap.
   e. federal funds rate and the core inflation rate.

3. Which of the following is the Fed's monetary policy instrument?
   a. the output gap
   b. the core inflation rate
   c. the federal funds rate
   d. the supply of reserves
   e. the demand for reserves

4. To lower the federal funds rate, the Fed conducts an open market _____ of securities which _____.
   a. sale; increases the demand for reserves
   b. sale; increases the supply of reserves
   c. purchase; increases the demand for reserves
   d. purchase; decreases the demand for reserves
   e. None of the above answers is correct

© 2015 Pearson Education, Inc.

Short Response Question

■ FIGURE 33.1

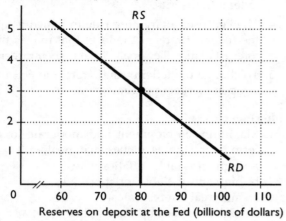

Federal funds rate (percent per year)

Reserves on deposit at the Fed (billions of dollars)

1. Figure 33.1 shows the market for reserves.
   a. What is the equilibrium federal funds rate?
   b. If the Fed wants to change the federal funds rate to 2 percent, what can the Fed do?
   c. Through what method will the Fed change the federal funds rate to 2 percent?

Long Response Questions

1. Why do stable prices help the Fed meet its goals for employment and long-term interest rates?

2. What are the Fed's objectives for employment and the price level? What does it use as operational goals for these targets?

3. What does the Fed use as its monetary policy instrument? How was this instrument used during the financial crisis of 2008?

4. What is the difference between an instrument rule and a target rule? Which rule does the Fed use?

5. How does the Fed change the supply of reserves? What happened in the market for reserves during the financial crisis of 2008?

Additional Exercises (also in MyEconLab Test A)

1. What does the Federal Reserve Act say that the Fed must try to achieve and the means that it must use?

2. If the price of housing was rising much faster than other prices, would the core inflation measure exclude housing costs?

3. Consider two situations, *A* and *B*: In *A*, the output gap is positive (an inflationary gap) and the core inflation rate is 3 percent a year; and in *B*, the output gap is negative (a recessionary gap) and the core inflation rate is 1 percent a year. In which situation is the Fed likely to have the higher federal funds rate target and why?

■ FIGURE 33.2

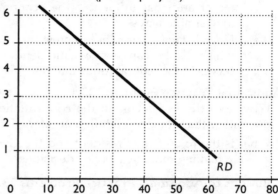

Federal funds rate (percent per year)

Reserves on deposit at the Fed (billions of dollars)

4. If in Figure 33.2 the quantity of reserves supplied is $40 billion and the Fed wants to set the federal funds rate at 5 percent a year, does it buy or sell securities in the open market? By how much must it change banks' reserves?

CHECKPOINT 33.2

■ **Explain the transmission channels through which the Fed influences real GDP and the inflation rate.**

Quick Review

- *Monetary policy transmission* When the Fed raises the federal funds rate, other short-term interest rates and the exchange rate rise. The quantity of money and supply of loanable funds decrease so

© 2015 Pearson Education, Inc.

that the long-term real interest rate rises. Consumption expenditure, investment, and net exports decrease so aggregate demand decreases. The real GDP growth rate and the inflation rate decrease.

Additional Practice Problems 33.2

1. The figure shows the market for reserves. Suppose the Fed becomes concerned that the inflation rate is too high and wants to change the quantity of reserves by $20 billion.

   a. Will the Fed want to raise or lower the federal funds rate? How will the Fed make this change? In the figure, show how the Fed's policy will the change the market for reserves.

   b. What will be the effect of the policy on the quantity of money, the supply of loanable funds and the real interest rate?

   c. What will be the effect of the policy on aggregate demand and on the growth rate real GDP and the inflation rate?

2. In reality, can monetary policy offset fluctuations in aggregate demand so that neither the price level nor real GDP changes? Explain your answer.

Solutions to Additional Practice Problems 33.2

1a. Because the Fed is concerned with inflation, the Fed will raise the federal funds rate. To do so, the Fed will use open market purchases of securities. The figure shows that the Fed will decrease the quanti-

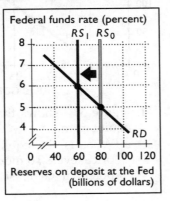

ty of reserves. The federal funds rate will rise from 5 percent to 6 percent.

1b. The quantity of money decreases as does the supply of loanable funds. The decrease in the supply of loanable funds raises the real long-term interest rate.

1c. The rise in the long-term real interest rate decreases consumption expenditure and investment. Net exports also decreases, so for these three reasons aggregate demand decreases. The growth rate of real GDP slows and the inflation rate falls.

2. It is not possible for monetary policy to offset fluctuations in aggregate demand so that neither the price level nor real GDP changes. Because monetary policy must work through many linkages before it affects the economy, there are long and variable lags between the Fed's policy action and its impact on the economy. As a consequence, policy that eliminates all changes in the price level and real GDP is impossible.

■ AP Self Test 33.2

True or false

1. When the Fed lowers the federal funds rate, other short-term interest rates quickly fall.

2. If the Fed raises the federal funds rate, the quantity of money and the supply of loanable funds both decrease

3. The Fed has immediate and direct control over the long-term real interest rate.

4. When the Fed lowers the federal funds rate, its policy affects real GDP and the price level by changing aggregate supply.

5. If the Fed raises the federal funds rate, it is aiming to decrease aggregate demand and thereby decrease the inflation rate.

6. On average, the Fed's actions take about 3 to 4 months before they have an impact on the inflation rate.

© 2015 Pearson Education, Inc.

Multiple choice

1. When the Fed lowers the federal funds rate, which of the following economic variables responds most rapidly?
   a. consumption expenditure
   b. the supply of loanable funds
   c. the long-term real interest rate
   d. other short-term interest rates
   e. the inflation rate

2. When the Fed lowers the federal funds rate, which of the following economic variables responds most slowly?
   a. consumption expenditure
   b. the supply of loanable funds
   c. the long-term real interest rate
   d. other short-term interest rates
   e. the inflation rate

3. When the Fed lowers the federal funds rate, in the short run the quantity of money ____ and the supply of loanable funds ____.
   a. increases; increases
   b. increases; decreases
   c. decreases; decreases
   d. decreases; increases
   e. increases; does not change

4. When the Fed raises the federal funds rate, consumption expenditure ____ and investment ____.
   a. does not change; does not change
   b. does not change; decreases
   c. increases; decreases
   d. increases; increases
   e. decreases; decreases

5. When the Fed raises the federal funds rate, the exchange rate ____ and net exports ____.
   a. does not change; does not change
   b. does not change; decreases
   c. increases; decreases
   d. increases; increases
   e. decreases; decreases

6. A change in the federal funds rate ____ the supply of loanable funds, ____ the long-term real interest rate, and ____ investment.
   a. affects; affects; affects
   b. affects; affects; does not affect
   c. does not affect; affect; does not affect
   d. affects; does not affect; affects
   e. does not affect; does not affect; does not affect

7. If the Fed wants to fight a recession, it will ____ the federal funds rate in order to ____.
   a. raise; increase aggregate demand
   b. raise; decrease aggregate supply
   c. raise; increase aggregate supply
   d. lower; increase aggregate supply
   e. lower; increase aggregate demand

8. If the Fed wants to fight inflation, it will ____ the federal funds rate in order to ____.
   a. raise; decrease aggregate demand
   b. raise; decrease aggregate supply
   c. raise; increase aggregate supply
   d. lower; increase aggregate supply
   e. lower; decrease aggregate demand

Short Response Question

■ **FIGURE 33.3**

Price level (GDP price index, 2009 = 100)

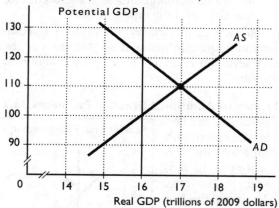

1. Figure 33.3 shows the economy in its initial equilibrium.
   a. What is the equilibrium real GDP and price level? To move the economy back to potential GDP, should the Fed raise or

© 2015 Pearson Education, Inc.

lower the federal funds rate? Why?

b. Supposing that the Fed undertakes the correct policy to restore real GDP to potential GDP. In Figure 33.3 show the effect of that policy.

Long Response Questions

1. Does the Fed's monetary policy aim to change aggregate demand or aggregate supply? Why?

2. How does monetary policy affect the exchange rate? In your answer, explain the case in which the Fed raises the interest rate and assume that the Fed's monetary policy is the only factor that changes.

3. Use Figures 33.4 through 33.7 to show the effect of the Fed conducting an open market purchase that increases the supply of reserves by $1 billion.

■ **FIGURE 33.4**

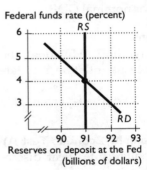

Federal funds rate (percent)

Reserves on deposit at the Fed (billions of dollars)

■ **FIGURE 33.6**

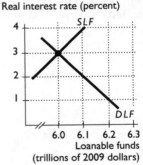

Real interest rate (percent)

Loanable funds (trillions of 2009 dollars)

4. Suppose the Fed is concerned that the economy is entering a recession. What policy can the Fed pursue and what is the effect of the

policy on real GDP and the price level?

5. Suppose it takes two years for monetary policy to have an effect and recessions last for only one year. What implication does this have for monetary policy?

Additional Exercises (also in MyEconLab Test A)

1. List the sequence of events in the transmission from a fall in the federal funds rate to a change in the inflation rate.

For the next two exercises, suppose the Fed thinks that an inflationary gap is emerging and takes actions to avoid its consequences.

2. What action does the Fed take? Illustrate the effects of the Fed's actions in the money market and the loanable funds market.

3. Explain how the Fed's actions change aggregate demand and real GDP.

CHECKPOINT 33.3

■ **Explain and compare alternative monetary policy strategies.**

Quick Review

- *Discretionary monetary policy* A monetary policy that is based on the expert assessment of the current economic situation.

- *k-percent rule* A monetary policy that makes the quantity of money grow at *k* percent per year, where *k* is the growth rate of potential GDP.

- *Inflation targeting* A monetary policy framework that combines an announced target range for the inflation rate with the publication of the central bank's economic forecasts and analysis.

Additional Practice Problems 33.3

1. What is the major drawback of discretionary monetary policy?

2. If a central bank is using a *k*-percent rule, how does it respond to a recession?

Solutions to Additional Practice Problems 33.3

1. People must make long-term plans for the future. Firms and workers must determine wages

■ **FIGURE 33.5**

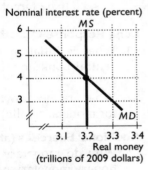

Nominal interest rate (percent)

Real money (trillions of 2009 dollars)

■ **FIGURE 33.7**

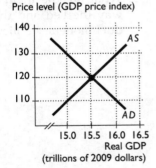

Price level (GDP price index)

Real GDP (trillions of 2009 dollars)

© 2015 Pearson Education, Inc.

while savers and borrowers must determine interest rates. These plans are best made when inflation is correctly anticipated. Discretionary monetary policy makes it difficult to correctly anticipate inflation, so this type of policy can lead to poor economic outcomes.

2. A *k*-percent rule calls for the central bank to ignore recessions and keep the quantity of money growing at *k* percent. So the central bank would not respond to a recession; the growth rate of the quantity of money would stay at *k* percent.

■ AP Self Test 33.3

True or false

1. Discretionary policy must be implemented using an inflation targeting rule.

2. Inflation targeting aims to keep the inflation rate within an announced target range.

3. The *k*-percent rule says that the growth rate of the quantity of money must equal the inflation rate minus *k* percent.

4. The United States is currently targeting nominal GDP.

Multiple choice

1. Discretionary monetary policy has the drawback that it
   a. must lead to very high inflation.
   b. is currently illegal in the United States.
   c. makes inflation expectations harder to manage.
   d. cannot be implemented using changes in the federal funds rate.
   e. None of the above answers is correct.

2. To work well, which monetary policy rule needs the demand for money to be stable?
   a. discretionary monetary policy
   b. nominal GDP targeting
   c. *k*-percent rule
   d. inflation targeting rule
   e. No monetary policy rule requires the demand for money to be stable.

3. Under a nominal GDP targeting rule, the Federal Reserve
   a. cannot use the federal funds rate to conduct monetary policy.
   b. lowers its interest rate when nominal GDP falls below the target.
   c. changes the interest rate only when real GDP, and hence nominal GDP, is off target.
   d. loses its ability to influence the inflation rate.
   e. must publish its expected inflation rate.

4. Inflation targeting requires the central bank to
   a. use a short-term interest rate as its policy instrument.
   b. adopt a *k*-percent rule for the inflation rate.
   c. avoid changing the amount of the monetary base.
   d. publicize its targeted inflation rate.
   e. set a fixed target for nominal GDP.

Long Response Questions

1. What is inflation targeting? Why does the central bank announce its inflation rate targets?

2. What are the drawbacks of the *k*-percent rule for monetary policy?

Additional Exercises (also in MyEconLab Test A)

1. Why do monetary policy rules beat discretionary monetary policy?

2. What are the main differences between the way the Fed and the Bank of England conduct monetary policy?

© 2015 Pearson Education, Inc.

SELF TEST ANSWERS

■ AP Self Test 33.1

True or false
1. False; page 844
2. False; page 845
3. True; page 846
4. True; page 848
5. True; page 849

Multiple choice
1. e; page 844
2. d; page 845
3. c; page 846
4. e; page 849

Short Response Questions

■ FIGURE 33.8

Federal funds rate (percent per year)

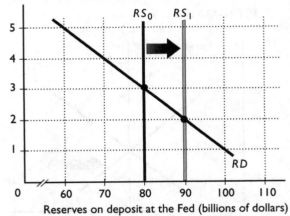

Reserves on deposit at the Fed (billions of dollars)

1. a. The equilibrium federal funds rate is 3 percent; page 849.
   b. As Figure 33.8 shows, for the Fed lower the federal funds rate to 2 percent, the Fed must increase the quantity of reserves to by $10 billion to $90 billion; pages 849-850.
   c. The Fed will increase the quantity of reserves by using an open market purchase of securities; page 849.

Long Response Questions
1. The Fed seeks "maximum employment" and "moderate long-term interest rates." If the Fed can achieve stable prices, then the inflation rate will be low. A low inflation rate helps people makes the best decisions about savings and investment and so helps promote economic growth and maximum employment. Because the long-term interest rate equals the real interest rate plus the inflation rate, low inflation also makes the long-term interest lower than otherwise; page 844.

2. The Fed seeks "maximum employment, stable prices …". For use as an operational "maximum employment" goal, the Fed uses percentage output gap. For use as an operational "stable prices" goal, the Fed uses the core inflation rate; page 845.

3. The Fed uses the federal funds rate—the interest rate at which banks can borrow and lend reserves—as its policy instrument. The federal funds rate has fluctuated since 1990. Since 2009 the Fed has set the federal funds at an unprecedentedly low level of near 0 percent; pages 846-847.

4. An instrument rule sets the policy instrument according to a formula. For instance, the Taylor rule sets the federal funds rate according to the inflation rate and the output gap. A targeting rule sets the policy instrument at the level that makes the forecasts of the ultimate policy goals equal to their targets. A targeting rule need not be a specific quantitative rule. The Fed currently uses a targeting rule; page 848.

5. The Fed changes the supply of reserves by using open market operations, its purchases or sales of securities. In the financial crisis of 2008, increased risk vastly raised banks' demand for reserves. To keep the interest rate low, the Fed responded with a huge increase in the quantity of reserves; pages 849-850.

Additional Exercises (also in MyEconLab Test A)
1. The Federal Reserve Act says that "The Board of Governors of the Federal Reserve System and the Federal Open Market Committee shall maintain long-run growth of the

© 2015 Pearson Education, Inc.

monetary and credit aggregates commensurate with the economy's long-run potential to increase production, so as to promote effectively the goals of maximum employment, stable prices, and moderate long-term interest rates." In this statement, the Fed's goals are specified as "maximum employment, stable prices, and moderate long-term interest rates." In order to reach these goals, the act specifies that the Fed should focus upon the "long-run growth of the monetary and credit aggregates"; page 844.

2. The core inflation is defined as excluding the effects from changes in the prices of food and fuel. So the core inflation rate does not exclude the effect of higher housing costs; page 845.

3. The Fed will have a higher federal funds rate target in situation *A*. A higher federal funds rate target aims to reduce aggregate demand and thereby lower the price level and inflation. In situation *A* the inflation rate is higher than in situation *B*, so the Fed efforts to lower the inflation rate will be more strenuous in situation *A*; page 849.

4. If the Fed wants the federal funds rate to equal its target of 5 percent a year, banks must posses $20 billion of reserves. Because banks presently have $40 billion of reserves, the Fed must decrease banks' reserves by $20 billion. In order to decrease reserves, the Fed sells securities in the open market. So to decrease reserves by $20 billion, the Fed must sell $20 billion of securities; page 849.

■ AP Self Test 33.2

True or false

1. True; page 852
2. True; pages 852-853
3. False; page 854
4. False; page 853
5. True; pages 858-859
6. False; page 860

Multiple choice

1. d; page 853
2. e; page 853
3. a; pages 854-855
4. e; pages 854-855
5. d; page 854
6. a; pages 854-855
7. e; pages 856-857
8. a; pages 858-859

Short Response Question

1. a. The equilibrium real GDP is $17 trillion and the equilibrium price level is 110. To move the economy back to potential GDP, $16 trillion, the Fed should raise the federal fund rate. By raising the federal funds rate, the Fed decreases aggregate demand, which decreases real GDP (and lowers the inflation rate); pages 858-859.

■ **FIGURE 33.9**

Price level (GDP price index, 2009 = 100)

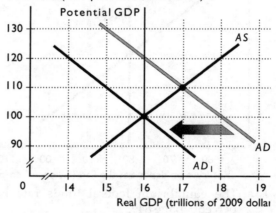

b. Figure 33.9 shows the effect of the Fed's policy. The increase in the federal funds rate and the multiplier effect shift the *AD* leftward to *AD₁* and real GDP falls back to potential GDP, $16 trillion; pages 858-859.

Long Response Questions

1. The Fed's monetary policy affects aggregate demand. The Fed controls the federal funds rate. Through this control the Fed can influence the exchange rate and the long-term real

© 2015 Pearson Education, Inc.

interest rate, which in turn affect net exports, consumption expenditure, and investment. Changes in all three of these variables change aggregate demand, so the Fed's policy allows it to influence aggregate demand. The Fed has no such influence over aggregate supply; page 852.

2. If the U.S. interest rate rises relative to the interest rate in other countries, some people will want to move funds into the United States from other countries to take advantage of the higher interest rate they can now earn on U.S. bank deposits and bonds. To move money into the United States, people must buy dollars and sell other currencies. With more dollars demanded, the U.S. exchange rate rises; page 854.

■ **FIGURE 33.10**

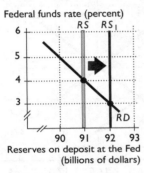

Federal funds rate (percent)

Reserves on deposit at the Fed
(billions of dollars)

■ **FIGURE 33.11**

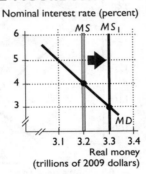

Nominal interest rate (percent)

Real money
(trillions of 2009 dollars)

■ **FIGURE 33.12**

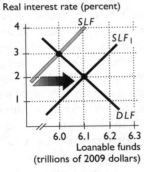

Real interest rate (percent)

Loanable funds
(trillions of 2009 dollars)

■ **FIGURE 33.13**

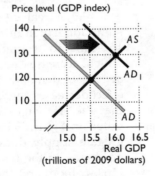

Price level (GDP index)

Real GDP
(trillions of 2009 dollars)

3. Figures 33.10 through 33.13 show the effects from the Fed's open market operation that increases the supply of reserves by $1 billion. In Figure 33.10 this policy shifts the supply of reserves curve rightward and the federal

funds rate falls from 4 percent to 3 percent. This policy also increases the supply of money, so in Figure 33.11, the quantity of money increases and the interest rate falls. The policy increases the supply of loanable funds. Figure 33.12 shows that the supply of loanable funds curve shifts rightward to SLF_1 so that the real interest rate falls to 2 percent. Finally, the fall in the real interest rate increases consumption expenditure and investment, so these increases, combined with the multiplier effect, increases aggregate demand. In Figure 33.13 the aggregate demand curve shifts rightward to AD_1. Real GDP increases and the price level rises; pages 856-857.

4. When the Fed is concerned that the economy is entering a recession, it makes an open market purchase of government securities in order to lower the federal funds rate and increases reserves. The quantity of money and the supply of loanable funds increase. The long-term real interest rate falls so that consumption expenditure and investment increase. The exchange rate falls so that net exports also increases. With the increase in consumption expenditure, investment, and net exports, the multiplier effect increases aggregate demand by even more. The increase in aggregate demand raises the growth rate of real GDP and also raises the inflation rate; pages 856-857.

5. If it takes two years for monetary policy to have an effect and recessions last for only one year, for the Fed to help offset a recession, the Fed must be able to predict recessions a year in advance. If it cannot, then the long and variable lags make it possible for monetary policy to boost inflation rather than fight recession; page 860.

Additional Exercises (also in MyEconLab Test A)

1. When the Fed lowers the federal funds rate, the Fed increases banks' reserves. Other short-term interest rates fall and the exchange rate falls. Because the Fed increases banks' reserves, the quantity of money and

© 2015 Pearson Education, Inc.

supply of loanable funds increase so that the long-term real interest rate falls. Consumption expenditure and investment increase because of the lower real interest rate. The U.S. exchange rate falls so that net exports increase. With the increase in consumption expenditure, investment, and net exports, aggregate demand increases, and eventually the real GDP growth rate and the inflation rate increase; page 853.

■ **FIGURE 33.14**

Federal funds rate (percent per year)

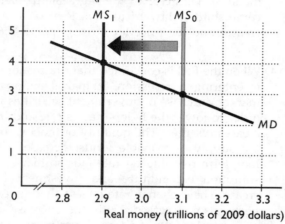

2. Because the Fed is worried about an inflationary gap, the Fed will raise the federal funds rate and decrease banks' reserves. Decreasing banks' reserves decreases the quantity of money so, as illustrated in Figure 33.14, the supply of money decreases, in the figure from $3.1 trillion to $2.9 trillion, and the interest rate rises, in the figure from 3 percent to 4 percent.

In the market for loanable funds, the higher federal funds rate and lower quantity of reserves decrease the supply of banks' loans, which decreases the supply of loanable funds. As Figure 33.15 then shows, the supply of loanable funds curve shifts leftward. The real interest rate rises, from 2 percent to 3 percent in the figure, and the quantity of loanable funds decreases, from $1.3 trillion to $1.1 trillion in the figure; page 858.

■ **FIGURE 33.15**

Real interest rate (percent per year)

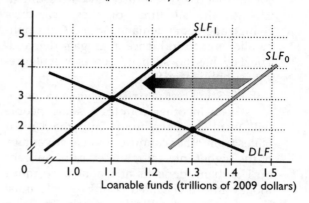

■ **FIGURE 33.16**

Price level (GDP price index, 2009 = 100)

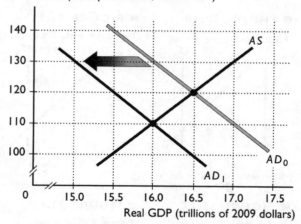

3. The higher real interest rate decreases consumption expenditure and investment. It also leads to a higher U.S. exchange rate, which decreases net exports. On all counts, aggregate demand decreases. The multiplier effect decreases aggregate demand by more so that the *AD* curve shifts leftward, as illustrated in Figure 33.16. In the short run, aggregate supply does not change. Real GDP decreases, in the figure from $16.5 trillion to $16.0 trillion, and the price level falls, in the figure from 120 to 110. In addition to the fall in the price level, the inflation rate also falls; pages 858-859.

© 2015 Pearson Education, Inc.

■ AP Self Test 33.3

True or false

1. False; page 862
2. True; page 862
3. False; page 863
4. False; page 865

Multiple choice

1. c; page 862
2. d; pages 862-863
3. c; page 865
4. b; page 865

Long Response Questions

1. Inflation targeting is a monetary policy framework in which the central bank announces a target range for the inflation rate and publicizes its economic forecasts and analysis. The central bank commits to keeping the inflation rate within its target zone. The target is announced because the announcement gives the people and businesses an anchor for their inflation expectations and thereby helps the central bank manage these expectations; pages 862-863.

2. For a *k*-percent rule to work well, the demand for money needs to be stable and predictable. If the demand for money is not stable, then the interest rate will fluctuate whenever the demand changes. In turn, the changes in the interest rate would lead to fluctuations in aggregate demand. The Fed believes that the demand for money is not stable. As a result, the Fed does not use this policy strategy because the Fed believes this policy would introduce undesirable fluctuations in the interest rate. And, ultimately, the policy would result in unnecessary fluctuations in real GDP growth and the inflation rate; page 865.

Additional Exercises (also in MyEconLab Test A)

1. Rules are superior to discretion because people make long-term plans. These plans, such as employment contracts and long-term loans depend on people's view of inflation. Rules help make future inflation more predictable, and so enable people to make better plans for the future. When people's expectations are more accurate, the economic outcomes are more desirable; page 862.

2. The Bank of England targets inflation, so it makes its inflation target public, commits to hitting the target, and explains how its policy actions will allow it to met its target. The Federal Reserve, however, does not make public its inflation target, does not commit to meeting its target, and does not explain how its actions will enable it to hit its (unannounced) target; pages 862-863.

© 2015 Pearson Education, Inc.

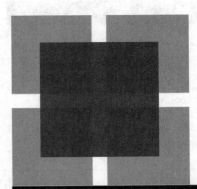

International Finance

Chapter 34

Chapter 34 studies how nations keep their international accounts, what determines the balance of payments, and how the value of the dollar is determined in the foreign exchange market.

1 Describe a country's balance of payments accounts and explain what determines the amount of international borrowing and lending.

There are three balance of payments accounts: the current account, the capital account, and the official settlements account. The current account balance equals exports minus imports, plus net interest and transfers received from abroad. The capital account is a record of foreign investment in the United States minus U.S. investment abroad. The official settlements account is a record of the change in U.S. official reserves. The sum of the balances on the three accounts always equals zero. We pay for imports that exceed the value of our exports by borrowing from the rest of the world. A net borrower is a country that is borrowing more from the rest of the world than it is lending to the rest of the world and a net lender is a country that is lending more to the rest of the world than it is borrowing from the rest of the world. A debtor nation is a country that during its entire history has borrowed more from the rest of the world than it has lent to it and a creditor nation is a country that during its entire history has invested more in the rest of the world than other countries have invested in it. Net exports, $X - M$, equals the sum of the private sector balance, $S - I$, and the government sector balance, $NT - G$.

2 Explain how the exchange rate is determined and why it fluctuates.

Foreign currency is needed to buy goods or invest in another country. The foreign exchange rate is the price at which one currency exchanges for another. It is determined by demand and supply in the foreign exchange market. The quantity of dollars demanded increases when the exchange rate falls. The demand for dollars changes and the demand curve for dollars shifts if the U.S. interest rate differential or the expected future exchange rate changes. A rise in either increases the demand for dollars. The quantity of dollars supplied increases when the exchange rate rises. The supply of dollars changes and the supply curve of dollars shifts if the U.S. interest rate differential or the expected future exchange rate changes. A rise in either decreases the supply of dollars. At the equilibrium exchange rate, the quantity of dollars demanded equals the quantity of dollars supplied. The exchange rate is volatile because factors that change the demand also change the supply. Exchange rate expectations are influenced by purchasing power parity, a situation in which money buys the same amount of goods and services in different currencies, and interest rate parity, a situation in which the interest rate in one currency equals the interest rate in another currency once exchange rate changes are taken into account. The Fed and other central banks can intervene directly in the foreign exchange market by pegging the exchange rate. If the peg overvalues the exchange rate, the central bank runs out of foreign reserves; if the peg undervalues the exchange rate, the central bank accumulates foreign reserves.

© 2015 Pearson Education, Inc.

YOUR AP TEST HINTS

AP Topics

Topic on your AP test	What to Know	Corresponding textbook section
Balance of payments accounts	Definition of current account, capital and financial account; official settlements account	Checkpoint 34.1
Exchange rates	Definition of currency appreciation and depreciation; factors that determine the demand and supply of dollars; different exchange rate regimes	Checkpoint 34.2

AP Vocabulary Covered

Terms	What to Know	Text Sections
Balance of payments account	How nations record international trading, borrowing, and lending	Checkpoint 33.1, p. 872
Current account	Receipts from the sale of exports sold to other countries, minus imports bought from other countries, plus net international interest payments and transfers	Checkpoint 34.1, p. 872
Capital and financial account	Foreign investment in the United States minus U.S. investment abroad	Checkpoint 34.1, p. 872
Official settlement account	Records changes in U.S. official reserves; sum of current account, capital and financial account, and official settlements account, so that they equal zero	Checkpoint 34.1, p. 872
U.S. official reserves	The U.S. government's holdings of foreign currencies	Checkpoint 34.1, p. 872
Net borrower	A country that borrows more from the rest of the world than it lends to the rest of the world	Checkpoint 34.1, p. 874
Net lender	A country that lends more to the rest of the world than it borrows	Checkpoint 34.1, p. 874
Debtor nation	A country that during its history has borrowed more from the rest of the world than it has lent to the rest of the world	Checkpoint 34.1, p. 874
Creditor nation	A country that during its history has loaned more to the rest of the world than it has borrowed from the rest of the world	Checkpoint 34.1, p. 874
Private sector balance	Saving minus investment	Checkpoint 34.1, p. 876
Government sector balance	Net taxes minus government expenditures on goods and services	Checkpoint 34.1, p. 876
Foreign exchange market	Currencies of one country being traded for those of other countries	Checkpoint 34.2. p. 879
Foreign exchange rate	The price at which one currency trades for another	Checkpoint 34.2, p. 879
Currency appreciation	Rise in the value of a currency (its price in other currencies)	Checkpoint 34.2, p. 879
Currency depreciation	Fall in the value of a currency	Checkpoint 34.2, p. 880
U.S. interest rate differential	The U.S. interest rate minus the foreign interest rate; affects the relative profitability of saving in the United States and abroad	Checkpoint 34.2, p. 882
Purchasing power parity, *PPP*	The situation in which a unit of money buys the same amount of goods and services in different nations	Checkpoint 34.2, p. 888
Interest rate parity	The situation in which interest rates in different nations are equal when exchange rate changes are taken into account	Checkpoint 34.2, p. 890

© 2015 Pearson Education, Inc.

Extra AP material

- The label *capital account* has been replaced in the official records by the term *capital and financial account*. The newest AP sources also just call this account the *financial account*.
- The AP test requires students to identify whether transactions, such as exports or U.S. investment abroad, are included in the current account <u>or</u> the capital and financial account.
- The foreign exchange markets are used on AP tests to connect appreciation and depreciation with changes in imports and exports, which then change a nation's aggregate demand and its real GDP and are part of the "net exports" effect.
- Fiscal policy influences capital flows and the exchange rate. An expansionary fiscal policy, such as an increase in government expenditure, raises the interest rate. The higher interest rate attracts capital inflows from abroad and appreciates the exchange rate. Monetary policy also influences capital flows and the exchange rate. An expansionary monetary policy lowers the interest rate. The lower interest rate attracts capital outflows from the nation to abroad and depreciates the exchange rate.
- On the AP test, exchange rates can be said to be "fixed," "floating," or "flexible." A fixed exchange rate is one for which the central bank (the Federal Reserve for the United States) actively intervenes to keep the exchange rate constant. A floating exchange rate is one that is not influenced by the central bank; that is, the central bank does not intervene in the foreign exchange market. A flexible exchange rate, often called a "managed flexible" exchange rate, is one for which the central bank intervenes to keep the exchange rate within certain bounds and/or from appreciating or depreciating too much or too rapidly.
- The AP test also describes *pegged exchange rates* as the historic system in which nations fixed their exchange rates to a single country's currency. This was the system used prior to the early 1970s. The currency to which other nations fixed their exchange rates was generally the U.S. dollar.

CHECKPOINT 34.1

■ **Describe a country's balance of payments accounts and explain what determines the amount of international borrowing and lending.**

Quick Review

- *Current account balance* The current account balance equals net exports plus net interest plus net transfers received from abroad.
- *Capital and financial account balance* The capital and financial account balance equals foreign investment in the United States minus U.S. investment abroad.

Additional Practice Problems 34.1

1. In 2006 the U.S. economy recorded the following transactions:

Imports of goods and services, $2,203 billion; net interest, $36 billion; net transfers −$90 billion; decrease in U.S. official reserves, −$2 billion; exports of goods and services, $1,446 billion; statistical discrepancy −$18 billion; foreign investment in the United States, $1,882 billion; and, U.S. investment abroad, $1,055 billion.

   a. Calculate the current account balance.
   b. Calculate the capital account balance.
   c. Calculate the official settlements account balance.
   d. To what do these balances sum?
   e. Was the United States a debtor or a creditor nation in 2006?

© 2015 Pearson Education, Inc.

2. Suppose the official settlements account equals zero. In this case, what is the relationship between the current account and the capital account? Why does this relationship exist?

Solutions to Additional Practice Problems 34.1

1a. The current account balance equals exports plus net interest plus net transfers minus imports. So the current account balance equals $1,446 billion + $36 billion + (−$90 billion) − $2,203 billion = −$811 billion.

1b. The capital account balance equals foreign investment in the United States minus U.S. investment abroad plus any statistical discrepancy. So the capital account balance equals $1,882 billion − $1,055 billion + (−$18 billion) = $809 billion.

1c. The official settlements account balance is the negative of the change in U.S. official reserves. When reserves decrease by $2 billion, the official settlements account balance is $2 billion.

1d. Keep in mind that the sum of the current account, capital account, and official settlements account is zero. So, if the previous answers are correct, they will sum to zero. Fortunately, they do: −$811 billion + $809 billion + $2 billion = $0.

1e. Interest payments reflect the value of outstanding debts. The United States is a debtor nation because the value of interest payments received from the rest of the world is less than the value of interest payments made to the rest of the world.

2. If the official settlements account equals zero, then the deficit in the current account equals the surplus in the capital account. Or, if the official settlements account equals zero, then the surplus in the current account equals the deficit in the capital account. This relationship exists because the sum of the current account, capital account, and the official settlements account equals zero. If the official settlements account equals zero, the current account balance must equal the negative of the capital account balance.

■ AP Self Test 34.1

True or false

1. If foreign investment in the United States increases, and U.S. investment in the rest of the world decreases, the current account shows an increase in exports and a decrease in imports.

2. The official settlements account balance is negative if U.S. official reserves increase.

3. If the United States has a surplus in its capital account and a deficit in its current account, the balance in its official settlements account is zero.

4. At the present time, the United States has a current account deficit.

5. The United States is a net lender and a debtor nation.

6. If the United States started to run a current account surplus that continued indefinitely, it would immediately become a net lender and would eventually become a creditor nation.

7. Net exports equals the private sector balance minus the government sector balance.

8. In 2010, U.S. borrowing from abroad financed investment.

Multiple choice

1. A country's balance of payments accounts records its
   a. tax receipts and expenditures.
   b. tariffs and nontariff revenue and government purchases.
   c. international trading, borrowing, and lending.
   d. its tariff receipts and what it pays in tariffs to other nations.
   e. international exports and imports and nothing else.

© 2015 Pearson Education, Inc.

2. Which of the following are balance of payments accounts?
   i. capital account
   ii. tariff account
   iii. current account
   a. i only.
   b. ii only.
   c. iii only.
   d. i and iii.
   e. ii and iii.

3. Which balance of payments account records payments for imports and receipts from exports?
   a. current account
   b. capital account
   c. official settlements account
   d. reserves account
   e. trade account

4. The current account balance is equal to
   a. imports − exports + net interest + net transfers.
   b. imports − exports + net interest − net transfers.
   c. exports − imports − net interest + net transfers.
   d. exports − imports + net interest + net transfers.
   e. exports − imports − net interest − net transfers.

5. If an investment of $100 million from the United Kingdom is made in the United States, in the U.S balance of payments accounts the $100 million is listed as a _____ entry in the _____ account.
   a. positive; current
   b. negative; capital
   c. positive; capital
   d. negative; current
   e. positive; official settlements

6. If the United States receives $200 billion of foreign investment and at the same time invests a total of $160 billion abroad, then the U.S.
   a. capital account balance increases by $40 billion.
   b. current account must be in surplus.
   c. balance of payments must be negative.
   d. capital account balance decreases by $40 billion.
   e. official settlements account balance increases by $40 billion.

7. In the balance of payments accounts, changes in U.S. official reserves are recorded in the
   a. current account.
   b. capital account.
   c. official settlements account.
   d. international currency account.
   e. international reserves account.

8. If a country has a current account balance of $100 billion and the official settlements account balance is zero, then the country's capital account balance must be
   a. equal to $100 billion.
   b. positive but not necessarily equal to $100 billion.
   c. equal to −$100 billion.
   d. negative but not necessarily equal to −$100 billion.
   e. zero.

9. A country that is borrowing more from the rest of the world than it is lending is called a
   a. net lender.
   b. net borrower.
   c. net debtor.
   d. net creditor.
   e. net loaner country.

© 2015 Pearson Education, Inc.

10. A debtor nation is a country that
   a. borrows more from the rest of the world than it lends to it.
   b. lends more to the rest of the world than it borrows from it.
   c. during its entire history has invested more in the rest of the world than other countries have invested in it.
   d. during its entire history has borrowed more from the rest of the world than it has lent to it.
   e. during its entire history has consistently run a capital account deficit.

11. Comparing the U.S. balance of payments in 2012 to the rest of the world, we see that the
   a. United States has the largest current account surplus.
   b. U.S. current account is similar in size to most developed nations.
   c. United States has the largest capital account deficit.
   d. United States has the largest current account deficit.
   e. U.S. current account is similar in size to most developed nations and has a deficit.

12. According to the U.S. balance of payments accounts in 2012, U.S. international borrowing is used for
   a. private and public investment.
   b. private consumption.
   c. government expenditure.
   d. private and public saving.
   e. private saving and public consumption.

Short Response Question
1. If its official settlements account equals zero, what will a country's capital account equal if it has a $350 billion current account deficit?

Long Response Questions
1. What is recorded in the U.S. current account? In its capital account? In its official settlements account?

Item	(billions of dollars)
U.S. investment abroad	400
Exports of goods and services	1,000
Net transfers	0
Change in official reserves	10
Net interest	0
Foreign investment in the United States	800

2. The table above has balance of payment data for the United States.
   a. What is the capital account balance?
   b. What is the official settlements balance?
   c. What is the current account balance?
   d. What is the value of imports of goods and services?

3. What is a net borrower? A debtor nation? Is it possible for a nation to be net borrower and yet not be a debtor nation?

Item	(billions of dollars)
Saving	1,600
Investment	1,900
Government expenditures	1,300
Net taxes	1,400

4. The table above has data for the United States.
   a. What is the private sector balance?
   b. What is the government sector balance?
   c. What is net exports?

Additional Exercises (also in MyEconLab Test A)
It is 2016, and the U.S. economy records the following transactions: Exports of goods and services, $1,800 billion; interest payments to the rest of the world, $550 billion; interest received from the rest of the world, $350 billion; decrease in U.S. official reserves, $10 billion; government sector balance, $200 billion; saving, $1,800 billion; investment, $2,000 billion; net transfers are zero.

1. Calculate the current account balance, the capital account balance, the official settlements account balance, and imports of goods and services.

2. Is the United States a debtor or creditor nation in 2016?

3. If net taxes increase by $100 billion, what happens to the capital account balance?

© 2015 Pearson Education, Inc.

CHECKPOINT 34.2

■ **Explain how the exchange rate is determined and why it fluctuates.**

Quick Review

- *U.S. interest rate differential* In the foreign exchange market, an increase in the U.S. interest rate differential increases the demand for dollars and decreases the supply of dollars.
- *Expected future exchange rate* In the foreign exchange market, a rise in the expected future exchange rate increases the demand for dollars and decreases the supply of dollars.

Additional Practice Problems 34.2

1. The figure shows the supply and demand curves for dollars in the foreign exchange market.

   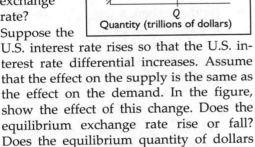

   a. What is the equilibrium exchange rate?

   b. Suppose the U.S. interest rate rises so that the U.S. interest rate differential increases. Assume that the effect on the supply is the same as the effect on the demand. In the figure, show the effect of this change. Does the equilibrium exchange rate rise or fall? Does the equilibrium quantity of dollars exchanged increase or decrease?

2. How and why does an increase in the expected future exchange rate change the *current* demand for U.S. dollars and the demand curve for dollars? How and why does an increase in the expected future exchange rate change the supply of U.S. dollars and the supply curve of dollars? What is the effect on the equilibrium exchange rate?

Solutions to Additional Practice Problems 34.2

1a. The figure shows that the initial equilibrium exchange rate is 0.8 euros per dollar.

1b. The increase in the U.S. interest rate differential increases the demand for U.S. dollars and simultaneously decreases the supply of U.S. dollars. As a result the demand curve for dollars shifts rightward, from D_0 to D_1 and the supply curve of dollars shifts leftward, from S_0 to S_1. The exchange rate rises. In the figure the exchange rate rises to 0.9 euros per dollar. Because the effect on the demand is the same as the effect on the supply, the curves shift by the same amount, so the equilibrium quantity of dollars exchanged does not change.

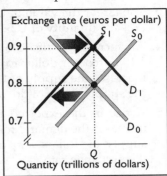

2. An increase in the expected future exchange rate increases the demand for U.S. dollars and shifts the demand curve rightward. The demand for U.S. dollars increases because at the current exchange rate people want to buy U.S. dollars now and sell them in the future at the higher expected exchange rate. An increase in the expected future exchange rate decreases the supply of U.S. dollars and shifts the supply curve leftward. The supply of U.S. dollars decreases because people would rather keep the dollars until they can sell them in the future at the higher expected exchange rate. Because the demand for dollars increases and the supply of dollars decreases, the current equilibrium exchange rate rises.

■ **AP Self Test 34.2**

True or false

1. The U.S. foreign exchange rate changes infrequently.

© 2015 Pearson Education, Inc.

2. If the exchange rate increases from 0.9 euros per dollar to 1.1 euros per dollar, the dollar has appreciated.

3. The larger the value of U.S. exports, the larger is the quantity of U.S. dollars demanded.

4. An increase in the U.S. exchange rate from 1.10 euros per dollar to 1.20 euros per dollar increases the supply of U.S. dollars and shifts the supply curve of dollars rightward.

5. A rise in the expected future exchange rate increases the demand for dollars and also the supply of dollars and might raise or lower the exchange rate.

6. The equilibrium U.S. exchange rate is the exchange rate that sets the quantity of dollars demanded equal to the quantity of dollars supplied.

7. An increase in the U.S. interest rate differential raises the U.S. exchange rate.

8. To prevent the price of the euro from falling, the European Central Bank might sell euros on the foreign exchange market.

Multiple choice

1. The foreign exchange market is the market in which
   a. all international transactions occur.
   b. currencies are exchanged solely by governments.
   c. goods and services are exchanged between governments.
   d. the currency of one country is exchanged for the currency of another.
   e. the world's governments collect their tariff revenue.

2. When Del Monte, an American company, purchases Mexican tomatoes, Del Monte pays for the tomatoes with
   a. Canadian dollars.
   b. Mexican pesos.
   c. gold.
   d. Mexican goods and services.
   e. euros.

3. If today the exchange rate is 1.00 euro per dollar and tomorrow the exchange rate is 0.98 euros per dollar, then the dollar ____ and the euro____.
   a. appreciated; appreciated
   b. appreciated; depreciated
   c. depreciated; appreciated
   d. depreciated; depreciated
   e. depreciated; did not change

4. In the foreign exchange market, as the U.S. exchange rate rises from 0.95 euros per dollar to 1.05 euros per dollar, other things remaining the same, the
   a. quantity of dollars demanded increases.
   b. demand curve for dollars shifts rightward.
   c. demand curve for dollars shifts leftward.
   d. quantity of dollars demanded decreases.
   e. supply curve of dollars shifts rightward.

5. In the foreign exchange market, the demand for dollars increases and the demand curve for dollars shifts rightward if the
   a. U.S. interest rate differential increases.
   b. expected future exchange rate falls.
   c. foreign interest rate rises.
   d. U.S. interest rate falls.
   e. exchange rate falls.

6. As the exchange rate ____, the quantity of U.S. dollars supplied ____.
   a. rises; increases
   b. falls; increases
   c. falls; remains the same
   d. rises; decreases
   e. rises; remains the same

7. In the foreign exchange market, the supply curve of dollars is
   a. upward sloping.
   b. downward sloping.
   c. vertical.
   d. horizontal.
   e. identical to the demand curve for dollars.

© 2015 Pearson Education, Inc.

8. Everything else remaining the same, in the foreign exchange market which of the following increases the supply of U.S. dollars?
   a. The European interest rate rises.
   b. The expected future exchange rate rises.
   c. The U.S. interest rate rises.
   d. The U.S. interest rate differential increases.
   e. The exchange rate falls.

9. When there is a shortage of dollars in the foreign exchange market, the
   a. demand curve for dollars shifts leftward to restore the equilibrium.
   b. U.S. exchange rate will appreciate.
   c. U.S. exchange rate will depreciate.
   d. supply curve of dollars shifts leftward to restore the equilibrium.
   e. supply curve of dollars shifts rightward to restore the equilibrium.

10. In the foreign exchange market, when the U.S. interest rate rises, the supply of dollars _____ and the foreign exchange rate _____.
    a. increases; rises
    b. increases; falls
    c. decreases; rises
    d. decreases; falls
    e. increases; does not change

11. A situation in which money buys the same amount of goods and services in different currencies is called
    a. exchange rate equilibrium.
    b. purchasing power parity.
    c. exchange rate surplus.
    d. exchange rate balance.
    e. a fixed exchange rate.

12. Interest rate parity occurs when
    a. the interest rate in one currency equals the interest rate in another currency when exchange rate changes are taken into account.
    b. interest rate differentials are always maintained across nations.
    c. interest rates are equal across nations.
    d. prices are equal across nations when exchange rates are taken into account.
    e. interest rates no longer affect the exchange rate.

Short Response Questions
1. Define "currency depreciation."
2. Define "currency appreciation."

Long Response Questions
1. If the exchange rate rises from 0.90 euros per dollar to 1.00 euros per dollar, has the dollar appreciated or depreciated? Has the euro appreciated or depreciated?

2. What is the relationship between the value of U.S. exports and the quantity of U.S. dollars demanded? Why does this relationship exist?

3. What is the relationship between the value of U.S. imports and the quantity of U.S. dollars supplied? Why does this relationship exist?

4. Everything else remaining the same, how will a rise in the European interest rate affect the demand for dollars, the supply of dollars, and the U.S. exchange rate?

5. If the Fed believes the exchange rate is too low and wants to raise it, what action does the Fed undertake in the foreign exchange market? What limits the extent to which the Fed can undertake this action?

■ **FIGURE 34.1**

Exchange rate (euros per dollar)

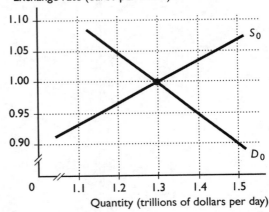

6. Figure 34.1 shows the foreign exchange market for U.S. dollars.
   a. What is the equilibrium exchange rate?
   b. The U.S. interest rate differential rises. In Figure 34.1, illustrate the effect of this change. What happens to the exchange rate?

© 2015 Pearson Education, Inc.

■ **FIGURE 34.2**

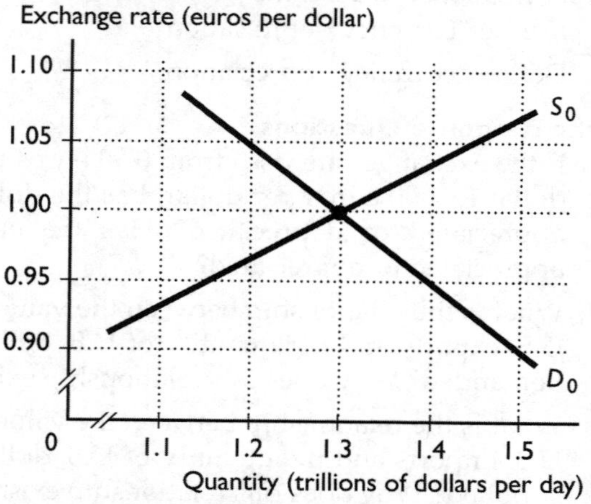

Exchange rate (euros per dollar)

Quantity (trillions of dollars per day)

7. Figure 34.2 shows the foreign exchange market for U.S. dollars. Suppose people expect that the future exchange rate will be lower. In Figure 34.2, illustrate the effect of this change. What happens to the exchange rate? Has the exchange rate appreciated or depreciated?

Additional Exercises (also in MyEconLab Test A)

Use the following for the next 3 exercises. Suppose that yesterday, the Canadian dollar ($C) was trading on the foreign exchange market at $0.85 U.S. per $C. Today, the Canadian dollar is trading at $0.80 U.S. per $C.

1. Which of the two currencies (the Canadian dollar or the U.S. dollar) has appreciated and which has depreciated today?

2. List the events that could have caused today's change in the value of the Canadian dollar on the foreign exchange market. Did the events on you list increase or decrease the demand for Canadian dollars, the supply of Canadian dollars, or both the demand for and supply of Canadian dollars?

3. If the Bank of Canada had tried to stabilize the value of the Canadian dollar at $0.85 U.S., what action would it have taken? What effect would the Bank of Canada's actions have had on Canadian official reserves?

© 2015 Pearson Education, Inc.

SELF TEST ANSWERS

■ AP Self Test 34.1

True or false

1. False; page 872
2. True; page 872
3. False; page 872
4. True; page 873
5. False; page 874
6. True; page 875
7. False; pages 876-877
8. True; page 877

Multiple choice

1. c; page 872
2. d; page 872
3. a; page 872
4. d; page 872
5. c; page 872
6. a; page 872
7. c; page 872
8. c; page 872
9. b; page 874
10. d; page 874
11. d; page 877
12. a; page 877

Short Response Question

1. The current account records payments for imports, receipts from exports, net interest and net transfers received from abroad. The capital and financial account records foreign investment in the United States minus U.S. investments abroad. The official settlements account records changes in U.S. official reserves, the government's holding of foreign currency; page 872.

Long Response Questions

1. The current account balance plus the capital and financial account balance plus official settlements account balance sums to zero. So if the official settlements account equals zero, a $350 billion current account deficit means there is a $350 billion capital account surplus; page 872.

2. a. The capital account balance equals foreign investment in the United States minus U.S. investment abroad, which is $400 billion; pages 872-873.

   b. The official settlements balance is the negative of the change in official reserves, or −$10 billion; pages 872-873.

   c. The sum of the current account balance, the capital account balance, and the official settlements account balance is zero. The capital account balance is $400 billion and the official settlements account balance is −$10 billion, so the current account balance is −$390 billion; pages 872-873.

   d. The current account balance equals exports minus imports plus net interest plus net transfers received from abroad. Net interest and net transfers are given as zero. The current account balance is −$390 billion and exports are $1,000 billion, so imports equal $1,390 billion; pages 872-873.

3. A net borrower is a country that is borrowing more from the rest of the world than it is lending to the rest of the world. A debtor nation is a country that during its entire history has borrowed more from the rest of the world than it has lent to it. It is possible for a nation to be a net borrower but not be a debtor nation. A country can be a creditor nation and a net borrower. This situation occurs if a creditor nation is, during a particular year, borrowing more from the rest of the world than it is lending to the rest of the world; page 874.

4. a. The private sector balance equals saving minus investment, so the private sector balance is −$300 billion; page 877.

   b. The government sector balance equals net taxes minus government expenditures on goods and services, so the government sector balance is $100 billion; page 877.

   c. The sum of the private sector balance plus the government sector balance equals net exports, so net exports equals −$200 billion; page 877.

© 2015 Pearson Education, Inc.

Additional Exercises (also in MyEconLab Test A)

1. The current account balance equals net exports plus net interest (which is −$200 billion) plus net transfers (which is zero). Net exports equals the government sector balance ($200 billion) plus the private sector balance. The private sector balance equals saving ($1,800 billion) minus investment ($2,000 billion), which is −$200 billion. So net exports equals ($200 billion) + (−$200 billion) = $0. So the current account balance equals −$200 billion.

   The capital account equals −(current account balance + official settlements account balance). The official settlements account equals $10 billion because official U.S. reserves decreased by $10 billion. So the capital account balance equals −(−$200 billion + $10 billion) = −(−$190 billion) = $190 billion.

   The official settlements account balance is $10 billion.

   Net exports equal exports minus imports. Exports are $1,800 billion and net exports are −$200 billion, so imports = $2,000 billion; pages 872-873.

2. The United States is a debtor nation because interest payments to the rest of the world exceed interest payments to the United States; pages 874-875 .

3. If net taxes increase by $100 billion, the government surplus increases by $100 billion and so the current account deficit shrinks. With no change in the official settlements account balance, the capital account surplus decreases; pages 876-877.

■ AP Self Test 34.2

True or false

1. False; page 879
2. True; page 879
3. True; page 880
4. False; page 884
5. False; pages 882, 885, 887
6. True; page 886
7. True; page 887
8. False; page 890

Multiple choice

1. d; page 879
2. b; page 879
3. c; pages 879-880
4. d; page 880
5. a; page 882
6. a; page 883
7. a; page 884
8. a; page 885
9. b; page 886
10. c; pages 885, 887
11. b; page 888
12. a; page 890

Short Response Questions

1. Currency depreciation is the fall in value of the currency on the foreign exchange market. For instance, if the U.S. dollar falls from 120 yen per dollar to 110 yen per dollar, the U.S. dollar has depreciated; page 879.

2. Currency appreciation is the rise in value of the currency on the foreign exchange market. For instance, if the U.S. dollar rises from 120 yen per dollar to 130 yen per dollar, the U.S. dollar has appreciated; page 879.

Long Response Questions

1. When the exchange rate rises from 0.90 euros per dollar to 1.00 euro per dollar, the dollar appreciates because the dollar buys more euros. The euro depreciates because it now takes 1 euro to buy a dollar instead of 0.9 euros to buy a dollar; pages 879-880.

2. The larger the value of U.S. exports, the larger is the quantity of U.S. dollars demanded. This relationship exists because U.S. firms want to be paid for their goods and services in dollars; page 880.

3. The larger the value of U.S. imports, the larger the quantity of U.S. dollars supplied. This relationship exists because U.S. consumers must pay for their imports in foreign

© 2015 Pearson Education, Inc.

currency. To obtain foreign currency, U.S. consumers supply dollars; page 883.

4. An increase in the European interest rate decreases the U.S. interest rate differential. The smaller the U.S. interest rate differential, the smaller is the demand for U.S. assets and the smaller the demand for dollars. And the smaller the U.S. interest rate differential, the greater is the demand for foreign assets and the greater is the supply of dollars. So when the European interest rate rises, the demand for dollars decreases, the supply of dollars increases, and the equilibrium exchange rate falls; pages 882, 885, 887.

5. If the Fed wants to raise the exchange rate, it will buy dollars. The Fed would have to sell U.S. official reserves to buy dollars. The Fed is limited by its quantity of official reserves. If the Fed persisted in this action, eventually it would run out of reserves and would be forced to stop buying dollars; page 880.

■ **FIGURE 34.3**

Exchange rate (euros per dollar)

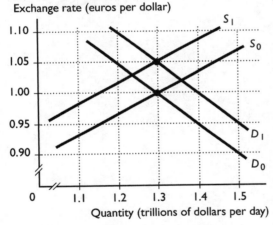

6. a. The equilibrium exchange rate is 1.00 euro per dollar; page 886.

   b. The increase in the U.S. interest rate differential increases the demand for dollars and shifts the demand curve from D_0 to D_1 in Figure 34.3. The increase in the U.S. interest rate differential also decreases the supply of dollars and shifts the supply curve from S_0 to S_1. The exchange rate ris-

es. In the figure, the exchange rate rises to 1.05 euros per dollar; pages 882, 885, 887.

■ **FIGURE 34.4**

Exchange rate (euros per dollar)

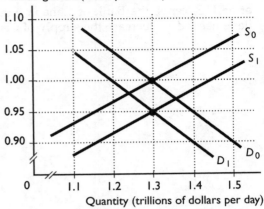

7. The fall in the expected future exchange rate decreases the demand for dollars and increases the supply of dollars. The demand curve shifts leftward from D_0 to D_1 and the supply curve shifts rightward from S_0 to S_1. The exchange falls from 1.00 euro per dollar to 0.95 euros per dollar in Figure 34.4. The exchange rate depreciates; pages 882, 885, 887.

Additional Exercises (also in MyEconLab Test A)

1. Yesterday a Canadian dollar purchased 85 U.S. cents; today a Canadian dollar buys only 80 U.S. cents. The Canadian dollar buys fewer U.S. cents and so the Canadian dollar has depreciated. The U.S. dollar has appreciated; pages 879-880.

2. The main events that might have caused the appreciation of the U.S. dollar and the depreciation of the Canadian dollar are an increase in the U.S. interest rate, a decrease in the Canadian interest rate, or concern that the Canadian dollar will depreciate (the U.S. dollar will appreciate) even more in the future.

   The foreign exchange market is unlike other markets because the factors that affect the supply also affect the demand. So the factors listed in part (b) all affected both the demand for Canadian dollars as well as the supply of Canadian dollars. All the factors listed de-

© 2015 Pearson Education, Inc.

creased the demand for Canadian dollars and increased the supply;   pages 879-882, 884-885.

3. To stabilize the value of the Canadian dollar at 85 U.S. cents, the Bank of Canada would have needed to decrease the supply of Cana-

dian dollars. The Bank of Canada would have needed to buy Canadian dollars.

When the Bank of Canada buys Canadian dollars, it decreases Canadian official reserves; pages 880-891.

© 2015 Pearson Education, Inc.

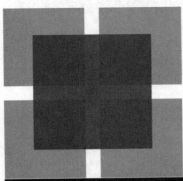

AP Graphing Questions

Chapter 35

■ MICROECONOMICS

1. Shoes are a normal good and people's incomes increase. Using an appropriate diagram, determine the effect on the equilibrium price and quantity of a pair of shoes.

2. The price of cheese used to produce pizza rises. Using an appropriate diagram, determine the effect on the equilibrium price and quantity of pizza.

3. Define consumer surplus and producer surplus. Illustrate the consumer surplus and producer surplus in a competitive market that is producing the allocatively efficient quantity of output.

4. Using an appropriate diagram, illustrate the result when the government imposes a $1 per cup tax on coffee paid by the suppliers. Define tax incidence and explain how the elasticity of demand affects tax incidence.

5. Using an appropriate diagram, explain the deadweight loss that results from an external cost, such as pollution, in an unregulated competitive market.

6. Illustrate the case of a perfectly competitive firm that is earning an economic profit. Indicate the amount of the economic profit.

7. Compare the price and quantity set by a single-price monopoly to the price and quantity set by a perfectly competitive market with the same costs as the monopoly.

■ MACROECONOMICS

1. Golf balls and golf clubs are complements. The price of golf clubs falls. Using an appropriate diagram, determine the effect on the equilibrium price and quantity of golf balls.

2. New technology for producing memory chips is developed. Using an appropriate diagram, determine the effect on the equilibrium price and quantity of memory chips.

3. The nation's population increases. Using a diagram of the labor market, determine the effect on the full-employment amount of employment.

4. The economy emerges from a recession so business firms believe that investment is more profitable. Using an appropriate diagram, determine the effect on the real interest rate.

5. The Federal Reserve increases the quantity of money. Using an appropriate diagram, explain the short-run effect on the interest rate. Tell what will be the short-run effect on real GDP and the price level.

6. Using an aggregate demand/aggregate supply model, determine the short-run effect on the price level and real GDP from an increase in government expenditures.

7. If the price of oil rises, using an aggregate demand/aggregate supply model, determine the short-run effect on the price level and real GDP.

© 2015 Pearson Education, Inc.

ANSWERS

■ MICROECONOMICS

■ FIGURE 35.1

Price (dollars per pair of shoes)

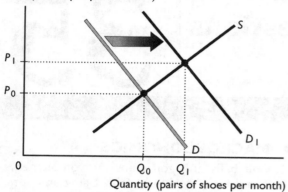

Quantity (pairs of shoes per month)

1. The increase in income increases the demand for a normal good. The demand curve shifts rightward and, as illustrated in Figure 35.1, the equilibrium price of a pair of shoes rises from P_0 to P_1 and the equilibrium quantity increases from Q_0 to Q_1; Chapter 4.

■ FIGURE 35.2

Price (dollars per pizza)

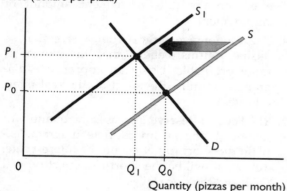

Quantity (pizzas per month)

2. The rise in the price of the cheese used to produce pizza increases the cost of producing pizza. The supply curve shifts leftward and, as illustrated in Figure 35.2, the equilibrium price of a pizza rises from P_0 to P_1 and the equilibrium quantity decreases from Q_0 to Q_1; Chapter 4.

■ FIGURE 35.3

Price (dollars per unit)

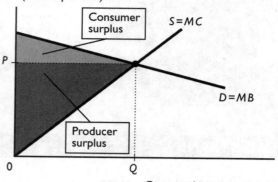

Quantity (units per month)

3. Consumer surplus is the marginal benefit of a good minus the price paid for it, summed over the quantity consumed. Producer surplus is the price of a good minus the marginal cost of producing it, summed over the quantity produced. The demand curve shows the marginal benefit and the supply curve shows the marginal cost. So, as illustrated above, the consumer surplus is the area below the demand curve and above the price and the producer surplus is the area below the price and above the supply curve; Chapter 6.

■ FIGURE 35.4

Price (dollars per cup of coffee)

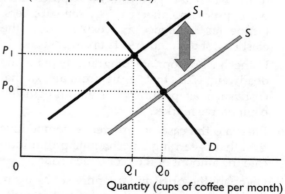

Quantity (cups of coffee per month)

4. The one dollar per cup tax on a cup of coffee paid by suppliers is like an increase in cost to the suppliers. The supply decreases and, as

© 2015 Pearson Education, Inc.

illustrated in Figure 35.4, the supply curve shifts leftward. The vertical distance between the initial supply curve, S, and the supply curve with the tax, S₁, indicated by the length of the grey arrow, equals the amount of the tax, $1 in this case. The price rises but not by the full amount of the tax. Tax incidence refers to the division of the burden of a tax between the buyers and the sellers. For a given elasticity of supply, the more inelastic the demand, the larger the share of a tax paid by the buyers; Chapter 8.

■ **FIGURE 35.5**

Price (dollars per unit)

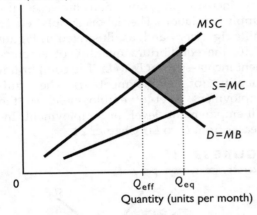

Quantity (units per month)

5. The quantity produced in an unregulated, competitive market is the equilibrium quantity, where the supply and demand curves intersect. In Figure 35.5, the quantity produced is Qeq. If there is an external cost, the marginal social cost curve, MSC, lies above the marginal private cost curve, MC, because the marginal social cost includes costs omitted (the external costs) from the marginal private cost. The allocatively efficient quantity is the quantity that sets the marginal social benefit equal to the marginal (social) cost, which is Qeff in the figure. The figure shows that an unregulated competitive market over-produces compared to the efficient quantity. There is a deadweight loss, equal to the area of the darkened triangle in the figure; Chapter 11.

■ **FIGURE 35.6**

Price and cost (dollars per unit)

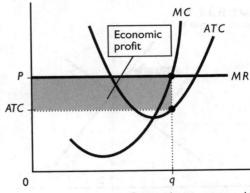

Output (units per month)

6. Figure 35.6 illustrates a perfectly competitive firm. To maximize its profit, the firm produces where MR equals MC, which means that the firm produces q. The price is P. The firm is earning an economic profit because P > ATC. The amount of the economic profit equals the amount of the gray area; Chapter 15.

■ **FIGURE 35.7**

Price and cost (dollars per unit)

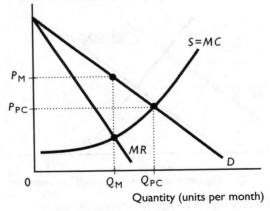

Quantity (units per month)

7. A perfectly competitive market produces where the demand and supply curves intersect, which is QPC in Figure 35.7. The equilibrium price is PPC. A monopoly produces where its marginal revenue and marginal cost curves intersect, which is QM in the figure. The price is set from the demand curve as PM. The monopoly produces less and sets a higher price; Chapter 16.

© 2015 Pearson Education, Inc.

■ **MACROECONOMICS**

■ **FIGURE 35.8**
Price (dollars per golf ball)

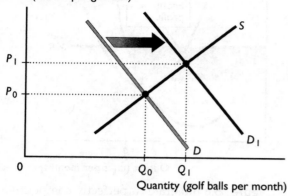

1. The fall in the price of a complement increases the demand for golf balls. The demand curve shifts rightward and, as illustrated in Figure 35.8, the equilibrium price of a golf ball rises from P_0 to P_1 and the equilibrium quantity increases from Q_0 to Q_1; Chapter 4.

■ **FIGURE 35.9**
Price (dollars per memory chip)

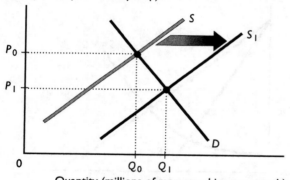

2. The new technology increases the supply of memory chips. The supply curve shifts rightward and, as illustrated in Figure 35.9, the equilibrium price of a memory chip falls from P_0 to P_1 and the equilibrium quantity increases from Q_0 to Q_1; Chapter 4.

■ **FIGURE 35.10**
Real wage rate (2009 dollars per hour)

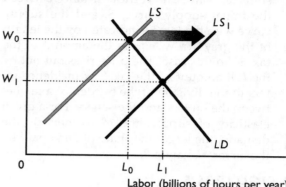

3. The increase in population increases the supply of labor. The labor supply curve shifts rightward and, as illustrated in Figure 35.10, the equilibrium quantity of employment increases from L_0 to L_1. The equilibrium quantity of employment *is* the full-employment level of employment, so the full-employment level of employment increases from L_0 to L_1; Chapter 24.

■ **FIGURE 35.11**
Real interest rate (percent per year)

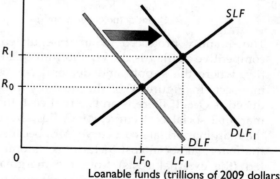

4. Because investment is more profitable, investment demand increases which increases the demand for loanable funds. The demand for loanable funds curve shifts rightward and, as illustrated in Figure 35.11, the equilibrium real interest rate rises from R_0 to R_1. The equilibrium quantity of investment increases; Chapter 26.

© 2015 Pearson Education, Inc.

■ FIGURE 35.12

Nominal interest rate (percent per year)

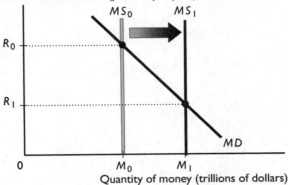

Quantity of money (trillions of dollars)

5. The increase in the quantity of money shifts the supply of money curve rightward from MS_0 to MS_1. As illustrated in Figure 35.12, the equilibrium (nominal) interest rate falls from R_0 to R_1. In the short run, the fall in the nominal interest rate lowers the real interest rate so that investment increases. In turn, the increase in investment increases aggregate demand so that in the short run, the price level rises and real GDP increases; Chapters 27, 28, and 33.

■ FIGURE 35.13

Price level (GDP deflator, 2009 = 100)

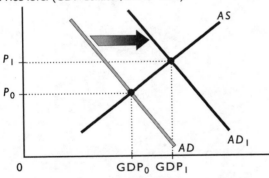

Real GDP (trillions of 2009 dollars)

6. An increase in government expenditures increases aggregate demand because government expenditures are a part of aggregate demand. The aggregate demand curve shifts rightward, as illustrated in Figure 35.13. In the short run, the price level rises, from P_0 to P_1 in the figure and real GDP increases, from GDP_0 to GDP_1 in the figure; Chapters 29 and 32.

■ FIGURE 35.14

Price level (GDP deflator, 2009 = 100)

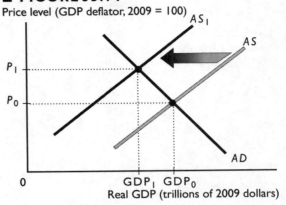

Real GDP (trillions of 2009 dollars)

7. An increase in the price of oil increases firms' costs and thereby decreases aggregate supply. The aggregate supply curve shifts leftward, as illustrated in Figure 35.14. In the short run, the price level rises, from P_0 to P_1 in the figure and real GDP decreases, from GDP_0 to GDP_1 in the figure; Chapter 29.

© 2015 Pearson Education, Inc.